Malignant Self Love

Narcissism Revisited

1ˢᵗ EDITION
8ᵗʰ Revised Impression

Sam Vaknin, Ph.D.

The Author is NOT a Mental Health Professional.
The Author is certified in Counselling Techniques by Brainbench.

Editing and Design:
Lidija Rangelovska

Narcissus Publications, Prague & Skopje 2007

To get FREE updates of this book JOIN the Narcissism Study List.
To JOIN, visit our Web sites:
http://www.geocities.com/samvaknin/narclist.html or
http://www.narcissistic-abuse.com/narclist.html or
http://health.groups.yahoo.com/group/narcissisticabuse

Visit the Author's Web site:

http://samvak.tripod.com

Buy other books about pathological narcissism and relationships with abusive narcissists here:

http://www.narcissistic-abuse.com/thebook.html

Further details on how to purchase these books at the end of this volume.

ISBN: 978-80-238-3384-3

"Sam Vaknin is the world's leading expert on narcissism."

Tim Hall, New York Press, Volume 16, Issue 7
February 12, 2003

"Vaknin's a respected expert on malignant narcissists...
He set about to know everything there is about the psychopathic narcissist."

Ian Walker, ABC Radio National Background Briefing
July 18, 2004

"Sam Vaknin is a leading authority on the topic of narcissism."

Lisa Angelettie M.S.W., BellaOnline's Mental Health Editor
"What is Narcissistic Personality Disorder"

"If you wish to get under the skin of a narcissist, if you wish
to get to know how he thinks and feels and why he behaves as
he does, then this is the book for you."

Dr. Anthony Benis, Mount Sinai Hospital, New York
Author "Towards Self and Sanity - On the Genetic
Origins of the Human Character"

"... This book has an important purpose. I am sure it will be
appreciated in a library, classroom or among the mental health
profession."

Katherine Theriault, Inscriptions Magazine, Vol. 2, Issue 20

"Sam Vaknin has written THE book on narcissism. Read
'Malignant Self Love' so you will understand that you are NOT
crazy, you are just embedded in a crazy making relationship."

Liane J. Leedom, M.D., psychiatrist and
Author of "Just Like His Father?"

"If you want to understand Narcissistic Personality Disorder from the best, don't look any further. I cannot recommend this book enough to those of you who have this disorder, to families and friends who are trying to understand. Dr. Vaknin has this disorder himself and examines this disorder closely."

Patty Pheil, MSW, Webmistress
www.mental-health-today.com

"Sam Vaknin's study of narcissism is truly insightful. The author has done probably more than anyone else to educate others to this poorly understood condition. In this, his twelfth book, he shares his considerable knowledge and experience of narcissism in a comprehensive yet easy to read style."

Tim Field, late Author and Webmaster
http://www.bullyonline.org/workbully

"Sam has plugged all the loopholes, exposed all the plots, and introduced a new language to confront the narcissist. Vaknin has composed OVER 100 Frequently Asked Questions, Essays and more, contained in a volume of 600 pages! Sam has designed Malignant Self Love as a 'hands-on' tool that can immediately bring relief. If you want to breathe again, if you are at your wits end, if everything has been tried and failed, if you NEED a change, then Malignant Self Love can give you your life back. This book is a lifesaver!"

Kathy Stringer, Webmistress of "Kathy's Mental Health Review"
http://www.toddlertime.com

"I love to read Dr. Sam's material. He lets you into his mind (and what a mind he has!). This book is required reading for any co-dependent - to understand how the other side works."

Dr. Irene Matiatos, Webmisress of Verbal Abuse
http://drirene.com

"For many years narcissism was extremely difficult to describe. But now, for the first time, Dr. Vaknin offers much-needed first hand account of what Narcissistic Personality Disorder is like. Malignant Self Love offers insight and clarity into a complex and difficult to describe disorder."

Howard Brown, Webmaster
www.4therapy.com

"The 6000+ members at our MSN learning, resource and discussion forums enthusiastically and unanimously recommend Dr. Vaknin's book Malignant Self Love Narcissism Revisited. It is an essential and crucial 'Must Read'. Dr. Vaknin dissects and describes not only the mind of the narcissist but what the narcissist's targets/victims can do about it. The result: Our members go zooming up the learning curve of understanding the Narcissistic Personality Disorder. Our members say the knowledge gained is essential for their lawyers who successfully counsel and litigate in cases where narcissists are involved, and our members' therapists who treat both narcissists and their victims and families."

Darla Boughton, Owner, Narcissistic Personality Disorder Board
http://groups.msn.com/NARCISSISTICPERSONALITYDISORDER

FIVE STAR rating at Barnes and Noble!

Read what more than 140 readers have to say:

http://search.barnesandnoble.com/bookSearch/
isbnInquiry.asp?r=1&ISBN=9788023833843

CONTENTS

Foreword 13

Prologue 21

Introduction - The Habit of Identity 23

The Narcissistic Personality Disorder

A Primer on Narcissism
And the Narcissistic Personality Disorder (NPD) 35

Bibliography 41

Frequently Asked Questions

Narcissism - The Disorder

FAQ # 1:   The Narcissist's Poor Prognosis 45
FAQ # 2:   Pathological Narcissism -
            A Dysfunction or a Blessing? 47
FAQ # 3:   The Energy of Self 49
FAQ # 4:   Self-Love and Narcissism 51
FAQ # 5:   Self-Defeating and Self-Destructive
            Behaviours 55
FAQ # 6:   Ideas of Reference 59
FAQ # 7:   Grandiose Fantasies 62
FAQ # 8:   Grandiosity Hangover and Narcissist Baiting 70
FAQ # 9:   Depression and the Narcissist 74
FAQ # 10:   Narcissistic Rage
            (Anger as a Source of Personality Disorder) 84
FAQ # 11:   Gender and the Narcissist 90
FAQ # 12:   Homosexual and Transsexual Narcissists 94
FAQ # 13:   Addiction to Fame and Celebrity 97
FAQ # 14:   Conspicuous Existence 101
FAQ # 15:   The Narcissist's Reaction to Deficient
            Narcissistic Supply 103

FAQ # 16:   The Delusional Way Out 106
FAQ # 17:   The Compulsive Acts of the Narcissist 113
FAQ # 18:   Narcissistic Routines 118
FAQ # 19:   The Unstable Narcissist 120
FAQ # 20:   Do Narcissists Have Emotions? 126
FAQ # 21:   The Inappropriate Affect 131
FAQ # 22:   The Ubiquitous Narcissist 133
FAQ # 23:   The Narcissist as a Sadist 135
FAQ # 24:   Other People's Pain 140
FAQ # 25:   The Psychology of Torture 144
FAQ # 26:   Multiple Grandiosity 150
FAQ # 27:   False Modesty 152
FAQ # 28:   Warped Reality and Retroactive Emotional
            Content 154
FAQ # 29:   Narcissistic Signal, Stimulus and Hibernation
            Mini-Cycles 157
FAQ # 30:   The Narcissistic Pendulum and the
            Pathological Narcissistic Space 160
FAQ # 31:   The Inanimate as a Source of Narcissistic Supply
            (Narcissistic Branding and Narcissistic Contagion) 163
FAQ # 32:   The Dual Role of the False Self 169
FAQ # 33:   The Stripped Ego 172
FAQ # 34:   The Split-off Ego 181
FAQ # 35:   The Serious Narcissist 188
FAQ # 36:   Narcissists, Disagreements and Criticism 191
FAQ # 37:   Transformations of Aggression 194
FAQ # 38:   Narcissistic Humiliation 198
FAQ # 39:   The Midlife Narcissist 201
FAQ # 40:   To Age with Grace 204
FAQ # 41:   The Narcissist and Introspection 207
FAQ # 42:   The Losses of the Narcissist 210
FAQ # 43:   Waiting for Him to Get Better 212
FAQ # 44:   Can a Narcissist Help Himself? 214
FAQ # 45:   Reconditioning the Narcissist 219
FAQ # 46:   Treatment Modalities and Therapies 223
FAQ # 47:   Narcissistic Mirroring 233
FAQ # 48:   The Development of the Narcissist 236
FAQ # 49:   The Narcissist's Mother 242
FAQ # 50:   The Inverted Narcissist 257
FAQ # 51:   Narcissists, Inverted Narcissists and Schizoids .. 289
FAQ # 52:   Narcissists, Medications and Chemical
            Imbalances 299
FAQ # 53:   Myths about Narcissism 302

FAQ # 54: The Selfish Gene
(The Genetic Underpinnings of Narcissism) 307
FAQ # 55: Narcissism – The Psychopathological Default ... 311
FAQ # 56: Narcissism, Other Mental Health Disorders,
Substance Abuse, and Reckless Behaviours
(Co-Morbidity and Dual Diagnosis) 317
FAQ # 57: Eating Disorders and the Narcissist 342
FAQ # 58: Can the Narcissist Have a Meaningful Life? 345
FAQ # 59: A Case Study of an Adolescent Narcissist 351
FAQ # 60: The Narcissist's Reactions to This Text 354

Narcissism and Society

FAQ # 61: A Dream Interpreted 356
FAQ # 62: How to Recognize a Narcissist? 364
FAQ # 63: Interacting with a Narcissist 370
FAQ # 64: The Weapon of Language 371
FAQ # 65: Exploitation by a Narcissist 374
FAQ # 66: The Narcissist's Victims 377
FAQ # 67: Narcissism by Proxy 380
FAQ # 68: Facilitating Narcissism 385
FAQ # 69: Narcissists in Positions of Authority 388
FAQ # 70: For the Love of God 397
FAQ # 71: The Narcissist and Social Institutions 400
FAQ # 72: Collective Narcissism
(Narcissism, Culture and Society) 403
FAQ # 73: The Narcissist in Court 407
FAQ # 74: The Narcissist in the Workplace 409
FAQ # 75: Responsibility and Other Matters 412
FAQ # 76: The Accountable Narcissist 414
FAQ # 77: Crime and Punishment:
The Never Repenting Narcissist 416
FAQ # 78: Narcissists, Group Behaviour and Terrorism 419
FAQ # 79: Is the Narcissist Ever Sorry? 422
FAQ # 80: A Letter about Trust 424
FAQ # 81: Traumas as Social Interactions 427
FAQ # 82: The Guilt of Others 435
FAQ # 83: Narcissistic Confinement 439
FAQ # 84: Narcissistic Allocation 442
FAQ # 85: Narcissistic Immunity 446
FAQ # 86: Narcissists, Love and Healing 450
FAQ # 87: Vindictive Narcissists 453
FAQ # 88: Narcissists as Mass and Serial Killers 457
FAQ # 89: Narcissists, Narcissistic Supply and
Sources of Supply 462

Narcissists and Family

FAQ # 90:   How to Cope with a Narcissist? 469
FAQ # 91:   Narcissists and Women 472
FAQ # 92:   The Spouse/Mate/Partner of the Narcissist 478
FAQ # 93:   Investing in a Narcissist 489
FAQ # 94:   The Double Reflection
            (Narcissistic Couples and Narcissistic Types) ... 490
FAQ # 95:   Narcissistic Parents 493
FAQ # 96:   Narcissists and Children 495
FAQ # 97:   The Narcissist and His Family 497
FAQ # 98:   Narcissists, Sex and Fidelity
            (The Somatic and the Cerebral Narcissist) 507
FAQ # 99:   The Extra-Marital Narcissist 511
FAQ # 100: Mourning the Narcissist 513
FAQ # 101: Surviving the Narcissist 518
FAQ # 102: The Dead Parents 532

The Mind of the Narcissist

Chapter I: The Soul of a Narcissist –
              The State of the Art 537
Chapter II: Being Special 549
Chapter III: Uniqueness and Intimacy 552
Chapter IV: The Workings of a Narcissist –
              A Phenomenology 567
Chapter V: The Tortured Self
              (The Inner World of the Narcissist) 573
Chapter VI: The Emotional Involvement
              Preventive Measures 577

The Author 593

Online index

Go here: http://samvak.tripod.com/siteindex.html

FOREWORD

Hello. Recognize me? No? Well, you see me all the time. You read my books, watch me on the big screen, feast on my art, cheer at my games, use my inventions, vote me into office, follow me into battle, take notes at my lectures, laugh at my jokes, marvel at my successes, admire my appearance, listen to my stories, discuss my politics, enjoy my music, excuse my faults, envy me my blessings. No? Still doesn't ring a bell? Well, you have seen me. Of that I am positive. In fact, if there is one thing I am absolutely sure of, it is that. You have seen me.

Perhaps our paths crossed more privately. Perhaps I am the one who came along and built you up when you were down, employed you when you needed a job, showed the way when you were lost, offered confidence when you were doubting, made you laugh when you were blue, sparked your interest when you were bored, listened to you and understood, saw you for what you really are, felt your pain and found the answers, made you want to be alive. Of course you recognize me. I am your inspiration, your role model, your saviour, your leader, your best friend, the one you aspire to emulate, the one whose favour makes you glow.

But I can also be your worst nightmare. First I build you up because that's what you need. Your skies are blue. Then, out of the blue, I start tearing you down. You let me do it because that's what you are used to. You are dumfounded. But I was wrong to take pity on you. You really *are* incompetent, disrespectful, untrustworthy, immoral, ignorant, inept, egotistical, constrained, disgusting. You are a social embarrassment, an unappreciative partner, an inadequate parent, a disappointment, a sexual flop, a financial liability. I tell you this to your face. I must. It is my right, because it is. I behave, at home and away, in any way I want to, with total disregard for conventions, mores, or the feelings of others. It is my right, because it is.

I lie to your face, without a twitch or a twitter, and there is absolutely nothing you can do about it. In fact, my lies are not lies at all. They are the truth, my truth. And you believe them, because you do, because they do not sound or feel like lies, because to do otherwise would make you question your own sanity, which you have a tendency to do anyway, because from the very beginning of our relationship you placed your trust and hopes in me, derived your energy, direction, stability, and confidence from me and from your association with me. So what's the problem if the safe haven I provide comes with a price? Surely I am worth it and then some.

Run to our friends. Go. See what that will get you. Ridicule. People believe what they see and what they see is the same wonderful me that you also saw and still do. What they also see is the very mixed up person that you have obviously become. The more you plead for understanding, the more convinced they are that the crazy one is you, the more isolated you feel, and the harder you try to make things right again, not by changing me but by accepting my criticisms and by striving to improve yourself. Could it be that you were wrong about me in the beginning? So wrong as that? How do you think our friends will react if you insist that they are also wrong about me? After all, they know that it really is you who have thwarted my progress, tainted my reputation, and thrown me off course.

I disappoint you? Outrageous! It is you who have disappointed me. Look at all he frustrations you cause me. Lucky for you, I have an escape from all this, and fortunately my reputation provides enough insulation from the outside world so I can indulge in this escape with impunity. What escape? Why, those eruptions of rage you dread and fear. Ah, it feels so good to rage. It is the expression of and the confirmation of my power over you, my absolute superiority. Lying feels good too, for the same reason, but nothing compares to the pleasure of exploding for no material reason and venting my anger with total abandon, all the time a spectator at my own show and at your helplessness, pain, fear, frustration, and dependence. In fact my raging is precisely what allows me to stay with you. Go ahead. Tell our friends about it. See if they can imagine what it's like, let alone believe it. The more outrageous the things you say about me, the more convinced they are that it is you who have taken a turn for the worse. And don't expect much more from your therapist either. You may tell him this or that, but what he sees when I visit him is something quite different. So what's the therapist to believe?

After all, it was you who came for help. No! That's what this is all about. No! That simple two-letter word that, regardless of how bad I am, you simply cannot say. Who knows? You might even acquire some of my behaviour yourself.

But you know what? This may come as a shock, but I can also be my own worst nightmare. I can and I am. You see, at heart my life is nothing more than illusion-clad confusion. I have no idea why I do what I do, nor do I care to find out. In fact, the mere notion of asking the question is so repulsive to me that I employ all of my resources to repel it. I reconstruct facts, fabricate illusions, act them out, and thus create my own reality. It is a precarious state of existence indeed, so I am careful to include enough demonstrable truth in my illusions to ensure their credibility. And I am forever testing that credibility on you and on the reactions of others. Fortunately my real attributes and accomplishments are in sufficient abundance to fuel my illusions seemingly forever. And modern society, blessed/cursed modern society, values most what I do best and thus serves as my accomplice. Even I get lost in my own illusions, swept away by my own magic.

So, not to worry if you still do not recognize me. I don't recognize me either. In fact, I am not really sure who I am. That's probably a question you never ask of yourself. Yet I wonder about it all the time. Perhaps I am not too different from everyone else, just better. After all, that's the feedback I get. My admirers certainly wish they were me. They just don't have the gifts I have, nor the courage I have to express them. That's what the universe is telling me.

Then again, *the* universe or *my* universe? As long as the magic of my illusions works on me too, there really is no need for distinction. All I need is an abundant fan club to stay on top of it all. So I am constantly taking fan club inventory, testing the loyalty of present members with challenges of abuse, writing off defectors with total indifference, and scouting the landscape for new recruits. Do you see my dilemma? I use people who are dependent on me to keep my illusions alive. So really it is I who am dependent on them. I need them to tell me that I don't need them. Sound crazy? It is. And at times it throws me into a rage. But even the rage, that orgasmic release of pain and anger, works better with an audience. On some level I am aware of my illusions, but to admit that would spoil the magic. And that I couldn't bear. So I proclaim that what I do is of no consequence and no different from what others do, and thus I create an illusion about my creating illusions. So, no, I don't recognize me any better than you do. I wouldn't dare. Like my fans, I marvel at my own being. Then again, sometimes I wish that I were not the person I am. You find that confusing? How do you think it makes me feel? I need my own magic to stay afloat. Sometimes others like me recruit me into their magic. But that's ok. As long as we feed off of each other, who's the worse for wear? It only confirms my illusion about my illusions: that I am no different from most other people, just a bit better.

But I *am* different and we both know it, although neither one of us dares to admit it. Therein lies the root of my hostility. I tear you down because in reality I am envious of you *because* I am different. At some haunting level, I see my magic for what it is and realize that people around me function just fine *without* any "magic". This terrifies me. Panic stricken, I try all my old tricks: displays of my talents, unnecessary deceptions, self-serving distortions, skilful seductions, ludicrous projections, frightening rages, whatever. Normally, that works. But if it fails, watch out. Like a solar-powered battery in darkness, my fire goes out and I cease to exist. Destruction sets in.

That is the key to understanding me. Most people strive for goals and feel good when they approach them. They move toward something positive. If they get there, or even close, receive recognition, enjoy the moment, and show their enjoyment, it is the genuine celebration of genuine self-worth. Even though it may invoke envy or criticism of self-aggrandizement, it is still a real expression of what they really appreciate in who they are and what they do. It is, in a word, real.

Not so for me. I move in the same direction but my movement is not toward something positive but away from something negative, something unreal. That's why I never stop, am never content, no matter what I achieve. I never get "there" because there is no "there" for me to get. That negative thing seems to follow me around like a shadow. I dowse myself in the light of praise and the light fades, but that's all it does. Like a moth, I renew the chase, again and again, and each time I succumb to it, again and again.

Can you tell the difference between the real thing and me, between people who genuinely enjoy celebrating themselves and someone like me who merely pretends to? Usually not. The difference, you see, is not in the behaviour you observe. It's in the motivation. Sure, I look like them and they look like me. But we are not the same. Not at all.

If by chance you are witness to one of my inexplicable Jeckyll-and-Hyde personality changes, you might suspect that something is amiss. But you quickly pass it off as an exception to the rule, for I am quick to revert to "normal". Witnessing several changes might make you pause a little longer. But it takes an awful lot before you truly entertain the frightening possibility that these abrupt changes might not be the exception, rather the rule. But then what? You - a self-doubter by nature - might be the only one to see behind the mask. Alone with your secret, it will drive you mad.

Where did it come from, this negativity? Probably from before I learned to talk. When you were exploring your world for the first time, with the usual little toddler mishaps, your mother kept a careful eye on you, intervened when she saw you heading for danger, and comforted you when you made a mistake, even if you cried. Well, that's not how it was for me. My mother's expectations of me were much higher. Mistakes were mistakes and crying was not the way to get her approval. That required being perfect, so that's exactly what I become. Not the little awkward toddler that I was, but my mother's model child. Not the brave and curious little person that I really was, but the fearful personification of my mother's ideal.

What you were experiencing through your little mishaps and mistakes were small doses of shame. What you were learning from your quick recoveries was shame repair. At first your mother did most of the repairing. Through repetition, you gradually learned how to do it by yourself. Shame repair brain circuitry was being laid down that would carry you for the rest of your life. I had no such luck. I simply did not acquire that skill when nature had intended my brain to acquire it.

Instead I acquired something else: a sense of needlessness. That's right, needlessness. Since Mother wouldn't help me where I needed it most, I learned to pretend that I did not need her. I became tough, self-assured, a know-it-all, a do-it-all, an achiever, a leader. And you know what? It worked. By pretending not to need Mother, I got what I needed from her, her love. Well, at least a semblance of love, in the form of approval and encouragement. Naturally, I tried this out on the rest of the world, and it worked again. All I needed to do was show others that I did not need them. How? By pretending, of course. Pretending that I knew more and could do more than they did, that I was above the rules of accepted behaviour, that I was special, that I, like Peter Pan, could do and get away with anything I wanted to.

And they played along, perfectly, with all the affirmations needed to sustain the show. It didn't work on everybody, of course. It was usually the neediest who were drawn to my needlessness, so I became an expert at sniffing them out within seconds. An illusion? Sure. But by then that's what I had become. Exploitation? Right again. But they were exploiting me too. I gave them what they needed and they followed behind me like obedient sheep. Just as you do to this day! Little did they know that I needed them every bit as much as they needed me. But there was no way I could ever admit that. For most people, to need others is normal, an accepted part of who they are, of being human. For me, to need anything is to accept that my needlessness is all a sham. If that dissolves, there is nothing left. At least that's what I fear. The sense of needlessness is my addiction. Am I ashamed of that? Yes, I am. But even greater is my fear of the shame I might experience in facing life without it. No one enjoys shame. But most people can deal with it. Not me. I fear it the way you fear snakes. You will go to great lengths to avoid stepping on a snake. I go to great lengths to avoid stepping on shame.

How many others like me are there? More than you might think, and our numbers are increasing. Take twenty people off the street and you might well find one whose mind ticks so much like mine that you could consider us clones. Impossible, you say. It is simply not possible for that many people - highly accomplished, respected, and visible people - to be out there replacing reality with illusions, each in the same way and for reasons they know not why. It is simply not possible for so many shame-phobic robots of havoc and chaos, all fitting the same description, to function daily midst other educated, intelligent, and experienced individuals, and pass for normal. It is simply not possible for such an aberration of human cognition and behaviour to infiltrate and infect the population in such numbers and such similarity, virtually undetected by the radar of mental health professionals. It is simply not possible for so much similar visible positive to contain so much concealed similar negative. It is simply not possible.

But it is. That is the enlightenment of *Narcissism Revisited* by Sam Vaknin. Sam is himself one such clone. What distinguishes him is his uncharacteristic courage to confront, and his uncanny understanding of, that which makes us tick, himself included. Not only does Sam dare ask and then answer the question we clones avoid like the plague, he does so with relentless, laser-

MALIGNANT SELF LOVE

SAM VAKNIN

like precision. Read his book. Take your seat at the double-headed microscope and let Sam guide you through the dissection. Like a brain surgeon operating on himself, Sam explores and exposes the alien among us, hoping beyond hope for a resectable tumour but finding instead each and every cell teeming with the same resistant virus. The operation is long and tedious, and at times frightening and hard to believe. Read on. The parts exposed are as they are, despite what may seem hyperbolic or farfetched. Their validity might not hit home until later, when coupled with memories of past events and experiences.

I am, as I said, my own worst nightmare. True, the world is replete with my contributions, and I am lots of fun to be around. And true, most contributions like mine are not the result of troubled souls. But many more than you might want to believe are. And if by chance you get caught in my web, I can make your life a living hell. But remember this. I am in that web too. The difference between you and me is that you can get out.

Ken Heilbrunn, M.D
Seattle, Washington, USA
ksbrunh@aol.com

PROLOGUE

I met Sam on an Internet list about 5 years ago. I'd been studying personality disorders and narcissism at the time, looking at
it from Jungian, spiritual, and literary points of view as well as
psychological, and I was just not too terribly impressed with the
psychological state of the art on those topics.

Sam invited me to visit his site, and without knowing him from
Adam, I just wrongly assumed that he was one more run-of the-
mill shrink writing standard stuff about narcissism. I replied
something like, "No, that won't be necessary I am the only person in the whole world who truly understands narcissism" - a
supremely narcissistic reply, in other words.

I went ahead and visited his site anyway, and was most
impressed. I e-mailed him back then, and told him of my mistake, and said I thought his work was way ahead of the standard
psychological writings on the subject. You just can't understand
something as complex and subtle as narcissism without inte-
grating your feelings, your soul and your heart with it, and the
supposedly "objective" stuff written by professionals was just
missing key dimensions that made it flat and cold 'dead information" instead of "living knowledge".

Sam's writing on the subject pulsated with heat, it ran red with
blood, it crackled with flames of passion, it cried out in agony.
Sam KNEW narcissism like the fish knows the water and the eagle
knows the air, because he had lived it. He described it's small
insignificant currents, he knew what it does when the weather
changes, he knew exactly what happens to little frogs, snakes
and crickets whenever they fall into the stream. Most psychologists only know ABOUT narcissism - Sam UNDERSTANDS it.

Paul Shirley, MSW

INTRODUCTION

The Habit of Identity

Warning and Disclaimer

The contents of this book are not meant to substitute for professional help and counselling. The readers are discouraged from using it for diagnostic or therapeutic ends. The diagnosis and treatment of the Narcissistic Personality Disorder can only be done by professionals specifically trained and qualified to do so - which the author is not. The author is NOT a mental health professional, though he is certified by Brainbench in Mental Health Counselling Techniques.

In a famous experiment, students were asked to take a lemon home and to get used to it. Three days later, they were able to single out "their" lemon from a pile of rather similar ones. They seemed to have bonded. Is this the true meaning of love, bonding, coupling? Do we simply get used to other human beings, pets, or objects?

Habit forming in humans is reflexive. We change ourselves and our environment in order to attain maximum comfort and well being. It is the effort that goes into these adaptive processes that forms a habit. The habit is intended to prevent us from constant experimenting and risk taking. The greater our well being, the better we function and the longer we survive.

Actually, when we get used to something or to someone - we get used to ourselves. In the object of the habit we see a part of our history, all the time and effort we had put into it. It is an encapsulated version of our acts, intentions, emotions and reactions. It is a mirror reflecting that part in us which formed the habit in the first place. Hence, the feeling of comfort: we really feel comfortable with our own selves through the agency of our habitual objects.

Because of this, we tend to confuse habits with identity. When asked WHO they are, most people resort to communicating their habits. They describe their work, their loved ones, their pets, their hobbies, or their material possessions. Yet, surely, all of these do not constitute identity! Removing them does not change who we are. They are habits and they make people comfortable and relaxed. But they are not part of one's identity in the truest, deepest sense.

Still, it is this simple mechanism of deception that binds people together. A mother feels that her offspring are part of her identity because she is so used to them that her well-being depends on their existence and availability. Thus, any threat to her children is perceived by her as a threat to her own Self. Her reaction is, therefore, strong and enduring and can be recurrently elicited.

The truth, of course, is that her children ARE a part of her identity in a superficial manner. Removing them will make her a different person, but only in the shallow, phenomenological sense of the word. Her deep-set, true identity will not change as a result. Children do die at times and the mother does go on living, essentially unchanged.

But what is this kernel of identity that I am referring to? This immutable entity which is who we are and what we are and which, ostensibly, is not influenced by the death of our loved ones? What can resist the breakdown of habits that die hard?

It is our personality. This elusive, loosely interconnected, interacting, pattern of reactions to our changing environment. Like the Brain, it is difficult to define or to capture. Like the Soul, many believe that it does not exist, that it is a fictitious convention.

Yet, we know that we do have a personality. We feel it, we experience it. It sometimes encourages us to do things - at other times, it prevents us from doing them. It can be supple or rigid, benign or malignant, open or closed. Its power lies in its networked looseness. It is able to combine, recombine and permute in hundreds of unforeseeable ways. It metamorphoses and the constancy of these changes is what gives us a sense of identity.

Actually, when the personality is rigid to the point of being unable to change in reaction to shifting circumstances - we say that it is disordered. One has a personality disorder when one's habits substitute for one's identity. Such a person identifies himself with his environment, taking behavioural, emotional, and cognitive cues exclusively from it. His inner world is, so to speak, vacated, his True Self merely an apparition.

Such a person is incapable of loving and of living. He is incapable of loving because to love another one must first love oneself. And, in the absence of a Self that is impossible. And, in the long-term, he is incapable of living because life is a struggle towards multiple goals, a striving, a drive at something. In other words: life is change. He who cannot change, does not live.

What is Personality and What is Normal?

In their opus magnum "Personality Disorders in Modern Life", Theodore Millon and Roger Davis define personality as:

"(A) complex pattern of deeply embedded psychological characteristics that are expressed automatically in almost every area of psychological functioning." [p. 2]

The Diagnostic and Statistical Manual (DSM)) IV-TR [2000], published by the American Psychiatric Association, defines personality traits as:

"(E)nduring patterns of perceiving, relating to, and thinking about the environment and oneself that are exhibited in a wide range of social and personal contexts." [p. 686]

Laymen often confuse and confute "personality" with "character" and "temperament".

25 Our temperament is the biological-genetic template that interacts with our environment.

Our temperament is a set of in-built dispositions we are born with. It is mostly unalterable (though recent studies demonstrate that the brain is far more plastic and elastic than we thought).

In other words, our temperament is our nature.

Our character is largely the outcome of the process of socialization, the acts and imprints of our environment and nurture on our psyche during the formative years (0-6 years and in adolescence).

Our character is the set of all acquired characteristics we posses, often judged in a cultural-social context.

Sometimes the interplay of all these factors results in an abnormal personality.

Personality disorders are dysfunctions of our whole identity, tears in the fabric of who we are. They are all-pervasive because our personality is ubiquitous and permeates each and every one of our mental cells.

In the background lurks the question: what constitutes normal behaviour? Who is normal?

There is the statistical response: the average and the common are normal. But it is an unsatisfactory and incomplete answer.

Conforming to social edicts and mores does not guarantee normalcy. Think about anomic societies and periods of history such as Hitler's Germany or Stalin's Russia. Model citizens in these hellish environments were the criminal and the sadist.

Rather than look to the outside for a clear definition, many mental health professionals ask: is the patient functioning and happy (ego-syntonic)? If he or she is both then all is well and normal. Abnormal traits, behaviours, and personalities are, therefore defined as those traits, behaviours, and personalities that are dysfunctional and cause subjective distress.

But, of course, this definition falls flat on its face at the slightest scrutiny. Many evidently mentally ill people are rather happy and reasonably functional.

Some scholars reject the concept of "normalcy" altogether. The anti-psychiatry movement object to the medicalization and pathologization of whole swathes of human conduct. Others prefer to study the disorders themselves rather to "go metaphysical" by trying to distinguish them from an imaginary and ideal state of being "mentally healthy".

I subscribe to the later approach. I much prefer to delve into the phenomenology of mental health disorders: their traits, characteristics, and impact on others.

Appendix for Mental Health Professionals

The Myth of Mental Illness

"You can know the name of a bird in all the languages of the world, but when you're finished, you'll know absolutely nothing whatever about the bird... So let's look at the bird and see what it's doing - that's what counts. I learned very early the difference between knowing the name of something and knowing something."

[Richard Feynman, Physicist and 1965 Nobel Prize laureate (1918-1988)]

"You have all I dare say heard of the animal spirits and how they are transfused from father to son etcetera etcetera - well you may take my word that nine parts in ten of a man's sense or his nonsense, his successes and miscarriages in this world depend on their motions and activities, and the different tracks and trains you put them into, so that when they are once set a-going, whether right or wrong, away they go cluttering like hey-go-mad."

[Lawrence Sterne (1713-1758), "The Life and Opinions of Tristram Shandy, Gentleman", 1759]

Overview

Someone is considered mentally "ill" if:

1. His conduct rigidly and consistently deviates from the typical, average behaviour of all other people in his culture and society that fit his profile (whether this conventional behaviour is moral or rational is immaterial), or
2. His judgement and grasp of objective, physical reality is impaired, and
3. His conduct is not a matter of choice but is innate and irresistible, and
4. His behaviour causes him or others discomfort, and is
5. Dysfunctional, self-defeating, and self-destructive even by his own yardsticks.

Descriptive criteria aside, what is the ESSENCE of mental disorders? Are they merely physiological disorders of the brain, or, more precisely of its chemistry? If so, can they be cured by restoring the balance of substances and secretions in that mysterious organ? And, once equilibrium is reinstated - is the illness "gone" or is it still lurking there, "under wraps", waiting to erupt? Are psychiatric problems inherited, rooted in faulty genes (though amplified by environmental factors) - or brought on by abusive or wrong nurturance?

These questions are the domain of the "medical" school of mental health.

Others cling to the spiritual view of the human psyche. They believe that mental ailments amount to the metaphysical discomposure of an unknown medium - the soul. Theirs is a holistic approach, taking in the patient in his or her entirety, as well as his milieu.

The members of the functional school regard mental health disorders as perturbations in the proper, statistically "normal", behaviours and manifestations of "healthy" individuals, or as dysfunctions. The "sick" individual - ill at ease with himself (ego-dystonic) or making others unhappy (deviant) - is "mended" when rendered functional again by the prevailing standards of his social and cultural frame of reference.

In a way, the three schools are akin to the trio of blind men who render disparate descriptions of the very same elephant. Still, they share not only their subject matter - but, to a counter intuitively large degree, a faulty methodology.

As the renowned anti-psychiatrist, Thomas Szasz, of the State University of New York, notes in his article "The Lying Truths of

Psychiatry", mental health scholars, regardless of academic predilection, infer the aetiology of mental disorders from the success or failure of treatment modalities.

This form of "reverse engineering" of scientific models is not unknown in other fields of science, nor is it unacceptable if the experiments meet the criteria of the scientific method. The theory must be all-inclusive (anamnetic), consistent, falsifiable, logically compatible, monovalent, and parsimonious. Psychological "theories" - even the "medical" ones (the role of Serotonin and Dopamine in mood disorders, for instance) - are usually none of these things.

The outcome is a bewildering array of ever-shifting mental health "diagnoses" expressly centred around Western civilization and its standards (example: the ethical objection to suicide). Neurosis, a historically fundamental "condition" vanished after 1980. Homosexuality, according to the American Psychiatric Association, was a pathology prior to 1973. Seven years later, narcissism was declared a "personality disorder", almost seven decades after it was first described by Freud.

The Biochemistry and Genetics of Mental Health

Certain mental health afflictions are either correlated with a statistically abnormal biochemical activity in the brain - or are ameliorated with medication. Yet the two FACTS are not ineludibly facets of THE SAME underlying phenomenon. In other words, that a given medicine reduces or abolishes certain symptoms does not necessarily mean they were CAUSED by the processes or substances affected by the drug administered. Causation is only one of many possible connections and chains of events.

To designate a pattern of behaviour as a mental health disorder is a value judgement, or at best a statistical observation. Such designation is effected regardless of the facts of brain science.

Moreover, correlation is not causation. Deviant brain or body biochemistry (once called "polluted animal spirits") do exist - but are they truly the roots of mental perversion? Nor is it clear which triggers what: do the aberrant neurochemistry or biochemistry cause mental illness - or the other way around?

That psychoactive medication alters behaviour and mood is indisputable. So do illicit and legal drugs, certain foods, and all interpersonal interactions. That the changes brought about by prescription are desirable - is debatable and involves tautological thinking. If a certain pattern of behaviour is described as (socially) "dysfunctional" or (psychologically) "sick" - clearly, every change would be welcomed as "healing" and every agent of transformation would be called a "cure".

The same applies to the alleged heredity of mental illness. Single genes or gene complexes are frequently "associated" with mental health diagnoses, personality traits, or behaviour patterns. But too little is known to establish irrefutable sequences of causes-and-effects. Even less is proven about the interaction of nature and nurture, genotype and phenotype, the plasticity of the brain and the psychological impact of trauma, abuse, upbringing, role models, peers, and other environmental elements.

Nor is the distinction between psychotropic substances and talk therapy that clear-cut. Words and the interaction with the therapist also affect the brain, its processes and chemistry - albeit more slowly and, perhaps, more profoundly and irreversibly. Medicines - as David Kaiser reminds us in "Against Biologic Psychiatry" [Psychiatric Times, Volume XIII, Issue 12, December 1996] - treat symptoms, not the underlying processes that yield them.

The Variance of Mental Disease

If mental illnesses are bodily and empirical, they should be invariant both temporally and spatially, across cultures and societies. This, to some degree, is, indeed, the case. Psychological diseases are not context dependent - but the pathologizing of certain behaviours is. Suicide, substance abuse, narcissism, eating disorders, antisocial ways, schizotypal symptoms, depression, even psychosis are considered sick by some cultures - and utterly normative or advantageous in others.

This was to be expected. The human mind and its dysfunctions are alike around the world. But values differ from time to time and from one place to another. Hence, disagreements about the propriety and desirability of human actions and inaction are bound to arise in a symptom-based diagnostic system.

As long as the PSEUDO-MEDICAL definitions of mental health disorders continue to rely exclusively on signs and symptoms - i.e., mostly on observed or reported behaviours - they remain vulnerable to such discord and devoid of much-sought universality and rigour.

Mental Disorders and the Social Order

The mentally sick receive the same treatment as carriers of AIDS or SARS or the Ebola virus or smallpox. They are sometimes quarantined against their will and coerced into involuntary treatment by medication, psychosurgery, or electroconvulsive therapy. This is done in the name of the greater good, largely as a preventive policy.

Conspiracy theories notwithstanding, it is impossible to ignore the enormous interests vested in psychiatry and psychopharmacology. The multibillion dollar industries involving drug companies, hospitals, managed healthcare, private clinics, academic departments, and law enforcement agencies rely, for their continued and exponential growth, on the propagation of the concept of "mental illness" and its corollaries: treatment and research.

Mental Ailment as a Useful Metaphor

Abstract concepts form the core of all branches of human knowledge. No one has ever seen a quark, or untangled a chemical bond, or surfed an electromagnetic wave, or visited the unconscious. These are useful metaphors, theoretical entities with explanatory or descriptive power.

"Mental health disorders" are no different. They are shorthand for capturing the unsettling quiddity of "the Other". Useful as taxonomies, they are also tools of social coercion and conformity, as Michel Foucault and Louis Althusser observed. Relegating both the dangerous and the idiosyncratic to the collective fringes is a vital technique of social engineering.

The aim is progress through social cohesion and the regulation of innovation and creative destruction. Psychiatry, therefore, is reifies society's preference of evolution to revolution, or, worse still, to mayhem. As is often the case with human endeavour, it is a noble cause, unscrupulously and dogmatically pursued.

The Insanity Defence

"It is an ill thing to knock against a deaf-mute, an imbecile, or a minor. He that wounds them is culpable, but if they wound him they are not culpable."
[Mishna, Babylonian Talmud]

If mental illness is culture-dependent and mostly serves as an organizing social principle - what should we make of the insanity defence (NGRI - Not Guilty by Reason of Insanity)?

A person is held not responsible for his criminal actions if s/he cannot tell right from wrong ("lacks substantial capacity either to appreciate the criminality (wrongfulness) of his conduct" - diminished capacity), did not intend to act the way he did (absent "mens rea") and/or could not control his behaviour ("irresistible impulse"). These handicaps are often associated with "mental disease or defect" or "mental retardation".

Mental health professionals prefer to talk about an impairment of a "person's perception or understanding of reality". They hold a "guilty but mentally ill" verdict to be contradiction in terms. All "mentally-ill" people operate within a (usually coherent) worldview, with consistent internal logic, and rules of right and wrong (ethics). Yet, these rarely conform to the way most people perceive the world. The mentally-ill, therefore, cannot be guilty because s/he has a tenuous grasp on reality.

Yet, experience teaches us that a criminal maybe mentally ill even as s/he maintains a perfect reality test and thus is held criminally responsible (Jeffrey Dahmer comes to mind). The "perception and understanding of reality", in other words, can and does co-exist even with the severest forms of mental illness.

This makes it even more difficult to comprehend what is meant by "mental disease". If some mentally ill maintain a grasp on reality, know right from wrong, can anticipate the outcomes of their actions, are not subject to irresistible impulses (the official position of the American Psychiatric Association) - in what way do they differ from us, "normal" folks?

This is why the insanity defence often sits ill with mental health pathologies deemed socially "acceptable" and "normal" - such as religion or love.

Consider the following case:

A mother bashes the skulls of her three sons. Two of them die. She claims to have acted on instructions she had received from God. She is found not guilty by reason of insanity. The jury determined that she "did not know right from wrong during the killings".

But why exactly was she judged insane?

Her belief in the existence of God - a being with inordinate and inhuman attributes - may be irrational.

But it does not constitute insanity in the strictest sense because it conforms to social and cultural creeds and codes of conduct in her milieu. Billions of people faithfully subscribe to the same ideas, adhere to the same transcendental rules, observe the same mystical rituals, and claim to go through the same experiences. This shared psychosis is so widespread that it can no longer be deemed pathological, statistically speaking.

She claimed that God has spoken to her.

As do numerous other people. Behaviour that is considered psychotic (paranoid-schizophrenic) in other contexts is lauded and admired in religious circles. Hearing voices and seeing visions - auditory and visual delusions - are considered rank manifestations of righteousness and sanctity.

Perhaps it was the content of her hallucinations that proved her insane?

She claimed that God had instructed her to kill her boys. Surely, God would not ordain such evil?

Alas, the Old and New Testaments both contain examples of God's appetite for human sacrifice. Abraham was ordered by God to sacrifice Isaac, his beloved son (though this savage command was rescinded at the last moment). Jesus, the son of God himself, was crucified to atone for the sins of humanity.

A divine injunction to slay one's offspring would sit well with the Holy Scriptures and the Apocrypha as well as with millennia-old Judeo-Christian traditions of martyrdom and sacrifice.

Her actions were wrong and incommensurate with both human and divine (or natural) laws.

Yes, but they were perfectly in accord with a literal interpretation of certain divinely-inspired texts, millennial scriptures, apocalyptic thought systems, and fundamentalist religious ideologies (such as the ones espousing the imminence of "rupture"). Unless one declares these doctrines and writings insane, her actions are not.

We are forced to the conclusion that the murderous mother is perfectly sane. Her frame of reference is different to ours. Hence, her definitions of right and wrong are idiosyncratic. To her, killing her babies was the right thing to do and in conformity with valued teachings and her own epiphany. Her grasp of reality - the immediate and later consequences of her actions - was never impaired.

It would seem that sanity and insanity are relative terms, dependent on frames of cultural and social reference, and statistically defined. There isn't - and, in principle, can never emerge - an "objective", medical, scientific test to determine mental health or disease unequivocally.

Adaptation and Insanity

"Normal" people adapt to their environment - both human and natural.

"Abnormal" ones try to adapt their environment - both human and natural - to their idiosyncratic needs/profile.

If they succeed, their environment, both human (society) and natural is pathologized.

Sam Vaknin

32

SAM VAKNIN   MALIGNANT SELF LOVE

Malignant Self Love

Narcissism Revisited

The Narcissistic Personality Disorder

A Primer on Narcissism
And the Narcissistic Personality Disorder

Most narcissists are men.
This is why I use male pronouns throughout this book.

What is Pathological Narcissism?

Pathological narcissism is a life-long pattern of traits and behaviours which signify infatuation and obsession with one's self to the exclusion of all others and the egotistic and ruthless pursuit of one's gratification, dominance and ambition.

As distinct from healthy narcissism which we all possess, pathological narcissism is maladaptive, rigid, persisting, and causes significant distress, and functional impairment.

Pathological narcissism was first described in detail by Freud in his essay "On Narcissism" [1915]. Other major contributors to the study of narcissism are: Melanie Klein, Karen Horney, Franz Kohut, Otto Kernberg, Theodore Millon, Elsa Roningstam, J.G. Gunderson, and Robert Hare.

What is Narcissistic Personality Disorder (NPD)?

The Narcissistic Personality Disorder (NPD) is a form of pathological narcissism. It is a Cluster B (dramatic, emotional, or erratic) Personality Disorder. Other Cluster B personality disorders are the Borderline Personality Disorder (BPD), the Antisocial Personality Disorder (APD), and the Histrionic Personality Disorder (HPD). The Narcissistic Personality Disorder (NPD) first appeared as a mental health diagnosis in the DSM-III-TR (Diagnostic and Statistical Manual) in 1980.

Diagnostic Criteria

The Narcissistic Personality Disorder (NPD) is not a new psychological construct. In previous centuries it was called "egotism" or "megalomania". It is an extreme form of pathological narcissism.

The ICD-10 (International Classification of Diseases), published by the World Health Organization in Geneva [1992], does not include the Narcissistic Personality Disorder (NPD). It regards it as *"a personality disorder that fits none of the specific rubrics"* and puts it together with other bizarre dysfunctions such as, "haltlose", immature, passive-aggressive, and psychoneurotic personality disorders and types in a catchall category: "Other Specific Personality Disorders".

The Diagnostic and Statistical Manual of Mental Disorders, fourth edition, Text Revision (DSM-IV-TR) [2000], published by the American Psychiatric Association, based in Washington D.C., USA, provides the diagnostic criteria for the Narcissistic Personality Disorder (NPD) [301.81] on page 717.

The DSM-IV-TR defines Narcissistic Personality Disorder (NPD) as *"an all-pervasive pattern of grandiosity (in fantasy or behaviour), need for admiration or adulation and lack of empathy, usually beginning by early adulthood and present in various contexts"*, such as family life and work.

Five or more of the DSM's nine diagnostic criteria must be met for a diagnosis of Narcissistic Personality Disorder (NPD) to be rendered.

[In the text below, I have proposed modifications to the language of these criteria to incorporate current knowledge about this disorder. My modifications appear in italics.]

[My amendments do not constitute a part of the text of the DSM-IV-TR, nor is the American Psychiatric Association (APA) associated with them in any way.]

[Download a bibliography of the studies and research regarding the Narcissistic Personality Disorder (NPD) on which I based my proposed revisions: http://www.suite101.com/files/topics/6514/files/NPDBibliography.zip]

Proposed Amended Criteria for the Narcissistic Personality Disorder

- Feels grandiose and self-important (e.g., exaggerates accomplishments, talents, *skills, contacts, and personality traits to the point of lying, demands* to be recognized as superior without commensurate achievements);
- Is *obsessed* with fantasies of unlimited success, *fame, fearsome* power or *omnipotence, unequalled* brilliance *(the cerebral narcissist), bodily* beauty *or sexual performance (the somatic narcissist),* or ideal, *everlasting, all-conquering* love *or passion;*

- Firmly convinced that he or she is unique and, being special, can only be understood by, *should only be treated by*, or associate with, other special or unique, or high-status people (or institutions);
- Requires excessive admiration, *adulation, attention and affirmation - or, failing that, wishes to be feared and to be notorious (Narcissistic Supply)*;
- Feels entitled. *Demands automatic and full compliance* with his or her unreasonable expectations for special and *favourable priority* treatment;
- Is "interpersonally exploitative", i.e., *uses* others to achieve his or her own ends;
- *Devoid* of empathy. Is *unable* or unwilling to identify with, *acknowledge, or accept* the feelings, needs, *preferences, priorities, and choices* of others;
- Constantly envious of others *and seeks to hurt or destroy the objects of his or her frustration. Suffers from persecutory (paranoid) delusions* as he or she believes that they feel the same about him or her *and are likely to act similarly*;
- Behaves arrogantly and haughtily. *Feels superior, omnipotent, omniscient, invincible, immune, "above the law", and omnipresent (magical thinking). Rages when frustrated, contradicted, or confronted* by people he or she considers inferior to him or her and unworthy.

Prevalence and Age and Gender Features

What is the difference between healthy narcissism and the pathological kind?

Luckily for us, we are all narcissists to some degree. But healthy narcissism is adaptive, flexible, empathic, causes elation and joy (happiness), and help us to function. Pathological narcissism is maladaptive, rigid, persisting, and causes significant distress, and functional impairment.

"The lifetime prevalence rate of NPD is approximately 0.5-1 percent; however, the estimated prevalence in clinical settings is approximately 2-16 percent. Almost 75 percent of individuals diagnosed with NPD are male (APA, DSM-IV-TR 2000)."

[Psychotherapeutic Assessment and Treatment of Narcissistic Personality Disorder by Robert C. Schwartz, Ph.D., DAPA and Shannon D. Smith, Ph.D., DAPA (American Psychotherapy Association, Article 3004 Annals July/August 2002)]

We must carefully distinguish between the narcissistic traits of adolescents - narcissism is an integral part of their healthy personal development - and the full-fledged disorder. Adolescence is about self-definition, differentiation, separation from one's parents, and individuation. These inevitably involve narcissistic assertiveness which is not to be conflated or confused with Narcissistic Personality Disorder (NPD).

Narcissistic Personality Disorder (NPD) is exacerbated by the onset of aging and the physical, mental, and occupational restrictions it imposes.

In certain situations, such as under constant public scrutiny and exposure, a transient and reactive form of the Narcissistic Personality Disorder (NPD) has been observed by Robert Milman and labelled "Acquired Situational Narcissism". ⟶ *What's this?*

There is only scant research regarding the Narcissistic Personality Disorder (NPD), but studies did not demonstrate any ethnic, social, cultural, economic, genetic, or professional predilection to it.

Co-Morbidity and Differential Diagnoses

Narcissistic Personality Disorder (NPD) is often diagnosed with other mental health disorders ("co-morbidity"), such as mood disorders, eating disorders, and substance-related disorders. Patients with Narcissistic Personality Disorder (NPD) are frequently abusive and prone to impulsive and reckless behaviours ("dual diagnosis").

Narcissistic Personality Disorder (NPD) is also commonly diagnosed with other personality disorders, such as the Histrionic, Borderline, Paranoid, and Antisocial Personality Disorder.

The personal style of those suffering from the Narcissistic Personality Disorder (NPD) should be distinguished from the personal styles of patients with other Cluster B personality disorders. The narcissist is grandiose, the histrionic coquettish, the antisocial (psychopath) callous, and the borderline needy.

As opposed to patients with the Borderline Personality Disorder, the self-image of the narcissist is stable, he or she is less impulsive and less self-defeating or self-destructive and less concerned with abandonment issues (not as clinging).

Contrary to the histrionic patient, the narcissist is achievements-orientated and proud of his or her possessions and accomplishments. Narcissists also rarely display their emotions as histrionics do and they hold the sensitivities and needs of others in contempt.

According to the DSM-IV-TR, both narcissists and psychopaths are "tough-minded, glib, superficial, exploitative, and unempathic". But narcissists are less impulsive, less aggressive, and less deceitful. Psychopaths rarely seek Narcissistic Supply. As opposed to psychopaths, few narcissists are criminals.

Patients suffering from the range of obsessive-compulsive disorders are committed to perfection and believe that only they are capable of attaining it. But, as opposed to narcissists, they are self-critical and far more aware of their own deficiencies, flaws, and shortcomings.

Clinical Features of the Narcissistic Personality Disorder

The onset of pathological narcissism is in infancy, childhood and early adolescence. It is commonly attributed to childhood abuse and trauma inflicted by parents, authority figures, or even peers. Pathological narcissism is a defence mechanism intended to deflect hurt and trauma from the victim's "True Self" into a "False Self" which is construed by the narcissist to be omnipotent, invulnerable, and omniscient. The narcissist uses the False Self to regulate his or her labile sense of self-worth by extracting from his environment Narcissistic Supply (any form of attention, both positive and negative).

There is a whole range of narcissistic reactions, styles, and personalities: from the mild, reactive and transient to the permanent personality disorder.

Patients with Narcissistic Personality Disorder (NPD) feel injured, humiliated and empty when criticized. They often react with disdain (devaluation), rage, and defiance to any slight, real or imagined. To avoid such situations, some patients with Narcissistic Personality Disorder (NPD) socially withdraw and feign false modesty and humility to mask their underlying grandiosity. Dysthymic and depressive disorders are common reactions to isolation and feelings of shame and inadequacy.

The interpersonal relationships of patients with Narcissistic Personality Disorder (NPD) are typically impaired due to their lack of empathy, disregard for others, exploitativeness, sense of entitlement, and constant need for attention (Narcissistic Supply).

Though often ambitious and capable, inability to tolerate setbacks, disagreement, and criticism make it difficult for patients with Narcissistic Personality Disorder (NPD) to work in a team or to maintain long-term professional achievements. The narcissist's fantastic grandiosity, frequently coupled with a hypomanic mood, is typically incommensurate with his or her real accomplishments (the "Grandiosity Gap").

Patients with Narcissistic Personality Disorder (NPD) are either "cerebral" (derive their Narcissistic Supply from their intelligence or academic achievements) or "somatic" (derive their Narcissistic Supply from their physique, exercise, physical or sexual prowess and romantic or physical "conquests").

Patients with Narcissistic Personality Disorder (NPD) are either "classic" (meet five of the nine diagnostic criteria included in the DSM), or they are "compensatory" (their narcissism compensates for deep-set feelings of inferiority and lack of self-worth).

Some narcissists are covert, or inverted narcissists. As co-dependents, they derive their Narcissistic Supply from their relationships with classic narcissists.

Treatment and Prognosis

The common treatment for patients with Narcissistic Personality Disorder (NPD) is talk therapy (mainly psychodynamic psychotherapy or cognitive-behavioural treatment modalities). Talk therapy is used to modify the narcissist's antisocial, interpersonally exploitative, and dysfunctional behaviours, often with some success. Medication is prescribed to control and ameliorate attendant conditions such as mood disorders or obsessive-compulsive disorders.

The prognosis for an adult suffering from the Narcissistic Personality Disorder (NPD) is poor, though his adaptation to life and to others can improve with treatment.

40

Bibliography

1. Alford, C. Fred. Narcissism: Socrates, the Frankfurt School and Psychoanalytic Theory. New Haven and London, Yale University Press, 1988
2. Devereux, George. Basic Problems of Ethno-Psychiatry. University of Chicago Press, 1980
3. Fairbairn, W. R. D. An Object Relations Theory of the Personality. New York, Basic Books, 1954
4. Freud S. Three Essays on the Theory of Sexuality (1905). Standard Edition of the Complete Psychological Works of Sigmund Freud. Vol. 7. London, Hogarth Press, 1964
5. Freud, S. On Narcissism. Standard Ed. Vol. 14, p. 73-107
6. Gelder, Michael, Gath, Dennis, Mayou, Richard, Cowen, Philip (eds.). Oxford Textbook of Psychiatry, third edition, 1996, reprinted 2000. Oxford University Press, Oxford
7. Goldman, Howard H. (Ed.). Review of General Psychiatry. 4th Ed. London, Prentice Hall International, 1995
8. Golomb, Elan. Trapped in the Mirror: Adult Children of Narcissists in Their Struggle for Self. Quill, 1995
9. Greenberg, Jay R. and Mitchell, Stephen A. Object Relations in Psychoanalytic Theory. Cambridge, Mass., Harvard University Press, 1983
10. Grunberger, Bela. Narcissism: Psychoanalytic Essays. New York, International Universities Press, 1979
11. Guntrip, Harry. Personality Structure and Human Interaction. New York, International Universities Press, 1961
12. Horowitz M. J. Sliding Meanings: A Defence against Threat in Narcissistic Personalities. International Journal of Psychoanalytic Psychotherapy, 1975; 4:167
13. Horovitz M. J. Stress Response Syndromes: PTSD, Grief and Adjustment Disorders. 3rd Ed. New York, NY University Press, 1998

14. Jacobson, Edith. The Self and the Object World. New York, International Universities Press, 1964
15. Jung, C.G. Collected Works. G. Adler, M. Fordham and H. Read (Eds.). 21 volumes. Princeton University Press, 1960-1983
16. Kernberg O. Borderline Conditions and Pathological Narcissism. New York, Jason Aronson, 1975
17. Klein, Melanie. The Writings of Melanie Klein. Roger Money-Kyrle (Ed.). 4 Vols. New York, Free Press, 1964-75
18. Kohut H. The Chicago Institute Lectures 1972-1976. Marian and Paul Tolpin (Eds.). Analytic Press, 1998
19. Kohut M. The Analysis of the Self. New York, International Universities Press, 1971
20. Lasch, Christopher. The Culture of Narcissism. New York, Warner Books, 1979
21. Levine, J. D., and Weiss, Rona H. The Dynamics and Treatment of Alcoholism. Jason Aronson, 1994
22. Lowen, Alexander. Narcissism: Denial of the True Self. Touchstone Books, 1997
23. Millon, Theodore (and Roger D. Davis, contributor). Disorders of Personality: DSM-IV and Beyond. 2nd ed. New York, John Wiley and Sons, 1995
24. Millon, Theodore. Personality Disorders in Modern Life. New York, John Wiley and Sons, 2000
25. Riso, Don Richard. Personality Types: Using the Enneagram for Self-Discovery. Boston: Houghton Mifflin 1987
26. Roningstam, Elsa F. (Ed.). Disorders of Narcissism: Diagnostic, Clinical, and Empirical Implications. American Psychiatric Press, 1998
27. Rothstein, Arnold. The Narcissistic Pursuit of Reflection. 2nd revised Ed. New York, International Universities Press, 1984
28. Schwartz, Lester. Narcissistic Personality Disorders – A Clinical Discussion. Journal of American Psychoanalytic Association – 22 (1974): 292-305
29. Salant-Schwartz, Nathan. Narcissism and Character Transformation. Inner City Books, 1985 – p. 90-91
30. Stern, Daniel. The Interpersonal World of the Infant: A View from Psychoanalysis and Developmental Psychology. New York, Basic Books, 1985
31. Vaknin, Sam. Malignant Self-Love – Narcissism Revisited. Skopje and Prague, Narcissus Publications, 1999-2007
32. Zweig, Paul. The Heresy of Self-Love: A Study of Subversive Individualism. New York, Basic Books, 1968

Malignant Self Love

Narcissism Revisited

Frequently Asked Questions

The Narcissist's Poor Prognosis

Question: What makes a narcissist tick?

Answer: Therapy, in most cases, cannot cure the Narcissistic Personality Disorder (NPD), only mitigate and ameliorate the condition by modifying some of the narcissist's behaviours.

Only narcissists, who go through a severe life crisis, tend to consider the possibility of therapy at all. When they attend the therapeutic sessions, they, usually, bring all their rigid defence mechanisms to the fore. The therapy quickly becomes a tedious - and useless - affair for both therapist and patient.

45

Most cerebral narcissists are very intelligent. They base their grandiose fantasies on this natural advantage. When faced with a reasoned analysis, which shows that they suffer from NPD, most of them accept and acknowledge the new information. But first they have to face it - and this is the difficult part: they all are deniers of reality.

Moreover, cognitively assimilating the information is a mere process of labelling. It has no psychodynamic effect. It does not affect the narcissist's behaviour patterns and interactions with his human environment. These are the products of well-entrenched and rigid mental mechanisms.

Narcissists are pathological liars. This means that they are either unaware of their lies - or feel completely justified and at ease when lying to others. Often, they believe their own confabulations and attribute to them "retroactive veracity". The very essence of the narcissist is a huge, contrived, lie: his FALSE Self, his grandiose FANTASIES, and his IDEALIZED objects.

Personality disorders are adaptive. This means that they help to resolve mental conflicts and the anxiety, which, normally, accompanies them.

Narcissists sometimes contemplate suicide (suicidal ideation) when they go through a crisis - but they are not very likely to follow through.

Narcissists are, in a way, sadists. They are likely to use verbal and psychological abuse and violence against their closest, nearest and "dearest".

The Narcissistic Personality Disorder (NPD) is a newcomer to the zoo of mental disorders. It was not fully defined and described until the late 1980's. The discussion, analysis and study of narcissism are as old as psychology - but there is a great difference between being a "mere" narcissist and having a Narcissistic Personality Disorder (NPD). So, it is not clear how widespread this particular personality disorder is - or, even, how widespread personality disorders are (recent estimates range between 3 and 15% of the population).

46

Pathological Narcissism
A Dysfunction or a Blessing?

Is pathological narcissism a blessing or a malediction?

The answer is: it depends. Healthy narcissism is a mature, balanced love of oneself coupled with a stable sense of self-worth and self-esteem. Healthy narcissism implies knowledge of one's boundaries and a proportionate and realistic appraisal of one's achievements and traits. Pathological narcissism is wrongly described as too much healthy narcissism (or too much self-esteem). Yet, these are two absolutely unrelated phenomena which, regrettably, came to bear the same name. Confusing pathological narcissism with healthy self-esteem betrays a fundamental ignorance of both.

Pathological narcissism involves an impaired, dysfunctional, immature (True) Self coupled with a compensatory fiction (the False Self). The sick narcissist's sense of self-worth and self-esteem derive entirely from audience feedback. The narcissist has no self-esteem or self-worth of his own (no such ego functions). In the absence of observers, the narcissist shrivels to non-existence and feels dead. Hence the narcissist's preying habits in his constant pursuit of Narcissistic Supply. Pathological narcissism is an addictive behaviour.

Still, dysfunctions are reactions to abnormal environments and situations (e.g., abuse, trauma, smothering, etc.).

Paradoxically, his dysfunction allows the narcissist to function. It compensates for his lacks, deficits, and deficiencies by exaggerating certain tendencies and traits. It is like the overdeveloped tactile sense of a blind person. In short: pathological narcissism is a result of over-sensitivity, the repression of overwhelming memories and experiences, and the suppression of inordinately strong negative feelings (e.g., hurt, envy, anger, or humiliation).

47

That the narcissist functions at all is because of his pathology
d thanks to it. The alternative is complete decompensation
d integration.

n time, the narcissist learns how to leverage his pathology,
w to use it to his advantage, how to deploy it in order to max-
ze benefits and utilities - in other words, how to transform
curse into a blessing.

Narcissists are obsessed with delusions of fantastic grandeur
and superiority. As a result they are very competitive. They are
strongly compelled - where others are merely motivated. They
are driven, relentless, tireless, and ruthless. They often make it
to the top. But even when they do not, they strive and fight and
learn and climb and create and think and devise and design and
conspire. Faced with a challenge, they are likely to do better
than non-narcissists.

Yet, we often find that narcissists abandon their efforts in
mid-stream, give up, vanish, lose interest, devalue former pursuits, or slump. Why is that?

Coping with a challenge, even with a guaranteed eventual triumph is meaningless in the absence of onlookers. The narcissist
needs an audience to applaud, affirm, recoil, approve, admire,
adore, fear, or even detest him. He craves the attention and
depends on the Narcissistic Supply only others can provide. The
narcissist derives sustenance only from the outside - his emotional innards are hollow and moribund.

The narcissist's enhanced performance is predicated on the
existence of a challenge (real or imaginary) and of an audience.

First published on the Suite 101 Narcissistic Personality Disorders Topic.

The Energy of Self

Question: The narcissists I know appear to be very lazy and laid-back. Is this part of the pathology?

Answer: The personality is not a static structure which immutably permeates our being. It is a dynamic, on-going, process. It is a series of cognitive and emotional interactions compounded by extraneous input and endogenous feedback. It is ever-evolving, though, following our formative years, all subsequent changes are subtle and infinitesimal. This labyrinthine **49** complex of reactions, behaviour patterns, beliefs, and defence mechanisms consumes a lot of psychic energy. The more primitive the personality, the less organized, the more disordered, the greater the amount of energy required to maintain it in a semblance of balance, however precarious.

The predicament of the narcissist, the histrionic, and the borderline is even more multifarious. People suffering from these all-pervasive and pernicious personality disorders externalize most of their available energy in an effort to secure Narcissistic Supply and, thus, regulate a vicissitudinal sense of self-worth.

Normally, one's energy is expended on the proper functioning of one's personality. The personality disordered devote any shred of vitality to the projection and maintenance of a False Self, whose sole purpose is to elicit attention, admiration, approval, acknowledgement, fear, or adulation from others. The Narcissistic Supply thus obtained helps these unfortunates to calibrate a wildly fluctuating self-esteem and, thus, fulfils critical ego functions.

Yet, the constant pursuit of this drug, the need to stay permanently attuned to one's human environment and to manipulate it ceaselessly, inevitably depletes the narcissist's vigour. His emotional exoskeleton - derived and Sisyphically constructed from the outside - is far more demanding than the normal endoskeletons that healthy people possess. To borrow from Freud, we can say that the narcissist sublimates his libido. He is an artist with himself as his sole work. His entire energy is committed to the theatre production that is his False Self.

Hence the narcissist's constant fatigue and ennui, his short attention span, his tendency to devalue Sources of Supply, even his transformed aggression.

The narcissist can afford to dedicate resources only to the most promising founts of Narcissistic Supply. The "path of least investment" - criminal shortcuts, violence, cheating, con-artistry, lies and confabulations - is always preferred by the narcissist because his ŭlan is so run down, his vitality so drenched, and his verve so exhausted by the unusual need to secure from the outside what most people effortlessly produce internally and take for granted.

First published on the Suite 101 Narcissistic Personality Disorders Topic.

Self-Love and Narcissism

Question: What is the difference between self-love and narcissism and how does it affect the capacity to love others?

Answer: There are two differences between healthy self-love and pathological narcissism: (a) in the ability to tell reality from fantasy, and (b) in the ability to empathize and, indeed, to fully and maturely love others. As we said, the narcissist does not love himself because he has very little True Self to love. Instead, a monstrous, malignant construct - the False Self - encroaches upon his True Self and devours it.

The narcissist loves an image which he projects onto others who reflect it to the narcissist (the False Self). This process reassures the narcissist of both the objective existence of his False Self and of the boundaries of his Ego. It blurs all distinctions between reality and fantasy.

The False Self leads to false assumptions and to a contorted personal narrative, to a false worldview, and to a grandiose, inflated sense of being. The latter is rarely grounded in real achievements or merit. The narcissist's feeling of entitlement is all-pervasive, demanding and aggressive. It easily deteriorates into open verbal, psychological and physical abuse of others.

Maintaining a distinction between who we really are and what we dream of becoming, knowing our limits, our advantages and faults and having a sense of true, realistic accomplishments in our life are of paramount importance in the establishment and maintenance of our self-esteem, sense of self-worth and self-confidence.

Reliant as he is on outside judgement, the narcissist feels miserably inferior and dependent. He rebels against this degrading state of things by escaping into a world of make-belief, day-dreaming, pretensions and delusions of grandeur. The narcissist knows little about himself and finds what he does know to be unacceptable.

Our familiarity with what it is like to be human - our very humanness - depends largely on our self-knowledge and on our experience of our selves. In other words: only through being oneself and through experiencing one's self can one fully appreciate the humanness of others.

The narcissist has precious little experience of his self. Instead, he lives in an invented world, of his own design, where he is a fictitious figure in a grandiose script. He, therefore, possesses no tools to enable him to cope with other human beings, share their emotions, put himself in their place (empathize) and, of course, love them - the most demanding task of inter-personal-relating.

The narcissist just does not know what it means to be human. He is a predator, rapaciously preying on others for the satisfaction of his narcissistic cravings and appetites for admiration, adoration, applause, affirmation and attention. Humans are Narcissistic Supply Sources and are (over- or de-) valued according to their contributions to this end.

Self-love is a precondition for the experience and expression of mature love. One cannot truly love someone else if one does not first love one's True Self. If we have never loved ourselves, we have never experienced unconditional love and, therefore, we do not know how to love.

If we keep living in a world of fantasy - how could we notice the very real people around us who ask for our love and who deserve it? The narcissist wants to love. In his rare moments of self-awareness, he feels ego-dystonic (unhappy with his situation and with his relationships with others). This is his predicament: he is sentenced to isolation precisely because his need of other people is so great.

Inner Dialog, Cognitive Deficits, and Introjects in Narcissism

"Man can will nothing unless he has first understood that he must count no one but himself; that he is alone, abandoned on earth in the midst of his infinite responsibilities, without help, with no other aim than the one he sets himself, with no other destiny than the one he forges for himself on this earth."

[Jean Paul Sartre, Being and Nothingness, 1943]

The narcissist lacks empathy. He is, therefore, unable to meaningfully relate to other people and to truly appreciate what it is to be human. Instead, he withdraws inside, into a universe populated by avatars - simple or complex representations of parents, peers, role models, authority figures, and other members of his social milieu. There, in this twilight zone of simulacra, he develops "relationships" and maintains an on-going internal dialog with them.

All of us generate such representations of meaningful others and internalize these objects. In a process called introjection, we adopt, assimilate, and, later, manifest their traits and attitudes (the introjects).

But the narcissist is different. He is incapable of holding an external dialog. Even when he seems to be interacting with someone else - the narcissist is actually engaged in a self-referential discourse. To the narcissist, all other people are cardboard cut-outs, two dimensional animated cartoon characters, or symbols. They exist only in his mind. He is startled when they deviate from the script and prove to be complex and autonomous.

But this is not the narcissist's sole cognitive deficit.

The narcissist attributes his failures and mistakes to circumstances and external causes. This propensity to blame the world for one's mishaps and misfortunes is called "alloplastic defence". At the same time, the narcissist regards his successes and achievements (some of which are imaginary) as proofs of his omnipotence and omniscience. This is known in attribution theory as "defensive attribution".

Conversely, the narcissist traces other people's errors and defeats to their inherent inferiority, stupidity, and weakness. Their successes he dismisses as "being in the right place at the right time" - i.e., the outcome of luck and circumstance.

Thus, the narcissist falls prey to an exaggerated form of what is known in attribution theory as the "fundamental attribution error". Moreover, these fallacies and the narcissist's magical thinking are not dependent on objective data and tests of distinctiveness, consistency, and consensus.

The narcissist never questions his reflexive judgements and never stops to ask himself: are these events distinct or are they typical? Do they repeat themselves consistently or are they unprecedented? And what do others have to say about them?

The narcissist learns nothing because he regards himself as born perfect. Even when he fails a thousand times, the narcissist still feels the victim of happenstance. And someone else's repeated outstanding accomplishments are never proof of mettle or merit. People who disagree with the narcissist and try to teach him differently are, to his mind, biased or morons or both.

But the narcissist pays a dear price for these distortions of perception. Unable to gauge his environment with accuracy, he develops paranoid ideation and fails the reality test. Finally, he lifts the drawbridges and vanishes into a state of mind that can best be described as borderline psychosis.

[First published on the Suite 101 Narcissistic Personality Disorders Topic]

Self-Defeating and Self-Destructive Behaviours

Question: The narcissist often engages in self-defeating and self-destructive behaviours. Can you tell me more about it?

Answer: The narcissist is besieged and tormented by a sadistic Superego which sits in constant judgement. It is an amalgamation of negative evaluations, criticisms, angry or disappointed voices, and disparagement meted out in the narcissist's formative years and adolescence by parents, peers, role models, and authority figures.

These harsh and repeated comments reverberate throughout the narcissist's inner landscape, berating him for failing to conform to his unattainable ideals, fantastic goals, and grandiose or impractical plans. The narcissist's sense of self-worth is, therefore, catapulted from one pole to another: from an inflated view of himself (incommensurate with real life accomplishments) to utter despair and self-denigration.

Hence the narcissist's need for Narcissistic Supply to regulate this wild pendulum. People's adulation, admiration, affirmation, and attention restore the narcissist's self-esteem and self-confidence.

The narcissist's sadistic and uncompromising Superego affects three facets of his personality:

1. The narcissist's sense of self-worth and worthiness (the deeply ingrained conviction that one deserves love, compassion, care, and empathy regardless of what one achieves). The narcissist feels worthless without Narcissistic Supply.

2. The narcissist's self-esteem (self-knowledge, the deeply ingrained and realistic appraisal of one's capacities, skills, limitations, and shortcomings). The narcissist lacks clear

boundaries and, therefore, is not sure of his abilities and weaknesses. Hence his grandiose fantasies.

3. The narcissist's self-confidence (the deeply ingrained belief, based on lifelong experience, that one can set realistic goals and accomplish them). The narcissist knows that he is a fake and a fraud. He, therefore, does not trust his ability to manage his own affairs and to set practical aims and realize them.

By becoming a success (or at least by appearing to have become one) the narcissist hopes to quell the voices inside him that constantly question his veracity and aptitude. The narcissist's whole life is a two-fold attempt to both satisfy the inexorable demands of his inner tribunal and to prove wrong its harsh and merciless criticism.

It is this dual and self-contradictory mission, to conform to the edicts of his internal enemies and to prove their very judgement wrong, that is at the root of the narcissist's unresolved conflicts.

On the one hand, the narcissist accepts the authority of his introjected (internalized) critics and disregards the fact that they hate him and wish him dead. He sacrifices his life to them, hoping that his successes and accomplishments (real or perceived) will ameliorate their rage.

On the other hand, he confronts these very gods with proofs of their fallibility. "You claim that I am worthless and incapable" - he cries - "Well, guess what? You are dead wrong! Look how famous I am, look how rich, how revered, and accomplished!"

But then much rehearsed self-doubt sets in and the narcissist feels yet again compelled to falsify the claims of his trenchant and indefatigable detractors by conquering another woman, giving one more interview, taking over yet another firm, making an extra million, or getting re-elected one more time.

To no avail. The narcissist is his own worst foe. Ironically, it is only when incapacitated that the narcissist gains a modicum of peace of mind. When terminally ill, incarcerated, or inebriated the narcissist can shift the blame for his failures and predicaments to outside agents and objective forces over which he has no control. "It's not my fault" - he gleefully informs his mental tormentors - "There was nothing I could do about it! Now, go away and leave me be."

And then - with the narcissist defeated and broken - they do and he is free at last.

We can group the narcissist's self-destructive and self-defeating behaviours according to their underlying motivation:

The Self-Punishing, Guilt-Purging Behaviours

Akin to compulsive rituals, these behaviours are intended to inflict punishment on the narcissist and thus instantly relieve him of his overwhelming anxiety.

The narcissist feels guilty. It could be an "ancient", early childhood, guilt, a "sexual" guilt (Freud), or a "social" guilt. In his infancy, the narcissist internalizes and introjects the voices of meaningful and authoritative others - parents, role models, peers, and authority figures - that consistently and convincingly judge him to be no good, blameworthy, deserving of punishment or retaliation, or corrupt.

The narcissist's life is thus transformed into an on-going trial. The constancy of this trial, the never adjourning tribunal IS the punishment. It is a Kafkaesque "process": meaningless, undecipherable and never-ending. It leads to no verdict, is subject to mysterious and fluid laws and presided over by a capricious tribunal.

Such a narcissist masochistically frustrates his deepest desires and drives, obstructs his own efforts, alienates his friends and sponsors, provokes figures of authority to punish, demote, or ignore him, actively seeks and solicits disappointment, failure, or mistreatment and relishes them, incites anger or rejection, bypasses or rejects opportunities, or engages in excessive self-sacrifice.

In their book "Personality Disorders in Modern Life", Theodore Millon and Roger Davis, describe the diagnosis of Masochistic or Self-Defeating Personality Disorder, found in the appendix of the DSM-III-R but excluded from the DSM-IV. While the narcissist is rarely a full-fledged masochist, many a narcissist exhibit some of the traits of this proposed personality disorder.

The Extracting Behaviours

Narcissists are very afraid of real, mature, intimacy. Intimacy forms not only within a couple, but also in a workplace, in a neighbourhood, with friends, or while collaborating on a project. Intimacy is another word for emotional involvement, which is the result of interactions with others in constant and predictable (safe) propinquity.

Narcissists interpret intimacy as co-dependence, emotional strangulation, the snuffing of freedom, a kind of death in installments. They are terrorized by it. To avoid it, their self-destructive and self-defeating acts are intended to dismantle the very foundation of a successful relationship, a career, a project, or a friendship. Narcissists feel elated and relieved after they unshackle these "chains". They feel that they broke a siege, that they are liberated, free at last.

The Default Behaviours

We are all, to some degree, inertial, somewhat intimidated by new situations, new opportunities, new challenges, new circumstances and new demands. Being successful, getting married, becoming a mother, or someone's boss often entail abrupt breaks with the past. Some self-defeating behaviours are intended to preserve the past, to restore it, to protect it from the winds of change, to self-deceptively skirt promising opportunities while seeming to embrace them.

Ideas of Reference

Question: My narcissist always suspects others of gossiping about him or mocking him. Is it paranoia?

Answer: The narcissist holds himself to be the centre of the world. He is not merely the centre of HIS world - as far as he can tell, he is the centre of THE world. This Archimedean delusion is one of the narcissist's most predominant and all-pervasive cognitive distortions. The narcissist feels certain that he is the source of all events around him, the origin of all the emotions of his nearest or dearest, the fount of all knowledge, both the first and the final causes, the beginning as well as the end.

59

The narcissist derives his sense of being, his experience of his own existence, and his self-worth from the outside. He mines others for Narcissistic Supply - adulation, attention, reflection, fear. Their reactions stalk his furnace. Absent Narcissistic Supply, the narcissist disintegrates and self-annihilates. When unnoticed, he feels empty and worthless. The narcissist MUST delude himself into believing that he is persistently the focus and object of the attentions, intentions, plans, feelings, and stratagems of other people. The narcissist faces a stark choice - either be (or become) the permanent centre of the world, or cease to be altogether.

This constant obsession with one's locus, with one's centrality, with one's position as a hub leads to referential ideation ("ideas of reference"). This is the conviction that one is at the receiving end of other people's behaviours, speech, and even thoughts. The person suffering from delusional ideas of reference is at the self-appointed centre of imaginary constant attention.

When people talk among themselves, the narcissist is convinced that he is the topic of discussion. When they quarrel - he is most probably the cause. When they smirk - he is the victim of their ridicule. If they are unhappy - he must have made them so. If they are happy - they are egotists for ignoring him. He is convinced that his behaviour is continuously monitored, criticized, compared, dissected, approved of, or imitated by others. He deems himself so indispensable and important, such a pivotal component of other people's lives, that his every act, his every word, his every omission - is bound to upset, hurt, uplift, or satisfy his audience.

And, to the narcissist, everyone is a member of his audience. Everything emanates from him and reverts to him. The narcissist's is a circular and closed universe. His ideas of reference are a natural extension of his primitive defence mechanisms (omnipotence, omniscience, omnipresence, projection, and narcissism).

Being omnipresent explains why everyone, everywhere is concerned with him. Being omnipotent and omniscient renders him the sole deserving recipient of the admiration, adulation, and attention of people.

Yet, the attrition afforded by years of tormenting ideas of reference inevitably yields paranoiac thinking.

To preserve his egocentric cosmology, the narcissist is compelled to attribute fitting motives and psychological dynamics to **60** others. Such motives and dynamics have little to do with reality. They are PROJECTED by the narcissist UNTO others so as to maintain his personal mythology.

In other words, the narcissist attributes to others and projects onto them HIS OWN motives and psychodynamics. Since narcissists are mostly besieged by transformations of aggression (rage, hatred, envy, fear), these they often ascribe to others as well. Thus, the narcissist tends to interpret other people's behaviour as motivated by anger, fear, hatred, or envy and as directed at him or revolving around him. The narcissist (often erroneously) believes that people discuss him, gossip about him, hate him, defame him, mock him, berate him, underestimate him, envy him, or fear him. He is (often rightly) convinced that he is, to others, the source of hurt, humiliation, impropriety, and indignation. The narcissist "knows" that he is a wonderful, powerful, talented, and entertaining person - but this only explains why people are so jealous of him and why they seek to undermine and destroy him.

Thus, since the narcissist is unable to secure the long-term love, admiration, or even attention of his Sources of Supply, he resorts to a mirror strategy - he becomes paranoid. Better to be the object of (often imaginary and always self-inflicted) derision, scorn, and bile than to be ignored. Being envied is preferable to being treated with indifference. If he cannot be loved, the narcissist would rather be feared or hated. His biggest nightmare is to be forgotten or ignored.

First published on the Suite 101 Narcissistic Personality Disorders Topic.

Grandiose Fantasies

Question: What happens to a narcissist who lacks even the basic potential and skills to realize some of his grandiose fantasies?

Answer: Such a narcissist resorts to deferred Narcissistic Supply which generates an effect of deferred grandiosity. He forgoes his grandiose schemes and gives up on the present. He supports his inflated Ego by postponing the fulfilment of his fantasies to the (indefinite) future.

Such narcissists engage in activities (or in daydreaming), which they fervently believe, will make them famous, powerful, influential, or superior in some unspecified future time. These keep their minds occupied and off their failures.

Such frustrated and bitter narcissists hold themselves answerable only to History, God, Eternity, Future Generations, Art, Science, the Church, the Country, the Nation and so on. They entertain notions of grandeur which are dependent upon the judgement or assessment of a fuzzily defined collective in an unspecified future. Thus, these narcissists find solace in the embrace of Chronos.

Deferred grandiosity is an adaptive mechanism which ameliorates dysphorias and Grandiosity Gaps. [See the next chapters for more on these]

It is healthy to daydream and fantasize. It is the antechamber of life and often anticipates its circumstances. It is a process of preparing for eventualities. But healthy daydreaming is different from grandiosity.

Grandiosity has four components:

Omnipotence

The narcissist believes in his omnipotence. "Believes" in this context is a weak word. The narcissist knows that he is omnipo-

62

tent. It is a cellular, biological, certainty, it flows in his blood and permeates every niche of his being. The narcissist "knows" that he can do anything he chooses to do and excel in it. What the narcissist does, what he excels at, what he achieves, depends only on his volition. To his mind, there is no other determinant.

Hence his rage when confronted with disagreement or opposition - not only because of the audacity of his, evidently inferior, adversaries. But because it threatens his world view, it challenges his feeling of omnipotence. The narcissist is often fatuously daring, adventurous, experimental and curious precisely due to this hidden assumption of "can-do". He is genuinely surprised and devastated when he fails, when the "universe" does not arrange itself, magically, to accommodate his unbounded fantasies, when the world (and people in it) does not comply with his whims and wishes.

He often denies away such discrepancies, deletes them from his memory. As a result of these selective erasures, the narcissist remembers his life as a patchy quilt of unrelated events and people.

Omniscience

63 The narcissist often pretends to know everything, in every field of human knowledge and endeavour.

"deception" He lies and prevaricates to avoid the exposure of his ignorance. He resorts to numerous subterfuges to support his God-like omniscience.

Where his knowledge fails him, he feigns authority, fakes superiority, quotes from non-existent sources, weaves threads of truth in a canvass of falsehoods. He transforms himself into an artist of intellectual prestidigitation. As he gets older, this invidious quality may recede, or, rather, metamorphose. He may now claim more limited (but deeper) expertise.

He may no longer be ashamed to admit his ignorance and his need to learn things outside the fields of his real or self-proclaimed knowledge. But this "improvement" is merely optical. Within his self-appropriated intellectual "territory", the narcissist is still as fiercely defensive and possessive as ever.

Many narcissists are avowed autodidacts, unwilling to subject their knowledge and insights to peer scrutiny, or, for that matter, to any scrutiny. The narcissist keeps re-inventing himself, adding new fields of knowledge as he goes. This creeping intellectual annexation is a round about way of reverting to his erstwhile image as the erudite "Renaissance man".

Omnipresence

Even the narcissist cannot pretend to actually physically be everywhere at once. Instead, he feels that he is the centre and the axis of his "universe", that all things and happenstances revolve around him, and that cosmic disintegration would ensue if he were to disappear or to lose interest in someone or in something.

The narcissist is convinced, for instance, that he is the main, if not the only, topic of conversation in his absence. He is often surprised and offended to learn that he was not even mentioned. When invited to a meeting with many participants, he assumes the position of the sage, the guru, or the teacher/guide whose words carry a special weight. His creations (books, articles, works of art) are widely-distributed and copied extensions of his self and, in this restricted sense, he does seem to exist everywhere. In other words, through his creative endeavours, the narcissist "stamps" his environment. He "leaves his mark" upon it. He "stigmatizes" it.

Narcissist the Omnivore
(Perfectionism and Completeness)

There is another "omni" component in grandiosity. The narcissist is an omnivore. He devours and digests experiences and people, sights and smells, bodies and words, books and films, sounds and achievements, his work and his leisure, his pleasure and his possessions. The narcissist is incapable of ENJOYING anything because he is in constant pursuit of perfection and completeness.

Classic narcissists interact with the world as predators do with their prey. They want to own it all, be everywhere, to experience everything. They cannot delay gratification. They do not take "no" for an answer. And they settle for nothing less than the ideal, the sublime, the perfect, the all-inclusive, the all-encompassing, the engulfing, the all-pervasive, the most beautiful, the cleverest, the richest, and the most brilliant.

The narcissist is shattered when he discovers that a collection he possesses is incomplete, that his colleague's wife is more glamorous, that his son is better than he is in math, that his neighbour has a new, flashy car, that his roommate got promoted, that the "love of his life" signed a recording contract. It is not plain old jealousy, not even pathological envy (though these are definitely a part of the psychological makeup of the narcissist). It is the discovery that the narcissist is NOT perfect, or ideal, or complete that does him in.

Ask anyone who shared a life with a narcissist, or knew one and they are likely to sigh: "What a waste". Waste of potential, waste of opportunities, waste of emotions, a wasteland of arid addiction and futile pursuit.

Narcissists are as gifted as they come. The problem is to disentangle their tales of fantastic grandiosity from the reality of their talents and skills. They always either over-estimate or devalue their potency. They often emphasize the wrong traits and invest in their mediocre or less than average capacities at the expense of their true and promising potential. Thus, they squander their advantages and under-rate their natural gifts.

The narcissist decides which aspects of his self to nurture and which to neglect. He gravitates towards activities commensurate with his pompous auto-portrait. He suppresses these tendencies and aptitudes in him which don't conform to his inflated view of his own uniqueness, brilliance, might, sexual prowess, or standing in society. He cultivates these flairs and predilections which he regards as befitting his overweening self-image and ultimate grandeur.

But, the narcissist, no matter how self-aware and well-meaning, is accursed. His grandiosity, his fantasies, the compelling, overriding urge to feel unique, invested with some cosmic significance, unprecedentedly bestowed - these thwart his best intentions. These structures of obsession and compulsion, these deposits of insecurity and pain, the stalactites and stalagmites of years of abuse and then abandonment, they all conspire to frustrate the gratification, however circumspect, of the narcissist's true nature.

An utter lack of self-awareness is typical of the narcissist. He is intimate only with his False Self, constructed meticulously from years of lying and deceit. The narcissist's True Self is stashed, dilapidated and dysfunctional, in the furthest recesses of his mind. The False Self is omnipotent, omniscient, omnipresent, creative, ingenious, irresistible, and glowing. The real narcissist - the True Self - often isn't.

Add combustible paranoia to the narcissist's divorce from himself, and his constant and recurrent failure to assess reality accurately becomes more understandable. The narcissist's overpowering sense of entitlement is rarely commensurate with his real life accomplishments or with his traits or skills. When the world fails to comply with his demands and to support his grandiose fantasies, the narcissist suspects a plot against him by his inferiors.

The narcissist rarely admits to a weakness, an ignorance, or a deficiency. He filters out information that contradicts his self-image - a cognitive impairment with serious consequences. Narcissists are likely to unflinchingly make inflated and inane claims about their sexual prowess, wealth, connections, history, or achievements.

All this is mighty embarrassing to the narcissist's nearest, dearest, colleagues, friends, neighbours, or even mere onlookers. The narcissist's tales are so patently absurd that he often catches people off-guard. Behind his back, the narcissist is derided and mockingly imitated. He fast makes a nuisance and an imposition of himself in every company.

But the narcissist's failure of the reality test can have more serious and irreversible consequences. Narcissists, unqualified to make life-and-death decisions often insist on rendering them. Narcissists pretend to be economists, engineers, or medical doctors when they are not. But they are not con-artists in the classic, premeditated sense. They firmly believe that, though self-taught at best, they are more qualified than even the properly accredited sort. Narcissists believe in magic and in fantasy. They are no longer with us.

Grandiosity Bubbles

As one Source of Narcissistic Supply dwindles, the narcissist finds himself trapped in a frantic (though, at times, unconscious) effort to secure alternatives. As one Pathological Narcissistic Space (the narcissist's stomping grounds) is rendered "uninhabitable" (too many people "see through" the narcissist's manipulation and machinations) - the narcissist wanders off to find another.

These hysterical endeavours sometimes lead to boom-bust cycles which involve, in the first stage, the formation of a Grandiosity Bubble.

A Grandiosity Bubble is an imagined, self-aggrandising, narrative involving the narcissist and elements from his real life: people around him, places he frequents, or conversations he is having. The narcissist weaves a story incorporating these facts, inflating them in the process and endowing them with bogus internal meaning and consistency. In other words: he confabulates - but, this time, his confabulation is loosely based on reality.

In the process, the narcissist re-invents himself and his life to fit the new-fangled tale. He re-casts himself in newly adopted roles. He suddenly fancies himself an actor, a guru, a political activist, an entrepreneur, or an irresistible hunk. He modifies his behaviour to conform to these new functions. He gradually morphs into the fabricated character and "becomes" the fictitious protagonist he has created.

All the mechanisms of pathological narcissism are at work during the bubble phase. The narcissist idealizes the situation, the other "actors", and the environment. He tries to control and manipulate his milieu into buttressing his false notions and perceptions. Faced with an inevitable Grandiosity Gap, he becomes disillusioned and bitter and devalues and discards the people, places, and circumstances involved in the bubble.

Still, Grandiosity Bubbles are not part of the normal narcissistic mini-cycle. They are rare events, much like trying on a new outfit for size and comfort. They fizzle out rapidly and the narcissist reverts to his regular pattern: idealizing new Sources of Supply, devaluing and discarding them, pursuing the next victims to be drained of emotional energy.

Actually, the deflation of a Grandiosity Bubble is met with relief by the narcissist. It does not involve a narcissistic injury. The narcissist views the bubble as merely an experiment at being someone else for a while. It is a safety valve, allowing the narcissist to effectively cope with negative emotions and frustration. Thus cleansed, the narcissist can go back to doing what he does best: projecting a False Self and garnering attention from others.

[First published on the Suite 101 Narcissistic Personality Disorders Topic]

The Narcissist's Confabulated Life

Confabulations are an important part of life. They serve to heal emotional wounds or to prevent ones from being inflicted in the first place. They prop-up the confabulator's self-esteem, regulate his (or her) sense of self-worth, and buttress his (or her) self-image. They serve as organizing principles in social interactions. Father's wartime heroism, mother's youthful good looks, one's oft-recounted exploits, erstwhile alleged brilliance, and past purported sexual irresistibility are typical examples of white, fuzzy, heart-warming lies wrapped around a shrivelled kernel of truth.

But the distinction between reality and fantasy is rarely completely lost. Deep inside, the healthy confabulator knows where facts end and wishful thinking takes over. Father acknowledges he was no war hero, though he did his share of fighting. Mother understands she was no ravishing beauty, though she may have been attractive. The confabulator realizes that his recounted exploits are overblown, his brilliance exaggerated, and his sexual irresistibility a myth.

Such distinctions never rise to the surface because everyone - the confabulator and his audience alike - have a common interest to maintain the confabulation. To challenge the integrity of the confabulator or the veracity of his confabulations is to threaten the very fabric of family and society. Human intercourse is built around such entertaining deviations from the truth.

This is where the narcissist differs from others (from "normal" people).

His very Self is a piece of fiction concocted to fend off hurt and to nurture the narcissist's grandiosity. The narcissist fails his "reality test": the ability to distinguish the actual from the imagined. He fervently believes in his own infallibility, brilliance, omnipotence, heroism, and perfection. He doesn't dare confront the truth and admit it even to himself.

Moreover, he imposes his personal mythology on his nearest and dearest. Spouse, children, colleagues, friends, neighbours - sometimes even perfect strangers - must abide by the narcissist's narrative or face his wrath. The narcissist countenances no disagreement, alternative points of view, or criticism. To him, confabulation IS reality.

The coherence of the narcissist's dysfunctional and precariously-balanced personality depends on the plausibility of his stories and on their acceptance by his Sources of Narcissistic Supply. The narcissist invests an inordinate time in substantiating his tales, collecting "evidence", defending his version of events, and in re-interpreting reality to fit his scenario. As a result, most narcissists are self-delusional, obstinate, opinionated, and argumentative.

The narcissist's lies are not goal-orientated. This is what makes his constant dishonesty both disconcerting and incomprehensible. The narcissist lies at the drop of a hat, needlessly, and almost ceaselessly. He lies in order to avoid the Grandiosity Gap - when the abyss between fact and (narcissistic) fiction becomes too gaping to ignore.

The narcissist lies in order to preserve appearances, uphold fantasies, support the tall (and impossible) tales of his False Self and extract Narcissistic Supply from unsuspecting sources, who are not yet on to him. To the narcissist, confabulation is not merely a way of life - it is life itself.

We are all conditioned to let other indulge in pet delusions and get away with white, not too egregious, lies. The narcissist

68

makes use of our socialization. We dare not confront or expose him, despite the outlandishness of his claims, the improbability of his stories, the implausibility of his alleged accomplishments and conquests. We meekly avert our eyes, often embarrassed.

Moreover, the narcissist makes clear, from the very beginning, that it is his way or the highway. His aggression - his violent streak - are close to the surface. He may be charming in a first encounter - but even then there are telltale signs of pent-up abuse. His interlocutors sense this impending threat and avoid conflict by acquiescing with the narcissist's fairy tales. Thus he imposes his private universe and virtual reality on his milieu - sometimes with disastrous consequences.

[First published on the Suite 101 Narcissistic Personality Disorders Topic]

Grandiosity Hangover
And Narcissist Baiting

Question: My mother doesn't want to grow up. She wears my stuff, flirts with my boyfriends, and insists on going out with us everywhere. What's wrong with her?

Answer: The grandiose fantasies of the narcissist inevitably and invariably clash with his drab, routine, and mundane reality. We call this constant dissonance the Grandiosity Gap. Sometimes the gap is so yawning that even the narcissist, however dimly, recognizes its existence. Still, this insight into his real situation fails to alter his behaviour. The narcissist knows that his grandiose fantasies are incommensurate with his accomplishments, knowledge, qualities, qualifications, skills, status, actual wealth (or lack thereof), physical constitution, or sex appeal - yet, he keeps behaving as though this were not the case.

The situation is further exacerbated by periods of relative success in the narcissist's past. Has-been and also-ran narcissists suffer from a Grandiosity Hangover. They may have once been rich, famous, powerful, brilliant, or sexually irresistible, but they no longer are. Still, they continue to behave as though little has changed.

The balding, potbellied, narcissist still courts women aggressively. The impoverished tycoon sinks deeper into debt, trying to maintain an unsustainable and lavish lifestyle. The one-novel author or one-discovery scholar still demands professional deference and expects attention by media and superiors. The once-potent politician maintains regal airs and holds court in great pomp. The wizened actress demands special treatment and throws temper tantrums when rebuffed. The ageing beauty wears her daughter's clothes and regresses emotionally as she progresses chronologically.

70

SAM VAKNIN   MALIGNANT SELF LOVE

Human collectives - firms, nations, clubs - develop Grandiosity Hangovers as easily and as frequently as do individuals. It is not uncommon to come across a group of people who still live in a bygone glorious past. This mass pathology is self-reinforcing. Members feed on each other's delusions, pretensions, and lies. Ostrich-like, they bury their collective head in the sands of time, harking back to happier moments of omnipotence, omniscience, and omnipresence.

The Grandiosity Hangover and the Grandiosity Gap are the two major vulnerabilities of the narcissist. By exploiting them, the narcissist can be effortlessly manipulated. This is especially true when the narcissist is confronted with authority, finds himself in an inferior position, or when his Narcissistic Supply is deficient or uncertain.

Abusing the Gullible Narcissist

"Such a one (the narcissist - SV) is encased, is he not, in an armour - such an armour! The armour of the crusaders was nothing to it - an armour of arrogance, of pride, of complete self-esteem. This armour, it is in some ways a protection, the arrows, the everyday arrows of life glance off it. But there is this danger; Sometimes a man in armour might not even know he was being attacked. He will be slow to see, slow to hear - slower still to feel."

["Dead Man's Mirror" by Agatha Christie in "Hercule Poirot - The Complete Short Stories", Great Britain, HarperCollins Publishers, 1999]

The irony is that narcissists, who consider themselves worldly, discerning, knowledgeable, shrewd, erudite, and astute are actually more gullible than the average person. This is because the narcissist is a fake. His self is false, his life a confabulation, his reality test gone. Narcissists live in a fantasy land all their own in which they are the centre of the universe, admired, feared, held in awe, and respected for their omnipotence and omniscience.

Narcissists are prone to magical thinking. They hold themselves immune to the consequences of their actions (or inaction) and, therefore, beyond punishment and the laws of Man. Narcissists are easily persuaded to assume unreasonable risks and expect miracles to happen. They often find themselves on the receiving end of investment scams, for instance.

Narcissists feel entitled to money, power, and honours incommensurate with their accomplishments or toil. The world, or God, or the nation, or society, or their families, co-workers, employers, even neighbours owe them a trouble-free, exalted, and luxurious existence. They are rudely shocked when they are penalized for their misconduct or when their fantasies remain just that.

The narcissist believes that he is destined to greatness - or at least the easy life. He wakes up every morning fully ready for a fortuitous stroke of luck. That explains the narcissist's reckless behaviours and his lazed lack of self-discipline. It also explains why he is so easily duped.

By playing on the narcissist's grandiosity and paranoia, it is possible to deceive and manipulate him effortlessly. Just offer him Narcissistic Supply - admiration, affirmation, adulation - and he is yours. Harp on his insecurities and his persecutory delusions, and he is likely to trust only you and cling to you for dear life.

Narcissists attract abuse. Haughty, exploitative, demanding, insensitive, and quarrelsome, they tend to draw opprobrium and provoke anger and even hatred. Sorely lacking in interpersonal skills, devoid of empathy, and steeped in irksome grandiose fantasies, they invariably fail to mitigate the irritation and revolt that they induce in others.

Successful narcissists are frequently targeted by erotomaniacs - usually mentally ill people who develop a fixation of a sexual and emotional nature on the narcissist. When these stalkers are inevitably rebuffed, they become vindictive and even violent.

Less prominent narcissists end up sharing life with co-dependents and inverted narcissists [see FAQ 50].

The narcissist's situation is exacerbated by the fact that, often, the narcissist himself is an abuser. Like the boy who cried "wolf", people do not believe that the perpetrator of egregious deeds can himself fall prey to maltreatment. They tend to ignore and discard the narcissist's cries for help and disbelieve his protestations.

The narcissist reacts to abuse as would any other victim. Traumatized, he goes through the phases of denial, helplessness, rage, depression, and acceptance. But, the narcissist's reactions are amplified by his shattered sense of omnipotence. Abuse breeds humiliation. To the narcissist, helplessness is a novel experience.

The narcissistic defence mechanisms and their behavioural manifestations - diffuse rage, idealization and devaluation, exploitation - are useless when confronted with a determined, vindictive, or delusional stalker. That the narcissist is flattered by the attention he receives from the abuser, renders him more vulnerable to the latter's manipulation.

SAM VAKNIN   MALIGNANT SELF LOVE

Nor can the narcissist come to terms with his need for help or acknowledge that wrongful behaviour on his part may have contributed somehow to the situation. His self-image as an infallible, mighty, all-knowing person, far superior to others, won't let him admit to shortfalls or mistakes.

As the abuse progresses, the narcissist feels increasingly cornered. His conflicting emotional needs - to preserve the integrity of his grandiose False Self even as he seeks much needed support - place an unbearable strain on the precarious balance of his immature personality. Decompensation (the disintegration of the narcissist's defence mechanisms) leads to acting out and, if the abuse is protracted, to withdrawal and even to psychotic micro-episodes.

First published on the Suite 101 Narcissistic Personality Disorders Topic.

Depression and the Narcissist

Question: My husband is a narcissist and is constantly depressed. Is there any connection between these two problems?

Answer: There is no proven high correlation between pathological narcissism and depression.

Depression is a form of aggression coupled with a self-defeating negative perception of oneself. Transformed, this aggression is directed at the depressed person rather than at his environment. This regime of repressed and mutated aggression is characteristic of both narcissism and depression.

Originally, the narcissist experiences "forbidden" thoughts and urges (sometimes to the point of an obsession). His mind is full of "dirty" words, curses, the remnants of magical thinking ("If I think or wish something it just might happen"), and denigrating and malicious thinking concerned with authority figures (mostly parents or teachers).

These are all proscribed by the narcissist's sadistic and capricious Superego (a result of the wrong kind of parenting). These thoughts and wishes do not fully surface. The individual is only aware of them in passing and vaguely. But they are sufficient to provoke intense guilt feelings and to set in motion a chain of self-flagellation and self-punishment.

The result is a constant feeling of imminent threat. This is what we call anxiety. It has no discernible external triggers and, therefore, it is unlike fear. It is the echo of a battle between one part of the personality, which viciously wishes to destroy the individual through excessive punishment and the individual's instinct of self-preservation.

Anxiety is not, as some scholars have it, an irrational reaction to internal dynamics involving imaginary threats and conflicts. Actually, anxiety is more rational than many fears. The powers

74

SAM VAKNIN   MALIGNANT SELF LOVE

unleashed by the Superego are so enormous, its intentions so fatal, the self-loathing and self-degradation that it brings with it so intense that the threat to the individual is real and the conflict ferocious.

The overly strict Superego is usually coupled with weaknesses and vulnerabilities in all other personality structures. Thus, there is no psychic structure able to fight back, to take the side of the depressed person. Small wonder that depressive patients manifest constant suicidal ideation (they toy with ideas of self-mutilation and suicide), or worse, commit such acts.

Confronted with a horrible internal enemy, lacking in defences, falling apart at the seams, depleted by previous inner turmoil, the depressed patient wishes himself dead. His anxiety is about survival, the alternatives being, usually, self-torture or self-annihilation.

Depression is how such people experience their overflowing reservoirs of aggression. They are like volcanoes, which are about to explode and bury them under their own ashes. Anxiety is how these patients experience the war raging inside them. Sadness is the name that they give to the resulting wariness, to the knowledge that the battle is lost and personal doom is at hand.

Depression is the acknowledgement by the depressed individual that something is so fundamentally wrong that there is no way he can win. The individual is depressed because he is fatalistic. As long as he believes that there is a chance, however slim, to better his position, he moves in and out of depressive episodes.

True, anxiety disorders and depression (mood disorders) do not belong in the same diagnostic category. But they are very often co-morbid. In many cases, the patient tries to exorcize his depressive demons by adopting ever more bizarre rituals. These are the compulsions, which - by diverting energy and attention away from the "bad" content in more or less symbolic (though totally arbitrary) ways, bring temporary relief and an easing of the anxiety. It is very common to come across all four: a mood disorder, an anxiety disorder, an obsessive-compulsive disorder and a personality disorder in one patient.

Depression is the most varied of all psychological illnesses. It assumes a myriad of guises and disguises. Many people are chronically depressed without even knowing it and without corresponding cognitive or affective contents. Some depressive episodes are part of a cycle of ups and downs (as is the case in the bipolar disorder as well as in a milder form, the cyclothymic disorder).

Other depressive illnesses are "built into" the characters and the personalities of the patients (e.g., the dysthymic disorder or what used to be known as depressive neurosis). One type of depression is even seasonal and can be cured by photo-therapy (gradual exposure to carefully timed artificial lighting). We all experience "adjustment disorders with depressed mood" (used to be called reactive depression, which occurs after a stressful life event and as a direct and time-limited reaction to it).

These poisoned garden varieties are all-pervasive. Not a single aspect of the human condition escapes them, not one element of human behaviour evades their grip. It is not wise (it has no predictive or explanatory value) to differentiate "good" or "normal" depressions from "pathological" ones. There are no "good" depressions.

Whether provoked by misfortune or endogenously (from the inside), whether during childhood or later in life, all depressive illnesses are one and the same. A depression is a depression is a depression no matter what its precipitating causes are or which stage in life it appears in.

The only valid distinction seems to be phenomenological: some depressives slow down (psychomotor retardation), their appetite, sex life (libido) and sleep (known together as the vegetative) functions are notably perturbed. Behaviour patterns change or disappear altogether. These patients feel dead: they are anhedonic (find pleasure or excitement in nothing) and dysphoric (sad).

The other type of depressive is psychomotorically active (at times, hyperactive). These are the patients that I described above: they report overwhelming guilt feelings, anxiety, even to the point of having delusions (delusional thinking, not grounded in reality but in a thwarted logic of an outlandish world).

The most severe cases exhibit paranoia (delusions of systematic conspiracies to persecute them), and seriously entertain ideas of self-destruction and the destruction of others (nihilistic delusions).

They hallucinate. Their hallucinations reveal their hidden contents: self-deprecation, the need to be (self) punished, humiliation, "bad" or "cruel" or "permissive" thoughts about authority figures. Depressives are almost never psychotic (psychotic depression does not belong to this family of afflictions). Depression does not necessarily entail a marked change in mood. "Masked depression" is, therefore, difficult to diagnose if we stick to the strict definition of depression as a "mood" disorder.

Depression can happen at any age, to anyone, with or without a preceding stressful event. It can set on gradually or erupt dramatically. The earlier it occurs, the more likely it is to recur. This apparently arbitrary and shifting nature of depression only enhances the guilt feelings of the patient. He refuses to accept that the source of his problems is beyond his control and could be biological, for instance. The depressive patient always blames himself, or events in his immediate past, for his "misconduct".

This is a vicious and self-fulfilling prophetic cycle. The depressive feels worthless, doubts his future and his abilities, feels guilty. This constant brooding alienates his dearest and nearest. His interpersonal relationships become distorted and disrupted and this dysfunction, in turn, exacerbates his depression.

The patient finally finds it most convenient and rewarding to avoid human contact altogether. He resigns from his job, shies away from social settings, sexually abstains, shuts out his few remaining friends and family members. Hostility, avoidance, histrionics all emerge and the co-existence of personality disorders only makes matters worse.

Freud said that the depressive person had lost a love object (was deprived of a properly functioning parent). The psychic trauma suffered early on can be alleviated only by inflicting self-punishment (thus implicitly "punishing" and devaluing the internalized version of the disappointing love object).

The development of the Ego is conditioned upon a successful resolution of the loss of these love objects (a phase all of us have to go through). When the love object fails, the child is furious, revengeful, and aggressive. Unable to direct these negative emotions at the frustrating parent, the child directs them at himself.

Narcissistic Identification means that the child prefers to love himself (direct his libido at himself) rather than to love an unpredictable, abandoning parent (mother, in most cases). Thus, the child becomes his own parent and directs his aggression at himself (at the parent that he has become). Throughout this wrenching process, the Ego feels helpless and this is another major source of depression.

When depressed, the patient becomes an artist of sorts. He tars his life, people around him, his experiences, places, and memories with a thick brush of maudlin, sentimental, and nostalgic longing. The depressive imbues everything with sadness: a tune, a sight, a colour, another person, a situation, a memory.

In this sense, the depressive is cognitively distorted. He interprets his experiences, evaluates his self and assesses the future totally negatively. He behaves as though he is constantly disenchanted, disillusioned, and hurting (dysphoric affect) and this helps to sustain the distorted perceptions.

No success, accomplishment, or support can break this cycle because it is so self-contained and self-enhancing. Dysphoric affect supports distorted perceptions, which enhance dysphoria, which encourages self-defeating behaviours, which bring about failure, which justifies depression.

This is a cosy little circle, charmed and emotionally protective because it is unfailingly predictable. Depression is addictive because it is a strong love substitute. Much like drugs, it has its own rituals, language and worldview. It imposes rigid order and behaviour patterns on the depressive. This is learned helplessness: the depressive prefers to avoid certain situations even if they hold the promise of improvement and pleasure.

The depressive patient has been conditioned by repeated aversive stimuli to freeze - he does not even have the energy needed to exit this cruel world by committing suicide. The depressive is devoid of the positive reinforcements, which are the building blocks of our self-esteem.

He is filled with negative thinking about his self, his (lack of) goals, his (lack of) achievements, his emptiness and loneliness and so on. And because his cognition and perceptions are deformed, no cognitive or rational input can alter the situation. Everything is immediately reinterpreted to fit the paradigm.

People often mistake depression for emotion. They say about the narcissist: "He is sad" and they mean: "He is human because he has emotions". This is wrong. True, depression is a big component in the narcissist's emotional makeup. But it mostly has to do with the absence of Narcissistic Supply. It mostly has to do with nostalgia for more plentiful days, full of adoration and attention and applause. It mostly occurs after the narcissist has depleted his Secondary Sources of Narcissistic Supply (spouse, mate, girlfriend, colleagues) with his constant demands for the "re-enactment" of his days of glory. Some narcissists even cry, but they cry exclusively for themselves and for their lost paradise. And they do so conspicuously and publicly, in order to attract attention.

The narcissist is a human pendulum hanging by the thread of the void that is his False Self. He swings between brutal and vicious abrasiveness and mellifluous, maudlin, and saccharine sentimentality. It is all an emotional simulacrum, a verisimilitude, a facsimile. Enough to fool the casual observer. Enough to extract the coveted drug: other people's attention, that reflection that somehow sustains his mental house of cards.

But the stronger and more rigid the defences - and nothing is more resilient than pathological narcissism - the greater and deeper the hurt the narcissist aims to compensate for. One's narcissism stands in direct relation to the seething abyss and the devouring vacuum that one harbours in one's True Self.

Perhaps narcissism is, indeed, as some scholars say, a reversible choice. But it is also a rational choice, guaranteeing self-preservation and survival. The paradox is that being a self-loathing narcissist may be the only act of true self-love the narcissist ever commits.

The Depressive Narcissist

Many scholars consider pathological narcissism to be a form of depressive illness. This is the position of the authoritative magazine "Psychology Today". The life of the typical narcissist is, indeed, punctuated with recurrent bouts of dysphoria (ubiquitous sadness and hopelessness), anhedonia (loss of the ability to feel pleasure), and clinical forms of depression (cyclothymic, dysthymic, or other). This picture is further obfuscated by the frequent presence of mood disorders, such as Bipolar I (co-morbidity).

While the distinction between reactive (exogenous) and endogenous depression is obsolete, it is still useful in the context of narcissism. Narcissists react with depression not only to life crises but to fluctuations in Narcissistic Supply.

The narcissist's personality is disorganized and precariously balanced. He regulates his sense of self-worth by consuming Narcissistic Supply from others. Any threat to the uninterrupted flow of said supply compromises his psychological integrity and his ability to function. It is perceived by the narcissist as life threatening.

Loss Induced Dysphoria

This is the narcissist's depressive reaction to the loss of one or more Sources of Narcissistic Supply, or to the disintegration of a Pathological Narcissistic Space (PN Space, his stalking or hunting grounds, the social unit whose members lavish attention or admiration on the narcissist).

Deficiency Induced Dysphoria

Deep and acute depression which follows the aforementioned losses of Supply Sources or a PN Space. Having mourned these losses, the narcissist now grieves their inevitable outcome - the absence or deficiency of Narcissistic Supply. Paradoxically, this dysphoria energises the narcissist and moves him to find new Sources of Supply to replenish his dilapidated stock (thus initiating a Narcissistic Cycle).

Self-Worth Dysregulation Dysphoria

The narcissist reacts with depression to criticism or disagreement, especially from a trusted and long-term Source of Narcissistic Supply. He fears the imminent loss of the source and the damage to his own, fragile, mental balance. The narcissist also resents his vulnerability and his extreme dependence on feedback from others. This type of depressive reaction is, therefore, a mutation of self-directed aggression.

Grandiosity Gap Dysphoria

The narcissist's firmly, though counterfactually, perceives himself as omnipotent, omniscient, omnipresent, brilliant, accomplished, irresistible, immune, and invincible. Any data to the contrary is usually filtered out, altered, or discarded altogether. Still, sometimes reality intrudes and creates a Grandiosity Gap. The narcissist is forced to face his mortality, limitations, ignorance, and relative inferiority. He sulks and sinks into an incapacitating but short-lived dysphoria.

Self-Punishing Dysphoria

Deep inside, the narcissist hates himself and doubts his own worth. He deplores his desperate addiction to Narcissistic Supply. He judges his actions and intentions harshly and sadistically. He may be unaware of these dynamics - but they are at the heart of the narcissistic disorder and the reason the narcissist had to resort to narcissism as a defence mechanism in the first place.

This inexhaustible well of ill will, self-chastisement, self-doubt, and self-directed aggression yields numerous self-defeating and self-destructive behaviours - from reckless driving and substance abuse to suicidal ideation and constant depression.

It is the narcissist's ability to confabulate that saves him from himself. His grandiose fantasies remove him from reality and prevent recurrent narcissistic injuries. Many narcissists end up delusional, schizoid, or paranoid. To avoid agonizing and gnawing depression, they give up on life itself.

Persecutory Anxiety - Note to Mental Health Practitioners

Positive feelings (about oneself or pertaining to one's accomplishments, assets, etc.) are never gained merely through conscious endeavour. They are the outcome of insight. Insight has a cognitive component (factual knowledge regarding one's achievements, assets, qualities, skills, etc.) plus an emotional correlate that is heavily dependent on past experience, the presence of defence mechanisms, and personality style or structure ("character").

People who consistently feel worthless or unworthy usually overcompensate cognitively for the lack of the aforementioned emotional component.

Such a person doesn't love himself, yet is trying to convince himself that he is loveable. He doesn't trust himself, yet he lectures to himself on how trustworthy he is (replete with supporting evidence from his experiences).

But such cognitive substitutes to emotional self-acceptance won't do.

The root of the problem is the inner dialog between disparaging voices and countervailing "proofs". Such self-doubting is, in principle, a healthy thing. It serves as an integral and critical part of the "checks and balances" that constitute the mature personality.

But, normally, some ground rules are observed and some facts are considered indisputable. When things go awry, however, the consensus breaks. Chaos replaces structure and the regimented update of one's self-image (via introspection) gives way to recursive loops of self-deprecation with diminishing insights.

In other words, normally, the dialog serves to augment some self-assessments and mildly modify others. When things go wrong, the dialog concerns itself with the very narrative, rather than with its content.

The dysfunctional dialog deals with questions that are far more fundamental (and typically settled early on in life):

"Who am I?"

"What are my traits, my skills, my accomplishments?"

"How reliable, loveable, trustworthy, qualified, truthful am I?"

"How can I separate fact from fiction?"

The answers to these questions consist of both cognitive (empirical) and emotional components. They are mostly derived from our social interactions, from the feedback we get and give. An inner dialog that is still concerned with these qualms indicates a problem with socialization.

It is not one's "psyche" that is delinquent but one's social functioning. One should direct one's efforts to "heal" outwards (to remedy one's interactions with others), not inwards (to cure one's "psyche").

Moreover, the disordered dialog is not time-synchronic.

The healthy internal discourse is between concurrent, equipotent, and same-age "entities" (psychological constructs). Its aim is to negotiate conflicting demands and reach a compromise based on a rigorous test of reality.

The pathological dialog, on the other hand, involves wildly disparate interlocutors. These are in different stages of maturation and possessed of unequal faculties. They are more interested to give monologues than to participate in a dialog. Because they are "stuck" in various ages and periods, they do not all relate to the same "host", "person", or "personality". They require time- and energy-consuming constant mediation. It is this depleting process of arbitration and "peacekeeping" that is consciously felt as nagging insecurity or, even, in extremis, self-loathing.

A constant and consistent lack of self-confidence and a fluctuating sense of self-worth are the conscious "translation" of the unconscious threat posed by the precariousness of the disordered personality. It is, in other words, a warning sign.

Thus, the first step is to clearly identify the various segments that, together, however incongruently, constitute the personality. This can be surprisingly easily done by noting down the "stream of consciousness" dialog and assigning "names" or "handles" to the various "voices" in it.

The next step is to "introduce" the voices to each other and form an internal consensus (a "coalition", or an "alliance"). This requires a prolonged period of "negotiations" and mediation, leading to the compromises that underlie such a consensus. The mediator can be a trusted friend, a lover, or a therapist.

The very achievement of such internal "ceasefire" reduces anxiety considerably and removes the "imminent threat". This, in turn, allows the patient to develop a realistic "core" or "kernel", wrapped around the basic understanding reached earlier between the contesting parts of his personality.

The development of such a nucleus of stable self-worth, however, is dependent on two things:

1. Sustained interactions with mature and predictable people who are aware of their boundaries and of their true identity (their traits, skills, abilities, limitations, and so on), and
2. The emergence of a nurturing and "holding" emotional correlate to every cognitive insight or breakthrough.

The latter is inextricably bound with the former.

Here is why:

Some of the "voices" in the internal dialog of the patient are bound to be disparaging, injurious, belittling, sadistically critical, destructively sceptical, mocking, and demeaning. The only way to silence these voices - or at least "discipline" them and make them conform to a more realistic emerging inner consensus - is by gradually (and sometimes surreptitiously) introducing countervailing "players".

Protracted exposure to the right people, in the framework of mature interactions, negates the pernicious effects of what Freud called a Superego gone awry. It is, in effect, a process of reprogramming and deprogramming.

There are two types of beneficial, altering, social experiences:

1. Structured - interactions that involve adherence to a set of rules embedded in authoritative structures, institutions, and enforcement mechanisms (example: attending psychotherapy, going through a spell in prison, convalescing in a hospital, serving in the army, being an aid worker or a missionary, studying at school, growing up in a family, participating in a 12-steps group), and

2. Non-structured - interactions which involve a voluntary exchange of information, opinion, goods, or services with others.

The problem with the disordered person is that, usually, his (or her) chances of freely interacting with mature adults (interactions of the non-structured kind) are limited to start with and dwindle with time. This is because few potential partners - interlocutors, lovers, friends, colleagues, neighbours - are willing to invest the time, effort, energy, and resources required to effectively cope with the patient and manage the often-arduous relationship. Disordered patients are typically hard to get along with, demanding, petulant, paranoid, and narcissistic.

Even the most gregarious and outgoing patient finally finds himself isolated, shunned, and misjudged. This only adds to his initial misery and amplifies the wrong kind of voices in the internal dialog.

Hence my recommendation to start with structured activities and in a structured, almost automatic manner. Therapy is only one - and at times not the most efficient - choice.

Narcissistic Rage

Anger as a Source of Personality Disorder

Question: Do all personality disorders have a common psycho-dynamic source? To what stage of personal development can we attribute this common source? Can the paths leading from that common source to each of these disorders be charted? Will positive answers to the above endow us with a new understanding of these pernicious conditions?

Answer:

84

Acute Anger

Anger is a compounded phenomenon. It has dispositional properties, expressive and motivational components, situational and individual variations, cognitive and excitatory interdependent manifestations and psycho-physiological (especially neuroendocrine) aspects. From the psychobiological point of view, it probably had its survival utility in early evolution, but it seems to have lost a lot of it in modern societies. Actually, in most cases it is counterproductive, even dangerous. Dysfunctional anger is known to have pathogenic effects (mostly cardiovascular).

Most narcissists are prone to be angry. Their anger is always sudden, raging, frightening and without an apparent provocation by an outside agent. It would seem that narcissists are in a CONSTANT state of rage, which is effectively controlled most of the time. It manifests itself only when the narcissist's defences are down, incapacitated, or adversely affected by circumstances, inner or external.

In a nutshell, a person presenting with such acute rage was, usually, unable to express anger and direct it at "forbidden" targets in his early, formative years (his parents, in most cases).

MALIGNANT SELF LOVE

SAM VAKNIN

The anger, however, was a justified reaction to abuses and mistreatment. The patient was, therefore, left to nurture a sense of profound injustice and frustrated rage. Healthy people experience anger, but as a transitory state. This is what sets the personality disordered apart: their anger is always acute, permanently present, often suppressed or repressed. Healthy anger has an external inducing agent (a reason). It is directed at this agent (coherence).

Pathological anger is neither coherent, not externally induced. It emanates from the inside and it is diffuse, directed at the "world" and at "injustice" in general. The narcissist is capable of identifying the IMMEDIATE cause of his fury. Still, upon closer scrutiny, the cause is likely to be found lacking and the anger excessive, disproportionate, and incoherent.

It might be more accurate to say that the narcissist is expressing (and experiencing) TWO layers of anger, simultaneously and always. The first layer, of superficial ire, is indeed directed at an identified target, the alleged cause of the eruption. The second layer, however, incorporates the narcissist's self-aimed wrath.

The patient is angry at himself for being unable to normally vent off normal anger. He feels like a miscreant. He hates himself. This second layer of anger also comprises strong and easily identifiable elements of frustration, irritation and annoyance.

Yet, normal anger results in taking some action regarding the source of frustration (or, at the very least, the planning or contemplation of such action). In contrast, pathological rage is mostly directed at oneself, displaced, or even lacks a target altogether.

The personality disordered are afraid to show to meaningful others that they are angry because they are afraid to lose them. The borderline personality disordered is terrified of being abandoned, the narcissist (NPD) needs his Narcissistic Supply Sources, the paranoid - his persecutors and so on. These people prefer to direct their anger at people who are meaningless to them, people whose withdrawal will not constitute a threat to their precariously balanced personalities. They yell at a waitress, berate a taxi driver, or explode at an underling. Alternatively, they sulk, feel anhedonic or pathologically bored, drink or do drugs - all forms of self-directed aggression.

From time to time, no longer able to pretend and to suppress their rage, they have it out with the real source of their anger. Then they lose all vestiges of self-control and rave like lunatics.

They shout incoherently, make absurd accusations, distort facts, and air long-suppressed grievances, allegations and suspicions.

These episodes are followed by periods of saccharine sentimentality and excessive flattering and submissiveness towards the victim of the latest rage attack. Driven by the mortal fear of being abandoned or ignored, the narcissist debases and demeans himself to the point of provoking repulsion in the beholder. These pendulum-like emotional swings make life with the personality disordered difficult.

It is not clear whether action diminishes anger or anger is used up in action - but anger in healthy persons is diminished through action and expression. It is an aversive, unpleasant emotion. It is intended to generate action in order to reduce frustration. Anger is coupled with physiological arousal. But it is not clear whether action diminishes anger or anger is used up in action. Similarly, it is not clear whether the consciousness of anger is dependent on a stream of cognition expressed in words? Do we become angry because we say that we are angry (we identify the anger and capture it) - or do we say that we are angry because we are angry to start with?

Anger is induced by numerous factors. It is almost a universal reaction. Any threat to one's welfare (physical, emotional, social, financial, or mental) is met with anger. So are threats to one's affiliates, nearest, dearest, nation, favourite football club, pet and so on. The territory of anger includes not only the angry person himself, but also his real and perceived environment and social milieu.

This does not sound like a very adaptative strategy. Threats are not the only situations met with anger. Anger is also the reaction to injustice (perceived or real), to disagreements, to inconvenience. But the two main sources of anger are the existence of a threat (even a disagreement is potentially threatening) and injustice (even inconvenience is injustice inflicted on the angry person by the world).

These are also the two sources of personality disorders. The personality disordered is moulded by recurrent and frequent injustice and he is constantly threatened both by his internal and by his external universes. No wonder that there is a close affinity between the personality disordered and the acutely angry person.

And, as opposed to common opinion, the angry person becomes angry whether he believes that what was done to him was deliberate or not. If we lose a precious manuscript, even unintentionally, we are bound to become angry at ourselves. If his home is devastated by an earthquake, the owner will surely rage, though the devastation was not premeditated. When we perceive an injustice in the distribution of wealth or love, we become angry because of moral reasoning, whether the injustice was deliberate or not. We retaliate and we punish as a result of our ability to morally reason and to get even. Sometimes even moral reasoning is lacking, as in when we simply wish to alleviate a diffuse anger.

What the personality disordered does is: he suppresses his anger, but has no effective mechanisms of redirecting it in order to correct the inducing conditions. His hostile expressions are not constructive - they are destructive because they are diffuse, excessive and, therefore, unclear. He does not lash out at people in order to restore his lost self-esteem, his prestige, his sense of power and control over his life, to recover emotionally, or to restore his well-being. He rages because he cannot help it and is in a self-destructive and self-loathing mode. His anger does not contain a signal, which could alter his environment in general and the behaviour of those around him, in particular. His anger is primitive, maladaptive, pent up.

Anger is a primitive, limbic emotion. Its excitatory components and patterns are shared with sexual excitation and with fear. It is cognition that guides our behaviour, aimed at avoiding harm and aversion or at minimizing them. Our cognition is in charge of attaining certain kinds of mental gratification. We cognitively analyse future values of relief-gratification versus repercussions (reward to risk ratio). Anger is provoked by aversive treatment, deliberately or unintentionally inflicted. Such treatment must violate either prevailing conventions regarding social interactions or some otherwise deeply ingrained sense of what is fair and what is just. The judgement of fairness or justice (namely, the appraisal of the extent of compliance with conventions of social exchange) is also cognitive.

Angry people - narcissists or not - suffer from a cognitive deficit and are worried and anxious. They are unable to conceptualize, to design effective strategies, and to execute them. They dedicate all their attention to the here and now and ignore the future consequences of their actions. Recent events are judged more relevant and weighted more heavily than any earlier ones. Anger impairs cognition, including the proper perception of time and space.

In other words, their attention and information processing faculties are distorted, skewed in favour of the here and now, biased on both the intake and the output. Time is "relativistically dilated": the present feels more protracted, "longer" than any future. Immediate facts and actions are judged more relevant and weighted more heavily than any remote aversive conditions. Anger impairs cognition.

The angry person is a worried person. The personality disordered patient is also excessively preoccupied with himself. Worry and anger are the cornerstones of the edifice of anxiety. This is where it all converges: people become angry because they are excessively concerned with bad things which might happen to them. Anger is a result of anxiety (or, when the anger is not acute, of fear).

In all people, whether narcissists or normal, anger is associated with a suspension of empathy. Irritated people cannot empathize. Actually, "counter-empathy" develops in a state of aggravated anger. All mitigating circumstances related to the source of the anger are taken as intended to devalue and belittle the suffering of the angry person. His anger thus increases the more mitigating circumstances are brought to his attention. The faculties of judgement and risk evaluation are also altered by anger. Later provocative acts are judged to be more serious than earlier ones - just by "virtue" of their chronological position. All this is also very typical of the personality disordered. An impairment of empathic sensitivities is a prime symptom in the narcissistic, antisocial, schizoid and schizotypal personality disorders, to mention but four.

Moreover, the aforementioned impairment of judgement (impairment of the proper functioning of the mechanism of risk assessment) appears in both acute anger and in many personality disorders. The illusion of omnipotence (power), immunity, and invulnerability, the partiality of judgement are typical of both states. Acute anger (rage attacks in personality disorders) is always incommensurate with the magnitude of the source of the emotion and is fuelled by extraneous experiences. An acutely angry person usually reacts to an ACCUMULATION, an amalgamation of aversive experiences, all enhancing each other in vicious feedback loops, many of them not directly related to the cause of the specific episode. The angry person may be reacting to stress, agitation, disturbance, drugs, violence or aggression witnessed by him, to a social or national conflict, to elation and even to sexual excitation.

The same is true of the personality disordered. His inner world is fraught with unpleasant, ego-dystonic, discomfiting, unsettling, worrisome experiences. His external environment - influenced and moulded by his distorted personality - is also transformed into a source of aversive, repulsive, or plainly unpleasant experiences. The personality disordered explodes in rage - because he implodes AND reacts to outside stimuli, simultaneously. Because he is a slave to magical thinking and, therefore, regards himself as omnipotent, omniscient and protected from the consequences of his own acts (immune), the personality disordered often acts in a self-destructive and self-defeating manner. The similarities are so numerous and so striking that it seems safe to say that the personality disordered is in a constant state of acute anger.

Finally, acutely angry people perceive anger to have been the result of intentional (or circumstantial) provocation with a hostile purpose (by the target of their anger). Their targets, on the other hand, invariably regard acutely angry people as incoherent, acting arbitrarily, in an unjustified manner.

Narcissistic Rage

Narcissists can be imperturbable, resilient to stress, and sangfroid. Narcissistic rage is not a reaction to stress - it is a reaction to a perceived slight, insult, criticism, or disagreement (in other words, to narcissistic injury). It is intense and disproportional to the "offence".

Narcissistic rage has two forms:

1. *Explosive* - The narcissist flares up, attacks everyone in his immediate vicinity, causes damage to objects or people, and is verbally and psychologically abusive.
2. *Pernicious or Passive-Aggressive (P/A)* - The narcissist sulks, gives the silent treatment, and is plotting how to punish the transgressor and put her in her proper place. These narcissists are vindictive and often become stalkers. They harass and haunt the objects of their frustration. They sabotage and damage the work and possessions of people whom they regard to be the sources of their mounting wrath.

Gender and the Narcissist

Question: Are female narcissists any different from male nar-cissists?

Answer: Throughout this book I keep using the male third per-son singular because most narcissists (75%) are males and more so because there is little difference between the male and female narcissist.

In the manifestations of their narcissism, female and male narcissists, inevitably, do tend to differ. They emphasize differ-ent things. They transform different elements of their personal-ities and of their lives into the cornerstones of their disorder.

Women concentrate on their body (many also suffer from eat-ing disorders: Anorexia Nervosa and Bulimia Nervosa). They flaunt and exploit their physical charms, their sexuality, and their socially and culturally determined "femininity". They often secure their Narcissistic Supply through their more tradi-tional gender roles: home making, child rearing, suitable careers, tending to their husbands ("the wife of..."), their fem-inine traits, taking part in social functions, charity work, etc.

It is no wonder than narcissists - both men and women - are chauvinistic and conservative. They depend to such an extent on the opinions of people around them that, with time, they are transformed into ultra-sensitive seismographs of public opinion, barometers of prevailing fads and fashions, and guardians of conformity. The narcissist cannot afford to seriously alienate his "constituency", those people who reflect his False Self back to him. The very functioning of the narcissist's Ego depends on the goodwill and the collaboration of his human environment.

True, besieged and consumed by pernicious guilt feelings, many a narcissist finally seek to be punished. Such self-destruc-tive narcissists pose as "bad guys" (or "bad girls"). But even

90

then they make themselves fit traditional, widely-accepted stereotypes. To ensure social opprobrium (read: attention), the narcissist exaggerates these roles to the point of a caricature.

A self-destructive female narcissist is likely to label herself a "whore" and her male counterpart to style himself a "vicious, unrepentant criminal". Yet, these again are traditional social roles. Even as they seek their masochistic punishment, men are likely to emphasize intellect, power, aggression, money, or social status. Women are likely to emphasize body, looks, charm, sexuality, feminine "traits", homemaking, children and childrearing.

Another difference between the genders is in the way they react to treatment. Women are more likely to resort to therapy because they are more likely to admit to having psychological problems. Women are also generally more likely to ask for help than men.

But while men may be less inclined to DISCLOSE or to expose their problems to others (the macho-man factor), this does not necessarily imply that they are less prone to acknowledge the existence of these issues to themselves.

Yet, the prime rule of narcissism must never be forgotten: the narcissist uses everything around him or her to obtain his (or her) Narcissistic Supply. Children happen to be more attached to the female narcissist due to the way our society is still structured and to the fact that women are the ones to give birth and to serve as primary caretakers. It is easier for a woman to think of her children as her extensions because they once indeed were her physical extensions and because her on-going interaction with them is both more intensive and more extensive.

This means that the male narcissist is more likely to regard his children as a nuisance than as a Source of rewarding Narcissist Supply - especially as they grow older and become autonomous. With less alternatives than men, the narcissistic woman fights to maintain her most reliable Source of Supply: her children. Through insidious indoctrination, guilt formation, emotional sanctions and blackmail, deprivation and other psychological mechanisms, she tries to induce in her offspring dependence, which cannot be easily unravelled.

But, from the psychodynamic point of view, there is no difference between children, money, or intellect, as Sources of Narcissistic Supply. So, there is no psychodynamic difference between male and female narcissists. The only difference is in their choices of Sources of Narcissistic Supply.

There are mental disorders, which afflict a specific sex more often. This has to do with hormonal or other physiological dispositions, with social and cultural conditioning (socialization), and with role assignment through the gender differentiation process. None of these seem to be strongly correlated to the formation of malignant narcissism. The Narcissistic Personality Disorder (as opposed, for instance, to the Borderline or the Histrionic Personality Disorders, which affect women more than men) seems to conform to social mores and to the prevailing ethos of capitalism. Social thinkers like Lasch speculated that modern American culture - a narcissistic, self-centred one - increases the rate of incidence of the Narcissistic Personality Disorder. As Kernberg observed:

"The most I would be willing to say is that society can make serious psychological abnormalities, which already exist in some percentage of the population, seem to be at least superficially appropriate."

Quotes from the Literature

"Specifically, past research suggests that exploitive tendencies and open displays of feelings of entitlement will be less integral to narcissism for females than for males. For females such displays may carry a greater possibility of negative social sanctions because they would violate stereotypical gender-role expectancies for women, who are expected to engage in such positive social behaviour as being tender, compassionate, warm, sympathetic, sensitive, and understanding.

In females, Exploitiveness/Entitlement is less well-integrated with the other components of narcissism as measured by the Narcissistic Personality Inventory (NPI) - Leadership/Authority, Self-absorption/Self-admiration, and Superiority/Arrogance - than in males - though 'male and female narcissists in general showed striking similarities in the manner in which most of the facets of narcissism were integrated with each other'."

[Gender differences in the structure of narcissism: a multi-sample analysis of the narcissistic personality inventory - Brian T. Tschanz, Carolyn C. Morf, Charles W. Turner - Sex Roles: A Journal of Research - Issue: May, 1998]

"Women leaders are evaluated negatively if they exercise their authority and are perceived as autocratic."

[Eagly, A. H., Makhijani, M. G., & Klonsky, B. G. (1992). Gender and the evaluation of leaders: A meta-analysis. Psychological Bulletin, 111, 3-22, and...

Butler, D., & Gels, F. L. (1990). Nonverbal affect responses to male and female leaders: Implications for leadership evaluations. Journal of Personality and Social Psychology, 58, 48-59.]

"Competent women must also appear to be sociable and likable in order to influence men - men must only appear to be competent to achieve the same results with both genders."

[Carli, L. L., Lafleur, S. J., & Loeber, C. C. (1995). Nonverbal behaviour, gender, and influence. Journal of Personality and Social Psychology, 68, 1030-1041.]

93

Homosexual and Transsexual Narcissists

Question: What is the typical profile of a homosexual narcissist? Why is he always on a lookout for new victims? Is he lying or is he telling the truth when he says that he "wants to get laid" by one and all? If he is not suicidal, is he not afraid of AIDS?

Answer: I am a heterosexual and thus deprived of an intimate acquaintance with certain psychological processes, which allegedly are unique to homosexuals. It is doubtful whether there are such processes, to begin with. Research failed to find any substantive difference between the psychological makeup of a narcissist who happens to have homosexual preferences and a heterosexual narcissist.

They both are predators, devouring Narcissistic Supply Sources as they go. Narcissists look for new victims for the same reason tigers look for prey: they are hungry. Hungry for adoration, admiration, acceptance, approval, and any other kind of attention. Old Sources of Supply (suppliers) die easy: once taken for granted, the narcissistic element of conquest vanishes.

Conquest is important because it proves the superiority of the narcissist. The very act of subduing, subjugating, or acquiring the power to influence someone provides the narcissist with Narcissistic Supply. The newly conquered idolize the narcissist and serve as trophies.

The act of conquering and subordinating is epitomized by the sexual encounter: an objective and atavistic interaction. Making love to someone means that the consenting partner finds the narcissist (or one or more of his traits, such as his intelligence, his physique, even his money) irresistible.

The distinction between passive and active sexual partners is mechanical, false, superfluous and superficial. Penetration does not make one of the parties "the stronger one". To cause some-

94

one to have sex with you is a powerful stimulus and always provokes a sensation of omnipotence. Whether one is physically
passive or active, one is always psychosexually active.

Anyone who practices unsafe sex is gambling with his life,
though the odds are much smaller than public hysteria would have
us believe. Reality does not matter, though - it is the perception
of reality that matters. Getting this close to (perceived) danger is
the equivalent of engaging in self-destruction (suicide). Indeed,
narcissists are, at times, suicidal and are always self-destructive.

There is, however, one element, which might be unique to
homosexuals: the fact that their self-definition hinges on their
sexual identity. Few heterosexuals would use their sexual preference to comprehensively define themselves. Homosexuality
has been inflated to the level of a sub-culture, a distinct psychology, or a myth. This kind of grandiose defence is typical of
persecuted minorities and it has an all-pervasive influence on
the individual. Preoccupation with body and sex makes most
homosexual narcissists SOMATIC narcissists.

Moreover, the homosexual makes love to a person of the SAME
sex - in a way, to his REFLECTION. In this respect, homosexual
relations are highly narcissistic and autoerotic affairs.

The somatic narcissist directs his libido at his body (as
opposed to the cerebral narcissist, who concentrates upon his
intellect). He cultivates it, nourishes and nurtures it, is often a
hypochondriac, dedicates an inordinate amount of time to its
needs (real and imaginary). It is through his body that this type
of narcissist tracks down and captures his Supply Sources.

The supply that the somatic narcissist so badly requires is
derived from his sex appeal, shape, his build, his profile, his
beauty, his physical attractiveness, his health, his age, and his
fitness. He downplays Narcissistic Supply directed at other
traits. He uses sex to reaffirm his prowess, his attractiveness,
his irresistibility, his omnipotence, or his youth. Love, to him, is
synonymous with sex and he focuses his learning skills on the
sexual act, the foreplay and the coital aftermath.

The act of seduction becomes addictive because it leads to a
quick succession of Supply Sources. Naturally, boredom (a form
of transmuted aggression) sets in once the going gets routine.
Routine is counter-narcissistic by definition because it threatens
the narcissist's sense of uniqueness.

An interesting side issue relates to transsexuals.

Philosophically, there is little difference between a narcissist who seeks to avoid his True Self (and positively to become

his False Self) and a transsexual who seeks to discard his true gender. But this similarity, though superficially appealing, is questionable.

People sometimes seek sex reassignment because of advantages and opportunities which, they believe, are enjoyed by the other sex. This rather unrealistic (fantastic) view of the other is faintly narcissistic. It includes elements of idealized over-valuation, of self-preoccupation, and of objectification of one's self. It demonstrates a deficient ability to empathize and some grandiose sense of entitlement ("I deserve to be taken care of") and omnipotence ("I can be whatever I want to be, despite nature/God").

This feeling of entitlement is especially manifest in some gender dysphoric individuals who aggressively pursue hormonal or surgical treatment. They feel that it is their inalienable right to receive it on demand and without any strictures or restrictions. For instance, they oftentimes refuse to undergo psychological evaluation or treatment as a condition for the hormonal or surgical intervention.

It is interesting to note that both narcissism and gender dysphoria are early childhood phenomena. This could be explained by problematic Primary Objects, dysfunctional families, or a common genetic or biochemical problem. It is too early to say which. As yet, there isn't even an agreed typology of gender identity disorders, let alone an in-depth comprehension of their sources.

A radical view, proffered by Ray Blanchard, seems to indicate that pathological narcissism is more likely to be found among non-core, ego-dystonic, autogynephilic transsexuals and among heterosexual transvestites. It is less manifest in core, ego-syntonic, homosexual transsexuals.

Autogynephilic transsexuals are subject to an intense urge to become the opposite sex and, thus, to be rendered the sexual object of their own desire. In other words, they are so sexually attracted to themselves that they wish to become both lovers in the romantic equation: the male and the female. It is the fulfilment of the ultimate narcissistic fantasy with the False Self as a fetish ("narcissistic fetish").

Autogynephilic transsexuals start off as heterosexuals and end up as either bisexual or homosexual. By shifting his/her attentions to men, the male autogynephilic transsexual "proves" to himself that he has finally become a "true" and desirable woman.

Addiction to Fame and Celebrity

Question: Are narcissists addicted to being famous?

Answer: Yes, they are. Narcissists are addicted to being famous. This, by far, is their predominant drive. Being famous encompasses a few important functions: it endows the narcissist with power, provides him with a constant Source of Narcissistic Supply (admiration, adoration, approval, awe), and fulfils important ego functions.

The image that the narcissist projects is hurled back at him, reflected by those exposed to his celebrity or fame. This way he feels alive, his very existence is affirmed and he acquires a sensation of clear boundaries (where he ends and the world begins).

There is a set of narcissistic behaviours typical to the pursuit of fame and celebrity. The narcissist will do almost anything and cross all boundaries achieve renown. To him, there is no such thing as "bad publicity" - what matters is to be in the public eye. Because the narcissist equally enjoys all types of attention and likes as much to be feared as to be loved, for instance - he doesn't mind if what is published about him is wrong ("As long as they spell my name correctly"). Fame and notoriety are equally welcome. The narcissist's only bad emotional stretches are when he lacks attention, publicity, or exposure.

The narcissist then feels empty, hollowed out, negligible, humiliated, wrathful, discriminated against, deprived, neglected, treated unjustly and so on. At first, he tries to obtain attention from ever narrowing groups of reference ("supply scale down"). But the feeling that he is compromising gnaws at his anyhow fragile self-esteem.

Sooner or later, the spring bursts. The narcissist plots, contrives, plans, conspires, thinks, analyses, synthesizes and does whatever else is necessary to regain the lost exposure and bask

97

in it. The more he fails to secure the attention of his target group, the more daring, eccentric and outlandish he becomes. A firm decision to become well-known is transformed into resolute action and then to a panicky pattern of attention seeking behaviours.

The narcissist is not really interested in publicity per se. Narcissists are misleading. The narcissist appears to love himself - and, really, he abhors himself. Similarly, he appears to be interested in becoming a celebrity while, in reality, he is concerned with the REACTIONS to his fame: people watch him, notice him, talk about him, debate his actions - therefore he exists.

The narcissist goes around "hunting and collecting" the way the expressions on people's faces change when they notice him. He places himself at the centre of attention, or even as a figure of controversy. He constantly and recurrently pesters those nearest and dearest to him in a bid to reassure himself that he is not losing his fame, his magic touch, the attention of his social milieu.

Truly, the narcissist is not choosy. If he can become famous as a writer - he writes, if as a businessman - he conducts business. He switches from one field to the other with ease and without remorse because in all of them he is present without conviction, bar the conviction that he must (and deserves to) get famous.

He grades activities, hobbies and people not according to the pleasure that they give him but according to their utility: can they or can't they make him famous and, if so, to what extent. The narcissist is one-track minded (not to say obsessive). His is a world of black (being unknown and deprived of attention) and white (being famous and celebrated).

Acquired Situational Narcissism

The Narcissistic Personality Disorder (NPD) is a systemic, all-pervasive condition, very much like pregnancy: either you have it or you don't. Once you have it, you have it day and night, it is an inseparable part of the personality, a recurrent set of behaviour patterns.

Recent research (1996) by E. Roningstam and others, however, shows that there is a condition which might be called "Transient or Temporary or Short-Term Narcissism" as opposed to the full-fledged version. Even prior to this discovery, "Reactive Narcissistic Regression" was well known: people regress to a transient narcissistic phase in response to a major life crisis which threatens their mental composure.

But can narcissism be acquired or learned? Can it be provoked by certain, well-defined, situations?

Robert B. Millman, professor of psychiatry at New York Hospital - Cornell Medical School thinks it can. In a paper published in 2000, he proposed to reverse the accepted chronology. According to him, pathological narcissism can be induced in adulthood by celebrity, wealth, and fame.

The "victims" - billionaire tycoons, movie stars, renowned authors, politicians, and other authority figures - develop grandiose fantasies, lose their erstwhile ability to empathize, react with rage to slights, both real and imagined and, in general, act like textbook narcissists.

But is the occurrence of Acquired Situational Narcissism (ASN) inevitable and universal - or are only certain people prone to it?

It is likely that ASN is merely an amplification of earlier narcissistic conduct, traits, style, and tendencies. Celebrities with ASN already possessed a narcissistic personality and have acquired it long before it "erupted". Being famous, powerful, or rich only "legitimized" and conferred immunity from social sanction on the unbridled manifestation of a pre-existing disorder. Indeed, narcissists tend to gravitate to professions and settings which guarantee fame, celebrity, power, and wealth.

As Millman correctly notes, the celebrity's life is abnormal. The adulation is often justified and plentiful, the feedback biased and filtered, the criticism muted and belated, social control either lacking or excessive and vitriolic. Such vicissitudinal existence is not conducive to mental health even in the most balanced person.

The confluence of a person's narcissistic predisposition and his pathological life circumstances gives rise to ASN. Acquired Situational Narcissism borrows elements from both the classic Narcissistic Personality Disorder - ingrained and all-pervasive - and from Transient or Reactive Narcissism.

Celebrities are, therefore, unlikely to "heal" once their fame or wealth or might are gone. Instead, their basic narcissism merely changes form. It continues unabated, as insidious as ever - but modified by life's ups and downs.

In a way, all narcissistic disturbances are acquired. Patients acquire their pathological narcissism from abusive or overbearing parents, from peers, and from role models. Narcissism is a defence mechanism designed to fend off hurt and danger brought on by circumstances - such as celebrity - beyond the person's control.

Social expectations play a role as well. Celebrities try to conform to the stereotype of a creative but spoiled, self-centred, monomaniacal, and emotive individual. A tacit trade takes place. We offer the famous and the powerful all the Narcissistic Supply they crave - and they, in turn, act the consummate, fascinating albeit repulsive, narcissists.

Conspicuous Existence

Question: My boyfriend's behaviour is so exaggerated and unnatural. It's like he is acting all the time. Can't he just be himself?

Answer: The narcissist is a shell. Uncertain of his own reality, he engages in "conspicuous existence".

"Conspicuous existence" is a form of "conspicuous consumption", in which the consumed commodity is Narcissistic Supply. The narcissist elaborately stage manages his very being. His every movement, his tone of voice, his inflection, his poise, his text and subtext and context are carefully orchestrated to yield the maximum effect and to garner the most attention.

Narcissists appear to be unpleasantly deliberate. They are somehow "wrong", like automata gone awry. They are too human, or too inhuman, or too modest, or too haughty, or too loving, or too cold, or too empathic, or too stony, or too industrious, or too casual, or too enthusiastic, or too indifferent, or too courteous, or too abrasive.

Narcissists are excess reified. They act their part and their acting shows. Their show invariably unravels at the seams under the slightest stress. Their enthusiasm is always manic, their emotional expression unnatural, their body language defies their statements, their statements belie their intentions, their intentions are focused on the one and only drug: securing Narcissistic Supply from other people.

The narcissist authors his life and scripts it. To him, time is the medium upon which he, the narcissist, records the narrative of his recherché biography. He is, therefore, always calculated, as though listening to an inner voice, to a "director", or a "choreographer" of his unfolding history. His speech is tumid. His motion stunted. His emotional palette, a mockery of true countenances.

But the narcissist's constant invention of his self is not limited to outward appearances.

The narcissist does nothing and says nothing - or even thinks nothing - without first having computed the quantity of Narcissistic Supply his actions, utterances, or thoughts may yield. The visible narcissist is the tip of a gigantic, submerged, iceberg of seething reckoning. The narcissist is incessantly engaged in energy draining gauging of other people and their possible reactions to him. He estimates, he counts, he weighs and measures, he determines, evaluates, and enumerates, compares, despairs, and re-awakens. His fatigued brain is bathed with the drowning noise of stratagems and fears, rage and envy, anxiety and relief, addiction and rebellion, meditation and premeditation. The narcissist is a machine which never rests, not even in his dreams, and it has one purpose only - the securing and maximization of Narcissistic Supply.

Small wonder the narcissist is tired. His exhaustion is all-pervasive and all-consuming. His mental energy depleted, the narcissist can hardly empathize with others, love, or experience emotions. "Conspicuous existence" malignantly replaces "real existence". The myriad, ambivalent, forms of life are supplanted by the single obsession-compulsion of being seen, being observed, being reflected, being by proxy, through the gaze of others. The narcissist ceases to exist when not in company. His being fades when not discerned. Yet, he is unable to return the favour. He is a captive, oblivious to everything but his preoccupation. Emptied from within, devoured by his urge, the narcissist blindly stumbles from one relationship to another, from one warm body to the next, forever in search of that elusive creature - himself.

First published on the Suite 101 Narcissistic Personality Disorders Topic.

The Narcissist's Reaction to Deficient Narcissistic Supply

Question: How does the narcissist react when he fails to obtain enough Narcissistic Supply?

Answer: Very much as a drug addict reacts to the absence of his drug of choice.

103 The narcissist constantly consumes (really, preys upon) adoration, admiration, approval, applause, attention and other forms of Narcissistic Supply. When lacking or deficient, a Narcissistic Deficiency Dysphoria sets in. The narcissist then appears to be lethargic or (more rarely) agitated, depressed or (infrequently) manic, his movements slow down or become frantic, his sleep patterns are disordered (he either sleeps too much or becomes insomniac), his eating patterns change (he gorges on food or is avoids it altogether).

Typically, when deprived of Narcissistic Supply, the narcissist is constantly dysphoric (sad) and anhedonic (finds no pleasure in anything, including his former pursuits, hobbies, and interests). He is subjected to violent mood swings (mainly rage attacks) and all his (visible and painful) efforts at self-control fail. He may compulsively and ritually resort to an alternative addiction: alcohol, drugs, reckless driving, shopaholism.

This gradual disintegration is the narcissist's futile effort both to escape his predicament and to sublimate his aggressive urges. His whole behaviour seems constrained, artificial, and effortful. The narcissist gradually turns more and more mechanical, detached, and "unreal". His thoughts constantly wander or become obsessive and repetitive, his speech may falter, he appears to be far away, in a world of his narcissistic fantasies, where Narcissistic Supply is aplenty.

He withdraws from his painful existence, where others fail to appreciate his greatness, special skills and talents, potential, or achievements. The narcissist thus ceases to bestow himself upon a cruel universe, punishing the world for its shortcomings, its inability to realize how unique the narcissist is.

The narcissist goes into a schizoid mode: he isolates himself, a hermit in the kingdom of his hurt. He minimizes his social interactions and uses "messengers" to communicate with the outside. Devoid of energy, the narcissist can no longer pretend to succumb to social conventions. His former compliance gives way to open withdrawal (a rebellion of sorts). Smiles are transformed to frowns, courtesy becomes rudeness, emphasized etiquette used as a weapon, an outlet of aggression, an act of violence.

The narcissist, blinded by pain, seeks to restore his balance, to take another sip of the narcissistic nectar. In this quest, the narcissist turns both to and upon those nearest to him. His real attitude emerges: for him, his nearest and dearest are nothing but tools, one-dimensional instruments of gratification, Sources of Supply or pimps of such supply, catering to his narcissistic lusts.

Having failed to procure for him his "drug" (Narcissistic Supply), the narcissist regards friends, colleagues, and even family members as dysfunctional, frustrating objects. In his wrath, he tries to "mend" them by forcing them to perform again, to function.

This is coupled with merciless self-flagellation, a deservedly self-inflicted punishment, the narcissist feels. In extreme cases of deprivation, the narcissist entertains suicidal thoughts, this is how deeply he loathes his self and his dependence.

Throughout, the narcissist is beset by a pervading sense of malignant nostalgia, harking back to a past, which never existed except in the thwarted fantastic grandiosity of the narcissist. The longer the lack of Narcissistic Supply, the more the narcissist glorifies, re-writes, misses and mourns this past.

This nostalgia serves to enhance other negative feelings, together amounting to clinical depression. The narcissist proceeds to develop paranoia. He concocts a prosecuting world, incorporating in it his life's events and his social milieu. This gives meaning to what is erroneously perceived by the narcissist to be a sudden shift (from over-supply to no supply).

These theories of conspiracy account for the decrease in Narcissistic Supply. The narcissist then - frightened, in pain, and in despair - embarks upon an orgy of self-destruction intended to generate "alternative Supply Sources" (attention) at all costs. The narcissist is poised to commit the ultimate narcissistic act: self-destruction in the service of self-aggrandizement.

When deprived of Narcissistic Supply - both Primary AND Secondary - the narcissist feels annulled, hollowed out, or mentally disembowelled. This is an overpowering sense of evaporation, disintegration into molecules of terrified anguish, helplessly and inexorably.

Without Narcissistic Supply the narcissist crumbles like the zombies or the vampires one sees in horror movies. It is terrifying and the narcissist will do anything to avoid it. Again, like the drug addict, the narcissist's withdrawal symptoms are: delusions, physiological effects, irritability, and emotional lability.

In the absence of regular Narcissistic Supply, narcissists often experience brief, decompensatory psychotic episodes. This also happens while in therapy or following a life-crisis accompanied by a major narcissistic injury.

These psychotic episodes may be closely allied to another feature of narcissism: magical thinking. Narcissists are like children in this sense. Many, for instance, fully believe in two things: that whatever happens, they will prevail and that good things will always happen to them. It is more than mere belief. Narcissists just KNOW it, the same way one "knows" about gravity: directly, immediately and assuredly.

The narcissist believes that, no matter what he does, he will always be forgiven, always prevail and triumph, always come on top. The narcissist is, therefore, fearless in a manner perceived by others to be both admirable and reckless. He attributes to himself divine and cosmic immunity: he cloaks himself in it, it renders him invisible to his enemies and to the powers of "evil". It is a childish phantasmagoria, but to the narcissist it is very real.

With equal certitude, the more self-aware narcissist knows that he will squander this good fortune time and again - a painful experience best avoided. So, no matter what serendipity or fortuity, what lucky circumstance, what blessing the narcissist receives, he always strives with blind fury to deflect them and, thus, to ruin his chances.

The Delusional Way Out

"The man abandoned by all gods escapes completely from reality and creates for himself another world in which he ... can achieve everything that he wants. as been unloved, even tormented, he now splits off from himself a part which in the form of a helpful, loving, often motherly minder commiserates with the tormented remainder of the self, nurses him and decides for him ... with the deepest wisdom and most penetrating intelligence..."
[Ferenczi and Sandor - "Notes and Fragments" - International Journal of Psychoanalysis - Vol XXX (1949), p. 234]

Question: When my husband goes through a bad spot, he shuts himself in his den all day long, doesn't talk to anyone, just surfs the Web. Is this typical? Should I be worried?

Answer: The study of narcissism is a century old and the two scholarly debates central to its conception are still undecided. Is there such a thing as HEALTHY adult narcissism (Kohut) - or are all the manifestations of narcissism in adulthood pathological (Freud, Kernberg)? Moreover, is pathological narcissism the outcome of verbal, sexual, physical, or psychological abuse (the prevailing view) - or, on the contrary, the sad result of spoiling the child and idolizing it (Millon, Freud in his alter writings)?

The second debate is easier to resolve if one agrees to adopt a more comprehensive definition of "abuse". Overweening, smothering, spoiling, overvaluing, and idolizing the child are all forms of parental abuse.

This is because, as Horney pointed out, the child is dehumanized and instrumentalized. His parents love him not for what he really is but for what they wish and imagine him to be: the fulfilment of their dreams and frustrated wishes. The child becomes the vessel of his parents' discontented lives, a tool,

SAM VAKNIN   MALIGNANT SELF LOVE

the magic wand with which they can transform their failures into successes, their humiliation into victory, and their frustrations into happiness. The child is taught to ignore reality and to occupy the parental fantastic space. Such an unfortunate child feels omnipotent and omniscient, perfect and brilliant, worthy of adoration and entitled to special treatment. The faculties that are honed by constantly brushing against bruising reality - empathy, compassion, a realistic assessment of one's abilities and limitations, realistic expectations of oneself and of others, personal boundaries, team work, social skills, perseverance and goal-orientation, not to mention the ability to postpone gratification and to work hard to achieve it - are all lacking or missing altogether. This kind of child turned adult sees no reason to invest in his skills and education, convinced as he is that his inherent genius should suffice. He feels entitled for merely being, rather than for actually doing (rather as the nobility in days gone by felt entitled not by virtue of its merits but as an inevitable, foreordained birth right). In other words, the budding narcissist is not meritocratic but aristocratic.

But such a mental structure is brittle, susceptible to criticism and disagreement, vulnerable to incessant encounters with a harsh and intolerant world. Deep inside, narcissists of both kinds (those wrought by "classic" abuse and those yielded by being idolized) feel inadequate, phoney, fake, inferior, and deserving of punishment.

Millon makes a distinction between several types of narcissists. He wrongly assumes that the "classic" narcissist is the outcome of overvaluation, idolization, and spoiling and, thus, is possessed of supreme, unchallenged, self-confidence, and is devoid of all self-doubt. According to Millon, it is the "compensatory" narcissist that falls prey to nagging self-doubts, feelings of inferiority, and a masochistic desire for self-punishment. Yet, the distinction is both wrong and unnecessary. There is only ONE type of narcissist - though there are TWO developmental paths to it. And ALL narcissists are besieged by deeply ingrained (though at times not conscious) feelings of inadequacy, fears of failure, masochistic desires to be penalized, a fluctuating sense of self-worth (regulated by Narcissistic Supply), and an overwhelming sensation of fraudulence.

The Grandiosity Gap (between a fantastically grandiose self-image and actual, limited, accomplishments and achievements) is grating. Its recurrence threatens the precariously balanced house of cards that is the narcissistic personality. The narcissist finds, to his chagrin that people are much less admiring, accommodating and accepting than his parents. As he grows old, the narcissist often becomes the target of constant derision and mockery, a sorry sight indeed. His claims to superiority appear less plausible and substantial the more often and the longer he makes them.

Pathological narcissism - originally a defence mechanism intended to shield the narcissist from an injurious world - becomes the main source of hurt, a generator of injuries, counterproductive and dangerous. Overwhelmed by negative or absent Narcissistic Supply, the narcissist is forced to let go of it.

The narcissist then resorts to self-delusion. Unable to completely ignore contrarian opinion and data, he transmutes them. Unable to face the dismal failure that he is, the narcissist partially withdraws from reality. To soothe and salve the pain of disillusionment, he administers to his aching soul a mixture of lies, distortions, half-truths and outlandish interpretations of events around him. These solutions can be classified thus:

The Delusional Narrative Solution

The narcissist constructs a narrative in which he figures as the hero: brilliant, perfect, irresistibly handsome, destined for great things, entitled, powerful, wealthy, the centre of attention, etc. The bigger the strain on this delusional charade - the greater the gap between fantasy and reality - the more the delusion coalesces and solidifies.

Finally, if it is sufficiently protracted, it replaces reality and the narcissist's reality test deteriorates. He withdraws his bridges and may become schizotypal, catatonic, or schizoid.

The Antisocial Solution

The narcissist renounces reality. To his mind, those who pusillanimously fail to recognize his unbounded talents, innate superiority, overarching brilliance, benevolent nature, entitlement, cosmically important mission, perfection, etc. do not deserve consideration. The narcissist's natural affinity with the criminal - his lack of empathy and compassion, his deficient social skills, his disregard for social laws and morals, and his poor impulse control - now erupt and blossom. He becomes a full fledged antisocial (sociopath or psychopath). He ignores the wishes and needs of others, he breaks the law, he violates all rights, both natural and legal, he holds people in contempt and disdain, he derides society and its codes, he punishes the ignorant ingrates who, to his mind, drove him to this state by acting criminally and by jeopardising their safety, lives, or property.

The Paranoid Schizoid Solution

The narcissist develops persecutory delusions. He perceives slights and insults where none were intended. He becomes subject to ideas of reference (he becomes convinced that people are gossiping about him, mocking him, prying into his affairs, hacking his e-mail, etc.). He is convinced that he is the centre of malign and mal-intentioned attention. People are conspiring to humiliate him, punish him, abscond with his property, delude him, impoverish him, confine him physically or intellectually, censor him, impose on his time, force him to action (or to inaction), frighten him, coerce him, surround and besiege him, change his mind, part with his values, victimize or even murder him, and so on.

Some narcissists withdraw completely from a world populated with such minacious and ominous objects (really projections of internal objects and processes). They avoid all social contact, except the most necessary. They refrain from meeting people, falling in love, having sex, talking to others, or even corresponding with them. In short: they become schizoids - not out of social shyness, but out of what they feel to be their choice. "This evil, hopeless world does not deserve me" - goes the inner refrain - "and I shall waste none of my time and resources on it."

The Paranoid Aggressive (Explosive) Solution

Other narcissists, who develop persecutory delusions, resort to an aggressive stance, a more violent resolution of their internal conflict. They become verbally, psychologically, situationally (and, very rarely, physically) abusive. They insult, castigate, chastise, berate, demean, and deride their nearest and dearest (often well wishers and loved ones). They explode in unprovoked displays of indignation, self-righteousness, condemnation, and blame. Theirs is an exegetic Bedlam. They interpret everything - even the most innocuous, inadvertent, and innocent comment - as designed to provoke and humiliate them. They sow fear, revulsion, hate, and malignant envy. They flail against the windmills of reality - a pathetic, forlorn, sight. But often they cause real and lasting damage - fortunately, mainly to themselves.

The Masochistic Avoidant Solution

The narcissist is angered by the lack of Narcissistic Supply. He directs some of this fury inwards, punishing himself for his "failure". This masochistic behaviour has the added "benefit" of forcing the narcissist's closest to assume the roles of dismayed spectators or of persecutors and thus, either way, to pay him the attention that he craves.

Self-administered punishment often manifests as self-handi-capping masochism - a narcissistic cop-out. By undermining his work, his relationships, and his efforts, the increasingly fragile narcissist avoids additional criticism and censure (negative sup-ply). Self-inflicted failure is the narcissist's doing and thus proves that he is the master of his own fate.

Masochistic narcissists keep finding themselves in self-defeat-ing circumstances which render success impossible and *"an objective assessment of their performance improbable"* [Millon, 2000]. They act carelessly, withdraw in mid-effort, are constantly fatigued, bored, or disaffected and thus passive-aggressively sabotage their lives. Their suffering is defiant and by "deciding to abort" they reassert their omnipotence.

The narcissist's pronounced and public misery and self-pity are compensatory and *"reinforce (his) self-esteem against over-whelming convictions of worthlessness"* [Millon, 2000]. His tribulations and anguish render him, in his eyes, unique, saint-ly, virtuous, righteous, resilient, and significant. They are, in other words, self-generated Narcissistic Supply.

Thus, paradoxically, the worst his anguish and unhappiness, the more relieved and elated such a narcissist feels!

[Additional reading: Millon, Theodore and Davis, Roger - Personality Disorders in Modern Life, 2nd Edition - New York, John Wiley and Sons, 2000]

Note: The Prodigy as Narcissistic Injury

The prodigy - the precocious "genius" - feels entitled to special treatment. Yet, his unrealistic expectations are rarely fulfilled. This frustrates him and renders him even more aggressive, dri-ven, and overachieving than he is by nature.

Not all precocious prodigies end up under-accomplished and petulant. Many of them go on to attain great stature in their communities and great standing in their professions. But, even then, the gap between the kind of treatment they believe that they deserve and the one they are getting is unbridgeable.

This is because narcissistic prodigies often misjudge the extent and importance of their accomplishments and, as a result, erro-neously consider themselves to be indispensable and worthy of special rights, perks, and privileges. When they find out other-wise, they are devastated and furious. Moreover, people are envious of the prodigy. The genius serves as a constant reminder to others of their mediocrity, lack of creativity, and mundane existence. Naturally, they try to "bring him down to their level" and "cut him down to size". The gifted person's haughtiness and high-handedness only exacerbate his strained relationships.

In a way, merely by existing, the prodigy inflicts constant and repeated narcissistic injuries on the less endowed and the pedestrian. This creates a vicious cycle. People try to hurt and harm the overweening and arrogant genius and he becomes defensive, aggressive, and aloof. This renders him even more obnoxious than before and others resent him more deeply and more thoroughly. Hurt and wounded, he retreats into fantasies of grandeur and revenge. And the cycle re-commences.

Grandiosity and Intimacy - The Roots of Paranoia

Paranoid ideation - the narcissist's deep-rooted conviction that he is being persecuted by his inferiors, detractors, or powerful ill-wishers - serves two psychodynamic purposes. It upholds the narcissist's grandiosity and it fends off intimacy.

Grandiosity Enhancing Paranoia

Being the target of relentless, ubiquitous, and unjust persecution proves to the paranoid narcissist how important and feared he is. Being hounded by the mighty and the privileged validates his pivotal role in the scheme of things. Only vital, weighty, crucial, essential principals are thus bullied and intimidated, followed and harassed, stalked and intruded upon goes his unconscious inner dialog. The narcissist consistently baits authority figures into punishing him and thus into upholding his delusional self-image as worthy of their attention. This provocative behaviour is called Projective Identification.

The paranoid delusions of the narcissist are always grandiose, "cosmic", or "historical". His pursuers are influential and formidable. They are after his unique possessions, out to exploit his expertise and special traits, or to force him to abstain and refrain from certain actions. The narcissist feels that he is at the centre of intrigues and conspiracies of colossal magnitudes.

Alternatively, the narcissist feels victimized by mediocre bureaucrats and intellectual dwarves who consistently fail to appreciate his outstanding - really, unparalleled - talents, skills, and accomplishments. Being hunted by his challenged inferiors substantiates the narcissist's comparative superiority. Driven by pathological envy, these pygmies collude to defraud him, badger him, deny him his due, denigrate, isolate, and ignore him.

The narcissist projects onto this second class of lesser persecutors his own deleterious emotions and transformed aggression: hatred, rage, and seething jealousy.

The narcissist's paranoid streak is likeliest to erupt when he lacks Narcissistic Supply. The regulation of his labile sense of self-worth is dependent upon external stimuli: adoration, adulation, affirmation, applause, notoriety, fame, infamy, and, in general, attention of any kind.

When such attention is deficient, the narcissist compensates by confabulating. He constructs ungrounded narratives in which he is the protagonist and uses them to force his human environment into complicity.

Put simply, he provokes people to pay attention to him by misbehaving or by behaving oddly.

Intimacy Retarding Paranoia

Paranoia is used by the narcissist to ward off or reverse intimacy. The narcissist is threatened by intimacy because it reduces him to ordinariness by exposing his weaknesses and shortcomings and by causing him to act "normally". The narcissist also dreads the encounter with his deep buried emotions - hurt, envy, anger, aggression - likely to be foisted on him in an intimate relationship.

The paranoid narrative legitimizes intimacy-retarding behaviours such as keeping one's distance, secrecy, aloofness, reclusion, aggression, intrusion on privacy, lying, desultoriness, itinerancy, unpredictability, and idiosyncratic or eccentric reactions. Gradually, the narcissist succeeds to alienate and wear down all his friends, colleagues, well-wishers, spouses, partners, and mates.

Even his closest, nearest, and dearest, his family, feel emotionally detached and "burnt out".

The paranoid narcissist ends life as an oddball recluse: derided, feared, and loathed in equal measures. His paranoia - exacerbated by repeated rejections and ageing - pervades his entire life and diminishes his creativity, adaptability, and functioning. The narcissist's personality, buffeted by paranoia, turns ossified and brittle. Finally, atomized and useless, it succumbs and gives way to a great void. The narcissist is consumed.

First published on the Suite 101 Narcissistic Personality Disorders Topic.

The Compulsive Acts of the Narcissist

Question: Are there compulsive acts unique to the narcissist?

Answer: The short and the long of it is: no. In general, there is a strong compulsive strand in the narcissist's behaviour. He is driven to exorcize internal demons by means of ritualistic acts. The narcissist's very pursuit of Narcissistic Supply is compulsive. The narcissist seeks to recreate and re-enact old traumas, ancient, unresolved conflicts with figures of (primary) importance in his life.

The narcissist feels that he is "bad" and guilty (in a diffuse, vague sort of way) and that, therefore, he should be punished. So, he makes sure that he is disciplined. This Repetition Complex possesses the tint and hue of compulsion. In many respects, narcissism can be defined as an all-pervasive obsessive-compulsive disorder.

The narcissist is faced with difficult conditions in his childhood: neglect, abandonment, capriciousness, arbitrariness, strictness, sadistic behaviour, abuse (physical, psychological, or verbal) - or doting, smothering, "annexation" and "appropriation" by a narcissistic and frustrated parent.

The narcissist develops a unique defence mechanism: a story, a narrative, another self. This False Self is possessed of all the qualities that can insulate the child from an ominous and hostile world. It is perfect, omnipotent, omniscient, and omnipresent. In short: it is divine.

The narcissist develops a private religion with the False Self at its centre. It is replete with rites, mantras, scriptures, and spiritual and physical exercises. The child worships this new deity. He succumbs to what he perceives to be its wishes and its needs. He caters to it and offers it sacrifices of Narcissistic Supply. He is awed by it because it possesses many of the traits of the hallowed tormentors, his parents.

The child reduces his True Self, minimizes it. He is looking to appease the new Divinity, not to incur its wrath. He does so by adhering to strict schedules and ceremonies, by reciting texts, by self-imposition of self-discipline. Henceforth, the child is transformed into the servant of his False Self. And he is rewarded for his efforts: he feels elated when in compliance with the creed, he emulates the characteristics of this entity.

Suffused with Narcissistic Supply, his False Self content, the child feels omnipotent, untouchable, invulnerable, immune to threats and insults and omniscient. On the other hand, when Narcissistic Supply is lacking, the child feels guilty, miserable, and unworthy. The Superego then takes over: sadistic, ominous, cruel, suicidal, it chastises the child for having failed, for having sinned, for being guilty. It demands a self-inflicted penalty to cleanse, to atone, to let go.

Caught between these two deities - the False Self and the Superego - the child is compulsively forced to seek Narcissistic Supply. Success in this pursuit holds both promises: an emotional reward, mediated by the False Self and protection from the murderous Superego.

Throughout, the child maintains the rhythms of regenerating his conflicts and traumas in order to try and resolve them. Such resolution can be either in the form of punishment or in the form of healing. But since healing means letting go of his system of beliefs and deities, the child is more likely to choose punishment.

The narcissist strives to re-enact old traumas and open old wounds. For instance, he behaves in ways that make people abandon him. Or he becomes rebellious in order to be chastised by figures of authority. Or he engages in criminal or antisocial activities. These types of self-defeating and self-destructive behaviours are in permanent interaction with and guided by the False Self. It is a marriage made in hell between dysfunctional impulse control and Projective Identification.

The False Self breeds compulsive acts. The narcissist seeks Narcissistic Supply compulsively. He wants to be punished compulsively. He generates resentment or hatred, switches sexual partners, becomes eccentric, writes articles and makes scientific discoveries - all compulsively. There is no joy in his life or in his actions - just relieved anxiety, the moment of liberation and soothing protection that he enjoys following a compulsive act.

As pressure builds inside the narcissist, threatening to upset the precarious balance of his personality, something warns him that danger is imminent. He reacts by developing an acute anxiety, which can be alleviated only with a compulsive act. If this act fails to materialize, the emotional outcome can be anything from absolute terror to deep-set depression.

The narcissist knows that his very life is at stake, that in his Superego lurks a mortal enemy. He knows that only his False Self stands between him and his Superego (the True Self is warped, depleted, immature and dilapidated).

Narcissists are characterized by reckless and impulsive behaviours: binge eating, compulsive shopping, pathological gambling, drinking, reckless driving. But what sets them apart from non-narcissistic compulsives is twofold:

1. With the narcissist, the compulsive acts constitute a part of a larger "grandiose" picture. When a narcissist shops, it is in order to build up a unique collection. If he gambles, it is to prove right a method that he has developed to defeat the casino, or to demonstrate his amazing mental or psychic powers. If he climbs mountains or races cars, it is to break records and if he binges, it is part of constructing a universal diet or bodybuilding and so on. The narcissist never does anything in a simple and straightforward manner for fear of becoming too mundane, not sufficiently grandiose. He invents a contextual narrative in order to lend outstanding proportions, perspectives, and purpose to his most common acts, including the compulsive ones. Where the regular compulsive patient feels that the compulsive act restores his control over himself and over his life, the narcissist feels that the compulsive act restores his control over his environment and secures his future Narcissistic Supply.

2. With the narcissist, the compulsive acts enhance the reward-penalty cycle. At their inception and for as long as they are committed, they reward the narcissist emotionally in the ways described above. But they also provide him with fresh ammunition against himself. His sins of indulgence lead the narcissist down the path of yet another self-inflicted punishment.

Finally, "normal" compulsions usually can be effectively treated. The (behaviourist or cognitive-behavioural) therapist reconditions the patient and helps him get rid of his constricting rituals, often with the aid of medication. This works only partly with the narcissist. His compulsive acts are merely an element in his complicated personality. They are the sick tips of very abnormal icebergs. Shaving them off does nothing to ameliorate the narcissist's titanic inner struggle.

The Cyber Narcissist

To the narcissist, the Internet is an alluring and irresistible combination of playground and hunting grounds, the gathering place of numerous potential Sources of Narcissistic Supply, a world where false identities are the norm and mind games the bon ton. And it is beyond the reach of the law, the pale of social norms, or the strictures of civilized conduct.

The somatic finds cyber-sex and cyber-relationships aplenty. The cerebral claims false accomplishments, sham skills, erudition and talents. Both, if minimally communicative, end up at the instantly gratifying epicentre of a cult of fans, followers, stalkers, erotomaniacs, denigrators, and plain nuts. The constant attention and attendant quasi-celebrity feed and sustain their grandiose fantasies and inflated self-image.

The Internet is an extension of the real-life Narcissistic Pathological Space but without its risks, injuries, and disappointments. In the virtual universe of the Web, the narcissist vanishes and reappears with ease, often adopting a myriad aliases and nicknames. He can thus fend off criticism, abuse, disagreement, and disapproval effectively and in real time while simultaneously preserving the precarious balance of his infantile personality. Narcissists are, therefore, prone to Internet addiction.

The positive characteristics of the Net are largely lost on the narcissist. He is not keen on expanding his horizons, fostering true relationships, or getting in real contact with other people. The narcissist is forever the provincial because he filters everything through the narrow lens of his addiction. He measures others - and idealizes or devalues them - according to one criterion only: how useful they might be as Sources of Narcissistic Supply.

The Internet is an egalitarian medium where people are judged by the consistency and quality of their contributions rather than by the content or bombast of their claims. But the narcissist is driven to distracting discomfiture by a lack of clear and commonly accepted hierarchy (with himself at the pinnacle). He fervently and aggressively tries to impose the "natural order" - either by monopolizing the interaction or, if that fails, by becoming a major disruptive influence.

But the Internet may also be the closest many narcissists get to psychodynamic therapy. Because it is still largely text-based, the Web is populated by disembodied entities. By interacting with these intermittent, unpredictable, ultimately unknowable, ephemeral, and ethereal voices the narcissist is compelled to project unto them his own experiences, fears, hopes, and prejudices.

Transference (and counter-transference) are quite common on the Net and the narcissist's defence mechanisms, notably projection and Projective Identification, are frequently aroused. The therapeutic process is set in motion by the unbridled, uncensored, and brutally honest reactions to the narcissist's repertory of antics, pretensions, delusions, and fantasies.

The narcissist - ever the intimidating bully - is not accustomed to such resistance. Initially, it may heighten and sharpen his paranoia and lead him to compensate by extending and deepening his grandiosity. Some narcissists withdraw altogether, reverting to the schizoid posture. Others become openly antisocial and seek to subvert, sabotage, and destroy the online sources of their frustration. A few retreat and confine themselves to the company of adoring sycophants and unquestioning groupies.

But a long exposure to the culture of the Net - irreverent, sceptical, and populist - usually exerts a beneficial effect even on the staunchest and most rigid narcissist. Far less convinced of his own superiority and infallibility, the online narcissist mellows and begins, albeit hesitantly, to listen to others and to collaborate with them.

Narcissistic Routines

Question: Narcissists are so predictable! I can tell what he will do next, what he will say, how he will react. It's sometimes boring.

Answer: The behaviour of the narcissist is regulated by a series of routines developed by rote learning and by repetitive patterns of experience. The narcissist finds change extremely distasteful and unsettling. He is a creature of habit. The function of these routines is to reduce his anxiety by transforming a hostile and arbitrary world into a hospitable and manageable one.

Granted, many narcissists are unstable: they often change jobs, residences, spouses, and vocations. But even these changes are predictable. The narcissistic personality is disorganized, but also rigid. The narcissist finds solace in certainty, in recurrence, in the familiar and the anticipated. It balances his inner precariousness, lability, and volatility.

Narcissists often strike their interlocutors as "machine-like", "artificial", "fake", "forced", "insincere", or "spurious". This is because even the narcissist's ostensibly spontaneous behaviours are either planned or automatic. The narcissist is continuously preoccupied with his Narcissistic Supply: how to secure its sources and the next dose. This preoccupation restricts the narcissist's attention span. As a result, he often appears to be aloof, absent-minded, and uninterested in other people, in events around him, and in abstract ideas - unless, of course, they have a direct bearing on his Narcissistic Supply.

The narcissist develops some of his routines to compensate for his inability to attend to his environment. Automatic reactions require much less investment of mental resources.

Narcissists may fake personal warmth and an outgoing personality: this is the routine of the "narcissistic mask". But as one gets to know the narcissist better, his mask falls, his "narcissistic

118

MALIGNANT SELF LOVE   SAM VAKNIN

makeup" wears off, his muscles relax and he reverts to the Narcissistic Tonus. The Narcissistic Tonus is a bodacious air of superiority mixed with disdain.

While routines, such as the various masks, are extraneous and require an often conscious investment of energy, the Tonus is the default position: it is effortless and frequent.

Many narcissists are obsessive-compulsive as well. They conduct daily "rituals", they are overly punctilious, they do things in a certain order, and adhere to numerous "laws", "principles", and "rules". They have rigid and oft-repeated opinions, uncompromising rules of conduct, unalterable views and judgements. These compulsions and obsessions are ossified routines.

Other routines involve paranoid, repetitive, thoughts. Yet others induce shyness and Social Phobia. The whole range of narcissistic behaviours can be traced to these routines and the various phases of their evolutionary cycles.

When these routines break down and are violated, when they become no longer defensible, or when the narcissist can no longer exercise them, a narcissistic injury occurs. The narcissist expects the outside world to conform to his inner universe. When a conflict between these two realms erupts, thus unsettling the ill-poised mental balance so painstakingly achieved by the narcissist (mainly by exercising his routines), the narcissist unravels. The narcissist's very defence mechanisms are routines, and so he is left defenceless in a hostile, cold world: the true reflection of his inner landscape.

119

First published on the Suite 101 Narcissistic Personality Disorders Topic.

The Unstable Narcissist

Question: Is the narcissist characterized by simultaneous instabilities in all the important aspects of his life?

Answer: The narcissist is a person who derives his Ego (and ego functions) from other people's reactions to an image he invents and projects, called the False Self (Narcissistic Supply). Since no absolute control over the quantity and quality of Narcissistic Supply is possible - it is bound to fluctuate - the narcissist's view of himself and of his world is correspondingly and equally volatile. As "public opinion" ebbs and flows, so do the narcissist's self-confidence, self-esteem, sense of self-worth, or, in other words, so does his Self. Even the narcissist's convictions are subject to a never-ending process of vetting by others.

The narcissistic personality is unstable in each and every one of its dimensions. It is the ultimate hybrid: rigidly amorphous, devoutly flexible, reliant for its sustenance on the opinion of people, whom the narcissist undervalues. A large part of this instability is subsumed under the Emotional Involvement Prevention Measures (EIPM), described in the Essay. The narcissist's lability is so ubiquitous and so dominant, that it might well be described as the ONLY stable feature of his personality.

The narcissist does everything with one goal in mind: to attract Narcissistic Supply (attention).

An example of this kind of behaviour:

The narcissist may study a given subject diligently and in great depth in order to impress people later with this newly acquired erudition. But, having served its purpose, the narcissist lets the knowledge thus acquired evaporate. The narcissist maintains a sort of a "short-term" cell or warehouse where he stores whatever may come handy in the pursuit of Narcissistic Supply. But he is almost never really interested in what he does, or studies, or experiences.

120

MALIGNANT SELF LOVE   SAM VAKNIN

From the outside, this might be perceived as instability. But think about it this way: the narcissist is constantly preparing for life's "exams" and feels that he is on a permanent trial. It is common to forget material studied only in preparation for an exam or for a court appearance.

Short-term memory is perfectly normal. What sets the narcissist apart is the fact that, with him, this short-termism is a CONSTANT state of affairs and affects ALL his functions, not only those directly related to learning, or to emotions, or to experience, or to any single dimension of his life.

Thus, the narcissist learns, remembers and forgets not in line with his real interests or hobbies; he loves and hates not the real subjects of his emotions but one dimensional, utilitarian, cartoons constructed by him. He judges, praises and condemns - all from the narrowest possible point of view: the potential to extract Narcissistic Supply.

He asks not what he can do with the world and in it - but what can the world do for him as far as Narcissistic Supply is concerned. He falls in and out of love with people, workplaces, residences, vocations, hobbies, and interests because they seem to be able to provide more or less Narcissistic Supply and for no other reason.

Still, narcissists belong to two broad categories: the "compensatory stability" and the "enhancing instability" types.

Compensatory Stability ("Classic") Narcissists

These narcissists isolate one or more (but never most) aspects of their lives and "make these aspect/s stable". They do not really emotionally invest themselves in maintaining these areas of their lives stable. Rather, this stability is safeguarded by artificial means: money, celebrity, power, fear. A typical example is a narcissist who changes numerous workplaces, a few careers, a myriad of hobbies, value systems or faiths. At the same time, he maintains (preserves) a relationship with a single woman (and even remains faithful to her). She is his "island of stability". To fulfil this role, she just needs to be physically present around him.

The narcissist is dependent upon "his" woman to maintain the stability lacking in all other areas of his life (to compensate for his instability). Yet, emotional closeness and intimacy are bound to threaten the narcissist. Thus, he is likely to distance himself from her and to remain detached and indifferent to most of her needs.

Despite this cruel emotional treatment, the narcissist considers her to be a source of sustenance and a fountain of empowerment.

This mismatch between what he wishes to receive and what he is able to give, the narcissist prefers to deny, repress and bury deep in his unconscious.

This is why he is always shocked and devastated to learn of his wife's estrangement, infidelity, or intentions to divorce him. Possessed of no emotional depth, being completely clueless and one track minded, he cannot fathom the needs of others. In other words, he cannot empathize.

Another, even more common case is the "career narcissist". This narcissist marries, divorces and remarries with dizzying speed. Everything in his life is in constant flux: friends, emotions, judgements, values, beliefs, place of residence, affiliations, hobbies. Everything, that is, except his work.

His career is the island of compensating stability in his otherwise mercurial existence. This kind of narcissist is dogged by unmitigated ambition and devotion. He perseveres in one workplace or one job, patiently, persistently and blindly climbing up the corporate ladder and treading the career path. In his pursuit of job fulfilment and achievements, the workaholic narcissist is ruthless and unscrupulous, and, very often, successful.

Enhancing Instability ("Borderline") Narcissist

The other kind of narcissist enhances instability in one aspect or dimension of his life by introducing instability in others. Thus, if such a narcissist resigns (or, more likely, is made redundant), he also relocates to another city or country. If he divorces, he is also likely to resign his job.

This added instability gives this type of narcissist the feeling that all the dimensions of his life are changing simultaneously, that he is being "unshackled", that a transformation is in progress. This, of course, is an illusion. Those who know the narcissist, no longer trust his frequent "conversions", "decisions", "crises", "transformations", "developments" and "periods". They see through his pretensions, protestations, and solemn declarations into the core of his instability. They know that he is not to be relied upon. They know that with narcissists, the temporary is the only permanence.

Narcissists hate routine. When a narcissist finds himself doing the same things over and over again, he gets depressed. He oversleeps, over-eats, over-drinks and, in general, engages in addictive, impulsive, reckless, and compulsive behaviours. This is his way of re-introducing risk and excitement into what he (emotionally) perceives to be a barren life.

The problem is that even the most exciting and varied existence becomes routine after a while. Living in the same country or apartment, meeting the same people, doing essentially the same things (even with changing content) all amount, in the eyes of the narcissist, to stultifying rote.

The narcissist feels entitled. He feels it is his right - due to his intellectual or physical superiority - to lead a thrilling, rewarding, kaleidoscopic life. He wants to force life itself, or at least people around him, to yield to his wishes and needs, supreme among them the need for stimulating variety.

This rejection of habit is part of a larger pattern of aggressive entitlement. The narcissist feels that the very existence of a sublime intellect (such as his) warrants concessions and allowances by others.

Thus, queuing in line is a waste of time better spent pursuing knowledge, inventing and creating. The narcissist feels that he deserves only the best medical treatment proffered by the most prominent medical authorities - lest the precious asset that he is should be lost to Mankind. The narcissist makes clear that he should not be bothered with trivial pursuits - these lowly functions are best assigned to the less gifted.

Entitlement is sometimes justified in a Picasso or an Einstein. But few narcissists are either. Their achievements are grotesquely incommensurate with their overwhelming sense of entitlement and with their grandiose self-image.

Of course, this overpowering sense of superiority often serves to mask and compensate for a cancerous complex of inferiority. Moreover, the narcissist infects others with his projected grandiosity and their feedback constitutes the edifice upon which he constructs his self-esteem. He regulates his sense of self-worth by rigidly insisting that he is above the madding crowd while deriving his Narcissistic Supply from the very people he holds in deep contempt.

But there is a second angle to this abhorrence of the predictable. Narcissists employ a host of Emotional Involvement Prevention Measures (EIPM's). Despising routine and avoiding it is one of these mechanisms. Their function is to prevent the narcissist from getting emotionally involved and, subsequently, hurt.

Their application results in an Approach-Avoidance Repetition Complex. The narcissist, fears and loathes intimacy, stability and security and yet craves them. Consequently, he approaches and then avoids significant others or important tasks in a rapid succession of apparently inconsistent and disconnected cycles.

The Two Loves of the Narcissist

Narcissists "love" their spouses or other significant others - as long as they continue to reliably provide them with Narcissistic Supply (in one word, with attention). Inevitably, they regard others as mere "sources", objects, or functions. Lacking empathy and emotional maturity, the narcissist's love is pathological. But the precise locus of the pathology depends on the narcissist's stability or instability in different parts of his life.

We are, therefore, faced with two pathological forms of narcissistic "love".

One type of narcissist "loves" others as one attaches to objects. He "loves" his spouse, for instance, simply because she exists and is available to provide him with Narcissistic Supply. He "loves" his children because they are part of his self-image as a successful husband and father. He "loves" his "friends" because - and only as long as - he can exploit them.

Such a narcissist reacts with alarm and rage to any sign of independence and autonomy in his "charges". He tries to "freeze" everyone around him in their "allocated" positions and "assigned roles". His world is rigid and immovable, predictable and static, fully under his control. He punishes for "transgressions" against this ordained order. He thus stifles life as a dynamic process of compromises and growth rendering it instead a mere theatre, a tableau vivant.

The other type of narcissist abhors monotony and constancy, equating them, in his mind, with death. He seeks upheaval, drama, and change, but only when they conform to his plans, designs, and views of the world and of himself. Thus, he does not encourage growth in his nearest and dearest. By monopolizing their lives, he, like the other kind of narcissist, also reduces them to mere objects, props in the exciting drama of his life. ·

This narcissist likewise rages at any sign of rebellion and disagreement. But, as opposed to the first sub-species, he seeks to animate others with his demented energy, grandiose plans, and megalomaniacal self-perception. An adrenaline junkie, his world is a whirlwind of comings and goings, reunions and separations, loves and hates, vocations adopted and discarded, schemes erected and dismantled, enemies turned friends and vice versa. His Universe is equally a theatre, but a more ferocious and chaotic one.

Where is love in all this? Where is the commitment to the loved one's welfare, the self-discipline, the extension of oneself to incorporate the beloved, the mutual growth?

These are nowhere to be seen. The narcissist's "love" is hate and fear disguised: fear of losing control and hatred of the very people his precariously balanced personality so depends on. The narcissist is egotistically committed only to his own well-being. To him, the objects of his "love" are interchangeable and inferior.

He idealizes his nearest and dearest not because he is smitten by emotion, but because he needs to captivate them and to convince himself that they are worthy Sources of Supply, despite their flaws and mediocrity. Once he deems them useless, he discards and devalues them cold-bloodedly. A predator, always on the lookout, he debases the coin of "love" as he corrupts everything else in himself and around him.

Do Narcissists Have Emotions?

Of course they do. All humans have emotions. It is how we choose to relate to our emotions that matters. The narcissist tends to repress them so deeply that, for all practical purposes, they play no conscious role in his life and conduct, though they play an extraordinarily large unconscious role in determining both.

The narcissist's positive emotions come bundled with very negative ones. This is the outcome of frustration and the consequent transformations of aggression. This frustration is connected to the Primary Objects of the narcissist's childhood (parents and caregivers).

126

Instead of being provided with the unconditional love that he craved, the narcissist was subjected to totally unpredictable and inexplicable bouts of temper, rage, searing sentimentality, envy, prodding, infusion of guilt and other unhealthy parental emotions and behaviour patterns.

The narcissist reacted by retreating to his private world, where he is omnipotent and omniscient and, therefore, immune to such vicious vicissitudes. He stashed his vulnerable True Self in a deep mental cellar and presented to the world a False Self in its stead.

But bundling is far easier than unbundling. The narcissist is unable to experience positive feelings without provoking negative emotions. Gradually, he becomes phobic: afraid to feel anything at all, lest it be accompanied by fearsome, guilt inducing, anxiety provoking, out of control emotional complements.

He is thus reduced to experiencing dull stirrings in his soul that he identifies to himself and to others as emotions. Even these are felt only in the presence of someone or something capable of providing the narcissist with his badly needed Narcissistic Supply.

Only when the narcissist is in the overvaluation (idealization) phase of his relationships, does he experience the convulsions that he calls "feelings". These are so transient and fake that they are easily replaced by rage, envy and devaluation. The narcissist thus recreates the behaviour patterns of his less than ideal Primary Objects.

Deep inside, the narcissist knows that something is amiss. He does not empathize with other people's feelings. Actually, he holds them in contempt and ridicule. He cannot understand how people are so sentimental, so "irrational" (he identifies being rational with being cool headed and cold blooded).

Often the narcissist believes that other people are "faking it", merely aiming to achieve a goal. He is convinced that their "feelings" are grounded in ulterior, non-emotional, motives. He becomes suspicious, embarrassed, feels compelled to avoid emotion-tinged situations, or, worse, experiences surges of almost uncontrollable aggression in the presence of genuinely expressed sentiments. They remind him how imperfect and poorly equipped he is.

The weaker variety of narcissist tries to emulate and simulate "emotions", or, at least their expression, the external facet (affect). Such narcissists mimic and replicate the intricate pantomime that they learn to associate with the existence of feelings. But there are no real emotions there, no emotional correlates.

The narcissist's is an empty affect, devoid of emotion. This being so, the narcissist quickly tires of it, becomes impassive and begins to display inappropriate affect (e.g., he remains indifferent when grief is the normal reaction). The narcissist subjects his feigned emotions to his cognition. He "decides" that it is appropriate to feel this or that way. His "emotions" are invariably the result of analysis, goal setting and planning.

The narcissist substitutes "remembering" for "sensing". He relegates his bodily sensations, feelings and emotions to a kind of memory vault. His short and medium-term memory is exclusively used to store his reactions to his (actual and potential) Narcissistic Supply Sources.

For the narcissist, as we saw, reacts only to such sources. The narcissist finds it hard to remember or recreate what he ostensibly - though ostentatiously - "felt" (even a short while back) towards a Narcissistic Supply Source once it has ceased to be one. In his attempts to recall his feelings, the narcissist draws mental blanks.

It is not that narcissists are incapable of expressing what we would tend to classify as "extreme emotional reactions". They mourn and grieve, rage and smile, excessively "love" and "care". But this is precisely what sets them apart: this rapid movement from one emotional extreme to another and the fact that they never occupy the emotional middle ground.

The narcissist is especially "emotional" when he is weaned off his drug of Narcissistic Supply. Breaking a habit is always difficult - especially one that defines (and engenders) oneself. Getting rid of an addiction is doubly taxing. The narcissist mistakes these psychological crises for emotional depth and his self-conviction is so immense, that he mostly succeeds to delude his environment, as well. But an "emotionally"-charged narcissistic crisis (losing a Source of Narcissistic Supply, obtaining an alternative one, moving from one Narcissistic Pathological Space to another) must never be confused with the real thing, which the narcissist never experiences: emotions.

Many narcissists have "emotional resonance tables". They use words as others use algebraic signs: with meticulousness, with caution, with the precision of the artisan. They sculpt in words the fine tuned reverberations of pain and love and fear. It is the mathematics of emotional grammar, the geometry of the syntax of passions. Devoid of all emotions, narcissists closely monitor people's reactions and adjust their verbal choices according to these cues, until their vocabulary resembles that of their listeners. This mimicry is as close as narcissists get to empathy.

To summarize, the emotional life of the narcissist is colourless and eventless, as rigidly blind as his disorder, as dead as he is. The narcissist does feel rage and hurt and inordinate humiliation, envy and fear. These are very dominant, prevalent and recurrent hues in the canvass of his emotional existence. But there is nothing there except these atavistic gut reactions.

Whatever the narcissist experiences as emotions, he experiences in reaction to slights and injuries, real or imagined. His emotions are all reactive, not active. He feels insulted - he sulks. He feels devalued - he rages. He feels ignored - he pouts. He feels humiliated - he lashes out. He feels threatened - he fears. He feels adored - he basks in glory. He is virulently envious of one and all.

The narcissist can appreciate beauty but in a cerebral, cold and "mathematical" way. Many have no mature, adult sex drive to speak of. Their emotional landscape is dim and grey, as though through a glass darkly.

Many narcissists can intelligently discuss emotions never experienced by them: empathy, love, or compassion. This is because they make it a point to read a lot and to communicate with people who claim to be experiencing them. Thus, they gradually construct working hypotheses as to what people feel. As far as the narcissist is concerned, it is pointless to try to really understand emotions, but at least these models he forms allow him to better predict people's behaviours and adjust to them.

Narcissists are not envious of others for having emotions. They disdain feelings and sentimental people because they deem them weak and vulnerable and they deride human frailties and vulnerabilities. Such derision makes the narcissist feel superior and is probably the ossified remains of a defence mechanism gone awry.

Narcissists are afraid of pain. Their pains do not come isolated: they constitute families of anguish, tribes of hurt, whole races of agony. The narcissist cannot experience various pains separately, only collectively.

Narcissism is an effort to contain the ominous onslaught of stale negative emotions, repressed rage, and one's childhood injuries.

Pathological narcissism is a useful survival strategy: this is why it is so resilient and resistant to change. When it is "conjured" by the tormented individual, it enhances his functionality and makes life bearable for him. Because it is so successful, it attains religious dimensions: it become rigid, doctrinaire, automatic and ritualistic.

In other words, pathological narcissism becomes a PATTERN of behaviour. This rigidity is like an outer shell, an exoskeleton. It constrains the narcissist and limits him. It is often prohibitive and inhibitive. As a result, the narcissist is afraid to do certain things. He is injured or humiliated when forced to engage in certain activities. He reacts with rage when the mental edifice underlying his disorder is subjected to scrutiny and criticism, no matter how benign or well-meaning.

Narcissism is ridiculous and embarrassing to behold. Narcissists are pompous, grandiose, repulsive and contradictory. There is a serious mismatch between who they really are, their true accomplishments, and how they regard themselves. The narcissist doesn't merely THINK that he is far superior to others. The perception of his superiority is ingrained in him, it is a part of his every mental cell, an all-pervasive sensation, an instinct and a drive.

He feels that he is entitled to special treatment and to outstanding consideration because he is such a unique specimen. He knows this to be true, the same way one knows that one is surrounded by air. It is an integral part of his identity.

This opens a gap - rather, an abyss - between the narcissist and other people. Because he considers himself so special and so superior, he has no way of knowing how it is to be human, neither the inclination to find out. In other words, the narcissist cannot and will not empathize with others.

Can you empathize with an ant? Empathy implies identity or equality with the empathized, both implications abhorrent to the narcissist. And being perceived by the narcissist to be so inferior, people are reduced to cartoonish, two-dimensional representations of functions. They become instrumental, or useful, or functional, or entertaining, gratifying or infuriating, frustrating or accommodating objects, rather than loving or emotionally responsive potential partners.

This state of mind leads to ruthlessness and exploitativeness. Narcissists are not "evil" - actually, the narcissist considers himself to be a good person. Many narcissists help people, professionally, or voluntarily. But narcissists are indifferent. They couldn't care less. The narcissist helps people because it is a way to secure attention, gratitude, adulation and admiration and because it is the fastest and surest method to get rid of them and their incessant nagging.

The narcissist may realize these unpleasant truths cognitively, but there is no corresponding emotional reaction (emotional correlate) to this realization. There is no resonance. To him, the act of introspection in order to gain psychological insight is like reading a boring users' manual pertaining to a computer you do not even own.

Still, to further insulate himself from the improbable possibility of confronting the inevitable gulf between reality and grandiose fantasy (the Grandiosity Gap), the narcissist comes up with the most elaborate mental structure, replete with mechanisms, levers, switches and flickering alarm lights.

Narcissism isolates the narcissist from the pain of facing reality and allows him to inhabit the fantasyland of ideal perfection and brilliance.

The Inappropriate Affect

Question: Why is there no connection between the behaviour of the narcissist and his emotions?

Answer: There is a weak correlation between the narcissist's behaviour and his professed or proclaimed emotions. The reason is that his emotions are merely professed or proclaimed, but not felt. The narcissist fakes feelings and their outer expression in order to impress others, to gain their sympathy or to motivate them to act in a manner benefiting the narcissist and promoting his interests.

131

In this, as in many other simulated behaviour patterns, the narcissist seeks to manipulate his human environment. Inside, he is barren, devoid of any inkling of true emotion, and disdainful of feelings and emotional people. He looks down upon those who succumb to the weakness of sentiment and holds them in contempt. He berates and debases them.

This is the heartless mechanism of "simulated affect". It lies at the core of the narcissist's inability to empathize with his fellow human beings.

The narcissist constantly lies to himself and to others. He defensively distorts facts and circumstances and provides consonant interpretations so as to preserve his delusions of grandeur and feelings of (unmerited) self-importance. This is the mechanism of the "sliding of meanings". This mechanism is part of the much larger set of Emotional Involvement Prevention Measures (EIPMs).

The EIPMs are intended to prevent the narcissist from getting emotionally involved or committed. This way he insures himself against getting hurt and abandoned, or so he erroneously believes. Actually, these mechanisms are self-defeating and lead directly to the results they were intended to forestall. They mostly operate through emotional denial. The narcissist is estranged from his own emotions as a means of self-defence.

Another characteristic of the narcissistic personality is the use that it makes of "emotional delegation". The narcissist, appearances notwithstanding, is human and is possessed of emotions and of emotional content. But, in an effort to defend himself against a repetition of past hurts, he "delegates" his emotions to a fictitious construct, the False Self.

It is the False Self that interacts with the world. It is the False Self that suffers and enjoys, gets attached and detached, joins and separates, develops likes and dislikes, preferences and prejudices, loves and hates. Whatever happens to the narcissist, his experiences, the setbacks that he (unavoidably) suffers, the humiliations, the adoration, the fears and the hopes - happens to one self removed, to the False Self.

The narcissist is shielded by this construction. He lives in a padded cell of his own creation, an eternal observer, unharmed, embryo-like in the womb of his False Self. No wonder that this duality, so entrenched, so fundamental to the narcissistic personality is also so evident, so discernible. This delegation of emotions is what unsettles those who interact with the narcissist: the feeling that his True Self is absent and that all the emoting is done by a false emanation.

The narcissist himself experiences this dichotomy, this break between his False Self which is his interface with the true world and his True Self which is forever dormant in a no-man's land. The narcissist lives in this warped reality, divorced from his own emotions, constantly feeling that he is an actor in a film about his own life.

[A more detailed description of this emotional break can be found in FAQ 28: Warped Reality and Retroactive Emotional Content]

The Ubiquitous Narcissist

Question: Nothing is sacred to him. He mocks everything and derides everyone. He does it publicly and privately and always loudly. It grates on my nerves. Is there anything I can do about it?

Answer: The narcissist feels omnipresent, all-pervasive, the prime mover and shaker, the cause of all things. Hence his constant projection of his own traits, fears, behaviour patterns, beliefs, and plans onto others. The narcissist is firmly convinced that he is the generator of other people's emotions, that they depend on him for their well-being, that without him their lives will degenerate into grey mediocrity. He regards himself as the most important part in the life of his nearest and dearest. To avoid painful realizations to the contrary, the narcissist aims to micromanage and control his human environment.

But this is only one aspect of the pathology.

The second aspect is malignant cynicism. A healthy modicum of doubt and caution is... well... healthy. But the narcissist is addicted to excess doses of both. He is convinced that everyone is a narcissist and that people are simply hypocritical when they pretend to be "normal". They are weak and fear society's reactions, so they adhere to its edicts and behavioural-moral codes. As opposed to these craven weaklings, the narcissist magically feels strong, immune to punishment, and invincible and thus able to express his true nature fearlessly and openly.

Consider generosity and altruism, the daughters of empathy - that which the narcissist is absolutely devoid of.

The narcissist cannot digest or fathom true generosity, especially when he is its recipient and beneficiary. He immediately suspects ulterior motives (though not necessarily sinister ones). He asks himself: "Why the helping hand?", "How come the trust placed in me?", "What do they really want from me?", "How

133

(unbeknownst to me) do I benefit them?", "What is the disguised self-interest which drives their perplexing behaviour?", "Don't these people know better?", "Don't they realize that everyone is, without exception, self-centred, interest-driven, unnecessarily malevolent, ignorant, and abusive?".

In other words, the narcissist is surprised that his true nature doesn't show through instantly. He feels like an incandescent lamp. He is sure that people can see through his transparent defences and that what they see must horrify and repel them.

When this does not happen, he is shocked.

He is shocked because altruistic, loving, caring, and generous behaviours expose as false the hidden assumptions underlying his mental edifice. Not everyone is a narcissist. People do care for each other for no immediate reward. And, most damaging of all to his worldview, he is loveable.

The Narcissist as a Sadist

Question: What would cause a narcissist to victimize a significant other sadistically versus just discarding her when no longer useful?

Answer: The narcissist discards people when he becomes convinced that they can no longer provide him with Narcissistic Supply. This conviction, subjective and emotionally charged, does not have to be grounded in reality. Suddenly, because of boredom, disagreement, disillusion, a fight, an act, inaction, **135** or a mood, the narcissist wildly swings from idealization to devaluation.

The narcissist then detaches immediately. He needs all the energy he can muster to obtain new Sources of Narcissistic Supply and would rather not spend these scarce resources over what he regards as human refuse, the pulp left after the extraction of Narcissistic Supply.

The narcissist would tend to display the sadistic aspect of his personality in one of two cases:

1. That the very acts of sadism generate Narcissistic Supply to be consumed by the narcissist ("I inflict pain, therefore I am superior"), or
2. That the victims of his sadism are still his only or major Sources of Narcissistic Supply but are perceived by him to be intentionally frustrating and withholding. Sadistic acts are his way of punishing them for not being docile, obedient, admiring and adoring as he expects them to be in view of his uniqueness, cosmic significance, and special entitlement.

The narcissist is not a full-fledged sadist, masochist, or paranoiac. He does not enjoy hurting his victims. He does not believe firmly that he is the focal point of persecution and the target of conspiracies.

But, he does enjoy punishing himself when it provides him with a sense of relief, exoneration and validation. This is his masochistic streak.

Because of his lack of empathy and his rigid personality, he often inflicts great (physical or mental) pain on meaningful others in his life and he enjoys their writhing and suffering. In this restricted sense he is a sadist.

To support his sense of uniqueness, greatness and (cosmic) significance, he is often hypervigilant. If he falls from grace, he attributes it to dark forces out to destroy him. If his sense of entitlement is not satisfied and he is ignored by others, he attributes it to the fear and feelings of inferiority that he provokes in them. So, to some extent, he is a paranoid.

The narcissist is as much an artist of pain as any sadist. The difference between them lies in their motivation. The narcissist tortures and abuses others as means to punish and to reassert superiority, omnipotence, and grandiosity. The sadist does it for pure (usually, sexually-tinged) pleasure. But both are adept at finding the chinks in people's armours. Both are ruthless and venomous in the pursuit of their prey. Both are unable to empathize with their victims, and are self-centred, and rigid.

The narcissist abuses his victim verbally, mentally, or physically (often, in all three ways). He infiltrates her defences, shatters her self-confidence, confuses and confounds her, demeans and debases her. He invades her territory, abuses her confidence, exhausts her resources, hurts her loved ones, threatens her stability and security, enmeshes her in his paranoid state of mind, frightens her out of her wits, withholds love and sex from her, prevents satisfaction and causes frustration, humiliates and insults her privately and in public, points out her shortcomings, criticizes her profusely and in a "scientific and objective" manner - and this is a partial list.

Very often, the narcissist's sadistic acts are disguised as an enlightened interest in the welfare of his victim. He plays the psychiatrist to her psychopathology (totally dreamt up by him). He acts the guru, the avuncular or father figure, the teacher, the only true friend, the old and the experienced - all these in order to weaken her defences and to lay siege to her disintegrating nerves. So subtle and poisonous is the narcissistic variant of sadism that it might well be regarded as the most dangerous of all.

Luckily, the narcissist's attention span is short and his resources and energy limited. In constant, effort-consuming and attention-diverting pursuit of Narcissistic Supply, the narcissist lets his victim go, usually before it had suffered irreversible damage. The victim is then free to rebuild her life from ruins. Not an easy undertaking, this but far better than the total obliteration which awaits the victims of the "true" sadist.

If one had to distil the quotidian existence of the narcissist in two pithy sentences, one would say:

The narcissist loves to be hated and hates to be loved.

Hate is the complement of fear and narcissists like being feared. It imbues them with an intoxicating sensation of omnipotence.

Many of them are veritably inebriated by the looks of horror or repulsion on people's faces: "They know that I am capable of anything."

The sadistic narcissist perceives himself as Godlike, ruthless and unscrupulous, capricious and unfathomable, devoid of emotions and asexual, omniscient, omnipotent and omnipresent, a plague, a devastation, an inescapable verdict.

He nurtures his ill-repute, stoking it and fanning the flames of gossip. It is an enduring asset. Hate and fear are sure-fire generators of attention. It is all about Narcissistic Supply, of course: the drug which narcissists consume and which, in turn, consumes them.

Deep inside, it is the horrid future and inescapable punishment that await the narcissist that are irresistibly appealing. Sadists are often also masochists. In sadistic narcissists, there is, actually, a burning desire - nay, need - to be punished. In the grotesque mind of the narcissist, his punishment is equally his vindication.

By being permanently on trial, the narcissist defiantly claims the high moral ground and the position of the martyr: misunderstood, discriminated against, unjustly roughed, outcast due to his very towering genius or other outstanding qualities.

To conform to the cultural stereotype of the "tormented artist", the narcissist provokes his own suffering. He is thus validated. His grandiose fantasies acquire a modicum of substance. "If I were not so special, they surely wouldn't have persecuted me so." The persecution of the narcissist proves to him his self-imputed uniqueness. To have "deserved" or to have provoked it, he must have been different and unique, for better or for worse.

The narcissist's aforementioned streak of paranoia makes his persecution inevitable. The narcissist is in constant conflict with "lesser beings": his spouse, his shrink, his boss, his colleague the police, the courts, his neighbours. Forced to stoop to their intellectual level, the narcissist feels like Gulliver: a giant shackled by Lilliputians. His life is a constant struggle against the self-contented mediocrity of his milieu. This is his fate which he accepts, though never stoically. It is his calling and the mission of his stormy life.

Deeper still, the narcissist has an image of himself as a worthless, bad and dysfunctional extension of others. In constant need of Narcissistic Supply, he feels humiliated by his dependency. The contrast between his grandiose fantasies and the reality of his habit, neediness and, often, failure (the Grandiosity Gap) is an emotionally corroding experience. It is a perpetual background noise of devilish, demeaning scorn. His inner voices "say" to him: "You are a fraud", "You are a nobody, a loser", "You deserve nothing", "If only they knew how worthless you are".

The narcissist attempts to silence these tormenting voices not by fighting them but by agreeing with them. Unconsciously - sometimes consciously - he "responds" to them: "I do agree with you. I am bad and worthless and deserving of the most severe punishment for my rotten character, disgraceful habits, my addiction and the constant sham that is my life. I will go and seek my doom. Now that I have complied, will you leave me alone? Will you let me be?"

Of course, they never do.

Sadistic Personality Disorder

The Sadistic Personality Disorder made its last appearance in the DSM-III-TR and was removed from the DSM-IV and from its text revision, the DSM-IV-TR. Some scholars, notably Theodore Millon, regard its removal as a mistake and lobby for its reinstatement in future editions of the DSM.

The Sadistic Personality Disorder is characterized by a pattern of gratuitous cruelty, aggression, and demeaning behaviours which indicate the existence of deep-seated contempt for other people and an utter lack of empathy. Some sadists are "utilitarian": they leverage their explosive violence to establish a position of unchallenged dominance within a relationship. Unlike psychopaths, they rarely use physical force in the commission of crimes. Rather, their aggressiveness is embedded in an interpersonal context and is expressed in social settings, such as the family or the workplace.

This narcissistic need for an audience manifests itself in other circumstances. Sadists strive to humiliate people in front of witnesses. This makes them feel omnipotent. Power plays are important to them and they are likely to treat people under their control or entrusted to their care harshly: a subordinate, a child, a student, a prisoner, a patient, or a spouse are all liable to suffer the consequences of the sadist's "control freakery" and exacting "disciplinary" measures.

Sadists like to inflict pain because they find suffering, both corporeal and psychological, amusing. They torture animals and people because, to them, the sights and sounds of a creature writhing in agony are hilarious and pleasurable. Sadists go to great length to hurt others: they lie, deceive, commit crimes, and even make personal sacrifices merely so as to enjoy the cathartic moment of witnessing someone else's anguish.

Sadists are masters of abuse by proxy and ambient abuse. They terrorize and intimidate even their nearest and dearest into doing their bidding. They create an aura and atmosphere of unmitigated yet diffuse dread and consternation. This they achieve by promulgating complex "rules of the house" that restrict the autonomy of their dependants (spouses, children, employees, patients, clients, etc.). They have the final word and are the ultimate law. They must be obeyed, no matter how arbitrary and senseless are their rulings and decisions.

Most sadists are fascinated by gore and violence. They are vicarious serial killers: they channel their homicidal urges in socially acceptable ways by "studying" and admiring historical figures such as Hitler, for instance. They love guns and other weapons, are fascinated by death, torture, and martial arts in all their forms.

Other People's Pain

Question: Do narcissists actually enjoy the taunting, the sadistic behaviour, and the punishment that always follows?

Answer: Most narcissists enjoy an irrational and brief burst of relief after having suffered emotionally ("narcissistic injury") or after having sustained a loss. It is a sense of freedom, which comes with being unshackled. Having lost everything, the narcissist often feels that he has found himself, that he has been re-born, that he has been charged with natal energy, able to take on new challenges and to explore new territories. This elation is so addictive, that the narcissist often seeks pain, humiliation, punishment, scorn, and contempt - as long as they are public and involve the attention of peers and superiors. Being penalized accords with the tormenting inner voices of the narcissist which keep telling him that he is bad, corrupt, and worthy of punishment.

This is the masochistic streak in the narcissist. But the narcissist is also a sadist, albeit an unusual one.

The narcissist inflicts pain and abuse on others. He devalues Sources of Supply, callously and offhandedly abandons them, and discards people, places, partnerships, and friendships unhesitatingly. Some narcissists, though by no means the majority, actually ENJOY abusing, taunting, tormenting, and freakishly controlling others ("gaslighting"). But most of them do these things absentmindedly, automatically, and, often, even without good reason.

What is unusual about the narcissist's sadistic behaviours - ᵖᵐeditated acts of tormenting others while enjoying their ᵘᵢshed reactions - is that they are goal orientated. "Pure" ˢ have no goal in mind except the pursuit of pleasure: pain ᵃʳt form (remember the Marquis de Sade?). Conversely,

MALIGNANT SELF LOVE

SAM VAKNIN

the narcissist haunts and hunts his victims for a reason: he wants them to reflect his inner state. It is all part of a psychological defence mechanism called Projective Identification.

When the narcissist is angry, unhappy, disappointed, injured, or hurt, he feels unable to express his emotions sincerely and openly since to do so would be to admit his frailty, his neediness, and his weaknesses. He deplores his own humanity: his emotions, his vulnerability, his susceptibility, his gullibility, his inadequacies, and his failures. So, he makes use of other people to express his pain and his frustration, his pent up anger and his aggression.

He achieves this by mentally torturing other people to the point of madness, by driving them to violence, by forcing them to search for an outlet, for closure, and, sometimes, revenge. He causes people to lose their own character traits and adopt his own instead.

In reaction to his constant and well-targeted abuse, they become abusive, vengeful, ruthless, lacking empathy, obsessed, and aggressive. They mirror him faithfully and thus relieve him of the need to express himself directly.

Having constructed this hall of writhing human mirrors, the narcissist withdraws. His goal achieved, he lets go. As opposed to the sadist, he is not in it, indefinitely, for the pleasure. He abuses and traumatizes, humiliates and abandons, discards and ignores, insults and provokes only for the purpose of purging his inner demons. By possessing others, he purifies himself, cathartically, and exorcizes his demented self.

This accomplished, he acts almost with remorse. An episode of extreme abuse is followed by an act of great care and by mellifluous apologies. The Narcissistic Pendulum swings between the extremes of torturing others and soothing the resulting pain.

This incongruous behaviour, these "sudden" shifts between sadism and compassion, abuse and "love", ignoring and caring, abandoning and clinging, viciousness and remorse, the harsh and the tender are, perhaps, the most difficult to comprehend and to accept.

These swings produce in people around the narcissist emotional insecurity, an eroded sense of self-worth, fear, stress, and anxiety (often described as "walking on eggshells"). Gradually emotional paralysis sets in and they come to occupy the same emotional wasteland inhabited by the narcissist, in effect prisoners and hostages in more ways than one and even wh is long out of their lives.

The Narcissism of Differences Big and Small

Freud coined the phrase "narcissism of small differences" in a paper titled "The Taboo of Virginity" that he published in 1917. Referring to earlier work by British anthropologist Ernest Crawley, he said that we reserve our most virulent emotions - aggression, hatred, envy - towards those who resemble us the most. We feel threatened not by the Other with whom we have little in common - but by the "nearly-we", who mirror and reflect us.

The "nearly-he" imperils the narcissist's selfhood and challenges his uniqueness, perfection, and superiority: the fundaments of the narcissist's sense of self-worth. It provokes in him primitive narcissistic defences and leads him to adopt desperate measures to protect, preserve, and restore his balance. I call it the Array of Gulliver Defence Mechanisms.

The very existence of the "nearly-he" constitutes a narcissistic injury. The narcissist feels humiliated, shamed, and embarrassed not to be unique after all and he reacts with envy and aggression towards this source of frustration.

In doing so, he resorts to splitting, projection, and Projective Identification. He attributes to other people personal traits that he dislikes in himself and he forces them to behave in conformity with his expectations. In other words, the narcissist sees in others those parts of himself that he cannot countenance. He forces people around him to become him and to reflect his shameful behaviours, hidden fears, and forbidden wishes.

But how does the narcissist avoid the realization that what he loudly decries and derides is actually part of him? By exaggerating, or even dreaming up and creatively inventing, differences between his qualities and conduct and other people's. The more hostile he becomes towards the "nearly-he", the easier it is to distinguish himself from "the Other".

To maintain this differentiating aggression, the narcissist stokes the fires of hostility by obsessively and vengefully nurturing grudges and hurts (some of them imagined). He dwells on injustice and pain inflicted on him by these stereotypically "bad or unworthy" people. He devalues and dehumanizes them and plots revenge to achieve closure. In the process, he indulges in grandiose fantasies, aimed to boost his feelings of omnipotence and magical immunity.

the process of acquiring an adversary, the narcissist blocks information that threatens to undermine his emerging self-tion as righteous and offended. He begins to base his entity on the brewing conflict which is by now a major preoccupation and a defining or even all-pervasive dimension of his existence.

Very much the same dynamic applies to coping with major differences between the narcissist and others. He emphasizes the large disparities while transforming even the most minor ones into decisive and unbridgeable.

Deep inside, the narcissist is continuously subject to a gnawing suspicion that his self-perception as omnipotent, omniscient, and irresistible is flawed, confabulated, and unrealistic. When criticized, the narcissist actually agrees with the critic. In other words, there are only minor differences of opinion between the narcissist and his detractors. But this threatens the narcissist's internal cohesion. Hence the wild rage at any hint of disagreement, resistance, or debate.

Similarly, intimacy brings people closer together: it makes them more similar. There are only minor differences between intimate partners. The narcissist perceives this as a threat to his sense of uniqueness. He reacts by devaluing the cause of his fears: the mate, spouse, lover, or partner. He re-establishes the boundaries and the distinctions that were removed by intimacy. Thus restored, he is emotionally ready to embark on another round of idealization (the Approach-Avoidance Repetition Complex).

143

First published on the Suite 101 Narcissistic Personality Disorders Topic.

The Psychology of Torture

There is one place in which one's privacy, intimacy, integrity and inviolability are guaranteed: one's body, a unique temple and a familiar territory of sensa and personal history. The torturer invades, defiles and desecrates this shrine. He does so publicly, deliberately, repeatedly and, often, sadistically and sexually, with undisguised pleasure. Hence the all-pervasive, long-lasting, and, frequently, irreversible effects and outcomes of torture.

In a way, the torture victim's own body is rendered his worse enemy. It is corporeal agony that compels the sufferer to mutate, his identity to fragment, his ideals and principles to crumble. The body becomes an accomplice of the tormentor, an uninterruptible channel of communication, a treasonous, poisoned territory.

It fosters a humiliating dependency of the abused on the perpetrator. Bodily needs denied - sleep, toilet, food, water - are wrongly perceived by the victim as the direct causes of his degradation and dehumanization. As he sees it, he is rendered bestial not by the sadistic bullies around him but by his own flesh.

The concept of "body" can easily be extended to "family", or "home". Torture is often applied to kin and kith, compatriots, or colleagues. This intends to disrupt the continuity of "surroundings, habits, appearance, relations with others", as the CIA put it in one of its manuals. A sense of cohesive self-identity depends crucially on the familiar and the continuous. By attacking both one's biological body and one's "social body", the victim's psyche is strained to the point of dissociation.

Beatrice Patsalides describes this transmogrification thus in "Ethics of the Unspeakable: Torture Survivors in Psychoanalytic Treatment":

144

SAM VAKNIN   MALIGNANT SELF LOVE

"As the gap between the 'I' and the 'me' deepens, dissociation and alienation increase... Thoughts and dreams attack the mind and invade the body."

Torture robs the victim of the most basic modes of relating to reality and, thus, is the equivalent of cognitive death. Space and time are warped by sleep deprivation. The self ("I") is shattered. The tortured have nothing familiar to hold on to: family, home, personal belongings, loved ones, language, name. Gradually, they lose their mental resilience and sense of freedom. They feel alien: unable to communicate, relate, attach, or empathize with others.

Torture splinters early childhood grandiose narcissistic fantasies of uniqueness, omnipotence, invulnerability, and impenetrability. But it enhances the fantasy of merger with an idealized and omnipotent (though not benign) other - the inflicter of agony. The twin processes of individuation and separation are reversed.

Torture is the ultimate act of perverted intimacy. The torturer invades the victim's body, pervades his psyche, and possesses his mind. Deprived of contact with others and starved for human interactions, the prey bonds with the predator. "Traumatic bonding", akin to the Stockholm Syndrome, is about hope and the search for meaning in the brutal and indifferent and nightmarish universe of the torture cell.

The abuser becomes the black hole at the centre of the victim's surrealistic galaxy, sucking in the sufferer's universal need for solace. The victim tries to "control" his tormentor by becoming one with him (introjecting him) and by appealing to the monster's presumably dormant humanity and empathy.

This bonding is especially strong when the torturer and the tortured form a dyad and "collaborate" in the rituals and acts of torture (for instance, when the victim is coerced into selecting the torture implements and the types of torment to be inflicted, or to choose between two evils).

The psychologist Shirley Spitz offers this powerful overview of the contradictory nature of torture in a seminar titled "The Psychology of Torture" [1989]:

"Torture is an obscenity in that it joins what is most private with what is most public... A further obscenity of torture is the inversion it makes of intimate human relationships."

Obsessed by endless ruminations, demented by pain and a continuum of sleeplessness, the victim regresses, shedding all but the most primitive defence mechanisms: splitting, narcissism, dissociation, Projective Identification, introjection, and cognitive dissonance. The victim constructs an alternative world, often suffering from depersonalization and derealization, hallucinations, ideas of reference, delusions, and psychotic episodes.

Sometimes the victim comes to crave pain - very much as self-mutilators do - because it is a proof and a reminder of his individuated existence otherwise blurred by the incessant torture. Pain shields the sufferer from disintegration and capitulation. It preserves the veracity of his unthinkable and unspeakable experiences.

This dual process of the victim's alienation and addiction to anguish complements the perpetrator's view of his quarry as "inhuman", or "subhuman". The torturer assumes the position of the sole authority, the exclusive fount of meaning and interpretation, the source of both evil and good.

Torture is about reprogramming the victim to succumb to an alternative exegesis of the world, proffered by the abuser. It is an act of deep, indelible, traumatic indoctrination. The abused also swallows whole and assimilates the torturer's negative view of him and often, as a result, is rendered suicidal, self-destructive, or self-defeating.

Thus, torture has no cut-off date. The sounds, the voices, the **146** smells, the sensations reverberate long after the episode has ended, both in nightmares and in waking moments. The victim's ability to trust other people - i.e., to assume that their motives are at least rational, if not necessarily benign - has been irrevocably undermined. Social institutions are perceived as precariously poised on the verge of an ominous, Kafkaesque mutation. Nothing is either safe, or credible anymore.

Victims typically react by undulating between emotional numbing and increased arousal: insomnia, irritability, restlessness, and attention deficits. Recollections of the traumatic events intrude in the form of dreams, night terrors, flashbacks, and distressing associations.

The tortured develop compulsive rituals to fend off obsessive thoughts. Other psychological sequelae reported include cognitive impairment, reduced capacity to learn, memory disorders, sexual dysfunction, social withdrawal, inability to maintain long-term relationships, or even mere intimacy, phobias, ideas of reference and superstitions, delusions, hallucinations, psychotic microepisodes, and emotional flatness.

Depression and anxiety are very common. These are forms and manifestations of self-directed aggression. The sufferer rages at his own victimhood and the resulting multiple dysfunctions. He feels shamed by his new disabilities and responsible, or even guilty, somehow, for his predicament and the dire consequences borne by his nearest and dearest. His sense of self-worth and self-esteem are crippled.

In a nutshell, torture victims suffer from a Post-Traumatic Stress Disorder (PTSD). Their strong feelings of anxiety, guilt, and shame are also typical of victims of childhood abuse, domestic violence, and rape. They feel anxious because the perpetrator's behaviour is seemingly arbitrary and unpredictable - or mechanically and inhumanly regular.

They feel guilty and disgraced because, to restore a semblance of order to their shattered world and a modicum of dominion over their chaotic life, they need to transform themselves into the cause of their own degradation and the accomplices of their tormentors.

The CIA, in its "Human Resource Exploitation Training Manual - 1983" [reprinted in the April 1997 issue of Harper's Magazine], summed up the theory of coercion thus:

"The purpose of all coercive techniques is to induce psychological regression in the subject by bringing a superior outside force to bear on his will to resist. Regression is basically a loss of autonomy, a reversion to an earlier behavioural level. As the subject regresses, his learned personality traits fall away in reverse chronological order. He begins to lose the capacity to carry out the highest creative activities, to deal with complex situations, or to cope with stressful interpersonal relationships or repeated frustrations."

Inevitably, in the aftermath of torture, its victims feel helpless and powerless. This loss of control over one's life and body is manifested physically in impotence, attention deficits, and insomnia. This is often exacerbated by the disbelief many torture victims encounter, especially if they are unable to produce scars, or other "objective" proof of their ordeal. Language cannot communicate such an intensely private experience as pain.

Spitz makes the following observation:

"Pain is also unsharable in that it is resistant to language... (W)hen we explore the interior state of physical pain we find that there is no object 'out there' - no external, referential content. Pain is not of, or for, anything. Pain is."

Bystanders resent the tortured because they make them feel guilty and ashamed for having done nothing to prevent the atrocity. The victims threaten their sense of security and their much-needed belief in predictability, justice, and rule of law. The victims, on their part, do not believe that it is possible to effectively communicate to "outsiders" what they have been through. The torture chambers are "another galaxy". This is how Auschwitz was described by the author K. Zetnik in his testimony in the Eichmann trial in Jerusalem in 1961.

Kenneth Pope in "Torture", a chapter he wrote for the "Encyclopaedia of Women and Gender: Sex Similarities and Differences and the Impact of Society on Gender", quotes Harvard psychiatrist Judith Herman:

"It is very tempting to take the side of the perpetrator. All the perpetrator asks is that the bystander do nothing. He appeals to the universal desire to see, hear, and speak no evil. The victim, on the contrary, asks the bystander to share the burden of pain. The victim demands action, engagement, and remembering."

But, more often, continued attempts to repress fearful memories result in psychosomatic illnesses (conversion). The victim wishes to forget the torture, to avoid re-experiencing the often life threatening abuse and to shield his human environment from the horrors. In conjunction with the victim's pervasive distrust, this is frequently interpreted as hypervigilance, or even paranoia. It seems that the victims can't win. Torture is forever.

Why Do People Torture?

We should distinguish functional torture from the sadistic variety. The former is calculated to extract information from the tortured or to punish them. It is measured, impersonal, efficient, and disinterested.

The latter - the sadistic variety - fulfils the emotional needs of the perpetrator.

People who find themselves caught up in anomic states - for instance, soldiers in war or incarcerated inmates - tend to feel helpless and alienated. They experience a partial or total loss of control. They have been rendered vulnerable, powerless, and defenceless by events and circumstances beyond their influence.

Torture amounts to exerting an absolute and all-pervasive domination over the victim's existence. It is a coping strategy employed by torturers who wish to reassert control over their lives and, thus, to re-establish their mastery and superiority. By subjugating the tortured, they regain their self-confidence and regulate their sense of self-worth.

Other tormentors channel their negative emotions - pent up aggression, humiliation, rage, envy, diffuse hatred - and displace them. The victim becomes a symbol of everything that's wrong in the torturer's life and the situation he finds himself caught in. The act of torture amounts to misplaced and violent venting.

Many perpetrate heinous acts out of a wish to conform. Torturing others is their way of demonstrating obsequious obeisance to authority, group affiliation, colleagueship, and adherence to the same ethical code of conduct and common values. They bask in the praise that is heaped on them by their superiors, fellow workers, associates, team mates, or collaborators. Their need to belong is so strong that it overpowers ethical, moral, or legal considerations.

Many offenders derive pleasure and satisfaction from sadistic acts of humiliation. To these, inflicting pain is fun. They lack empathy and so their victim's agonized reactions are merely cause for much hilarity.

Moreover, sadism is rooted in deviant sexuality. The torture inflicted by sadists is bound to involve perverted sex (rape, homosexual rape, voyeurism, exhibitionism, paedophilia, fetishism, and other paraphilias). Aberrant sex, unlimited power, excruciating pain, these are the intoxicating ingredients of the sadistic variant of torture.

149 Still, torture rarely occurs where it does not have the sanction and blessing of the authorities, whether local or national. A permissive environment is sine qua non. The more abnormal the circumstances, the less normative the milieu, the further the scene of the crime is from public scrutiny - the more is egregious torture likely to occur. This is especially true in totalitarian societies where the use of physical force to discipline or eliminate dissent is an acceptable practice.

First published on the Suite 101 Narcissistic Personality Disorders Topic.

Multiple Grandiosity

Question: Is the narcissist confined in his grandiose fantasies to one subject?

Answer: The narcissist is bound to make use of his more pronounced traits and qualities in both the design of his False Self and the extraction of Narcissistic Supply from others. Thus, a cerebral narcissist is likely to emphasize his intellect, his brainpower, his analytical skills and his rich and varied fund of knowledge. A somatic narcissist accentuates his body, his physical strength, his appearance, his sex appeal and so on. But this is only one facet of the answer. It seems that narcissists engage in what could best be described as Narcissistic Hedges.

A Narcissistic Hedge is when a narcissist colours more than one field of activity (or one person) with his narcissistic hues. He infuses the selected subjects with narcissistic investment (cathexis). He prepares them as auxiliary Sources of Narcissistic Supply and as backup options in case of a major system failure.

These ostensibly redundant activities and interests constitute a fallback option during a life crisis. In the majority of cases, the chosen subjects or fields all belong to the same "family". A cerebral narcissist might select mathematics and art, but not mountain climbing. A sportsman might choose to be a radio sports commentator but not a philosopher of science, and so on. Still, the correlation between the various selections may not be very strong (which is why they can be used as hedges).

Experience shows that this hedging mechanism is not very effective. The narcissist responds to events in his life as a rigid unit. His reactions are not differentiated or scaled. A failure (or a success) in one domain contagiously spreads to all the others. This narcissistic contagion effect dominates the narcissist's life. The narcissist measures his personal history in terms of fluctuations in

150

MALIGNANT SELF LOVE

SAM VAKNIN

Narcissistic Supply. He is blind to all other aspects, angles and points of view. He is like a thermometer which reacts to human warmth, admiration, adoration, approval, applause and attention.

The narcissist perceives his life in gradations of narcissistic temperature. When a Source of Supply ceases to exist or is threatened or diminished, all the other parts of the narcissist's world (including his backup options) are affected. The dysphoric and euphoric moods, which are related to the absence or to the presence of Narcissistic Supply, engulf the entire personality and consume it.

A case study to illustrate these economic principles of the narcissist's soul:

A narcissist has a successful career as an economic commentator in several mass media. As a result of his criticism of the policies of the government, he is threatened and there are signs that a book that he was about to publish, will not be published after all. The narcissist has other subjects from which he is able to derive Narcissistic Supply (Narcissistic Hedges). What would the likely reaction of such a narcissist be?

Being threatened endangers this narcissist's feelings of omnipotence and superiority. He is "reduced to size". The special treatment that he believed himself to be entitled to has all but evaporated. This is a narcissistic injury. Worse, it looks as if the very availability and existence of his main and "serious" Narcissistic Supply Sources (the media, the book) are at risk.

Dysphoria ensues. The narcissist reacts hysterically and with paranoia. The paranoid streaks in his reaction serve to re-establish the perturbed balance of his own grandiosity. Only important people are persecuted, he soothes himself: "I am being persecuted, therefore I must be important". The hysteria is the result of panic at the prospect of remaining bereft of Narcissistic Supply Sources. A drug addict would have reacted the same way.

In theory, this would be the perfect time to revert to the alternatives, to the hedges. But the narcissist's energy is too depleted to make this switch. He is depressed, dysphoric, anhedonic, in extreme cases even suicidal. He jumps to radical and sweeping conclusions ("If this happened to me once, it could well happen again"). His output and achievements deteriorate. As a result, his Narcissistic Supply is further reduced and a vicious circle is set in motion.

This is the absurdity of the narcissistic mental household: the hedges are brought into play only when they are not needed. Once a crisis erupts, the violently reduced narcissist, a faltering shadow of his former False Self, is too depleted to make use of them.

False Modesty

Question: I met many narcissists who are modest - even self-effacing. This seems to conflict with your observations. How do you reconcile the two?

Answer: The "modesty" evinced by the narcissist is false. It is mostly and merely verbal. It is couched in flourishing phrases, emphasized to absurdity, repeated unnecessarily, usually to the point of causing gross inconvenience to the listener. The real aim of such behaviour and its subtext are exactly the opposite of common modesty.

It is intended to either aggrandize the narcissist or to protect his grandiosity from scrutiny and possible erosion. Such outbursts of "modesty" frequently precede inflated, grandiosity-laden statements made by the narcissist and pertaining to fields of human knowledge and activity in which his accomplishments are meagre.

Devoid of systematic and methodical education, the narcissist tries to make do with pompous, or aggressive mannerisms, bombastic announcements, and the unnecessary and wrong usage of professional jargon. He attempts to dazzle his surroundings with apparent "brilliance" and to put possible critics on the defence.

Beneath all this he is shallow, ignorant, improvising, and fearful of being exposed as deceitful. The narcissist is a conjurer of verbosity, using sleight of mouth rather than sleight of hand. He is ever possessed by the fear that he is really a petty crook about to be unearthed and reviled by society.

This is a horrible feeling to endure and a taxing, onerous way to live. The narcissist has to protect himself from his own premonitions, from his internal semipternal trial, his guilt, shame, and anxiety. One of the more efficacious defence mechanisms is false modesty.

SAM VAKNIN   MALIGNANT SELF LOVE

The narcissist publicly chastises himself for being unfit, unworthy, lacking, not trained and not (formally) schooled, not objective, cognisant of his own shortcomings and vain. This way, if (or, rather, when) exposed he could always say: "But I told you so in the first place, haven't I?" False modesty is, thus an insurance policy. The narcissist "hedges his bets" by placing a side bet on his own fallibility, weakness, deficiencies and proneness to err.

Yet another function is to extract Narcissistic Supply from the listener. By contrasting his own self-deprecation with a brilliant, dazzling display of ingenuity, wit, intellect, knowledge, or beauty, the narcissist aims to secure an adoring, admiring, approving, or applauding protestation from the listener.

The person to whom the narcissist addresses his statement of false modesty statement is expected to vehemently deny the narcissist's assertions: "But, really, you are more of an expert than you say!", or "Why did you tell me that you are unable to do (this or that)? Truly, you are very gifted!", "Don't put yourself down so much - you are a generous man!"

The narcissist then shrugs, smirks, blushes and moves uncomfortably from side to side. This was not his intention, he assures his interlocutor. He did not mean to fish for compliments (exactly what he did mean to do). He really does not deserve the praise. But the aim has, thus, been achieved: the Narcissistic Supply has been doled out and avidly consumed. Despite the narcissist's protestations, he feels much better now.

The narcissist is a dilettante and a charlatan. He glosses over complicated subjects and situations in life. He sails through them powered by shallow acquaintance with rapidly acquired verbal and behavioural vocabularies (which he then promptly proceeds to forget).

False modesty is only one of a series of feigned behaviours. The narcissist is a pathological liar, either implicitly or explicitly. His whole psychological existence is premised on a False Self, his deceitful invention and its reflections. With false modesty he seeks to involve others in his mind games, to co-opt them, to force them to collaborate while making ultimate use of social conventions of conduct.

The narcissist, above all, is a shrewd manipulator, well-acquainted with human nature and its fault lines. Still, no narcissist will ever admit to it. In this sense, narcissists are really modest.

Warped Reality
And Retroactive Emotional Content

Question: How does a narcissist experience his own life?

Answer: As a prolonged, incomprehensible, unpredictable, frequently terrifying and deeply saddening nightmare. This is a result of the functional dichotomy, fostered by the narcissist himself, between his False Self and his True Self.

The False Self is nothing but a concoction, a figment of the narcissist's disorder, a reflection in the narcissist's hall of mirrors. It is incapable of feeling, or experiencing anything. Yet, it is fully the master of the psychodynamic processes which rage within the narcissist's psyche.

This inner battle is so fierce that the True Self experiences it as a diffuse, though imminent and eminently ominous, threat. Anxiety ensues and the narcissist finds himself constantly ready for the next blow. He commits acts and he knows not why or wherefrom. He says things and behaves in ways, which, he knows, endanger him and put him in line for punishment and humiliation - but he can't control himself.

The narcissist hurts people around him, or breaks the law, or violates accepted morality. He knows that he is in the wrong and feels ill at ease on the rare moments that he does feel. He wants to stop but knows not how. Gradually, he is estranged from himself, possessed by some kind of demon, a puppet on invisible, mental strings. He resents this feeling, he wants to rebel, he is repelled by this part in him with which he is not acquainted. In his efforts to exorcize this devil from his soul, he sometimes dissociates.

An eerie sensation sets in and pervades the psyche of the narcissist. At times of crisis, of danger, of depression, of failure, and of narcissistic injury, the narcissist feels that he is watching himself from the outside (twin pathological mental processes known as

154

MALIGNANT SELF LOVE

SAM VAKNIN

depersonalization and derealization). This is not an out-of-body experience. The narcissist does not really "exit" his body. It is just that he assumes, involuntarily, the position of a spectator, a polite observer mildly interested in the whereabouts of one, Mr. Narcissist.

It is akin to watching a movie, the illusion is not complete, neither is it precise. This detachment continues for as long as the narcissist's ego-dystonic behaviour persists, for as long as the crisis goes on, for as long as the narcissist cannot face who he is, what he is doing and the consequences of his actions.

Since this is the case most of the time, the narcissist gets used to seeing himself in the role of the protagonist (usually the hero) of a motion picture or of a novel. It also sits well with his grandiosity and fantasies. Sometimes, he talks about himself in the third person singular. Sometimes he calls his "other", narcissistic, self by a different name.

The narcissist describes his life, its events, ups and downs, pains, elation and disappointments in the most remote, "professional" and coldly analytical voice, as though delineating (though with a modicum of involvement) the life of some exotic insect (echoes of Kafka's "Metamorphosis").

The metaphor of "life as a movie", gaining control by "writing a scenario" or by "inventing a narrative" is not a modern invention. Cavemen narcissists have, probably, done the same. But this is only the external, superficial, facet of the disorder.

The crux of the problem is that the narcissist really FEELS this way. He actually experiences his life as belonging to someone else, his body as dead weight (or as an instrument in the service of some entity), his deeds as a-moral and not immoral (he cannot be judged for something he didn't do, can he?).

As time passes, the narcissist accumulates a mountain of mishaps, conflicts unresolved, pains well hidden, abrupt separations and bitter disappointments. He is subjected to a constant barrage of social criticism and condemnation. He is ashamed and fearful. He knows that something is wrong but there is no correlation between his cognition and his emotions.

He prefers to run away and hide, as he did when he was a child. Only this time he hides behind another self, a false one. People reflect to him this mask of his making, until even he believes its existence and acknowledges its dominance, until he forgets the truth and knows no different. The narcissist is only dimly aware of the decisive battle, which rages inside him. He feels threatened, very sad, perhaps suicidal, but there seems to be no outside cause of all this and it makes it even more mysteriously menacing.

This dissonance, these negative emotions, these nagging anxieties, transform the narcissist's "motion picture" solution into a permanent one. It becomes a feature of the narcissist's life. Whenever confronted by an emotional or by an existential threat, he retreats into this haven, this mode of coping: he relegates responsibility, submissively assuming a passive role. He who is not responsible cannot be punished runs the subtext of this capitulation.

The narcissist is thus conditioned to annihilate himself, both in order to avoid (emotional) pain and to bask in the glow of his impossibly grandiose fantasies.

This he does with fanatic zeal and with efficacy. He assigns his very life (decisions to be made, judgements to be passed, agreements to be reached) to the False Self. He re-interprets his past life in a manner consistent with the current needs of the False Self.

It is no wonder that there is no connection between what the narcissist did feel in a given period in his life, or in relation to a specific event or person and the way he sees or remembers his emotions later on. He may describe certain occurrences or phases in his life as "tedious, painful, sad, burdening" even though he experienced them entirely differently at the time.

The same retroactive colouring occurs with regards to people. The narcissist completely distorts the way he regarded certain people and felt about them. This re-writing of his personal history is aimed to directly and fully accommodate the requirements of his False Self.

In sum, the narcissist does not occupy his own soul, nor does he inhabit his own body. He is the servant of an apparition, of a reflection, of an ego function. To please and appease his Master, the narcissist sacrifices to it his very essence. From that moment onwards, the narcissist lives vicariously, through the good offices of the False Self.

Throughout, the narcissist feels detached, alienated and estranged from his (False) Self. He constantly harbours the sensation that he is an actor a movie with a plot over which he has little control. It is with a certain interest - even fascination - that he watches it unfold. Still, mostly, he is a mere, passive observer.

Thus, not only does the narcissist relinquish control of his future life (the movie) - he gradually loses ground to the False Self in the battle to preserve the integrity and genuineness of his past experiences. Eroded by these two processes, the narcissist incrementally disappears and is replaced by his disorder to the fullest extent.

Narcissistic Signal, Stimulus And Hibernation Mini-Cycles

Question: I know a narcissist intimately. Sometimes he is hyperactive, full of ideas, optimism, and plans. At other times, he is somnolent, almost zombie-like.

Answer: You are witnessing the narcissistic signal-stimulus-hibernation mini-cycle. Narcissists go through long euphoric and dysphoric cycles. These cycles are dilated, all-encompassing, all-pervasive, and all-consuming. They are different from manic-depressive cycles (in the bipolar disorder) in that they are reactive, caused by easily identifiable external events or circumstances.

For instance: the narcissist reacts with dysphoria and anhedonia when he loses his Pathological Narcissistic Space, or to major life crises (financial problems, divorce, imprisonment, loss of social status and peer appreciation, death in the family, crippling illness, etc.).

But the narcissist also goes through much shorter and much weaker cycles. He experiences brief periods of mania. Then he can be entertaining, charming, and charismatic. Then he is "full of ideas and plans", attractive and leader-like. In the manic phase, he is restless (often insomniac), full of pent up energy, explosive, dramatic, creative, an excellent performer and manager.

Suddenly, and often for no apparent reason, he becomes subdued, depressed, devoid of energy, pessimistic, and "zombie-like". He oversleeps, his eating patterns change, he is slow and pays no attention to his external appearance or to the impression that he leaves on others.

The contrast is very sharp and striking. While in the manic phase, the narcissist is talkative and gregarious. In the depressive phase he is passively-aggressively silent and schizoid. He vacillates between being imaginative and being dull, being social and being asocial or even antisocial, being obsessed with time management and achievement and lying in bed for hours, being a leader and being led.

These mini-cycles, though outwardly manic-depressive (or cyclothymic) are not. They are the result of subtle fluctuations in the volatile flow of Narcissistic Supply.

The narcissist is addicted to Narcissistic Supply: admiration, adoration, approval, and other forms of attention. All his activities, thoughts, plans, aspirations, inspiration, and daydreams - in short, all the aspects of his life - are dedicated to regulating the flow of such supply and to rendering it relatively stable and predictable.

The narcissist even resorts to Secondary Narcissistic Supply Sources (a spouse, his colleagues, or his business - SNSSs) in order to "accumulate" a reserve of past Narcissistic Supply for times of short supply. The SNSSs do this by witnessing the narcissist's accomplishments and moments of grandeur and recounting what they saw when he is down and low. Thus, the SNSSs smooth and regulate the vicissitudes of the supply emanating from the Primary Narcissistic Supply Sources (PNSSs).

But the very process of obtaining and securing Narcissistic Supply, in the first place, is complex and multi-phased. **158**

First there is a depressive phase. To obtain Narcissistic Supply, the narcissist has to toil. He has to work hard to create Sources of Supply (PNSSs, SNSSs) and to maintain them. These are demanding tasks. They are often very tiring. Exhaustion plays a major role in the mini-cycles. His energy depleted, his creativity at an end, his resources stretched to the maximum, the narcissist reposes, "plays dead", withdraws from life. This is the phase of Narcissistic Hibernation.

The narcissist invariably goes into Narcissistic Hibernation before the emission of a Narcissistic Signal [see below]. He does so in order to gather the energies that he knows are going to be needed in the later phases. During his hibernation, he surveys the terrain, in an effort to determine the richest and most rewarding sources, veins and venues of Narcissistic Supply. He contemplates the possible content of various signals, in order to ensure that the most effective one is emitted.

Building up his energy reserves during the hibernation phase is crucial. The narcissist knows that even the manic phase of the mini-cycle, following the receipt of the Narcissistic Stimulus [see below] is taxing and laborious.

Having thus reposed, the narcissist is ready to proceed. He jump starts the cycle by emitting a Narcissistic Signal. It is a message - written, verbal, or behavioural - intended to foster the generation of Narcissistic Supply. The narcissist may send letters to magazines, offering to write for them (for free, if need be). He may dress, behave, or make statements intended to elicit admiration or opprobrium (in short, attention). He may consistently and continuously describe himself in glamorous and flattering terms (or, conversely, fish for compliments by berating himself and his achievements).

Anything goes in order to become well known and to impress people.

Narcissistic Signals are automatically triggered and emitted whenever an important element changes in a narcissist's life: his workplace, his domicile, his position, or his spouse. They are intended to re-establish the equilibrium between the uncertainty which inevitably follows such changes and the narcissist's inner turmoil which is the result of the disruption of the patterns and flows of Narcissistic Supply caused by said shifts.

Ideally, the Narcissistic Signal elicits a Narcissistic Stimulus. This is a positive sign or response from the recipients of the signal indicating their willingness to swallow the narcissist's bait and to provide him with Narcissistic Supply. Such a stimulus brings the narcissist back to life. It energizes him. Once more, he becomes a fountain of ideas, plans, visions and dreams.

The Narcissistic Stimulus pushes the narcissist into the manic phase of the mini-cycle.

Thus, caught between mini-cycles of mania and depression, and bigger cycles of euphoria and dysphoria the narcissist leads his tumultuous life. It is no wonder that he gradually evolves into a paranoid. It is easy to feel persecuted and at the mercy of forces mysterious, capricious and powerful when this, indeed, is the case.

The Narcissistic Pendulum
And the Pathological Narcissistic Space

Question: The behaviour of the narcissist is very inconsistent. It is as though he has multiple personalities. How can you explain this?

Answer: The narcissist is chronically depressed and anhedonic (finds no pleasure in life). Unable to love and, in the long run (as a result), unloved, the narcissist is ever in the pursuit of excitement and drama intended to alleviate his all-pervasive boredom and melancholy. The narcissist is a drama queen.

Needless to say that both the pursuit itself and its goals must conform to the grandiose vision that the narcissist has of his (False) Self. They must be commensurate with his view of his own uniqueness and entitlement.

The process of seeking excitement and drama cannot be deemed by the narcissist or by others to be humiliating, belittling or common. The excitement and drama generated must be truly unique, ground breaking, breathtaking, overwhelming, unprecedented, and, under no circumstances, routine.

Actually, the very act of dramatization is intended to secure ego-syntony. "Surely, the dramatic is special, meaningful, eternal, and memorable, just like me" - says the narcissist to himself - "I, myself, am dramatic (therefore I exist)." The narcissist - always a pathological liar and the chief victim of his own stratagems and deceit - can (and does) convince himself that his antics and exploits are significant.

Thus, existential boredom, self-directed aggression (depression), and the compulsive quest for excitement and titillating drama lead to the relentless pursuit of Narcissistic Supply (NS).

The processes of obtaining, preserving, accumulating and recalling Narcissistic Supply take place in the Pathological

160

MALIGNANT SELF LOVE

SAM VAKNIN

Narcissistic Space (PN Space). This is an imaginary environment, a comfort zone, demarcated by the narcissist. The PN Space has clear geographical and physical boundaries: a home, a neighbourhood, a workplace, a club, a city, a country.

The narcissist strives to maximize the amount of Narcissistic Supply that he derives from people within the PN Space. There, he seeks admiration, adoration, approval, applause, or, as a minimum: attention. If not fame - then notoriety. If not real achievements - then contrived or imagined ones. If not real distinction - then concocted and forced "uniqueness".

Narcissistic Supply substitutes for having a real vocation or avocation and actual achievements. It displaces the emotional rewards of intimacy in mature relationships. The narcissist is ruefully aware of this substitutive nature, of his inability to have a go at "the real thing". His permanent existence in fantasyland, intended to shield him from his self-destructive urges, paradoxically only enhances them.

This state of things makes him feel sad, enraged at his helplessness in the face of his disorder, and at the discrepancy between his delusions of grandeur and reality (the Grandiosity Gap). It is the engine of his growing disappointment and disillusionment, his anhedonia and impotence, his degeneration and ultimate ugly decadence.

The narcissist ages disgracefully, ungraciously. He is not a becoming sight as his defences crumble and harsh reality intrudes: the reality of his self-imposed mediocrity and wasted life. These flickers of sanity, these reminders of his downhill path get more ubiquitous with every day of confabulated existence.

The more fiercely the narcissist fights this painfully realistic appraisal of himself, the more apparent its veracity. The narcissist's intellect overwhelms the narcissist's defences and this is followed by either spontaneous healing or a complete meltdown.

The narcissist's PN Space incorporates people whose role is to applaud, admire, adore, approve and attend to the narcissist. Extracting Narcissistic Supply from them calls for emotional and cognitive investments, stability, perseverance, long-term presence, attachment, collaboration, emotional agility, people skills and so on.

But all this inevitable toil contradicts the deeply ingrained conviction of the narcissist that he is entitled to special and immediate preferential treatment. The narcissist expects to be instantaneously recognized as outstanding, talented, and unique. He does not see why this recognition should depend on his achievements and efforts. He feels that he is unique by virtue of his sheer existence. He feels that his very life is meaningful, that it encapsulates some cosmic message, mission, or process.

Narcissistic Supply obtained through the mundane and grinding investment of efforts and resources, such as time, money and energy is nothing special or unexpected. This renders it useless. Useful Narcissistic Supply is obtained miraculously, dramatically, excitingly, surprisingly, shockingly, unexpectedly and simply by virtue of the narcissist being there. No action is called for, as far as the narcissist is concerned. Cajoling, requesting, initiating, convincing, demonstrating, and begging for supply are all acts which starkly contrast with the grandiose delusions of the narcissist.

Additionally, the narcissist is simply unable to behave in certain ways, even if he wanted to. He cannot get attached, be intimate, persevere, be stable, predictable, or reliable because such conduct contradicts the Emotional Involvement Prevention Measures (EIPM). This is a group of destabilising behaviours intended to forestall future emotional pain inflicted on the narcissist when he is abandoned or when he fails.

If the narcissist does not get attached - he cannot be hurt. If he is not intimate with anyone - he cannot be emotionally (or otherwise) blackmailed. If he does not persevere - he has nothing to lose. If he does not stay put - he cannot be expelled. If he rejects or abandons - he cannot be rejected or abandoned.

The narcissist anticipates the inevitable schisms and emotional abysses in a life fraught with gross dishonesty. He shoots first. Indeed, it is only when he is itinerant and besieged by problems that the narcissist has a respite from his maddeningly nagging addiction to Narcissistic Supply.

This is the basic conflict of the narcissist. The two mechanisms underlying his distorted personality are incompatible. One calls for the establishment of a PN Space and for continuous gratification. The other urges the narcissist not to embark on any long-term project, to move, to disconnect, and to dissociate.

Only others can provide the narcissist with his badly needed doses of Narcissistic Supply. But he is loath to communicate and to associate with them in an emotionally meaningful way. The narcissist lacks the basic skills required in order to obtain his drug. The very people who are supposed to sustain his grandiose fantasies through their adoration and attention - mostly find him too repulsive, eccentric (weird) or dangerous to interact with. This predicament can be aptly called The Narcissistic Condition.

The Inanimate as a Source of Narcissistic Supply

Narcissistic Branding and Narcissistic Contagion

Question: Can inanimate objects serve as Sources of Narcissistic Supply?

Answer:

The Discarder

163 Any thing can serve as a Source of Narcissistic Supply, providing that it has the potential to attract people's attention and be the subject of their admiration. This is why narcissists are enamoured of status symbols, i.e., objects, which comprehensively encapsulate and concisely convey a host of data regarding their owners. These data generate a reaction in people: they make them look on, admire, envy, dream, compare, or aspire. In short: they elicit Narcissistic Supply.

But, generally, discarder narcissists do not like souvenirs and the memories they evoke. They are afraid to get emotionally attached to such mementos and then get hurt if the objects are lost or stolen or taken. Narcissists are sad people. Almost anything can depress them: a tune, a photograph, a work of art, a book, a mental image, or a voice. Narcissists are people who divorced their emotions because their emotions are mostly negative and painful, coloured by their basic trauma, by the early abuses that they had suffered.

Objects, situations, voices, sights, or colours provoke unwanted memories. The narcissist tries to avoid them. The discarder narcissist callously discards or gives away hard-won assets, memorabilia, gifts, and property. This behaviour sustains his sense of omnipotent control and lack of vulnerability. It also proves to him that he is unique, not like "other people", hoarders who are attached to their material belongings. He is above it.

The Accumulator

This kind of narcissist jealously guards his possessions: his collections, his furniture, his cars, his children, his women, his money, his credit cards...

Objects comfort this type of narcissist. They remind him of his status. They are linked to gratifying events and, thus, constitute Secondary Sources of Narcissistic Supply. They attest to the narcissist's wealth, his connections, his achievements, his friendships, his conquests, and his glorious past. No wonder he is so attached to them. Objects connected with failures or embarrassments have no place in his abode. They get cast out.

Moreover, owning the right objects often guarantees the uninterrupted flow of Narcissistic Supply. A flashy car or an ostentatious house help the somatic narcissist attract sexual partners. Owning a high powered computer and a broadband connection, or a sizable and expensive library, facilitate the intellectual pursuits of the cerebral narcissist. Sporting a glamorous wife and politically correct kids is indispensable in the careers of the narcissistic politician, or diplomat.

The narcissist parades his objects, flaunts them, consumes them conspicuously, praises them vocally, draws attention to them compulsively, and brags about them incessantly. When they fail to elicit Narcissistic Supply - admiration, adulation, marvel - the narcissist feels wounded, humiliated, deprived, discriminated against, the victim of a conspiracy, and generally unloved.

Objects make the accumulator narcissist. They are an integral part of his pathology. This type of narcissist is possessive. He obsesses about his belongings and collects them compulsively. He "brands" them as his own. He infuses them with his spirit and his personality (in other words, he cathexes them, he invest in them emotionally). He attributes to them his traits. He projects onto them his thwarted emotions, his fears, his hopes. They are an inseparable part of him and provide him with emotional succour.

Such a narcissist anthropomorphises objects (imbues them with human qualities). He is likely to say: "My car is daring and unstoppable", or "How clever is my computer!", or "My dog is cunning". He often compares people to the inanimate. Himself he regards, literally, not only figuratively or metaphorically, as a computer or sex machine. His wife he views as some kind of luxury good.

SAM VAKNIN   MALIGNANT SELF LOVE

The narcissist loves objects and relates to them - which he fails to do with humans. This is why he objectifies people: it makes it easier for him to interact with them. Objects are predictable, reliable, always there, obedient, easy to control and manipulate, universally desired.

Accumulators and Narcissistic Handles

Still, not all narcissists are like this. Accumulator narcissists take to objects and memorabilia, to voices and tunes, to sights and to works of art as reminders of their past glory and of their potential future grandeur. Many narcissists collect proofs and trophies of their sexual prowess, dramatic talent, past wealth, or intellectual achievements. They file them away almost compulsively. These are the Narcissistic Handles.

The Narcissistic Handle operates through the mechanism of narcissistic branding.

An example: as far as the narcissist is concerned, objects, which belonged to former lovers, are "stamped" by them and become their full-fledged representations. They become fetishes. By interacting with these objects, the narcissist recreates the narcissistic-supply-rich situation, within which the objects were introduced into his life in the first place.

This is a form of magical thinking. Some clairvoyants claim to be able to extract from an object all the information regarding the present, past and future states of its successive owners. It is as though the object, the memory, or the sound carry the narcissist back to where and when Narcissistic Supply was abundant.

This powerful combination of branding and evidencing is what gives rise to the Narcissistic Contagion. This is the ability of the narcissist to objectify people and to anthropomorphise objects in order to derive the maximum Narcissistic Supply from both.

On the one hand, the narcissist invests as much affection and emotions in inanimate objects as healthier people do in human beings. On the other hand, he transforms people around him into functions, or objects.

In their effort to cater to the needs of the narcissist, his closest, nearest and dearest very often neglect their own. They feel that something is sorely amiss or even sick in their lives. But they are so entrapped, so much part of the narcissist's personal mythology that they cannot cut loose. Manipulated through guilt, leveraged through fear, they become a shadow of their former selves. They have contracted the disease of narcissism. They have been infected and poisoned. They have been branded.

The Misanthropic Altruist

Some narcissists are ostentatiously generous - they donate to charity, lavish gifts on their closest, abundantly provide for their nearest and dearest, and, in general, are open-handed and unstintingly benevolent. How can this be reconciled with the pronounced lack of empathy and with the pernicious self-preoccupation that is so typical of narcissists?

The act of giving enhances the narcissist's sense of omnipotence, his fantastic grandiosity, and the contempt he holds for others. It is easy to feel superior to the supplicating recipients of one's largesse. Narcissistic altruism is about exerting control and maintaining it by fostering dependence in the beneficiaries.

But narcissists give for other reasons as well.

The narcissist flaunts his charitable nature as bait. He impresses others with his selflessness and kindness and thus lures them into his lair, entraps them, and manipulates and brainwashes them into subservient compliance and obsequious collaboration. People are attracted to the narcissist's larger than life posture - only to discover his true personality traits when it is far too late. "Give a little to take a lot" - is the narcissist's creed.

This does not prevent the narcissist from assuming the role of the exploited victim. Narcissists always complain that life and people are unfair to them and that they invest far more than their "share of the profit". The narcissist feels that he is the sacrificial lamb, the scapegoat, and that his relationships are asymmetric and imbalanced. "She gets out of our marriage far more than I do" - is a common refrain. Or: "I do all the work around here - and they get all the perks and benefits!"

Faced with such (mis)perceived injustice - and once the relationship is clinched and the victim is "hooked" - the narcissist tries to minimize his contributions. He regards his input as a contractual maintenance chore and the unpleasant and inevitable price he has to pay for his Narcissistic Supply.

After many years of feeling deprived and wronged, some narcissists lapse into "sadistic generosity" or "sadistic altruism". They use their giving as a weapon to taunt and torment the needy and to humiliate them. In the distorted thinking of the narcissist, donating money gives him the right and license to hurt, chastise, criticize, and berate the recipient. His generosity, feels the narcissist, elevates him to a higher moral ground.

Most narcissists confine their giving to money and material goods. Their munificence is an abusive defence mechanism, intended to avoid real intimacy. Their "big-hearted" charity renders all their relationships - even with their spouses and children - "business-like", structured, limited, minimal, non-emotional, unambiguous, and non-ambivalent. By doling out bounteously, the narcissist "knows where he stands" and does not feel threatened by demands for commitment, emotional investment, empathy, or intimacy.

In the narcissist's wasteland of a life, even his benevolence is spiteful, sadistic, punitive, and distancing.

The Compulsive Giver

To all appearances, the compulsive giver is an altruistic, empathic, and caring person. Actually, he or she is a people-pleaser and a co-dependent. The compulsive giver is trapped in a narrative of his own confabulation: how his nearest and dearest need him because they are poor, young, inexperienced, lacking in intelligence or good looks, and are otherwise inferior to him. Compulsive giving, therefore, involves pathological narcissism.

In reality, it is the compulsive giver who coerces, cajoles, and tempts people around him to avail themselves of his services or money. He forces himself on the recipients of his ostentatious largesse and the beneficiaries of his generosity or magnanimity. He is unable to deny anyone their wishes or requests, even when these are not explicit or expressed and are mere figments of his own neediness and grandiose imagination.

Inevitably, he develops unrealistic expectations. He feels that people should be immensely grateful to him and that their gratitude should translate into a kind of obsequiousness. Internally, he seethes and rages against the lack of reciprocity he perceives in his relationships with family, friends, and colleagues. He mutely castigates everyone around him for being so ungenerous. To the compulsive giver, giving is perceived as sacrifice and taking is exploitation. Thus, he gives without grace, always with visible strings attached. No wonder he is always frustrated and often aggressive.

In psychological jargon, we would say that the compulsive giver has alloplastic defences with an external locus of control. This simply means that he relies on input from people around him to regulate his fluctuating sense of self-worth, his precarious self-esteem, and his ever shifting moods. It also means that he blames the world for his failures. He feels imprisoned in a hostile and mystifying universe, entirely unable to influence events, circumstances, and outcomes. He thus avoids assuming responsibility for the consequences of his actions.

Yet, it is important to realize that the compulsive giver cherishes and relishes his self-conferred victimhood and nurtures his grudges by maintaining a meticulous accounting of everything he gives and receives. This mental operation of masochistic bookkeeping is a background process of which the compulsive giver is sometimes unaware. He is likely to vehemently deny such meanness and narrow-mindedness.

The compulsive giver is an artist of Projective Identification. He manipulates his closest into behaving exactly the way he expects them to. He keeps lying to them and telling them that the act of giving is the only reward he seeks. All the while he secretly yearns for reciprocity. He rejects any attempt to rob him of his sacrificial status - he won't accept gifts or money and he avoids being the recipient or beneficiary of help or compliments. These false asceticism and fake modesty are mere baits. He uses them to prove to himself that his nearest and dearest are nasty ingrates. "If they wanted to (give me a present or help me), they would have insisted" - he bellows triumphantly, his worst fears and suspicions yet again confirmed.

Gradually, people fall into line. They begin to feel that they are the ones who are doing the compulsive giver a favour by succumbing to his endless and overweening charity. "What can we do?" - they sigh - "It means so much to him and he has put so much effort into it! I just couldn't say no." The roles are reversed and everyone is happy: the beneficiaries benefit and the compulsive giver goes on feeling that the world is unjust and people are self-centred exploiters. Just as he has always suspected.

The Dual Role of the False Self

Question: Why does the narcissist conjure up another Self? Why not simply transform his True Self into a False one?

Answer: Once formed and functioning, the False Self stifles the growth of the True Self and paralyses it. Henceforth, the True Self is virtually non-existent and plays no role (active or passive) in the conscious life of the narcissist. It is difficult to "resuscitate" it, even with psychotherapy.

169 This substitution is not only a question of alienation, as Horney observed. She said that because the Idealized (False) Self sets impossible goals to the narcissist, the results are frustration and self hate which grow with every setback or failure. But the constant sadistic judgement, the self-berating, the suicidal ideation emanate from the narcissist's idealized, sadistic, Superego regardless of the existence or functioning of a False Self.

There is no conflict between the True Self and the False Self.

First, the True Self is much too weak to do battle with the overbearing False Self. Second, the False Self is adaptive (though maladaptive). It helps the True Self to cope with the world. Without the False Self, the True Self would be subjected to so much hurt that it will disintegrate. This happens to narcissists who go through a life crisis: their False Ego becomes dysfunctional and they experience a harrowing feeling of annulment.

The False Self has many functions. The two most important ones are:

1. It serves as a decoy, it "attracts the fire". It is a proxy for the True Self. It is tough as nails and can absorb any amount of pain, hurt and negative emotions. By inventing it, the child develops immunity to the indifference, manipulation, sadism, smothering, or exploitation - in short: to the abuse

- inflicted on him by his parents (or by other Primary Objects in his life). It is a cloak, protecting him, rendering him invisible and omnipotent at the same time.

2. The False Self is misrepresented by the narcissist as his True Self. The narcissist is saying, in effect: "I am not who you think I am. I am someone else. I am this (False) Self. Therefore, I deserve a better, painless, more considerate treatment." The False Self, thus, is a contraption intended to alter other people's behaviour and attitude towards the narcissist.

These roles are crucial to survival and to the proper psychological functioning of the narcissist. The False Self is by far more important to the narcissist than his dilapidated, dysfunctional, True Self.

The two Selves are not part of a continuum, as the neo-Freudians postulated. Healthy people do not have a False Self which differs from its pathological equivalent in that it is more realistic and closer to the True Self.

It is true that even healthy people wear a mask (Goffman), or a persona (Jung), which they consciously present to the world. But these are a far cry from the False Self, which is mostly subconscious, depends on outside feedback, and is compulsive.

The False Self is an adaptive reaction to pathological circumstances. But its dynamics make it predominate, devour the psyche and prey upon the True Self. Thus, it prevents the efficient, flexible functioning of the personality as a whole.

That the narcissist possesses a prominent False Self as well as a suppressed and dilapidated True Self is common knowledge. Yet, how intertwined and inseparable are these two? Do they interact? How do they influence each other? And what behaviours can be attributed squarely to one or the other of these protagonists? Moreover, does the False Self assume traits and attributes of the True Self in order to deceive the world?

Let's start by referring to an oft-recurring question:

Why are narcissists not prone to suicide?

The simple answer is that they had died a long time ago. Narcissists are the true zombies of the world.

Many scholars and therapists tried to grapple with the void at the core of the narcissist. The common view is that the remnants of the True Self are so ossified, shredded, cowed into submission and repressed that, for all practical purposes, the True Self is dysfunctional and useless. In treating the narcissist, the therapist often tries to construct and nurture a completely new healthy self, rather than build upon the distorted wreckage strewn across the narcissist's psyche.

But what of the rare glimpses of True Self oft reported by those who interact with the narcissist?

Pathological narcissism is frequently co-morbid with other disorders. The narcissistic spectrum is made up of gradations and shades of narcissism. Narcissistic traits or style or even personality (overlay) often attach to other disorders (co-morbidity). A person may well appear to be a full-fledged narcissist - may well appear to be suffering from the Narcissistic Personality Disorder (NPD) - but is not, in the strict, psychiatric, sense of the word. In such people, the True Self is still there and can sometimes be observed.

In a full-fledged narcissist, the False Self imitates the True Self.

To do so artfully, it deploys two mechanisms:

Re-Interpretation

The False Self causes the narcissist to re-interpret certain emotions and reactions in a flattering, socially acceptable, light. The narcissist may, for instance, interpret fear as compassion. Example: if the narcissist hurts someone that he fears (e.g., an authority figure), he may feel bad afterwards and interpret his discomfort as empathy and compassion. To be afraid is humiliating, but to be compassionate is commendable and earns the narcissist acclamation and understanding (Narcissistic Supply).

Emulation

The narcissist is possessed of an uncanny ability to psychologically penetrate others. Often, this gift is abused and put at the service of the narcissist's control freakery and sadism. The narcissist uses it liberally to pulverize the natural defences of his victims by faking empathy.

This capacity is coupled with the narcissist's eerie ability to imitate emotions and their attendant behaviours (affect). The narcissist possesses "emotional resonance tables". He keeps records of every action and reaction, every utterance and consequence, every datum provided by others regarding their state of mind and emotional makeup. From these data he constructs a set of formulas, which often result in impeccably accurate renditions of emotional behaviour. This can be enormously deceiving.

The Stripped Ego

Question: Sometimes you say that the narcissist's True Self had relegated its functions to the outside world and at other times you say that it is not in touch with the outside world (or that only the False Self is in touch with it). How do you settle this apparent contradiction?

Answer: The narcissist's True Self is introverted and dysfunctional. In healthy people, ego functions are generated from the inside, from the Ego. In narcissists, the Ego is dormant, comatose. The narcissist needs input from the outside to perform the most basic ego functions (examples of such functions: recognizing reality, setting boundaries, differentiation, self-esteem and regulation of a sense of self-worth). Only the False Self gets in touch with the world. The True Self is isolated, repressed, unconscious, a shadow.

Forcing the narcissist's False Self to acknowledge and interact with his True Self is not only difficult but may also be counter-productive and dangerously destabilizing. The narcissist's disorder is adaptive and functional, though rigid. The alternative to this (mal)adaptation can be self-destructive (suicidal). Bottled-up, self-directed venom is bound to resurface if the narcissist's various personality structures are coerced into making contact.

That a personality structure (such as the True Self) is in the unconscious does not automatically mean that it is conflict-generating, or that it is involved in conflict, or that it has the potential to provoke conflict. As long as the True Self and the False Self remain out of touch, conflict is avoided.

The False Self pretends to be the only Self and denies the existence of a True Self. It is also extremely useful (adaptive). Rather than risk constant conflict, the narcissist opts for a solution of "disengagement".

172

MALIGNANT SELF LOVE

SAM VAKNIN

The classical Ego, as proposed by Freud, is partly conscious and partly preconscious and unconscious. The narcissist's Ego is completely submerged. The preconscious and conscious parts are detached from it by early traumas and form the False Ego.

The Superego in healthy people constantly compares the Ego to the Ego Ideal. The narcissist has a different psychodynamic. The narcissist's False Self serves as a buffer and as a shock absorber between the True Ego and the narcissist's sadistic, punishing, immature Superego. The narcissist aspires to become pure Ideal Ego.

The narcissist's Ego cannot develop because it is deprived of contact with the outside world and, therefore, endures no growth-inducing conflict. The False Self is rigid. The result is that the narcissist is unable to respond and to adapt to threats, illnesses, and to other life crises and circumstances. He is brittle and more likely to be broken than bent by life's trials and tribulations.

The Ego remembers, evaluates, plans, responds to the world and acts in it and on it. It is the locus of the "executive functions" of the personality. It integrates the inner world with the outer world, the Id with the Superego. It acts under a "reality principle" rather than a "pleasure principle".

This means that the Ego is in charge of delaying gratification. It postpones pleasurable acts until they can be carried out both safely and successfully. The Ego is, therefore, in an ungrateful position. Unfulfilled desires produce unease and anxiety. Reckless fulfilment of desires is diametrically opposed to self-preservation. The Ego has to mediate these tensions.

In an effort to thwart anxiety, the Ego deploys psychological defence mechanisms. On the one hand the Ego channels fundamental drives. It has to "speak their language". It must possess a primitive, infantile, component. On the other hand, the Ego is in charge of negotiating with the outside world and of securing realistic and optimal "bargains" for its "client", the Id. These intellectual and perceptual functions are supervised by the exceptionally strict court of the Superego.

Persons with a strong Ego can objectively comprehend both the world and themselves. In other words, they are possessed of insight. They are able to contemplate longer time spans, plan, forecast and schedule. They choose decisively among alternatives and follow their resolve. They are aware of the existence of their drives, but control them and channel them in socially acceptable ways. They resist pressures, social or otherwise. They choose their course and pursue it.

The weaker the Ego is, the more infantile and impulsive its owner, the more distorted his or her perception of self and reality. A weak Ego is incapable of productive work.

The narcissist is an extreme case. His Ego is non-existent. The narcissist has a fake, substitute Ego. This is why his energy is drained. He spends most of it on maintaining, protecting and preserving the warped, unrealistic images of his (False) Self and of his (fake) world. The narcissist is a person exhausted by his own absence.

The healthy Ego preserves some sense of continuity and consistency. It serves as a point of reference and of departure. It relates events of the past to actions at present and to plans for the future. It incorporates memory, anticipation, imagination and intellect. It defines where the individual ends and the world begins. Though not coextensive with the body or with the personality, it is a close approximation.

In the narcissistic condition, all these functions are relegated to the False Ego, essentially a confabulation, a falsity. Inevitably, the narcissist is bound to develop false memories, conjure up false fantasies, anticipate the unrealistic and work his intellect to justify them by dissembling.

The fraudulence of the False Self is dual: not only is it not "the real thing" - it also operates on false premises. It is a fake and wrong gauge of the world. It falsely and inefficiently regulates the drives. It fails to thwart anxiety.

The False Self provides a false sense of continuity and of a "personal centre". It weaves an enchanted and grandiose fable as a substitute to reality. The narcissist gravitates out of his self and into a plot, a narrative, a story. He continuously feels that he is a character in a film, a concocted figment of his own imagination, or a con artist to be momentarily exposed and summarily socially excommunicated.

Moreover, the narcissist cannot be consistent or coherent. His False Self is preoccupied with the pursuit of Narcissistic Supply. The narcissist has no boundaries because his Ego is not sufficiently defined or fully differentiated. The only constancy is the narcissist's feelings of diffusion or atomization. This is especially true in life crises, when the False Ego ceases to function.

From the developmental point of view, all this is easily accounted for. The child reacts to stimuli, both internal and external. He cannot, however, control, alter, or anticipate them. Instead, he develops mechanisms to regulate the resulting tensions and anxieties.

The child's pursuit of mastery of his environment is compulsive. He is obsessed with securing gratification. Any postponement of his actions and responses forces him to tolerate added tension and anxiety. It is very surprising that, as he grows older, the child ultimately learns to separate stimulus and response and delay the latter. This miracle of expedient self-denial has to do with the development of intellectual skills, on the one hand and with the socialization process, on the other hand.

The intellect is a representation of the world. Through it, the Ego examines reality vicariously without suffering the consequences of possible errors. The Ego uses the intellect to simulate various courses of action and their consequences and to decide how to achieve its ends and the attendant gratification.

The intellect is what allows the child to anticipate the world and what makes him believe in the accuracy and high probability of his own predictions. It is through the intellect that the concepts of the "laws of nature", "predictability", and "order" are introduced. Causality and consistency are all mediated through the intellect. But the intellect must be sustained by an emotional complement. Our picture of the world and of our place in it emerges from experience, both cognitive and emotional.

Socialization has a verbal-communicative element but, decoupled from a strong emotional component, it remains a dead letter.

An example: the child is likely to learn from his parents and from other adults that the world is a predictable, law abiding place. However, if his Primary Objects (most importantly, his mother) behave in a capricious, discriminating, unpredictable, unlawful, abusive, or indifferent manner, it hurts and the conflict between cognition and emotion is powerful. It is bound to paralyse the ego functions of the child.

The accumulation and retention of past events is a prerequisite for both thinking and judgement. Both are impaired if one's personal history contradicts the content of the Superego and the lessons of the socialization process. Narcissists are victims of such a glaring discrepancy between what adult figures in their lives preached and their contradictory course of action.

Once victimized, the narcissist swears "no more". Henceforth, he will be the one doing the victimizing. And as a decoy, he presents to the world his False Self. But he falls prey to his own devices. Internally impoverished and undernourished, isolated and cushioned to the point of suffocation, the True Ego degenerates and decays. The narcissist wakes up one day to find that he is at the mercy of his False Self as much as his victims are.

start

Defence Mechanisms

According to Freud and his followers, our psyche is a battlefield between instinctual urges and drives (the Id), the constraints imposed by reality on the gratification of these impulses (the Ego), and the norms of society (the Superego). This constant infighting generates what Freud called "neurotic anxiety" (fear of losing control) and "moral anxiety" (guilt and shame).

But these are not the only types of anxiety. "Reality anxiety" is the fear of genuine threats and it combines with the other two to yield a morbid and surrealistic inner landscape.

These multiple, recurrent, "mini-panics" are potentially intolerable, overwhelming, and destructive. Hence the need to defend against them. There are dozens of defence mechanisms. An overview of the most common defence mechanisms:

Acting Out

When an inner conflict (most often, frustration) translates into aggression. It involves acting with little or no insight or reflection and in order to attract attention and disrupt other people's cozy lives.

Denial

Perhaps the most primitive and best known defence mechanism. People simply ignore unpleasant facts, they filter out data and content that contravene their self-image, prejudices, and pre-conceived notions of others and of the world.

Devaluation

Attributing negative or inferior traits or qualifiers to self or others. This is done in order to punish the person devalued and to mitigate his or her impact on and importance to the devaluer. When the self is devalued, it is a self-defeating and self-destructive act.

Displacement

When we cannot confront the real sources of our frustration, pain, and envy, we tend to pick a fight with someone weaker or irrelevant and, thus, less menacing. Children often do it because they perceive conflicts with parents and caregivers as life-threatening. Instead, they go out and torment the cat or bully someone at school or lash out at their siblings.

Dissociation

Our mental existence is continuous. We maintain a seamless flow of memories, consciousness, perception, and representation of both inner and external worlds. When we face horrors and unbearable truths, we sometimes "disengage". We lose track of space, time, and the continuum of our identity. We become "someone else" with minimal awareness of our surroundings, of incoming information, and of circumstances. In extreme cases, some people develop a permanently rent personality and this is known as Dissociative Identity Disorder (DID).

Fantasy

Everyone fantasizes now and then. It helps to fend off the dreariness and drabness of everyday life and to plan for an uncertain future. But when fantasy becomes a central feature of grappling with conflict, it is pathological. Seeking gratification - the satisfaction of drives or desires - mainly by fantasizing is an unhealthy defence. Narcissists, for instance, often indulge in grandiose fantasies which are incommensurate with their accomplishments and abilities. Such fantasy life retards personal growth and development because it substitutes for true coping.

Idealization

Another defence mechanism in the arsenal of the narcissist (and, to lesser degree, the borderline and histrionic) is the attribution of positive, glowing, and superior traits to self and (more commonly) to others. Again, what differentiates the healthy from the pathological is the reality test. Imputing positive characteristics to self or others is good, but only if the attributed qualities are real and grounded in a firm grasp of what's true and what's not.

Isolation of Affect

Cognition (thoughts, concepts, ideas) is never divorced from emotion. Conflict can be avoided by separating the cognitive content (for instance, a disturbing or depressing idea) from its emotional correlate. The subject is fully aware of the facts or of the intellectual dimensions of a problematic situation but feels numb. Casting away threatening and discomfiting feelings is a potent way of coping with conflict in the short-term. It is only when it become habitual that it rendered self-defeating.

Omnipotence

When one has a pervading sense and image of oneself as incredibly powerful, superior, irresistible, intelligent, or influential. This is not an adopted affectation but an ingrained, ineradicable inner conviction which borders on magical thinking. It is intended to fend off expected hurt in having to acknowledge one's shortcomings, inadequacies, or limitations.

Projection

We all have an image of how we "should be". Freud called it the "Ego Ideal". But sometimes we experience emotions and drives or have personal qualities which don't sit well with this idealized construct. Projection is when we attribute to others these unacceptable, discomfiting, and ill-fitting feelings and traits that we possess. This way we disown these discordant features and secure the right to criticize and chastise others for having or displaying them. When entire collectives (nations, groups, organizations, firms) project, Freud calls it the "narcissism of small differences".

Projective Identification

Projection is unconscious. People are rarely aware that they are projecting onto others their own ego-dystonic and unpleasant characteristics and feelings. But, sometimes, the projected content is retained in the subject's awareness. This creates a conflict. On the one hand, the patient cannot admit that the emotions, traits, reactions, and behaviours that he so condemns in others are really his. On the other hand, he can't help but being self-aware. He fails to erase from his consciousness the painful realization that he is merely projecting.

So, instead of denying it, the subject explains unpleasant emotions and unacceptable conduct as reactions to the recipient's behaviour. "She made me do it!" is the battle cry of Projective Identification.

We all have expectations regarding the world and its denizens. Some people expect to be loved and appreciated - others to be feared and abused. The latter behave obnoxiously and thus force their nearest and dearest to hate, fear, and "abuse" them. Thus vindicated, their expectations fulfilled, they calm down. The world is rendered once more familiar by making other people behave the way they expect them to. "I knew you would cheat on me! It was clear I couldn't trust you!"

Rationalization or Intellectualization

To cast one's behaviour after the fact in a favourable light. To justify and explain one's conduct or, more often, misconduct by resorting to "rational, logical, socially-acceptable" explications and excuses. Rationalization is also used to re-establish ego-syntony (inner peace and self-acceptance).

178

Though not strictly a defence mechanism, cognitive dissonance may be considered a variant of rationalization. It involves the devaluation of things and people very much desired but frustratingly out of one's reach and control. In a famous fable, a fox, unable to snag the luscious grapes he covets, says: "These grapes are probably sour anyhow!" This is an example of cognitive dissonance in action.

Reaction Formation

Adopting a position and mode of conduct that defy personally unacceptable thoughts or impulses by expressing diametrically opposed sentiments and convictions. Example: a latent (closet) homosexual finds his sexual preference deplorable and acutely shameful (ego-dystonic). He resorts to homophobia. He public berates, taunts, and baits homosexuals. Additionally, he may flaunt his heterosexuality by emphasizing his sexual prowess, or by prowling singles bars for easy pick-ups and conquests. This way he contains and avoids his unwelcome homosexuality.

Repression

The removal from consciousness of forbidden thoughts and wishes. The removed content does not vanish and it remains as potent as ever, fermenting in one's unconscious. It is liable to create inner conflicts and anxiety and provoke other defence mechanisms to cope with these.

Splitting

This is a "primitive" defence mechanism. In other words, it begins to operate in very early infancy. It involves the inability to integrate contradictory qualities of the same object into a coherent picture.

Mother has good qualities and bad, sometimes she is attentive and caring and sometimes distracted and cold. The baby is unable to grasp the complexities of her personality. Instead, the infant invents two constructs (entities), "Bad Mother" and "Good Mother". It relegates everything likable about mother to the "Good Mother" and contrasts it with "Bad Mother", the repository of everything it dislikes about her.

This means that whenever mother acts nicely, the baby relates to the idealized "Good Mother" and whenever mother fails the test, the baby devalues her by interacting, in its mind, with "Bad Mother". These cycles of idealization followed by devaluation are common in some personality disorders, notably the narcissistic and borderline.

Splitting can also apply to one's self. Patients with personality disorders often idealize themselves fantastically and grandiosely, only to harshly devalue, hate, and even harm themselves when they fail or are otherwise frustrated.

Sublimation

The conversion and channelling of unacceptable emotions into socially-condoned behaviour. Freud described how sexual desires and urges are transformed into creative pursuits or politics.

Undoing

Trying to rid oneself of gnawing feelings of guilt by compensating the injured party either symbolically or actually.

Finish

The Split-off Ego

In the previous chapter ("The Stripped Ego") I have dealt with the classical, Freudian, concept of the Ego. It is partly conscious, partly preconscious and unconscious. It operates on a "reality principle" (as opposed to the Id's "pleasure principle"). It maintains an inner equilibrium between the onerous (and unrealistic, or ideal) demands of the Superego and the almost irresistible (and unrealistic) drives of the Id. It also has to fend off the unfavourable consequences of comparisons between itself and the Ego Ideal (comparisons that the Superego is only too eager to repeatedly make). In many respects, therefore, the Ego in Freudian psychoanalysis is the Self. Not so in Jungian psychology.

The famous, though controversial, psychoanalyst, C. G. Jung, postulated the existence of two "personalities" (actually, two selves), one of them being the Shadow. Technically, the Shadow is a part (though an inferior part) of one's overarching personality (one's chosen conscious attitude).

The Shadow develops thus:

Inevitably, some personal and collective psychic elements are found wanting or incompatible with one's personality (narrative). Their expression is suppressed and they coalesce into an almost autonomous "splinter personality".

This second personality is contrarian: it negates the official, chosen, personality, though it is totally relegated to the unconscious. Jung believes, therefore, in a system of "checks and balances": the Shadow balances the Ego (consciousness). This is not necessarily negative. The behavioural and attitudinal compensation offered by the Shadow can be positive.

Jung [all quotes from C.G. Jung. Collected Works. G. Adler, M. Fordham and H. Read (Eds.). 21 volumes. Princeton University Press, 1960-1983]:

"The shadow personifies everything that the subject refuses to acknowledge about himself and yet is always thrusting itself upon him directly or indirectly - for instance, inferior traits of character and other incompatible tendencies."

[The Archetypes and the Collective Unconscious, Collected Writings. Volume 9, i. p. 284 f.]

It would seem fair to conclude that there is a close affinity between the Jungian complexes (split-off materials) and the Shadow:

"Complexes are psychic fragments which have split off owing to traumatic influences or certain incompatible tendencies. As the association experiments prove, complexes interfere with the intentions of the will and disturb the conscious perfor-mance; they produce disturbances of memory and blockages in the flow of associations; they appear and disappear according to their own laws; they can temporarily obsess consciousness, or influence speech and action in an unconscious way."

[The Structure and Dynamics of the Psyche, Collected Writings, Volume 8, p. 121]

Perhaps the complexes (also the result of incompatibility with the conscious personality) are the negative part of the Shadow. Perhaps they just reside in it, on closely collaborate with it, in a feedback mechanism. Perhaps whenever the Shadow manifests itself in a manner obstructive, destructive or disruptive to the Ego, Jung calls it a complex. Complexes and the Shadow may really be one and the same, the result of a massive split-off of material and its relegation to the realm of the unconscious.

This is part and parcel of the individuation-separation phase of our early childhood development. Prior to this phase, the infant, in its exploration of the world, begins to differentiate between self and everything that is not self.

The child begins to form and store images of his self and of the World (initially, as represented by the Primary Object in his life, normally his mother). These images are distinct from the child himself. To the infant, this is revolutionary stuff, nothing short of a breakdown of an erstwhile unitary universe and its substi-tution with fragmented, unconnected, entities. It is traumatic.

Moreover, these images are themselves split. The child has separate images of a "good" mother and a "bad" mother, respectively associated with the gratification of his needs and desires and with their frustration. He also constructs separate images of a "good" self and a "bad" self, linked to the ensuing states of being gratified (by the "good" mother) and being frus-trated (by the "bad" mother).

At this stage, the child is unable to see that people are both good and bad (that an entity with a single identity can be both gratifying and frustrating). He derives his own sense of being good or bad from the outside. The "good" mother inevitably and invariably leads to a "good", satisfied, self and the "bad", frustrating mother always engenders the "bad", frustrated, self.

But the image of the "bad" mother is very threatening. It is anxiety provoking. The child is afraid that, if he is found out by his mother, she will abandon him. Moreover, the "bad" mother is a forbidden subject of negative feelings (one must not think about mother in bad terms!).

Thus, the child splits the bad images off and uses them to form a separate collage of "bad objects". This process is called "object splitting". It is the most primitive defence mechanism. When still used by adults it is an indication of pathology.

This is followed by the phases of "separation" and "individuation" (18-36 months). The child no longer splits his objects (bad objects to one, repressed side and good objects to another, conscious, side). He learns to relate to objects (people) as integrated wholes, with the "good" and the "bad" aspects coalesced. An integrated self-concept inevitably follows.

183   The child internalizes the mother (he memorizes her roles). He becomes his own parent (mother) and performs her functions by himself. He acquires "object constancy" (he learns that the existence of objects does not depend on his presence or on his vigilance). Mother always returns to him after she disappears from sight. A major reduction in anxiety follows and this permits the child to dedicate his energy to the development of stable, consistent, and independent senses of self and introjects (internalized images) of others.

This is the juncture at which personality disorders form. Between the ages of 15 months and 22 months, a sub-phase in this stage of separation-individuation is known as "rapprochement".

The child, at this stage, is still exploring the world. This is a terrifying and anxiety-inducing process. The child needs to know that he is protected, that he is doing the right thing, and that he is gaining the approval of his mother. The child periodically returns to his mother for reassurance, affirmation, and admiration, as if making sure that his mother endorses his newfound autonomy and independence and accepts his separate individuality.

When the mother is immature, narcissistic, or suffers from a mental pathology, she withholds from the child what he needs: approval, admiration, and reassurance. She feels threatened by his independence. She feels that she is losing him. She does not let go sufficiently. She smothers him with over-protection and indulgence. She offers him overpowering emotional incentives to remain "mother-bound", dependent, undeveloped, a part of a mother-child symbiotic dyad.

The child, in turn, develops mortal fears of being abandoned, of losing his mother's love and support. His unspoken dilemma is: to become independent and lose mother - or to retain mother and never have a self?

The child is enraged (because he is frustrated in his quest for his self). He is anxious (fearful of losing mother), he feels guilty (for being angry at mother), he is attracted and repelled. In short, he is in a chaotic state of mind.

Whereas healthy people experience such eroding dilemmas now and then, to the personality disordered they are a constant, characteristic emotional state.

To defend himself against this intolerable vortex of emotions, the child bars them from his consciousness. The "bad" mother and the "bad" self plus all the negative feelings of abandonment, anxiety, and rage are "split-off".

But the child's over-reliance on this primitive defence mechanism obstructs his orderly development: he fails to integrate the split images. The Bad parts are so laden with negative emotions that they remain virtually untouched throughout life (in the Shadow, as complexes). It proves impossible to integrate such explosive Bad material with the more benign Good parts.

Thus, some adults remain fixated at this earlier stage of development. Such a person is unable to integrate and to see people as whole objects. They are either all "good" or all "bad" (idealization and devaluation cycles). He is terrified (unconsciously) of abandonment, actually feels abandoned, or under threat of being abandoned and subtly plays it out in his/her interpersonal relationships.

Is the reintroduction of split-off material in any way helpful? Is it likely to lead to an integrated Ego (or self)?

To ask this is to confuse two issues. With the exception of schizophrenics and some types of psychotics, the Ego (or self) is always integrated. That the patient cannot integrate the images of objects, both libidinal and non-libidinal, does not mean that he has a non-integrated or a disintegrative Ego.

The inability to integrate the world (as is the case in the Borderline or in the Narcissistic personality disorders) relates to the patient's choice of defence mechanisms. It is a secondary layer. The crux of the matter is not what state the self is in (integrated or not) but what is the state of one's perception of the self.

Thus, from the theoretical point of view, the reintroduction of split-off material does nothing to "increase" the Ego's integration. This is especially true if we adopt the Freudian concept of the Ego as inclusive of all split-off material.

But does the transfer of the split-off material from one part of the Ego (the unconscious) to another (the conscious) in any way affect the integration of the Ego?

Confronting split-off, repressed material is still an important part of many psychodynamic therapies. It has been shown to reduce anxiety, cure conversion symptoms and, generally, have a beneficial and therapeutic effect on the individual. Yet, this has nothing to do with integration. It has to do with conflict resolution.

That various parts of the personality are in constant conflict is an integral principle of all psychodynamic theories. Dredging split-off material to our consciousness reduces the scope or the intensity of these conflicts. This is so by definition: split-off material introduced to consciousness is no longer split-off material and, therefore, can no longer participate in the "war" raging in the unconscious.

But is it always recommended?

Consider personality disorders.

Personality disorders are adaptive solutions to given circumstances. It is true that, as circumstances change, these "solutions" usually don't and, thus, prove to be rigid straitjackets, maladaptive rather than adaptive. But the patient has no substitutive coping strategies available. No therapy can provide him with such substitutes because the whole personality is affected by his pathology, not just an aspect or an element of it.

Bringing up split-off material may constrain or even eliminate the patient's personality disorder. And then what? How is the patient supposed to cope with the world then, a world that has suddenly reverted to being hostile, abandoning, capricious, whimsical, cruel and devouring - just like it was in the patient's infancy, before he stumbled across the magic of his personality disorder?

The Narcissist's Object Constancy

Narcissists often carry on talking (rather, lecturing) long after their interlocutors, bored stiff and resentful, have physically departed or mentally switched off. They are shocked to discover that they have been conversing with thin air for awhile. They are equally astounded when they are abandoned or shunned by spouses, friends, colleagues, the media, their fans, or audiences.

The root of this recurrent astonishment is the narcissist's perverse object constancy.

According to the great developmental psychologist, Margaret Mahler, between the ages of 24 and 36 months of life, the infant is finally able to cope with the mother's absence (by finding appropriate substitutes to her presence). It knows that she will return and trusts her to do so time and again.

The psychic image of the mother is internalized as a stable, reliable, and predictable object. As the infant's sense of time and verbal skills evolve, it becomes more immune to delayed gratification and tolerant of inevitable separation.

Piaget, the renowned child psychologist, concurred with Mahler and coined the term "object constancy" to describe the dynamics she observed.

As opposed to Mahler, Daniel Stern, another prominent psychoanalyst, proposes that the child is born with a sense of Self:

"Infants begin to experience a sense of an emergent self from birth. They are pre-designed to be aware of self - organizing processes. They never experience a period of total self / other lack of differentiation. There is no confusion of self and other in the beginning or at any point during infancy."

But even Stern accepts the existence of a distinct and separate "other" versus the nascent "self".

Pathological narcissism is a reaction to deficient bonding and dysfunctional attachment (Bowlby). Object relations in narcissists are infantile and chaotic (Winnicott, Guntrip). Many narcissists have no psychological-object constancy at all. In other words, many of them do not feel that other people are benign, reliable, helpful, constant, predictable, and trustworthy.

To compensate for this lack in ability (or willingness) to relate to real, live people, the narcissist invents and moulds substitute-objects or surrogate-objects.

These are mental representations of meaningful or significant others (Sources of Narcissistic Supply). They have little or nothing to do with reality. These imagoes - images - are confabulations, works of fiction. They respond to the narcissist's needs and fears and do not correspond to the persons they purport to stand for.

The narcissist internalizes these pliable representations, manipulates them, and interacts with them - not with the originals. The narcissist is entirely immersed in his world, talking to these "figurines", arguing with these substitutes, contracting with these surrogates, being admired by them.

Hence his dismay when confronted with real people, their needs, feelings, preferences, and choices.

Thus, the typical narcissist refrains from any meaningful discourse with his spouse and children, friends and colleagues. Instead, he spins a narrative in which these people - represented by mental avatars - admire him, find him fascinating, fervently wish to oblige him, love him, or fear him.

These "avatars" have little or nothing to do with the way his kin and kith REALLY feel about him. The protagonists in the narcissist's yarns do not incorporate veritable data about his wife, or offspring, or colleagues, or friends. They are mere projections of the narcissist's inner world. Thus, when the narcissist faces the real thing - he refuses to believe and accept the facts:

"My wife has always been so cooperative - whatever happened to her lately?"

She was never cooperative - she was subservient or frightened into submission. But the narcissist didn't notice because he never actually "saw her".

"My son always wanted to follow in my footsteps - I don't know what possesses him!"

The narcissist's poor son never wanted to be a lawyer or a doctor. He always dreamed of being an actor or an artist. But the narcissist was not aware of it.

"My friends used to listen to my stories enraptured - I have no idea why they no longer do so!"

At first, his friends politely listened to the narcissist's interminable rants and ravings. Finally, they dropped from his social circle, one by one.

"I was admired by the media - now I am constantly ignored!"

At first, an object of derision and morbid fascination, the novelty wore off and the media moved on to other narcissists.

Puzzled, hurt, and clueless - the narcissist withdraws further and further with every narcissistic injury. Finally, he is forced into choosing the delusional way out.

The Serious Narcissist

Question: Do narcissists have an exceptional sense of humour?

Answer: I am sure that some of them do. In this, they are no different to healthier specimen of the human species. The narcissist, though, rarely engages in self-directed, self-deprecating humour. If he does, he expects to be contradicted, rebuked and rebuffed by his listeners ("Come on, you are actually quite handsome!"), or to be commended or admired for his courage or for his wit and intellectual acerbity ("I envy your ability to laugh at yourself!"). As everything else in a narcissist's life, his sense of humour is deployed in the interminable pursuit of Narcissistic Supply.

The absence of Narcissistic Supply (or the impending threat of such an absence) is, indeed, a serious matter. It is the narcissistic equivalent of mental death. If prolonged and unmitigated, such absence can lead to the real thing: physical death, a result of suicide, or of a psychosomatic deterioration of the narcissist's health.

Yet, to obtain Narcissistic Supply, one must be taken seriously and to be taken seriously one must be the first to take oneself seriously. Hence the gravity with which the narcissist contemplates himself. These lacks of levity and of perspective and proportion characterize the narcissist and set him apart.

The narcissist firmly believes that he is unique and that he has a mission to fulfil, a destined life. The narcissist's biography is part of Mankind's legacy, spun by a cosmic plot which constantly thickens. Such a life deserves only the most somber consideration.

Moreover, every particle of the narcissist's existence, every action or inaction, every utterance, creation, or composition, indeed every thought, are bathed in this self-imputed universal

188

SAM VAKNIN   MALIGNANT SELF LOVE

significance. The narcissist treads the paths of glory, of achievement, of perfection, or of brilliance. It is all part of a design, a pattern, a plot, which inexorably lead the narcissist on to the fulfilment of his task.

The narcissist may subscribe to a religion, to a belief, or to an ideology in his effort to understand the source of this ubiquitous conviction of uniqueness. He may attribute his sense of direction to God, to history, to society, to culture, to a calling, to his profession, to a value system, or even to his life's circumstances. But he always does it with a straight face and with deadly seriousness.

And because, to the narcissist, the part is a reflection of the whole, he tends to generalize, to resort to stereotypes, to induct (to learn about the whole from the detail), to exaggerate, finally to pathologically lie to himself and to others. This self-importance, this belief in a grand design, in an all embracing and all-pervasive pattern make him an easy prey to all manner of logical fallacies and con artistry. Despite his avowed and proudly expressed rationality the narcissist is besieged by superstition and prejudice. Above all, he is a captive of the false conviction that his uniqueness destines him to fulfil a mission of cosmic significance.

All these make the narcissist a volatile person. Not merely mercurial, but labile, fluctuating, histrionic, unreliable, and disproportional. That which has cosmic implications calls for cosmic reactions. A person with an inflated sense of self-importance reacts with exaggeration to threats, greatly inflated by his imagination and by his personal mythology.

On the narcissist's cosmic scale, the daily vagaries of life, the mundane, the routine are not important, even damagingly distracting. This is the source of his feeling of exceptional entitlement. Surely, engaged as he is in benefiting humanity through the exercise of his unique faculties, the narcissist deserves special treatment!

This is the source of his violent swings between opposite behaviour patterns and between devaluation and idealization of others. To the narcissist, every minor development is nothing less than a portentous omen, every adversity is a conspiracy to upset his progress, every setback an apocalyptic calamity, every irritation the cause for outlandish outbursts of rage.

He is a man of the extremes and only the extremes. He may learn to efficiently suppress or hide his feelings or reactions, but never for long. In the most inappropriate and inopportune moment, you can count on the narcissist to explode, like a wrongly wound time bomb. And in between eruptions, the narcissistic volcano daydreams, indulges in delusions, plans his victories over an increasingly hostile and alienated environment. Gradually, the narcissist becomes paranoid, aloof, detached and dissociative.

In such a personal setting, one must admit, there is not much room for a sense of humour.

Narcissists, Disagreements and Criticism

Question: How do narcissists react to criticism?

Answer: Narcissistic injury is any threat (real or imagined) to the narcissist's grandiose and fantastic self-perception (False Self) as brilliant, perfect, omnipotent, omniscient, and entitled to special treatment and recognition, regardless of his actual accomplishments (or lack thereof).

The narcissist is forever trapped in the unresolved conflicts of his childhood (including the famous Oedipus Complex). This compels him to seek resolution by re-enacting these conflicts with significant others. But he is likely to return to the Primary Objects in his life (parents, authority figures, role models, or caregivers) to do either of two:

1. To "re-charge" the conflict "battery", or
2. When he fails to re-enact the conflict with another person.

The narcissist relates to his human environment through his unresolved conflicts. The energy of the tension thus created sustains him.

The narcissist is a person driven by parlously imminent eruptions, by the unsettling prospect of losing his precarious balance. Being a narcissist is a tightrope act. The narcissist must remain alert and on-edge. Only in a constant state of active conflict does he attain the requisite levels of mental arousal.

This periodical interaction with the objects of his conflicts sustains his inner turmoil, keeps the narcissist on his toes, infuses him with the intoxicating feeling that he is alive.

The narcissist perceives every disagreement, let alone criticism, as nothing short of a threat. Most narcissists react defensively to criticism and disagreement. They become conspicuously indignant, aggressive, and cold. They detach emotionally for fear of yet another (narcissistic) injury. They devalue the person who made the disparaging remark, the critical comment, the unflattering observation, the innocuous joke at the narcissist's expense.

By holding the critic in contempt, by diminishing the stature of the discordant conversant, the narcissist minimizes the impact of the disagreement or criticism on himself. This is known as cognitive dissonance.

The narcissist actively solicits Narcissistic Supply - adulation, compliments, admiration, subservience, attention, being feared - from others in order to sustain his fragile and dysfunctional Ego. Thus, he constantly courts possible rejection, criticism, disagreement, and even mockery.

The narcissist is, therefore, dependent on other people. He is aware of the risks associated with such all-pervasive and essential dependence. He resents his weakness and dreads possible disruptions in the flow of his drug: Narcissistic Supply. He is caught between the rock of his habit and the hard place of his frustration. No wonder he is prone to raging, lashing and acting out, and to pathological, all-consuming envy (all of these being expressions of pent-up aggression).

Like a trapped animal, the narcissist is constantly on the look-out for slights. He is hypervigilant: was this comment meant to demean him? Was this utterance a deliberate attack? He perceives every disagreement as criticism and every critical remark as complete and humiliating rejection - nothing short of a threat or a challenge. Gradually, his mind turns into a chaotic battlefield of paranoia and ideas of reference until he loses touch with reality and retreats to his own world of fantasized and unchallenged grandiosity.

When the disagreement or criticism or disapproval or approbation are public, though, the narcissist tends to regard them as Narcissistic Supply! Only when they are expressed in private does the narcissist rage against them.

The cerebral narcissist is as competitive and intolerant of criticism or disagreement as his somatic counterpart. The subjugation and subordination of others demand the establishment of his undisputed intellectual superiority or professional authority.

Alexander Lowen wrote an excellent exposition of this "hidden or tacit competition". The cerebral narcissist aspires to perfection. Thus, even the slightest and most inconsequential challenge to his authority is inflated by him. Hence, the disproportionateness of his reactions.

When confronting adversity fails, some narcissists resort to denial, which they apply to their "extensions" (family, business, workplace, friends) as well.

Take, for example, the narcissist's family. Narcissists often instruct, order, or threaten their children into hiding the truth of abuse, malfunction, maladaptation, fear, pervasive sadness, violence, mutual hatred and mutual repulsion which are the hallmarks of the narcissistic family.

"Not to wash the family's dirty linen in public" is a common exhortation. The whole family conforms to the fantastic, grandiose, perfect and superior narrative invented by the narcissist. The family becomes an extension of the False Self. This is an important function of these Sources of Secondary Narcissistic Supply.

Criticizing, disagreeing, or exposing these fictions and lies, penetrating the family's facade, are considered to be mortal sins. The sinner is immediately subjected to severe and constant emotional harassment, guilt trips and blame games, and to abuse, including physical abuse. This state of things is especially typical of families with sexual abuse.

Behaviour modification techniques are liberally used by the narcissist to ensure that the skeletons do stay in the family closets. An unexpected by-product of this atmosphere of concealment and falsity is mutiny. The narcissist's spouse or his adolescent children are likely to exploit the narcissist's vulnerabilities - his proneness to secrecy, self-delusion, and aversion to the truth - to rebel against him. The first thing to crumble in the narcissist's family is this shared psychosis: the mass denial and the secretiveness so diligently cultivated by him.

[Learn more about Narcissistic Rage in FAQ 10]

Interesting

Transformations of Aggression

Question: Why is he so aggressive? Is it pent-up sadism? Is he born this way? It's like he hates everyone, all the time. How can I avoid this aspect of his personality?

Answer: Prone to magical thinking, the narcissist is deeply convinced of the transcendental meaning of his life. He fervently believes in his own uniqueness and "mission". He constantly searches for clues regarding the hidden, though inevitable, meaning of his personal life. The narcissist is forever a "public persona", even when alone, in the confines of his bedroom. His every move, his every act, his every decision and every scribbling is of momentous consequence. The narcissist often documents his life with vigil, for the benefit of future biographers. His every utterance and shred of correspondence are carefully orchestrated as befitting a historical figure of import.

This grandiose background leads to an exaggerated sense of entitlement. The narcissist feels that he is worthy of special and immediate treatment by the most qualified persons. His time is too precious to be wasted on bureaucratic trifles, misunderstandings, underlings, and social conventions. His mission is urgent. Other people are expected both to share the narcissist's self-assessment and to behave accordingly: to accommodate his needs, instantly comply with his wishes, and succumb to his whims.

But the world does not always accommodate, comply, and succumb. It often resists the wishes of the narcissist, mocks his comportment, or, worst of all, ignores him. The narcissist reacts to this with a cycle of frustration and aggression.

Still, it is not always possible to express naked aggression. It may be dangerous, or counterproductive, or plain silly. Even the narcissist cannot attack his boss, or a policeman, or the neigh-

194

MALIGNANT SELF LOVE

SAM VAKNIN

bourhood bully with impunity. So, the narcissist's aggression wears many forms. The narcissist suddenly becomes brutally "honest", or bitingly "humorous", or smotheringly "helpful", or sexually "experimental", or socially "reclusive", or behaviourally "different", or finds yet another way to express his scathing and repressed hostility.

The narcissist's favourite sadistic cocktail is brutal honesty coupled with "helpful advice" and "concern" for the welfare of the person thus attacked. The narcissist blurts out, often unprovoked, hurtful observations. These statements are invariably couched in a socially impeccable context.

For instance, "Do you know you have bad breath? You will be much more popular had you treated it", "You are really too fat, you should take care of yourself, you are not young, you know, who knows what this is doing to your heart", "These clothes do not complement you. Let me give you the name of my tailor...", "You are behaving very strangely lately, I think that talk therapy combined with medication may do wonders", and so on.

The misanthropic and schizoid narcissist at once becomes sociable and friendly when he spots an opportunity to hurt someone or to avenge himself. He then resorts to humour: black, thwarted, poignant, biting, sharpened and agonizing. Thinly disguises barbs follow thinly disguised threats cloaked in "jokes" or "humorous anecdotes".

Another favourite trick is to harp on the insecurities, fears, weaknesses, and deficiencies of the target of aggression. If married to a jealous spouse, the narcissist emphasizes his newfound promiscuity and need to experiment sexually. If his business partner has been traumatized by a previous insolvency, the narcissist berates him for being too cautious or insufficiently entrepreneurial while forcing the partnership to assume outlandish and speculative business risks. If co-habiting with a gregarious mate, the narcissist acts the recluse, the hermit, the social misfit, or the misunderstood visionary, thus forcing the partner to give up her social life.

The narcissist is seething with enmity and venom. He is a receptacle of unbridled hatred, animosity, and hostility. When he can, the narcissist often turns to physical violence. But the non-physical manifestations of his pent-up bile are even more terrifying, more all-pervasive, and more lasting. Beware of narcissists bearing gifts. They are bound to explode in your face, or poison you. The narcissist hates you wholeheartedly and thoroughly simply because you are. Remembering this has a survival value.

195

The Adrenaline Junkie

Narcissistic Supply is exciting. When it is available, the narcissist feels elated, omnipotent, omniscient, handsome, sexy, adventurous, invincible, and irresistible. When it is missing, the narcissist first enters a manic phase of trying to replenish his supply and, if he fails, the narcissist shrivels, withdraws and is reduced to a zombie-like state of numbness.

Some people - and all narcissists - are addicted to excitement, to the adrenaline rush, to the danger inevitably and invariably involved. They are the adrenaline junkies. All narcissists are adrenaline junkies, but not all adrenaline junkies are narcissists. Narcissistic Supply is the narcissist's particular sort of thrill. Deficient Narcissistic Supply is tantamount to the absence of excitement and thrills in non-narcissistic adrenaline junkies.

Originally, in early childhood, Narcissistic Supply is meant to help the narcissist regulate his volatile sense of self-worth and self-esteem. But Narcissistic Supply, regardless of its psychodynamic functions, also simply feels good. The narcissist grows addicted to the gratifying effects of Narcissistic Supply. He reacts with anxiety when constant, reliable provision is absent or threatened.

Thus, Narcissistic Supply always comes with excitement, on the one hand and with anxiety on the other hand.

When unable to secure "normal" Narcissistic Supply - adulation, recognition, fame, celebrity, notoriety, infamy, affirmation, or mere attention - the narcissist resorts to "abnormal" Narcissistic Supply. He tries to obtain his drug - the thrills, the good feeling that comes with Narcissistic Supply - by behaving recklessly, by succumbing to substance abuse, or by living dangerously.

Narcissists faced with a chronic state of deficient Narcissistic Supply become criminals, or race car drivers, or gamblers, or soldiers, or investigative journalists. They defy authority. They avoid safety, routine and boredom: no safe sex, no financial prudence, no stable marriage or career. They become peripatetic and itinerant. They change jobs, or lovers, or vocations, or avocations, or residences, or friendships often.

But sometimes even these extreme and demonstrative steps are not enough. When confronted with a boring, routine existence, with a chronic and permanent inability to secure Narcissistic Supply and excitement, these people compensate by inventing thrills where there are none.

They become paranoid, full of delusional persecutory notions and ideas of reference. Or they develop phobias: fear of flying, of heights, of enclosed or open spaces, of cats or spiders. Fear is a good substitute to the excitement they so crave and that eludes them.

Anxiety leads to the frenetic search for Narcissistic Supply. Obtaining the supply causes a general, albeit transient, sense of wellbeing, relief and release as the anxiety is alleviated. This cycle is addictive.

But what generates the anxiety in the first place? Are people born adrenaline junkies or do they become ones?

No one knows for sure. It may be genetically determined. We may discover one day that adrenaline junkies, conditioned by defective genes, develop special neural and biochemical paths, an unusual sensitivity to adrenaline. Or, it may indeed be the sad outcome of abuse and trauma during the formative years. The brain is plastic and easily influenced by recurrent bouts of capricious and malicious treatment.

First published on the Suite 101 Narcissistic Personality Disorders Topic.

Narcissistic Humiliation

Question: How do narcissists react to humiliation?

Answer: As do normal people - only more so. The narcissist feels regularly and strongly humiliated by things, which, normally, do not amount to slights or insults. It would be safe to say that the emotional life of the narcissist is tinted with ubiquitous and recurrent humiliation.

Any event, action, inaction, utterance, or thought, which negate or can be construed to negate the uniqueness or the grandiose superiority of the narcissist humiliate him. Living in a big city, belonging to a group of peers, any sign of disapproval, disagreement, criticism, or remonstrance reduce him to a state of sulking petulance and agitation.

The narcissist interprets everything as addressed to his person ("ad hominem") rather than to his actions. The list of things, real or imagined, which might slight the narcissist is dizzying indeed. When contradicted, when deprived of special treatment, when subjected to an attitude or comment which he judges to contravene his grandiose, superior self-image or his sense of entitlement, he is beside himself with indignant rage.

It is as though the narcissist has a need to be humbled, reduced, minimized and otherwise trampled upon. It is the eternal quest for punishment that is thus satisfied. The narcissist is on a never-ending trial, which, itself, constitutes his punishment.

The initial reaction of the narcissist to a perceived humiliation is a conscious rejection of the humiliating input. The narcissist tries to ignore it, talk it out of existence, or belittle its importance. If this crude mechanism of cognitive dissonance fails, the narcissist resorts to denial and repression of the humiliating material. He "forgets" all about it and, when reminded of it, denies it.

MALIGNANT SELF LOVE

SAM VAKNIN

But these are usually merely stopgap measures. The disturbing data are bound to impinge on the narcissist's tormented consciousness. Once aware of their re-emergence, the narcissist uses fantasy to counteract and counterbalance it. He imagines all the horrible things that he would do to the sources of his frustration.

It is through fantasy that the narcissist seeks to redeem his pride and dignity and to re-establish his damaged sense of uniqueness and grandiosity. Paradoxically, the narcissist does not mind being humiliated if this were to make him more unique or draw more attention to his person.

For instance: if the injustice involved in the process of humiliation is unprecedented, or if the humiliating acts or words place the narcissist in a unique position, or if they transform him into a public figure, the narcissist tries to encourage such behaviours and to elicit them from others.

In this case, he fantasizes how he would defiantly demean and debase his opponents by forcing them to behave even more barbarously than before, so that their unjust conduct is universally recognized as such and condemned and the narcissist is publicly vindicated and his self-respect restored. In short: martyrdom is as good a method of obtaining Narcissist Supply as any.

Fantasy, though, has its limits and once reached, the narcissist is likely to experience waves of self-hatred and self-loathing, the outcomes of helplessness and of realizing the depths of his dependence on Narcissistic Supply. These feelings culminate in severe self-directed aggression: depression, destructive, self-defeating behaviours or suicidal ideation.

These self-negating reactions, inevitably and naturally, terrify the narcissist. He tries to project them on to his environment. He may decompensate by developing obsessive-compulsive traits or by going through a psychotic microepisode.

At this stage, the narcissist is suddenly besieged by disturbing, uncontrollable violent thoughts. He develops ritualistic reactions to them: a sequence of motions, an act, or obsessive counter-thoughts. Or he might visualize his aggression, or experience auditory hallucinations. Humiliation affects the narcissist this deeply.

Luckily, the process is entirely reversible once Narcissistic Supply is resumed. Almost immediately, the narcissist swings from one pole to another, from being humiliated to being elated, from being put down to being reinstated, from being at the bottom of his own, imagined, pit to occupying the top of his own, imagined, Everest.

This metamorphosis is very typical: the narcissist has only an inner world. He does not accept, nor does he recognize reality. To him, reality is but a shadow cast by the fire, which burns inside him. He is consumed by it, by the wish to be loved, to be recognized, to control, to avoid hurt. And by succumbing to this internal conflagration, the narcissist all but cements his inability to attain even the modest goals that are achieved by others at a minimal cost and almost effortlessly.

The Midlife Narcissist

Question: Are narcissists likely to go through a midlife crisis and, if so, to what extent does such a crisis ameliorate or exacerbate their condition?

Answer: The sometimes severe crises experienced by persons of both sexes in middle age (a.k.a. the "midlife crisis" or the "change of life") is a much discussed though little understood phenomenon. It is not even certain that the beast exists.

201   Women go through menopause between the ages of 42-55 (the average age of onset in the USA is 51.3). The amount of the hormone oestrogen in their bodies decreases sharply, important parts of the reproductive system shrink and menstruation ceases. Many women suffer from "hot flashes" and a thinning and fracturing of the bones (osteoporosis).

The "male menopause" is a more contentious issue. Men do experience a gradual decline in testosterone levels but nothing as sharp as the woman's deterioration of her oestrogen supply. No link has been found between these physiological and hormonal developments and the mythical "midlife crisis".

This fabled turning point has to do with the gap between earlier plans, dreams and aspirations and one's life and reality. Come middle age, men are supposed to be less satisfied with life, career, or spouse. People get disappointed and disillusioned. They understand that they are not likely to have a second chance, that they largely missed the train, and that their dreams will remain just that. They have nothing to look forward to. They feel spent, bored, fatigued and trapped.

Some adults embark on a transition. They define new goals, look for new partners, form new families, engage in new hobbies, change vocation and avocation alike, or relocate. They regenerate and reinvent themselves and the structures of their lives. Others just grow bitter. Unable to face the shambles, they resort to alcoholism, workaholism, emotional absence, abandonment, escapism, degeneration, or a sedentary lifestyle.

Another pillar of discontent is the predictability of adult life. Following a brief flurry, in early adulthood, of excitement and vigour, of dreams and hopes, fantasies and aspirations, we succumb to and sink into the mire of mediocrity. The mundane engulfs us and digests us. Routines consume our energy and leave us dilapidated and empty. We know with a dull certainty what awaits us and this ubiquitous rut is maddening.

Paradoxically, the narcissist is best equipped to successfully tackle these problems. The narcissist suffers from mental progeria. Subject to childhood abuse, he ages prematurely and finds himself in a time warp, in the throes of a constant midlife crisis.

On the one hand, the narcissist keeps dreaming, hoping, planning, conspiring, scheming and fighting all his life. As far as he is concerned, reality, with its sobering feedback, does not exist. He occupies a world of his own where hope springs eternal. It is a universe of recurrent serendipity, inevitable fortuity, auspiciousness, lucky chances, strikes, and coincidences, no downs and uplifting ups. It is an unpredictable, titillating, and exciting universe. The narcissist may feel bored for long stretches of time but only because he can't wait for the ultimate, inevitable thrill.

On the other hand, the narcissist experiences a constant midlife crisis. His reality is always way short of his dreams and aspirations. He suffers from a constant Grandiosity Gap: the same Gap that plagues the healthy midlife adult. But the narcissist has one advantage: he is used to being disappointed and disillusioned as he habitually inflicts setbacks and defeats upon himself by devaluing persons and situations that he had previously idealized.

The narcissist regularly employs a host of psychological mechanisms to cope with this simmering, festering incessant "crisis". Cognitive dissonance, over- and de- valuation cycles, abrupt mood swings, changes in behaviour patterns, goals, companions, mates, jobs and locations are the narcissist's daily bread and escapist weapons.

Whereas the healthy and mature adult confronts the abyss between his image of himself and his real self, his dreams and his achievements, his fantasyland and his reality only late in life, the narcissist straddles this chasm constantly and from an early age.

The healthy and mature adult recoils from the predictability of his routine and abhors it. The narcissist's life is not predictable or routine in any sense of the word.

The mature adult in his forties tries to remedy the structural and emotional deficits of his existence either by a renewed commitment to it or by a cataclysmic break with it. The narcissist regularly and habitually does both.

The narcissist's personality is rigid but his life is changeable and tumultuous, his typical day riddled with surprises and unpredictable, his grandiose fantasies so far removed from his reality that even his disillusionment and disappointments are fantastic and, thus, easily overcome.

Soon enough, the narcissist is engaged in a new project, as exciting, as grandiose and as impossible as the ones that came before. The gap between his confabulations and the truth is so yawning that he chooses to ignore his reality. He recruits people around him to affirm this choice and to confirm to him that reality is illusory and that his fantasyland is real.

Such pretensions are counterproductive and self-defeating, but they also serve as perfect defences. The narcissist does not go through a midlife crisis because he is forever the child, forever dreaming and fantasizing, forever enamoured with himself and with the narrative that is his life.

To Age with Grace

"Ships at a distance have every man's wish on board. For some they come in with the tide. For others they sail forever on the horizon, never out of sight, never landing until the Watcher turns his eyes away in resignation, his dreams mocked to death by Time."
[Zora Neale Hurston, Their Eyes Were Watching God, 1937]

"Do not go gentle into that good night, / Old age should burn and rave at close of day; / Rage, rage against the dying of the light."
[Dylan Thomas, Do Not Go Gentle Into That Good Night]

"The permanent temptation of life is to confuse dreams with reality. Then permanent defeat of life comes when dreams are surrendered to reality."
[James Michener, Author]

The narcissist ages without mercy and without grace. His withered body and his overwrought mind betray him all at once. He stares with incredulity and rage at cruel mirrors. He refuses to accept his growing fallibility. He rebels against his decrepitude and mediocrity. Accustomed to being awe-inspiring and the recipient of adulation, the narcissist cannot countenance his social isolation and the pathetic figure that he cuts in his senescence.

As a child prodigy, a sex symbol, a stud, a public intellectual, an actor, an idol, the narcissist was at the centre of attention, the eye of his personal twister, a black hole which sucked people's energy and resources dry and spat out with indifference their mutilated carcasses. No longer. With old age comes disillusionment. Old charms wear thin.

Having been exposed for what he is - a deceitful, treacherous, malignant egotist - the narcissist's old tricks now fail him. People are on their guard, their gullibility reduced. The narcissist - being the rigid, precariously balanced structure that he is - can't change. He reverts to old forms, re-adopts hoary habits, succumbs to erstwhile temptations. He is made a mockery by his accentuated denial of reality, by his obdurate refusal to grow up, an eternal, malformed child in the sagging body of a decaying man.

It is the fable of the grasshopper and the ant revisited.

The narcissist - the grasshopper - having relied on supercilious stratagems throughout his life, is singularly ill-adapted to life's rigours and tribulations. He feels entitled, but fails to elicit Narcissistic Supply. Wrinkled time makes child prodigies lose their magic, lovers exhaust their potency, philanderers waste their allure, and geniuses lose their touch. The longer the narcissist lives, the more average he becomes. The wider the gulf between his pretensions and his accomplishments, the more he is the object of derision and contempt.

Yet, few narcissists save for rainy days. Few bother to study a trade, or get an academic degree, pursue a career, maintain a business, keep their jobs, or raise functioning families, nurture their friendships, or broaden their horizons. Narcissists are perennially ill-prepared. Those who succeed in their vocation, end up bitterly alone having squandered the love of spouse, offspring, and mates. The more gregarious and family-orientated often flunk at work, leap from one job to another, relocate erratically, forever itinerant and peripatetic.

The contrast between his youth and prime and his dilapidated present constitutes a permanent narcissistic injury. The narcissist retreats deeper into himself to find solace. He withdraws into the penumbral universe of his grandiose fantasies. There, on the verge of psychosis, he salves his wounds and comforts himself with trophies of his past. A rare minority of narcissists accept their fate with fatalism or good humour. These precious few are healed mysteriously by the deepest offence to their megalomania: old age. They lose their narcissism and confront the outer world with the poise and composure that they lacked when they were captives of their own, distorted, narrative.

Such changed narcissists develop new, more realistic, expectations and hopes, commensurate with their talents, skills, accomplishments and education. Ironically, it is invariably too late. They are avoided and ignored, rendered transparent by their checkered past. They are passed over for promotion, never invited to professional or social gatherings, cold-shouldered by the media. They are snubbed and disregarded. They are never the recipients of perks, benefits, or awards. They are blamed when not blameworthy and rarely praised when deserving. They are being constantly and consistently punished for who they once were. It is poetic justice in more than one way. They are being treated narcissistically by their erstwhile victims. They are finally getting to taste their own medicine, the bitter harvest of their erstwhile wrath and arrogance.

First published on the Suite 101 Narcissistic Personality Disorders Topic.

The Narcissist and Introspection

*

Question: Are narcissists capable of introspection? Can they distinguish their False Self from who they really are? Can this help them in the therapeutic process?

Answer: The Jungian scholar Nathan Salant-Schwartz wrote this in his book "Narcissism and Character Transformation" [p. 90-91. Inner City Books, 1985]:

207 *"It is interesting and even psychotherapeutically useful to have persons suffering from NPD study their face in a mirror. Often they will see someone of great power and effectiveness, precisely the qualities they feel a lack of. For even though they may overwhelm others with their energy and personal qualities, they themselves feel ineffective."*

This passage captures the basic relationship between the True Self and the False Self. No theoretician has ignored this dichotomy, most basic to malignant narcissism.

The True Self is synonymous with the (Freudian) Ego. It is shrivelled, dilapidated, stifled and marginalized by the False Self. The narcissist draws no distinction between his Ego and his Self. He is incapable of doing so. He relegates his ego functions to the outside world. His False Self is an invention and the reflection of an invention.

Narcissists, therefore, do not "exist". The narcissist is a loose coalition, based on a balance of terror, between a sadistic, idealized Superego and a grandiose and manipulative False Ego. These two interact only mechanically. Narcissists are Narcissistic Supply seeking androids. No robot is capable of introspection, not even with the help of mirroring.

Narcissists often think of themselves as machines (the "automata metaphor"). They say things like "I have an amazing brain" or "I am not functioning today, my efficiency is low".

They measure things, and constantly compare performance. They are acutely aware of time and its use. There is a meter in the narcissist's head, it ticks and tocks, a metronome of self-reproach and grandiose, unattainable, fantasies.

The narcissist likes to consider himself in terms of automata because he finds that machines are aesthetically compelling in their precision, in their impartiality, in their harmonious reification of the abstract. Machines are so powerful and so emotionless, not hurting weaklings, like humans are.

The narcissist often talks to himself and about himself in the third person singular. He feels that it lends objectivity to his thoughts and makes them appear to be emanating from an external source. The narcissist's self-esteem is so low that, to be trusted, he feels that he has to disguise himself, to hide himself from himself. It is the narcissist's pernicious and all-pervasive art of un-being.

Thus, the narcissist carries within him his metal constitution, his robot countenance, his superhuman knowledge, his inner timekeeper, his theory of morality and his very own divinity: himself.

Sometimes the narcissist does gain self-awareness and knowledge of his predicament, typically in the wake of a life crisis (divorce, bankruptcy, incarceration, accident, serious illness, or the death of a loved one). But, in the absence of an emotional correlate, of feelings, such merely cognitive awakening is useless. It does not gel into an insight. The dry facts alone cannot bring about any transformation, not to mention healing.

Narcissists often go through "soul searching". But they do so only in order to optimize their performance, to maximize the number of Sources of Narcissistic Supply, and to better manipulate their environment. They regard introspection as an inevitable and intellectually enjoyable maintenance chore.

The introspection of the narcissist is emotionless, akin to an inventory of his "good" and "bad" sides and without any commitment to change. It does not enhance his ability to empathize, nor does it inhibit his propensity to exploit others and discard them when their usefulness is over. It does not tamper his overpowering and raging sense of entitlement, nor does it deflate his grandiose fantasies.

The narcissist's introspection is a futile and arid exercise at bookkeeping, a soulless bureaucracy of the psyche and, in its own way, even more chilling that the alternative: a narcissist blissfully unaware of his own disorder.

Still, if the narcissist becomes self-aware, if he accepts that he is a narcissist, isn't this the first, important step, towards healing?

Alas, No. self-awareness, though a necessary condition for healing, is not a sufficient one.

Narcissism defines the narcissist's waking moments and his nocturnal dreams. It is all-pervasive. Everything the narcissist does is motivated by it. Everything he avoids is its result. Every utterance, decision, his very body language are all manifestations of narcissism. It is rather like being abducted by an alien and ruthlessly indoctrinated ever since. The alien is the narcissist's False Self, a defence mechanism constructed in order to shield his True Self from hurt and inevitable abandonment.

Cognitive understanding of the disorder does not constitute a transforming INSIGHT. In other words, it has no emotional correlate. The narcissist does not INTERNALIZE what he understands and learns about his disorder. This new gained knowledge does not become a motivating part of the narcissist. It remains an inert and indifferent piece of knowledge, with minor influence on the narcissist's psyche.

Sometimes, when the narcissist first learns about the Narcissistic Personality Disorder (NPD), he really believes he could change (usually, following a period of violent rejection of the "charges" against him). He fervently wants to. This is especially true when his whole world is in shambles. Time in prison, a divorce, a bankruptcy, the death of a major Source of Narcissistic Supply are all transformative life crises. The narcissist admits to having a problem only when abandoned, when he has hit rock bottom, when he is destitute, and devastated. Then he feels that he had had enough. He wants to change. And often there are signs that he IS changing. And then it fades. He reverts to old form. The "progress" he had made evaporates virtually overnight. Many narcissists report the same process of progression followed by recidivist remission and many therapists refuse to treat narcissists because of the Sisyphean frustration involved.

The Losses of the Narcissist

Question: Don't narcissists care that they may lose everything with their obnoxious behaviour? Aren't they scared of accumulating a lifetime's crop of enemies? Are they oblivious to the risks?

Answer: Narcissists are accustomed to loss. Their obnoxious personality and intolerable behaviours make them lose friends and spouses, mates and colleagues, jobs and family. Their peripatetic nature, their constant mobility and instability cause them to lose everything else: their place of residence, their property, their businesses, their country, and their mother tongue.

There is always a locus of loss in the narcissist's life. He may be faithful to his wife and a model family man - but then he is likely to change jobs frequently and renege on his financial and social obligations. Or, he may be a top achiever - scientist, doctor, CEO, actor, pastor, politician, or journalist - with a steady, long-term and successful career, but a lousy homemaker, thrice divorced, unfaithful, unstable, always on the lookout for better or more plentiful Narcissistic Supply.

The narcissist is aware of his propensity to lose everything of value, meaning, and significance in his life. If he is inclined to magical thinking and alloplastic defences, he blames life, or fate, or country, or his boss, or his nearest and dearest for his uninterrupted string of losses. Otherwise, he attributes it to people's inability to cope with his outstanding talents, towering intellect, or rare abilities. His losses, he convinces himself, are the outcomes of pettiness, pusillanimity, envy, malice, and ignorance. It would all have turned out the same even had he behaved differently, he consoles himself.

In time, the narcissist develops defence mechanisms against the inevitable pain and hurt that he incurs with every loss and defeat. He ensconces himself in an ever thicker skin, an impenetrable

210

SAM VAKNIN   MALIGNANT SELF LOVE

shell, a make belief environment in which his sense of in-bred superiority and entitlement is preserved. He appears indifferent to the most harrowing and agonizing experiences, inhuman in his unperturbed composure, emotionally detached and cold, inaccessible, and invulnerable. Deep inside, he, indeed, feels nothing.

The narcissist cruises through his life as a tourist would through an exotic island. He observes events and people, his own experiences and loved ones, as a spectator would a movie that at times is mildly exciting and at other times mildly boring. He is never fully there, entirely present, irreversibly committed. He is constantly with one hand on his emotional escape hatch, ready to bail out, to absent himself, to re-invent his life in another place, with other people. The narcissist is a coward, terrified of his True Self and protective of the deceit that is his existence. He feels no pain. He feels no love. He feels no life.

First published on the Suite 101 Narcissistic Personality Disorders Topic.

211

Waiting for Him to Get Better

Question: Can a narcissist ever get better and, if not, how should his partner end a relationship with him?

Answer: The Narcissistic Personality Disorder is a systemic, all-pervasive condition, very much like pregnancy: either you have it or you don't. Once you have it, you have it day and night, it is an inseparable part of the personality, a recurrent set of behaviour patterns.

Recent research shows that there is a condition, which might be called "Transient or Temporary or Short-Term Narcissism" as opposed to the full-fledged Narcissistic Personality Disorder (NPD), [Ronningstam, 1996]. The phenomenon of "reactive narcissistic regression" or Acquired Situational Narcissism is well known: people regress to a transient narcissistic phase in reaction to a major life crisis which threatens their mental composure.

There are narcissistic touches in every personality and in this sense all of us are narcissists to some extent. But this is a far cry from the full-fledged (NPD) pathology.

One bit of good news: no one knows why, but, in certain cases, though rarely, with age (in one's forties), the disorder seems to mutate into a subdued version of its former self. This does not universally occur, though.

Should a partner remain with a narcissist in the hope that his disorder will be ameliorated by ripe old age? This is a matter of value judgement, preferences, priorities, background, emotions and a host of other "non-scientific" matters. There could be no one "correct" answer. It would seem that the only valid criterion is the partner's well-being. If he or she feels bad in a relationship (and no amount of self-help or professional help changes that), then looking for the exit door sounds like a viable and healthy strategy.

A typical relationship with a narcissist has elements of dependence, even symbiosis. Moreover, the narcissist is a superb emotional manipulator and extortionist. In some cases, abandonment poses a real threat to his mental stability. Even "demonstrative" (failed) suicide cannot be ruled out in the repertory of narcissistic reactions to the dissolution of a relationship. And even a modest amount of residual love harboured by the narcissist's partner makes the separation very difficult for him or her.

But there is a magic formula.

The partner is the narcissist's pusher and the drug that she is proffering - Narcissistic Supply - is stronger than any other drug because it sustains the narcissist's very essence (his False Self).

Without Narcissistic Supply the narcissist disintegrates, crumbles and shrivels, very much as vampires do in horror movies when exposed to sunlight.

The narcissist teams up with his partner because he regards IT as a Source of Narcissistic Supply. He values the partner as such a source. Put differently: the minute the partner ceases to supply the narcissist with what he needs, the narcissist loses all interest in IT. (I use IT judiciously: the narcissist objectifies his partners, he treats them as one does inanimate objects.)

213 The transition from over-valuation (bestowed upon potential and actual Sources of Narcissistic Supply) to devaluation (reserved for other mortals) is so swift that it is likely to inflict pain upon the narcissist's partner, even if she previously prayed for the narcissist to depart and leave her alone.

Here lies the partner's salvation: if you wish to sever your relationship with the narcissist, stop providing him with what he needs. Do not adore, admire, approve, applaud, or confirm anything that he does or says. Disagree with his views, belittle him, reduce him to size, compare him to others, tell him that he is not unique, criticize him, make suggestions, offer help. In short, deprive him of that illusion which holds his personality together.

The narcissist is a delicately attuned piece of equipment. At the first sign of danger to his inflated, fantastic and grandiose self, he will quit and disappear on you.

Can a Narcissist Help Himself?

In the book describing the fabulous tales of Baron Munchausen, there is a story about how the legendary nobleman succeeded to pull himself out of a quicksand marsh by his own hair. Such a miracle is not likely to recur. Narcissists cannot cure themselves.

It is not a question of determination or resilience. It is not a function of the time invested by the narcissist, the effort expended by him, the lengths to which he is willing to go, the depth of his commitment and his professional knowledge. All these are very important precursors and good predictors of the success of an eventual therapy. However, they are no substitutes for one.

The best - really, the only way - a narcissist can help himself is by seeing a mental health professional. Even then, sadly, the prognosis (the healing prospects) is dim. It seems that only time can bring on a limited remission (or, more often, an aggravation of the condition).

Therapy can tackle the more pernicious aspects of this disorder. It can help the patient adapt to his condition, accept it and learn to conduct a more functional life. Learning to live with one's disorder is a great achievement and the narcissist should be happy that even this modicum of success is, in principle, possible.

But just to get the narcissist to see a therapist is difficult. The therapeutic situation implies a superior-inferior relationship. The therapist is supposed to help him and, to the narcissist, this means that he is not as omnipotent as he imagines himself to be. The therapist is supposed to know more (in his field) than the narcissist - a presumption which seems to undermine the second pillar of narcissism, that of omniscience.

Attending therapy (of whatever nature) implies both imperfection (something is wrong) and need (read: weakness, inferiority). The therapeutic setting (the client visits the therapist,

214

MALIGNANT SELF LOVE

SAM VAKNIN

has to be punctual, and to pay for the service) implies subservience. The process itself is also threatening: it involves transformation, losing one's identity (read: uniqueness) and one's long cultivated and familiar defences.

The narcissist must shed his False Self and face the world naked, defenceless, and (to his mind) pitiful. He is inadequately equipped to deal with his old hurts, traumas and unresolved conflicts. His True Self is infantile, fossilized, incapable of confronting the almighty Superego (the narcissist's inner, chastising, voice). The narcissist knows this and recoils. Therapy demands of him to finally place full, unmitigated, trust in another human being.

Moreover, the transaction implicitly offered to him is the most unappealing imaginable. He is to give up decades of emotional investment in an elaborate, adaptive and, mostly, functioning, mental hyper structure. In return, he stands to become "normal" - an anathema to a narcissist. Being normal, to him, means, being average, not unique, non-existent. Why should the narcissist commit himself to such a move when it doesn't even guarantee him happiness (he sees many unhappy "normal" people around)?

But is there anything the narcissist can do by himself, "in the meantime", until he reaches a final decision whether to attend therapy or not?

The first step involves self-awareness. The narcissist often notices that something is wrong with him and with his life but he never owns up to his role in and responsibility for his misfortune and discomfort. He prefers to come up with elaborate rationalizations as to why that which is wrong with him is really quite OK and even cool!

Cognitive dissonance, rationalization, and intellectualization are the narcissist's allies in the task of insulating him from reality. The narcissist consistently convinces himself that everyone else is wrong, deficient, lacking, and incapable (in other words, he has alloplastic defences and an outside locus of control). He tells himself that he is exceptional and made to suffer for it - not that he is in the wrong. On the contrary, history will surely prove him right as it has done so many other towering figures.

This is the first and, by far, the most critical step on the way to coping with the disorder: will the narcissist admit, be forced, or convinced to concede that he is absolutely and unconditionally wrong, that something is very amiss in his life, that he is in need of urgent, professional, help and that, in the absence of such help, things will only get worse? Having crossed this

Rubicon, the narcissist is more open and amenable to constructive suggestions and assistance.

The second important leap forward is when the narcissist begins to confront a more REALISTIC version of himself. A good friend, a spouse, a therapist, a parent, or a combination of these people can decide not to collaborate with the narcissist's confabulations anymore, to stop fearing the narcissist and not to acquiesce in his folly any longer.

When they confront the narcissist with the truth about himself, they help demolish the grandiose phantom that "runs" the narcissist. They no longer succumb to his whims or accord him special treatment. They reprimand him when needed. They disagree with him and show him why and where he is mistaken. In short: they deprive him of many of his Sources of Narcissistic Supply. They refuse to take part in the elaborate game that is the narcissist. They rebel.

The third Do It Yourself element involves the decision to commit to a regime of therapy. This is a tough one. The narcissist must not decide to embark on therapy only because he is (currently) feeling bad (mostly, owing to a life crisis), or because he is subjected to pressure by family or peers, or because he wants to get rid of a few disturbing issues while preserving the otherwise awesome totality.

His attitude towards the therapist must not be judgemental, cynical, critical, disparaging, competitive, or superior. He must not view the therapy as a contest or a tournament. There are many winners in therapy but only one loser if it fails. He must decide not to try to co-opt the therapist, not to threaten him, or humiliate him.

In short: he must adopt a humble frame of mind, open to the new experience of encountering one's self. Finally, he must resolve to be constructively and productively active in his own therapy, to assist the therapist without condescending, to provide information without distorting, to try to change without consciously resisting.

The end of therapy is really only the beginning of a new, more vulnerable life. This terrifies the narcissist. He knows that maybe he can get better, but he can rarely get well ("heal"). The reason is the narcissist's enormous life-long, irreplaceable and indispensable emotional investment in his disorder.

The narcissist's disorder serves two critical functions, which together maintain the precariously balanced house of cards that is his personality. His disorder endows the narcissist with a sense of uniqueness, of "being special" and it provides him with a rational explanation of his behaviour (an "alibi").

Most narcissists reject the notion or diagnosis that they are mentally disturbed. Absent powers of introspection and a total lack of self-awareness are part and parcel of the disorder. Pathological narcissism is founded on alloplastic defences: the firm conviction that the world or others are to blame for one's behaviour, misfortune, and failures.

The narcissist simply "knows" that his closest, nearest and dearest should be held responsible for his reactions because they have triggered them. With such an entrenched state of mind, the narcissist is constitutionally incapable of admitting that something is wrong with HIM.

But that is not to say that the narcissist does not experience the pernicious outcomes of his disorder. He does. But he re-interprets this experience. He regards his dysfunctional behaviours - social, sexual, emotional, mental - as conclusive and irrefutable proof of his superiority, brilliance, distinction, prowess, might, or success.

Rudeness to others and bullying are reinterpreted as efficiency. Abusive behaviours are cast as educational. Sexual abstinence as proof of preoccupation with higher functions. His rage is always justified and a reaction to injustice or to being misunderstood by intellectual dwarves.

Thus, paradoxically, the disorder becomes an integral and inseparable part of the narcissist's inflated self-esteem and vacuous grandiose fantasies.

His False Self (the pivot of his pathological narcissism) is a self-reinforcing mechanism. The narcissist believes that he is unique BECAUSE he has a False Self. His False Self IS the centre of his "specialness". Any therapeutic "attack" on the integrity and functioning of the False Self constitutes a threat to the narcissist's ability to regulate his wildly fluctuating sense of self-worth and an effort to "reduce" him to other people's mundane and mediocre existence.

The few narcissists who are willing to admit that something is terribly wrong with them, displace their alloplastic defences. Instead of blaming the world, other people, or circumstances beyond their control - they now blame their "disease". Their disorder becomes a catch-all, universal explanation for everything that is wrong in their lives and every derided, indefensible and inexcusable behaviour. Their narcissism becomes a "licence to kill", a liberating force which sets them outside and above human rules and codes of conduct. Such freedom is so intoxicating and empowering that it is difficult to give up.

The narcissist is emotionally attached to only one thing: his disorder. The narcissist loves his disorder, desires it passionately, cultivates it tenderly, he is proud of its "achievements". His emotions are misdirected. Where normal people love others and empathize with them, the narcissist loves his False Self and identifies with it to the exclusion of everything else, including his True Self.

Reconditioning the Narcissist

Question: You seem to be very sceptical that someone with a Narcissistic Personality Disorder can be treated successfully.

Answer: The Narcissistic Personality Disorder has been recognized as a distinct mental health diagnosis a little more than two decades ago. There are few who can honestly claim expertise or even in-depth understanding of this complex condition.

No one knows whether therapy works. What is known is that therapists find narcissists repulsive, overbearing and unnerving. It is also known that narcissists try to co-opt, idolize, or humiliate the therapist.

But what if the narcissist really wants to improve? Even if complete healing is out of the question - behaviour modification is not.

To a narcissist, I would recommend a functional approach, along the following lines:

a. Know and accept yourself. This is who you are. You have good traits and bad traits and you are a narcissist. These are facts. Narcissism is an adaptive mechanism. It is dysfunctional now, but, once, it saved you from a lot more dysfunction or even non-function. Make a list: what does it mean to be a narcissist in your specific case? What are your typical behaviour patterns? Which types of conduct do you find to be counterproductive, irritating, self-defeating or self-destructive? Which are productive, constructive and should be enhanced despite their pathological origin?

b. Try to suppress the first type of behaviours and to promote the second. Construct lists of self-punishments, negative feedback and negative reinforcements. Impose them upon yourself when you have behaved negatively. Make a list of prizes, little indulgences, positive feedbacks and positive reinforcements. Use them to reward yourself when you adopt a behaviour of the second kind.

c. Keep doing this with the express intent of conditioning yourself. Be objective, predictable and just in the administration of both punishments and awards, positive and negative reinforcements and feedback. Learn to trust your "inner court". Constrain the sadistic, immature and ideal parts of your personality by applying a uniform codex, a set of immutable and invariably applied rules.

d. Once sufficiently conditioned, monitor yourself incessantly. Narcissism is sneaky and it possesses all your resources because it is you. Your disorder is intelligent because you are. Beware and never lose control. With time this onerous regime will become a second habit and supplant the narcissistic (pathological) superstructure.

You might have noticed that all the above can be amply summed by suggesting to you to become your own parent. This is what parents do and the process is called "education" or "socialization". Re-parent yourself. If therapy is helpful or needed, go ahead.

The heart of the beast is the inability of the narcissist to distinguish true from false, appearances from reality, posing from being, Narcissistic Supply from genuine relationships, and compulsive drives from true interests and avocations. Narcissism is about deceit. It blurs the distinction between authentic actions, true motives, real desires, and original emotions and their malignant verisimilitudes.

Narcissists are not capable of knowing themselves. Terrified by their internal apparitions, paralyzed by their lack of authenticity, suppressed by the weight of their repressed emotions, they occupy a hall of mirrors. Edvard Munch-like, their elongated figures stare at them, on the verge of a scream, yet somehow, soundless.

The narcissist's childlike, curious, vibrant, and optimistic True Self is dead. His False Self is, well, false. How can anyone on a permanent diet of echoes and reflections ever acquaint himself with reality? How can the narcissist ever love - he, whose essence is to devour meaningful others?

The answer is: discipline, decisiveness, clear targets, conditioning, and justice. The narcissist is the product of unjust, capricious and cruel treatment. He is the finished product off a production line of self-recrimination, guilt and fear. He needs to take the antidote to counter the narcissistic poison.

Unfortunately, there is no drug which can ameliorate pathological narcissism.

Confronting one's parents about one's childhood is a good idea if the narcissist feels that he can cope with new and painful truths. But the narcissist must be careful. He is playing with fire. Still, if he feels confident that he can withstand anything revealed to him in such a confrontation, it is a good and wise move in the right direction.

My advice to the narcissist would then be: dedicate a lot of time to rehearsing this critical encounter and define well what is it exactly that you want to achieve. Do not turn this reunion into a monodrama, group therapy, or trial. Get some answers and get at the truth. Don't try to prove anything, to vindicate, to exact revenge, to win the argument, or to exculpate. Talk to your erstwhile abusers, heart to heart, as you would with yourself. Do not try to sound professional, mature, intelligent, knowledgeable and distanced. There is no "problem to solve" - just a condition to adjust yourself to.

More generally, try to take life and yourself much less seriously. Being immersed in one's self and in one's mental health condition is never the recipe for full functionality, let alone happiness. The world is an absurd place. It is indeed a theatre to be enjoyed. It is full of colours and smells and sounds to be treasured and cherished. It is varied and it accommodates and tolerates everyone and everything, even narcissists.

You, the narcissist, should try to see the positive aspects of your disorder. In Chinese, the ideogram for "crisis" includes a part that stands for "opportunity". Why don't you transform the curse that is your life into a blessing? Why don't you tell the world your story, teach people in your condition and their victims how to avoid the pitfalls, how to cope with the damage? Why don't you do all this in a more institutionalized manner?

For instance, you can start a discussion group or put up a Website on the Internet. You can establish a "narcissists anonymous" in some community shelter. You can open a correspondence network, a help centre for men in your condition, for women abused by narcissists ... the possibilities are endless. And it will instil in you a regained sense of self-worth, give you a purpose, endow you with self-confidence and reassurance. It is only by helping others that we help ourselves. This is, of course, a suggestion, not a prescription. But it demonstrates the ways in which you can draw strength from adversity.

It is easy for the narcissist to think about pathological narcissism as the source of all that is evil and wrong in his life. Narcissism is a catchphrase, a conceptual scapegoat, an evil seed. It conveniently encapsulates the predicament of the narcissist. It introduces logic and causal relations into his baffling, tumultuous world. But this is a trap.

The human psyche is too complex and the brain too plastic to be captured by a single, all-encompassing label, however all-pervasive the disorder is. The road to self-help and self-betterment passes through numerous junctions and stations. Except for pathological narcissism, there are many other elements in the complex dynamics that is the soul of the narcissist. The narcissist should take responsibility for his life and not relegate it to some hitherto rather obscure psychodynamic concept. This is the first and most important step towards healing.

Treatment Modalities and Therapies

Question: Is the Narcissistic Personality Disorder (NPD) more amenable to Cognitive-Behavioural Therapies or to psychodynamic/psychoanalytic ones?

Answer: Narcissism pervades the entire personality. It is all-pervasive. Being a narcissist is akin to being an alcoholic. Alcoholism is an impulsive behaviour. Narcissists exhibit dozens of similarly reckless behaviours, some of them uncontrollable (like their rage, the outcome of their wounded grandiosity). Narcissism is not a vocation. Narcissism resembles depression or other disorders and cannot be changed at will.

Adult pathological narcissism is no more "curable" than the entirety of one's personality is disposable. The patient IS a narcissist. Narcissism is more akin to the colour of one's skin rather than to one's choice of subjects at the university.

Moreover, the Narcissistic Personality Disorder (NPD) is frequently diagnosed with other, even more intractable personality disorders, mental illnesses, and substance abuse.

Cognitive-Behavioural Therapies (CBTs)

CBTs postulate that insight, even when merely verbal and intellectual, is sufficient to induce an emotional outcome. The therapist uses verbal cues, analyses the mantras we keep repeating ("I am ugly", "I am afraid that no one would like to be with me"), itemizes inner dialogues and narratives and notes repeated behavioural patterns (learned behaviours). He provides positive (and, rarely, negative) reinforcements to induce a cumulative emotional effect tantamount to healing.

Psychodynamic theories reject the notion that cognition can influence emotion. Healing requires access to and the study of much deeper strata by both patient and therapist. The very

223

exposure of these strata to the therapeutic process is considered sufficient to induce a dynamic of healing.

The therapist's role is either to interpret the material revealed to the patient (psychoanalysis) by allowing the patient to transfer past experience and superimpose it on the therapist - or to provide a safe emotional and holding environment conducive to changes in the patient.

The sad fact is that no known therapy is effective with narcissism ITSELF, though a few therapies are reasonably successful in coping with some of its effects (behavioural modification).

Dynamic Psychotherapy
Or Psychodynamic Therapy, Psychoanalytic Psychotherapy

This is NOT psychoanalysis. It is an intensive psychotherapy BASED on psychoanalytic theory WITHOUT the (very important) element of free association. This is not to say that free association is not used in these therapies, only that it is not a pillar of the technique. Dynamic therapies are usually applied to patients not considered "suitable" for psychoanalysis (such as those suffering from personality disorders, except the Avoidant Personality Disorder).

Typically, different modes of interpretation are employed and other techniques borrowed from other treatments modalities. But the material interpreted is not necessarily the result of free association or dreams and the psychotherapist is a lot more active than the psychoanalyst.

Psychodynamic therapies are open-ended. At the commencement of the therapy, the therapist (analyst) makes an agreement (a "pact" or "alliance") with the analysand (patient or client). The pact says that the patient undertakes to explore his problems for as long as may be needed. This is supposed to make the therapeutic environment much more relaxed because the patient knows that the analyst is at his/her disposal no matter how many meetings would be required in order to broach painful subject matter.

Sometimes, these therapies are divided to expressive versus supportive.

Expressive therapies seek to uncover (make conscious) the patient's conflicts and study his/her defences and resistances. The analyst interprets the conflict in view of the new knowledge gained and guides the therapy towards a resolution of the conflict. The conflict, in other words, is "interpreted away" through insight and the change in the patient motivated by his/her insights.

The supportive therapies seek to strengthen the Ego. Their premise is that a strong Ego can cope better (and later on, alone) with external (situational) or internal (instinctual, related to drives) pressures. Supportive therapies seek to increase the patient's ability to REPRESS conflicts (rather than bring them to the surface of consciousness).

When the patient's painful conflicts are suppressed, the attendant dysphorias and symptoms vanish or are ameliorated. This is somewhat reminiscent of behaviourism (the main aim is to change behaviour and to relieve symptoms). It usually makes no use of insight or interpretation (though there are exceptions).

Modern Therapy and Treatment of Personality Disorders

The dogmatic schools of psychotherapy (such as psychoanalysis, psychodynamic therapies, and behaviourism) more or less failed in ameliorating, let alone curing or healing personality disorders. Disillusioned, most therapists now adhere to one or more of three modern methods: brief therapies, the Common Factors approach, and eclectic techniques.

Conventionally, brief therapies, as their name implies, are short-term but effective. They involve a few rigidly structured sessions, directed by the therapist. The patient is expected to be active and responsive. Both parties sign a therapeutic contract (or alliance) in which they define the goals of the therapy and, consequently, its themes. As opposed to earlier treatment modalities, brief therapies actually encourage anxiety because they believe that it has a catalytic and cathartic effect on the patient.

Supporters of the Common Factors approach point out that all psychotherapies are more or less equally efficient (or rather similarly inefficient) in treating personality disorders. As Garfield noted in 1957, the first step perforce involves a voluntary action: the subject seeks help because he or she experiences intolerable discomfort, ego-dystony, dysphoria, and dysfunction. This act is the first and indispensable factor associated with all therapeutic encounters, regardless of their origins.

Another common factor is the fact that all talk therapies revolve around disclosure and confidences. The patient confesses his or her problems, burdens, worries, anxieties, fears, wishes, intrusive thoughts, compulsions, difficulties, failures, delusions, and, generally invites the therapist into the recesses of his or her innermost mental landscape.

The therapist leverages this torrent of data and elaborates on it through a series of attentive comments and probing, thought-provoking queries and insights. This pattern of give and take should, in time, yield a relationship between patient and healer, based on mutual trust and respect. To many patients this may well be the first healthy relationship they experience and a model to build on in the future.

Good therapy empowers the client and enhances her ability to properly gauge reality (her reality test). It amount to a comprehensive rethink of oneself and one's life. With perspective comes a stable sense of self-worth, well-being, and competence (self-confidence).

In 1961, a scholar, Frank, made a list of the important elements in all psychotherapies regardless of their intellectual provenance and technique:

1. The therapist should be trustworthy, competent, and caring;
2. The therapist should facilitate behavioural modification in the patient by fostering hope and "stimulating emotional arousal" (as Millon puts it). In other words, the patient should be re-introduced to his repressed or stunted emotions and thereby undergo a "corrective emotional experience";
3. The therapist should help the patient develop insight about himself: a new way of looking at himself and his world and of understanding who he is;
4. All therapies must weather the inevitable crises and demoralization that accompany the process of confronting oneself and one's shortcomings. Loss of self-esteem and devastating feelings of inadequacy, helplessness, hopelessness, alienation, and even despair are an integral, productive, and important part of the sessions if handled properly and competently.

Eclectic Psychotherapy

The early days of the emerging discipline of psychology were inevitably rigidly dogmatic. Clinicians belonged to well-demarcated schools and practiced in strict accordance with canons of writings by "masters" such as Freud, or Jung, or Adler, or Skinner. Psychology was less a science than an ideology or an art form. Freud's work, for instance, though incredibly insightful, is closer to literature and cultural studies than to proper, evidence-based, medicine.

Not so nowadays. Mental health practitioners freely borrow tools and techniques from myriad therapeutic systems. They refuse to be labelled and boxed in. The only principle that guides modern therapists is "what works": the effectiveness of treatment modalities, not their intellectual provenance. The therapy, insist these eclecticists, should be tailored to the patient, not the other way around.

This sounds self-evident but as Lazarus pointed out in a series of articles in the 1970s, it is nothing less than revolutionary. The therapist today is free to match techniques from any number of schools to presenting problems without committing himself to the theoretical apparatus (or baggage) that is associated with them. He can use psychoanalysis or behavioural methods while rejecting Freud's ideas and Skinner's theory, for instance.

Lazarus proposed that the appraisal of the efficacy and applicability of a treatment modality should be based on seven data: BASIC IB (Behaviour, Affect, Sensation, Imagery, Cognition, Interpersonal Relationships, and Biology). What are the patient's dysfunctional behaviour patterns? How is his sensorium? In what ways does the imagery connect with his problems, presenting symptoms, and signs? Does he suffer from cognitive deficits and distortions? What is the extent and quality of the patient's interpersonal relationships? Does the subject suffer from any medical, genetic, or neurological problems that may affect his or her conduct and functioning?

Once the answers to these questions are collated, the therapist should judge which treatment options are likely to yield the fastest and most durable outcomes, based on empirical data. As Beutler and Chalkin noted in a groundbreaking article in 1990, therapists no longer harbour delusions of omnipotence. Whether a course of therapy succeeds or not depends on numerous factors such as the therapist's and the patient's personalities and past histories and the interactions between the various techniques used.

So what's the use of theorizing in psychology? Why not simply revert to trial and error and see what works?

Beutler, a staunch supporter and promoter of eclecticism, provides the answer:

Psychological theories of personality allow us to be more selective. They provide guidelines as to which treatment modalities we should consider in any given situation and for any given patient. Without these intellectual edifices we would be lost in a sea of "everything goes". In other words, psychological theories are organizing principles. They provide the practitioner with selection rules and criteria that he or she would do well to apply if they don't want to drown in a sea of ill-delineated treatment options.

Group Therapies

Narcissists are notoriously unsuitable for collaborative efforts and team work of any kind, let alone group therapy. They immediately size up others as potential Sources of Narcissistic Supply or as potential competitors. They idealize the first (suppliers) and devalue the latter (competitors). This, obviously, is not very conducive to group therapy.

Moreover, the dynamic of the group is bound to reflect the interactions of its members. Narcissists are individualists. They regard coalitions with disdain and contempt. The need to resort to team work, to adhere to group rules, to succumb to a moderator, and to honour and respect the other members as equals is perceived by them to be humiliating and degrading (a contemptible weakness). Thus, a group containing one or more narcissists is likely to fluctuate between short-term, very small size, coalitions (based on "superiority" and contempt) and narcissistic outbreaks (acting outs) of rage and coercion.

Can Narcissism Be Cured?

ADULT narcissists can rarely be "cured", though some scholars think otherwise. Still, the earlier the therapeutic intervention, the better the prognosis. A correct diagnosis and a proper mix of treatment modalities in early adolescence guarantees success without relapse in anywhere between one third and one half the cases. Additionally, ageing moderates or even vanquishes some antisocial behaviours.

In their seminal tome, "Personality Disorders in Modern Life" [New York, John Wiley & Sons, 2000], Theodore Millon and Roger Davis write [p. 308]:

"Most narcissists strongly resist psychotherapy. For those who choose to remain in therapy, there are several pitfalls that are difficult to avoid... Interpretation and even general assessment are often difficult to accomplish..."

The third edition of the "Oxford Textbook of Psychiatry" [Oxford, Oxford University Press, reprinted 2000], cautions [p. 128]:

"...(P)eople cannot change their natures, but can only change their situations. There has been some progress in finding ways of effecting small changes in disorders of personality, but management still consists largely of helping the person to find a way of life that conflicts less with his character... Whatever treatment is used, aims should be modest and considerable time should be allowed to achieve them."

The fourth edition of the authoritative "Review of General Psychiatry" [London, Prentice-Hall International, 1995], says [p. 309]:

"(People with personality disorders) ... cause resentment and possibly even alienation and burnout in the healthcare professionals who treat them... [p. 318] Long-term psychoanalytic psychotherapy and psychoanalysis have been attempted with (narcissists), although their use has been controversial."

The reason narcissism is under-reported and healing overstated is that therapists are being fooled by smart narcissists. Most narcissists are expert manipulators and consummate actors and they learn how to deceive their therapists.

Even a complete battery of tests, administered by experienced professionals sometimes fails to identify abusers and their personality disorders. Offenders are uncanny in their ability to deceive their evaluators. They often succeed in transforming therapists and diagnosticians into four types of collaborators: the adulators, the blissfully ignorant, the self-deceiving, and those deceived by the narcissist's conduct or statements.

[See the FAQ 68: "Facilitating Narcissism"]

Narcissists co-opt mental health and social welfare workers and compromise them, even when the diagnosis is unequivocal, by flattering them, by emphasizing common traits or a common background, by forming a joint front against the victim of abuse ("shared psychosis"), or by emotionally bribing them. Abusers are master manipulators and exploit the vulnerabilities, traumas, prejudices, and fears of the practitioners to "convert" them to the offender's cause. Here are some hard facts:

- There are gradations and shades of narcissism. The differences between two narcissists can be great. The existence of grandiosity and empathy or the lack thereof are not minor variations. They are serious predictors of future psychodynamics. The prognosis is much better if they do exist.
- There are cases of spontaneous healing, Acquired Situational Narcissism, and of "short-term NPD" [see Gunderson and Ronningstam's work (1996) as well as Milman, 2000].
- The prognosis for a classical narcissist (grandiosity, lack of empathy and all) is decidedly not good as far as long-term, lasting, and complete healing. Moreover, narcissists are intensely disliked by therapists.

BUT...

- Side effects, co-morbid disorders (such as obsessive-compulsive behaviours) and some aspects of NPD (the dysphorias, the persecutory delusions, the sense of entitlement, the pathological lying) can be modified (using talk therapy and, depending on the problem, medication). These are not long-term or complete solutions - but some of them do have long-term effects.

- The Diagnostic and Statistical Manual (DSM) is a billing and administration oriented diagnostic tool. It is intended to "tidy" up the psychiatrist's desk. The Axis II personality disorders are ill demarcated. The differential diagnoses are vaguely defined. There are some cultural biases and judgements [see, for example, the diagnostic criteria of the Schizotypal and Antisocial personality disorders]. The result is sizeable confusion and multiple diagnoses ("co-morbidity"). NPD was introduced to the DSM in 1980 (DSM-III). There isn't enough research to substantiate any view or hypothesis about NPD. Future DSM editions may abolish it altogether within the framework of a cluster or a single "personality disorder" category. When we ask: "Can NPD be healed?" we need to realize that we don't know for sure what is NPD and what constitutes long-term healing in the case of NPD. There are those who seriously claim that NPD is a cultural disease (culture-bound) with a societal determinant. The ICD-10 (the DSM's equivalent outside the United States) does not recognize NPD as a distinct mental health disorder.

Narcissists in Therapy

The narcissist has a dilapidated and dysfunctional True Self, overtaken and suppressed by a False Self. In therapy, the general idea is to create the conditions for the True Self to resume its growth: safety, predictability, justice, love and acceptance. To achieve this ambience, the therapist tries to establish a mirroring, re-parenting, and holding environment. Therapy is supposed to provide these conditions of nurturance and guidance (through transference, cognitive re-labelling or other methods). The narcissist must learn that his bitter past experiences are not laws of nature, that not all adults are abusive, that relationships can be nurturing and supportive.

Some therapists try to stroke the narcissist's grandiosity. By doing so, they hope to modify or counter cognitive deficits, thinking errors, and the narcissist's victim-stance. They contract with the narcissist to alter his conduct. Psychiatrists tend to medicalize the disorder by attributing it to genetic or biochemical causes. Narcissists like this approach as it absolves them from responsibility for their actions.

Most therapists try to co-opt the narcissist's inflated Ego (False Self) and defences. They compliment the narcissist and challenge him to prove his omnipotence by overcoming his disorder. They appeal to his quest for perfection, brilliance, and eternal love - and his paranoid tendencies - in an attempt to get rid of counterproductive, self-defeating, and dysfunctional behaviour patterns.

But, the narcissist regards therapy as a competitive sport. In therapy the narcissist usually immediately insists that he (or she) is equal to the psychotherapist in knowledge, in experience, or in social status. To substantiate this claim and "level the playing field", the narcissist in the therapeutic session spices his speech with professional terms and lingo.

The narcissist sends a message to his psychotherapist: there is nothing you can teach me, I am as intelligent as you are, you are not superior to me, actually, we should both collaborate as equals in this unfortunate state of things in which we, inadvertently, find ourselves involved. The narcissist at first idealizes and then devalues the therapist. His internal dialogue is:

"I know best, I know it all, the therapist is less intelligent than I, I can't afford the top level therapists who are the only ones qualified to treat me (as my equals, needless to say), I am actually as good as a therapist myself..."

"He (my therapist) should be my colleague, in certain respects it is he who should accept my professional authority, why won't he be my friend, after all I can use the lingo (psychobabble) even better than he does? It's us (him and me) against a hostile and ignorant world (shared psychosis, folie a deux)..."

"Just who does he think he is, asking me all these questions? What are his professional credentials? I am a success and he is a nobody therapist in a dingy office, he is trying to negate my uniqueness, he is an authority figure, I hate him, I will show him, I will humiliate him, prove him ignorant, have his licence revoked (transference). Actually, he is pitiable, a zero, a failure..."

Therapists with unresolved issues and narcissistic defences of their own sometimes feel compelled to confront the narcissist head on and to engage in power politics, for instance by instituting disciplinary measures. They compete with the narcissist and try to establish their superiority: "I am cleverer than you are", "My will should prevail", and so on. This form of immaturity is decidedly unhelpful and could lead to rage attacks and a deepening of the narcissist's persecutory delusions, bred by his humiliation in the therapeutic setting.

These self-delusions and fantastic grandiosity are, really, the narcissist's defences and resistance to treatment. This abusive internal exchange becomes more vituperative and pejorative as therapy progresses.

The narcissist distances himself from his painful emotions by generalising and analyzing them, by slicing his life and hurt into neat packages of what he thinks are "professional insights".

Narcissists generally are averse to being medicated as this amounts to an admission that something is, indeed, wrong and "needs fixing". Narcissists are control freaks and hate to be "under the influence" of "mind altering" drugs prescribed to them by others.

Additionally, many of them believe that medication is the "great equalizer": it will make them lose their uniqueness, superiority and so on. That is unless they can convincingly present the act of taking their medicines as "heroism", a daring enterprise of self-exploration, part of a breakthrough clinical trial, and so on.

They often claim that the medicine affects them differently than it does other people, or that they have discovered a new, exciting way of using it, or that they are part of someone's (usually themselves) learning curve ("part of a new approach to dosage", "part of a new cocktail which holds great promise"). Narcissists must dramatize their lives to feel worthy and special. Aut nihil aut unique - either be special or don't be at all. Narcissists are drama queens.

Successes have been reported by applying 12-step techniques (as modified for patients suffering from the Antisocial Personality Disorder), and with treatment modalities as diverse as NLP (Neurolinguistic Programming), Schema Therapy, and EMDR (Eye Movement Desensitization).

Very much like in the physical world, change is brought about only through incredible powers of torsion and breakage. Only when the narcissist's elasticity gives way, only when he is wounded by his own intransigence - only then is there hope.

It takes nothing less than a real crisis to move the narcissist to tackle his problems. Ennui is not enough.

Narcissistic Mirroring

Question: Do narcissists tend to react with paranoia when threatened (or when they feel threatened) and how long do these "attacks" last? Does the narcissist forever decry and fear the subjects of his paranoia (his "persecutors")?

Answer: Specific paranoid reactions tend to fade and the narcissist frequently homes in on new "agents of persecution".

Arguably the most hurtful thing about a relationship with a narcissist is the ultimate realization of how interchangeable one is, as far as the narcissist is concerned. The narcissist is hungry for Narcissistic Supply. Thus, even his paranoia is a "grandiose" fantasy aimed at regulating his sense of self-worth.

It is through his paranoia that the narcissist proves to himself that he is sufficiently important, interesting, and enough of a threat to be threatened back, to have people conspire and worry over him, in other words: to be the subject of incessant attention. Yet, this untoward mode of attracting Narcissistic Supply wanes easily if not fed constantly.

It is true, however, that many narcissists are paranoid by nature. Narcissism is the deformed emotional reaction to the narcissist's perception of the world as unpredictably hostile, precariously balanced, and illusory. In such a universe, the inclination to see enemies everywhere, to guard against them and to imagine the worst is almost adaptive and functional.

Moreover, the narcissist falls prey to delusions of grandeur. Important Men deserve Important Enemies. The narcissist attributes to himself influence and power much greater than he actually possesses. His claims for such overreaching power would look dubious without a proper set of opponents. The victories that the narcissist scores over his (mostly imagined) foes serve to emphasize his superiority. An unfriendly environment and the

233

threats it poses, overcome by his superior skills and traits, are an integral part of the personal myth of the narcissist.

The narcissist's partner (mate, spouse) usually craves and encourages his (paranoid, or threatening) attention. Her behaviour and reactive patterns tend to reinforce his. This is a game of two.

But the narcissist is not a full-fledged paranoiac. He maintains his reality test. His paranoid reactions are triggered by reality itself, and egged on by the ostensibly innocent (the narcissist's partner or mate or spouse or colleague, etc.). Actually, the narcissist's partner is likely to feel barren and vacuous when these games are over (for instance, after she divorces him).

The paranoid lives in constant fear and tribulation. This fact and the deficient structure of the narcissistic personality allow the partner to assume a position of superiority, high moral ground and sound mental health. The partner feels justified in regarding the narcissist in inferior terms: a child, a monster, an invalid, or a misfit.

She tends to play the missing parent or, more often, the "psychologist" in the relationships. In this mind game (which passes for a relationship), the narcissist is assigned the role of the "patient" in need of care and of being "objectively mirrored" (for his own good) by the partner.

These emergent roles endow the partner with authority and provide her with a way to distance herself from her own emotions (and from the narcissist's). This presumption of superiority is, therefore, analgesic. The partner is permanently enmeshed in a battle to prove herself (both to the ever critical and humiliating narcissist and to herself) as worthwhile. To restore her shattered sense of security and self-esteem, the partner must resort to narcissistic techniques.

This phenomenon is "narcissistic mirroring". It happens because the narcissist succeeds in turning himself into the partner's preferred - or even exclusive - frame of reference, the axis around which all her judgements revolve, the fountain of common sense and prevailing logic, the source of all knowledge and an authority on everything of importance.

Finally, the partner gathers enough courage to confront the narcissist with the facts (as seen from the partner's vantage point). The threshold of tolerance is crossed, the measure of suffering exceeded.

The partner does not expect to induce changes in the narcissist (though, if asked, she is most likely to insist otherwise). Her motivation is more basic: to exact revenge for a period of mental slavery, subservience, subjugation, subordination, exploitation, humiliation and objectification. The aim is to rattle the narcissist, and, thus, to make him vulnerable, inferior for just a minute. It is a mini-rebellion (which does not last long), sometimes possessed of sadistic elements.

Living with a narcissist is a harrowing experience. It can tilt one's mind toward abnormal reactions (actually, normal reactions to an abnormal situation). The capriciousness, volatility, arbitrariness and vicissitudinal character of the narcissist's behaviour can facilitate the formation of paranoid reactions in both the narcissist and his closest.

The less predictable the world, the more ominous and precarious it is and the more paranoid the reactions to it are. Sometimes, through the mechanism of narcissistic mirroring, the partner reacts to a prolonged period of emotional deprivation and stress by emulating the narcissist himself. The narcissist is then likely to reproach the partner by saying: "You became I and I became you!!! I do not know you anymore!"

The narcissist has a way of getting under his partners' skin. They cannot evade him because he is part of their lives and part of their selves, as internalized as any parent is. Even after a long sought separation, his partners typically still care for the narcissist greatly, enough to be mulling over the expired relationship endlessly. The partner discovers to her horror that she may be able to exit the narcissist's life, but he is unlikely exit hers.

The Development of the Narcissist

Question: Why does the narcissist behave childishly and immaturely?

Answer: "Puer Aeternus" - the eternal adolescent, the semipternal Peter Pan - is a phenomenon often associated with
pathological narcissism. People who refuse to grow up strike
others as self-centred and aloof, petulant and brattish, haughty
and demanding - in short: as childish or infantile.

The narcissist is a partial adult. He seeks to avoid adulthood.
Infantilization - the discrepancy between one's advanced
chronological age and one's retarded behaviour, cognition, and
emotional development - is the narcissist's preferred art form.
Some narcissists even use a childish tone of voice occasionally
and adopt a toddler's body language.

But most narcissist resort to more subtle means.

They reject or avoid adult chores and functions. They refrain
from acquiring adult skills (such as driving) or an adult's formal
education. They evade adult responsibilities towards others,
including and especially towards their nearest and dearest. They
hold no steady jobs, never get married, raise no family, cultivate
no roots, maintain no real friendships or meaningful relationships.

Many a narcissist remains attached to his family of origin. By
clinging to his parents, the narcissist continues to act in the role
of a child. He thus avoids the need to make adult decisions and
(potentially painful) choices. He transfers all adult chores and
responsibilities - from laundry to baby-sitting - to his parents,
siblings, spouse, or other relatives. He feels unshackled, a free
spirit, ready to take on the world (in other words omnipotent
and omnipresent).

Alternatively, by acting as surrogate caregiver to his siblings
or parents, the narcissist displaces his adulthood into a fuzzier

and less demanding territory. The social expectations from a husband and a father are clear-cut. Not so from a substitute, mock, or ersatz parent. By investing his efforts, resources, and emotions in his family of origin, the narcissist avoids having to establish a new family and face the world as an adult. His is an "adulthood by proxy", a vicarious imitation of the real thing.

The ultimate in dodging adulthood is finding God (long recognized as a father-substitute), or some other "higher cause". The believer allows the doctrine and the social institutions that enforce it to make decisions for him and thus relieve him of responsibility. He succumbs to the paternal power of the collective and surrenders his personal autonomy. In other words, he is a child once more. Hence the allure of faith and the lure of dogmas such as nationalism or communism or liberal democracy.

But why does the narcissist refuse to grow up? Why does he postpone the inevitable and regard adulthood as a painful experience to be avoided at a great cost to personal growth and self-realization? Because remaining essentially a toddler caters to all his narcissistic needs and defences and nicely tallies with the narcissist's inner psychodynamic landscape.

Pathological narcissism is an infantile defence against abuse and trauma, usually occurring in early childhood or early adolescence. Thus, narcissism is inextricably entwined with the abused child's or adolescent's emotional makeup, cognitive deficits, and worldview. To say "narcissist" is to say "thwarted, tortured child".

It is important to remember that overweening, smothering, spoiling, overvaluing, and idolizing the child are all forms of parental abuse. There is nothing more narcissistically-gratifying than the admiration and adulation (Narcissistic Supply) garnered by precocious child-prodigies (Wunderkinder). Narcissists who are the sad outcomes of excessive pampering and sheltering become addicted to it.

In a paper published in Quadrant in 1980 and titled "Puer Aeternus: The Narcissistic Relation to the Self", Jeffrey Satinover, a Jungian analyst, offers these astute observations:

"The individual narcissistically bound to (the image or archetype of the divine child) for identity can experience satisfaction from a concrete achievement only if it matches the grandeur of this archetypal image. It must have the qualities of greatness, absolute uniqueness, of being the best and ... prodigiously precocious."

The simple truth is that children get away with narcissistic traits and behaviours. Narcissists know that. They envy children, hate them, try to emulate them and, thus, compete with them for scarce Narcissistic Supply.

Children are forgiven for feeling grandiose and self-important or even encouraged to develop such emotions as part of "building up their self-esteem". Kids frequently exaggerate with impunity accomplishments, talents, skills, contacts, and personality traits - exactly the kind of conduct that narcissists are chastised for!

As part of a normal and healthy development trajectory, young children are as obsessed as narcissists are with fantasies of unlimited success, fame, fearsome power or omnipotence, and unequalled brilliance. Adolescent are expected to be pre-occupied with bodily beauty or sexual performance (as is the somatic narcissist), or ideal, everlasting, all-conquering love or passion. What is normal in the first 16 years of life is deemed pathological later on.

Children are firmly convinced that they are unique and, being special, can only be understood by, should only be treated by, or associate with, other special or unique, or high-status people. In time, through the process of socialization, young adults learn the benefits of collaboration and acknowledge the innate value of each and every person. Narcissists never do. They remain fixated in the earlier stage.

Preteens and teenagers require excessive admiration, adulation, attention and affirmation. It is a transient phase that gives place to the self-regulation of one's sense of inner worth. Narcissists, however, remain dependent on others for their self-esteem and self-confidence. They are fragile and fragmented and thus very susceptible to criticism, even if it is merely implied or imagined.

Well into pubescence, children feel entitled. As toddlers, they demand automatic and full compliance with their unreasonable expectations for special and favourable priority treatment. They grow out of it as they develop empathy and respect for the boundaries, needs, and wishes of other people. Again, narcissists never mature, in this sense.

Children, like adult narcissists, are "interpersonally exploitative", i.e., use others to achieve their own ends. During the formative years (0-6 years old), children are devoid of empathy. They are unable to identify with, acknowledge, or accept the feelings, needs, preferences, priorities, and choices of others.

Both adult narcissists and young children are envious of others and sometimes seek to hurt or destroy the sources of their frustration. Both groups behave arrogantly and haughtily, feel superior, omnipotent, omniscient, invincible, immune, "above the law", and omnipresent (magical thinking), and rage when frustrated, contradicted, challenged, or confronted.

The narcissist seeks to legitimize his child-like conduct and his infantile mental world by actually remaining a child, by refusing to mature and to grow up, by avoiding the hallmarks of adulthood, and by forcing others to accept him as the Puer Aeternus, the Eternal Youth, a worry-free, unbounded, Peter Pan.

Question: Isn't such infantile behaviour the result of extreme and unhealthy attachment to one's mother?

Answer: We are born with abilities of the first order (abilities to do) and of the second order (potentials, abilities to develop abilities to do). Our environment, though, is critical to the manifestation of these abilities. It is through socialization and comparison with others that we bring our capacities into full fruition and put them to use. We are further constrained by cultural and normative dictates. Generally speaking, we are faced with four scenarios as we grow up:

1. We possess an ability and society recognizes and encourages it. The result is a positive reinforcement of the capacity or talent.

2. We possess an ability but society is either indifferent to it, or outright hostile to it, or does not recognize it as such. Weak persons tend to suppress such socially undesirable potentials and talents as a result of social (peer and other) pressures. Stronger souls go on defiantly, adopting a nonconformist, or even rebellious stance.

3. We have no ability and our milieu insists that we do. We usually succumb to society's superior judgement and develop the talent in question, sliding inexorably into mediocrity.

4. We have no ability or talent, we know it and society concurs. This is the easiest case: no propensity to explore the irrelevant capacity will develop.

Parents (Primary Objects) and, more specifically, mothers are the first agents of socialization. It is through his mother that the child explores the answers to the most important existential questions, which shape his entire life: how loved one is, how loveable, how independent one becomes, how guilty one should feel for wanting to become autonomous, how predictable is the world, how much abuse should one expect in life and so on.

To the infant, the mother is not only an object of dependence (as his survival is at stake), love and adoration. She is a representation of the "universe" itself. It is through her that the child first exercises his senses: the tactile, the olfactory, and the visual. Later on, she becomes the subject of his nascent sexual cravings of her male offspring: a diffuse sense of wanting to merge, physically, as well as spiritually. This object of love is idealized and internalized and becomes part of the child's conscience (Superego). For better or worse, she is the yardstick, the benchmark against which everything in his future is measured. One forever compares oneself, one's identity, one's actions and omissions, one's achievements, one's fears and hopes and aspirations to this mythical figure.

Growing up entails the gradual separation from one's mother. At first, the child begins to form a more realistic view of her and incorporates the mother's shortcomings and disadvantages into this modified version. The more ideal, less realistic and earlier picture of the mother is stored and becomes part of the child's psyche. The later, less cheerful, more realistic view enables the infant to define his own identity and gender identity and to "go out to the world".

Thus, partly "abandoning" mother is the key to an independent exploration of the world, to personal autonomy and to a strong sense of self. Resolving the sexual complex and the resulting conflict of being attracted to a forbidden figure is the second, determining, step.

The (male) child must realize that his mother is "off-limits" to him sexually (and emotionally, or psychosexually) and that she "belongs" to his father (or to other males). He must thereafter choose to imitate his father ("become a man") in order to win, in the future, someone like his mother.

The third (and final) stage of letting go of the mother is reached during the delicate period of adolescence. One then seriously ventures out and, finally, builds and secures one's own world, replete with a new "mother-lover". If any of these phases is thwarted, the process of differentiation is not successfully completed, no autonomy or coherent self are achieved and dependence and "infantilism" characterize the unlucky person.

What determines the success or failure of these phases in one's personal history? Mostly, one's mother. If the mother does not "let go", the child does not go. If the mother herself is the dependent, narcissistic type, the growth prospects of the child are, indeed, dim. There are numerous mechanisms, which mothers use to ensure the continued presence and emotional dependence of their offspring (of both sexes).

The mother can cast herself in the role of the eternal victim, a sacrificial figure, who dedicated her life to the child (with the implicit or explicit proviso of reciprocity: that the child dedicates his life to her). Another strategy is to treat the child as an extension of the mother or, conversely, to treat herself as an extension of the child.

Yet another tactic is to create a situation of shared psychosis or "folie-a-deux" (the mother and child united against external threats), or an atmosphere suffused with sexual and erotic insinuations, leading to an illicit psychosexual bonding between mother and child ("emotional incest").

In this, latter case, the adult's ability to interact with members of the opposite sex is gravely impaired and the mother is perceived as envious of any feminine influence other than hers. Such a mother is frequently critical of the women in her offspring's life pretending to do so in order to protect him from dangerous liaisons or from ones which are "beneath him" ("You deserve more").

Other mothers exaggerate their neediness: they emphasize their financial dependence and lack of resources, their health problems, their emotional barrenness without the soothing presence of the child, their need to be protected against this or that (mostly imaginary) enemy. Guilt is a prime mover in the perverted relationships of such mothers and their children.

The death of the mother is, therefore, both a devastating shock and a deliverance. It generates ambivalent emotional reactions. Even a "normal" adult who mourns his dead mother is usually exposed to such emotional duality. This ambivalence is the source of great guilt feelings.

With a person who is abnormally attached to his mother, the situation is more complicated. He feels that he has a part in her death, that he is to blame, somehow responsible, that he could have done more for her. He is glad to be liberated and feels guilty and punishable because of it. He feels sad and elated, naked and powerful, exposed to dangers and omnipotent, about to disintegrate and to be newly integrated. These, precisely, are the emotional reactions to a successful therapy. With the death of his mother, the narcissist embarks on a process of healing.

The Narcissist's Mother

The Loved Enemies - An Introduction

An oft-overlooked fact is that the child is not sure that it exists. It avidly absorbs cues from its human environment. "Am I present?", "Am I separate?", "Am I being noticed?" - these are the questions that compete in his mind with his need to merge, to become an extension of his caregivers.

Granted, the infant (ages 0 to 2) does not verbally formulate these "thoughts" (which are part cognitive, part instinctual). His nagging uncertainty is more akin to a discomfort, like being thirsty or wet. The infant is torn between its need to differentiate and distinguish its self and its no less urgent urge to be assimilated and integrated.

"We ... know ... that (the child) requires an empathic environment, specifically, an environment that responds (a) to his need to have his presence confirmed by the glow of parental pleasure, and (b) to his need to merge into the reassuring calmness of the powerful adult, if he is to acquire a firm and resilient self."

[J. D. Levine and Rona H. Weiss. The Dynamics and Treatment of Alcoholism. Jason Aronson, 1994]

The child's nascent self must first overcome its feelings of diffusiveness, of being an extension of its caregivers (to include parents, in this text), or a part of them. Kohut says that parents perform the functions of the self for their child. More likely, a battle is joined from the child's first breath: a battle to gain autonomy, to usurp the power of the parents, to become a distinct entity.

The child refuses to let the parents continue to serve as its self. It rebels and seeks to depose them and take over their functions. The better the parents are at being self-objects (in lieu of the child's self), the stronger the child's self becomes, the more vigorously it fights for its independence.

The parents, in this sense, are like a benign, benevolent and enlightened colonial power, which performs the tasks of governance on behalf of the uneducated and uninitiated natives. The more lenient the colonial regime, the more likely it is to be supplanted by an indigenous, successful, government.

"The crucial question then is whether the parents are able to reflect with approval at least some of the child's proudly exhibited attributes and functions ... to respond with genuine enjoyment to his budding skills ... to remain in touch with him throughout his trials and errors ...to provide the child with a reliable embodiment of calmness and strength into which he can merge and with a focus for his need to find a target for his admiration." [Ibid.]

The Narcissistic Personality

"When the habitual narcissistic gratifications that come from being adored, given special treatment, and admiring the self are threatened, the results may be depression, hypochondriasis, anxiety, shame, self-destructiveness, or rage directed toward any other person who can be blamed for the troubled situation. The child can learn to avoid these painful emotional states by acquiring a narcissistic mode of information processing. Such learning may be by trial-and-error methods, or it may be internalized by identification with parental modes of dealing with stressful information."

[Jon Mardi Horowitz. Stress Response Syndromes: PTSD, Grief and Adjustment Disorders. Third edition. New York, NY University Press, 1998]

243

Narcissism is fundamentally an evolved version of the psychological defence mechanism known as splitting. The narcissist does not regard people, situations, entities (political parties, countries, races, his workplace) as a compound of good and bad elements. He is an "all or nothing" primitive "machine" (a common self-metaphor among narcissists).

He either idealizes his objects or devalues them. At any given time, the objects are either all good or all bad. The bad attributes are always projected, displaced, or otherwise externalized. The good ones are internalized in order to support the inflated ("grandiose") self-concepts of the narcissist and his grandiose fantasies and to avoid the pain of deflation and disillusionment.

The narcissist's earnestness and his (apparent) sincerity make people wonder whether he is simply detached from reality, unable to appraise it properly or willingly and knowingly distorts reality and reinterprets it, subjecting it to his self-imposed censorship. The truth is somewhere in between: the narcissist is dimly aware of the implausibility of his own constructions. He has not lost touch with reality. He is just less scrupulous in remoulding it and in ignoring its uncomfortable angles.

"The disguises are accomplished by shifting meanings and using exaggeration and minimization of bits of reality as a nidus for fantasy elaboration ... When the individual is faced with such stress events as criticism, withdrawal of praise, or humiliation, the information involved may be denied, disavowed, negated, or shifted in meaning to prevent a reactive state of rage, depression, or shame." [Ibid.]

The second psychological defence mechanism which characterizes the narcissist is the active pursuit of Narcissistic Supply. The narcissist seeks to secure a reliable and continuous stream of admiration, adulation, affirmation and attention. As opposed to common opinion, the narcissist is content to have any kind of attention, whether good or bad. If fame cannot be had, notoriety would do. The narcissist is obsessed with his Narcissistic Supply, he is addicted to it. His behaviour in its pursuit is impulsive and compulsive.

"(A)ny loss of a good and coherent self-feeling is associated with intensely experienced emotions such as shame and depression, plus an anguished sense of helplessness and disorientation. To prevent this state, the narcissistic personality slides the meanings of events in order to place the self in a better light ... Persons who function as accessories to the self may also be idealized by exaggeration of their attributes. Those who counter the self are depreciated." [Ibid.]

Freud versus Jung

Sigmund Freud (1856-1939) was the first to present a coherent theory of narcissism. He described transitions from subject-directed libido to object-directed libido through the intermediation and agency of the parents. To be healthy and functional, these transitions must be smooth and unperturbed. Neuroses are the outcomes of bumpy or incomplete transitions.

Freud conceived of each stage as the default (or fallback) of the next one. Thus, if a child reaches out to his objects of desire and fails to attract their love and attention, it regresses to the previous phase, to the narcissistic phase.

The first occurrence of narcissism is adaptive. It "trains" the child to love an object, (his self). It secures gratification through the availability, predictability and permanence of the loved object (oneself). But regressing to "secondary narcissism" is maladaptive. It is an indication of failure to direct the libido at the "right" targets (at objects, such as the parents).

If this pattern of regression persists and prevails, it leads to a narcissistic neurosis. The narcissist stimulates his self habitually in order to derive pleasure. He prefers this mode of deriving gratification to others. He is "lazy" because he takes the "easy" route of resorting to his self and reinvesting his libidinal resources "in-house" rather than making an effort (and risking failure) to seek out libidinal objects other than his self. The narcissist prefers fantasyland to reality, grandiose self-conception to realistic appraisal, masturbation to mature adult sex and daydreaming to real life achievements.

Carl Gustav Jung (1875-1961) suggested a mental picture of the psyche as a repository of archetypes (the conscious representations of adaptative behaviours). Fantasies are just a way of accessing these archetypes and releasing them.

Jungian psychology does not allow for regression. Any reversion to earlier phases of mental life, to earlier coping strategies, or to earlier choices is interpreted by Jungians as simply the psyche's way of using yet another, hitherto untapped, adaptation strategy. Regressions are compensatory processes intended to enhance adaptation and not methods of obtaining or securing a steady flow of gratification.

It would seem, though, that there is only a semantic difference between Freud and his disciple-turned-adversary, Jung. When libido investment in objects (esp. the Primary Object) fails to produce gratification, the result is maladaptation. This is dangerous and the default option - secondary narcissism - is activated.

This default option enhances adaptation (is adaptative) and is functional. It triggers adaptative behaviours. As a by-product, it secures gratification. We are gratified when we exert reasonable control over our environment, i.e., when our behaviours are adaptative. Thus, the compensatory process has two results: enhanced adaptation and inevitable gratification.

Perhaps the more serious disagreement between Freud and Jung is with regards to introversion.

Freud regards introversion as an instrument in the service of a pathology (introversion is indispensable to narcissism, as opposed to extroversion which is a necessary condition for libidinal object-orientation).

As opposed to Freud, Jung regards introversion as a useful tool in the service of the psychic quest for adaptation strategies (narcissism being one such strategy). The Jungian adaptation repertoire does not discriminate against narcissism. To Jung narcissism is a legitimate choice.

But even Jung acknowledged that the very need to look for new adaptation strategies means that adaptation has failed. In other words, the search itself is indicative of a pathological state of affairs. It does seem that introversion per se is not pathological (because no psychological mechanism is pathological per se). Only the use made of it can be pathological. One tends to agree with Freud, though, that when introversion becomes a permanent feature of the psychic landscape of a person, it facilitates pathological narcissism.

Jung distinguished introverts (who habitually concentrate on their selves rather than on outside objects) from extroverts (the converse preference). According to him, not only is introversion a totally normal and natural function, it remains normal and natural even if it predominates one's mental life.

But surely the habitual and predominant focussing of attention upon one's self, to the exclusion of others, is the very definition of pathological narcissism. What differentiates the pathological from the normal and even the welcome is, of course, a matter of degree.

Pathological narcissism is all-pervasive. Other forms of narcissism are not. So, although there is no healthy state of habitual, predominant introversion, it remains a question of form and degree of introversion. Often a healthy, adaptative mechanism goes awry. When it does, as Jung himself recognized, neuroses form.

Last but not least, Freud regards narcissism as a point while Jung regards it as a continuum (from health to sickness). Modern views of narcissism tend to agree with Jung in this respect.

Kohut's Approach

In a way, Heinz Kohut took Jung a step further. He said that pathological narcissism is not the result of excessive narcissism, libido or aggression. It is the result of defective, deformed or incomplete narcissistic (self) structures. Kohut postulated the existence of core constructs which he named the "grandiose exhibitionistic self" and the "idealized parent imago" [see below].

Children entertain notions of greatness (primitive or naive grandiosity) mingled with magical thinking, feelings of omnipotence and omniscience and a belief in their immunity to the consequences of their actions. These elements and the child's feelings regarding its parents (whom it tars with the same brush of omnipotence and grandiosity) coalesce and form these constructs.

The child's feelings towards its parents are reactions to their responses (affirmation, buffering, modulation or disapproval, punishment, even abuse). The parents' responses help maintain the child's self-structures. Without appropriate parental responses, infantile grandiosity, for instance, cannot be transformed into healthy adult ambitions and ideals.

According to Kohut, grandiosity and idealization are positive childhood development mechanisms. Even their reappearance in transference should not be considered a pathological narcissistic regression.

Kohut's contention is nothing less than revolutionary. He says that narcissism (subject-love) and object-love coexist and interact throughout life. True, they wear different guises with age and psychological maturation, but they always cohabitate.

"It is not that the self-experiences are given up and replaced by ... a more mature or developmentally more advanced experience of objects."

[H. Kohut. The Chicago Institute Lectures 1972-1976. Marian and Paul Tolpin (Eds.). Analytic Press, 1998]

This dichotomy inevitably leads to a dichotomy of disorders. Kohut agreed with Freud that neuroses are conglomerates of defence mechanisms, formations, symptoms, and unconscious conflicts. He even did not object to identifying unresolved Oedipal Conflicts (ungratified unconscious wishes and their objects) as the root of neuroses. But he identified a whole new class of disorders: the self-disorders. These are the results of the perturbed development of narcissism.

This is not a cosmetic or superficial distinction. Self-disorders are the outcomes of childhood traumas very much different to Freud's Oedipal, castration and other conflicts and fears. These are the traumas of a child that is either not being "seen" (not being affirmed by objects, especially the Primary Objects, his parents) - or is being regarded merely as an object for gratification or abuse.

Such children grow up to become adults who are not sure that they exist (lack a sense of self-continuity) or that they are worth anything (labile sense of self-worth and fluctuating or bipolar self-esteem). They suffer from depressions, as neurotics do. But the source of these depressions is existential (a gnawing sensation of emptiness) as opposed to the "guilty conscience" depressions of neurotics.

Such depressions: *"...are interrupted by rages because things are not going their way, because responses are not forthcoming in the way they expected and needed. Some of them may even search for conflict to relieve the pain and intense suffering of the poorly established self, the pain of the discontinuous, fragmenting, undercathected self of the child not seen or responded to as a unit of its own, not recognized as an independent self who wants to feel like somebody, who wants to go its own way"* [see Lecture 22]

[Paul and Marian Tolpin (Eds.). The Preface to the "Chicago Institute Lectures 1972-1976 of H. Kohut", 1996]

One note: "constructs" or "structures" are permanent psychological patterns. But this is not to say that they do not change, for they are capable of slow change. Kohut and his self-psychology disciples believed that the only viable constructs are comprised of self self-object experiences and that these structures are lifelong ones.

Melanie Klein regarded psychic structures as amalgams of archaic drives, splitting defences and archaic internal objects and part objects. Winnicott [and Balint and other, mainly British researchers] as well as other ego-psychologists thought that only infantile drive wishes and hallucinated oneness with archaic objects qualify as structures.

Karen Horney's Contributions

Horney is one of the precursors of the "object relations" school of psychodynamics. She observed that one's personality was shaped mostly by one's environment, society, or culture. She believed that one's relationships and interactions with others in one's childhood determine both the shape and functioning of one's personality.

She expanded the psychoanalytic repertoire. She added needs to drives. Where Freud believed in the exclusivity of the sex drive as an agent of transformation (to which he later added other drives) - Horney believed that people (children) needed to feel secure, to be loved, protected, emotionally nourished and so on.

She believed that the satisfaction of these needs or their frustration early in childhood are important determinants in shaping one's personality - as crucial as any drive. Horney said that society enters the process of personal development through the parental door. Biology converges with social injunctions to yield human values such as the nurturance of children.

Horney's great contribution was the concept of anxiety. Freudian anxiety is a rather primitive mechanism, a reaction to imaginary threats arising from early childhood sexual conflicts. Horney argued convincingly that anxiety is a primary reaction to the child's dependence on adults for his survival.

Children are uncertain (of love, protection, nourishment, nurturance), so they become anxious. They develop psychological defences to compensate for the intolerable and gradual realization that adults are merely human and are, at times, capricious, arbitrary, unpredictable, and unreliable. These defences provide both gratification and a sense of security. The problem of dangerous dependence still exists, but it is "one stage removed". When the defences are attacked or perceived to be attacked (such as in therapy), anxiety is reawakened.

Karen B. Wallant wrote in "Creating Capacity for Attachment: Treating Addictions and the Alienated Self" [Jason Aronson, 1999]:

"The addict has had so few loving attachments in his life that when alone he is returned to his detached, alienated self. This feeling-state can be compared to a young child's fear of monsters without a powerful other to help him, the monsters continue to live somewhere within the child or his environment."

So, the child learns to sacrifice a part of his autonomy and of his identity in order to feel secure.

Horney identified three neurotic strategies: submission, aggression and detachment. The choice of strategy determines the type of neurotic personality. The submissive (or compliant) type is a fake. He hides aggression beneath a facade of friendliness. The aggressive type is fake as well: at heart he is submissive. The detached neurotic withdraws from people. This cannot be considered an adaptative strategy.

Horney's is an optimistic outlook. Because biology is only one of the forces shaping our adulthood - culture and society being the predominant ones - she believes in reversibility and in the power of insight to heal. She believes that when an adult understands his problem (his anxiety) he also acquires the ability to eliminate it altogether.

Yet, clinical experience shows that childhood trauma and abuse are difficult to completely erase. Modern brain research tends to support this sad view and, yet, offer some hope. The brain seems to be more plastic than previously imagined, but no one knows when this "window of plasticity" shuts. What has been established is that the brain is physically impressed with abuse and trauma.

It is conceivable that the brain's plasticity continues well into adulthood and that later "reprogramming" (by loving, caring, compassionate and empathic experiences) remoulds the brain permanently. Clearly, the patient has to accept his disorder as a given and work around it rather than confront it directly.

After all, our disorders are adaptive and help us to function. Their removal may not always be wise or necessary to attain a full and satisfactory life. We should not all conform to the same mould and experience life the same. Idiosyncrasies are a good thing, both on the individual level and on the level of the species.

The Issue of Separation and Individuation

It is by no means universally accepted that children go through a phase of separation from their parents and through subsequent individuation. Yet, most psychodynamic theories (especially Klein, Mahler) are virtually constructed upon this foundation. The child is considered to be merged with his parents until it differentiates itself (through object-relations).

But researchers like Daniel N. Stern dispute this hypothesis. Based on many studies, it appears that, as always, what seems intuitively right is not necessarily right.

In "The Interpersonal World of the Infant: A View from Psychoanalysis and Developmental Psychology" [New York, Basic Books - 1985], Stern seems to, inadvertently, support Kohut by concluding that children possess selves and separate from their caregivers from the very start.

In effect, he says that the picture of the child, as proffered by psychodynamic theories, is biased by the way adults see children and childhood in retrospect. Adult disorders (for instance, the pathological need to merge) are attributed to children and to childhood.

This view is in stark contrast to the belief that children accept any kind of parents (even abusive) because they depend on them for their survival and self-definition. Attachment to and dependence on significant others is the result of the non-separateness of the child, go the classical psychodynamic/object-relations theories.

The self is a construct (within a social context, some add), an assimilation of the oft-imitated and idealized parents plus the internalization of the way others perceive the child in social interactions. The self is, therefore, an internalized reflection, an imitation, a series of internalized idealizations. This kind of self-ness sounds close to pathological narcissism. The difference between a healthy self and a narcissistically corrupted one may, indeed, be a matter of quantity rather than quality.

Childhood Traumas and the Development of the Narcissistic Personality

Traumas are inevitable. They are an integral and important part of life. But in early childhood, especially in infancy (ages 0 to 4 years), they acquire an ominous aura and an evil interpretation. No matter how innocuous the event and the surrounding circumstances, the child's vivid imagination is likely to embed it in the framework of a highly idiosyncratic horror story.

Parents sometimes have to be absent due to medical or economic conditions. They may be too preoccupied to stay attuned at all times to the child's emotional needs. The family unit itself may be disintegrating with looming divorce or separation. The values of the parent may stand in radical contrast to those of society.

To adults, such mundane and common traumas do not amount to abuse. Verbal and psychological-emotional abuse or neglect are judged by us to be more serious "offences". But this distinction is lost on the child. To him, all traumas - deliberately inflicted or inevitable and inadvertent life crises - are of equal abusive standing, though their severity may differ together with the permanence of their emotional outcomes.

Sometimes even abuse and neglect are the results of circumstances beyond the abusive or neglecting parent's control. Consider a physically or mentally handicapped parent or caregiver, for instance. But the child cannot see this as a mitigating circumstance because he cannot appreciate it or even plainly understand the causal linkage.

Where even a child can tell the difference is with physical and sexual abuse. These are marked by a co-operative effort (offending parent and abused child) at concealment and strong emotions of shame and guilt, repressed to the point of producing anxiety and "neurosis". The child perceives the injustice of the situation, though it rarely dares to express its views, lest it be abandoned or severely punished by its abusers.

This type of trauma, which involves the child actively or passively, is qualitatively different and is bound to yield long-term effects such as dissociation or severe personality disorders. These are violent, premeditated traumas, not traumas by default, and the reaction is bound to be violent and active. The child becomes a reflection of its dysfunctional family: it represses emotions, denies reality, resorts to violence and escapism, disintegrates.

One of the abused and traumatized child's coping strategies is to withdraw inwards, to seek gratification from a secure, reliable and permanently-available source: from one's self. The child, fearful of further rejection and abuse, refrains from further interaction with others. Instead, it builds its own kingdom of grandiose fantasies where it is always loved, respected, and self-sufficient. This is the narcissistic strategy which leads to the development of a narcissistic personality.

The Narcissist's Family

"(According to) Cassidy's (1988) study ... the construction of the self is derived from early daily experience with attachment figures ... Bednar, Wells, and Peterson (1989) suggest that feelings of competence and the self-esteem associated with them are enhanced in children when their parents provide an optimum mixture of acceptance, affection, rational limits and controls, and high expectations."

[Lilian G. Katz - Distinctions between Self-Esteem and Narcissism: Implications for Practice, October 1993, ERIC/EECE Publications]

The Narcissist's Mother
A Suggestion for an Integrative Framework

The whole structure of the narcissistic disorder reflects a relationship with problematic and dysfunctional Primary Objects (usually, the mother or main caregiver).

The narcissist's mother is typically inconsistent and frustrating. She thus thwarts the narcissist's ability to trust others and to feel safe. By emotionally abandoning him, she fosters in him fears of being abandoned and the nagging sensation that the world is a dangerous, hostile, and unpredictable place. She becomes a negative, devaluing voice, which is duly incorporated into the narcissist's Superego

But there is a less traditional view.

Our natural state is anxiety, the readiness - physiological and mental - to "fight or flee". Research indicates that the Primary Object (PO) is really the child, rather than its mother. The child identifies itself as an object almost at birth. It explores itself and reacts to and interacts with itself. The infant monitors its bodily reactions to internal and external inputs and stimuli: the flow of blood, the peristaltic movement, the swallowing reflex, the texture of saliva, the experience of excretion, being wet, thirsty, hungry or content.

The child assumes the position of observer and integrator early on. As Kohut said, it has both a self and the ability to relate to objects. This intimacy with a familiar and predictable object (oneself) is a primary source of security and the precursor to emerging narcissism. The mother is only a Secondary Object (SO). It is this Secondary Object that the child learns to relate to and it has the indispensable developmental advantage of being transcendental, external to the child. All meaningful others are Auxiliary Objects (AO).

A "good enough" SO helps the child to extend the lessons he had learned from his interaction with the PO (his self) and apply them to the world at large. The child learns that the external environment can be as predictable and safe as the internal one.

This titillating discovery leads to a modification of naive or primitive narcissism. It recedes to the background allowing more prominent and adaptative strategies to the fore. In due time, and subject to an accumulation of the right positively reinforcing experiences, a higher form of narcissism develops: self-love, a stable sense of self-worth, and self-esteem.

If, however, SO fails or is abusive, the child reverts back to the PO and to its primitive form of narcissism. This is regression in the chronological sense. But it is also an adaptative strategy.

The emotional consequences of rejection and abuse are harsh. Narcissism ameliorates them by providing a substitute object. This is an adaptative, survival-orientated defence mechanism. It provides the child with time to "come to grips with its thoughts and feelings" and perhaps to revert with a different strategy more suited to the new - unpleasant and threatening - data.

So the interpretation of this regression as a failure of object love may be wrong. The child merely deduces that the SO, the object chosen as the first target of object love, was the wrong object. Object love continues to look for a different, familiar, object. The child merely replaces one object (his mother) with another (his self). The child does not relinquish his capacity for object-love.

If this failure to establish a proper object-relation persists and is not alleviated, all future objects are perceived either as extensions of the Primary Object (the self), or as external objects to be merged with one's self, because they are perceived narcissistically.

There are, therefore, two modes of object perception:

The narcissistic (all objects are perceived as variations of the perceiving self) and the social (all objects are perceived as others or self-objects).

The core (narcissistic) self precedes language or interaction with others. As the core self matures it develops either into a

True Self or into a False Self. The two are mutually exclusive (a person possessed by a False Self has no functioning True Self). The distinction of the False Self is that it perceives others narcissistically. As opposed to it, the True Self perceives others socially.

The child constantly compares his first experience with an object (with his internalized PO, his self) to his experience with his SO. The internalizations of both the PO and the SO are modified as a result of this process of comparison. The SO is idealized and internalized to form what I call the SEGO (loosely, the equivalent of Freud's Superego plus the internalized outcomes of social interactions throughout life). The internalized PO is constantly modified to conform to feedback from the SO (for example: "You are loved", or "You are a bad boy"). This is the process by which the Ideal Ego is created.

The internalizations of the PO, of the SO and of the outcomes of their interactions (for instance, of the results of the aforementioned constant comparison between them) form what Bowlby calls "working models". These are constantly updated representations of both the self and of Meaningful Others (what I call Auxiliary Others).

The narcissist's working models are defective. They pertain both to his self and to ALL others. As far as the narcissist is concerned, ALL people are meaningful because NO ONE really is.

The narcissist is forced to dehumanize, objectify, generalize, idealize, devalue, or stereotype in order to cope with the sheer volume of potential interactions with meaningful objects (i.e., with everyone!). Trying not to be overwhelmed, the narcissist feels superior and inflated - because he is the only REAL three-dimensional character in his mind.

Moreover, the narcissist's working models are rigid and never updated because he does not feel that he is interacting with real objects. How can one feel empathic, for instance, towards a representation or an abstraction or an object of gratification? How can such representations or abstractions grow or change?

Follows a matrix of possible axes (dimensions) of interaction between child and mother.

The first term in each of these equations of interaction describes the child, the second the mother.

The Mother can be:
- Accepting ("good enough");
- Domineering;
- Doting/Smothering;
- Indifferent;

- Rejecting;
- Abusive.

The Child can be:
- Attracted;
- Repelled (due to unjust mistreatment, for instance).

The possible axes or dimensions are:

Child / Mother
[How to read this table - an example:
Attraction - Attraction/Accepting
Means that the child is attracted to his mother, his mother is attracted to him and she is a "good enough" (accepting) mother.]

1. Attraction – Attraction/Accepting
   (Healthy axis, leads to self-love)
2. Attraction – Attraction/Domineering
   (Could lead to Schizoid, Avoidant, or other personality disorders, or to Social Phobia)
3. Attraction – Attraction/Doting or Smothering
   (Could lead to Cluster B personality disorders)
4. Attraction – Repulsion/Indifferent
   [passive-aggressive, frustrating]
   (Could lead to narcissism, Cluster B disorders)
5. Attraction – Repulsion/Rejecting
   (Could lead to Paranoid, Borderline, or other personality disorders)
6. Attraction – Repulsion/Abusive
   (Could lead to Dissociative Identity Disorder, Attention Deficit Hyperactivity Disorder, Narcissistic, Borderline, Antisocial, or Paranoid personality disorders)
7. Repulsion – Repulsion/Indifferent
   (Could lead to Avoidant, Schizoid, or Paranoid personality disorders)
8. Repulsion – Repulsion/Rejecting
   (Could lead to personality, mood, or anxiety disorders and to impulsive behaviours, such as eating disorders)
9. Repulsion – Attraction/Accepting
   (Could lead to unresolved Oedipal Conflicts and to neuroses)
10. Repulsion – Attraction/Domineering
    (Could have the same results as axis 6)
11. Repulsion – Attraction/Doting
    (Could have the same results as axis 9)

This, of course, is a very rough sketch. Many of the axes can be combined to yield more complex clinical pictures.

It provides an initial, coarse, map of the possible interactions between the PO and the SO in early childhood and the unsavoury results of internalized bad objects.

This PO/SO matrix continues to interact with AO to form the person's self-evaluation (self-esteem or sense of self-worth).

This process - the formation of a coherent sense of self-worth - starts with PO/SO interactions within the matrix and continues roughly till the age of 8, all the time gathering and assimilating interactions with AO (meaningful others).

First, the child forms a model of attachment in relationships (approximately captured by the matrix above). This model is based on the internalization of the Primary Object (later, the self). Attachment interactions with SO follow and in the wake of a critical mass of interactions with AO, the self is formed.

This process of the formation of self rests on a few critical principles:

1. The child, as we said earlier, develops a sense of "mother-constancy". This is crucial. If the child is unable to predict the behaviour (let alone the presence) of his mother from one moment to another, it finds it hard to trust anything or anyone, predict anything and expect anything. Because the self, to some extent (some say: to a large extent), is comprised of the internalized outcomes of the interactions with others, negative experiences are incorporated in the budding self as well as positive ones. In other words, a child feels loveable and desirable if it is indeed loved and wanted. If it is rejected, it is bound to feel worthless and worthy only of rejection. In due time, the child develops behaviours which yield rejection by others and the outcomes of which are thus soothingly familiar and conform to his self-perception.

2. The adoption and assimilation of the judgement of others and its incorporation into a coherent sense of self-worth and self-esteem.

3. The discounting or filtering-out of contrarian information. Once Bowlby's "working models" are formed, they act as selective membranes. No amount of external information to the contrary alters these models significantly. Granted, shifts in relative positions may and do occur in later stages of life. A person can feel more or less accepted, more or less competent, more or less integrated into a given social setting. But these are changes in the values of parameters within a set equation (the working model). The equation itself is rarely altered and only by very serious life crises.

The Inverted Narcissist

With contributions by
the members of the Narcissism List

THE CLINICAL PICTURE AND DEVELOPMENTAL ROOTS -
OPENING REMARKS

Terminology

Co-Dependents

257 There is great confusion regarding the terms co-dependent, counter-dependent, and dependent.

Like dependents (people with the Dependent Personality Disorder), co-dependents depend on other people for their emotional gratification and the performance of both inconsequential and crucial daily and psychological functions.

Co-dependents are needy, demanding, and submissive. They suffer from abandonment anxiety and, to avoid being overwhelmed by it, they cling to others and act immaturely. These behaviours are intended to elicit protective responses and to safeguard the "relationship" with their companion or mate upon whom they depend. Co-dependents appear to be impervious to abuse. No matter how badly they are mistreated, they remain committed.

This is where the "co" in "co-dependence" comes into play. By accepting the role of victims, co-dependents seek to control their abusers and manipulate them. It is a danse macabre in which both members of the dyad collaborate.

The Dependent Personality Disorder is a much disputed mental health diagnosis.

We are all dependent to some degree. We all like to be taken care of. When is this need judged to be pathological, compulsive, pervasive, and excessive? Clinicians who contributed to the study of this disorder use words such as "craving", "clinging", "stifling" (both the dependent and her partner), and "humiliating", or "submissive". But these are all subjective terms, open to disagreement and differences of opinion.

Moreover, virtually all cultures encourage dependency to varying degrees. Even in developed countries, many women, the very old, the very young, the sick, the criminal, and the mentally-handicapped are denied personal autonomy and are legally and economically dependent on others (or on the authorities). Thus, the Dependent Personality Disorder is diagnosed only when such behaviour does not conform to social or cultural norms.

Co-dependents, as they are sometimes known, are possessed with fantastic worries and concerns and are paralyzed by their abandonment anxiety and fear of separation. This inner turmoil renders them indecisive. Even the simplest everyday decision becomes an excruciating ordeal. This is why co-dependents rarely initiate projects or do things on their own.

Dependents typically go around eliciting constant and repeated reassurances and advice from myriad sources. This recurrent solicitation of succour is proof that the co-dependent seeks to transfer responsibility for his or her life to others, whether they have agreed to assume it or not.

This recoil and studious avoidance of challenges may give the wrong impression that the dependent is indolent or insipid. Yet, most dependents are neither. They are often fired by repressed ambition, energy, and imagination. It is their lack self-confidence that holds them back. They don't trust their own abilities and judgement.

Absent an inner compass and a realistic assessment of their positive qualities on the one hand and limitations on the other hand, dependents are forced to rely on crucial input from the outside. Realizing this, their behaviour becomes self-negating: they never disagree with meaningful others or criticizes them. They are afraid to lose their support and emotional nurturance.

Consequently, as I have written in the Open Site Encyclopedia entry on this disorder:

"The co-dependent moulds himself/herself and bends over backward to cater to the needs of his nearest and dearest and satisfy their every whim, wish, expectation, and demand. Nothing is too unpleasant or unacceptable if it serves to secure the uninterrupted presence of the co-dependent's family and friends and the emotional sustenance s/he can extract (or extort) from them.

The co-dependent does not feel fully alive when alone. S/he feels helpless, threatened, ill-at-ease, and child-like. This acute discomfort drives the co-dependent to hop from one relationship to another. The sources of nurturance are interchangeable. To the co-dependent, being with someone, with anyone, no matter whom - is always preferable to solitude."

Inverted Narcissist

Also called "covert narcissist", this is a co-dependent who depends exclusively on narcissists (narcissist-co-dependent). If you are living with a narcissist, have a relationship with one, if you are married to one, if you are working with a narcissist, etc. - it does NOT mean that you are an inverted narcissist.

To "qualify" as an inverted narcissist, you must CRAVE to be in a relationship with a narcissist, regardless of any abuse inflicted on you by him/her. You must ACTIVELY seek relationships with narcissists and ONLY with narcissists, no matter what your (bitter and traumatic) past experience has been. You must feel EMPTY and UNHAPPY in relationships with ANY OTHER kind of person. Only then, and if you satisfy the other diagnostic criteria of a Dependent Personality Disorder, can you be safely labelled an "inverted narcissist".

Counter-Dependents

Counter-dependents reject and despise authority (they are contumacious) and often clash with authority figures (parents, bosses, or the law). Their sense of self-worth and their very self-identity are premised on and derived from (in other words, are dependent on) these acts of bravura and defiance. Counter-dependents are fiercely independent, controlling, self-centred, and aggressive.

These behaviour patterns are often the result of a deep-seated fear of intimacy. In an intimate relationship, the counter-dependent feels enslaved, ensnared, and captive. Counter-dependents are locked into Approach-Avoidance Repetition Complex cycles. Hesitant approach is followed by avoidance of commitment. They are "lone wolves" and bad team players.

Most "classical" (overt) narcissists are counter-dependents. Their emotions and needs are buried under a "scar tissue" which had formed, coalesced, and hardened during years of one form of abuse or another. Grandiosity, a sense of entitlement, a lack of empathy, and overweening haughtiness usually hide gnawing insecurity and a fluctuating sense of self-worth.

Counter-dependence is a reaction formation. The counter-dependent dreads his own weaknesses. He seeks to overcome them by projecting an image of omnipotence, omniscience, success, self-sufficiency, and superiority.

Introduction

Co-dependence is an important and integral part of narcissism. Narcissists are either counter-dependent or co-dependent (inverted). The DSM-IV-TR uses 9 criteria to define the Narcissistic Personality Disorder (NPD). It is sufficient to show signs of 5 of them to be diagnosed as a narcissist. Thus, theoretically, it is possible to have NPD without being grandiose.

Many scholars (Alexander Lowen, Jeffrey Satinover, Theodore Millon and others) suggested a "taxonomy" of pathological narcissism. They divided narcissists to sub-groups (very much as I do with my somatic versus cerebral narcissist dichotomy).

Lowen, for instance, talks about the "phallic" narcissist versus others. Satinover and Millon make a very important distinction between narcissists who were raised by "classically" abusive parents and those who were raised by doting and smothering or domineering mothers.

Glenn O. Gabbard in "Psychodynamic Psychiatry in Clinical Practice" [The DSM-IV-TR Edition. Comments on Cluster B Personality Disorders - Narcissistic. American Psychiatric Press, Inc., 2000] we find this:

"...These criteria (the DSM-IV-TR's) identify a certain kind of narcissistic patient - specifically, the arrogant, boastful, 'noisy' individual who demands to be in the spotlight. However, they fail to characterize the shy, quietly grandiose, narcissistic individual whose extreme sensitivity to slights leads to an assiduous avoidance of the spotlight."

The DSM-III-R alluded to at least two types of narcissists, but the DSM-IV-TR committee chose to delete this portion of the text:

"...included criterion, 'reacts to criticism with feelings of rage, shame, or humiliation (even not if expressed)' due to lack of 'specificity'."

Other theoreticians, clinicians and researchers similarly suggested a division between "the oblivious narcissist" (a.k.a. overt) and "the hypervigilant narcissist" (a.k.a. covert).

The Inverted Narcissist

It is clear that there is, indeed, a hitherto neglected type of narcissist. It is the "self-effacing" or "introverted" narcissist. I call it the "inverted narcissist" (hereinafter: IN). Others call it "narcissist-co-dependent", "co-narcissist", or "N-magnet" (which erroneously implies the inverted narcissist's passivity and victimhood).

The Inverted Narcissist is a narcissist who, in many respects, is the mirror image of the "classical" narcissist. The psychodynamics of the inverted narcissist are not clear, nor are its developmental roots. Perhaps it is the product of an overweening Primary Object (parent) or caregiver. Perhaps excessive abuse leads to the repression of even the narcissistic and other defence mechanisms. Perhaps the IN's parents suppress every manifestation of grandiosity and of narcissism (very common in early childhood and adolescence), so that the narcissistic defence mechanism is "inverted" and internalized in this unusual form.

These narcissists are self-effacing, sensitive, emotionally fragile, and sometimes socially phobic. They derive all their self-esteem and sense of self-worth from the outside (from others), are pathologically envious (a transformation of aggression), are likely to intermittently engage in aggressive/violent behaviours, and are more emotionally labile than the classic narcissist.

There are, therefore, three "basic" types of narcissists:

1. *The offspring of neglecting parents* who default to narcissism as the predominant form of object relations (with themselves as the exclusive love object);

2. *The offspring of doting or domineering parents (often narcissists themselves)* - These children internalize their parents' voices in the form of a sadistic, ideal, immature Superego and spend their lives trying to be perfect, omnipotent, omniscient and to be judged "a success" by these parent-images and their later representations and substitutes (authority figures);

3. *The offspring of abusive parents* internalize the abusing, demeaning and contemptuous voices and spend their lives in an effort to elicit "counter-voices" from other people and thus to regulate their labile self-esteem and sense of self-worth.

All three types experience recurrent and Sisyphean failures. Shielded by their defence mechanisms, they constantly gauge reality wrongly, their actions and reactions become more and more rigid and the damage inflicted by them on themselves and on others is ever greater.

The narcissistic parent seems to employ a myriad primitive defence in his or her dealings with his or her children:

1. *Splitting, idealization, and devaluation* - Idealizing the child and devaluing him in cycles, which reflect the internal dynamics of the parent rather than anything the child does.
2. *Projective Identification* - Forcing the child to behave in a way which vindicates the parent's fears regarding himself or herself, his or her self-image and his or her self-worth. This is a particularly powerful and pernicious mechanism. If the narcissist parent fears his or her own deficiencies ("defects"), vulnerability, perceived weaknesses, susceptibility, gullibility, or emotions, he or she is likely to force the child to "feel" these rejected and (to him or her) repulsive emotions, to behave in ways strongly abhorred by the parent, to exhibit character traits the parent strongly rejects in himself or herself.
3. *Projection* - The child, in a way, becomes the "trash bin", the reflecting mirror of the parents' inhibitions, fears, self-loathing, self-contempt, perceived lack of self-worth, sense of inadequacy, rejected traits, repressed emotions, failures and emotional reticence. They attribute all these unwanted traits and emotions to the child.

Coupled with the parent's treatment of the child as the parent's extension, these psychological defences totally inhibit the psychological growth and emotional maturation of the child. The child becomes a reflection of the parent, a conduit through which the parent experiences and realizes himself or herself for better (hopes, aspirations, ambition, life goals) and for worse (weaknesses, "undesirable" emotions, "negative" traits).

Relationships between such parents and their progeny easily deteriorate to sexual or other modes of abuse because there are no functioning boundaries between them.

It seems that the child's reaction to a narcissistic parent can be either accommodation and assimilation, or rejection.

Accommodation and Assimilation

The child accommodates, idealizes and internalizes (introjects) the narcissistic and abusive Primary Object (parent) successfully. This means that the child's "internal voice" is also narcissistic and abusive. The child tries to comply with its directives and with its explicit and perceived wishes.

The child becomes a masterful provider of Narcissistic Supply, a perfect match to the parent's personality, an ideal source, an accommodating, understanding and caring caterer to all the needs, whims, mood swings and cycles of the narcissist parent.

The child learns to endure devaluation and idealization with equanimity and adapt to the narcissist's cultish world view. The child, in short, becomes the ultimate extension. This is what we call an inverted narcissist.

We must not neglect the abusive aspect of such a relationship. The narcissistic parent always alternates between idealization and devaluation of his or her offspring. The child is likely to internalize these devaluing, abusive, critical, demeaning, berating, diminishing, minimizing, upbraiding, chastising voices.

The abusive parent (or caregiver) goes on to survive inside the child-turned-adult (as part of a sadistic and ideal Superego and an fantastic Ego Ideal). These internalized voices are so powerful that they inhibit even the development of reactive narcissism, the child's typical defence mechanism.

The child-turned-adult keeps looking for narcissists in order to feel whole, alive and wanted. He craves to be treated by a narcissist narcissistically. What others call abuse is, to him or her, familiar territory and constitutes Narcissistic Supply. To the inverted narcissist, the classic narcissist is a Source of Supply (Primary or Secondary) and his narcissistic behaviours constitute Narcissistic Supply. The IN feels dissatisfied, empty and unwanted when not "loved" by a narcissist.

The roles of Primary Source of Narcissistic Supply (PSNS) and Secondary Source of Narcissistic Supply (SSNS) are reversed. To the inverted narcissist, her narcissistic spouse is a Source of PRIMARY Narcissistic Supply.

But the child can also reject the narcissistic parent rather than accommodate him or her.

Rejection

The child may react to the narcissism of the Primary Object (parent) with a peculiar type of rejection. He develops his own narcissistic personality, replete with grandiosity and lack of empathy - but his personality is antithetical to that of the narcissistic parent.

If the parent were a somatic narcissist, the child is likely to grow up to be a cerebral one. If his father prided himself on being virtuous, the son turns out sinful. If his narcissistic mother bragged about her frugality, her daughter would tend towards profligacy.

An Attempted DSM-Style List of Criteria

It is possible to compose a DSM-IV-TR-like set of criteria for the inverted narcissist, using the classic narcissist's as a template.

The two are, in many ways, flip sides of the same coin, or "the mould and the moulded" - hence the neologisms "mirror narcissist" or "inverted narcissist".

The narcissist tries to merge with an idealized but badly internalized object. He does so by "digesting" the meaningful others in his life and transforming them into extensions of his self. He uses various techniques to achieve this.

The inverted narcissist (IN), on the other hand, does not attempt, except in fantasy or in dangerous, masochistic sexual practice, to merge with an idealized external object. This is because she so successfully internalized the narcissistic Primary Object to exclude everyone else. The IN feels ill at ease in her relationships with non-narcissists because these dalliances are unconsciously perceived by her to constitute "betrayal", "cheating", an abrogation of the exclusivity clause she has with the narcissistic Primary Object.

This is the big difference between classical narcissists and their inverted sisters.

Classic narcissists of all stripes reject the Primary Object in particular (and object relations in general) in favour of a handy substitute: themselves. Inverted narcissists accept the (narcissist) Primary Object and internalize it to the exclusion of all others (unless they are perceived to be faithful renditions, replicas of the narcissistic Primary Object).

Criterion ONE

Possesses a rigid sense of lack of self-worth.

The classic narcissist has a badly regulated sense of self-worth. However this is not conscious. He goes through cycles of self-devaluation (and experiences them as dysphorias).

The IN's sense of self-worth does not fluctuate. It is rather stable - but it is very low. Whereas the narcissist devalues others - the IN devalues herself as an offering, a sacrifice to the narcissist. The IN pre-empts the narcissist by devaluing herself, by actively berating her own achievements, or talents. The IN is exceedingly distressed when singled out because of actual accomplishments or a demonstration of superior skills.

The inverted narcissist is compelled to filter all of her narcissistic needs through the primary narcissist in her life. Independence or personal autonomy are not permitted. The IN feels amplified by the narcissist's running commentary (because nothing can be accomplished by the IN without the approval of a primary narcissist in her life).

Criterion TWO

Pre-occupied with fantasies of unlimited success, power, brilliance and beauty or of an ideal love.

This is the same as the DSM-IV-TR criterion for Narcissistic Personality Disorder but, with the IN, it manifests absolutely differently, i.e. the cognitive dissonance is sharper here because the IN is so absolutely and completely convinced of her worthlessness that these fantasies of grandeur are extremely painful "dissonances".

With the classical narcissist, the dissonance exists on two levels:
1. Between the unconscious feeling of lack of stable self-worth and the grandiose fantasies;
2. AND between the grandiose fantasies and reality (the Grandiosity Gap).

In comparison, the inverted narcissist can only vacillate between a sense of lack of self-worth and reality. No grandiosity is permitted, except in dangerous, forbidden fantasy. This shows that the IN is psychologically incapable of fully realizing her inherent potentials without a primary narcissist to filter the praise, adulation or accomplishments through. She must have someone to whom praise can be redirected.

The dissonance between the IN's certainty of self-worthlessness and genuine praise that cannot be deflected is likely to emotionally derail the inverted narcissist every time.

Criterion THREE

Believes that she is absolutely un-unique and un-special (i.e., worthless and not worthy of merger with the fantasized ideal) and that no one at all could understand her because she is innately unworthy of being understood. The IN becomes very agitated the more one tries to understand her because that also offends against her righteous sense of being properly excluded from the human race.

A sense of worthlessness is typical of many other personality disorders (as well as the feeling that no one could ever understand them). The narcissist himself endures prolonged periods of self-devaluation, self-deprecation and self-doubt. This is part of the Narcissistic Cycle.

In this sense, the inverted narcissist is a partial narcissist. She is permanently fixated in a part of the Narcissistic Cycle, never to experience its complementary half: the narcissistic grandiosity and sense of entitlement.

The "righteous sense of being properly excluded" comes from the sadistic Superego in concert with an "overbearing, externally reinforced, conscience".

Criterion FOUR

Demands anonymity (in the sense of seeking to remain excluded at all costs) and is intensely irritated and uncomfortable with any attention being paid to her - similar to the Avoidant or the Schizoid.

Criterion FIVE

Feels that she is undeserving and not entitled.

Feels that she is inferior to others, lacking, insubstantial, unworthy, unlikable, unappealing, unlovable, someone to scorn and dismiss, or to ignore.

Criterion SIX

Is extinguishingly selfless, sacrificial, even unctuous in her interpersonal relationships and avoids the assistance of others at all costs. Can only interact with others when she can be seen to be giving, supportive, and expending an unusual effort to assist.

Some narcissists behave the same way but only as a means to obtain Narcissistic Supply (praise, adulation, affirmation, attention). This must not be confused with the behaviour of the IN.

Criterion SEVEN

Lacks empathy. Is intensely attuned to others' needs, but only in so far as it relates to her own need to perform the required self-sacrifice, which in turn is necessary in order for the IN to obtain her Narcissistic Supply from the primary narcissist.

By contrast, narcissists are never empathic. They are intermittently attuned to others only in order to optimise the extraction of Narcissistic Supply from them.

Criterion EIGHT

Envies others. Cannot conceive of being envied and becomes extremely agitated and uncomfortable if even brought into a situation where comparison might occur. Loathes and avoids competition at all costs, if there is any chance of actually winning it, or being singled out.

Criterion NINE

Displays extreme shyness, lack of any real relational connections, is publicly self-effacing in the extreme, is internally high-

ly moralistic and critical of others; is a perfectionist and engages in lengthy ritualistic behaviours, which can never be perfectly performed (is obsessive-compulsive, though not necessarily to the full extent exhibited in Obsessive-Compulsive Personality Disorder). Notions of being individualistic are anathema.

The Reactive Patterns of the Inverted Narcissist

The inverted narcissist does not suffer from a "milder" form of narcissism. Like the "classic" narcissists, inverted narcissism has degrees and shades. But it is much rarer and the DSM-IV-TR classical variety is the more prevalent.

The inverted narcissist is liable to react with rage whenever threatened, or...

...When envious of other people's achievements, their ability to feel wholeness, happiness, to accept rewards and successes; when her sense of self-worthlessness is diminished by a behaviour, a comment, an event, when her lack of self-worth and voided self-esteem is threatened. Thus, this type of narcissist might surprisingly react violently or wrathfully to GOOD things: a kind remark, a mission accomplished, a reward, a compliment, a proposition, or a sexual advance.

...When thinking about the past, when emotions and memories are evoked (usually negative ones) by certain music, a given smell, or sight.

...When her pathological envy leads to an all-pervasive sense of injustice and being discriminated against or deprived by a spiteful world.

...When she believes that she failed (and she always entertains this belief), that she is imperfect and useless and worthless, a good for nothing half-baked creature.

...When she realizes to what extent her inner demons possess her, constrain her life, torment her, and deform her and the hopelessness of it all.

When the inverted narcissist rages, she becomes verbally and emotionally abusive. She uncannily spots and attacks the vulnerabilities of her target, and mercilessly drives home the poisoned dagger of despair and self-loathing until it infects her adversary.

The calm after such a storm is even eerier, a thundering silence. The inverted narcissist regrets her behaviour and admits her feelings while apologizing profusely.

The inverted narcissist nurtures her negative emotions as yet another weapon of self-destruction and self-defeat. It is from this repressed self-contempt and sadistic self-judgement that the narcissistic rage springs forth.

One important difference between inverted narcissists and non-narcissists is that the former are less likely to react with PTSD (Post-Traumatic Stress Disorder) following the break-up of their relationships with their narcissists. They seem to be "desensitized" to the narcissist's unpredictable ways by their early upbringing.

Whereas the reactions of normal people to narcissistic behaviour patterns (and especially to the splitting and Projective Identification defence mechanisms and to the idealization devaluation cycles) is shock, profound hurt and disorientation - inverted narcissists show none of the above.

The Life of the Inverted Narcissist

The IN is, usually, exceedingly and painfully shy as a child. Despite this Social Phobia, her grandiosity (absorbed from the parent) might direct her to seek "limelight" professions and occupations, which involve exposure, competition, "stage fright" and social friction.

The setting can vary from the limited (family) to the expansive (national media) - but, whatever it is, the result is constant conflict and feelings of discomfort, even terror and extreme excitement and thrill ("adrenaline rush"). This is because the IN's grandiosity is "imported" and not fully integrated. It is, therefore, not supportive of her "grandiose" pursuits (as is the case with the classical narcissist). On the contrary, the IN feels awkward, pitted on the edge of a precipice, contrived, and deceitful.

The inverted narcissist grows up in a stifling environment, whether it is an orthodox, hyper-religious, collectivist, or traditionalist culture, a monovalent, "black and white", doctrinarian and indoctrinating society - or a family which manifests all the above in a microcosm.

The inverted narcissist is cast in a negative (emergent) role within her family. Her "negativity" is attributed to her gender, the order of her birth, religious, social, or cultural dictates and commandments, her "character flaws", her relation to a specific person or event, her acts or inaction and so on.

In the words of one such IN:

"In the religious culture I grew up in, women are SO suppressed, their roles are so carefully restricted. They are the representation, in the flesh, of all that is sinful, degrading, of all that is wrong with the world.

These are the negative gender/cultural images that were force fed to us the negative 'otherness' of women, as defined by men, was fed to me. I was so shy, withdrawn, unable to really relate to people at all from as early as I can remember."

The IN is subjected and exposed either to an overbearing, overvalued parent, or to an aloof, detached, emotionally unavailable one - or to both - at an early stage of her life:

"I grew up in the shadow of my father who adored me, put me on a pedestal, told me I could do or be anything I wanted because I was incredibly bright, BUT, he ate me alive, I was his property and an extension of him.

I also grew up with the mounting hatred of my narcissist brother who got none of this attention from our father and got no attention from our mother either. My function was to make my father look wonderful in the eyes of all outsiders, the wonderful parent with a genius Wunderkind as his last child, and the only child of the six that he was physically present to raise from the get go.

The overvaluation combined with being abjectly ignored or raged at by him when I stepped out of line even the tiniest bit, was enough to warp my personality."

The IN is prevented from developing full-blown secondary narcissism. The IN is so heavily preoccupied in her pre-school years with satisfying the narcissistic parent, that the traits of grandiosity and self-love, even the need for Narcissistic Supply, remain dormant or repressed.

The IN simply "knows" that only the narcissistic parent can provide the requisite amount of Narcissistic Supply. The narcissistic parent is so controlling that any attempt to garner praise or adulation from any other source (without the approval of the parent) is severely punished by swift devaluation and even the occasional spanking or abuse (physical, emotional, or sexual).

This is a vital part of the conditioning that gives rise to inverted narcissism. Where the classical narcissist exhibits grandiosity, the IN is intensely uncomfortable with personal praise, and always wishes to divert praise away from herself onto her narcissist. This is why the IN can only truly feel anything when she is in a relationship with another narcissist. The IN is conditioned and programmed from the very beginning to be the perfect companion to the narcissist: to feed his Ego, to be purely his extension, to seek only praise and adulation if it brings greater praise and adulation to her narcissist.

The Inverted Narcissist's Survival Guide

- Listen attentively to everything the narcissist says and agree with it all. Don't believe a word of it but let it slide as if everything is just fine, business as usual.
- Offer something absolutely unique to the narcissist which they cannot obtain anywhere else. Also be prepared to line up future Sources of Primary NS for your narcissist because you will not be IT for very long, if at all. If you take over the procuring function for the narcissist, they become that much more dependent on you which makes it a bit tougher for them to pull their haughty stuff - an inevitability, in any case.
- Be endlessly patient and go way out of your way to be accommodating, thus keeping the Narcissistic Supply flowing liberally, and keeping the peace (relatively speaking).
- Get tremendous personal satisfaction out of endlessly giving. This one may not be attractive to you, but it is a take it or leave it proposition.
- Be absolutely emotionally and financially independent of the narcissist. Take what you need: the excitement and engulfment (i.e., NS) and refuse to get upset or hurt when the narcissist does or says something dumb. Yelling back works really well but should be reserved for special occasions when you fear your narcissist may be on the verge of leaving you; the silent treatment is better as an ordinary response, but it must be devoid of emotional content, more with the air of boredom and "I'll talk to you later, when I am good and ready, and when you are behaving in a more reasonable fashion."
- If your narcissist is cerebral and not interested in having much sex, give yourself ample permission to have sex with other people. Your cerebral narcissist is not indifferent to infidelity, so discretion and secrecy is of paramount importance.
- If your narcissist is somatic and you don't mind, join in on group sex encounters but make sure that you choose properly for your narcissist. They are heedless and very undiscriminating in respect of sexual partners and that can get very problematic.
- If you are a "fixer", which most inverted narcissists are, focus on fixing situations, preferably before they become "situations". Don't for one moment delude yourself that you can actually fix the narcissist - it simply will not happen. Not because they are being stubborn - they just simply can't be fixed.

- If there is any fixing that can be done, it is to help your narcissist become aware of their condition, and (this is very important) with no negative implications or accusations in the process at all. It is like living with a physically handicapped person and being able to discuss, calmly, unemotionally, what the limitations and benefits of the handicap are and how the two of you can work with these factors, rather than trying to change them.
- Finally, and most important of all for the inverted narcissist: get to know yourself. What are you getting from the relationship? Are you actually a masochist? Why is this relationship attractive and interesting?

  Define for yourself what good and beneficial things you believe you are receiving in this relationship. Define the things that you find harmful to you. Develop strategies to minimize the harm to yourself.

  Don't expect that you will cognitively be able to reason with the narcissist to change who he is. You may have some limited success in getting your narcissist to tone down on the really harmful behaviours that affect you, which emanate from the unchangeable essence of the narcissist. This can only be accomplished in a very trusting, frank and open relationship.

The inverted narcissist can have a reasonably good, long lasting relationship with the narcissist. You must be prepared to give your narcissist a lot of space and leeway.

You don't really exist for him as a fully realized person - no one does. They are not fully realized people so they cannot possibly have the skills, no matter how small or sexy, to be a complete person in the sense that most adults are complete.

Somatic versus Cerebral Inverted Narcissists

The inverted narcissist is really an erstwhile narcissist internalized by the IN. Inevitably, we are likely to find among the inverted the same propensities, predilections, preferences and inclinations that we do among proper narcissists.

The cerebral IN is an IN whose Source of vicarious Primary Narcissistic Supply lies - through the medium and mediation of a narcissist - in the exercise of his intellectual faculties. A somatic IN would tend to make use of her body, sex, shape or health in trying to secure NS for "her" narcissist.

The inverted narcissist feeds on the primary narcissist and this is her Narcissistic Supply. So these two typologies can essentially become a self-supporting, symbiotic system.

In reality though, both the narcissist and the inverted narcissist need to be quite well aware of the dynamics of this relationship in order to make it work as a successful long-term arrangement. It might well be that this symbiosis would only work between a cerebral narcissist and a cerebral invert. The somatic narcissist's incessant sexual dalliances would be far too threatening to the equanimity of the cerebral invert for there to be much chance of this succeeding, even for a short time.

It would seem that only opposing types of narcissist can get along when two classic narcissists are involved in a couple. It follows, syllogistically, that only identical types of narcissist and inverted narcissist can survive in a couple. In other words: the best, most enduring couples of narcissist and his inverted narcissist mate would involve a somatic narcissist and a somatic IN - or a cerebral narcissist and a cerebral IN.

Coping with Narcissists and Non-Narcissists

The inverted narcissist is a person who grew up enthralled by the narcissistic parent. This parent engulfed and subsumed the child's being to such an extent that the child's personality was irrevocably shaped by this immersion, damaged beyond hope of repair. The child was not even able to develop defence mechanisms such as narcissism to cope with the abusive parent.

The end result is an inverted narcissistic personality. The traits of this personality are primarily evident in the context of romantic relationships. The child was conditioned by the narcissistic parent to only be entitled to feel whole, useful, happy, and productive when the child augmented or mirrored to the parent the parent's False Self. As a result the child is shaped by this engulfment and cannot feel complete in any significant adult relationship unless they are with narcissists.

The Inverted Narcissist in Relationship with the Narcissist

The inverted narcissist is drawn to significant relationships with other narcissists in her adulthood. These relationships are usually spousal primary relationships but can also be friendships with narcissists outside of the primary love relationship.

In a primary relationship, the inverted narcissist attempts to re-create the parent-child relationship. The IN thrives on mirroring to the narcissist his grandiose fantasies and in so doing the IN obtains her own Narcissistic Supply (which is the dependence of the narcissist upon the IN for his Secondary Narcissistic Supply).

The IN must have this form of relationship with a narcissist in order to feel whole. The IN goes as far as needed to ensure that the narcissist is happy, cared for, properly adored, as she feels is the narcissist's right. The IN glorifies and lionizes her narcissist, places him on a pedestal, endures any and all narcissistic devaluation with calm equanimity, impervious to the overt slights of the narcissist.

Narcissistic rage is handled deftly by the inverted narcissist. The IN is exceedingly adept at managing every aspect of her life, tightly controlling all situations, so as to minimize the potential for the inevitable narcissistic rages of her narcissist.

The IN wishes to be subsumed by the narcissist. The IN only feels truly loved and alive in this kind of relationship. The IN is loath to abandon her relationships with narcissists. The relationship only ends when the narcissist withdraws completely from the symbiosis. Once the narcissist has determined that the IN is of no further use, and withholds all Narcissistic Supply from the IN, only then does the IN reluctantly move on to another relationship.

The IN is most likely to equate sexual intimacy with engulfment. This can be easily misread to mean that the IN is herself a somatic narcissist, but it would be incorrect. The IN can endure years of minimal sexual contact with her narcissist and still be able to maintain the self-delusion of intimacy and engulfment. The IN finds a myriad of other ways to "merge" with the narcissist, becoming intimately, though only in support roles, involved with the narcissist's business, career, or any other activity where the IN can feel that they are needed by the narcissist and are indispensable.

The IN is an expert at doling out Narcissistic Supply and even goes as far as procuring Primary Narcissistic Supply for their narcissist (even where this means finding another lover for the narcissist, or participating in group sex with the narcissist).

Usually though, the IN seems most attracted to the cerebral narcissist and finds him easier to manage than the somatic narcissist. The cerebral narcissist is uninterested in sex and this makes life considerably easier for the IN, i.e., the IN is less likely to "lose" her cerebral narcissist to another primary partner. A somatic narcissist may be prone to changing partners with greater frequency or wish to have no partner, preferring to have multiple, casual sexual relationships of no apparent depth which never last very long.

The IN regards relationships with narcissists as the only true and legitimate form of primary relationship. The IN is capable of having primary relationships with non-narcissists. But without the engulfment and the drama, the IN feels unneeded, unwanted and emotionally uninvolved.

When Can a Classic Narcissist Become an Inverted Narcissist?

A classic narcissist can become an inverted narcissist in one (or more) of the following (typically cumulative) circumstances:

1. Immediately following a life crisis and a narcissistic injury (divorce, devastating financial loss, death of a parent, or a child, imprisonment, loss of social status and, in general, any other narcissistic injury); or

2. When the injured narcissist then meets another classic narcissist who restores a sense of meaning and superiority (uniqueness) to his life. The injured narcissist derives Narcissistic Supply vicariously, by proxy, through the "dominant" narcissist.

3. As part of an effort to secure a particularly desired Source of Narcissistic Supply. The conversion from classic to inverted narcissism serves to foster an attachment (bonding) between the narcissist and his source. When the narcissist judges that the source is his and can be taken for granted, he reverts to his former, classically narcissistic self.

Such a "conversion" is always temporary. It does not last and the narcissist reverts to his "default" or dominant state.

When Can an Inverted Narcissist Become a Classic Narcissist?

The inverted narcissist can become a classic narcissist in one (or more) of the following (typically cumulative) circumstances:

1. Immediately following a life crisis that involves the incapacitation or dysfunction of the inverted narcissist's partner (sickness, accident, demotion, divorce, devastating financial loss, death of a parent, or a child, imprisonment, loss of social status and, in general, any other narcissistic injury); or

2. When the inverted narcissist, injured and disillusioned, then meets another inverted narcissist who restores a sense of meaning and superiority (uniqueness) to her life. The injured narcissist derives Narcissistic Supply from the inverted narcissist.

3. As part of an effort to secure a particularly desired Source of Narcissistic Supply. The conversion from inverted to clas-

274

sic narcissism serves to foster an attachment (bonding) between the narcissist and her source. When the narcissist judges that the source is hers and can be taken for granted, she reverts to her former, inverted narcissistic self.

Such a "conversion" is always temporary. It does not last and the narcissist reverts to her "default" or dominant state.

Relationships between the Inverted Narcissist and Non-Narcissists

The inverted narcissist can maintain relationships outside of the symbiotic primary relationship with a narcissist. But the IN does not "feel" loved because she finds the non-narcissist not "engulfing" or not "exciting". Thus, the IN tends to devalue her non-narcissistic primary partner as less worthy of the IN's love and attention.

The IN may be able to sustain a relationship with a non-narcissist by finding other narcissistic symbiotic relationships outside of this primary relationship. The IN may, for instance, have a narcissistic friend or lover, to whom she pays extraordinary attention, ignoring the real needs of the non-narcissistic partner.

Consequently, the only semi-stable primary relationship between the IN and the non-narcissist occurs where the non-narcissist is very easy going, emotionally secure and not needing much from the IN at all by way of time, energy or commitment to activities requiring the involvement of both parties. In a relationship with this kind of non-narcissist, the IN may become a workaholic or very involved in outside activities that exclude the non-narcissist spouse.

It appears that the inverted narcissist in a relationship with a non-narcissist is behaviourally indistinguishable from a true narcissist. The only important exception is that the IN does not rage at his non-narcissist partner - she instead withdraws from the relationship even further. This passive-aggressive reaction has been noted, though, with narcissists as well.

INVERTED AND OTHER ATYPICAL / PARTIAL (NOS) NARCISSISTS

Inverted Narcissists Talk about Themselves

Competition and (Pathological) Envy

"I have a dynamic that comes up with every single person I get close to, where I feel extremely competitive toward and envious of the other person. But I don't ACT competitive, because at the very outset, I see myself as the loser in the competition.

I would never dream of trying to beat the other person, because I know deep in my heart that they would win and I would be utterly humiliated. There are fewer things on earth that feel worse to me than losing a contest and having the other person gloat over me, especially if they know how much I cared about not losing. This is one thing that I actually feel violent about. I guess I tend to project the grandiosity part of the NPD package onto the other person rather than on a False Ego of my own.

So most of the time I'm stuck in a state of deep resentment and envy toward her. To me, she's always far more intelligent, likable, popular, talented, self-confident, emotionally developed, morally good, and attractive than I am. And I really hate her for that, and feel humiliated by it. So it's incredibly hard for me to feel happy for this person when she has a success, because I'm overcome with humiliation about myself.

This has ruined many a close relationship. I tend to get this way about one person at a time, usually the person who is playing the role of 'my better half', best friends or lovers/partners. So it's not like I'm unable to be happy for anyone, ever, or that I envy every person I meet. I don't get obsessed with how rich or beautiful movie stars are or anything like that. It only gets projected onto this partner-person, the person I'm depending on the most in terms of supplies (attention, reassurance, security, building up my self-esteem, etc.)...

...The really destructive thing that happens is, I see her grandiose traits as giving her the power to have anything and anyone she wants. So I feel a basic insecurity, because why should she stay with a loser like me, when she's obviously so out of my league? So really, what I'm envious of is the power that all that talent, social ability, beauty, etc., gives her to have CHOICES - the choice to stay or leave me. Whereas I am utterly dependent on her. It's this emotional inequality that I find so humiliating."

"I agree with the inverted narcissist designation - sometimes I've called myself a 'closet narcissist'. That is, I've internalised the value system of grandiosity, but have not applied the grandiose identity to myself.

I believe I SHOULD BE those grandiose things, but at the same time, I know I'm not and I'm miserable about it. So people don't think of me as having an inflated Ego - and indeed I don't - but scratch the surface, and you'll find all these inflated expectations. I mean to say that perhaps the parents suppressed every manifestation of grandiosity (very common in early childhood) and of narcissism - so that the defence mechanism that narcissism is was 'inverted' and internalised in this unusual form."

"Maybe there aren't two discrete states (NPD vs. 'regular' low self-esteem) - maybe it's more of a continuum. And maybe it's just the degree and depth of the problem that distinguishes one from the other.

My therapist describes NPD as 'the inability to love oneself'. As she defines it, the 'narcissistic wound' is a deep wounding of the sense of self, the image of oneself. That doesn't mean that other disorders - or for that matter, other life stressors - can't also cause low self-esteem. But I think NPD IS low self-esteem...

That's what the disorder is really about - an image of yourself that is profoundly negative, and the inability to attain a normal and healthy self-image..."

"Yes, I'm a survivor of child abuse. But remember that not all abuse is alike. There are different kinds of abuse, and different effects. My XXX's style of abuse had to do with trying to annihilate me as a separate person. It also had to do with the need to put all his negative self-image onto me - to see in me what he hated in himself. So I got to play the role of the loser that he secretly feared he was. I was flipped back and forth in those roles - sometimes I'd be a Source of NS for him, and other times I was the receptacle of all his pain and rage. Sometimes my successes were used to reflect back on him, to show off to the rest of the family. Other times, my successes were threatening to my father, who suddenly feared that I was superior to him and had to be squelched.

277

I experience emotions that most people I know don't feel. Or maybe they do feel them, but to far less extreme intensity. For example, the envy and comparison/competition I feel toward others. I guess most of us have experienced rivalry, jealousy, being compared to others. Most of us have felt envy at another's success. Yet most people I know seem able to overcome those feelings to some extent, to be able to function normally. In a competition, for example, they may be driven to do their best so they can win. For me, the fear of losing and being humiliated is so intense that I avoid competition completely. I am terrified of showing people that I care about doing well, because it's so shaming for me if I lose. So I underachieve and pretend I don't care.

Most people I know may envy another person's good luck or success, but it doesn't prevent them from also being happy for them and supporting them. But for me, when I'm in a competitive dynamic with someone, I can't hear about any of their suc-

cesses, or compliments they've received, etc. I don't even like to see the person doing good things, like bringing Thanksgiving leftovers to the sick old guy next door, because those things make me feel inferior for not thinking of doing that myself (and not having anyone in my life that I'd do that for). It's just so incredibly painful for me to see evidence of the other person's good qualities, because it immediately brings up my feeling of inferiority. I can't even stand to date someone, who looks really good, because I'm jealous of their good looks! So this deep and obsessive envy has destroyed my joy in other people. All the things about other people that I love and take pleasure in is a double-edged sword because I also hate them for it, for having those good qualities (while, presumably, I don't).

I don't know - do you think this is garden-variety low self-esteem? I know plenty of people who suffer from lack of confidence, from timidity, social awkwardness, hatred of their body, feeling unlovable, etc. But they don't have this kind of hostile, corrosive resentment of another person for being all the wonderful things that they can't be, or aren't allowed to be, etc. And one thing I hate is when people are judgemental of me about how I feel, as though I can help it. It's like, 'You shouldn't be so selfish, you should feel happy for her that she's successful', etc. They don't understand that I would love to feel those things, but I can't. I can't stop the incredible pain that explodes in me when these feelings get triggered, and I often can't even HIDE the feelings. It's just so overwhelming. I feel so damaged sometimes. There's more, but that's the crux of it for me, anyway."

Getting Compliments

"I love getting compliments and rewards, and do not react negatively to them. In some moods, when my self-hate has gotten triggered, I can sometimes get to places where I'm inconsolable, because I get stuck in bitterness and self-pity, and so I doubt the sincerity or the reliability of the good thing that someone is saying to me (to try to cheer me up or whatever). But, if I'm in a reasonable mood and someone offers me something good, I'm all too happy to accept it! I don't have a stake in staying miserable."

The Partiality of the Condition

"I do agree that it's (atypical or inverted narcissism) not MILDER. But how I see it is that it's PARTIAL. The part that's there is just as destructive as it is in the typical narcissist. But there are parts missing from that total, full-blown disorder -

and I see that as healthy, actually. I see it as parts of myself that WEREN'T infected by the pathology, that are still intact.

In my case, I did not develop the overweening Ego part of the disorder. So in a sense, what you have with me is the naked pathology, with no covering: no suaveness, no charm, no charisma, no confidence, no persuasiveness, but also no excuses, no lies, no justifications for my feelings. Just the ugly self-hate, for all to see. And the self-hate part is just as bad as it is with a full-blown narcissist, so again, it's not milder.

But because I don't have the denial part of the disorder, I have a lot more insight, a lot more motivation to do something about my problems (i.e., I 'self-refer' to therapy), and therefore, I think, a lot more hope of getting better than people whose defence involves totally denying they even have a problem."

"When my full-blown XXX's pathological envy would get triggered, he would respond by putting down the person he was envious of - or by putting down the accomplishment itself, or whatever good stuff the other person had. He'd trivialise it, or outright contradict it, or find some way to convince the other person (often me) that the thing they're feeling good about isn't real, or isn't worthwhile, or is somehow bad, etc. He could do this because the inflated ego defence was fully formed and operating with him.

When MY pathological envy gets triggered, I will be bluntly honest about it. I'll say something self-pitying, such as: 'You always get the good stuff, and I get nothing'; 'You're so much better than I'; 'People like you better - you have good social skills and I'm a jerk'; and so on. Or I might even get hostile and sarcastic: 'Well, it must be nice to have so many people worshipping you, isn't it?' I don't try to convince myself that the other person's success isn't real or worthwhile, etc. Instead, I'm totally flooded with the pain of feeling utterly inferior and worthless - and there's no way for me to convince myself or anyone else otherwise.

I'm not saying that the things I say are pleasant to hear - and it is still manipulative of me to say them, because the other person's attention is drawn away from their joy and onto my pain and hostility. And instead of doubting their success's worth or reality, they feel guilty about it, or about talking about it, because it hurts me so much. So from the other person's point of view, maybe it's not any easier to live with a partial narcissist than with a full-blown, in that their joys and successes lead to pain in both cases. It's certainly not easier for me, being flooded with rage and pain instead of being able to hide behind a delusion of grandeur. But from my therapist's point of view, I'm much better off because I know I'm unhappy - it's in my face all the time. So I'm motivated to work on it and change it. And time has borne her words out.

Over the past several years that I've worked on this issue, I have changed a great deal in how I deal with it. Now when the envy gets triggered, I don't feel so entwined with the other person - I recognise that it's my OWN pain getting triggered, not something they are doing to me. And so I can acknowledge the pain in a more responsible way, taking ownership of it by saying, 'The jealousy feelings are getting triggered again, and I'm feeling worthless and inferior. Can you reassure me that I'm not?' That's a lot better than making some snide, hostile, or self-pitying comment that puts the other person on the defensive or makes them feel guilty... I do prefer the term 'partial' because that's what it feels like to me. It's like a building that's partially built - the house of narcissism. For me, the structure is there, but not the outside, so you can see inside the skeleton to all the junk that's inside. It's the same junk that's inside a full-blown narcissist, but their building is completed, so you can't see inside. Their building is a fortress, and it's almost impossible to bring it down. My defences aren't as strong ... which makes my life more difficult in some ways because I REALLY feel my pain. But it also means that the house can be brought down more easily, and the junk inside cleaned out..."

Thinking about the Past and the World

"I don't usually get rageful about the past. I feel sort of emotionally cut-off from the past, actually. I remember events very clearly, but usually can't remember the feelings. When I do remember the feelings, my reaction is usually one of sadness, and sometimes of relief that I can get back in touch with my past. But not rage. All my rage seems to get displaced on the current people in my life."

"...When I see someone being really socially awkward and geeky, passive-aggressive, indirect and victim-like, it does trigger anger in me because I identify with that person and I don't want to. I try to put my negative feelings onto them, to see that person as the jerk, not me - that's what a narcissist does, after all. But for me it doesn't completely work because I know, consciously, what I'm trying to do. And ultimately, I'm not kidding anyone, least of all myself."

Self-Pity and Depression

"More self-pity and depression here - not so much rage. One of the things that triggers my rage more than anything else is the inability to control another person, the inability to dominate them and force my reality on them. I feel impotent, humiliated, forced back on my empty self. Part of what I'm feeling here is envy: that person who can't be controlled clearly has a self and I don't, and I just hate them for it. But it's also a power struggle - I want to get Narcissistic Supply by being in control and on top and having the other person submissive and compliant..."

Regretting, Admitting Mistakes

"I regret my behaviour horribly, and I DO admit my feelings. I am also able, in the aftermath, to have empathy for the feelings of the person I've hurt, and I'm horribly sad about it, and ashamed of myself. It's as though I'd been possessed by a demon, acted out all this abusive horrible stuff, and then, after the departure of the demon, I'm back in my right mind and it's like, 'What have I DONE???' I don't mean I'm not responsible for what I did (i.e., a demon made me do it). But when I'm triggered, I have no empathy - I can only see my projection onto that person, as a huge threat to me, someone who must be demolished. But when my head clears, I see that person's pain, hurt, fear - and I feel terrible. I want to make it up to them. And that feeling is totally sincere - it's not an act. I'm genuinely sorry for the pain I've caused the other person."

Rage

"I wouldn't say that my rage comes from repressed self-contempt (mine is not repressed - I'm totally aware of it). And it's not missing atonement either, since I do atone. The rage comes from feeling humiliated, from feeling that the other person has somehow sadistically and gleefully made me feel inferior, that they're getting off on being superior, that they're mocking me and ridiculing me, that they have scorn and contempt for me and find it all very amusing. That - whether real or imagined (usually imagined) - is what causes my rage."

Pursuing Relationships with Narcissists

"There are some very few of us who actually seek out relationships with narcissists. We do this with the full knowledge that we are not wanted, despised even. We persist and pursue no matter the consequences, no matter the cost.

I am an 'inverted narcissist'. It is because as a child I was 'imprinted/fixated' with a particular pattern involving relationships. I was engulfed so completely by my father's personality and repressed so severely by various other factors in my childhood that I simply didn't develop a recognisable personality. I existed purely as an extension of my father. I was his genius Wunderkind. He ignored my mother and poured all his energy and effort into me. I did not develop full-blown secondary narcissism... I developed into the perfect 'other half' of the narcissists moulding me. I became the perfect, eager co-dependent. And this is an imprint, a pattern in my psyche, a way of (not) relating to the world of relationships by only being able to truly relate to one person (my father) and then one kind of person - the narcissist.

He is my perfect lover, my perfect mate, a fit that is so slick and smooth, so comfortable and effortless, so filled with meaning and actual feelings - that's the other thing. I cannot feel on my own. I am incomplete. I can only feel when I am engulfed by another (first it was my father) and now - well now it has to be a narcissist. Not just any narcissist either. He must be exceedingly smart, good looking, have adequate reproductive equipment and some knowledge on how to use it and that's about it.

When I am engulfed by someone like this I feel completed, I can actually FEEL. I am whole again. I function as a sibyl, an oracle, an extension of the narcissist. His fiercest protector, his purveyor/procurer of NS, the secretary, organiser, manager, etc. I think you get the picture and this gives me INTENSE PLEASURE.

So the answer to your question: 'Why would anyone want to be with someone who doesn't want them back?' The short answer is, 'Because there is no one else remotely worth looking at.'"

Making Amends

"I mostly apologise, and I give the person space to talk about what hurt them so that (1) they get to express their anger or hurt to me, and (2) I can understand better and know better how not to hurt them (if I can avoid it) the next time there's a conflict. Sometimes the hurt I cause is unintentional - maybe I've been insensitive or forgetful or something, in which case I feel more certain that I can avoid repeating the hurtful behaviour, since I didn't want to hurt them in the first place. If the hurt I caused has to do with my getting my trigger pulled and going into a rage, then that hurt was quite deliberate, although at the time I was unable to experience the other person as vulnerable

or capable of being hurt by me. And I do realise that if that trig-
ger is pulled again, it might happen again. But I also hope that
there'll be a LITTLE TINY window where the memory of the con-
versation will come back to me while I'm in my rage, and I'll
remember that the person really IS vulnerable. I hope that by
hearing over and over that the person actually does feel hurt by
what I say while in rages, that I might remember that when I am
triggered and raging. So, mostly I apologise and try to commu-
nicate with the other person. I don't verbally self-flagellate,
because that's manipulative. Not to say I never do that - in fact
I've had a dynamic with people where I verbally put myself down
and try to engage the other person into arguing me out of it.

But if I'm in the middle of apologising to the other person for
hurting them, then I feel like this is their moment, and I don't
want to turn the focus toward getting them to try to make me
feel better. I will talk about myself, but only in an attempt to
communicate, so that we can understand each other better. I
might say, 'I got triggered about such-and-such, and you
seemed so invulnerable that it enraged me', etc. - and the
other person might react with, 'But I was feeling vulnerable, I
just couldn't show it', etc. - and we'll go back and forth like
that. So it's not like I don't think my feelings count, and I do
want the other person to UNDERSTAND my feelings, but I don't
want to put the other person in the role of taking care of my
feelings in that moment, because they have just been hurt by
me and I'm trying to make it up to them, not squeeze more
stuff OUT of them..."

"So when I've been a real jerk to someone, I want them to feel
like it's OK to be pissed off at me, and I want them to know that
I am interested in and focused on how they feel, not just on how
I feel. As for gifts - I used to do that, but eventually I came to
feel that that was manipulative, too, that it muddled things
because then the other person would feel like they couldn't be
angry anymore, since after all, I've just brought them this nice
gift. I also feel that in general, gift-giving is a sweet and tender
thing to do, and I don't want to sully that tenderness by associ-
ating it with the hurt that comes from abusive behaviour."

Why Narcissists?

"I am BUILT this way. I may have overstated it by saying that I
have 'no choice' because, in fact I do.

The choice is - live in an emotionally deadened monochrome
world where I can reasonably interact with normal people OR I

can choose to be with a narcissist in which case my world is Technicolor, emotionally satisfying, alive and wondrous (also can be turbulent and a real roller coaster ride for the unprepared, not to mention incredibly damaging for people who are not inverted narcissists and who fall into relationships with narcissists). As I have walked on both sides of the street, and because I have developed coping mechanisms that protect me really quite well, I can reasonably safely engage in a primary, intimate relationship with a narcissist without getting hurt by it.

The real WHY of it all is that I learned, as a young child, that being 'eaten alive' by a narcissist parent, to the point where your existence is but an extension of his own, was how all relationships ought to work. It is a psychological imprint - my 'love map', it is what feels right to me intrinsically. A pattern of living - I don't know how else to describe it so you and others will understand how very natural and normal this is for me. It is not the torturous existence that most of the survivors of narcissism are recounting on this list.

My experiences with narcissists, to me, ARE NORMAL for me. Comfortable like an old pair of slippers that fit perfectly. I don't expect many people to attempt to do this, to 'make themselves into' this kind of person. I don't think anyone could, if they tried.

It is my need to be engulfed and merged that drives me to these relationships and when I get those needs met I feel more normal, better about myself. I am the outer extension of the narcissist. In many ways I am a vanguard, a public two-way warning system, fiercely defending my narcissist from harm, and fiercely loyal to him, catering to his every need in order to protect his fragile existence. These are the dynamics of my particular version of engulfment. I don't need anyone to take care of me. I need only to be needed in this very particular way, by a narcissist who inevitably possesses the ability to engulf in a way that normal, fully realised adults cannot. It is somewhat paradoxical - I feel freer and more independent with a narcissist than without one. I achieve more in my life when I am in this form of relationship. I try harder, work harder, am more creative, think better of myself, excel in most every aspect of my life."

"...I go ahead and cater to him and pretend that his words don't hurt, and later, I engage in an internal fight with myself for being so damned submissive. It's a constant battle and I can't seem to decide which voice in my head I should listen to... I feel like a fool, yet, I would rather be a fool with him than a *lonely, well-rounded woman without him. I've often said that the only way that we can stay together is because we feed off of each other. I give him everything he needs and he takes it. Seeing him happy and pleased is what gives me pleasure. I feel very successful then."*

Partial NPD

"I do think it's uncommon for girls to develop these patterns, as they are usually trained to be self-effacing. I certainly was! However, I have a lot of the very same underlying patterns that full-blown, obnoxiously egotistical NP's have, but I am not egotistical because I didn't develop the pattern of inflated Ego and grandiosity. All the rest of it is there, though: fragile Ego, lack of a centre or self, super-sensitive to criticism and rejections, pathological, obsessive envy, comparisons and competitive attitudes toward others, a belief that everyone in the world is either superior or inferior to me, and so on.

Sometimes I kind of wish I had developed the inflated Ego of a complete NP, because then I would at least be able to hide from all the pain I feel. But at the same time, I'm glad I didn't, because those people have a much lower chance of recovery - how can they recover if they don't acknowledge anything is wrong? Whereas it's pretty clear to me I have problems, and I've spent my life working on them and trying to change myself and heal."

Narcissist-Non Narcissist
And Narcissist-Inverted Narcissist Couples

"Can a N and a non-N ever maintain a long lasting marriage? It would seem that a non-N would have too much self-esteem to lend himself to a lifetime of catering and pandering to an N's unending need for unearned adoration and glory. I, as a non-N... got tired of these people and their unremitting attempts to drain my psyche within a relatively short period of time and abandoned them as soon as I realised what I was dealing with to preserve my own sanity."

"It depends on the non-narcissist, really. Narcissism is a RIGID, systemic pattern of responses. It is so all-pervasive and all-encompassing that it is a PERSONALITY disorder. If the non-narcissist is co-dependent, for instance, then the narcissist is a perfect match for him and the union will last..."

"You have to pimp for the narcissist, intellectually, and sexually. If your narcissist is somatic, you are much better off lin-

ing up the sex partners than leaving it to him. Intellectual pimping is more varied. You can think of wonderful things and then subtly string out the idea, in the most delicate of packages and watch the narcissist cogitate their way to 'their' brilliant discovery whilst you bask in the glow of their perfection and success... The point of this entire exercise is to assure YOUR supply, which is the narcissist himself, not to punish yourself by giving away a great idea or abase yourself because, of course, YOU are not worthy of having such a great idea on your own - but who knows, it may seem that way to the inverted narcissist. It really depends on how self-aware the inverted is."

"The only rejection you need to fear is the possibility of losing the narcissist and if one is doing everything else right, this is very unlikely to happen! So by 'emotionally independent' I am talking about being self-assured, doing your own thing, having a life, feeling strong and good about yourself, getting emotional sustenance from other people. I mean, let's face it, a drug is a drug is a habit. Habits just are, and what they ARE NOT are the be all and end all of love, commitment and serene symmetrical, balanced emotional perfection that is the ideal of the romanticised 'love-for-a-lifetime' all-American relationship dream."

"(I am) terribly turned on by narcissists. The most exciting moments of my life in every venue have been with narcissists. It is as if living and loving with normal people is a grey thing by comparison, not fuelled by sufficient adrenaline. I feel like a junkie, now, that I no longer permit myself the giddy pleasure of the RUSH I used to know when I was deeply and hopelessly involved with an N. I am like a lotus-eater. And I always felt guilty about this and also sorry that I ever succumbed that first time to my first narcissist lover."

"I am exactly this way and I feel exactly as you do, that the world is a sepia motion picture but when I am intimately involved with a narcissist, it breaks out into three-dimensional Technicolor and I can see and feel in ways that are not available to me otherwise. In my case I developed this (inverted narcissism) as a result of being the favourite of my father who so completely absorbed me into his personality that I was not able to develop a sense of separation. So I am stuck in this personality matrix of needing to be engulfed, adored by and completely taken over by a narcissist in my life. In turn, I worship, defend, regulate and procure Narcissistic Supply for my narcissist. It is like the mould and the moulded."

"In my case, I realise that while I can't stop loving my current narcissist, it isn't necessary for me to avoid as long as I can understand. In my way of looking at it, he is deserving of love, and since I can give him love without it hurting me, then as long as he needs it, he shall have it."

"My personal theory is that dogmatic religious culture is a retarding influence on the growth and maturation of those heavily involved - more and more autonomy (and hence personal responsibility) seems to be blithely sacrificed to the group mind/spirit. It is as though the church members become one personality and that personality is narcissistic and the individual just folds under the weight of that kind of group pressure - particularly if you are a child."

"If I displayed behaviour that made my XXX look good to others, I was insipidly overvalued. When I dared be something other than who she wanted me to be, the sarcastic criticism and total devaluation was unbelievable. So, I learned to be all things to all people. I get a heavenly high from surrendering my power to a narcissist, to catering to them, in having them overvalue and need me, and it is the only time that I truly feel alive..."

"We have very little choice in all of this. We are as vacant and warped as the narcissist. XXX is wont to say, 'I don't HAVE a personality disorder, I AM a personality disorder.' It defines who we are and how we will respond. You will always and ONLY have real feelings when you are with a narcissist. It is your love map, it is the programming within your psyche. Does it need to control your behaviour? Not necessarily. Knowing what you are can at least give you the opportunity to forecast the effect of an action before you take it. So, loveless black and white may be the very healthiest thing for you for the foreseeable future. I tend to think of these episodes with narcissists as being cyclic. You will likely need to cut loose for a while when your child is older.

DO NOT feel ashamed please! Should a physically handicapped person feel ashamed of their handicap? No and neither should we. The trouble with us is that we are fooled into thinking that these relationships are 'guilty pleasures'. They feel so very good for a time but they are more akin to addiction satisfaction rather than being the 'right match' or an 'appropriate relationship'. I am still very conflicted myself about this. I wrote a few months ago that it was like having a caged very dangerous animal inside of me. When I get near narcissists, the animal smells its own kind and it wants out. I very carefully 'micro-manage' my life. This means that I daily do fairly regular reality checks and keep a very tight reign on my self and my behaviours. I am also obsessive-compulsive."

"I feel as though I'm constantly on an emotional roller coaster. I may wake up in a good mood, but if my N partner does or says something, which is hurtful to me, my mood changes immediately. I now feel sad, empty, afraid. All I want to do at this point is anything that will make him say something NICE to me.

Once he does, I'm back on top of the world. This pattern of mood changes, or whatever you may call them, can take place several times a day. Each and every day. I've gotten to the point where I'm not sure that I can trust myself to feel any one way, because I know that I have no control over myself. He has the control. It's scary, yet I've sort of come to depend on him determining how I am going to feel."

"When I was first involved with my cerebral narcissist I was like this but after awhile I just learned to become more emotionally distant (the ups and downs were just too much) and find emotional gratification with other people, mostly girl friends and one of two male friends. I make a point of saying ... that the invert must be or become emotionally and financially independent (if you don't do this he will eat you up and when he has finished with you and you are nothing but a husk, you will be expelled from his life in one big vomit). It is really important for you to start to take responsibility for your own emotional wellness without regard to how he treats you. Remember that the narcissist has the emotional maturity of a two-year old! Don't expect much in the way of emotional depth or support in your relationship - he simply is not capable of anything that sophisticated."

Narcissists, Inverted Narcissists and Schizoids

Question: Some narcissists are not gregarious. They avoid social events and are stay-at-home recluses. Doesn't this behaviour go against the grain of narcissism?

Answer: Schizoids enjoy nothing and seemingly never experience pleasure (they are anhedonic). Even their nearest and dearest often describe them as "automata", "robots", or "machines". But the schizoid is not depressed or dysphoric, merely indifferent. Schizoids are uninterested in social relationships and bored or puzzled by interpersonal interactions. They are incapable of intimacy and have a very limited range of emotions and affect. Rarely does the schizoid express feelings, either negative (anger) or positive (happiness).

289

Schizoids never pursue an opportunity to develop a close relationship. Schizoids are asexual - not interested in sex. Consequently, they appear cold, aloof, bland, stunted, flat, and "zombie"-like. They derive no satisfaction from belonging to a close-knit group: family, church, workplace, neighbourhood, or nation. They rarely marry or have children.

Schizoids are loners. Given the option, they invariably pursue solitary activities or hobbies. Inevitably, they prefer mechanical or abstract tasks and jobs that require such skills. Many computer hackers, crackers, and programmers are schizoids, for instance - as are some mathematicians and theoretical physicists. Schizoids are inflexible in their reactions to changing life circumstances and developments - both adverse and opportune. Faced with stress they may disintegrate, decompensate, and experience brief psychotic episodes or a depressive illness.

Schizoids have few friends or confidants. They trust only first-degree relatives - but, even so, they maintain no close bonds or associations, not even with their immediate family.

Schizoids pretend to be indifferent to praise, criticism, disagreement, and corrective advice (though, deep inside, they are not). They are creatures of habit, frequently succumbing to rigid, predictable, and narrowly restricted routines. From the outside, the schizoid's life looks "rudderless" and adrift.

Like people with Asperger's Syndrome, schizoids fail to respond appropriately to social cues and rarely reciprocate gestures or facial expressions, such as smiles. As the DSM-IV-TR puts it: *"They seem socially inept or superficial and self-absorbed."*

Or, as the Howard H. Goldman (Ed.) in the "Review of General Psychiatry" [4th Edition. London, Prentice Hall International, 1995] puts it:

"The person with Schizoid Personality Disorder sustains a fragile emotional equilibrium by avoiding intimate personal contact and thereby minimising conflict that is poorly tolerated."

Intuitively, a connection between SPD and the Narcissistic Personality Disorder (NPD) seems plausible. After all, narcissists are people who self-sufficiently withdraw from others. They love themselves in lieu of loving others. Lacking empathy, they regard others as mere instruments, objectified "Sources" of Narcissistic Supply.

The inverted narcissist (IN) is a narcissist who "projects" his narcissism onto another narcissist. The mechanism of Projective Identification allows the IN to experience his own narcissism vicariously, through the agency of a classic narcissist. But the IN is no less a narcissist than the classical one. She is no less socially dysfunctional.

A distinction must be made between social interactions and social relationships. The schizoid, the narcissist and the inverted narcissist all interact socially. But they fail to form human and social relationships (bonds). The schizoid is uninterested and the narcissist is both uninterested and incapable due to his lack of empathy and pervasive sense of haughty superiority.

The psychologist H. Deutsch first suggested the construct of "as-if personality" in the context of schizoid patients (in an article, published in 1942 and titled "Some forms of emotional disturbance and their relationship to schizophrenia"). A decade later, Winnicott named the very same idea: the "False-self Personality". The False Self has thus been established as the driving engine of both pathological narcissism and pathological schizoid states.

Both C. R. Cloninger and N. McWilliams (in "Psychoanalytic Diagnosis", 1994) observed the "faintly contemptuous (attitude)

... (and) isolated superiority" of the schizoid - clearly narcissistic traits.

Theodore Millon and Roger Davis summed it up in their seminal tome, "Personality Disorders in Modern Life" (2000):

"Where withdrawal has an arrogant or oppositional quality, fantasy in a schizoidlike person sometimes betrays the presence of a secret grandiose self that longs for respect and recognition while offsetting fears that the person is really an iconoclastic freak. These individuals combine aspects of the compensating narcissist with the autistic isolation of the schizoid, while lacking the asocial and anhedonic qualities of the pure prototype." [p. 328]

Cultural and Social Considerations

The ethno-psychologist George Devereux [Basic Problems of Ethno-Psychiatry, University of Chicago Press, 1980] proposed to divide the unconscious into the Id (the part that is instinctual and unconscious) and the "ethnic unconscious" (repressed material that was once conscious). The latter includes all the defence mechanisms and most of the Superego.

Society dictates what is to be repressed. Mental illness is either idiosyncratic (cultural directives are not followed and the individual is unique, eccentric, and schizophrenic) - or conformist, abiding by the cultural dictates of what is allowed and disallowed.

Our culture, according to Christopher Lasch, teaches us to withdraw inwards when confronted with stressful situations. It is a vicious circle. One of the main stressors of modern society is alienation and a pervasive sense of isolation. The solution our culture offers - to further withdraw - only exacerbates the problem.

Richard Sennett expounded on this theme in "The Fall of Public Man: On the Social Psychology of Capitalism" [Vintage Books, 1978]. One of the chapters in Devereux's aforementioned tome is entitled "Schizophrenia: An Ethnic Psychosis, or Schizophrenia without Tears". To him, the United States is afflicted by what came later to be called a "schizoid disorder".

C. Fred Alford [in Narcissism: Socrates, the Frankfurt School and Psychoanalytic Theory, Yale University Press, 1988] enumerates the symptoms:

"...withdrawal, emotional aloofness, hyporeactivity (emotional flatness), sex without emotional involvement, segmentation and partial involvement (lack of interest and commitment to things outside oneself), fixation on oral-stage issues, regression,

infantilism and depersonalization. These, of course, are many of the same designations that Lasch employs to describe the culture of narcissism. Thus, it appears, that it is not misleading to equate narcissism with schizoid disorder." [p. 19]

Common Psychodynamic Roots

The first to seriously consider the similarity, if not outright identity, between the schizoid and the narcissistic disorders was Melanie Klein. She broke ranks with Freud in that she believed that we are born with a fragile, brittle, weak and unintegrated Ego. The most primordial human fear is the fear of disintegration (death), according to Klein.

Thus, the infant is forced to employ primitive defence mechanisms such as splitting, projection and introjection to cope with this fear (actually, with the aggression generated by the Ego). The Ego splits and projects both its constituent parts: the part that includes death, disintegration, and aggression and the part that is life-related, constructive, and integrative.

As a result of all these mechanics, the infant views the world as either utterly "good" (satisfying, complying, responding, gratifying) or universally "bad" (frustrating). Klein called it the good and the bad "breasts". The child then proceeds to introject (internalize and assimilate) the good object while keeping out (defending against) the bad object. The good object becomes the nucleus of the forming Ego. The bad object is felt as fragmented. But it has not vanished, it is there.

The fact that the bad object is "out there", persecutory and threatening gives rise to the first schizoid defence mechanisms, foremost amongst them the mechanism of Projective Identification (so often employed by narcissists). The infant projects parts of himself (his organs, his behaviours, his traits) unto the bad object. This is the famous Kleinian "paranoid-schizoid position". The Ego is split.

This is as terrifying as it sounds but it allows the baby to make a clear distinction between the "good object" (inside him) and the "bad object" (out there, split from him). If this phase is not transcended the individual develops schizophrenia and a fragmentation of the self.

Around the third or fourth month of life, the infant realizes that the good and the bad objects are really facets of one and the same object. He develops the depressive position. This depression (Klein believes that the two positions continue throughout life) is a reaction of fear and anxiety.

The infant feels guilty (at his own rage) and anxious (lest his aggression harms the object and eliminates the source of good things). He experiences the loss of his own omnipotence since the object is now outside his self. The infant wishes to erase the results of his own aggression by "making the object whole again". By recognizing the wholeness of other objects, the infant comes to realize and to experience his own wholeness. The Ego re-integrates.

But the transition from the paranoid-schizoid position to the depressive one is by no means smooth and assured. Excess anxiety and envy can delay it or prevent it altogether. Envy seeks to destroy all good objects, so that other people don't have them. It, therefore, hinders the split between the good and the bad "breasts". Envy destroys the good object but leaves the persecutory, bad object intact.

Moreover, envy does not allow re-integration ("reparation" in Kleinian jargon) to take place. The more whole the object, the greater the destructive envy. Thus, envy feeds on its own outcomes. The more envy, the less integrated the Ego is, the weaker and more inadequate it is and the more reason for envying the good object and other people.

Both the narcissist and the schizoid are examples of development arrested due to envy and other transformations of aggression.

Consider pathological narcissism.

Envy is the hallmark of narcissism and the prime source of what is known as narcissistic rage. The schizoid self - fragmented, weak, and primitive - is intimately connected with narcissism through envy. Narcissists prefer to destroy themselves and to deny themselves rather than endure someone else's happiness, wholeness and "triumph".

The narcissist fails his exams in order to frustrate the teacher he adores and envies. He aborts his therapy in order not to give the therapist a reason to feel gratified. By self-defeating and self-destructing, narcissists deny the worth of others. If the narcissist fails in therapy - his analyst must be inept. If he destroys himself by consuming drugs - his parents are blameworthy and should feel guilty and bad. One cannot exaggerate the importance of envy as a motivating power in the narcissist's life.

The psychodynamic connection is obvious. Envy is a rage reaction to not controlling or "having" or engulfing the good, desired object. Narcissists defend themselves against this acidulous, corroding sensation by pretending that they do control, possess, subsume, and engulf the good object. These are the narcissist's "grandiose fantasies (of omnipotence or omniscience)".

But, in so doing, the narcissist must deny the existence of any good outside himself. The narcissist defends himself against raging, all consuming envy by solipsistically claiming to be the only good object in the world. This is an object that cannot be had by anyone, except the narcissist and, therefore, is immune to the narcissist's threatening, annihilating envy.

In order to refrain from being "owned" by anyone (and, thus, avoid self-destruction at the hands of his own envy), the narcissist reduces others to "non-entities" (the narcissistic solution), or completely avoids all meaningful contact with them (the schizoid solution).

The suppression of envy is at the core of the narcissist's being. If he fails to convince his self that he is the only good object in the universe, he is bound to be exposed to his own murderous envy. If there are others out there who are better than him, he envies them, he lashes out at them ferociously, uncontrollably, madly, hatefully and spitefully, he tries to eliminate them.

If someone tries to get emotionally intimate with the narcissist, she threatens the grandiose belief that no one but the narcissist can possess the good object (that is the narcissist himself). Only the narcissist can own himself, have access to himself, possess himself. This is the only way to avoid seething envy and certain self-annihilation. Perhaps it is clearer now why narcissists react as raving madmen to anything, however minute, however remote that seems to threaten their grandiose fantasies, the only protective barrier between themselves and their lethal, seething envy.

There is nothing new in trying to link narcissism to schizophrenia. Freud did as much in his "On Narcissism" (1914). Klein's contribution was the introduction of immediately postnatal internal objects. Schizophrenia, she proposed, was a narcissistic and intense relationship with internal objects (such as fantasies or images, including fantasies of grandeur).

Freud suggested a transition from (primary, object-less) narcissism (self-directed libido) to objects relations (objects directed libido). Klein suggested a transition from internal objects to external ones. While Freud thought that the denominator common to narcissism and schizoid phenomena is a withdrawal of libido from the world - Klein suggested it was a fixation on an early phase of relating to internal objects.

But is the difference not merely semantic?

"The term 'narcissism' tends to be employed diagnostically by those proclaiming loyalty to the drive model (Otto Kernberg and Edith Jacobson, for instance - SV) and mixed model theorists (Kohut), who are interested in preserving a tie to drive theory. 'Schizoid' tends to be employed diagnostically by adherents of relational models (Fairbairn, Guntrip), who are interested in articulating their break with drive theory... These two differing diagnoses and accompanying formulations are applied to patients who are essentially similar, by theorists who start with very different conceptual premises and ideological affiliations."

[Greenberg and Mitchell. Object Relations in Psychoanalytic Theory. Harvard University Press, 1983]

Klein, in effect, said that drives (e.g., the libido) are relational flows. A drive is the mode of relationship between an individual and his objects (internal and external). Thus, a retreat from the world (Freud) into internal objects (as postulated by object relations theorists and especially the British school of Fairbairn and Guntrip) - is the drive itself.

Drives are orientations (to external or internal objects). Both narcissism and schizoid phenomena are orientations (preferences, actually) towards internal objects. This is why narcissists feel empty, fragmented, "unreal", and diffuse. It is because their Ego is still split (never integrated) and because they had withdrawn from the world (of external objects).

Kernberg identifies these internal objects with which the narcissist maintains a special relationship with the idealized, grandiose images of the narcissist's parents. He believes that the narcissist's very Ego (self-representation) had fused with these parental images.

Fairbairn's work - even more than Kernberg's, not to mention Kohut's - integrates all these insights into a coherent framework. Guntrip elaborated on it and together they created one of the most impressive theoretical bodies in the history of psychology.

Fairbairn incorporated Klein's insights that drives are object-orientated and their goal is the formation of relationships and not primarily the attainment of pleasure. Pleasurable sensations are the means to achieve relationships. The Ego does not seek to be stimulated and pleased but to find the right, "good", supporting object.

The infant is fused with his Primary Object, the mother. Life is not about using objects for pleasure under the supervision of the Ego and Superego, as Freud suggested. Life is about separating, differentiating, individuating, and achieving independence from the Primary Object and the initial state of fusion with it. Dependence on internal objects is narcissism. Freud's post-narcissistic (anaclitic) phase of life can be either dependent (immature) or mature.

The newborn's Ego is looking for objects with which to form relationships. Inevitably, some of these objects and some of these relationships frustrate the infant and disappoint him. He compensates for these setbacks by creating compensatory internal objects. The initially unitary Ego thus fragments into a growing group of internal objects. Reality breaks our hearts and minds, according to Fairbairn. The Ego and its objects are "twinned" and the Ego is split in three (or four, according to Guntrip, who introduced a fourth Ego). A schizoid state ensues.

The "original" (Freudian or libidinal) Ego is unitary, instinctual, needy and object seeking. It then fragments as a result of the three typical interactions with the mother (gratification, disappointment and deprivation). The central Ego idealizes the "good" parents. It is conformist and obedient. The antilibidinal Ego is a reaction to frustrations. It is rejecting, harsh, unsatisfying, dead set against one's natural needs. The libidinal Ego is the seat of cravings, desires and needs. It is active in that it keeps seeking objects to form relationships with. Guntrip added the regressed Ego, which is the True Self in "cold storage", the "lost heart of the personal self".

Fairbairn's definition of psychopathology is quantitative. How much of the Ego is dedicated to relationships with internal objects rather than with external ones (e.g., real people)? In other words: how fragmented (how schizoid) is the Ego?

To achieve a successful transition from focusing on internal objects to seeking external ones, the child needs to have the right parents (in Winnicott's parlance, the "good enough mother" - not perfect, but "good enough"). The child internalizes the bad aspects of his parents in the form of internal, bad objects and then proceeds to suppress them, together ("twinned") with portions of his Ego.

Thus, his parents become a part of the child (though a repressed part). The more bad objects are repressed, the "less Ego is left" for healthy relationships with external objects. To Fairbairn, the source of all psychological disturbances is in these schizoid phenomena. Later developments (such as the Oedipus Complex) are less crucial.

Fairbairn and Guntrip think that if a person is too attached to his compensatory internal objects, he finds it hard to mature psychologically. Maturing is about letting go of internal objects. Some people just don't want to mature, or are ambivalent about it. This reluctance, this withdrawal to an internal world of representations, internal objects and broken Ego - is narcissism itself. Narcissists simply don't know how to be themselves, how to be and act independent while managing their relationships with other people.

Fred Alford in "Narcissism: Socrates, the Frankfurt School and Psychoanalytic Theory" [Yale University Press, 1988]:

"That narcissism is such a confusing category is in large part because its drive-theoretic definition, the libidinal cathexis of the self - in a word, self-love - seems far removed from the experience of narcissism, as characterized by a loss of, or split-in, the self. Fairbairn's and Guntrip's view of narcissism as an excessive attachment of the Ego to internal objects (roughly analogous to Freud's narcissistic, as opposed to object, love), resulting in various splits in the Ego necessary to maintain these attachments, allows us to penetrate this confusion." [p. 67]

Both Otto Kernberg and Franz Kohut contended that narcissism is somewhere between neurosis and psychosis. Kernberg thought that it was a borderline phenomenon, on the verge of psychosis (where the Ego is completely shattered). In this respect Kernberg, more than Kohut, identifies narcissism with schizoid phenomena and with schizophrenia. This is not the only difference between them.

They also disagree on the developmental locus of narcissism. Kohut thinks that narcissism is an early phase of development, fossilized, and doomed to be repeated (a Repetition Complex) while Kernberg maintains that the narcissistic self is pathological from its very inception.

Kohut believes that the narcissist's parents failed to provide him with assurances that he does possess a self (in his words, they failed to endow him with a self-object). They did not explicitly recognize the child's nascent self, its separate existence, and its boundaries. The child learned to have a schizoid, split, fragmented self, rather than a coherent and integrated one. To Kohut, narcissism is really all-pervasive, at the very core of being (whether in its mature form, as self-love, or in it regressive, infantile form as a narcissistic disorder).

Kernberg regards "mature narcissism" (also espoused by neo-Freudians like Grunberger and Chasseguet-Smirgel) as a contradiction in terms, an oxymoron. He observes that narcissists are already grandiose and schizoid (they are detached, cold, aloof, asocial) at an early age (three years old, according to him!).

Like Klein, Kernberg believes that narcissism is a last ditch effort (defence) to halt the emergence of the paranoid-schizoid position described by Klein. In an adult, such an emergence is known as "psychosis" and this is why Kernberg classifies narcissists as borderline (almost) psychotics.

Even Kohut, who is an opponent of Kernberg's classification, uses Eugene O'Neill's famous sentence (in "The Great God Brown"): "Man is born broken. He lives by mending. The grace of God is glue." Kernberg himself sees a clear connection between schizoid phenomena (such as alienation in modern society and subsequent withdrawal) and narcissistic phenomena (inability to form relationships or to make commitments or to empathize).

Fred Alford wrote in "Narcissism: Socrates, the Frankfurt School and Psychoanalytic Theory" [Yale University Press, 1988]:

"Fairbairn and ... see a schizoid split in the self as characteristic of virtually all-emotional disorder ... Greenberg and Mitchell ... (pointed) out that what American analysts label 'narcissism', British analysts tend to call 'Schizoid Personality Disorder'. This insight allows us to connect the symptomatology of narcissism - feelings of emptiness, unreality, alienation and emotional withdrawal - with a theory that sees such symptoms as an accurate reflection of the experience of being split-off from a part of oneself." [p. 67]

Narcissists, Medications
And Chemical Imbalances

Question: Can pathological narcissism be induced by substance abuse or biochemical imbalances in the brain?

Answer: The narcissist's moods change abruptly in the wake of a narcissistic injury. One can easily manipulate the moods of a narcissist by making a disparaging remark, by disagreeing with him, by criticizing him, or by doubting his grandiosity or fantastic claims.

299   Such REACTIVE mood shifts are not provoked by the fluctuations in the narcissist's body chemistry (for instance, his blood sugar levels), or by the presence or absence of any substance or chemical in his brain. It is possible to reduce the narcissist to a state of rage and depression AT ANY MOMENT, simply by employing the above "techniques". He can be elated, even manic - and in a split second, following a narcissistic injury, depressed, sulking or raging.

The opposite is also true. The narcissist can be catapulted from the bleakest despair to utter euphoric mania (or at least to an increased and marked feeling of well-being) by being provided with the flimsiest Narcissistic Supply (attention).

These swings are totally correlated to external events (narcissistic injury or Narcissistic Supply) and not to cycles of hormones, enzymes, neurotransmitters, sugar, or other substances in the body. It is conceivable, though, that a third, unrelated problem causes chemical imbalances in the brain, metabolic diseases such as diabetes, pathological narcissism, and other mental health syndromes. There may be a common cause, a hidden common denominator (perhaps a group of genes).

Certain medical conditions can activate the narcissistic defence mechanism. Chronic ailments are likely to lead to the emergence of narcissistic traits or a narcissistic personality style. Traumas (such as brain injuries) have been known to induce states of mind akin to full-blown personality disorders.

Phineas Gage was a 25 years old construction foreman who lived in Vermont in the 1860s. While working on a railroad bed, he packed powdered explosives into a hole in the ground, using tamping iron. The powder heated and blew in his face. The tamping iron rebounded and pierced the top of his skull, ravaging the frontal lobes.

In 1868, Harlow, his doctor, reported the changes to his personality following the accident:

"He became fitful, irreverent, indulging at times in the grossest profanity (which was not previously his customs), manifesting but little deference to his fellows, impatient of restraint or advice when it conflicts with his desires, at times pertinaciously obstinate yet capricious and vacillating, devising many plans for future operation which are no sooner arranged than they are abandoned in turn for others appearing more feasible... His mind was radically changed, so that his friends and acquaintances said he was no longer Gage."

In other words, his brain injury turned him into a psychopathic narcissist.

Similarly startling transformations have been recorded among soldiers with penetrating head injuries suffered in World War I. Orbitomedial wounds made people "pseudopsychopathic": grandiose, euphoric, disinhibited, and puerile. When the dorsolateral convexities were damaged, those affected became lethargic and apathetic ("pseudodepressed"). As Geschwind noted, many had both syndromes.

Such "narcissism", though, is reversible and tends to be ameliorated or disappear altogether when the underlying medical problem does.

The DSM is clear: the brain-injured may acquire traits and behaviours typical of certain personality disorders but head trauma never results in a full-fledged personality disorder.

From the general diagnostic criteria for a personality disorder:

"The enduring pattern is not due to the direct physiological effects of a substance (e.g., a drug of abuse, a medication) or a general medical condition (e.g., head trauma)." [DSM-IV-TR, p. 689]

Other disorders, like the Bipolar Disorder (mania-depression) are characterized by mood swings that are not brought about by external events (endogenous, not exogenous). But the narcissist's mood swings are strictly the results of external events (as he perceives and interprets them, of course).

Narcissists are absolutely insulated from their emotions. They are emotionally flat or numb.

The narcissist does not have pendular (cyclical) mood swings on a regular, almost predictable basis, from depression to euphoria (mania), as is the case in biochemically induced mental disorders.

Additionally, the narcissist goes through mega-cycles which last months or even years. These cannot, of course, be attributed to blood sugar levels or to Dopamine and Serotonin secretions in the brain.

The Narcissistic Personality Disorder (NPD) per se is not treated with medication.

But phenomena, which are often associated with NPD, such as depression or OCD (Obsessive-Compulsive Disorder), are treated with medication. Rumour has it that SSRI's (such as Fluoxetine, known as Prozac) might have adverse effects if the primary disorder is NPD. They sometimes lead to the Serotonin Syndrome, which includes agitation and exacerbates the rage attacks typical of a narcissist. The use of SSRI's is associated at times with delirium and the emergence of a manic phase and even with psychotic microepisodes.

This is not the case with the heterocyclics, MAO and mood stabilizers, such as lithium. Blockers and inhibitors are regularly applied without discernible adverse side effects (as far as NPD is concerned).

To summarise:

Not enough is known about the biochemistry of NPD. There seems to be some vague link to Serotonin but no one knows for sure. There isn't a reliable non-intrusive method to measure brain and central nervous system Serotonin levels anyhow, so it is mostly guesswork at this stage.

Thus, as of now, the typical and recommended treatment for pathological narcissism and the co-morbid depression and OCD is talk therapy of one kind (psychodynamic) or another (cognitive-behavioural).

Antidepressants can be used moderately (with SSRI being currently under critical scrutiny).

Myths about Narcissism

Question: Is there such a thing as a "typical narcissist"? Is narcissism a "pure" mental disorder or a "cocktail" of psychological problems? Is there a typical way in which narcissists react to life crises? Is it true that they are prone to suicide?

Answer: There is no such thing as a typical narcissist. One must always specify whether one is referring to a cerebral narcissist or to a somatic one, a classical narcissist or an inverted one.

The cerebral narcissist uses his intelligence, intellect, and knowledge to obtain Narcissistic Supply. The somatic narcissist uses his body, his looks and his sexuality towards the same end. Inevitably, each type is likely to react very differently to life and its changing circumstances.

Somatic narcissists are a variation on the HPD (Histrionic Personality Disorder). They are seductive, provocative and obsessive-compulsive when it comes to their bodies, their sexual activities and their health (they are likely to be hypochondriacs as well).

Still, certain behavioural and character traits are common to all narcissists.

Pathological lying seems to be such a trait. Even the Diagnostic and Statistical Manual (DSM) defines the Narcissistic Personality Disorder (NPD) with words such as "fantasy", "grandiose" and "exploit", which imply the usage of half-truths, inaccuracies and lies on a regular basis. Kernberg, Winnicott, and others coined the term False Self not in vain.

Narcissists are not gregarious. Actually, many narcissists are schizoid (recluses) and paranoid [for more on this, see FAQ 51].

Naturally, narcissists love to have an audience - but only because and as long as it provides them with Narcissistic Supply. Otherwise, they are not interested in people. All narcissists lack empathy which makes others much less fascinating than they appear to be to empathic people.

Narcissists are terrified of introspection. I am not referring to intellectualization or rationalization or the straightforward application of their intelligence to themselves: these do not constitute introspection. Proper introspection must include an emotional element, an insight and the ability to emotionally integrate the insight so that it affects behaviour.

Some people are narcissists and they know it (cognitively). They even think about it from time to time. But this does not amount to useful introspection. Narcissists do some real introspection and even attend therapy following a life crisis, though.

So, while there are no "typical" narcissists, there are traits and behaviour patterns typical to all narcissists.

The second "myth" is that pathological narcissism is a pure phenomenon that can be dealt with experimentally. This is not the case. Actually, due to the fuzziness of the whole field, diagnosticians are both forced and encouraged to render multiple diagnoses ("co-morbidity"). NPD usually appears in tandem with some other Cluster B personality disorders (such as the Antisocial, Histrionic, and, most often, the Borderline Personality Disorder).

Regarding the third myth (that narcissists are prone to suicide, especially in the wake of a life crisis involving a grave narcissistic injury):

Narcissists very rarely commit suicide. They may well react with suicidal ideation and reactive psychosis to severe stress, but to commit suicide runs against the grain of narcissism. Suicide and self-mutilation are Borderline Personality Disorder (BPD) behaviours. The differential diagnosis of NPD (as distinct from BPD) rests on the absence of attempted suicide and self-mutilation in NPD.

In response to a life crisis (divorce, public disgrace, imprisonment, accident, bankruptcy, terminal or disfiguring illness) the narcissist is likely to adopt either of two reactions:

1. The narcissist may finally refer himself to therapy, realizing that something is dangerously wrong with him. Statistics show that talk therapies are rather ineffective with narcissism. Soon enough, the therapist is bored, fed up or actively repelled by the grandiose fantasies and open contempt of the narcissist. The therapeutic alliance crumbles and the narcissist emerges "triumphant" having sucked the therapist's energy dry.

2. The narcissist frantically gropes for alternative Sources of Narcissistic Supply. Narcissists are very creative. If all else fails, they exhibitionistically make use of their own misery. Or they lie, create a fantasy, confabulate, harp on people's emotions, fake a medical condition, pull a stunt, fall in ideal love, make a provocative move or commit a crime... The narcissist is bound to come up with a surprising angle to extract his Narcissistic Supply from a begrudging and mean world.

Experience shows that most narcissists go through (1) and then through (2).

The exposure of the False Self for what it is - false - is a major narcissistic injury. The narcissist is likely to react with severe self-deprecation and self-flagellation even to the point of suicidal ideation. This - on the inside.

On the outside, he is likely to appear assertive and confident. This is his way of channelling his life-threatening aggression. Rather than endure its assault and its frightening outcomes, he redirects his aggression, transforms it and hurls it at others.

What form this conversion assumes is nigh impossible to predict without knowing the narcissist in question intimately. It could be anything from cynical humour, through brutal honesty, verbal abuse, passive-aggressive behaviours (frustrating others) and down to actual physical violence.

Narcissism and Evil

In his bestselling "People of the Lie", Scott Peck claims that narcissists are evil. Are they?

The concept of "evil" in this age of moral relativism is slippery and ambiguous. The "Oxford Companion to Philosophy" [Oxford University Press, 1995] defines it thus:

"The suffering which results from morally wrong human choices."

To qualify as evil a person (Moral Agent) must meet these requirements:

a. That he can and does consciously choose between the (morally) right and wrong and constantly and consistently prefers the latter;

b. That he acts on his choice irrespective of the consequences to himself and to others.

Clearly, evil must be premeditated. Francis Hutcheson and Joseph Butler argued that evil is a by-product of the pursuit of one's interest or cause at the expense of other people's interests or causes. But this ignores the critical element of conscious choice among equally efficacious alternatives. Moreover, people often pursue evil even when it jeopardizes their well-being and obstructs their interests. Sadomasochists even relish this orgy of mutual assured destruction.

Narcissists satisfy both conditions only partly. Their evil is utilitarian. They are evil only when being malevolent secures a certain outcome. Sometimes, they consciously choose the morally wrong - but not invariably so. They act on their choice even if it inflicts misery and pain on others. But they never opt for evil if they are to bear the consequences. They act maliciously because it is expedient to do so, not because it is "in their nature".

The narcissist is able to tell right from wrong and to distinguish between good and evil. In the pursuit of his interests and causes, he sometimes chooses to act wickedly. Lacking empathy, the narcissist is rarely remorseful. Because he feels entitled, exploiting others is second nature. The narcissist abuses others absent-mindedly, offhandedly, as a matter of fact.

The narcissist objectifies people and treats them as expendable commodities to be discarded after use. Admittedly, that, in itself, is evil. Yet, it is the mechanical, thoughtless, heartless face of narcissistic abuse - devoid of human passions and of familiar emotions - that renders it so alien, so frightful and so repellent.

We are often shocked less by the actions of narcissist than by the way he acts. In the absence of a vocabulary rich enough to capture the subtle hues and gradations of the spectrum of narcissistic depravity, we default to habitual adjectives such as "good" and "evil". Such intellectual laziness does this pernicious phenomenon and its victims little justice.

Why are We Fascinated by Evil and Evildoers?

The common explanation is that one is fascinated with evil and evildoers because, through them, one vicariously expresses the repressed, dark, and evil parts of one's own personality. Evildoers, according to this theory, represent the "shadow" nether lands of our selves and, thus, they constitute our antisocial alter egos. Being drawn to wickedness is an act of rebellion against social strictures and the crippling bondage that is modern life. It is a mock synthesis of our Dr. Jekyll with our Mr. Hyde. It is a cathartic exorcism of our inner demons.

Yet, even a cursory examination of this account reveals its flaws.

Far from being taken as a familiar, though suppressed, element of our psyche, evil is mysterious. Though preponderant, villains are often labelled "monsters" - abnormal, even super-natural aberrations. It took Hanna Arendt two thickset tomes to remind us that evil is banal and bureaucratic, not fiendish and omnipotent.

In our minds, evil and magic are intertwined. Sinners seem to be in contact with some alternative reality where the laws of Man are suspended. Sadism, however deplorable, is also admirable because it is the reserve of Nietzsche's Supermen, an indicator of personal strength and resilience. A heart of stone lasts longer than its carnal counterpart.

Throughout human history, ferocity, mercilessness, and lack of empathy were extolled as virtues and enshrined in social insti-tutions such as the army and the courts. The doctrine of Social Darwinism and the advent of moral relativism and deconstruc-tion did away with ethical absolutism. The thick line between right and wrong thinned and blurred and, sometimes, vanished.

Evil nowadays is merely another form of entertainment, a species of pornography, a sanguineous art. Evildoers enliven our gossip, colour our drab routines and extract us from dreary exis-tence and its depressive correlates. It is a little like collective self-injury. Self-mutilators report that parting their flesh with razor blades makes them feel alive and reawakened. In this syn-thetic universe of ours, evil and gore permit us to get in touch with real, raw, painful life.

The higher our desensitized threshold of arousal, the more profound the evil that fascinates us. Like the stimuli-addicts that we are, we increase the dosage and consume added tales of malevolence and sinfulness and immorality. Thus, in the role of spectators, we safely maintain our sense of moral supremacy and self-righteousness even as we wallow in the minutest details of the vilest crimes.

The Selfish Gene

The Genetic Underpinnings of Narcissism

Question: Is pathological narcissism the outcome of inherited traits - or the sad result of abusive and traumatizing upbringing? Or, maybe it is the confluence of both? It is a common occurrence, after all, that, in the same family, with the same set of parents and an identical emotional environment - some siblings grow to be malignant narcissists, while others are perfectly "normal". Surely, this indicates a predisposition of some people to developing narcissism, a part of one's genetic heritage.

307

Answer: To identify the role of heredity, researchers have resorted to a few tactics: they studied the occurrence of similar psychopathologies in identical twins separated at birth, in twins and siblings who grew up in the same environment, and in relatives of patients (usually across a few generations of an extended family).

Tellingly, twins - both those raised apart and together - show the same correlation of personality traits, 0.5 [Bouchard, Lykken, McGue, Segal, and Tellegan, 1990]. Even attitudes, values, and interests have been shown to be highly affected by genetic factors [Waller, Kojetin, Bouchard, Lykken, et al., 1990].

A review of the literature demonstrates that the genetic component in certain personality disorders (mainly the Antisocial and Schizotypal) is strong [Thapar and McGuffin, 1993]. Nigg and Goldsmith found a connection in 1993 between the Schizoid and Paranoid personality disorders and schizophrenia.

The three authors of the Dimensional Assessment of Personality Pathology (Livesley, Jackson, and Schroeder) joined forces with Jang in 1993 to study whether 18 of the personality dimensions were heritable. They found that 40 to 60% of the recurrence of certain personality traits across generations can be explained by heredity: anxiousness, callousness, cognitive distortion, compulsivity, identity problems, oppositionality, rejection, restricted expression, social avoidance, stimulus seeking, and suspiciousness. Each and every one of these qualities is associated with a personality disorder. In a roundabout way, therefore, this study supports the hypothesis that personality disorders are hereditary.

This would go a long way towards explaining why in the same family, with the same set of parents and an identical emotional environment, some siblings grow to have personality disorders, while others are perfectly "normal". Surely, this indicates a genetic predisposition of some people to developing personality disorders.

Still, this oft-touted distinction between nature and nurture may be merely a question of semantics.

When we are born, we are not much more than the sum of our genes and their manifestations. Our brain - a physical object - is the residence of mental health and its disorders. Mental illness cannot be explained without resorting to the body and, especially, to the brain. And our brain cannot be contemplated without considering our genes. Thus, any explanation of our mental life that leaves out our hereditary makeup and our neurophysiology is lacking. Such lacking theories are nothing but literary narratives. Psychoanalysis, for instance, is often accused of being divorced from corporeal reality.

Our genetic baggage makes us resemble a personal computer. We are an all-purpose, universal, machine. Subject to the right programming (conditioning, socialization, education, upbringing), we can turn out to be anything and everything. A computer can imitate any other kind of discrete machine, given the right software. It can play music, screen movies, calculate, print, paint. Compare this to a television set: it is constructed and expected to do one, and only one, thing. It has a single purpose and a unitary function. We, humans, are more like computers than like television sets.

True, single genes rarely account for any behaviour or trait. An array of coordinated genes is required to explain even the minutest human phenomenon. "Discoveries" of a "gambling gene" here and an "aggression gene" there are derided by the more serious and less publicity-prone scholars. Yet, it would seem that even complex behaviours such as risk taking, reckless driving, and compulsive shopping have genetic underpinnings.

What about the Narcissistic Personality Disorder?

It would seem reasonable to assume - though, at this stage, there is not a shred of proof - that the narcissist is born with a propensity to develop narcissistic defences. These are triggered by abuse or trauma during the formative years in infancy or during early adolescence [see FAQ: Narcissist's Mother].

By "abuse" I am referring to a spectrum of behaviours which objectify the child and treat it as an extension of the caregiver (parent) or as an instrument. Dotting and smothering are as abusive as beating and starving. And abuse can be dished out by peers as well as by adult role models.

Still, the development of the Narcissistic Personality Disorder (NPD) is attributed mostly to nurture. The Narcissistic Personality Disorder is an extremely complex battery of phenomena: behaviour patterns, cognitions, emotions, conditioning, and so on. NPD is a PERSONALITY disorder and even the most ardent proponents of the school of genetics do not attribute the development of the whole personality to genes.

From my article "The Interrupted Self"

[http://samvak.tripod.com/sacks.html]:

"'Organic' and 'mental' disorders (a dubious distinction at best) have many characteristics in common (confabulation, antisocial behaviour, emotional absence or flatness, indifference, psychotic episodes and so on)."

From an essay I wrote "On Dis-ease"

[http://samvak.tripod.com/disease.html]:

"Moreover, the distinction between the psychic and the physical is hotly disputed, philosophically. The psychophysical problem is as intractable today as it ever was (if not more so). It is beyond doubt that the physical affects the mental and the other way around. This is what disciplines like psychiatry are all about. The ability to control 'autonomous' bodily functions (such as heartbeat) and mental reactions to pathogens of the brain are proof of the artificialness of this distinction. It is a result of the reductionist view of nature as divisible and summable...

The distinction between the patient and the outside world is superfluous and wrong. The patient AND his environment are ONE and the same. Disease is a perturbation in the operation and management of the complex ecosystem known as patient-world. Humans absorb their environment and feed it in equal measures. This on-going interaction IS the patient. We cannot exist without the intake of water, air, visual stimuli and food. Our environment is defined by our actions and output, physical and mental.

Thus, one must question the classical differentiation between 'internal' and 'external'. Some illnesses are considered 'endogenic' (generated from the inside). Natural, 'internal', causes - a heart defect, a biochemical imbalance, a genetic mutation, a metabolic process gone awry - cause disease. Aging and deformities also belong in this category.

In contrast, problems of nurturance and environment - early childhood abuse, for instance, or malnutrition - are 'external' and so are the 'classical' pathogens (germs and viruses) and accidents.

But this, again, is a counter-productive approach. Exogenic and Endogenic pathogenesis is inseparable. Mental states increase or decrease the susceptibility to externally induced disease. Talk therapy or abuse (external events) alter the biochemical balance of the brain (an internal event).

The inside constantly interacts with the outside and is so intertwined with it that all distinctions between them are artificial and misleading. The best example is, of course, medication: it is an external agent, it influences internal processes and it has a very strong mental correlate (its efficacy is influenced by mental factors as in the placebo effect).

The very nature of dysfunction and sickness is highly culture-dependent.

Societal parameters dictate right and wrong in health (especially mental health). It is all a matter of statistics. Certain diseases are accepted in certain parts of the world as a fact of life or even a sign of distinction (e.g., the paranoid schizophrenic as chosen by the gods). If there is no dis-ease there is no disease. That the physical or mental state of a person CAN be different - does not imply that it MUST be different or even that it is desirable that it should be different. In an over-populated world, sterility might be the desirable thing - or even the occasional epidemic. There is no such thing as ABSOLUTE dysfunction. The body and the mind ALWAYS function. They adapt themselves to their environment and if the latter changes - they change. Personality disorders are the best possible responses to abuse."

First published on the Suite 101 Narcissistic Personality Disorders Topic.

Narcissism
The Psychopathological Default

Question: Many of the symptoms and signs that you describe apply to other personality disorders as well (for instance, the Histrionic, the Antisocial and the Borderline Personality Disorder). Are we to think that all personality disorders are interrelated?

Answer: Are all personality disorders the outcomes of frustrated narcissism?

311   During our formative years (6 months to 6 years old), we are all "narcissists". As infants, we feel that we are the centre of the universe, omnipotent and omniscient. Our parents, those mythical figures, immortal and awesomely powerful, are there only to protect and serve us. Both self and others are viewed immaturely, as idealizations.

Primary narcissism is a useful and critically important defence mechanism. As the infant separates from his mother and becomes an individual, it is likely to experience great apprehension, fear, and pain. Narcissism shields the child from these negative emotions. By pretending to be omnipotent, the toddler fends off the profound feelings of isolation, unease, pending doom, and helplessness that are attendant on the individuation-separation phase of personal development.

Well into early adolescence, the empathic support of parents, caregivers, role models, authority figures, and peers is indispensable to the evolution of a stable sense of self-worth, self-esteem, and self-confidence. Traumas and abuse, smothering and doting, and the constant breach of emerging boundaries yield the entrenchment of rigid adult narcissistic defences.

What happens when we face disappointments, setbacks, failures, criticism and disillusionment?

Some people "resolve" these recurrent frustrations by developing personality disorders.

Back to infancy:

Inevitably, the inexorable processes and conflicts of life grind the ideal images of our parents into the fine dust of the real. Disappointments follow disillusionment. When these are gradual and tolerable, they are adaptative. If abrupt, capricious, arbitrary, and intense, the injuries sustained by the child's tender, budding self-esteem, are irreversible.

Moreover, the empathic support of the caretakers (the Primary Objects, the parents) is crucial. In its absence, self-esteem in adulthood tends to fluctuate, to alternate between over-valuation (idealization) and devaluation of both self and others.

Narcissistic adults are the result of bitter disappointments, of radical disillusionment with parents, role models, or peers. Healthy adults accept their limitations (the boundaries of their selves). They accept disappointments, setbacks, failures, criticism and disillusionment with grace and tolerance. Their sense of self-worth is constant and positive, minimally affected by outside events, no matter how severe.

The common view is that we go through the stages of a linear development. We are propelled forward by various forces: the Libido (force of life) and the Thanatos (force of death) in Freud's tripartite model, Meaning in Frenkel's work, socially mediated phenomena in both Adler's thinking and in Behaviourism, our cultural context in Horney's opera, or by interpersonal relations (Sullivan) and neurobiological and neurochemical processes, to mention but a few schools of developmental psychology.

Some scholars say that personal development ends in childhood, others - during adolescence. Yet others say that development is a process which continues throughout the life of the individual.

Common to all these schools of thought are the mechanics and dynamics of the process of personal growth. Forces - inner or external - facilitate the development of the individual. When an obstacle to development is encountered, development is stunted or arrested - but not for long. A distorted pattern of development, a bypass appears.

Psychopathology is the outcome of perturbed growth. Humans can be compared to trees. When a tree encounters a physical obstacle to its expansion, its branches or roots curl around it. Deformed and ugly, they still reach their destination, however late and partially.

Psychopathologies are, therefore, adaptative mechanisms. They allow the individual to continue to grow around obstacles. The nascent personality twists and turns, deforms itself, and is transformed until it reaches a functional equilibrium, which is not too ego-dystonic.

Having reached that point, it settles down and continues its more or less linear pattern of growth. The forces of life (as expressed in the development of the personality) are stronger than any hindrance. The roots of trees crack mighty rocks, microbes live in the most poisonous and extreme environments.

Similarly, humans form those personality structures which are optimally suited to their needs and outside constraints. Such personality configurations may be abnormal, but their mere existence proves that they have triumphed in the delicate task of successful adaptation.

Only death puts a stop to personal growth and development. Life's events, crises, joys and sadness, disappointments and surprises, setbacks and successes, all contribute to the weaving of the delicate fabric called "personality".

When an individual (at any age) encounters an obstacle to the orderly progression from one stage of development to another, he retreats at first to his early childhood's narcissistic phase rather than circumvent or "go around" the hindrance.

The process is three-phased:

1. The person encounters an obstacle;
2. The person regresses to the infantile narcissistic phase;
3. Thus having recuperated, the person confronts the obstacle again.

While in step (2), the person displays childish, immature behaviours. He feels that he is omnipotent and misjudges his powers and the strength of the opposition. He underestimates challenges facing him and pretends to be "Mr. Know-All". His sensitivity to the needs and emotions of others and his ability to empathize with them deteriorate sharply. He becomes intolerably haughty with sadistic and paranoid tendencies.

Above all, he then demands unconditional admiration, even when he does not deserve it. He is preoccupied with fantastic, magical, thinking and daydreams. He tends to exploit others, to envy them, to be edgy and explode with unexplained rage.

To put it succinctly: whenever we experience a major life crisis (which hinders our personal growth and threatens it), we suffer from a mild and transient form of the Narcissistic Personality Disorder.

This fantasy world, full of falsity and hurt feelings, serves as a springboard from which the rejuvenated individual resumes his progress towards the next stage of personal growth. This time around, faced with the same obstacle, he feels sufficiently potent to ignore it or to tackle it.

In most cases, the chances of success of this second onslaught are enhanced by the delusional assessment that the obstacle's fortitude and magnitude are diminished. This, indeed, is the main function of this reactive, episodic, and transient narcissism: to encourage magical thinking, to wish the problem away or to enchant it or to confront and overcome it from a position of omnipotence.

A structural abnormality of personality arises only when recurrent attacks fail constantly and consistently to eliminate the obstacle, or to overcome the hindrance. The contrast between the fantastic world (temporarily) occupied by the individual and the real world in which he keeps being frustrated is too acute to countenance for long without a resulting deformity.

This dissonance - the gap between grandiose fantasy and frustrating reality - gives rise to the unconscious "decision" to go on living in the world of fantasy, grandiosity and entitlement. It is better to feel special than to feel inadequate. It is better to be omnipotent than psychologically impotent. To (ab)use others is preferable to being (ab)used by them. In short: it is better to remain a pathological narcissist than to face harsh, unyielding reality.

Not all personality disorders are fundamentally narcissistic. Yet, I think that the default, when growth is stunted by the existence of a persistent obstacle, is remission to the narcissistic phase of early personal development. I further believe that this is the ONLY default available to the individual: whenever he comes across an obstacle, he regresses to the narcissistic phase. How can this be reconciled with the diversity of mental illnesses?

"Narcissism" is the substitution of a False Self for the True Self. This, arguably, is the predominant feature of narcissism: the True Self is repressed, relegated to irrelevance and obscurity, left to degenerate and decay. In its stead, a psychological structure is formed and projected unto the outside world: the False Self.

The narcissist's False Self is reflected at him by other people. This "proves" to the narcissist that the False Self indeed exists independently, that it is not entirely a figment of the narcissist's imagination and, therefore, that it is a legitimate successor to the True Self. It is this characteristic which is common to all psychopathologies: the emergence of false psychic structures which usurp the powers and capacities of the previous, legitimate and authentic ones.

Horrified by the absence of a clearly bounded, cohesive, coherent, reliable, and self-regulating self, the mentally abnormal person resorts to one of the following solutions, all of which involve reliance upon sham and invented personality constructs:

a. *The Narcissistic Solution* - The patient creates and projects an omnipotent, omniscient, and omnipresent False Self that largely replaces and represses the discredited and dilapidated True Self. He uses the False Self to garner Narcissistic Supply (attention, both positive and negative) and thus support his inflated fantasies. Both the Narcissistic and the Schizotypal personality disorders belong here because both involve grandiose, fantastic, and magical thinking. When the narcissistic solution fails, we have the Borderline Personality Disorder (BPD). The Borderline patient's awareness that the solution that she had opted for is "not working" generates in her an overwhelming separation anxiety (fear of abandonment), an identity disturbance, affective and emotional lability, suicidal ideation, and suicidal action, chronic feelings of emptiness, rage attacks, and transient (stress related) paranoid ideation.

b. *The Appropriation Solution* - This solution involves the appropriation of someone else's imagined (and, therefore, confabulated and false) self instead of one's dysfunctional True Self. Such people live vicariously, through others, and by proxy. Consider the Histrionic Personality Disorder. Histrionics sexualize and objectify others and then internalize (introject) them. Lacking an inner reality (True Self) they over-rate and over-emphasize their bodies. Histrionics and other "appropriators" misjudge the intimacy of their faux relationships and the degree of commitment involved. They are easily suggestible and their senses of self and self-worth shift and fluctuate with input from the outside (Narcissistic Supply). Another example of this type of solution is the Dependent Personality Disorder (co-dependents). Manipulative mothers who "sacrifice" their lives for their children, "drama queens", and people with factitious disorders (for instance, Munchausen Syndrome) also belong to this category.

c. *The Schizoid Solution* - Sometimes the emergence of the False Self is stunted or disrupted. The True Self remains immature and dysfunctional but it is not replaced by a functioning narcissistic defence mechanism. Such patients are mental zombies, trapped forever in the no-man's land between infancy and adulthood. They lack empathy, their psychosexual life is impoverished, they prefer to avoid contact with others, and withdraw from the world. The Schizotypal Personality Disorder is a mixture of the narcissistic and the schizoid solutions. The Avoidant Personality Disorder is a close kin.

d. *The Aggressive Destructive Solution* - These people suffer from hypochondriasis, depression, suicidal ideation, dysphoria, anhedonia, compulsions and obsessions and other expressions of internalized and transformed aggression directed at a self which is perceived to be inadequate, guilty, disappointing and worthy of nothing but elimination. Many of the narcissistic elements are present in an exaggerated form. Lack of empathy becomes reckless disregard for others, irritability, deceitfulness and criminal violence. Undulating self-esteem is transformed into impulsiveness and failure to plan ahead. The Antisocial Personality Disorder is a prime example of this solution, whose essence is: the total control of a False Self, without the mitigating presence of a shred of True Self.

Perhaps this common feature - the replacement of the original structures of the personality by new, invented, ersatz ones - is what causes one to see narcissists everywhere. This common denominator is most accentuated in the Narcissistic Personality Disorder.

The interaction, really, the battle, between the struggling original remnants of the personality and the malignant and omnivorous new structures can be discerned in all forms of psychic abnormality. The question is: if many phenomena have one thing in common, should they be considered one and the same, or, at least, caused by the same?

The answer in the case of personality disorders may well be in the affirmative. All the known personality disorders are forms of malignant self-love. In each personality disorder, different attributes are differently emphasized, different weights attach to different behaviour patterns. But these are all matters of quantity, not of quality. The myriad deformations of the reactive patterns collectively known as "personality" all belong to the same family.

Narcissism, Other Mental Health Disorders, Substance Abuse, and Reckless Behaviours

Co-Morbidity and Dual Diagnosis

Question: The symptoms that you describe are common to so many people that I know... Does this mean that they are all narcissists?

Answer: The classification of Axis II personality disorders - deeply ingrained, maladaptive, lifelong behaviour patterns - in the Diagnostic and Statistical Manual, fourth edition, text revision [American Psychiatric Association. DSM-IV-TR, Washington, 2000] - or the DSM-IV-TR for short - has come under sustained and serious criticism from its inception in 1952.

The DSM-IV-TR adopts a categorical approach, postulating that personality disorders are "qualitatively distinct clinical syndromes" [p. 689]. This is widely doubted. Even the distinction made between "normal" and "disordered" personalities is increasingly being rejected. The "diagnostic thresholds" between normal and abnormal are either absent or weakly supported.

The polythetic form of the DSM's Diagnostic Criteria - only a subset of the criteria is adequate grounds for a diagnosis - generates unacceptable diagnostic heterogeneity. In other words, people diagnosed with the same personality disorder may have only one diagnostic criterion in common.

The DSM fails to clarify the exact relationship between Axis II and Axis I disorders and the way chronic childhood and developmental problems interact with personality disorders.

The differential diagnoses are vague and the personality disorders are insufficiently demarcated. The result is excessive co-morbidity (multiple Axis II diagnoses in the same patient).

317

The DSM contains little discussion of what distinguishes normal character (personality), personality traits, or personality style (Millon) from personality disorders. The DSM does not incorporate personality disorders induced by circumstances (reactive personality disorders, such as Milman's proposed "Acquired Situational Narcissism"). Nor does it efficaciously cope with personality disorders that are the result of medical conditions (such as brain injuries, metabolic conditions, or protracted poisoning).

The DSM suffers from a dearth of documented clinical experience regarding both the disorders themselves and the utility of various treatment modalities.

A few personality disorders are "not otherwise specified": a catchall, basket "category".

Cultural bias is evident in certain personality disorders (such as the Antisocial and the Schizotypal).

The emergence of dimensional alternatives to the categorical approach is acknowledged in the DSM-IV-TR itself:

"An alternative to the categorical approach is the dimensional perspective that personality disorders represent maladaptive variants of personality traits that merge imperceptibly into normality and into one another." [p.689]

The following issues - long neglected in the DSM - are likely to be tackled in future editions as well as in current research:

- The longitudinal course of the disorder(s) and their temporal stability from early childhood onwards;
- The genetic and biological underpinnings of personality disorder(s);
- The development of personality psychopathology during childhood and its emergence in adolescence;
- The interactions between physical health and disease and personality disorders;
- The effectiveness of various treatments: talk therapies as well as psychopharmacology.

The Diagnostic and Statistical Manual [American Psychiatric Association. DSM-IV-TR, Washington, 2000] defines "personality" as: *"...enduring patterns of perceiving, relating to, and thinking about the environment and oneself ... exhibited in a wide range of important social and personal contexts."*

Patients suffering from personality disorders have these things in common:

They are persistent, relentless, stubborn, and insistent (except those suffering from the Schizoid or the Avoidant personality disorders).

They feel entitled to - and vociferously demand - preferential treatment and privileged access to resources and personnel. They often complain about multiple symptoms. They get involved in "power plays" with authority figures (such as physicians, therapists, nurses, social workers, bosses, and bureaucrats) and rarely obey instructions or observe rules of conduct and procedure.

They hold themselves to be superior to others or, at the very least, unique. Many personality disorders involve an inflated self-perception and grandiosity. Such subjects are incapable of empathy (the ability to appreciate and respect the needs and wishes of other people). In therapy or medical treatment, they alienate the physician or therapist by treating her as inferior to them.

Patients with personality disorders are self-centred, self-preoccupied, repetitive, and, thus, boring.

Subjects with personality disorders seek to manipulate and exploit others. They trust no one and have a diminished capacity to love or intimately share because they do not trust or love themselves. They are socially maladaptive and emotionally unstable.

No one knows whether personality disorders are the tragic outcomes of nature or the sad follow-up to a lack of nurture by the patient's environment.

Generally speaking, though, most personality disorders start out in childhood and early adolescence as mere problems in personal development. Exacerbated by repeated abuse and rejection, they then become full-fledged dysfunctions. Personality disorders are rigid and enduring patterns of traits, emotions, and cognitions. In other words, they rarely "evolve" and are stable and all-pervasive, not episodic. By "all-pervasive", I mean to say that they affect every area in the patient's life: his career, his interpersonal relationships, his social functioning.

Personality disorders cause unhappiness and are usually co-morbid with mood and anxiety disorders. Most patients are ego-dystonic (except narcissists and psychopaths). They dislike and resent who they are, how they behave, and the pernicious and destructive effects they have on their nearest and dearest. Still, personality disorders are defence mechanisms writ large. Thus, few patients with personality disorders are truly self-aware or capable of life transforming introspective insights.

Patients with personality disorder typically suffer from a host of other psychiatric problems (example: depressive illnesses, or obsessions-compulsions). They are worn-out by the need to reign in their self-destructive and self-defeating impulses.

319

Patients with personality disorders have alloplastic defences and an external locus of control. In other words: rather than accept responsibility for the consequences of their actions, they tend to blame other people or the outside world for their misfortune, failures, and circumstances. Consequently, they fall prey to paranoid persecutory delusions and anxieties. When stressed, they try to pre-empt (real or imaginary) threats by changing the rules of the game, introducing new variables, or by trying to manipulate their environment to conform to their needs. They regard everyone and everything as mere instruments of gratification.

Patients with Cluster B personality disorders (Narcissistic, Antisocial, Borderline, and Histrionic) are mostly ego-syntonic, even though they are faced with formidable character and behavioural deficits, emotional deficiencies and lability, and overwhelmingly wasted lives and squandered potentials. Such patients do not, on the whole, find their personality traits or behaviour objectionable, unacceptable, disagreeable, or alien to their selves.

There is a clear distinction between patients with personality-disorders and patients with psychoses (schizophrenia-paranoia and the like). As opposed to the latter, the former have no hallucinations, delusions or thought disorders. At the extreme, subjects who suffer from the Borderline Personality Disorder experience brief psychotic "microepisodes", mostly during treatment. Patients with personality disorders are also fully oriented, with clear senses (sensorium), good memory and a satisfactory general fund of knowledge.

Question: Does narcissism often occur with other mental health disorders (co-morbidity) or with substance abuse (dual diagnosis)?

Answer: NPD (Narcissistic Personality Disorder) is often diagnosed with other mental health disorders (such as the Borderline, Histrionic, or Antisocial Personality Disorders). This is called "co-morbidity". NPD is also often accompanied by substance abuse and other reckless and impulsive behaviours and this co-occurrence is called "dual diagnosis".

The Schizoid and Paranoid Personality Disorders

The basic dynamic of this particular brand of co-morbidity goes like this:

1. The narcissist feels superior, unique, entitled and better than his fellow men. He thus tends to despise them, to hold them in contempt and to regard them as lowly and subservient beings.

2. The narcissist feels that his time is invaluable, his mission of cosmic importance, his contributions to humanity priceless. He, therefore, demands total obedience and catering to his ever-changing needs. Any demands on his time and resources are deemed to be both humiliating and wasteful.
3. But the narcissist is DEPENDENT on input from other people for the performance of certain ego functions (such as the regulation of his sense of self-worth). Without Narcissistic Supply (adulation, adoration, attention), the narcissist shrivels and withers and is dysphoric (depressed).
4. The narcissist resents this dependence. He is furious at himself for his neediness and - in a typical narcissistic manoeuvre (called "alloplastic defence") - he blames OTHERS for his anger. He displaces his rage and its roots.
5. Many narcissists are also paranoid. This means that they are afraid of people and of what people might do to them. Wouldn't you be scared and paranoid if your very life depended continually on the goodwill of others? The narcissist's very life depends on others providing him with Narcissistic Supply. He becomes suicidal if they stop doing so.
6. To counter this overwhelming feeling of helplessness (dependence on Narcissistic Supply), the narcissist becomes a control freak. He sadistically manipulates others to satisfy his needs. He derives pleasure from the utter subjugation of his human environment.
7. Finally, the narcissist is a latent masochist. He seeks punishment, castigation and ex-communication. This self-destruction is the only way to validate powerful voices he had internalized as a child ("You are a bad, rotten, hopeless child").

The narcissistic landscape is fraught with contradictions. The narcissist depends on people - but hates and despises them. He wants to control them unconditionally - but is also looking to punish himself savagely. He is terrified of persecution ("persecutory delusions") - but seeks the company of his own "persecutors" compulsively.

The narcissist is the victim of incompatible inner dynamics, ruled by numerous vicious circles, pushed and pulled simultaneously by irresistible forces. A minority of narcissists choose the Schizoid Solution. They choose, in effect, to disengage, both emotionally and socially.

[Read more about the narcissist's reactions to deficient Narcissistic Supply in FAQ 16: The Delusional Way Out]

[Read more about Schizoid Narcissists in FAQ 51]

HPD (Histrionic Personality Disorder) and Somatic NPD

Somatic narcissists acquire their Narcissistic Supply by making use of their bodies, of sex, of physical of physiological achievements, traits, health, exercise, or relationships. They possess many Histrionic features.

[Read the DSM-IV-TR (2000) definition of the Histrionic Personality Disorder: http://behavenet.com/capsules/disorders/histrionicpd.htm]

Narcissists and Depression

[Read Frequently Asked Question 9 to learn more about depression and the narcissist]

Dissociative Identity Disorder and NPD

Is the True Self of the narcissist the equivalent of the host personality in the DID (Dissociative Identity Disorder) - and the False Self one of the fragmented personalities, also known as "alters"?

The False Self is a mere construct rather than a full-fledged self. It is the locus of the narcissist's fantasies of grandiosity, his feelings of entitlement, omnipotence, magical thinking, omniscience and magical immunity. But it lacks many other functional and structural elements.

Moreover, it has no "cut-off" date. DID alters have a date of inception, usually as a reaction to trauma or abuse (they have an "age"). The False Self is a process, not an entity, it is a reactive pattern and a reactive formation. The False Self is not a self, nor is it false. It is very real, more real to the narcissist than his True Self.

As Kernberg observed, the narcissist actually vanishes and is replaced by a False Self. There is NO True Self inside the narcissist. The narcissist is a hall of mirrors - but the hall itself is an optical illusion created by the mirrors. Narcissism is reminiscent of a painting by Escher.

In DID, the patient's emotions are segregated into personality-like internal constructs ("entities"). The notion of "unique separate multiple whole personalities" is untrue. DID is a continuum. The subject's inner language breaks down into polyglottal chaos. In DID, emotions cannot communicate with each other for fear of provoking overwhelming pain (and its fatal consequences). So, they are being kept apart by various mechanisms (a host or birth personality, a facilitator, a moderator and so on).

All personality disorders involve a modicum of dissociation. But the narcissistic solution is to emotionally disappear altogether. Hence, the tremendous, insatiable need of the narcissist for external approval. The narcissist exists ONLY as a reflection. Since he is forbidden to love his True Self, he chooses to have no self at all. It is not dissociation - it is a vanishing act.

NPD is a total, "pure" solution: self-extinguishing, self-abolishing, and entirely fake.

NPD and Attention Deficit Hyperactivity Disorder

NPD has been associated with Attention Deficit / Hyperactivity Disorder (ADHD, or ADD) and with RAD (Reactive Attachment Disorder). The rationale is that children suffering from ADHD are unlikely to develop the attachment necessary to prevent a narcissistic regression (Freud) or adaptation (Jung).

Bonding and object relations ought to be affected by ADHD. Research to supports this intuitive linkage has yet to come to light, though. Still, many psychotherapists and psychiatrists use it as a working hypothesis. Another proposed dynamic is between autistic disorders (such as Asperger's Syndrome) and narcissism.

Narcissism and Bipolar Disorder

The manic phase of Bipolar I Disorder is often misdiagnosed as Narcissistic Personality Disorder (NPD).

Bipolar patients in the manic phase exhibit many of the signs and symptoms of pathological narcissism: hyperactivity, self-centredness, lack of empathy, and control freakery. During this recurring chapter of the disease, the patient is euphoric, has grandiose fantasies, spins unrealistic schemes, and has frequent rage attacks (is irritable) if her or his wishes and plans are (inevitably) frustrated.

The manic phases of the bipolar disorder, however, are limited in time while NPD is not. Furthermore, the mania is followed by - usually protracted - depressive episodes. The narcissist is also frequently dysphoric. But whereas the bipolar sinks into deep self-deprecation, self-devaluation, unbounded pessimism, all-pervasive guilt and anhedonia, the narcissist, even when depressed, never forgoes his narcissism: his grandiosity, sense of entitlement, haughtiness, and lack of empathy.

Narcissistic dysphorias are much shorter and reactive: they constitute a response to the Grandiosity Gap. In plain words, the narcissist is dejected when confronted with the abyss between his inflated self-image and grandiose fantasies and the drab reality of his life: his failures, lack of accomplishments, disintegrating interpersonal relationships, and low status. Yet, one dose of Narcissistic Supply is enough to elevate the narcissists from the depth of misery to the heights of manic euphoria.

Not so with the bipolar. The source of her or his mood swings is assumed to be brain biochemistry - not the availability of Narcissistic Supply. Whereas the narcissist is in full control of his faculties, even when maximally agitated, the bipolar often feels that s/he has lost control of his/her brain ("flight of ideas"), his/her speech, his/her attention span (distractibility), and his/her motor functions.

The bipolar is prone to reckless behaviours and substance abuse only during the manic phase. The narcissist does drugs, drinks, gambles, shops on credit, indulges in unsafe sex or in other compulsive behaviours both when elated and when deflated.

As a rule, the bipolar's manic phase interferes with his/her social and occupational functioning. Many narcissists, in contrast, reach the highest rungs of their community, church, firm, or voluntary organization. Most of the time, they function flawlessly - though the inevitable blowups and the grating extortion of Narcissistic Supply usually put an end to the narcissist's career and social liaisons.

The manic phase of bipolar sometimes requires hospitalization and, more frequently than admitted, involves psychotic features. Narcissists are never hospitalized as the risk for self-harm is minute. Moreover, psychotic microepisodes in narcissism are decompensatory in nature and appear only under unendurable stress (e.g., in intensive therapy).

The bipolar's mania provokes discomfort in both strangers and in the patient's nearest and dearest. His/her constant cheer and compulsive insistence on interpersonal, sexual, and occupational, or professional interactions engenders unease and repulsion. Her/his lability of mood - rapid shifts between uncontrollable rage and unnatural good spirits - is downright intimidating. The narcissist's gregariousness, by comparison, is calculated, "cold", controlled, and goal-orientated (the extraction of Narcissistic Supply). His cycles of mood and affect are far less pronounced and less rapid.

The bipolar's swollen self-esteem, overstated self-confidence, obvious grandiosity, and delusional fantasies are akin to the narcissist's and are the source of the diagnostic confusion. Both types of patients purport to give advice, carry out an assignment, accomplish a mission, or embark on an enterprise for which they are uniquely unqualified and lack the talents, skills, knowledge, or experience required.

But the bipolar's bombast is far more delusional than the narcissist's. Ideas of reference and magical thinking are common and, in this sense, the bipolar is closer to the schizotypal than to the narcissistic.

There are other differentiating symptoms:

Sleep disorders - notably acute insomnia - are common in the manic phase of bipolar and uncommon in narcissism. So is "manic speech": pressured, uninterruptible, loud, rapid, dramatic (includes singing and humorous asides), sometimes incomprehensible, incoherent, chaotic, and lasts for hours. It reflects the bipolar's inner turmoil and his/her inability to control his/her racing and kaleidoscopic thoughts.

As opposed to narcissists, bipolar in the manic phase are often distracted by the slightest stimuli, are unable to focus on relevant data, or to maintain the thread of conversation. They are "all over the place" - simultaneously initiating numerous business ventures, joining a myriad organization, writing umpteen letters, contacting hundreds of friends and perfect strangers, acting in a domineering, demanding, and intrusive manner, totally disregarding the needs and emotions of the unfortunate recipients of their unwanted attentions. They rarely follow up on their projects.

The transformation is so marked that the bipolar is often described by his/her closest as "not himself/herself". Indeed, some bipolars relocate, change name and appearance, and lose contact with their "former life". Antisocial or even criminal behaviour is not uncommon and aggression is marked, directed at both others (assault) and oneself (suicide). Some biploars describe an acuteness of the senses, akin to experiences recounted by drug users: smells, sounds, and sights are accentuated and attain an unearthly quality.

As opposed to narcissists, bipolars regret their misdeeds following the manic phase and try to atone for their actions. They realize and accept that "something is wrong with them" and seek help. During the depressive phase they are ego-dystonic and their defences are autoplastic (they blame themselves for their defeats, failures, and mishaps).

Finally, pathological narcissism is already discernible in early adolescence. The full-fledged bipolar disorder - including a manic phase - rarely occurs before the age of 20. The narcissist is consistent in his pathology - not so the bipolar. The onset of the manic episode is fast and furious and results in a conspicuous metamorphosis of the patient.

[More about this topic here:

Stormberg, D., Roningstam, E., Gunderson, J., & Tohen, M. (1998) Pathological Narcissism in Bipolar Disorder Patients. Journal of Personality Disorders, 12, 179-185;

Roningstam, E. (1996), Pathological Narcissism and Narcissistic Personality Disorder in Axis I Disorders. Harvard Review of Psychiatry, 3, 326-340]

Narcissism and Asperger's Disorder

Asperger's Disorder is often misdiagnosed as Narcissistic Personality Disorder (NPD), though evident as early as age 3 (while pathological narcissism cannot be safely diagnosed prior to early adolescence).

In both cases, the patient is self-centred and engrossed in a narrow range of interests and activities. Social and occupational interactions are severely hampered and conversational skills (the give and take of verbal intercourse) are primitive. The Asperger's patient's body language - eye to eye gaze, body posture, facial expressions - is constricted and artificial, akin to the narcissist's. Nonverbal cues are virtually absent and their interpretation in others lacking.

Yet, the gulf between Asperger's and pathological narcissism is vast.

The narcissist switches between social agility and social impairment voluntarily. His social dysfunctioning is the outcome of conscious haughtiness and the reluctance to invest scarce mental energy in cultivating relationships with inferior and unworthy others. When confronted with potential Sources of Narcissistic Supply, however, the narcissist easily regains his social skills, his charm, and his gregariousness.

Many narcissists reach the highest rungs of their community, church, firm, or voluntary organization. Most of the time, they function flawlessly - though the inevitable blowups and the grating extortion of Narcissistic Supply usually put an end to the narcissist's career and social liaisons.

The Asperger's patient often wants to be accepted socially, to have friends, to marry, to be sexually active, and to sire offspring. He just doesn't have a clue as to how to go about it. His affect is limited. His initiative - for instance, to share his experiences with nearest and dearest or to engage in foreplay - is thwarted. His ability to divulge his emotions stilted. He is incapable or reciprocating and is largely unaware of the wishes, needs, and feelings of his interlocutors or counterparties.

Inevitably, Asperger's patients are perceived by others to be cold, eccentric, insensitive, indifferent, repulsive, exploitative or emotionally-absent. To avoid the pain of rejection, they confine themselves to solitary activities - but, unlike the schizoid, not by choice. They limit their world to a single topic, hobby, or person and dive in with the greatest, all-consuming intensity, excluding all other matters and everyone else. It is a form of hurt-control and pain regulation.

Thus, while the narcissist avoids pain by excluding, devaluing, and discarding others, the Asperger's patient achieves the same result by withdrawing and by passionately incorporating in his universe only one or two people and one or two subjects of interest. Both narcissists and Asperger's patients are prone to react with depression to perceived slights and injuries, but Asperger's patients are far more at risk of self-harm and suicide.

The use of language is another differentiating factor.

The narcissist is a skilled communicator. He uses language as an instrument to obtain Narcissistic Supply or as a weapon to obliterate his "enemies" and discarded sources with. Cerebral narcissists derive Narcissistic Supply from the consummate use they make of their innate verbosity.

Not so the Asperger's patient. He is equally verbose at times (and taciturn on other occasions) but his topics are few and, thus, tediously repetitive. He is unlikely to obey conversational rules and etiquette (for instance, to let others speak in turn). Nor is the Asperger's patient able to decipher nonverbal cues and gestures or to monitor his own misbehaviour on such occasions. Narcissists are similarly inconsiderate - but only towards those who cannot possibly serve as Sources of Narcissistic Supply.

[More about Autism Spectrum Disorders here:

McDowell, Maxson J. (2002) The Image of the Mother's Eye: Autism and Early Narcissistic Injury, Behavioural and Brain Sciences (Submitted);

Benis, Anthony - "Toward Self & Sanity: On the Genetic Origins of the Human Character" - Narcissistic-Perfectionist Personality Type (NP) with special reference to infantile autism;

Stringer, Kathi (2003) An Object Relations Approach to Understanding Unusual Behaviours and Disturbances;

James Robert Brasic, MD, MPH (2003) Pervasive Developmental Disorder: Asperger Syndrome]

Narcissism and Generalised Anxiety Disorder (GAD)

Anxiety disorders - and especially Generalized Anxiety Disorder (GAD) - are often misdiagnosed as Narcissistic Personality Disorder (NPD).

Anxiety is uncontrollable and excessive apprehension. Anxiety disorders usually come replete with obsessive thoughts, compulsive and ritualistic acts, restlessness, fatigue, irritability, difficulty concentrating, and somatic manifestations (such as an increased heart rate, sweating, or, in Panic Attacks, chest pains).

By definition, narcissists are anxious for social approval or attention (Narcissistic Supply). The narcissist cannot control this need and the attendant anxiety because he requires external feedback to regulate his labile sense of self-worth. This dependence makes most narcissists irritable. They fly into rages and have a very low threshold of frustration.

Like patients who suffer from panic attacks and Social Phobia (another Anxiety Disorder), narcissists are terrified of being embarrassed or criticized in public. Consequently, most narcissists fail to function well in various settings (social, occupational, romantic, etc.).

Many narcissists develop obsessions and compulsions. Like sufferers of GAD, narcissists are perfectionists and preoccupied with the quality of their performance and the level of their competence. As the Diagnostic and Statistical Manual [DSM-IV-TR, p. 473] puts it, GAD patients (especially children):

"... (A)re typically overzealous in seeking approval and require excessive reassurance about their performance and their other worries."

This applies equally well to narcissists. Both classes of patients are paralyzed by the fear of being judged as imperfect or lacking. Narcissists as well as patients with anxiety disorders constantly fail to measure up to an inner, harsh, and sadistic critic and a grandiose, inflated self-image.

The narcissistic solution is to avoid comparison and competition altogether and to demand special treatment. The narcissist's sense of entitlement is incommensurate with the narcissist's true accomplishments. He withdraws from the rat race because he does not deem his opponents, colleagues, or peers worthy of his efforts. As opposed to narcissists, patients with anxiety disorders are invested in their work and their profession. To be exact, they are over-invested. Their preoccupation with perfection is counter-productive and, ironically, renders them underachievers.

It is easy to mistake the presenting symptoms of certain anxiety disorders as pathological narcissism. Both types of patients are worried about social approbation and seek it actively. Both present a haughty or impervious facade to the world. Both are dysfunctional and weighed down by a history of personal failure on the job and in the family.

But the narcissist is ego-dystonic: he is proud and happy of who he is. The anxious patient is distressed and is looking for help and a way out of his or her predicament. Hence the differential diagnosis.

[Bibliography:

Goldman, Howard G. - Review of General Psychiatry, 4th ed. - London, Prentice-Hall International, 1995 - p. 279-282;

Gelder, Michael et al., eds. - Oxford Textbook of Psychiatry, 3rd ed. - London, Oxford University Press, 2000 - p. 160-169;

Klein, Melanie - The Writings of Melanie Klein - Ed. Roger Money-Kyrle, 4 vols. - New York, Free Press, 1964-75;

Kernberg O. - Borderline Conditions and Pathological Narcissism - New York, Jason Aronson, 1975;

Millon, Theodore (and Roger D. Davis, contributor) - Disorders of Personality: DSM IV and Beyond, 2nd ed. - New York, John Wiley and Sons, 1995;

Millon, Theodore - Personality Disorders in Modern Life - New York, John Wiley and Sons, 2000;

Schwartz, Lester - Narcissistic Personality Disorders - A Clinical Discussion - Journal of American Psychoanalytic Association, 22 (1974) - p. 292-305;

Vaknin, Sam - Malignant Self Love - Narcissism Revisited, 8th revised impression - Skopje and Prague, Narcissus Publications, 2007]

BPD, NPD and Other Cluster B Personal Disorders

In the DSM, there are 10 distinct personality disorders (Paranoid, Schizoid, Schizotypal, Antisocial, Borderline, Histrionic, Narcissistic, Avoidant, Dependent, Obsessive-Compulsive) and one catchall category, Personality Disorders NOS (Not Otherwise Specified).

Personality disorders with marked similarities are grouped into clusters.

Cluster A (the Odd or Eccentric Cluster) includes the Paranoid, Schizoid, and Schizotypal personality disorders.

Cluster B (the Dramatic, Emotional, or Erratic Cluster) is comprised of the Antisocial, Borderline, Histrionic, and Narcissistic personality disorders.

Cluster C (the Anxious or Fearful Cluster) encompasses the Avoidant, Dependent, and Obsessive-Compulsive personality disorders.

The Clusters are not valid theoretical constructs and have never been verified or rigorously tested. They constitute merely convenient shorthand and so provide little additional insight into their component personality disorders.

The personality disorders in Cluster B are ubiquitous. You are far more likely to have come across a Borderline or a Narcissist or a Psychopath than across a Schizotypal, for instance.

First, an overview of Cluster B:

Borderline Personality Disorder is marked by instability. The patient is a roller-coaster of emotions (this is called emotional lability). She (most Borderlines are women) fails to maintain stable relationships and dramatically attaches to, clings, and violently detaches from a seemingly inexhaustible stream of lovers, spouses, intimate partners, and friends. Self-image is volatile, one's sense of self-worth is fluctuating and precarious, affect is unpredictable and inappropriate, and impulse control is impaired (the patient's threshold of frustration is low).

The Antisocial Personality Disorder involves contemptuous disregard for others. The psychopath ignores or actively violates other people's rights, choices, wishes, preferences, and emotions.

The Narcissistic Personality Disorder is founded on a sense of fantastic grandiosity, brilliance, perfection, and power (omnipotence). The narcissist lacks empathy, is exploitative, and compulsively seeks Narcissistic Supply (attention, admiration, adulation, being feared, etc.) to buttress his False Self - a confabulated "person" aimed at inspiring awe and extracting compliance and subservience from others.

Finally, the Histrionic Personality Disorder also revolves around attention-seeking but is usually confined to sexual conquests and displays of the histrionic's capacity to irresistibly seduce others.

Each personality disorder (PD) has its own form of Narcissistic Supply:

- *HPD (Histrionic PD)* - Derive their supply from their heightened sexuality, seductiveness, flirtatiousness, from serial romantic and sexual encounters, from physical exercises, and from the shape and state of their body;
- *NPD (Narcissistic PD)* - Derive their supply from garnering attention, both positive (adulation, admiration) and negative (being feared, notoriety);

- *BPD (Borderline PD)* - Derive their supply from the presence of others (they suffer from separation anxiety and are terrified of being abandoned);
- *AsPD (Antisocial PD)* - Derive their supply from accumulating money, power, control, and having (sometimes sadistic) "fun".

Seductive behaviour alone is NOT necessarily indicative of Histrionic PD. Somatic narcissists behave this way as well.

The differential diagnoses between the various personality disorders are blurred. It is true that some traits are much more pronounced (or even qualitatively different) in specific disorders. For example: delusional, expansive, and all-pervasive grandiose fantasies are typical of the narcissist. But, in a milder form, they also appear in many other personality disorders, such as the Paranoid, the Schizotypal, and the Borderline. A sense of entitlement is common to ALL Cluster B disorders.

It would seem that personality disorders occupy a continuum.

Abandonment, NPDs and Other Personality Disorders

Both narcissists and borderlines are afraid of abandonment. Only their coping strategies differ. Narcissists do everything they can to bring about their own rejection (and thus "control" it and "get it over with"). Borderlines do everything they can either to avoid relationships in the first place, or to prevent abandonment once in a relationship by clinging to the partner or by emotionally extorting his continued presence and commitment.

331

NPD and BPD - Suicide

Narcissists almost never act on their suicidal ideation, while borderlines do so incessantly (by cutting, self injury, or mutilation). But both tend to become suicidal under severe and prolonged stress.

NPDs can suffer from brief reactive psychoses in the same way that borderlines suffer from psychotic microepisodes.

There are some differences between NPD and BPD, though:
a. The narcissist is way less impulsive;
b. The narcissist is less self-destructive, rarely self-mutilates, and practically never attempts suicide;
c. The narcissist is more stable (displays reduced emotional lability, maintains stability in interpersonal relationships and so on).

Narcissist vs. Psychopath

We all heard the terms "psychopath" or "sociopath". These are the old names for a patient with the Antisocial Personality

Disorder (AsPD). It is hard to distinguish narcissists from psychopaths. The latter may simply be a less inhibited and less grandiose form of the former. Indeed, the DSM-V Committee is considering to abolish this differential diagnosis altogether.

Still, there are some important nuances setting the two disorders apart:

As opposed to most narcissists, psychopaths are either unable or unwilling to control their impulses or to delay gratification. They use their rage to control people and manipulate them into submission.

Psychopaths, like narcissists, lack empathy but many of them are also sadistic: they take pleasure in inflicting pain on their victims or in deceiving them. They even find it funny!

Psychopaths are far less able to form interpersonal relationships, even the twisted and tragic relationships that are the staple of the narcissist.

Both the psychopath and the narcissist disregard society, its conventions, social cues and social treaties. But the psychopath carries this disdain to the extreme and is likely to be a scheming, calculated, ruthless, and callous career criminal. Psychopaths are deliberately and gleefully evil while narcissists are absent-mindedly and incidentally evil.

Psychopaths really do not need other people while narcissists are addicted to Narcissistic Supply (the admiration, attention, and envy of others).

Millon and Davis (supra) add [p. 299-300]:

"When the egocentricity, lack of empathy, and sense of superiority of the narcissist cross-fertilize with the impulsivity, deceitfulness, and criminal tendencies of the antisocial, the result is a psychopath, an individual who seeks the gratification of selfish impulses through any means without empathy or remorse."

As opposed to what Scott Peck says, narcissists are not evil - they lack the intention to cause harm (mens rea). As Millon notes, certain narcissists *"incorporate moral values into their exaggerated sense of superiority. Here, moral laxity is seen (by the narcissist) as evidence of inferiority, and it is those who are unable to remain morally pure who are looked upon with contempt."*

[Millon, Th., Davis, R. - Personality Disorders in Modern Life, John Wiley and Sons, 2000]

Narcissists are simply indifferent, callous and careless in their conduct and in their treatment of others. Their abusive conduct is off-handed and absent-minded, not calculated and premeditated like the psychopath's.

NPD and Neuroses

The personality disordered patient maintains ALLOPLASTIC defences (reacts to stress by attempting to change the external environment or by shifting blame to it). Neurotics have AUTO-PLASTIC defences (react to stress by attempting to change their internal processes, or by assuming blame). Many personality disorders also TEND to be ego-syntonic (i.e., to be perceived by the patient as acceptable, unobjectionable and part of the self) while neurotics tend to be ego-dystonic (the opposite).

The Hated-Hating Personality Disordered

One needs only to read scholarly texts to learn how despised, derided, hated and avoided patients with personality disorders are even by mental health practitioners. Many people don't even realize that they have a personality disorder. Their social ostracism makes them feel victimized, wronged, discriminated against and hopeless. They don't understand why they are so detested, shunned and abandoned.

They cast themselves in the role of victims and attribute mental disorders to others ("pathologizing"). They employ the primitive defence mechanisms of splitting and projection augmented by the more sophisticated mechanism of Projective Identification.

In other words:

They "split off" from their personality the bad feelings of hating and being hated because they cannot cope with negative emotions. They project these undesirable emotions unto others ("He hates me, I don't hate anyone", "I am a good soul, but he is a psychopath", "He is stalking me, I just want to stay away from him", "He is a con-artist, I am the innocent victim").

Then they FORCE others to behave in a way that JUSTIFIES their expectations and their view of the world (Projective Identification followed by counter Projective Identification).

Some narcissists, for instance, firmly "believe" that women are evil predators, out to suck their lifeblood and then abandon them. So, they try and make their partners fulfil this prophecy. They try and make sure that the women in their lives behave exactly in this manner, that they do not abnegate and ruin the narcissist's craftily, elaborately, and studiously designed Weltanschauung (worldview).

Such narcissists tease women and betray them and bad mouth them and taunt them and torment them and stalk them and haunt them and pursue them and subjugate them and frustrate them until these women do, indeed, abandon them. The narcissist then feels vindicated and validated - totally ignoring HIS contribution to this recurrent pattern.

The personality disordered patient is full of negative emotions, with aggression and its transmutations, hatred and pathological envy. He is constantly seething with rage, jealousy, and other corroding sentiments. Unable to release these emotions (personality disorders are defence mechanisms against "forbidden" feelings), such patients split them, project them and force others to behave in a way which LEGITIMIZES and RATIONALIZES this overwhelming negativity. "No wonder I hate everyone - look how people repeatedly mistreat me." The personality disordered are doomed to incur self-inflicted injuries. They generate the very hate that legitimizes their hatred, which fosters their social ex-communication.

The Negativistic (Passive-Aggressive) Personality Disorder

The Negativistic (Passive-Aggressive) Personality Disorder is not yet recognized by the DSM Committee. It makes its appearances in Appendix B of the Diagnostic and Statistical Manual, titled "Criteria Sets and Axes Provided for Further Study".

Some people are perennial pessimists and have "negative energy" and negativistic attitudes ("good things don't last", "it doesn't pay to be good", "the future is behind me"). Not only do they disparage the efforts of others, but they make it a point to resist demands to perform in workplace and social settings and to frustrate people's expectations and requests, however reasonable and minimal they may be. Such persons regard every requirement and assigned task as impositions, reject authority, resent authority figures (boss, teacher, parent-like spouse), feel shackled and enslaved by commitment, and oppose relationships that bind them in any manner.

Passive-aggressiveness wears a multitude of guises: procrastination, malingering, perfectionism, forgetfulness, neglect, truancy, intentional inefficiency, stubbornness, and outright sabotage. This repeated and advertent misconduct has far reaching effects. Consider the Negativist in the workplace: he or she invests time and efforts in obstructing their own chores and in undermining relationships. But, these self-destructive and self-defeating behaviours wreak havoc throughout the workshop or the office.

People diagnosed with the Negativistic (Passive-Aggressive) Personality Disorder resemble narcissists in some important respects. Despite the obstructive role they play, passive-aggressives feel unappreciated, underpaid, cheated, and misunder-

334

SAM VAKNIN   MALIGNANT SELF LOVE

stood. They chronically complain, whine, carp, and criticize. They blame their failures and defeats on others, posing as martyrs and victims of a corrupt, inefficient, and heartless system (in other words, they have alloplastic defences and an external locus of control).

Passive-aggressives sulk and give the "silent treatment" in reaction to real or imagined slights. They suffer from ideas of reference (believe that they are the butt of derision, contempt, and condemnation) and are mildly paranoid (the world is out to get them, which explains their personal misfortune). In the words of the DSM: *"They may be sullen, irritable, impatient, argumentative, cynical, sceptical and contrary."* They are also hostile, explosive, lack impulse control, and, sometimes, reckless.

Inevitably, passive-aggressives are envious of the fortunate, the successful, the famous, their superiors, those in favour, and the happy. They vent this venomous jealousy openly and defiantly whenever given the opportunity. But, deep at heart, passive-aggressives are craven. When reprimanded, they immediately revert to begging forgiveness, kowtowing, or maudlin protestations, turning on their charm, and promising to behave and perform better in the future.

335 The Borderline Narcissist – A Psychotic?

Kernberg suggested a "borderline" diagnosis. It is somewhere between psychotic and neurotic (actually between the psychotic and the personality disordered):

- The neurotic has autoplastic defences ("Something's wrong with me");
- The personality disordered has alloplastic defences ("Something's wrong with the world");
- Psychotics believe that "something's wrong with those who say that something's wrong with me".

Some personality disorders have a psychotic streak. Borderlines have psychotic episodes. Narcissists react with psychosis to life crises and in treatment ("psychotic microepisodes" which can last for days).

Pathological Narcissism, Psychosis and Delusions

One of the most important symptoms of pathological narcissism (the Narcissistic Personality Disorder) is grandiosity. Grandiose fantasies (megalomaniac delusions of grandeur) permeate every aspect of the narcissist's personality. They are the reason that the narcissist feels entitled to special treatment which is typically incommensurate with his real accomplishments. The

Grandiosity Gap is the abyss between the narcissist's self-image (as reified by his False Self) and reality.

When Narcissistic Supply is deficient, the narcissist de-compensates and acts out in a variety of ways. Narcissists often experience psychotic micro-episodes during therapy and when they suffer narcissistic injuries in a life crisis. But can the narcissist "go over the edge"? Do narcissists ever become psychotic?

Some terminology first:

The narrowest definition of PSYCHOSIS, according to the DSM-IV-TR, is *"restricted to delusions or prominent hallucinations, with the hallucinations occurring in the absence of insight into their pathological nature"*.

And what are delusions and hallucinations?

A DELUSION is *"a false belief based on incorrect inference about external reality that is firmly sustained despite what almost everyone else believes and despite what constitutes incontrovertible and obvious proof or evidence to the contrary"*.

A HALLUCINATION is a *"sensory perception that has the compelling sense of reality of a true perception but that occurs without external stimulation of the relevant sensory organ"*.

Granted, the narcissist's hold on reality is tenuous (narcissists sometimes fail the reality test). Admittedly, narcissists often seem to believe in their own confabulations. They are unaware of the pathological nature and origin of their self-delusions and are, thus, technically delusional (though they rarely suffer from hallucinations, disorganized speech, or disorganized or catatonic behaviour). In the strictest sense of the word, narcissists appear to be psychotic.

But, actually, they are not. There is a qualitative difference between benign (though well-entrenched) self-deception or even malignant con-artistry - and "losing it".

Pathological narcissism should not be construed as a form of psychosis because:

1. The narcissists is usually fully aware of the difference between true and false, real and make-belief, the invented and the extant, right and wrong. The narcissist consciously chooses to adopt one version of the events, an aggrandising narrative, a fairy-tale existence, a "what-if" counterfactual life. He is emotionally invested in his personal myth. The narcissist feels better as fiction than as fact - but he never loses sight of the fact that it is all just fiction.

2. Throughout, the narcissist is in full control of his faculties, cognisant of his choices, and goal-orientated. His beha-

viour is intentional and directional. He is a manipulator and his delusions are in the service of his stratagems. Hence his chameleon-like ability to turn his guises, his conduct, and his convictions on a dime.

3. Narcissistic delusions rarely persist in the face of blanket opposition and reams of evidence to the contrary. The narcissist usually tries to convert his social milieu to his point of view. He attempts to condition his nearest and dearest to positively reinforce his delusional False Self. But, if he fails, he modifies his profile on the fly. He "plays it by ear". His False Self is extemporaneous: a perpetual work of art, permanently reconstructed in a reiterative process designed around intricate and complex Feedback Loops.

Though the narcissistic personality is rigid, its content is always in flux. Narcissists forever re-invent themselves, adapt their consumption of Narcissistic Supply to the "marketplace", attuned to the needs of their "suppliers". Like the performers that they are, they resonate with their "audience", giving it what it expects and wants. They are efficient instruments for the extraction and consumption of human reactions.

As a result of this interminable process of fine tuning, narcissists have no loyalties, no values, no doctrines, no beliefs, no affiliations, and no convictions. Their only constraint is their addiction to human attention, positive or negative.

Psychotics, by comparison, are fixated on a certain view of the world and of their place in it. They ignore any and all information that might challenge their delusions. Gradually, they retreat into the inner recesses of their tormented mind and become dysfunctional.

Narcissists can't afford to shut out the world because they so heavily depend on it for the regulation of their labile sense of self-worth. Owing to this dependence, they are hypersensitive and hypervigilant, alert to every bit of new data. They are continuously busy rearranging their self-delusions to incorporate new information in an ego-syntonic manner.

This is why the Narcissistic Personality Disorder is insufficient grounds for claiming a "diminished capacity" (insanity) defence. Narcissists are never divorced from reality - they crave it, and need it, and consume it in order to maintain the precarious balance of their disorganized, borderline-psychotic personality. All narcissists, even the freakiest ones, can tell right from wrong, act with intent, and are in full control of their faculties and actions.

Masochism and Narcissism

Isn't seeking punishment a form of assertiveness and self-affirmation? Author Cheryl Glickauf-Hughes, in the American Journal of Psychoanalysis [June 97, 57:2, p. 141-148] wrote:

"Masochists tend to defiantly assert themselves to the narcissistic parent in the face of criticism and even abuse. For example, one masochistic patient's narcissistic father told him as a child that if he said 'one more word' that he would hit him with a belt and the patient defiantly responded to his father by saying 'One more word!'. Thus, what may appear, at times, to be masochistic or self-defeating behaviour may also be viewed as self-affirming behaviour on the part of the child toward the narcissistic parent."

Masochistic Personality Disorder

The Masochistic Personality Disorder made its last appearance in the DSM-III-TR and was removed from the DSM-IV and from its text revision, the DSM-IV-TR. Some scholars, notably Theodore Millon, regard its removal as a mistake and lobby for its reinstatement in future editions of the DSM.

The masochist has been taught from an early age to hate himself and consider himself unworthy of love and worthless as a person. Consequently, he or she is prone to self-destructive, punishing, and self-defeating behaviours. Though capable of pleasure and possessed of social skills, the masochist avoids or undermines pleasurable experiences. He does not admit to enjoying himself, seeks suffering, pain, and hurt in relationships and situations, rejects help and resents those who offer it. He actively renders futile attempts to assist or ameliorate or mitigate or solve his problems and predicaments.

These self-penalizing behaviours are self-purging: they intend to relieve the masochist of overwhelming, pent-up anxiety. The masochist's conduct is equally aimed at avoiding intimacy and its benefits: companionship and support.

Masochists tend to choose people and circumstances that inevitably and predictably lead to failure, disillusionment, disappointment, and mistreatment. Conversely, they tend to avoid relationships, interactions, and circumstances that are likely to result in success or gratification. They reject, disdain, or even suspect people who consistently treat them well. Masochists find caring, loving persons sexually unattractive.

The masochist typically adopts unrealistic goals and thus guarantees underachievement. Masochists routinely fail at mundane

338

tasks, even when these are crucial to their own advancement and personal objectives and even when they adequately carry out similar assignments on behalf of others. The DSM gives this example: *"Helps fellow students write papers, but is unable to write his or her own."*

When the masochist fails at these attempts at self-sabotage, he reacts with rage, depression, and guilt. He is likely to "compensate" for his undesired accomplishments and happiness by having an accident or by engaging in behaviours that produce abandonment, frustration, hurt, illness, or physical pain. Some masochists make harmful self-sacrifices, uncalled for by the situation and unwanted by the intended beneficiaries or recipients.

The Projective Identification defence mechanism is frequently at play. The masochist deliberately provokes, solicits, and incites angry, disparaging, and rejecting responses from others in order to feel on "familiar territory": humiliated, defeated, devastated, and hurt.

The Inverted Narcissist – A Masochist?

[The inverted narcissist (IN) is described in great detail in FAQ 50].

The inverted narcissist (IN) is more of a co-dependent than a masochist. Strictly speaking masochism is sexual (as in sado-masochism). But the colloquial term means "seeking gratification through self-inflicted pain or punishment". This is not the case with co-dependents or IN's.

The inverted narcissist is a specific variant of co-dependent that derives gratification from her relationship with a narcissistic or a psychopathic (antisocial personality disordered) partner. But her gratification has nothing to do with the (very real) emotional (and, at times, physical) pain inflicted upon her by her mate.

Rather the IN is gratified by the re-enactment of past abusive relationships. In the narcissist, the IN feels that she has found a lost parent. The IN seeks to re-create old unresolved conflicts through the agency of the narcissist. There is a latent hope that this time the IN will get it "right", that THIS emotional liaison or interaction will not end in bitter disappointment and lasting agony. Yet, by choosing a narcissist for her partner, the IN ensures an identical outcome time and again. Why should one choose to repeatedly FAIL in her relationships is an intriguing question. Partly, it has to do with the comfort of familiarity. The IN is used since childhood to failing relationships. It seems that the IN prefers predictability to emotional gratification and to personal development. There are also strong elements of self-punishment and self-destruction added to the combustible mix that is the dyad narcissist-inverted narcissist.

Narcissists and Sexual Perversions

Narcissism has long been thought to be a form of paraphilia (sexual deviation or perversion). It has been closely associated with incest and paedophilia.

Incest is an AUTOEROTIC act and, therefore, narcissistic. When a father makes love to his daughter - he is making love to himself because she IS 50% himself. It is a form of masturbation and reassertion of control over oneself.

[I analyzed the relationship between narcissism and homosexuality in FAQ 12]

Narcissism, Substance Abuse, and Reckless Behaviours

Pathological narcissism is an addiction to Narcissistic Supply, the narcissist's drug of choice. It is, therefore, not surprising that other addictive and reckless behaviours: workaholism, alcoholism, drug abuse, pathological gambling, compulsory shopping, or reckless driving - piggyback on this primary dependence.

The narcissist - like other types of addicts - derives pleasure from these exploits. But they also sustain and enhance his grandiose fantasies as "unique", "superior", "entitled", and "chosen". They place him above the laws and pressures of the mundane and away from the humiliating and sobering demands of reality. They render him the centre of attention - but also place him in "splendid isolation" from the madding and inferior crowd.

Such compulsory and wild pursuits provide a psychological exoskeleton. They are a substitute to quotidian existence. They afford the narcissist with an agenda, with timetables, goals, and faux achievements. The narcissist - the adrenaline junkie - feels that he is in control, alert, excited, and vital. He does not regard his condition as dependence. The narcissist firmly believes that he is in charge of his addiction, that he can quit at will and on short notice.

The narcissist denies his cravings for fear of "losing face" and subverting the flawless, perfect, immaculate, and omnipotent image he projects. When caught red handed, the narcissist underestimates, rationalizes, or intellectualizes his addictive and reckless behaviours - converting them into an integral part of his grandiose and fantastic False Self.

Thus, a drug abusing narcissist may claim to be conducting first hand research for the benefit of humanity - or that his substance abuse results in enhanced creativity and productivity.

The dependence of some narcissists becomes a way of life: busy corporate executives, race car drivers, athletes, or professional gamblers come to mind.

The narcissist's addictive behaviours take his mind off his inherent limitations, inevitable failures, painful and much-feared rejections, and the Grandiosity Gap: the abyss between the image he projects (the False Self) and injurious reality. They relieve his anxiety and resolve the tension between his unrealistic expectations and inflated self-image and his incommensurate achievements, position, status, recognition, intelligence, wealth, and physique.

Thus, there is no point in treating the dependence and recklessness of the narcissist without first treating the underlying personality disorder. The narcissist's addictions serve deeply ingrained emotional needs. They intermesh seamlessly with the pathological structure of his disorganized personality, with his character faults, and primitive defence mechanisms.

Techniques such as "12 steps" may prove efficacious in treating the narcissist's grandiosity, rigidity, sense of entitlement, exploitativeness, and lack of empathy. This is because - as opposed to traditional treatment modalities - the emphasis is on tackling the narcissist's psychological makeup, rather than on mere behaviour modification.

The narcissist's overwhelming need to feel omnipotent and superior can be co-opted in the therapeutic process. Overcoming an addictive behaviour can be - truthfully - presented by the therapist as a rare and impressive feat, worthy of the narcissist's unique mettle.

Narcissists fall for these transparent pitches surprisingly often. But this approach can backfire. Should the narcissist relapse - an almost certain occurrence - he will feel ashamed to admit his fallibility, need for emotional sustenance, and impotence. He is likely to avoid treatment altogether and convince himself that now, having succeeded once to get rid of his addiction, he is self-sufficient and omniscient.

Eating Disorders and the Narcissist

Question: Do narcissists also suffer from eating disorders such as Bulimia Nervosa or Anorexia Nervosa?

Answer: Patients suffering from eating disorders either binge on food or refrain from eating and sometimes are both anorectic and bulimic. This is an impulsive behaviour as defined by the DSM and is sometimes co-morbid with Cluster B Personality Disorder, particularly with the Borderline Personality Disorder.

Some patients develop eating disorders as the convergence and confluence of two pathological behaviours: self-mutilation and an impulsive (rather, obsessive-compulsive or ritualistic) behaviour. **342**

The key to improving the mental state of patients who have been diagnosed with both a personality disorder and an eating disorder lies in focusing at first upon their eating and sleeping disorders.

By controlling his eating disorder, the patient reasserts control over his life. This newfound power is bound to reduce depression, or even eliminate it altogether as a constant feature of his mental life. It is also likely to ameliorate other facets of his personality disorder.

It is a chain reaction: controlling one's eating disorders leads to a better regulation of one's sense of self-worth, self-confidence, and self-esteem. Successfully coping with one challenge - the eating disorder - generates a feeling of inner strength and results in better social functioning and an enhanced sense of well-being.

As opposed to eating disorders, personality disorders are intricate and intractable. They are rarely curable (though certain aspects, like obsessive-compulsive behaviours, or depression can be ameliorated with medication or modified). The treatment of personality disorders requires enormous, persistent and continuous investment of resources of every kind by everyone involved.

From the patient's point of view, the treatment of her personality disorder is not an efficient allocation of scarce mental resources. Neither are personality disorders the real threat. If one's personality disorder is cured but one's eating disorders are left untouched, one might die.

An eating disorder is both a signal of distress ("I wish to die, I feel so bad, somebody help me") and a message: "I think I lost control. I am very afraid of losing control. I will control my food intake and discharge. This way I can control at least ONE aspect of my life."

This is where we can and should begin to help the patient: by letting her regain control of her life. The family or other supporting figures must think what they can do to make the patient feel that she is in control, that she is managing things her own way, that she is contributing, has her own schedules, her own agenda, and that she, her needs, preferences, and choices matter.

Eating disorders indicate the strong combined activity of an underlying sense of lack of personal autonomy and an underlying sense of lack of self-control. The patient feels inordinately, paralyzingly helpless and ineffective. His eating disorders are an effort to exert and reassert mastery over his own life.

At the early stage of an eating disorder, the patient is unable to differentiate his own feelings and needs from those of others. His cognitive and perceptual distortions and deficits (for instance, regarding his body image - a phenomenon known as a Somatoform or Body Dysmorphic Disorder) only increase his feeling of personal ineffectualness and his need to exercise even more self-control (by way of his diet).

The patient does not trust himself in the slightest. He rightly considers himself to be his worst enemy, a mortal adversary. Therefore, any effort to collaborate with the patient against his own disorder is perceived by the patient as self-destructive. The patient is emotionally invested in his disorder - his vestigial mode of self-control.

The patient views the world in terms of black and white, of absolutes ("splitting"). Thus, he cannot let go even to a very small degree. He is constantly anxious. This is why he finds it impossible to form relationships: he mistrusts (himself and by extension others), he does not want to become an adult, he does not enjoy sex or love (which both entail a modicum of loss of control).

All this leads to low self-esteem. These patients like their disorder. Their eating disorder is their only achievement. Otherwise they are ashamed of themselves and disgusted by their shortcomings (expressed through the distaste with which they hold their body).

Eating disorders are amenable to treatment, though co-morbidity with a personality disorder presages a poorer prognosis. The patient should be referred to talk therapy, medication, and enrol in online and offline support groups (such as Overeaters Anonymous).

Recovery prognosis is good after 2 years of treatment and support. The family must be heavily involved in the therapeutic process. Family dynamics usually contribute to the development of such disorders.

The change in the patient following a successful course of treatment is VERY MARKED. His major depression disappears together with his sleeping disorders. He becomes socially active again and gets a life. His personality disorder might make it difficult for him, but, in isolation, without the exacerbating circumstances of his other disorders, he finds it easier to cope with.

Patients with eating disorders may be in mortal danger. Their behaviour is ruining their bodies relentlessly and inexorably. They might attempt suicide. They might do drugs. The therapist's goal is to buy them time. The older they get, the more experienced they become, the more their body chemistry changes with age, the better their chances to survive and thrive.

Can the Narcissist Have a Meaningful Life?

We all have a scenario of our life. We invent, adopt, are led by and measure ourselves against our personal narratives. These are, normally, commensurate with our personal histories, our predilections, our abilities, limitations, and our skills. We are not likely to invent a narrative which is wildly out of synch with our selves.

We rarely judge ourselves by a narrative which is not somehow correlated to what we can reasonably expect to achieve. In other words, we are not likely to frustrate and punish ourselves knowingly. As we grow older, our narrative changes. Parts of it are realized and this increases our self-confidence, sense of self-worth and self-esteem and makes us feel fulfilled, satisfied, and at peace with ourselves.

The narcissist differs from normal people in that his is a HIGHLY unrealistic personal narrative. This choice of a frustrating Ego Ideal could be imposed and inculcated by a sadistic and hateful Primary Object (a narcissistic, domineering mother, for instance) - or it could be the product of the narcissist's own tortured psyche. Instead of realistic expectations, the narcissist has grandiose fantasies. The latter cannot be effectively pursued. They are elusive, ever receding targets.

This constant failure (the Grandiosity Gap) leads to dysphorias (bouts of sadness) and to losses. Observed from the outside, the narcissist is perceived to be odd, prone to illusions and self-delusions and, therefore, lacking in judgement.

The dysphorias - the bitter fruits of the narcissist's impossible demands of himself - are painful. Gradually the narcissist learns to avoid them by eschewing a structured narrative altogether. Life's disappointments and setbacks condition him to understand that his specific "brand" of unrealistic narrative inevitably leads to frustration, sadness and agony and is a form of self-punishment (inflicted on him by his sadistic, rigid Superego). This incessant punishment serves another purpose: to support and confirm the negative judgement meted out by the narcissist's Primary Objects (usually, by his parents or care-givers) in his early childhood (a negative judgement that is now an inseparable part of his Superego).

The narcissist's mother, for instance, may have consistently insisted that the narcissist is bad, rotten, or useless. Surely, she could not have been wrong, goes the narcissist's internal dialog. Even raising the possibility that she may have been wrong proves her right! The narcissist feels compelled to validate her verdict by making sure that he indeed BECOMES bad, rotten and useless.

Yet, no human being - however deformed - can live without a narrative. The narcissist develops circular, ad-hoc, circumstan-tial, and fantastic "life-stories" (the Contingent Narratives). Their role is to avoid confrontation with (often disappointing and disillusioning) reality. He thus reduces the number of dys-phorias and their strength, though he usually fails to avoid the Narcissistic Cycle [see FAQ 29].

The narcissist pays a heavy price for accommodating his dys-functional narratives: emptiness, existential loneliness (he shares no common psychic ground with other people), sadness, drifting, emotional absence, emotional platitude, mechaniza-tion/robotization (lack of anima, excess persona in Jung's terms) and meaninglessness. This fuels his envy and the result-ing rage and amplifies the EIPM (Emotional Involvement Preventive Measures) [see Chaapter VI].

The narcissist develops a "Zu Leicht - Zu Schwer" ("Too Easy - Too Difficult") syndrome:

On the one hand, the narcissist's life is unbearably difficult. The few real achievements he does have should normally have mitigated his harsh existence. But, in order to preserve his sense of omnipotence, the narcissist is forced to dismiss and "down-grade" these accomplishments by labelling them as "too easy".

The narcissist cannot admit that he had toiled to achieve some-thing and, with this confession, shatter his alleged omnipotence and grandiose False Self. He must belittle every achievement of his and make it appear to have been a routine triviality. This is intended to support the dreamland quality of his fragmented per-sonality. But it also prevents him from deriving the psychological benefits which usually accrue to goal attainment: an enhance-ment of self-confidence, a more realistic self-assessment of one's capabilities and abilities, a strengthening sense of self-worth.

The narcissist is doomed to roam a circular labyrinth. When he does achieve something - he underestimates it in order to enhance his own sense of omnipotence, perfection, and brilliance. When he fails, he dares not face reality. He escapes to the land of no narratives where life is nothing but a meaningless wasteland. The narcissist whiles his life away.

But what is it like to be a narcissist?

The narcissist is often anxious. This anxiety is usually unconscious, like a nagging pain, a permanence, like being immersed in a gelatinous liquid, trapped and helpless, or as the DSM puts it, narcissism is "all-pervasive". Still, these anxieties are never diffuse. The narcissist worries about specific people, or possible events, or more or less plausible scenarios. He seems to constantly conjure up some reason or another to be worried or offended.

Positive past experiences do not ameliorate this preoccupation. The narcissist believes that the world is hostile, a cruelly arbitrary, ominously contrarian, contrivingly cunning and indifferently crushing place. The narcissist simply "knows" it will all end badly and for no good reason. Life is too good to be true and too bad to endure. Civilization is an ideal and the deviations from it are what we call "history". The narcissist is incurably pessimistic, an ignoramus by choice and incorrigibly blind to any evidence to the contrary.

Underneath all this, there is a Generalized Anxiety. The narcissist fears life and what people do to each other. He fears his fear and what it does to him. He knows that he is a participant in a game whose rules he will never master and which places his very existence at stake. He trusts no one, believes in nothing, knows only two certainties: evil exists and life is meaningless. He is convinced that no one cares about him.

This existential angst that permeates his every cell is atavistic and irrational. It has no name or likeness. It is like the monsters that lurk in every child's bedroom when the lights are turned off. But being the rationalizing and intellectualizing creatures that cerebral narcissists are, they instantly label this unease, explain it away, analyse it and attempt to predict its onset.

They attribute this poisonous inner presence to some external cause. They set it in a pattern, embed it in a context, transform it into a link in the great chain of being. Thus, they translate diffuse anxiety into focused worries. Worries are known and measurable quantities. They have reasons which can be tackled and eliminated. They have a beginning and an end. They are linked to names, to places, faces and to people. Worries are human.

Thus, the narcissist transforms his demons into compulsive notations in his real or mental diary: check this, do that, apply preventive measures, do not allow, pursue, attack, avoid. The narcissist ritualizes both his discomfort and his attempts to cope with it.

But such excessive worrying - whose sole intent is to convert irrational anxiety into mundane and tangible preoccupations - is the stuff of paranoia.

For what is paranoia if not the attribution of inner disintegration to external persecution, the assignment of malevolent agents from the outside to the figments of turmoil inside? The paranoid seeks to alleviate his voiding by irrationally clinging to rationality. "Things are so bad", he says, mainly to himself, "because I am a victim, because 'they' are after me and I am hunted by the juggernaut of state, or by the Freemasons, or by the Jews, or by the neighbourhood librarian". This is the path that leads from anxiety through worry to the consuming darkness of paranoia.

Paranoia is a defence against anxiety and against aggression. In the paranoid state, the latter is projected unto imaginary others, the agents of one's imminent crucifixion.

Anxiety is also a defence against aggressive impulses. Therefore, anxiety and paranoia are related, the latter merely a variant of the former. The mentally disordered patient defends against his aggressive propensities by either being anxious or by becoming paranoid.

Yet, aggression has numerous guises, not only anxiety and paranoia. One of its favourite disguises is boredom. Like its relation, depression, boredom is aggression directed inwards. It threatens to drown the bored person in a primordial soup of inaction and energy depletion. It is anhedonic (pleasure depriving) and dysphoric (leads to profound sadness). But it is also threatening, perhaps because it is so reminiscent of death.

Not surprisingly, the narcissist is most worried when bored. The narcissist is aggressive. He channels his aggression and internalizes it. He experiences his bottled wrath as boredom.

When the narcissist is bored, he feels threatened by his ennui in a vague, mysterious way. Anxiety ensues. He rushes to construct an intellectual edifice to accommodate all these primitive emotions and their transubstantiations. He identifies reasons, causes, effects and possibilities in the outer world. He builds scenarios. He spins narratives. As a result, he feels no more anxiety. He has identified the enemy (or so he thinks). And now, instead of being anxious, he is simply worried or paranoid.

The narcissist often strikes people as "laid back" - or, less charitably: lazy, parasitic, spoiled, and self-indulgent. But, as usual with narcissists, appearances deceive. Narcissists are either compulsively driven over-achievers or chronic under-achieving wastrels. Most of them fail to make full and productive use of their potential and capacities. Many avoid even the now standard paths of an academic degree, a career, or family life.

The disparity between the accomplishments of the narcissist and his grandiose fantasies and inflated self image - the Grandiosity Gap - is staggering and, in the long run, unsustainable. It imposes onerous exigencies on the narcissist's grasp of reality and on his meagre social skills. It pushes him either to reclusion or to a frenzy of "acquisitions": cars, women, wealth, power.

Yet, no matter how successful the narcissist is - many of them end up being abject failures - the Grandiosity Gap can never be bridged. The narcissist's False Self is so unrealistic and his Superego so sadistic that there is nothing the narcissist can do to extricate himself from the Kafkaesque trial that is his life.

The narcissist is a slave to his own inertia. Some narcissists are forever accelerating on the way to ever higher peaks and ever greener pastures. Others succumb to numbing routines, the expenditure of minimal energy, and to preying on the vulnerable. But either way, the narcissist's life is out of control, at the mercy of pitiless inner voices and internal forces.

349

Narcissists are one-state machines, programmed to extract Narcissistic Supply from others. To do so, they develop early on a set of immutable routines. This propensity for repetition, inability to change and rigidity confine the narcissist, stunt his development, and limit his horizons. Add to this his overpowering sense of entitlement, his visceral fear of failure, and his invariable need to both feel unique and be perceived as such - and one often ends up with a recipe for inaction.

The under-achieving narcissist dodges challenges, eludes tests, shirks competition, sidesteps expectations, ducks responsibilities, and evades authority because he is afraid to fail and because doing something everyone else does endangers his sense of uniqueness. Hence the narcissist's apparent "laziness" and "parasitism". His sense of entitlement - with no commensurate accomplishments or investment - irritates his social milieu. People tend to regard such narcissists as "spoiled brats".

In specious contrast, the over-achieving narcissist seeks challenges and risks, provokes competition, embellishes expectations, aggressively bids for responsibilities and authority and seems to be possessed with an eerie self-confidence. People tend to regard such specimen as "entrepreneurial", "daring", "vision-ary", or "tyrannical". Yet, these narcissists too are mortified by potential failure, driven by a strong conviction of entitlement, and strive to be unique or at least to be perceived as such.

Their hyperactivity is merely the flip side of the under-achiev-er's inactivity: it is as fallacious and as empty and as doomed to miscarriage and disgrace. It is often sterile or illusory, all smoke and mirrors rather than substance. The precarious "achieve-ments" of such narcissists invariably unravel. They often act outside the law or social norms. Their industriousness, worka-holism, ambition, and commitment are intended to disguise their essential inability to produce and build. Theirs is a whistle in the dark, a pretension, a Potemkin life, all make-believe and thunder.

A Philosophical Comment about Shame

The Grandiosity Gap is the difference between self-image - the way the narcissist perceives himself - and contravening cues from reality. The greater the conflict between grandiosity and reality, the bigger the gap and the greater the narcissist's feel-ings of shame and guilt.

There are two varieties of shame:

Narcissistic Shame, which is the narcissist's experience of the Grandiosity Gap. It is a pervasive feeling of worthlessness (the dysfunctional regulation of the sense of self-worth is the crux of pathological narcissism), "invisibleness" and ridiculousness. The patient feels pathetic and foolish, deserving of mockery and humiliation.

Narcissists adopt all kinds of defences to counter narcissistic shame. They develop addictive, reckless, or impulsive behav-iours. They deny, withdraw, rage, or engage in the compulsive pursuit of some kind of (unattainable, of course) perfection. They display haughtiness and exhibitionism and so on. All these defences are primitive and involve splitting, projection, Projective Identification, and intellectualization.

The second type of shame is *Self-Related*. It is a result of the gap between the narcissist's grandiose Ego Ideal and his Self or Ego. This is a well-known concept of shame and it has been explored widely in the works of Freud (1914), Reich (1960), Jacobson (1964), Kohut (1977), Kingston (1983), Spero (1984) and Morrison (1989). One must draw a clear distinction between GUILT (or control)-related shame and CONFORMITY-related shame.

A Case Study of an Adolescent Narcissist

Donovan, 16 years old, is incapable of loving and, therefore, has never loved you, his stepmother (or, for that matter, anyone else, himself included) in his entire life. His natural capacity to love and to return love was all but eliminated by his horrid childhood. We practice loving first and foremost through our parents. If they fail us, if they turn out to be unpredictable, capricious, violent, or unjust - this capacity is stunted forever. This is what happened to Donovan: the ideal figures of his childhood proved to be much less than ideal. Abuse is a very poor breeding ground for healthy emotions.

351

Granted, Donovan - being the brilliant and manipulative person that he is - knows how to perfectly simulate and emulate LOVE. He acts lovingly - but this is a mere act and it should not be confused with the real thing. Donovan shows love in order to achieve goals: money, a warm house, food on the table, adoration (Narcissistic Supply). Once these are available from other sources, the first ones are discarded callously, cold-heartedly, cruelly and abruptly.

You have been a temporary stopover for Donovan, the equivalent of a full board hotel (no chores, no requirements on his time). Not only was he able to secure his material needs from you - he also found in you a perfect Source of Narcissistic Supply: adoring, submissive, non-critical, wide-eyed, approving, admiring, the perfect narcissistic fix.

You describe a very disturbed young man. He values intelligence above all else, he uses foul language to vent his aggression (the narcissist resents his dependence on his Sources of Supply). The narcissist knows it all and best, is judgemental (without merit), hates all people (though he calls upon them if he needs something), and is never above exploiting and manipulation.

When not in need, he does not contact his "friends", not even his "girlfriend". After all, emotions ("sensitivity") are a deplorable weakness.

In the pursuit of narcissistic gratification, there is no place for hesitation or pause. You put it succinctly: he will do nothing for others, nothing matters to him if it is not in his interest. As a result, he lets people down and refrains almost religiously from keeping promises and obligations.

The narcissist is above such mundane things as obligations undertaken. They counter his conviction that he is above the law - social or other - and this threatens his grandiosity.

The narcissist, being above reproach (who is qualified to judge him, to teach him, to advise him?), inevitably reverts to blaming others for his misdeeds: they should have warned/reminded/alerted him. For instance: they should have waked him up if they desired his precious company and wanted him to keep a date.

The narcissist is above normal people and their daily chores: he doesn't think that he needs to attend classes that others attend. They should go to school because they are inferior (stupid). This is the natural order of things - read Nietzsche. Most narcissists are predictable and, therefore, boring.

To love a narcissist is to love a reflection, not a real person. Donovan is the most basic, primitive type: the somatic (or anal) narcissist, whose disorder is centred on his body, his skin, his hair, his dress, his food, his health. Some of these preoccupations border on the phobic ("freaky with germs") and that is a bad sign.

Hypochondriasis could be the next mental step. But Donovan is in great danger. He should seek help immediately. His narcissism - as is usually the case - has been and is still being compounded by other, more serious disorders. He is led down a path of no return. Donovan is constantly depressed. Maybe he has had few major depressive episodes but he is distinctly dysphoric (sad) and anhedonic (hates the world and finds pleasure in nothing). He alternates between hypersomnia (sleeping too much) and insomnia (not sleeping for two days). This is one of the surest signs of depression.

Narcissists suffer, by their nature, from an undulating sense of self-worth and from all-pervasive feelings of guilt and recrimination. They punish themselves: they dress in ragged clothes contrary to their primary predilections and they direct their pent up aggression at themselves. The result is depression.

Donovan also seems to suffer from a schizoid personality. Such people prefer staying and working in their rooms, in solitary confinement, chained to their computers and books, to any social encounter or diversion. They rarely trust others and they lack the requisite emotional baggage to develop stable interpersonal relationships. They are miserable failures at communicating with people and confine their interactions to first degree relatives.

The total picture is that of a young person suffering from a Borderline Personality Disorder with strong narcissistic and schizoid traits. His reckless and self-destructive spending and his eating irregularities point in this direction. So does the inappropriate affect (for instance, smiling while pretending to shoot people). Donovan is a menace above all to himself.

Borderline patients have suicidal ideation (contemplate suicide) and tend finally to act upon these ruminations. Donovan might direct this aggression elsewhere with catastrophic consequences. But, at best, Donovan will continue to make people around him miserable and ill-at-ease.

Treatment is not very effective. My advice to you is to immediately stop your "unconditional love". Narcissists sense blood where others see only love and altruism. If, for masochistic reasons, you still wish to engage this young person, my advice to you is to condition your love. Sign a contract with him: You want my adoration, admiration, approval, and warmth, you want access to my home and money? If you do - these are my conditions. And if he says that he doesn't want to have anything to do with you anymore - count your blessings and let go.

The Narcissist's Reactions to This Text

Question: What is the reaction of a narcissist likely to be when confronted with your text?

Answer: It takes a major life crisis to force the narcissist to face up to his False Self: a painful breakdown of a close (symbiotic) relationship, a failure (in business, in a career, in the pursuit of a goal), the death of a parent, imprisonment, or a disease.

Under normal circumstances, the narcissist denies that he is one (denial is a defence mechanism) and reacts with rage to any hint of a diagnosis. The narcissist employs a host of intricate and interwoven defence mechanisms (intellectualization, projection, Projective Identification, splitting, repression and denial, to name but a few) to sweep his narcissism under the psychological rug.

When at risk of getting in touch with the reality of his mental disorder (and, as a result, with his emotions), the narcissist displays the whole spectrum of reactions usually associated with bereavement. At first he denies the facts, ignores them and distorts them to fit an alternative, coherent, "healthy", interpretation.

Then, he becomes enraged. Wrathful, he attacks the people and social institutions that are the constant reminders of his true state. Then he sinks into depression and sadness. This phase is, really, a transformation of his aggression into self-destructive impulses.

Horrified by the potential consequences of being aggressive towards the Sources of his Narcissistic Supply, the narcissist redirects his rage and resorts to self-attack, or self-annihilation. Yet, if the evidence is hard and still coming, the narcissist accepts himself as such and tries to make the best of it (in other words, to use his very narcissism to obtain Narcissistic Supply).

354

SAM VAKNIN MALIGNANT SELF LOVE

The narcissist is a survivor and (while rigid in most parts of his personality) very inventive and flexible when it comes to securing Narcissistic Supply. The narcissist can channel this force (of narcissism) positively (by helping people or by leading and guiding them) - or defiantly caricature and exaggerate the main aspects of narcissism so as to attract attention.

But in most cases, the reflex of avoidance prevails. The narcissist feels disenchanted with the person who presented him with proof of his narcissism. He swiftly and cruelly parts ways with the "messenger" often without as much as an explanation.

He then proceeds to develop paranoid theories to explain why people, events, institutions and circumstances tend to confront him with his narcissism and he, bitterly and cynically, opposes or avoids them. As anti-narcissistic agents they constitute a threat to the very coherence and continuity of his personality and this probably serves to explain the ferocity, malice, obduracy, consistency and exaggeration which characterize his reactions. Faced with the potential collapse or dysfunctioning of his False Self, the narcissist risks the terrible consequences of being left alone and defenceless with his sadistic, maligned, self-destructive Superego.

A Dream Interpreted

Background

This dream was related to me by a male, 46 years old, who claims to be in the throes of a major personal transformation. Whether he is a narcissist (as he believes himself to be) or not is quite irrelevant. Narcissism is a language. A person can choose to express himself in it, even if he is not possessed by the disorder. The dreamer made this choice.

Henceforth, I will treat him as a narcissist, though insufficient information renders a "real" diagnosis impossible. Moreover, the subject feels that he is confronting his disorder and that this could be a significant turning point on his way to being healed. It is in this context that this dream should be interpreted. Evidently, if he chose to write to me, he is very preoccupied with his internal processes. There is every reason to believe that such conscious content invaded his dream.

The Dream

"I was in a run-down restaurant/bar with two friends sitting at a table in a large open area with a few other tables and a bar. I did not like the music or the smoky atmosphere or other customers or greasy food, but we were travelling and were hungry and it was open and the only place we could find.

There was a woman with other people at a table about 10 feet in front of me that I found attractive, and noticed she was noticing me as well. There was also another woman with other people at a table about 30 feet to my right, old with heavy makeup and poorly dyed hair, loud, obnoxious, drunk, who noticed me. She started saying negative things to me, and I tried to ignore her. She just got louder and more derogatory, with horrible rude and jabbing comments. I tried to ignore her, but my other friends looked at me with raised eyebrows, as if to ask: 'How much more are you going to take before you stand up for yourself?' I felt sick to my stomach, and did not want to confront her, but everyone in the place was now noticing her confrontation of me, and she was almost screaming at me. I couldn't believe no one was telling her to stop it, to be civil, to be nice.

I finally looked over at her and raised my voice and told her to shut up. She looked at me and seemed to get even angrier, and then looked at her plate and picked up a piece of food and threw it at me! I couldn't believe it. I told her I wasn't going to take one more thing, and to stop it now or I would call the police. She got up, walked towards me, picking up a plate of popcorn from another table, and upended it flat upon the top of my head. I stood up and said: 'That's it! That's assault! You're going to jail!' and went to the cash register area by the door and called the police.

The police instantly appeared and took her away, with her resisting arrest the whole time. I sat down and someone at the table next to me said: 'Now you can open up the dam gate.' I said: 'What?', and he explained how the woman was actually pretty powerful and owned a dam and had shut the gate down years ago, but that now she was locked up we could go open it up.

We piled into a truck and I was led into a cavernous room and shown a small room with a glass wall in it and a big wheel, a control valve. I was told that I could turn it whenever I wanted. So I started to turn it and the water started flowing. I could easily see it through the glass, and the level on the glass rose higher the more I turned the wheel. Soon there was a torrent, and it was thrilling. I had never seen such an incredible roar of water. It was like the Niagara Falls flowing through the huge room. I got frightened along with being thrilled, but discovered I could lessen the water with the valve if it got to be too much. It went on for a long time, and we whooped and laughed and felt so excited. Finally, the water grew less no matter how wide I opened the valve, and it reached a steady flow.

I noticed the pretty woman from the grill way across the huge area, and she seemed to be looking for someone. I hoped it was me. I opened the door, and went out to go meet her. On the way out, I got grease on my hand, and picked up a rag on the table to wipe it off. The rag had even more grease on it, and so now my hands were completely covered in grease. I picked up another rag on top of a box, and there were wet spark plugs stuck with globs of grease to the underside of the rag, lined up in *order as if they used to be in an engine and someone stuck them in this order on purpose, and some of it got on my clothes. The guys with me laughed and I laughed with them, but I left without going to meet the woman, and we went back to the grill.*

I found myself in a tiny room with a table in it and a picture window looking out into the area where everyone was sitting and eating. The door was open into a back hallway. I started to go out, but a man was coming into the room. For some reason he frightened me, and I backed up. However, he was robot-like, and walked to the window and looked out to the dining area, making no indication that he even noticed me, and stared blandly at the people having fun. I left and went out into the dining area. I noticed everyone staring at me in an unfriendly way. I started for the exit, but one of the policemen who had arrested the woman from the night before was off-duty in plain clothes and grabbed my arm and twisted me around and shoved me face down on a table. He told me that what I did to the woman was wrong, and that no one liked me because of it. He said that just because I had the law on my side and was in the right didn't mean anyone would like me. He said if I was smart I would leave town. Others were around me and spit on me.

He let me go, and I left. I was driving in a car alone out of town. I didn't know what became of the friends I was with. I felt both elated and ashamed at the same time, crying and laughing at the same time, and had no idea where to go and what I was doing."

The Interpretation

As the dream unfolds, the subject finds himself with two friends. These friends vanish towards the end of the dream and he doesn't seem to find this worrisome. *"I didn't know what became of the friends I was with."* This is a strange way to treat one's friends. It seems that we are dealing not with three dimensional, full-blown, flesh and blood friends but with FRIENDLY MENTAL FUNCTIONS. Indeed, they are the ones who encourage the subject to react to the old woman's antics. *"How much more are you going to take before you stand up for yourself?"*, they ask him, cunningly. All the other people present at the bar-restaurant do not even bother to tell the woman *"to stop, to be civil, to be nice"*. This eerie silence contributes to the subject's reaction of disbelief that mushrooms throughout this nightmare. At first, he tries to emulate their behaviour and to ignore the woman himself. She says negative things about him, grows louder and more derogatory, horribly rude and jab-bing and he still tries to ignore her. When his friends push him to react: *"I felt sick to my stomach and did not want to con-front her."* He finally does confront her because *"everyone was noticing"* as she was almost screaming at him.

The subject emerges as the plaything of others. A woman screams at him and debases him, friends prod him to react, and motivated by *"everyone"* he does react. His actions and reac-tions are determined by input from the outside. He expects oth-ers to do for him the things that he finds unpleasant to do by himself (to tell the woman to stop, for instance). His feeling of entitlement (*"I deserve this special treatment, others should take care of my affairs"*) and his magical thinking (*"If I want something to happen, it surely will"*) are so strong that he is stunned when people do not do his (silent) bidding. This depen-dence on others is multi-faceted. They mirror the subject. He modifies his behaviour, forms expectations, gets disbelievingly disappointed, punishes and rewards himself and takes behav-ioural cues from them (*"The guys with me laughed and I laughed with them"*). When confronted with someone who does not notice him, he describes him as robot-like and is frightened by him. The word *"look"* disproportionately recurs throughout the text. In one of the main scenes, his confrontation with the rude, ugly woman, both parties do not do anything without first *"look-ing"* at each other. He looks at her before he raises his voice and tells her to shut up. She looks at him and gets angrier.

359

The dream opens in a *"run down"* restaurant/bar with the wrong kind of music and of customers, a smoky atmosphere and greasy food. The subject and his friends were travelling and hun-gry and the restaurant was the only open place. The subject takes great pains to justify his (lack of) choice. He does not want us to believe that he is the type of person to willingly patronize such an establishment. What we think of him is very important to him. Our look still tends to define him. Throughout the text, he goes on to explain, justify, excuse, reason and persuade us. Then, he suddenly stops. This is a crucial turning point.

It is reasonable to assume that the subject is relating to his personal Odyssey. At the end of his dream, he continues his trav-els, goes on with his life *"ashamed and elated at the same time"*. We are ashamed when our sense of propriety is offended and we are elated when it is reaffirmed. How can these contra-dictory feelings coexist? This is what the dream is all about: the battle between, on the one hand, what the dreamer had been taught to regard as true and proper, the "shoulds" and the "oughts" of his life, usually the result of overly strict upbringing - and, on the other hand, what he feels is good for him. These two do not overlap and they foster in the subject a sense of escalating conflict, enacted before us. The first domain (the "shoulds" and the "oughts") is embedded in his Superego (to borrow Freud's quasi-literary metaphor). Critical voices constantly resound in his mind, an uproarious opprobrium, sadistic criticism, destructive chastising, uneven and unfair comparisons to unattainable ideals and goals. But the powers of life are also reawakening in him with the ripening and maturation of his personality. He vaguely realizes what he missed and misses, he regrets it, and he wants out of his virtual prison. In response, his disorder feels threatened and flexes its tormenting muscles, a giant awakened, Atlas shrugged. The subject wants to be less rigid, more spontaneous, more vivacious, less sad, less defined by the gaze of others, and more hopeful. His disorder dictates rigidity, emotional absence, automatism, fear and loathing, self-flagellation, dependence on Narcissistic Supply, a False Self. The subject does not like his current locus in life: it is dingy, it is downtrodden, it is shabby, and inhabited by vulgar, ugly people, the music is wrong, it is fogged by smoke, polluted. Yet, even while there, he knows that there are alternatives, that there is hope: a young, attractive lady, mutual signalling. And she is closer to him (10 feet) than the old, ugly woman of his past (30 feet). His dream will not bring them together, but he feels no sorrow. He leaves, laughing with the guys, to revisit his previous haunt. He owes it to himself. Then he goes on with his life.

He finds himself, in the middle of the road of life, in the ugly place that is his soul. The young woman is only a promise. There is another woman *"old, with heavy makeup, poorly dyed hair, loud, obnoxious, drunk"*. This is his mental disorder. It can scarcely sustain the deception. Its makeup is heavy, its hair dyed poorly, its mood a result of intoxication. It could well be the False Self or the Superego, but I rather think it is the whole sick personality. She notices him, she berates him with derogatory remarks, she screams at him. The subject realizes that his disorder is not friendly, that it seeks to humiliate him, it is out to degrade and destroy him. It gets violent, it hurls food at him, it buries him under a dish of popcorn (a cinema theatre metaphor?). The war is out in the open. The fake coalition, which glued the shaky structures of the fragile personality together, exists no longer. Notice that the subject does not recall what insults and pejorative remarks were directed at him. He deletes all the expletives because they really do not matter. The enemy is vile and ignoble and will make use and excuse of any weakness, mistake and doubt to crack the defence set up by the subject's budding healthier mental structures (the young woman). The end justifies all means and it is the subject's end that is sought. There is no self-hate more insidious and pernicious than the narcissist's.

But, to fight his illness, the subject still resorts to old solutions, to old habits and to old behaviour patterns. He calls the police because they represent the Law and What Is Right. It is through the rigid, unflinching, framework of a legal system that he hopes to suppress what he regards as the unruly behaviour of his disorder. Only at the end of his dream he comes to realize his mistake: *"He said that just because I had the law on my side and I was in the right didn't mean that anyone would like me."* The Police (who appear instantly because they were always present) arrest the woman, but their sympathy is with her. His true aides can be found only among the customers of the restaurant/bar, whom he initially found not to his liking (*"I did not like ... the other customers..."*). It is someone in the next table who tells him about the dam. The way to health is through enemy territory, information about healing can be gotten only from the sickness itself. The subject must leverage his own disorder to disown it.

The dam is a potent symbol in this dream. It represents all the repressed emotions, the now forgotten traumas, the suppressed drives and wishes, fears and hopes. These are natural elements, primordial and powerful. And they are dammed by the disorder (the vulgar, now-imprisoned, lady). It is up to him to open the dam. No one will do it for him: *"Now YOU can open the dam gate."* The powerful woman is no more, she owned the dam and guarded its gates for many years. This is a sad passage about the subject's inability to communicate with himself, to experience his feelings unmediated, to let go. When he does finally encounter the water (his emotions), they are safely contained behind glass, visible but described in a kind of scientific manner (*"the level on the glass rose higher the more I turned the wheel"*) and absolutely regulated by the subject (using a valve). The language chosen is detached and cold, protective. The subject must have been emotionally overwhelmed but his sentences are borrowed from the texts of laboratory reports and travel guides (*"Niagara Falls"*). The very existence of the dam comes as a surprise to him. *"I said: What?, and he explained."*

Still, this is nothing short of a revolution. It is the first time that the subject acknowledges that there is something hidden behind a dam in his brain (*"cavernous room"*) and that it is entirely up to him to release it (*"I was told that I could turn it whenever I wanted"*). Instead of turning around and running in panic, the subject turns the wheel (it is a control valve, he hurries to explain to us, the dream must be seen to obey the rules of logic and of nature). He describes the result of his first encounter with his long repressed emotions as "thrilling", "incredible" "roar(ing)", "torrent(ial)". It did frighten him but he wisely learned to make use of the valve and to calibrate the flow of his emotions to accord with his emotional capacity. And what were his reactions? "Whooped", "laughed", "excited". Finally, the flow became steady and independent of the valve. There was no need to regulate the water anymore. There was no threat. The subject learned to live with his emotions. He even diverted his attention to the attractive, young woman, who reappeared and seemed to be looking for someone (he hoped it was for him).

But, the woman belonged to another time, to another place and there was no turning back. The subject had yet to learn this final lesson. His past was dead, the old defence mechanisms unable to provide him with the comfort and illusory protection that he hitherto enjoyed. He had to move on, to another plane of existence. But it is hard to bid farewell to part of you, to metamorphose, to disappear in one sense and reappear in another. A break in one's consciousness and existence is traumatic no matter how well controlled, well intentioned and beneficial.

So, our hero goes back to visit his former self. He is warned not to. Moreover, it is not with clean hands that he proceeds. They get greasier the more he tries to clean them. Even his clothes are affected. Rags, wet (useless) spark plugs, the ephemeral images of a former engine all star in this episode. Those are passages worth quoting (in parentheses my comments):

*"I noticed the pretty woman from the grill (*from my past*) way across the huge area (*my brain*), and she seemed to be looking for someone. I hoped it was me. I opened the door, and went out to go meet her (*back to my past*). On the way out, I got grease on my hand (*dirt, warning*), and picked up a rag on the table to wipe it off. The rag had even more grease on it (*no way to disguise the wrong move, the potentially disastrous decision*), and so now my hands were completely covered in grease (*dire warning*). I picked up another rag on top of a box, and*

there were wet (dead) *spark plugs stuck with globs of grease to the underside of the rag, lined up in order as if they used to be in an engine* (an image of something long gone) *and someone stuck them in this order on purpose, and some of it got on my clothes. The guys with me laughed and I laughed with them* (he laughed because of peer pressure, not because he really felt like it)*, but I left without going to meet the woman, and we went back to the grill* (to the scene of his battle with his mental disorder)*."*

But, he goes on to the grill, where it all started, this undefined and untitled chain of events that changed his life. This time, he is not allowed to enter, only to observe from a tiny room. Actually, he does not exist there anymore. The man who enters his observation post, does not even see him or notice him. There are grounds to believe that this man is the previous, sick version of the subject himself. The subject was frightened and backed up. The robot-like person (?) looked through the window, stared blandly at people having fun. The subject then proceeded to commit the error of revisiting his past, the restaurant. Inevitably, the very people that he debunked and deserted (the elements of his mental disorder, the diseased occupants of his mind) were hostile. The policeman, this time off duty (not representing the Law), assaults him and advises him to leave. Others spit on him. This is reminiscent of a religious ritual of excommunication. The philosopher Baruch Spinoza was spat on in a synagogue, judged to have committed heresy. This reveals the religious (or ideological) dimension of mental disorders. Not unlike religion, they have their own catechism, compulsive rituals, set of rigid beliefs and "adherents" (mental constructs) motivated by fear and prejudice. Mental disorders are like churches. They employ institutions of inquisition and punish heretical views with a severity befitting the darkest ages.

But these people, this setting, exert no more power over him. He is free to go. There is no turning back now, all bridges burnt, all doors shut firmly, he is a persona non grata in his former disordered psyche. The traveller resumes his travels, not knowing where to go and what he is doing. But he is laughing and crying and ashamed and elated. In other words, he, finally, after many years, experiences emotions. On his way to the horizon, the dream leaves the subject with a promise, veiled as a threat *"If you were smart you would leave town."* If you know what is good for you, you will get healthy. And the subject seems to be doing just that.

How to Recognize a Narcissist?

Question: How to recognize a narcissist before it is "too late"?

Answer: Many complain of the incredible deceptive powers of the narcissist. They find themselves involved with narcissists (emotionally, in business, or otherwise) before they have a chance to discover their true character. Shocked by the later revelation, they mourn their inability to separate from the narcissist and their erstwhile gullibility.

Narcissists are an elusive breed, hard to spot, harder to pinpoint, impossible to capture. Even an experienced mental health diagnostician with unmitigated access to the record and to the person examined would find it fiendishly difficult to determine with any degree of certainty whether someone suffers from a full fledged Narcissistic Personality Disorder - or merely possesses narcissistic traits, a narcissistic style, a personality structure ("character"), or a narcissistic "overlay" superimposed on another mental health problem.

Moreover, it is important to distinguish between traits and behaviour patterns that are independent of the patient's cultural-social context (i.e., which are inherent, or idiosyncratic) and reactive patterns that conform to cultural and social morals and norms.

Additionally, reactions to severe life crises or circumstances are sometimes characterized by transient pathological narcissism [Ronningstam and Gunderson, 1996; Milman, 2000]. But such reactions do not a narcissist make.

When a person is a member of a society or culture that has often been described as narcissistic by scholars (such as Theodore Millon) and social thinkers (e.g., Christopher Lasch) - how much of his behaviour can be attributed to his milieu and which of his traits are really his?

The Narcissistic Personality Disorder is rigorously defined in the DSM-IV-TR with a set of strict criteria and differential diagnoses. But narcissism is regarded by many scholars to be an adaptive strategy ("healthy narcissism"). It is considered pathological in the clinical sense only when it becomes a rigid personality structure replete with a series of primitive defence mechanisms (such as splitting, projection, Projective Identification, or intellectualization) and when it leads to (mainly occupational or interpersonal) dysfunctions in one or more areas of the patient's life.

Pathological narcissism is the art of deception. The narcissist projects a False Self and manages all his social interactions through this concocted fictional construct.

When the narcissist reveals his true colours, it is usually far too late. His victims are unable to separate from him. They are frustrated by this acquired helplessness and angry at themselves for having failed to see through the narcissist earlier on.

But the narcissist does emit subtle, almost subliminal, signals ("presenting symptoms") even in a first or casual encounter.

Imagine a first or second date. You can already tell if he is a would-be narcissist. Here's how:

- Perhaps the first telltale sign is the narcissist's alloplastic defences - his tendency to blame every mistake of his, every failure, or mishap on others, or on the world at large. Be tuned: does he assume personal responsibility? Does he admit his faults and miscalculations? Or does he keep blaming you, the cab driver, the waiter, the weather, the government, or outrageous fortune for his predicament?

- Is he hypersensitive, picks up fights, feels constantly slighted, injured, and insulted? Does he rant incessantly? Does he treat animals and children impatiently or cruelly and does he express negative and aggressive emotions towards the weak, the poor, the needy, the sentimental, and the disabled? Does he confess to having a history of battering or violent offences or behaviour? Is his language vile and infused with expletives, threats, and hostility?

- Next thing: is he too eager? Does he push you to marry him having dated you only twice? Is he planning on having children on your first date? Does he immediately cast you in the role of the love of his life? Is he pressing you for exclusivity, instant intimacy, almost rapes you and acts jealous when you as much as cast a glance at another male? Does he inform you that, once you get hitched, you should abandon your studies or resign your job (forgo your personal autonomy)?

- Does he respect your boundaries and privacy? Does he ignore your wishes (for instance, by choosing from the menu or selecting a movie without as much as consulting you)? Does he treat you as an object or an instrument of gratification (materializes on your doorstep unexpectedly or calls you often prior to your date)? Does he go through your personal belongings while waiting for you to get ready?
- Does he control the situation and you compulsively? Does he insist to ride in his car, holds on to the car keys, the money, the theatre tickets, and even your bag? Does he disapprove if you are away for too long (for instance when you go to the powder room)? Does he interrogate you when you return ("Have you seen anyone interesting") - or make lewd "jokes" and remarks? Does he hint that, in future, you would need his permission to do things - even things as innocuous as meeting a friend or visiting with your family?
- Does he act in a patronizing and condescending manner and criticize you often? Does he emphasize your minutest faults (devalues you) even as he exaggerates your talents, traits, and skills (idealizes you)? Is he wildly unrealistic in his expectations from you, from himself, from the budding relationship, and from life in general?
- Does he tell you constantly that you "make him feel" good? Don't be impressed. Next thing, he may tell you that you "make" him feel bad, or that you make him feel violent, or that you "provoke" him. "Look what you made me do!" is the narcissist's ubiquitous catchphrase.
- Does he find sadistic sex exciting? Does he have fantasies of rape or paedophilia? Is he too forceful with you in and out of the sexual intercourse? Does he like hurting you physically or finds it amusing? Does he abuse you verbally - does he curse you, demeans you, calls you ugly or inappropriately diminutive names, or persistently criticizes you? Does he then switch to being saccharine and "loving", apologizes profusely and buys you gifts?

If you have answered "yes" to any of the above - stay away! He is a narcissist.

Then there is the narcissist's body language. It comprises an unequivocal series of subtle - but discernible - warning signs. Pay attention to the way your date comports himself - and save yourself a lot of trouble!

"Haughty" body language - The narcissist adopts a physical posture which implies and exudes an air of superiority, seniori-

ty, hidden powers, mysteriousness, amused indifference, etc. Though the narcissist usually maintains sustained and piercing eye contact, he often refrains from physical proximity (he protects his personal territory).

The narcissist takes part in social interactions - even mere banter - condescendingly, from a position of supremacy and faux "magnanimity and largesse". But even when he feigns gregariousness, he rarely mingles socially and prefers to remain the "observer", or the "lone wolf".

Entitlement markers - The narcissist immediately asks for "special treatment" of some kind. Not to wait his turn, to have a longer or a shorter therapeutic session, to talk directly to authority figures (and not to their assistants or secretaries), to be granted special payment terms, to enjoy custom tailored arrangements. This tallies well with the narcissist's alloplastic defences: his tendency to shift responsibility to others, or to the world at large, for his needs, failures, behaviours, choices, and mishaps ("Look what you made me do!").

The narcissist is the one who - vocally and demonstratively - demands the undivided attention of the head waiter in a restaurant, or monopolizes the hostess, or latches on to celebrities in a party. The narcissist reacts with rage and indignantly when denied his wishes or when treated the same as others whom he deems inferior. Narcissists frequently and embarrassingly publicly and volubly "dress down" service providers such as waiters, shop clerks, or cab drivers.

Idealisation or devaluation - The narcissist instantly idealizes or devalues his interlocutor. He flatters, adores, admires and applauds the "target" in an embarrassingly exaggerated and profuse manner - or sulks, abuses, and humiliates her.

Narcissists are polite only in the presence of a potential Source of Narcissistic Supply: a "mate", or a "collaborator". But they are unable to sustain even perfunctory civility and fast deteriorate to barbs and thinly-veiled hostility, to verbal or other violent displays of abuse, rage attacks, or cold detachment.

The "membership" posture - The narcissist always tries to "belong". Yet, at the very same time, he maintains his stance as an outsider. The narcissist seeks to be admired for his ability to integrate and ingratiate himself without investing the efforts commensurate with such an undertaking.

For instance: if the narcissist talks to a psychologist, the narcissist first states emphatically that he has never studied psychology. He then proceeds to make seemingly effortless use of obscure professional terms, thus demonstrating that he had mastered the discipline all the same - which is supposed to prove that he is exceptionally intelligent or introspective.

In general, the narcissist always prefers show-off to substance. One of the most effective methods of exposing a narcissist is by trying to delve deeper. The narcissist is shallow, a pond pretending to be an ocean. He likes to think of himself as a Renaissance man, a Jack of all trades, or a genius. Narcissists never admit to ignorance or to failure in any field - yet, typically, they are ignorant and losers. It is surprisingly easy to penetrate the gloss and the veneer of the narcissist's self-proclaimed omniscience, success, wealth, and omnipotence.

Bragging and false autobiography - The narcissist brags incessantly. His speech is peppered with "I", "my", "myself", and "mine". He describes himself as intelligent, or rich, or modest, or intuitive, or creative - but always excessively, implausibly, and extraordinarily so.

The narcissist's biography sounds unusually rich and complex. His self-proclaimed achievements are incommensurate with his age, education, or renown. Yet, his actual condition is evidently and demonstrably incompatible with his claims. Very often, the narcissist's lies or fantasies are easily discernible as such. He always name-drops and appropriates other people's experiences and accomplishments as his own.

Emotion-free language - The narcissist likes to talk about himself and only about himself. He is not interested in others or what they have to say, unless they constitute potential Sources of Supply and in order to obtain said supply. He acts bored, disdainful, or even angry if he feels that they are intruding on his precious time and, thus, abusing him.

In general, the narcissist is very impatient, easily bored, with strong attention deficits - unless and until he is the topic of discussion. One can publicly dissect all aspects of the intimate life of a narcissist without repercussions, providing the discourse is not "emotionally tinted".

When asked to relate directly to his emotions, the narcissist intellectualizes, rationalizes, speaks about himself in the third person and in a detached "scientific" tone or composes a narrative with a fictitious character in it, suspiciously autobiographical. Narcissists like to refer to themselves in mechanical terms, as efficient automata or machines.

Seriousness and sense of intrusion and coercion - The narcissist is dead serious about himself. He may possess a subtle, wry, and riotous sense of humour, scathing and cynical, but rarely is he self-deprecating. The narcissist regards himself as being on a constant mission, whose importance is cosmic and whose consequences are global. If a scientist - he is always in the throes of revolutionizing his discipline. If a journalist - he is in the middle of the greatest story ever. If a novelist - he is on his way to a Booker or Nobel Prize.

This self-misperception is not amenable to light-headedness or self-effacement. The narcissist is easily hurt and insulted (narcissistic injury). Even the most innocuous remarks or acts are interpreted by him as belittling, intruding, or coercive. His time is more valuable than others' - therefore, it cannot be wasted on unimportant matters such as mere banter or going out for a walk.

Any suggested help, advice, or concerned inquiry are immediately cast by the narcissist as intentional humiliation, implying that the narcissist is in need of help and counsel and, thus, imperfect and less than omnipotent. Any attempt to set an agenda is, to the narcissist, an intimidating act of enslavement. In this sense, the narcissist is both schizoid and paranoid and often entertains ideas of reference.

Finally, narcissists are sometimes sadistic and have inappropriate affect. In other words, they find the obnoxious, the heinous, and the shocking funny or even gratifying. They are sexually sado-masochistic or deviant. They like to taunt, to torment, and to hurt people's feelings ("humorously" or with bruising "honesty").

While some narcissists are "stable" and "conventional", others are antisocial and their impulse control is flawed. These are very reckless (self-destructive and self-defeating) and just plain destructive and typically succumb to workaholism, alcoholism, drug abuse, pathological gambling, compulsory shopping, or reckless driving.

These - the lack of empathy, the aloofness, the disdain, the sense of entitlement, the constricted sense of humour, the unequal treatment and the paranoia - render the narcissist a social misfit. The narcissist is able to provoke in his milieu, in his casual acquaintances, even in his psychotherapist, the strongest, most avid and furious hatred and revulsion. To his shock, indignation and consternation, he invariably induces in others unbridled aggression.

He is perceived to be asocial at best and, often, antisocial. This, perhaps, is the strongest presenting symptom. One feels ill at ease in the presence of a narcissist for no apparent reason. No matter how charming, intelligent, thought provoking, outgoing, easy going and social the narcissist is, he fails to secure the sympathy of others, a sympathy he is never ready, willing, or able to reciprocate.

Interacting with a Narcissist

Question: When interacting with a narcissist, how can one tell, at any given moment, whether one is interacting with the IMAGE, or with the REAL PERSON? Or is it ALWAYS the image that is to the fore, and NEVER the real person?

Answer: The short and the long of it is that one always interacts with the False Self (the Image, in your question) and not with the True Self or (luckily) with the Superego (the Real Person, to use your coinage).

The latter emerge and become observable and discernible **370** only in times of severe stress induced by life crises. The maintenance of the False Self is so demanding and takes up so much energy that it crumbles when that energy is used up to tackle another situation.

[A much more detailed analysis of these psychodynamics can be found in the Essay.]

The Weapon of Language

Question: My wife was diagnosed as a narcissist. She twists everything and turns it against me. She distorts everything I ever said, ignores the context, and even invents her own endings. It is impossible to have a meaningful conversation with her because she won't commit to anything she says.

Answer: In the narcissist's surrealistic world, even language is pathologized. It mutates into a weapon of self-defence, a verbal fortification, a medium without a message, replacing words with duplicitous and ambiguous vocables.

Narcissists (and, often, by contagion, their unfortunate victims) don't talk, or communicate. They fend off. They hide and evade and avoid and disguise. In their planet of capricious and arbitrary unpredictability, of shifting semiotic and semantic dunes - they perfect the ability to say nothing in lengthy, Castro-like speeches.

The ensuing convoluted sentences are arabesques of meaninglessness, acrobatics of evasion, a lack of commitment elevated to an ideology. The narcissist prefers to wait and see what waiting brings. It is the postponement of the inevitable that leads to the inevitability of postponement as a strategy of survival.

It is often impossible to really understand a narcissist. The evasive syntax fast deteriorates into ever more labyrinthine structures. The grammar tortured to produce the verbal Doppler shifts essential to disguise the source of the information, its distance from reality, the speed of its degeneration into rigid "official" versions.

Buried under the lush flora and fauna of idioms without an end, the language erupts, like some exotic rash, an autoimmune reaction to its infection and contamination. Like vile weeds it spreads throughout, strangling with absent minded persistence the ability to understand, to feel, to agree, to disagree and to debate, to present arguments, to compare notes, to learn and to teach.

Narcissists, therefore, never talk to others - rather, they talk at others, or lecture them. They exchange subtexts, camouflage-wrapped by elaborate, florid, texts. They read between the lines, spawning a multitude of private languages, prejudices, superstitions, conspiracy theories, rumours, phobias and hysterias. Theirs is a solipsistic world: where communication is permitted only with oneself and the aim of language is to throw others off the scent or to obtain Narcissistic Supply.

This has profound implications. Communication through unequivocal, unambiguous, information-rich symbol systems is such an integral and crucial part of our world that its absence is not postulated even in the remotest galaxies which grace the skies of science fiction. In this sense, narcissists are nothing short of aliens. It is not that they employ a different language, a code to be deciphered by a new Freud. Their linguistic deficiency is also not the outcome of upbringing or socio-cultural background.

It is the fact that language is put by narcissists to a different use - not to communicate but to obscure, not to share but to abstain, not to learn but to defend and resist, not to teach but to preserve ever less tenable monopolies, to disagree without incurring wrath, to criticize without commitment, to agree without appearing to do so. Thus, an "agreement" with a narcissist is a vague expression of intent at a given moment - rather than the clear listing of long-term, iron-cast and mutual commitments.

The rules that govern the narcissist's universe are loopholed incomprehensibles, open to an exegesis so wide and so self-contradictory that it renders them meaningless. The narcissist often hangs himself by his own verbose Gordic knots, having stumbled through a minefield of logical fallacies and endured self-inflicted inconsistencies. Unfinished sentences hover in the air, like vapour above a semantic swamp.

In the case of the inverted narcissist, who had been suppressed and abused by overbearing caregivers, there is the strong urge not to offend. Intimacy and co-dependence are companions. Parental or peer pressures are irresistible and result in conformity and self-deprecation. Aggressive tendencies, strongly repressed in the social pressure cooker, teem under the veneer of forced civility and violent politeness. Constructive ambiguity, a non-committal "everyone is good and right", an atavistic variant of moral relativism and tolerance bred of fear and of contempt - are all at the service of this eternal vigilance against aggressive drives, at the disposal of a never ending peacekeeping mission.

With the classic narcissist, language is used cruelly and ruthlessly to ensnare one's enemies, to saw confusion and panic, to move others to emulate the narcissist (Projective Identification), to leave the listeners in doubt, in hesitation, in paralysis, to gain control, or to punish. Language is enslaved and forced to lie. The language is appropriated and expropriated. It is considered to be a weapon, an asset, a piece of lethal property, a traitorous mistress to be gang raped into submission.

To cerebral narcissists, language is a lover. The infatuation with its very sound leads to a pyrotechnic type of speech which sacrifices its meaning to its music. Its speakers pay more attention to the composition than to the content. They are swept by it, intoxicated by its perfection, inebriated by the spiralling complexity of its forms. Here, language is an inflammatory process. It attacks the very tissues of the narcissist's relationships with artistic fierceness. It invades the healthy cells of reason and logic, of cool headed argumentation and level headed debate.

Language is a leading indicator of the psychological and institutional health of social units, such as the family, or the workplace. Social capital can often be measured in cognitive (hence, verbal-lingual) terms. To monitor the level of comprehensibility and lucidity of texts is to study the degree of sanity of family members, co-workers, friends, spouses, mates, and colleagues. There can be no hale society without unambiguous speech, without clear communications, without the traffic of idioms and content that is an inseparable part of every social contract. Our language determines how we perceive our world. It IS our mind and our consciousness. The narcissist, in this respect, is a great social menace.

First published on the Suite 101 Narcissistic Personality Disorders Topic.

373

Exploitation by a Narcissist

Question: In his drive for Narcissistic Supply, would the narcissist be callous enough to exploit the tragedy of others, if this were to secure him a new Supply Source?

Answer: Yes, he would. I compare Narcissistic Supply to drugs because of the almost involuntary and always-unrestrained nature of the pursuit involved in securing it. The narcissist is no better or worse (morally speaking) than others. But he lacks the ability to empathize precisely because he is obsessed with the maintenance of his delicate inner balance through the (ever-increasing) consumption of Narcissistic Supply.

The narcissist rates people around him according to whether they can provide him with Narcissistic Supply or not. As far as the narcissist is concerned, those who fail this simple test do not exist. They are two-dimensional cartoon figures. Their feelings, needs and fears are of no interest or importance.

Those identified as potential Sources of Narcissistic Supply are then subjected to a meticulous examination and probing of the volume and quality of the Narcissistic Supply that they are likely to provide. The narcissist nurtures and cultivates these people. He caters to their needs, desires, and wishes. He considers their emotions. He encourages those aspects of their personality that are likely to enhance their ability to provide him with his much needed supply.

In this very restricted sense, he regards and treats them as "human". This is his way of "maintaining and servicing" his Supply Sources. Needless to say that he loses any and all interest in them and in their needs once he decides that they are no longer able to supply him with what he needs: an audience, attention, and the witnessing of his accomplishments and moments of glory (in order to serve as his external memory).

374

MALIGNANT SELF LOVE

SAM VAKNIN

The same reaction is provoked by any behaviour judged by the narcissist to be narcissistically injurious.

The narcissist coldly evaluates tragic circumstances. Will the regrettable events allow him to extract Narcissistic Supply from people affected by the tragedy?

A narcissist, for instance, may give a helping hand, console, guide, and encourage another person if that person is important, powerful, has access to other important or powerful people, or to the media, or has a following - in other words, if the bereaved, once recovered, can provide the narcissist with benefits or Narcissistic Supply.

The same applies if helping, consoling, guiding, or encouraging that person is likely to win the narcissist applause, approval, adoration, a following, or some other kind of Narcissist Supply from on-lookers and witnesses to the interaction. The act of helping another person must be documented and thus transformed into narcissistic nourishment.

Otherwise the narcissist is not concerned or interested in the problems and suffering of others. The narcissist has no time or energy for anything, except for obtaining his next narcissistic fix, no matter what the price and who is trampled upon.

375 The Pathological Charmer

The narcissist is confident that people find him irresistible. His unfailing charm is part of his self-imputed omnipotence. This inane conviction is what makes the narcissist a "pathological charmer".

The somatic narcissist and the histrionic flaunt their sex appeal, virility or femininity, sexual prowess, musculature, physique, training, or athletic achievements. The cerebral narcissist seeks to enchant and entrance his audience with intellectual pyrotechnics. Many narcissists brag about their wealth, health, possessions, collections, spouses, children, personal history, family tree - in short: anything that garners them attention and renders them alluring.

Both types of narcissists firmly believe that, being unique, they are entitled to special treatment by others. They deploy their "charm offensives" to manipulate their nearest and dearest (or even complete strangers) and use them as instruments of gratification. Exerting personal magnetism and charisma become ways of asserting control and obviating other people's personal boundaries.

The pathological charmer feels superior to the person he captivates and fascinates. To him, charming someone means having power over her, controlling her, or even subjugating her. It is all a mind game intertwined with a power play. The person to be thus enthralled is an object, a mere prop, and of dehumanized utility.

In some cases, pathological charm involves more than a grain of sadism. Inflicting the "pain" of subjugation on his beguiled victims who "cannot help" but be enchanted sexually arouses the narcissist. Conversely, the pathological charmer engages in infantile magical thinking. He uses charm to help maintain object constancy and fend off abandonment - in other words, to ensure that the person he "bewitched" won't disappear on him.

Pathological charmers react with rage and aggression when their intended targets prove to be impervious and resistant to their lure. This kind of narcissistic injury - being spurned and rebuffed - makes them feel threatened, rejected, and denuded. Being ignored amounts to a challenge to their uniqueness, entitlement, control, and superiority. Narcissists wither without constant Narcissistic Supply. When their charm fails to elicit it, they feel annulled, non-existent, and "dead".

Expectedly, they go to great lengths to secure said supply. It is only when their efforts are frustrated that the mask of civility and congeniality drops and reveals the true face of the narcissist: a predator on the prowl.

The Narcissist's Victims

Question: You describe the narcissist as a cunning, immoral extortionist. How does the narcissist affect people around him?

Answer: Sooner, or later, everyone around the narcissist is bound to become his victim. People are sucked - voluntarily or involuntarily - into the turbulence that constitutes his life, into the black hole that is his personality, into the whirlwind, which makes-up his interpersonal relationships.

Different people are adversely affected by different aspects of the narcissist's life and psychological makeup. Some trust him and rely on him, only to be bitterly disappointed. Others love him and discover that he cannot reciprocate. Yet others are forced to live vicariously, through him.

There are three categories of victims:

Victims of the narcissist's instability - The narcissist leads an unpredictable, vicissitudinal, precarious, often dangerous life. His ground is ever shifting: geographically as well as mentally. He changes addresses, workplaces, vocations, avocations, interests, friends and enemies with a bewildering speed. He baits authority and challenges it.

He is, therefore, prone to conflict: likely to be a criminal, a rebel, a dissident, or a critic. He gets bored easily, trapped in cycles of idealization and devaluation of people, places, hobbies, jobs, values. He is mercurial, unstable, and unreliable. His family suffers: his spouse and children have to wander with him in his private desert, endure the Via Dolorosa that he incessantly walks.

They live in constant fear and trepidation: what next? where next? who is next? To a lesser extent, this is the case with the narcissist's friends, bosses, colleagues, or with his country. These biographical vacillations and mental oscillations deny the

377

people around him autonomy, unperturbed development and self-fulfilment, their path to self-recognition and contentment.

To the narcissist, other humans are mere instruments, Sources of Narcissistic Supply. He sees no reason to consider their needs, wishes, wants, desires and fears. He derails their life with ease and ignorance. Deep inside he knows that he is wrong to do so because they might retaliate - hence, his persecutory delusions.

Victims of the narcissist's misleading signals - These are the victims of the narcissist's deceiving emotional messages. The narcissist mimics real emotions artfully. He exudes the air of someone really capable of loving or of being hurt, of one passionate and soft, empathic and caring. Most people are misled into believing that he is even more humane than average.

They fall in love with the mirage, the fleeting image, with the fata morgana of a lush emotional oasis in the midst of their emotional desert. They succumb to the luring proposition that he is. They give in, give up, and give everything only to be discarded ruthlessly when deemed by the narcissist to be no longer useful.

Riding high on the crest of the narcissist's over-valuation only to crash into the abysmal depths of his devaluation, these victims lose control over their emotional life. The narcissist drains them, exhausts their resources, sucks the blood-life of Narcissistic Supply out of their dwindling, depleted selves.

This emotional roller coaster is so harrowing that the experience borders on the truly traumatic. To remove doubt: this behaviour pattern is not confined to matters of the heart. The narcissist's employer, for instance, is misled by his apparent seriousness, industriousness, ambition, willing to sacrifice, honesty, thoroughness and a host of other utterly fake qualities.

These apparent traits are false because they are directed at securing Narcissistic Supply rather than at doing a good job. The narcissist's clients and suppliers may suffer from the same illusion.

The narcissist's fraudulent emanations are not restricted to messages with emotional content. They may contain wrong or false or partial information. The narcissist does not hesitate to lie, deceive, or "reveal" (misleading) half-truths. He appears to be intelligent, charming and, therefore, reliable. He is a convincing conjurer of words, signs, behaviours, and body language.

The above two classes of victims are casually exploited and then discarded by the narcissist. As far as the narcissist is concerned, no more malice is involved in this behaviour pattern than in any other interaction with an instrument. No more premeditation and contemplation than in breathing. These are victims of narcissistic reflexes. Perhaps this is what makes it all so repulsively horrific: the offhanded nature of the damage inflicted.

Not so the third category of victims.

These are the *victims upon whom the narcissist designs*, maliciously and intentionally, to inflict his wrath and bad intentions. The narcissist is both sadistic and masochistic. In hurting others he always seeks to hurt himself. In punishing them he wishes to be penalized. Their pains are his.

Thus, he attacks figures of authority and social institutions with vicious, uncontrolled, almost insane rage - only to accept his due punishment (their reaction to his venomous diatribes or antisocial actions) with incredible complacency, or even relief. He engages in vitriolic humiliation of his kin and folk, of regime and government, of his firm or of the law - only to suffer pleasurably in the role of the outcast, the ex-communicated, the exiled, and the imprisoned martyr or dissident.

The punishment of the narcissist does little to compensate his randomly (rather incomprehensibly) selected victims. The narcissist forces individuals and groups of people around him to pay a heavy toll, materially, in reputation, and emotionally. He is ruinous, and disruptive.

379 In behaving so, the narcissist seeks not only to be punished, but also to maintain emotional detachment (Emotional Involvement Preventive Measures, EIPMs). Threatened by intimacy and by the predatory cosiness of routine and mediocrity, the narcissist lashes back at what he perceives to be the sources of this dual threat. He attacks those whom he thinks take him for granted, those who fail to recognize his superiority, those who consider him "average" and "normal".

And they, alas, include just about everyone he knows.

Narcissism by Proxy

Question: Is narcissism "contagious"? Can one "catch" narcissism by living with a narcissist?

Answer: Clinicians use the word "epidemiology" to describe the prevalence of psychopathologies. There is some merit in examining the incidence of personality disorders in the general population. Mental health is the visible outcome of an intricate interplay between nature and nurture, genetics and culture, the brain and one's upbringing and socialization.

Yet are personality disorders communicable diseases?

The answer is more complex than a simple "yes" or "no". Personality disorders are not contagious in the strict, rigorous, medical sense. They are not communicated by pathogens from one individual to another. They lack many of the basic features of biological epidemics. Still, they are communicated.

First, there is the direct, interpersonal, influence.

A casual encounter with a narcissist is likely to leave a bad aftertaste, bewilderment, hurt, or anger. But these transient reactions have no lasting effect and they fade with time. Not so with a more protracted exposure: marriage, partnership, cohabitation, working or studying together and the like.

Narcissism brushes off. Our reactions to the narcissist, the initial ridicule, the occasional rage, or the frustration tend to accumulate and form the sediment of deformity. Gradually, the narcissist distorts the personalities of those he is in constant touch with, casts them in his defective mould, limits them, redirects them, and inhibits them. When sufficiently cloned, the narcissist uses the people he affected as narcissistic proxies, narcissistic vehicles of vicarious narcissism.

The narcissist provokes in us emotions, which are predominantly negative and unpleasant. The initial reaction, as we said, is likely to be ridicule. The narcissist is pompous, incredibly self-centred, falsely grandiose, spoiled and odd (even his manner of speech is likely to be constrained and archaic). Thus, he often elicits smirks in lieu of admiration.

But the entertainment value is fast over. The narcissist's behaviour becomes tiresome, irksome and cumbersome. Ridicule is supplanted by ire and, then, by overt anger. The narcissist's inadequacies are so glaring and his denial and other defence mechanisms so primitive that we constantly feel like screaming at him, reproaching him, or even striking at him literally as well as figuratively.

Ashamed of these reactions, we begin to feel guilty. We find ourselves attached to a mental pendulum, swinging between repulsion and guilt, rage and pity, lack of empathy and remorse. Slowly we acquire the very characteristics of the narcissist that we so deplore. We become as tactless as he is, as devoid of empathy and of consideration, as ignorant of the emotional makeup of other people, and as one track minded. Exposed to the sick halo of the narcissist, we are "infected".

The narcissist invades our personality. He makes us react the way he would have liked to have reacted, had he dared, or had he known how (a mechanism known as Projective Identification). We are exhausted by his eccentricity, by his extravagance, by his grandiosity, by his constant entitlement.

The narcissist incessantly, adamantly, even aggressively makes demands upon his human environment. He is addicted to his Narcissistic Supply: admiration, adoration, approval, attention. He forces others to lie to him and over-rate his achievements, his talents, and his merits. Living in a narcissistic cult or fantasyland, he compels his closest, nearest and dearest to join him there.

The resulting depletion, exhaustion, desperation and weakening of the will are fully taken advantage of by the narcissist. He penetrates these reduced defences and, like a Trojan horse, spews forth his lethal charge. Gradually, those in proximity to him, find themselves imitating and emulating his personality traits. The narcissist also does not refrain from intimidating them into compliance with his commands.

The narcissist coerces people around him by making subtle uses of processes such as reinforcement and conditioning. As they seek to avoid the unpleasant consequences of not succumbing to his wishes, people put up with his demands and are subjected to his whims. Not to endure his terrifying rages, they "cut corners", pretend, participate in his charade, lie, and become subsumed in his grandiose fantasies.

Rather than be aggressively nagged, they reduce themselves and minimize their profiles, rendering themselves invisible. By doing all this they delude themselves into believing that they have escaped the worst consequences.

But the worst is yet to come. The narcissist is confined, constrained, restrained and inhibited by the unique structures of his personality and of his disorder. There are many behaviours which he cannot engage in, many reactions and actions "prohibited", many desires stifled, many fears insurmountable.

The narcissist uses others as an outlet for all these repressed emotions and behaviour patterns. Having invaded their personalities, having altered them by methods of attrition and erosion, having made them compatible with his own disorder, having secured the submission and compliance of his victims, he moves on to occupy their shells. Then he makes them do what he has always dreamt of doing, what he has often desired, what he has constantly feared to do.

Using the same compelling procedures, he drives his mates, spouse, partners, colleagues, children, or co-workers into collaborating in the expression of the repressed side of his personality. At the same time, he negates their vague suspicion that their personality has been replaced by his when committing these acts.

The narcissist can, thus, derive, vicariously, through the lives of others, the Narcissistic Supply that he so craves. He induces in his army of zombies criminal, romantic, or heroic, impulses. He makes his bots travel far and fast, breach all norms, gamble against all odds, fear none and nothing - in short: he transforms them into that which he could never be.

The narcissist thrives on the attention, admiration, fascination, or horrified reactions lavished upon his proxies. He consumes the Narcissistic Supply flowing through these human conduits of his own making. Such a narcissist is likely to use sentences like "I made him", "He was nothing before he met me", "He is my creation", "She learned everything she knows from me and at my expense", and so on.

Sufficiently detached - both emotionally and legally - the narcissist flees the scene when the going gets tough. Often, these behaviours, acts and emotions induced by the proximity to the narcissist result in harsh consequences. An emotional or legal crisis, a physical or material catastrophe are common outcomes of doing the narcissist's bidding.

The narcissist's prey is not equipped to deal with the crises that are the narcissist's daily bread and which, now, he or she are forced to confront as the narcissist's proxy. The behaviour and emotions induced by the narcissist are alien and the victim experiences a cognitive dissonance. This only aggravates the situation. But the narcissist is rarely there to watch his clones writhe and suffer.

At the first sign of trouble, he goes missing. This vanishing act is not necessarily physical or geographical. The narcissist is actually better at disappearing emotionally and at evading his moral and legal obligations (despite his constant self-righteous moralizing).

It is then and there that his family and coterie discover his true colours: he uses and discards people offhandedly. To him, people are either "functional" and "useful" in his pursuit of Narcissistic Supply - or they are not. But, in both cases, he regards them not as human but as objects, or mere abstractions. Of all the hurts that the narcissist inflicts on his nearest and ostensibly dearest, this abrupt and contemptuous disregard is, probably, the strongest and most enduring one.

When Victims Become Narcissists

Some people adopt the role of a professional victim. In doing so, they become self-centred, devoid of empathy, abusive, and exploitative. In other words, they become narcissists. The role of "professional victims" - people whose existence and very identity rest solely and entirely on their victimhood - is well researched in victimology. It doesn't make for nice reading.

These victim "pros" are often more cruel, vengeful, vitriolic, lacking in compassion and violent than their abusers. They make a career of it. They identify with this role to the exclusion of all else. This is precisely what I call "Narcissistic Contagion" or "Narcissism by Proxy".

Those affected entertain the (false) notion that they can compartmentalize their narcissistic behaviour and direct it only at the narcissist. In other words, they trust in their ability to segregate their conduct and to be verbally abusive towards the narcissist while civil and compassionate with others, to act with malice where the narcissist is concerned and with Christian charity towards all others.

They cling to the "faucet theory". They believe that they can turn on and off their negative feelings, their abusive outbursts, their vindictiveness and vengefulness, their blind rage, their non-discriminating judgement. This, of course, is untrue. These behaviours spill over into daily transactions with innocent neighbours, colleagues, family members, co-workers, or customers.

One cannot be partly or temporarily vindictive and judgemental any more than one can be partly or temporarily pregnant. To their horror, these victims discover that they have been transmuted and transformed into their worst nightmare: into narcissists.

Facilitating Narcissism

"The new narcissist is haunted not by guilt but by anxiety. He seeks not to inflict his own certainties on others but to find a meaning in life."
[Christopher Lasch - The Culture of Narcissism: American Life in an Age of Diminishing Expectations, 1979]

"A characteristic of our times is the predominance, even in groups traditionally selective, of the mass and the vulgar. Thus, in intellectual life, which of its essence requires and presupposes qualification, one can note the progressive triumph of the pseudo-intellectual, unqualified, unqualifiable..."
[Jose Ortega y Gasset - The Revolt of the Masses, 1932]

We are surrounded by malignant narcissists. How come this disorder has hitherto been largely ignored? How come there is such a dearth of research and literature regarding this crucial family of pathologies? Even mental health practitioners are woefully unaware of it and unprepared to assist its victims.

The sad answer is that narcissism meshes well with our culture. [See: "Lasch - The Cultural Narcissist" http://samvak.tripod.com/lasch.html]

It is a kind of a "background narcissistic radiation", permeating every social and cultural interaction. It is hard to distinguish pathological narcissists from ambitious, self-assertive, self-confident, self-promoting, eccentric, or highly individualistic persons. Hard sell, greed, envy, self-centredness, exploitativeness, diminished empathy are all socially condoned features of Western civilization.

Our society is atomized, the outcome of individualism gone awry. It encourages narcissistic leadership and role models. [Read about Narcissistic Leaders in FAQ 69]

Its sub-structures - institutionalized religion, political parties, civic organizations, the media, corporations - are all suffused with narcissism and pervaded by its pernicious outcomes. [See FAQ 72: Collective Narcissism]

The very ethos of materialism and capitalism upholds certain narcissistic traits, such as reduced empathy, exploitation, a sense of entitlement, or grandiose fantasies ("vision"). [More about this here: http://samvak.tripod.com/journal37.html]

Narcissists are aided, abetted and facilitated by four types of people and institutions: the adulators, the blissfully ignorant, the self-deceiving and those deceived by the narcissist.

The adulators are fully aware of the nefarious and damaging aspects of the narcissist's behaviour but believe that they are more than offset by his positive traits and by the benefits - to themselves, to their collective, or to society at large. They engage in an explicit trade-off between some of their principles and values and their personal profit, or the greater good. In a curious inversion of judgement, they cast the perpetrator as the victim of a smear campaign orchestrated by the abused or attribute the offender's predicament to bigotry.

They seek to help the narcissist, promote his agenda, shield him from harm, connect him with like-minded people, do his chores for him and, in general, create the conditions and the environment for his success. This kind of alliance is especially prevalent in political parties, the government, multinationals, religious organizations and other hierarchical collectives.

The blissfully ignorant are simply unaware of the "bad sides" of the narcissist - and make sure they remain oblivious to them. They look the other way, or pretend that the narcissist's behaviour is normative, or turn a blind eye to his egregious misbehaviour. They are classic deniers of reality. Some of them maintain a generally rosy outlook premised on the inbred benevolence of Mankind. Others simply cannot tolerate dissonance and discord. They prefer to live in a fantastic world where everything is harmonious and smooth and evil is banished. They react with rage to any information to the contrary and block it out instantly. Once they form an opinion that the accusations against the narcissist are overblown, malicious, and false - it becomes immutable. "I have made up my mind, - they seem to be broadcasting - now don't confuse me with the facts." This type of denial is well evidenced in dysfunctional families.

The self-deceivers are fully aware of the narcissist's transgressions and malice, his indifference, exploitativeness, lack of empathy, and rampant grandiosity - but they prefer to displace the causes, or the effects of such misconduct. They attribute it to externalities ("a rough patch"), or judge it to be temporary. They even go as far as accusing the victim for the narcissist's lapses, or for defending herself ("she provoked him").

In a feat of cognitive dissonance, they deny any connection between the acts of the narcissist and their consequences ("His wife abandoned him because she was promiscuous, not because of anything he did to her"). They are swayed by the narcissist's undeniable charm, intelligence, or attractiveness. But the narcissist needs not invest resources in converting them to his cause: he does not deceive them. They are self-propelled into the abyss that is narcissism. The inverted narcissist, for instance, is a self-deceiver. [See FAQ 50: The Inverted Narcissist]

The deceived are people - or institutions, or collectives - deliberately taken for a premeditated ride by the narcissist. He feeds them false information, manipulates their judgement, proffers plausible scenarios to account for his indiscretions, soils the opposition, charms them, appeals to their reason, or to their emotions, and promises the Moon.

Again, the narcissist's incontrovertible powers of persuasion and his impressive personality play a part in this predatory ritual. The deceived are especially hard to deprogram. They are often themselves encumbered with narcissistic traits and find it impossible to admit a mistake, or to atone.

They are likely to stay on with the narcissist to his - and their - bitter end.

Regrettably, the narcissist rarely pays the price for his offences. His victims pick up the tab. But even here the malignant optimism of the abused never ceases to amaze [read: The Malignant Optimism of the Abused in FAQ 92].

First published on the Suite 101 Narcissistic Personality Disorders Topic.

Narcissists in Positions of Authority

"He knows not how to rule a kingdom, that cannot manage a province; nor can he wield a province, that cannot order a city; nor he order a city, that knows not how to regulate a village; nor he a village, that cannot guide a family; nor can that man govern well a family that knows not how to govern himself; neither can any govern himself unless his reason be lord, will and appetite her vassals; nor can reason rule unless herself be ruled by God, and be obedient to Him."

[Hugo Grotius, Jurist]

Question: Are narcissists in position of authority likely to take advantage of their patients/students/subordinates?

Answer: Being in a position of authority secures the uninterrupted flow of Narcissistic Supply. Fed by the awe, fear, subordination, admiration, adoration and obedience of his underlings, parish, students, or patients, the narcissist thrives in such circumstances. The narcissist aspires to acquire authority by any means available to him. He may achieve it by making use of some outstanding traits or skills such as his intelligence, or through an asymmetry built into a relationship. The narcissistic medical doctor or mental health professional and his patients, the narcissistic guide, teacher, or mentor and his students, the narcissistic leader, guru, pundit, or psychic and his followers or admirers, or the narcissistic business tycoon, boss, or employer and his subordinates - all are instances of such asymmetry. The rich, powerful, more knowledgeable narcissists occupy a Pathological Narcissistic Space.

These types of relationships - based on the unidirectional and unilateral flow of Narcissistic Supply - border on abuse. The narcissist, in pursuit of an ever-increasing supply, of an ever-larger

388

SAM VAKNIN   MALIGNANT SELF LOVE

dose of adoration, and an ever-bigger fix of attention, gradually loses his moral constraints. With time, it gets harder to obtain Narcissistic Supply. The sources of such supply are human and they become weary, rebellious, tired, bored, disgusted, repelled, or plainly amused by the narcissist's incessant dependence, his childish craving for attention, his exaggerated or even paranoid fears which lead to obsessive-compulsive behaviours. To secure their continued collaboration in the procurement of his much-needed supply the narcissist might resort to emotional extortion, straight blackmail, abuse, or misuse of his authority.

The temptation to do so, though, is universal. No doctor is immune to the charms of certain female patients, nor are university professors asexual. What prevent them from immorally, cynically, callously and consistently abusing their positions are ethical imperatives embedded in them through socialization and empathy. They have learned the difference between right and wrong and, having internalized it, they choose right when they face a moral dilemma. They empathize with other human beings, "putting themselves in their shoes", and refrain from doing unto others what they do not wish to be done to them.

In these two crucial points narcissists differ from other humans.

Their socialization process - usually the product of problematic early relationships with Primary Objects (parents, or caregivers) - is often perturbed and results in social dysfunctioning. And they are incapable of empathizing: as far as they are concerned, people exist only to supply them with Narcissistic Supply. Those unfortunate few who do not comply with this overriding dictum must be made to alter their ways and if even this fails, the narcissist loses interest in them and classifies them as "sub-human, animals, service-providers, functions, symbols" and worse. Hence the abrupt shifts from over-valuation to devaluation of others. While bearing the gift of Narcissistic Supply the "other" is idealized by the narcissist. The narcissist shifts to the opposite pole (devaluation) when Narcissistic Supply dries up or when he estimates that it is about to.

As far as the narcissist is concerned, there is no moral dimension to abusing others - only a pragmatic one: will he be punished for doing so? The narcissist is atavistically responsive to fear and lacks any in-depth understanding of what it is to be a human being. Trapped in his pathology, the narcissist resembles an alien on drugs, a junkie of Narcissistic Supply devoid of the kind of language, which renders human emotions intelligible and communicable.

Narcissistic Leaders

"It was precisely that evening in Lodi that I came to believe in myself as an unusual person and became consumed with the ambition to do the great things that until then had been but a fantasy."

[Napoleon Bonaparte, "Thoughts"]

"They may all e called Heroes, in as much as they have derived their purposes and their vocation not from the calm regular course of things, sanctioned by the existing order, but from a concealed fount, from that inner Spirit, still hidden beneath the surface, which impinges on the outer world as a shell and bursts it into pieces - such were Alexander, Caesar, Napoleon... World-historical men - the Heroes of an epoch - must therefore be recognized as its clear-sighted ones: their deeds, their words are the best of their time... Moral claims which are irrelevant must not be brought into collision with World-historical deeds... So mighty a form must trample down many an innocent flower - crush to pieces many an object in its path."

[G.W.F. Hegel, "Lectures on the Philosophy of History"]

"Such beings are incalculable, they come like fate without cause or reason, inconsiderately and without pretext. Suddenly they are here like lightning too terrible, too sudden, too compelling and too 'different' even to be hated... What moves them is the terrible egotism of the artist of the brazen glance, who knows himself to be justified for all eternity in his 'work' as the mother is justified in her child...

In all great deceivers a remarkable process is at work to which they owe their power. In the very act of deception with all its preparations, the dreadful voice, expression, and gestures, they are overcome by their belief in themselves; it is this belief which then speaks, so persuasively, so miracle-like, to the audience."

[Friedrich Nietzsche, "The Genealogy of Morals"]

The narcissistic leader is the culmination and reification of his period, culture, and civilization. He is likely to rise to prominence in narcissistic societies.

The malignant narcissist invents and then projects a False, fictitious, Self for the world to fear, or to admire. He maintains a tenuous grasp on reality to start with and this is further exacerbated by the trappings of power. The narcissist's grandiose self-delusions and fantasies of omnipotence and omniscience are supported by real life authority and the narcissist's predilection to surround himself with obsequious sycophants.

The narcissist's personality is so precariously balanced that he cannot tolerate even a hint of criticism and disagreement. Most narcissists are paranoid and suffer from ideas of reference (the delusion that they are being mocked or discussed when they are not). Thus, narcissists often regard themselves counterfactually as "victims of persecution".

The narcissistic leader fosters and encourages a personality cult with all the hallmarks of an institutional religion: priesthood, rites, rituals, temples, worship, catechism, mythology. The leader is this religion's ascetic saint. He monastically denies himself earthly pleasures (or so he claims) in order to be able to dedicate himself fully to his calling.

The narcissistic leader is a monstrously inverted Jesus, sacrificing his life and denying himself so that his people - or humanity at large - should benefit. By surpassing and suppressing his humanity, the narcissistic leader becomes a distorted version of Nietzsche's "Superman".

But being a-human or super-human also means being a-sexual and a-moral.

In this restricted sense, narcissistic leaders are post-modernist and moral relativists. They project to the masses an androgynous figure and enhance it by engendering the adoration of nudity and all things "natural" - or by strongly repressing these feelings. But what they refer to as "nature" is not natural at all.

The narcissistic leader invariably proffers an aesthetic of decadence and evil carefully orchestrated and artificial - though it is not perceived this way by him or by his followers. Narcissistic leadership is about reproduced copies, not about originals. It is about the manipulation of symbols - not about veritable atavism or true conservatism.

In short: narcissistic leadership is about theatre, not about life. To enjoy the spectacle (and be subsumed by it), the leader demands the suspension of judgement, depersonalization, and de-realization. Catharsis is tantamount, in this narcissistic dramaturgy, to self-annulment.

Narcissism is nihilistic not only operationally, or ideologically. Its very language and narratives are nihilistic. Narcissism is conspicuous nihilism - and the cult's leader serves as a role model, annihilating the Man, only to re-appear as a pre-ordained and irresistible Force of Nature.

Narcissistic leadership often poses as a rebellion against the "old ways": against the hegemonic culture, the upper classes, the established religions, the superpowers, the corrupt order.

Narcissistic movements are puerile, a reaction to narcissistic injuries inflicted upon a narcissistic (and rather psychopathic) toddler nation-state, or group, or upon the leader.

Minorities or "others" - often arbitrarily selected - constitute a perfect, easily identifiable, embodiment of all that is "wrong". They are accused of being antiquated, of being eerily disembodied, cosmopolitan, part of the establishment, or "decadent". They are hated on religious and socio-economic grounds, or because of their race, sexual orientation, origin... They are castigated as different, as narcissistic (feel and act as morally superior), they are everywhere, they are defenceless, they are credulous, they are adaptable (and thus can be co-opted to collaborate in their own destruction). They are the perfect hate figures. Narcissists thrive on hatred and pathological envy.

This is precisely the source of the fascination with Hitler, diagnosed by Erich Fromm - together with Stalin - as a malignant narcissist. He was an inverted human. His unconscious was his conscious. He acted out our most repressed drives, fantasies, and wishes. He provides us with a glimpse of the horrors that lie beneath our social veneer, the barbarians at our personal gates, and what it was like before we invented civilization. Hitler forced us all through a time warp and many did not emerge. He was not the devil. He was one of us. He epitomized what Arendt aptly called the banality of evil: just an ordinary, mentally disturbed failure, a member of a mentally disturbed and failing nation, who lived through disturbed and failing times. He was the perfect mirror, a channel, a voice, and the very depth of our souls.

The narcissistic leader prefers the sparkle and glamour of well-orchestrated illusions to the tedium and method of real accomplishments. His reign is all smoke and mirrors, devoid of substances, consisting of mere appearances and mass delusions. In the aftermath of his regime - the narcissistic leader having died, been deposed, or voted out of office - it all unravels. The tireless and constant prestidigitation ceases and the entire edifice crumbles. What looked like an economic miracle turns out to have been a fraud-laced bubble. Loosely-held empires disintegrate. Laboriously assembled business conglomerates go to pieces. "Earth shattering" and "revolutionary" scientific discoveries and theories are discredited. Social experiments end in mayhem.

It is important to understand that the use of violence must be ego-syntonic. It must accord with the self-image of the narcissist. It must abet and sustain his grandiose fantasies and feed his sense of entitlement. It must conform to the narcissistic narrative.

Thus, a narcissist who regards himself as the benefactor of the poor, a member of the common folk, the representative of the disenfranchised, the champion of the dispossessed against the corrupt elite - is more unlikely to resort to violence against the poor, the disenfranchised, and the dispossessed.

The pacific mask crumbles when the narcissist becomes convinced that the very people he purported to speak for, his constituency, his grassroots fans, the Prime Sources of his Narcissistic Supply have turned against him. At first, in a desperate effort to maintain the fiction underlying his chaotic personality, the narcissist strives to explain away the sudden reversal of sentiment. "The people are being duped by (the media, big industry, foreign powers, the military, the elite, etc.)", "They don't really know what they are doing", "They will have a rude awakening and revert to form", etc. When these flimsy attempts to patch a tattered personal mythology fail, the narcissist is injured. Narcissistic injury inevitably leads to narcissistic rage and to a terrifying display of unbridled aggression. The pent-up frustration and hurt translate into devaluation. That which was previously idealized is now discarded with contempt and hatred.

This primitive defence mechanism is called "splitting". To the narcissist, things and people are either entirely bad (evil) or entirely good. "You are either with me or against me" is a common refrain. The narcissist projects onto others his own shortcomings and negative emotions, thus transforming himself, in his mind, into a totally good object. A narcissistic leader is likely to justify the butchering of his own people by claiming that they intended to kill him, undo the revolution, devastate the economy, or the country, etc.

The "small people", the "rank and file", the "loyal soldiers" of the narcissist - his flock, his nation, his employees - they pay the price. The disillusionment and disenchantment are agonizing. The process of reconstruction, of rising from the ashes, of overcoming the trauma of having been deceived, exploited and manipulated - is drawn-out. It is difficult to trust again, to have faith, to love, to be led, to collaborate. Feelings of shame and guilt engulf the erstwhile followers of the narcissist. This is his sole legacy: a massive Post-Traumatic Stress Disorder.

The Cult of the Narcissist

The narcissist is the guru at the centre of a cult. Like other gurus, he demands complete obedience from his flock: his spouse, his offspring, other family members, friends, and colleagues. He feels entitled to adulation and special treatment by his followers. He punishes the wayward and the straying lambs. He enforces discipline, adherence to his teachings, and common goals. The less accomplished he is in reality - the more stringent his mastery and the more pervasive the brainwashing.

The - often involuntary - members of the narcissist's mini-cult inhabit a twilight zone of his own construction. He imposes on them a shared psychosis, replete with persecutory delusions, "enemies", mythical narratives, and apocalyptic scenarios if he is flouted.

The narcissist's control is based on ambiguity, unpredictability, fuzziness, and ambient abuse. His ever-shifting whims exclusively define right versus wrong, desirable and unwanted, what is to be pursued and what to be avoided. He alone determines the rights and obligations of his disciples and alters them at will.

The narcissist is a micro-manager. He exerts control over the minutest details and behaviours. He punishes severely and abuses withholders of information and those who fail to conform to his wishes and goals.

The narcissist does not respect the boundaries and privacy of his reluctant adherents. He ignores their wishes and treats them as objects or instruments of gratification. He seeks to control both situations and people compulsively.

He strongly disapproves of others' personal autonomy and independence. Even innocuous activities, such as meeting a friend or visiting one's family require his permission. Gradually, he isolates his nearest and dearest until they are fully dependent on him emotionally, sexually, financially, and socially.

He acts in a patronizing and condescending manner and criticizes often. He alternates between emphasizing the minutest faults (devaluation) and exaggerating the talents, traits, and skills (idealization) of the members of his cult. He is wildly unrealistic in his expectations - which, when he is inevitably let down, legitimizes his subsequent abusive conduct.

The narcissist claims to be infallible, superior, talented, skilful, omnipotent, and omniscient. He often lies and confabulates to support these unfounded claims. Within his cult, he expects awe, admiration, adulation, and constant attention commensurate with his outlandish stories and assertions. He reinterprets reality to fit his fantasies.

His thinking is dogmatic, rigid, and doctrinaire. He does not countenance free thought, pluralism, or free speech and doesn't brook criticism and disagreement. He demands - and often gets -

complete trust and the relegation to his capable hands of all decision-making. He forces the participants in his cult to be hostile to critics, the authorities, institutions, his personal enemies, or the media - if they try to uncover his actions and reveal the truth. He closely monitors and censors information from the outside, exposing his captive audience only to selective data and analyses.

The narcissist's cult is "missionary" and "imperialistic". He is always on the lookout for new recruits - his spouse's friends, his daughter's girlfriends, his neighbours, new colleagues at work. He immediately attempts to "convert" them to his "creed" - to convince them how wonderful and admirable he is. In other words, he tries to render them Sources of Narcissistic Supply.

Often, his behaviour on these "recruiting missions" is different to his conduct within the "cult". In the first phases of wooing new admirers and proselytizing to potential "conscripts" - the narcissist is attentive, compassionate, empathic, flexible, self-effacing, and helpful. At home, among the "veterans" he is tyrannical, demanding, wilful, opinionated, aggressive, and exploitative.

As the leader of his congregation, the narcissist feels entitled to special amenities and benefits not accorded the "rank and file". He expects to be waited on hand and foot, to make free use of everyone's money and dispose of their assets liberally, and to be cynically exempt from the rules that he himself established (if such violation is pleasurable or gainful).

In extreme cases, the narcissist feels above the law - any kind of law. This grandiose and haughty conviction leads to criminal acts, incestuous or polygamous relationships, and recurrent friction with the authorities.

Hence the narcissist's panicky and sometimes violent reactions to "dropouts" from his cult. There's a lot going on that the narcissist wants kept under wraps. Moreover, the narcissist stabilizes his fluctuating sense of self-worth by deriving Narcissistic Supply from his victims. Abandonment threatens the narcissist's precariously balanced personality.

Add to that the narcissist's paranoid and schizoid tendencies, his lack of introspective self-awareness, and his stunted sense of humour (lack of self-deprecation) and the risks to the grudging members of his cult are clear.

The narcissist sees enemies and conspiracies everywhere. He often casts himself as the heroic victim (martyr) of dark and stupendous forces. In every deviation from his tenets he espies malevolent and ominous subversion. He, therefore, is bent on disempowering his devotees. By any and all means.

The Professions of the Narcissist

The narcissist naturally gravitates towards those professions which guarantee the abundant and uninterrupted provision of Narcissistic Supply. He seeks to interact with people from a position of authority, advantage, or superiority. He thus elicits their automatic admiration, adulation, and affirmation - or, failing that, their fear and obedience.

Several vocations meet these requirements: teaching, the priesthood, show business, corporate management, the medical professions, politics, and sports. It is safe to predict that narcissists would be over-represented in these occupations.

The cerebral narcissist is likely to emphasize his intellectual prowess and accomplishments (real and imaginary) in an attempt to solicit supply from awe-struck students, devoted parishioners, admiring voters, obsequious subordinates, or dependent patients. His somatic counterpart derives his sense of self-worth from body building, athletic achievements, tests of resilience or endurance, and sexual conquests.

The narcissistic medical doctor or mental health professional and his patients, the narcissistic guide, teacher, or mentor and his students, the narcissistic leader, guru, pundit, or psychic and his followers or admirers, and the narcissistic business tycoon, boss, or employer and his underlings are all instances of Pathological Narcissistic Spaces.

This is a worrisome state of affairs. Narcissists are liars. They misrepresent their credentials, knowledge, talents, skills, and achievements. A narcissist medical doctor would rather let patients die than expose his ignorance. A narcissistic therapist often traumatizes his clients with his acting out, rage, exploitativeness, and lack of empathy. Narcissistic businessmen bring ruin on their firms and employees.

Nor is the narcissist deterred by possible punishment or regards himself subject to Man-made laws. His sense of entitlement coupled with the conviction of his own superiority lead him to believe in his invincibility, invulnerability, immunity, and divinity. The narcissist holds human edicts, rules, and regulations in disdain and human penalties in contempt. He regards human needs and emotions as weaknesses to be predatorily exploited.

For the Love of God

"1 But know this, that in the last days perilous times will come: 2 For men will be lovers of themselves, lovers of money, boasters, proud, blasphemers, disobedient to parents, unthankful, unholy, 3 unloving, unforgiving, slanderers, without self-control, brutal, despisers of good, 4 traitors, headstrong, haughty, lovers of pleasure rather than lovers of God, 5 having a form of godliness but denying its power. And from such people turn away! 6 For of this sort are those who creep into households and make captives of gullible women loaded down with sins, led away by various lusts, 7 always learning and never able to come to the knowledge of the truth. 8 Now as Jan'nes and Jam'bres resisted Moses, so do these also resist the truth: men of corrupt minds, disapproved concerning the faith; 9 but they will progress no further, for their folly will be manifest to all, as theirs also was."

[The Second Epistle of Paul the Apostle to Timothy 3:1-9]

Question: I think that my priest is a narcissist. Can men of God be narcissists?

Answer: God is everything the narcissist ever wants to be: omnipotent, omniscient, omnipresent, admired, much discussed, and awe inspiring. God is the narcissist's wet dream, his ultimate grandiose fantasy. But God comes handy in other ways as well.

The narcissist alternately idealizes and devalues figures of authority.

In the idealization phase, he strives to emulate them, he admires them, imitates them (often ludicrously), and defends them. They cannot go wrong, or be wrong. The narcissist regards them as bigger than life, infallible, perfect, whole, and brilliant. But as the narcissist's unrealistic and inflated expectations are inevitably frustrated, he begins to devalue his former idols.

Now they are "human" (to the narcissist, a derogatory term). They are small, fragile, error-prone, pusillanimous, mean, dumb, and mediocre. The narcissist goes through the same cycle in his relationship with God, the quintessential authority figure.

But often, even when disillusionment and iconoclastic despair set in, the narcissist continues to pretend to love God and follow Him. The narcissist maintains this deception because his continued proximity to God confers on him authority. Priests, leaders of the congregation, preachers, evangelists, cultists, politicians, intellectuals - all derive authority from their allegedly privileged relationship with God.

Religious authority allows the narcissist to indulge his sadistic urges and to exercise his misogynism freely and openly. Such a narcissist is likely to taunt and torment his followers, hector and chastise them, humiliate and berate them, abuse them spiritually, or even sexually. The narcissist whose source of authority is religion is looking for obedient and unquestioning slaves upon whom to exercise his capricious and wicked mastery. The narcissist transforms even the most innocuous and pure religious sentiments into a cultish ritual and a virulent hierarchy. He preys on the gullible. His flock become his hostages.

Religious authority also secures the narcissist's Narcissistic Supply. His coreligionists, members of his congregation, his parish, his constituency, his audience are transformed into loyal and stable Sources of Narcissistic Supply. They obey his commands, heed his admonitions, follow his creed, admire his personality, applaud his personal traits, satisfy his needs (sometimes even his carnal desires), revere and idolize him.

Moreover, being a part of an immanent "bigger thing" is very gratifying narcissistically. Being a particle of God, being immersed in His grandeur, experiencing His power and blessings first hand, communing with him are all Sources of unending Narcissistic Supply. The narcissist becomes God by observing His commandments, following His instructions, loving Him, obeying Him, succumbing to Him, merging with Him, communicating and communing with Him, or even by defying Him (the greater the narcissist's adversary - the more grandiosely important the narcissist feels).

Like everything else in the narcissist's life, he mutates God into a kind of inverted narcissist. God becomes his dominant

Source of Supply. He forms a personal relationship with this overwhelming and overpowering entity in order to overwhelm and overpower others. He becomes God vicariously, by the proxy of his relationship with Him. He idealizes God, then devalues Him, then abuses Him. This is the classic narcissistic pattern and even God himself cannot escape it.

First published on the Suite 101 Narcissistic Personality Disorders Topic.

The Narcissist and Social Institutions

Question: Can narcissism be reconciled with a belief in any values?

Answer: The narcissist is prone to magical thinking. He regards himself in terms of "being chosen" or of "being destined for greatness". He believes that he has a "direct line" to God, even, perversely, that God "serves" him in certain junctions and conjunctures of his life, through divine intervention. He believes that his life is of such momentous importance, that it is micro-managed by God. The narcissist likes to play God to his human environment. In short, narcissism and religion go well together, because religion allows the narcissist to feel unique and to exert moral and institutional authority over others.

This is a private case of a more general phenomenon. The narcissist likes to belong to groups or to frameworks of allegiance. He derives easy and constantly available Narcissistic Supply from them. Within them and from their members he is certain to garner attention, to gain adulation, to be castigated or praised. His False Self is bound to be reflected by his colleagues, co-members, or fellows.

This is no mean feat and it cannot be guaranteed in other circumstances. Hence the narcissist's fanatic and proud emphasis of his membership. If a military man, he shows off his impressive array of medals, his impeccably pressed uniform, the status symbols of his rank. If a clergyman, he is overly devout and orthodox and places great emphasis on the proper conduct of rites, rituals and ceremonies.

The narcissist develops a reverse (benign) form of paranoia: he feels constantly watched over by senior members of his group or frame of reference, the subject of permanent (avuncular) criticism, the centre of attention. If a religious man, he calls it divine providence. This self-centred perception also caters to

MALIGNANT SELF LOVE   SAM VAKNIN

the narcissist's streak of grandiosity, proving that he is, indeed, worthy of such incessant and detailed attention, supervision and intervention.

From this mental junction, the way is short to entertaining the delusion that God (or the equivalent institutional authority) is an active participant in the narcissist's life in which constant intervention by Him is a key feature. God is subsumed in a larger picture, that of the narcissist's destiny and mission. God serves this cosmic plan by making it possible.

Indirectly, therefore, God is perceived by the narcissist to be at his service. Moreover, in a process of holographic appropriation, the narcissist views himself as a microcosm of his affiliation, of his group, of the collective or frame of reference. The narcissist is likely to say that he IS the army, the nation, the people, the struggle, history, or (a part of) God.

As opposed to healthier people, the narcissist believes that he both represents and reifies his class, his people, his race, history, his God, his art - or anything else he feels a part of. This is why individual narcissists feel completely comfortable to assume roles usually reserved to groups of people or to some transcendental, divine (or other), authority.

This kind of "personal inflation" also sits well with the narcissist's all-pervasive feelings of omnipotence and omniscience. In playing God, for instance, the narcissist is completely convinced that he is merely being himself. The narcissist does not hesitate to put people's lives or fortunes at risk. He preserves his sense of infallibility in the face of mistakes and misjudgements by distorting the facts, by blaming others, by evoking mitigating or attenuating circumstances, by repressing memories, or by simply lying.

In the overall design of things, small setbacks and defeats matter little, says the narcissist. The narcissist is haunted by the feeling that he is possessed of a mission, of a destiny, that he is the destined conveyor of fate, of history. He is convinced that his uniqueness is purposeful, that he is meant to lead, to chart new ways, to innovate, to modernize, to reform, to set precedents, or to create something unprecedented from scratch.

Every act of the narcissist is perceived by him to be significant, every utterance of momentous consequence, every thought of revolutionary calibre. He feels part of a grand design, a world plan and the frame of affiliation, the group, of which he is a member, must be commensurately grand. Its proportions and properties must resonate with his. Its characteristics must justify his and its ideology must conform to his pre-conceived opinions and prejudices.

In short: the group must magnify the narcissist, echo and amplify his life, his views, his knowledge, and his personal history. This intertwining, this enmeshing of individual and collective is what makes the narcissist the most devout and loyal of all members.

The narcissist is always the most fanatical, the most extreme, the most dangerous adherent. At stake is never merely the preservation of his group but his very own survival. As with other Narcissistic Supply Sources, once the group is no longer instrumental, the narcissist loses all interest in it, devalues it and ignores it.

In extreme cases, he might even wish to destroy it (as a punishment or revenge for its incompetence in securing his emotional needs). Narcissists switch groups and ideologies with ease (as they do partners, spouses and value systems). In this respect, narcissists are narcissists first and members of their groups only in the second place.

Collective Narcissism

Narcissism, Culture and Society

"It is always possible to bind together a considerable number of people in love, so long as there are other people left over to receive the manifestations of their aggressiveness."
[Sigmund Freud, Civilization and its Discontents]

403

Question: I believe that (ethnic group deleted) are all narcissists. Can it be that a group of people are all narcissists or am I your average bigot and racist?

Answer: In their book "Personality Disorders in Modern Life", Theodore Millon and Roger Davis state, as a matter of fact, that pathological narcissism was the preserve of *"the royal and the wealthy"* and that it *"seems to have gained prominence only in the late twentieth century"*. Narcissism, according to them, may be associated with *"higher levels of Maslow's hierarchy of needs... Individuals in less advantaged nations ... are too busy trying (to survive) ... to be arrogant and grandiose"*.

They - like Christopher Lasch before them - attribute pathological narcissism to *"a society that stresses individualism and self-gratification at the expense of community, namely the United States"*. They assert that the disorder is more prevalent among certain professions with "star power" or respect. *"In an individualistic culture, the narcissist is 'God's gift to the world'. In a collectivist society, the narcissist is 'God's gift to the collective'."*

Millon quotes Warren and Caponi's "The Role of Culture in the Development of Narcissistic Personality Disorders in America, Japan and Denmark":

"Individualistic narcissistic structures of self-regard (in individualistic societies) ... are rather self-contained and independent...

(In collectivist cultures) narcissistic configurations of the we-self ... denote self-esteem derived from strong identification with the reputation and honour of the family, groups, and others in hierarchical relationships."

But Millon and Davis are wrong. Theirs is, indeed, the quintessential American point of view which lacks an intimate knowledge of other parts of the world. Millon even wrongly claims that the DSM's international equivalent, the ICD, does not include the Narcissistic Personality Disorder (it does, though not as a separate mental health diagnosis).

Pathological narcissism is a ubiquitous phenomenon because every human being - regardless of the nature of his society and culture - develops healthy narcissism early in life. Healthy narcissism is rendered pathological by abuse - and abuse, alas, is a universal human behaviour. By "abuse" we mean any refusal to acknowledge the emerging boundaries of the individual - smothering, doting, and excessive expectations are as abusive as beating and incest.

There are malignant narcissists among subsistence farmers in Africa, nomads in the Sinai desert, day labourers in East Europe, and intellectuals and socialites in Manhattan. Malignant narcissism is all-pervasive and independent of culture and society.

It is true, though that the WAY pathological narcissism manifests and is experienced is dependent on the particulars of societies and cultures. In some cultures, it is encouraged, in others suppressed. In some societies it is channelled against minorities - in others it is tainted with paranoia. In collectivist societies, it may be projected onto the collective, in individualistic societies it is an individual's trait.

Yet, can families, organizations, ethnic groups, churches, and even whole nations be safely described as "narcissistic" or "pathologically self-absorbed"? Wouldn't such generalizations be a trifle racist and more than a trifle wrong? The answer is: it depends.

Human collectives - states, firms, households, institutions, political parties, cliques, bands - acquire a life and a character all their own. The longer the association or affiliation of the members, the more cohesive and conformist the inner dynamics of the group, the more persecutory or numerous its enemies, the more intensive the physical and emotional experiences of the individuals it is comprised of, the stronger the bonds of locale, language, and history - the more rigorous might an assertion of a common pathology be.

Such an all-pervasive and extensive pathology manifests itself in the behaviour of each and every member. It is a defining - though often an implicit or underlying - mental structure. It has explanatory and predictive powers. It is recurrent and invariable: a pattern of conduct melded with distorted cognition and stunted emotions. And it is often vehemently denied.

A possible DSM-like list of criteria for narcissistic organizations or groups:

An all-pervasive pattern of grandiosity (in fantasy or behaviour), need for admiration or adulation and lack of empathy, usually beginning at the group's early history and present in various contexts. Persecution and abuse are often the causes - or at least the antecedents - of the pathology.

Five (or more) of the following criteria must be met:

- The group as a whole, or members of the group - acting as such and by virtue of their association and affiliation with the group - feel grandiose and self-important (e.g., they exaggerate the group's achievements and talents to the point of lying, demand to be recognized as superior simply for belonging to the group and without commensurate achievement).

- The group as a whole, or members of the group - acting as such and by virtue of their association and affiliation with the group - are obsessed with group fantasies of unlimited success, fame, fearsome power or omnipotence, unequalled brilliance, bodily beauty or performance, or ideal, everlasting, all-conquering ideals or political theories.

- The group as a whole, or members of the group - acting as such and by virtue of their association and affiliation with the group - are firmly convinced that the group is unique and, being special, can only be understood by, should only be treated by, or associate with, other special or unique, or high-status groups (or institutions).

- The group as a whole, or members of the group - acting as such and by virtue of their association and affiliation with the group - require excessive admiration, adulation, attention and affirmation - or, failing that, wish to be feared and to be notorious (Narcissistic Supply).

- The group as a whole, or members of the group - acting as such and by virtue of their association and affiliation with the group - feel entitled. They expect unreasonable or special and favourable priority treatment. They demand automatic and full compliance with expectations. They rarely accept responsibility for their actions ("alloplastic defences"). This often leads to anti-social behaviour, cover-ups, and criminal activities on a mass scale.

- The group as a whole, or members of the group - acting as such and by virtue of their association and affiliation with the group - are "interpersonally exploitative", i.e., use others to achieve their own ends. This often leads to anti-social behaviour, cover-ups, and criminal activities on a mass scale.

- The group as a whole, or members of the group - acting as such and by virtue of their association and affiliation with the group - are devoid of empathy. They are unable or unwilling to identify with or acknowledge the feelings and needs of other groups. This often leads to anti-social behaviour, cover-ups, and criminal activities on a mass scale.

- The group as a whole, or members of the group - acting as such and by virtue of their association and affiliation with the group - are constantly envious of others or believe that they are being equally envied. This often leads to anti-social behaviour, cover-ups, and criminal activities on a mass scale.

- The group as a whole, or members of the group - acting as such and by virtue of their association and affiliation with the group - are arrogant and sport haughty behaviours or attitudes coupled with rage when frustrated, contradicted, punished, limited, or confronted. This often leads to anti-social behaviour, cover-ups, and criminal activities on a mass scale.

The Narcissist in Court

Question: How can I expose the lies of the narcissist in a court of law? He acts so convincing!

Answer: You should distinguish the factual pillar from the psychological pillar of any cross-examination of a narcissist or a deposition made by him.

It is essential to be equipped with absolutely unequivocal, first rate, thoroughly authenticated and vouched for information. The reason is that narcissists are superhuman in their capacity to distort reality by offering highly "plausible" alternative scenarios, which fit most of the facts.

It is very easy to "break" a narcissist - even a well-trained and well-prepared one.

Here are a few of the things the narcissist finds devastating:
- Any statement or fact, which seems to contradict his inflated perception of his grandiose self.
- Any criticism, disagreement, exposure of fake achievements, belittling of "talents and skills" which the narcissist fantasizes that he possesses.
- Any hint that he is subordinated, subjugated, controlled, owned or dependent upon a third party.
- Any description of the narcissist as average and common, indistinguishable from others.
- Any hint that the narcissist is weak, needy, dependent, deficient, slow, not intelligent, naive, gullible, susceptible, not in the know, manipulated, a victim, an average person of mediocre accomplishments.

The narcissist is likely to react with rage to all these and, in an effort to re-establish his fantastic grandiosity, he is likely to expose facts and stratagems he had no conscious intention of exposing.

407

The narcissist reacts indignantly, with wrath, hatred, aggression, or even overt violence to any infringement of what he perceives to be his natural entitlement.

Narcissists believe that they are so unique and that their lives are of such cosmic significance that others should defer to their needs and cater to their every whim without ado. The narcissist feels entitled to interact or be treated (or questioned) only by unique individuals. He resents being doubted and "ridiculed".

Any insinuation, hint, intimation, or direct declaration that the narcissist is not special at all, that he is average, common, not even sufficiently idiosyncratic to warrant a fleeting interest inflame the narcissist. He holds himself to be omnipotent and omniscient.

Tell the narcissist that he does not deserve the best treatment, that his desires are not everyone's priority, that he is boring or ignorant, that his needs can be catered to by any common practitioner (medical doctor, accountant, lawyer, psychiatrist), that he and his motives are transparent and can be easily gauged, that he will do what he is told, that his temper tantrums will not be tolerated, that no special concessions will be made to accommodate his inflated sense of self, that he is subject to court procedures, etc. - and the narcissist will likely lose control.

The narcissist believes that he is the cleverest of all, far above the madding crowd.

Contradict him often, disagree with him and criticize his judgement, expose his shortcomings, humiliate and berate him: "You are not as intelligent as you think you are", "Who is really behind all this? It takes sophistication which you don't seem to posses", "So, you have no formal education", "You are (mistake his age, make him much older)", "What did you do in your life? Did you study? Do you have an academic degree? Did you ever establish or run a business? Would you define yourself as a success?", "Would your children share your view that you are a good father?", "You were last seen with a certain Ms. ... who is (suppressed grin) a stripper (in demeaning disbelief)."

I know that many of these questions cannot be asked outright in a court of law. But you can insinuate them or hurl these sentences at him during the breaks, inadvertently during the examination or deposition phase, etc. Narcissists hate innuendos even more than they detest direct attacks.

The Narcissist in the Workplace

Question: The narcissist turns the workplace into a duplicitous hell. What to do?

Answer: To a narcissistic employer, the members of his "staff" are Secondary Sources of Narcissistic Supply. Their role is to accumulate Narcissistic Supply (i.e., to remember events that support the grandiose self-image of the narcissist) and to regulate the Narcissistic Supply of the narcissist during dry spells: to adulate, adore, admire, agree, provide attention and approval, and, generally, serve as an audience to him. The staff (or should we say "stuff"?) is supposed to remain passive. The narcissist is not interested in anything but the simplest function of mirroring. When the mirror acquires a personality and a life of its own, the narcissist is incensed. When independent-minded, an employee might be in danger of being sacked by his narcissistic employer (an act which demonstrates the employer's omnipotence).

409

The employee's presumption to be the employer's equal by trying to befriend him (friendship is possible only among equals) injures the employer narcissistically. He is willing to accept his employees only as underlings, whose very position serves to support his grandiose fantasies.

But his grandiosity is so tenuous and rests on such fragile foundations, that any hint of equality, disagreement or need (any intimation that the narcissist "needs" friends, for instance) threatens the narcissist profoundly. The narcissist is exceedingly insecure. It is easy to destabilize his impromptu "personality". His harsh reactions are merely in self-defence.

Classic narcissistic behaviour is when idealization is followed by devaluation. The devaluing attitude develops as a result of disagreements or simply because time has eroded the employee's capacity to serve as a FRESH Source of Supply.

The veteran employee, now taken for granted by his narcissistic employer, becomes uninspiring as a source of adulation, admiration and attention. The narcissist always seeks new thrills and stimuli.

The narcissist is notorious for his low threshold of resistance to boredom. His behaviour is impulsive and his biography tumultuous precisely because of his need to introduce uncertainty and risk to what he regards as "stagnation" or "slow death" (i.e., routine). Most interactions in the workplace are part of the rut - and thus constitute a reminder of this routine - deflating the narcissist's grandiose fantasies.

Narcissists do many unnecessary, wrong and even dangerous things in pursuit of the stabilization of their inflated self-image.

Narcissists feel suffocated by intimacy, or by the constant reminders of the REAL, nitty-gritty world out there. It reduces them, makes them realize the Grandiosity Gap between their fantasies and reality. It is a threat to the precarious balance of their personality structures ("false" and invented) and treated by them as a menace or a nuisance.

Narcissists forever shift the blame, pass the buck, and engage in cognitive dissonance. They "pathologize" the other, foster feelings of guilt and shame in her, demean, debase and humiliate in order to preserve their sense of superiority.

Narcissists are pathological liars. They think nothing of it because their very Self is False and their own confabulation.

Here are a few useful guidelines:

- Never disagree with the narcissist or contradict him;
- Never offer him any intimacy;
- Look awed by whatever attribute matters to him (for instance: by his professional achievements or by his good looks, or by his success with women and so on);
- Never remind him of life out there and if you do, connect it somehow to his sense of grandiosity. You can aggrandize even your office supplies, the most mundane thing conceivable by saying: "These are the BEST art materials ANY workplace is going to have", "We get them EXCLUSIVELY", etc.;
- Do not make any comment, which might directly or indirectly impinge on the narcissist's self-image, omnipotence, superior judgement, omniscience, skills, capabilities, professional record, or even omnipresence. Bad sentences start with: "I think you overlooked ... made a mistake here ... you don't know ... do you know ... you were not here yesterday so ... you cannot ... you should ... (interpreted as rude impo-

sition, narcissists react very badly to perceived restrictions placed on their freedom) ... I (never mention the fact that you are a separate, independent entity, narcissists regard others as extensions of their selves)..."

Manage your narcissistic boss. Notice patterns in his bullying. Is he more aggressive on Monday mornings and more open to suggestions on Friday afternoon? Is he amenable to flattery? Can you modify his conduct by appealing to his morality, superior knowledge, good manners, cosmopolitanism, or upbringing? Manipulating the narcissist is the only way to survive in such a tainted workplace.

Can the narcissist be harnessed? Can his energies be channelled productively?

This would be a deeply flawed - and even dangerous - strategy.. Various management gurus purport to teach us how to harness this force of nature known as malignant or pathological narcissism. Narcissists are driven, visionary, ambitious, exciting and productive, says Michael Maccoby, for instance. To ignore such a resource is a criminal waste. All we need to do is learn how to "handle" them.

Yet, this prescription is either naive or disingenuous. Narcissists cannot be "handled", or "managed", or "contained", or "channelled". They are, by definition, incapable of team work. They lack empathy, are exploitative, envious, haughty and feel entitled, even if such a feeling is commensurate only with their grandiose fantasies and when their accomplishments are meagre.

Narcissists dissemble, conspire, destroy and self-destruct. Their drive is compulsive, their vision rarely grounded in reality, their human relations a calamity. In the long run, there is no enduring benefit to dancing with narcissists - only ephemeral and, often, fallacious, "achievements".

Responsibility and Other Matters

Question: The narcissist is not entirely responsible for his actions. Should we judge him, get angry at him, be upset by him? Above all, should we communicate to him our displeasure?

Answer: The narcissist knows to tell right from wrong. He is perfectly capable of anticipating the results of his actions and their influence on his human environment. The narcissist is very perceptive and sensitive to the subtlest nuances. He has to be: the very integrity of his personality depends upon input from others.

But the narcissist does not care. Unable to empathize, he does not fully experience the outcomes of his deeds and decisions. For him, people are dispensable, rechargeable, reusable, and interchangeable. They are there to fulfil a function: to supply him with Narcissistic Supply (adoration, admiration, approval, affirmation, etc.) They do not have an existence apart from the carrying out of this duty.

True: it is the disposition of the narcissist to treat people in the inhuman way that he does. However, this propensity is absolutely controllable. The narcissist has a choice - he just doesn't think anyone is worth making it.

It is a fact that the narcissist can behave completely differently (under identical circumstances) - depending on who else is involved. He is not likely to be enraged by the behaviour of an important person (with a potential to supply him narcissistically). But, he might become absolutely violent with his nearest and dearest under the same circumstances. This is because they are captives, they do not have to be won over, the Narcissistic Supply emanating from them is taken for granted.

Being a narcissist does not exempt one from the obligation to act civil, lawfully, and humanely. A person afflicted with the Narcissistic Personality Disorder (NPD) must be subjected to the same moral treatment and judgement as the rest of us, less privileged ones. The courts do not recognize NPD as a mitigating circumstance - why should we? Treating the narcissist specially will only exacerbate the condition by supporting the grandiose, fantastic image the narcissist has of himself.

By all means: be angry, be upset with the narcissist (for good and just reasons) and don't hesitate to communicate your displeasure. The narcissist needs guidance (he is disorientated) and this is one of the best ways of providing him with one.

413

The Accountable Narcissist

Question: Should the narcissist be held accountable for his actions?

Answer: Narcissists of all shades can usually control their behaviour and actions. They simply don't care to, they regard it as a waste of their precious time, or a humiliating chore. The narcissist feels both superior and entitled, regardless of his real gifts or achievements. Other people are inferior, his slaves, there to cater to his needs and make his existence seamless, flowing and smooth.

The narcissist holds himself to be cosmically significant and thus entitled to the conditions needed to realize his talents and to successfully complete his mission (which changes fluidly and about which he hasn't got a clue except that it has to do with brilliance and fame).

What the narcissist cannot control is his inner void, his emotional black hole, the fact that he doesn't know what it is like to be human (because he lacks empathy). As a result, narcissists are awkward, tactless, painful, taciturn, abrasive and insensitive.

The narcissist should be held accountable for most of his actions, even taking into account his sometimes uncontrollable rage and the backdrop of his grandiose fantasies.

Admittedly, at times, the narcissist finds it hard control his rage.

But at all times, even during the worst explosive episode:
a. The narcissist can tell right from wrong, but...
b. He simply doesn't care about the other person sufficiently to refrain from deleterious action.

Similarly, the narcissist cannot "control" his grandiose fantasies. He firmly believes that they constitute an accurate representation of reality. Still:

414

MALIGNANT SELF LOVE   SAM VAKNIN

a. He knows that lying is wrong and not done, but...
b. He simply doesn't care enough about society and others to refrain from confabulating.

To summarize, narcissists should be held accountable for most of their actions because they can tell wrong from right and they can refrain from acting antisocially. They simply don't care enough about others to put to good use these twin abilities. Others are not sufficiently important to dent the narcissist's indifference or to alter his abusive conduct.

Crime and Punishment:
The Never Repenting Narcissist

Question: Do narcissists feel guilty and if so, do they ever repent?

Answer: The narcissist has no criminal intent ("mens rea"), though he may commit criminal acts ("acti rei"). Unlike the psychopath, he does not victimize, plunder, terrorize and abuse others in a cold, calculating manner. He does so offhandedly, as a manifestation of his genuine character. The narcissist is not morally repugnant because he is not purposeful, he is not deliberate and he does not contemplate the options and then prefers evil to good or chooses wrong over right. No ethical or moral judgement is possible without an act of choice.

The narcissist's perception of his life and his existence is discontinuous. The narcissist is a walking compilation of "personalities", each with its own history. The narcissist does not feel that he is, in any way, related to his former "selves". He, therefore, does not understand why he has to be punished for "someone else's" actions or inaction.

This "injustice" surprises, hurts, and enrages him.

The narcissist is taken aback by society's insistence that he should be held accountable and punished for his transgressions. He feels wronged, hurt, the victim of pettiness, bigotry, bias, discrimination and injustice. He rebels and rages. Unable to link his act (perpetrated, as far as he is concerned, by a previous phase of his self, alien to his "current" self) to its outcomes, the narcissist is constantly baffled. Depending upon how pervasive his magical thinking is, the narcissist may develop persecutory delusions making him the quarry of powers cosmic and intrinsically ominous. He may develop compulsive rites to fend off this impending threat.

416

SAM VAKNIN   MALIGNANT SELF LOVE

The narcissist is an assemblage. He plays host to many personas. One of the personas is always in the "limelight". This is the persona, which interfaces with the outside world, and which guarantees an optimal inflow of Narcissistic Supply. This is the persona which minimizes friction and resistance in the narcissist's daily dealings and, thus, the energy which the narcissist needs to expend in the process of obtaining his supply.

The "limelight persona" is surrounded by "shade personas". These are potential personas, ready to surface as soon as needed. Their emergence depends on their usefulness.

An old persona might be rendered useless or less useful by a confluence of events. The narcissist is in the habit of constantly and erratically changing his circumstances. He switches between vocations, marriages, "friendships", countries, residences, lovers, and even enemies with startling and dazzling swiftness. He is a machine whose sole aim is to optimize its input, rather than its output: the input of Narcissistic Supply.

To achieve its goal, this machine stops at nothing, and does not hesitate to alter itself beyond recognition. The narcissist is the true shape-shifter. To achieve ego-syntony (to feel good despite all these upheavals), the narcissist uses the twin mechanisms of idealization and devaluation. The first is intended to help him to tenaciously attach to his newfound Source of Supply - the second to detach from it, once its usefulness has been exhausted.

417

This is why and how the narcissist is able to pick up where he had left off so easily. It is common for a narcissist to return to haunt an old or defunct PN Space (Pathological Narcissistic Space, the hunting grounds of the narcissist). This happens when a narcissist can no longer occupy - physically or emotionally - his current PN Space.

Consider a narcissist who is imprisoned or exiled, divorced or fired. He can no longer obtain Narcissistic Supply from his old sources. He has to reinvent and reshape a new PNS. In his new settings (new family, new country, different city, new neighbourhood, new workplace) he tries out a few personas until he strikes gold and finds the one that provides him with the best results: Narcissistic Supply aplenty.

But if the narcissist is forced to return to his previous PN Space, he has no difficulty adjusting. He immediately assumes his old persona and begins to extract Narcissistic Supply from his old sources. The personas of the narcissist, in other words, bond with his respective PN Spaces. These couplets are both interchangeable and inseparable in the narcissist's mind. Every time he moves, the narcissist changes the narcissistic couplet: his PN Space and the persona attached thereto.

Thus, the narcissist is spatially and temporally discontinuous. His different personas are mostly in "cold storage". He does not feel that they are part of his current identity. They are "warehoused" or repressed, rigidly attached to four-dimensional PN Spaces. We say "four dimensional" because, to a narcissist, a PN Space is "frozen" both in space and in time.

This slicing of the narcissist's life is what stands behind the narcissist's apparent inability to predict the inevitable outcomes of his actions. Coupled with his inability to empathize, it renders him amoral and resilient - in short: a "survivor". His daredevil approach to life, his callousness, his ruthlessness, his maverick-ness, and, above all, his shock at being held accountable are all partly the results of his uncanny ability to reinvent himself so completely.

418

Narcissists, Group Behaviour and Terrorism

Human Collectives (Nations, Professions, Ethnic Groups) And Narcissism - Stereotyping or Racism?

The members of a sufficiently cohesive group tend to react similarly to circumstances. By "cohesive" I mean that they share the same mental world ("Weltanschauung"), possibly the same history, the same language or dialect, the same hopes, folklore, fears, and aspirations ("agenda"), the same enemies and so on.

419 Thus, if recurrently traumatized or abused by external or internal forces, a group of people may develop the mass equivalent of pathological narcissism as a defence or compensatory mechanism. By "abuse" and "trauma" I mean any event, or series of events, or circumstances, which threaten the self-identity, self-image, sense of self-worth, and self-esteem of the collective consistently and constantly - though often arbitrarily and unpredictably. Human collectives go through formation, individuation, separation - all the phases in individual psychological development. A disturbance in the natural and unhindered progression of these phases is likely to result in a shared psychopathology of all the members of the collective. Being subjugated to another nation, being exiled, enduring genocide, being destitute, being defeated in warfare are all traumatic experiences with far reaching consequences.

The members of the collective form a "condensate" (in physical terms) - a "substance" in which all the atoms vibrate with the same frequency. Under normal circumstances, group behaviour resembles diffuse light. Subject to trauma and abuse, it forms a malignant laser - a strong, same wavelength, potentially destructive beam. The group becomes abusive to others, exploitative, detached from reality, basked in grandiose fantasies, xenophobic, lacking empathy, prone to uncontrolled rages, over-sensitive, convinced of its superiority and entitlement. Force and coercion are often required to disabuse such a group of its delusions. But, this of course, only cements its narcissism and justifies its distorted perception of the world.

Are All Terrorists and Serial Killers Narcissists?

Terrorists can be phenomenologically described as narcissists in a constant state of deficient Narcissistic Supply. The Grandiosity Gap - the painful and narcissistically injurious gap between their grandiose fantasies and their dreary and humiliating reality - becomes emotionally insupportable. They decompensate and act out. They bring "down to their level" (by destroying it) the object of their pathological envy, the cause of their seething frustration, the symbol of their dull achievements, always incommensurate with their inflated self-image.

They seek omnipotence through murder, control (not least self-control) through violence, prestige, fame and celebrity by defying the authorities, challenging them, and humbling them. Unbeknownst to them, they seek self-punishment. They are at heart suicidal. They aim to cast themselves as victims by forcing others to punish them. This is called Projective Identification. They attribute evil and corruption to their enemies and foes. These forms of paranoia are called "projection" and "splitting". These are all primitive, infantile, and often persecutory, defence mechanisms.

When coupled with narcissism - the inability to empathize, the exploitativeness, the sense of entitlement, the rages, the dehumanization and devaluation of others - this mindset yields abysmal contempt. The overriding emotion of terrorists and serial killers, the amalgam and culmination of their tortured psyche is deep seated disdain for everything human, the flip side of envy. It is cognitive dissonance gone amok. On the one hand the terrorist derides as "false", "meaningless", "dangerous", and "corrupt" common values, institutions, human intercourse, and society. On the other hand, he devotes his entire life (and often risks it) to the elimination and pulverization of these "insignificant" entities. To justify this apparent contradiction, the terrorists casts himself as an altruistic saviour of a group of people "endangered" by his foes. He is always self-appointed and self-proclaimed, rarely elected.

The serial killer rationalizes and intellectualizes his murders similarly, by purporting to "liberate" or "deliver" his victims from a fate worse than death.

420

The terrorist's global reach, the secrecy, the impotence and growing panic of his victims, of the public, and of his pursuers, the damage he wreaks all serve as external ego functions. The terrorist and serial killer regulate their sense of self-esteem and self-worth by feeding slavishly on the reactions to their heinous deeds. Their cosmic significance is daily enhanced by media exposure, ever increasing bounties, admiring imitators, successful acts of blackmail, the strength and size of their opponents, and the devastation of human life and property. Appeasement works only to aggravate their drives and strengthen their appetites by emboldening them and by raising the threshold of excitation and Narcissistic Supply. Terrorists and killers are addicted to this drug of being acknowledged and reflected. They derive their sense of existence, parasitically, from the reactions of their (often captive) audience.

Is the Narcissist Ever Sorry?

Question: Doesn't the narcissist ever feel sorry for his "victims"?

Answer: The narcissist always feels "bad". He experiences all manner of depressive episodes and lesser dysphoric moods. He goes through a panoply of mood disorders and anxiety disorders. He experiences panic from time to time. It is not pleasant to be a narcissist.

But he has a diminished capacity to empathize, so he rarely feels sorry for what he does. He almost never puts himself in the shoes of his "victims". Actually, he doesn't regard them as victims at all! It is very common for the narcissist to feel victimized, deprived and discriminated against. He projects his own moods, cognitions, emotions, and actions onto others.

Sure, he feels distressed because he is intelligent enough to realize that something is wrong with him in a major way. He compares himself to others and the outcome is never favourable. His grandiosity is one of the defence mechanisms that he uses to cover up for this disagreeable state of things.

But its efficacy is partial and intermittent. The rest of the time, when it's not working, the narcissist is immersed in self-loathing and self-pity. He is under duress and distress most of his waking hours. In a vague way, he is also sorry for those upon whom he inflicts the consequences of his personality disorder.

He knows that they are not happy and he understands that it has something to do with him. Mostly, he uses even this to aggrandize himself: poor things, they can never fully understand him, they are so inferior. It is no wonder that they are so depressed. He puts himself at the centre of their world, the axis around which everything and everyone revolves.

When confronted with major crises (a traumatic divorce, a financial entanglement, a demotion), the narcissist experiences

422

MALIGNANT SELF LOVE   SAM VAKNIN

real, excruciating, life-threatening pain. This is the narcissist's "cold turkey", his withdrawal symptoms. Narcissistic Supply is, like any other drug, habit forming (psychologically). Its withdrawal has broad implications, all severely painful.

Only then is the answer unqualified, unequivocal and unambiguous: yes, the narcissist is in pain - when devoid of his stream of adoration and other positive reinforcements.

A Letter about Trust

For millions of years nature embedded in us the notion that the past can teach us a lot about the future. This is very useful for survival. And it is also mostly true with inanimate objects. With people the story is less straightforward: though it is reasonable to project someone's future behaviour from his past conduct, this proves erroneous some of the time.

Our natural tendency is to trust, because we trust our parents. It feels good to really trust. It is also an essential component of love and an important test thereof. Love without trust is dependence masquerading as love.

We must trust, it is an almost biological urge. Most of the time, we do trust. We trust the universe to behave according to the laws of physics, soldiers not to go mad and shoot at us, our nearest and dearest not to betray us.

When trust is broken, we feel as though a part of us has died, is hollowed out.

Not to trust is abnormal and is the outcome of bitter or even traumatic life experiences. Mistrust and distrust are induced not by our own thoughts, nor by some device or machination of ours - but by life's sad circumstances. To continue not to trust is to reward the people who wronged us and made us distrustful in the first place. Those people have long abandoned us and yet they still have a great, malignant, influence on our lives. This is the irony of the lack of trust.

So, some of us prefer not to experience this sinking feeling of trust violated. They choose not to trust and not to be disappointed. This is both a fallacy and a folly. Trusting releases enormous amounts of mental energy, which is better invested elsewhere. But trust - like knives - can be dangerous to your health if used improperly.

You have to discern WHOM to trust, you have to learn HOW to trust and you have to know HOW to CONFIRM the existence of mutual, functional trust.

People often disappoint and are not worthy of trust. Some people act arbitrarily, treacherously and viciously, or, worse, offhandedly. You have to select the targets of your trust carefully. He who has the most common interests with you, who is invested in you for the long haul, who is incapable of breaching trust ("a good person"), who doesn't have much to gain from betraying you is not likely to mislead you. These people you can trust.

You should not trust indiscriminately. No one is completely trustworthy in all fields. Most often our disappointments stem from our inability to separate one area of life from another. A person could be sexually faithful - but utterly irresponsible when it comes to money (for instance, a pathological gambler). Or a good, reliable father - but a womanizer.

You can trust someone to carry out some activities - but not others, because they are more complicated, more boring, or do not conform to his values. We should not trust with reservations: this is the kind of "trust" that is common in business and among criminals and its source is rational. Game Theory in mathematics deals with questions of calculated trust. We should trust wholeheartedly but know who to entrust with what. Then we will be rarely disappointed.

425

As opposed to popular opinion, trust must be put to the test, lest it goes stale and staid. We are all somewhat paranoid. The world is complex, inexplicable and overwhelming. Some forces are benign, some arbitrary, others downright evil. There must be an explanation, we feel, for all these amazing coincidences, for our existence, for events around us.

This tendency to introduce external powers and ulterior motives into our reality permeates human relations, as well. We gradually grow suspicious, inadvertently hunt for clues of infidelity or worse, masochistically relieved, even happy when we find some.

The more often we successfully test the trust we had established, the stronger our pattern-prone brain embraces it. Constantly in a precarious balance, our brain needs and devours reinforcements. Such testing should not be explicit but circumstantial.

Your husband could easily have had a lover or your partner could easily have embezzled your money - and, behold, they haven't. They passed the test. They resisted temptation.

Trust is based on the ability to predict the future. It is not so much the act of betrayal that we react to - as it is the feeling that the very foundations of our world are crumbling, that it is no longer safe because it is no longer predictable. When betrayed, we are in the throes of death of one theory and the birth of another, as yet untested.

Here is another important lesson: whatever the act of betrayal (with the exception of grave criminal corporeal acts), it is frequently limited, reversible, and, ultimately, negligible. Naturally, we tend to exaggerate the importance of the event. This serves a double purpose: indirectly it aggrandizes us. If we are "worthy" of such an unprecedented, unheard of, major betrayal, we must be worthwhile and unique. The magnitude of the betrayal reflects on us and re-establishes the fragile balance of powers between us and the universe.

The second purpose of exaggerating the act of perfidy is simply to gain sympathy and empathy, mainly from ourselves, but also from others. Catastrophes are a dozen a dime and in today's world it is difficult to provoke anyone to regard your personal disaster as anything exceptional.

Amplifying the event has, therefore, some very utilitarian purposes. But, finally, these lies poison the mental circulation of the liar. Putting the event in perspective goes a long way towards the commencement of a healing process. No betrayal stamps the world irreversibly or eliminates other possibilities, opportunities, chances, and people. Time goes by, people meet and part, lovers quarrel and make love, dear ones live and die. It is the very essence of time that it reduces us all to the finest dust. Our only weapon - however crude and naive - against this unstoppable process is to trust each other.

Traumas as Social Interactions

We react to serious mishaps, life altering setbacks, disasters, abuse, and death by going through the phases of grieving. Traumas are the complex outcomes of psychodynamic and biochemical processes. But the particulars of traumas depend heavily on the interaction between the victim and his social milieu.

It would seem that while the victim moves from denial to helplessness, rage, depression and thence to acceptance of the traumatizing events - society demonstrates a diametrically opposed progression. This incompatibility, this mismatch of psychological phases is what leads to the formation and crystallization of trauma.

427

PHASE I

Victim - DENIAL

The magnitude of unfortunate events is often so overwhelming, their nature so alien, and their message so menacing that denial sets in as a defence mechanism aimed at self-preservation. The victim denies that the event occurred, that he or she is being abused, that a loved one had passed away, and so on.

Society - ACCEPTANCE, MOVING ON

The victim's nearest ("society") - his colleagues, his employees, his clients, even his spouse, children, and friends - rarely experience the traumatizing events with the same shattering intensity. They are likely to accept the bad news and move on. Even at their most considerate and empathic, they are likely to lose patience with the victim's state of mind. They tend to ignore the victim, or chastise him, to mock, or to deride his feelings or behaviour, to collude to repress the painful memories, or to trivialize them.

Summary

The mismatch between the victim's reactive patterns and emotional needs and society's matter-of-fact attitude hinders growth and healing. The victim requires society's help in avoiding a head-on confrontation with a reality he cannot digest. Instead, society serves as a constant and mentally destabilizing reminder of the root of the victim's unbearable agony (the Job Syndrome).

PHASE II

Victim - HELPLESSNESS

Denial gradually gives way to a sense of all-pervasive and humiliating helplessness, often accompanied by debilitating fatigue and mental disintegration. These are among the classic symptoms of PTSD (Post-Traumatic Stress Disorder). These are the bitter results of the internalization and integration of the harsh realization that there is nothing one can do to alter the outcomes of a natural, or man-made, catastrophe. The horror in confronting one's finiteness, meaninglessness, negligibility, and powerlessness is overpowering.

Society - DEPRESSION

The more the members of society come to grips with the magnitude of the loss, or evil, or threat represented by the grief inducing events, the sadder they become. Depression is often little more than suppressed or self-directed anger. The anger, in this case, is belatedly induced by an identified or diffuse source of threat, or of evil, or by a loss. It is a higher level variant of the "fight or flight" reaction, tampered by the rational understanding that the "source" of the trauma is often impossible to tackle directly and to contain.

428

Summary

Thus, when the victim is most in need, terrified by his helplessness and adrift, society is immersed in depression and unable to provide a holding and supporting environment. Growth and healing is again retarded by social interaction. The victim's innate sense of annulment is enhanced by the self-addressed anger (depression) of those around him.

PHASE III

Both the victim and society react with RAGE to their predicaments. In an effort to narcissistically reassert himself, the victim develops a grandiose sense of anger directed at paranoidally selected, unreal, diffuse, and abstract targets (frustration sources). By being aggressive, the victim re-acquires mastery of the world and of himself.

Members of society use rage to re-direct the root cause of their depression (which is, as we said, self-directed anger) and to channel it safely. To ensure that this expressed aggression alleviates their depression, real targets are selected and real punishments meted out. In this respect, "social rage" differs from the victim's. The former is intended to sublimate aggression and channel it in a socially acceptable manner - the latter to reassert narcissistic self-love as an antidote to an all-devouring sense of helplessness.

In other words, society, by itself being in a state of rage, positively reinforces the narcissistic rage reactions of the grieving victim. This, in the long run, is counter-productive, inhibits personal growth, and prevents healing. It also erodes the reality test of the victim and encourages self-delusions, paranoidal ideation, and ideas of reference.

PHASE IV

Victim - DEPRESSION

As the consequences of narcissistic rage - both social and personal - grow more unacceptable, depression sets in. The victim internalizes his aggressive impulses. Self directed rage is safer but is the cause of great sadness and even suicidal ideation. The victim's depression is his way of conforming to social norms. It is also instrumental in ridding the victim of the unhealthy residues of narcissistic regression. It is when the victim acknowledges the malignancy of his rage (and its anti-social nature) that he adopts a depressive stance.

Society - HELPLESSNESS

People around the victim ("society") also emerge from their phase of rage transformed. As they realize the futility of their rage, they feel more and more helpless and devoid of options. They grasp their limitations and the irrelevance of their good intentions. They accept the inevitability of loss and evil and Kafkaesquely agree to live under an ominous cloud of arbitrary judgement, meted out by impersonal powers.

Summary

Again, the members of society are unable to help the victim to emerge from a self-destructive phase. His depression is enhanced by their apparent helplessness. Their introversion and inefficacy induce in the victim a feeling of nightmarish isolation and alienation. Healing and growth are once again retarded or even inhibited.

PHASE V

Victim - ACCEPTANCE, MOVING ON

Depression - when pathologically protracted and in conjunction with other mental health problems - sometimes leads to suicide. But more often, it allows the victim to process mentally hurtful and potentially harmful material and paves the way to acceptance. Withdrawal from social pressures enables the direct transformation of anger into other emotions, some of them socially unacceptable. The honest encounter between the victim and his own (possible) death often becomes a cathartic and self-empowering inner dynamic. The victim emerges ready to move on.

Society - DENIAL

Society, on the other hand, having exhausted its reactive arsenal, resorts to denial. As memories fade and as the victim recovers and abandons his obsessive-compulsive dwelling on his pain, society feels morally justified to forget and forgive. This mood of historical revisionism, of moral leniency, of effusive forgiveness, of re-interpretation, and of a refusal to remember in detail leads to a repression and denial of the painful events by society.

Summary

This final mismatch between the victim's emotional needs and society's reactions is less damaging to the victim. He is now more resilient, more flexible, and more willing to forgive and forget. Society's denial is really a denial of the victim. But, having ridden himself of more primitive narcissistic defences, the victim can do without society's acceptance and approval. Having endured the purgatory of grieving, he has now re-acquired his self, independent of society's acknowledgement.

How Victims are Affected by Abuse

Repeated abuse has long lasting pernicious and traumatic effects such as panic attacks, hypervigilance, sleep disturbances, flashbacks (intrusive memories), suicidal ideation, and psychosomatic symptoms. The victims experience shame, depression, anxiety, embarrassment, guilt, humiliation, abandonment, and an enhanced sense of vulnerability.

In "Stalking - An Overview of the Problem" [Can J Psychiatry 1998;43:473-476], authors Karen M Abrams and Gail Erlick Robinson write:

"Sometimes the victim develops an almost fatal resolve that, inevitably, one day she will be murdered. Victims, unable to live a normal life, describe feeling stripped of self-worth and dignity. Personal control and resources, psychosocial development, social support, premorbid personality traits, and the severity of the stress may all influence how the victim experiences and responds to it..."

Surprisingly, verbal, psychological, and emotional abuse have the same effects as the physical variety [Psychology Today, September/October 2000 issue, p. 24]. Abuse of all kinds also interferes with the victim's ability to work. Abrams and Robinson wrote this [in "Occupational Effects of Stalking", Can J Psychiatry 2002;47:468-472]:

"... (B)eing stalked by a former partner may affect a victim's ability to work in 3 ways. First, the stalking behaviours often interfere directly with the ability to get to work (for example, flattening tires or other methods of preventing leaving the home). Second, the workplace may become an unsafe location if the offender decides to appear. Third, the mental health effects of such trauma may result in forgetfulness, fatigue, lowered concentration, and disorganization. These factors may lead to the loss of employment, with accompanying loss of income, security, and status."

Still, it is hard to generalize. Victims are not a uniform lot. In some cultures, abuse is commonplace and accepted as a legitimate mode of communication, a sign of love and caring, and a boost to the abuser's self-image. In such circumstances, the victim is likely to adopt the norms of society and avoid serious trauma.

Deliberate, cold-blooded, and premeditated torture has worse and longer-lasting effects than abuse meted out by the abuser in rage and loss of self-control. The existence of a loving and accepting social support network is another mitigating factor. Finally, the ability to express negative emotions safely and to cope with them constructively is crucial to healing.

Typically, by the time the abuse reaches critical and all-pervasive proportions, the abuser had already, spider-like, isolated his victim from family, friends, and colleagues. She is catapulted into a nether land, cult-like setting where reality itself dissolves into a continuing nightmare.

When she emerges on the other end of this wormhole, the abused woman (or, more rarely, man) feels helpless, self-doubting, worthless, stupid, and a guilty failure for having botched her relationship and "abandoned" her "family". In an effort to regain perspective and avoid embarrassment, the victim denies the abuse or minimizes it.

No wonder that survivors of abuse tend to be clinically depressed, neglect their health and personal appearance, and succumb to boredom, rage, and impatience. Many end up abusing prescription drugs or drinking or otherwise behaving recklessly.

Some victims even develop Post-Traumatic Stress Disorder (PTSD).

Post-Traumatic Stress Disorder (PTSD)

Contrary to popular misconceptions, Post-Traumatic Stress Disorder (PTSD) and Acute Stress Disorder (or Reaction) are not typical responses to prolonged abuse. They are the outcomes of sudden exposure to severe or extreme stressors (stressful events). Some victims whose life or body have been directly and unequivocally threatened by an abuser react by developing these syndromes. PTSD is, therefore, typically associated with the aftermath of physical and sexual abuse in both children and adults.

One's (or someone else's) looming death, violation, personal injury, or powerful pain are sufficient to provoke the behaviours, cognitions, and emotions that together are known as PTSD. Even learning about such mishaps may be enough to trigger massive anxiety responses.

The first phase of PTSD involves incapacitating and overwhelming fear. The victim feels like she has been thrust into a nightmare or a horror movie. She is rendered helpless by her own terror. She keeps re-living the experience through recurrent and intrusive visual and auditory hallucinations ("flashbacks") or dreams. In some flashbacks, the victim completely lapses into a dissociative state and physically re-enacts the event while being thoroughly oblivious to her whereabouts.

In an attempt to suppress this constant playback and the attendant exaggerated startle response (jumpiness), the victim tries to avoid all stimuli associated, however indirectly, with the traumatic event. Many develop full-scale phobias (Agoraphobia, Claustrophobia, fear of heights, aversion to specific animals, objects, modes of transportation, neighbourhoods, buildings, occupations, weather, and so on).

Most PTSD victims are especially vulnerable on the anniversaries of their abuse. They try to avoid thoughts, feelings, conversations, activities, situations, or people who remind them of the traumatic occurrence ("triggers").

This constant hypervigilance and arousal, sleep disorders (mainly insomnia), the irritability ("short fuse"), and the inability to concentrate and complete even relatively simple tasks erode the victim's resilience. Utterly fatigued, most patients manifest protracted periods of numbness, automatism, and, in radical cases, near-catatonic posture. Response times to verbal cues increase dramatically. Awareness of the environment decreases, sometimes dangerously so. The victims are described by their nearest and dearest as "zombies", "machines", or "automata".

The victims appear to be sleepwalking, depressed, dysphoric, anhedonic (not interested in anything and find pleasure in nothing). They report feeling detached, emotionally absent, estranged, and alienated. Many victims say that their "life is over" and expect to have no career, family, or otherwise meaningful future.

The victim's family and friends complain that she is no longer capable of showing intimacy, tenderness, compassion, empathy, and of having sex (due to her post-traumatic "frigidity"). Many victims become paranoid, impulsive, reckless, and self-destructive. Others somatize their mental problems and complain of numerous physical ailments. They all feel guilty, shameful, humiliated, desperate, hopeless, and hostile.

433

PTSD need not appear immediately after the harrowing experience. It can be - and often is - delayed by days or even months. It lasts more than one month (usually much longer). Sufferers of PTSD report subjective distress (the manifestations of PTSD are ego-dystonic). Their functioning in various settings - job performance, grades at school, sociability - deteriorates markedly.

The DSM-IV-TR (Diagnostic and Statistical Manual) criteria for diagnosing PTSD are far too restrictive. PTSD seems to also develop in the wake of verbal and emotional abuse and in the aftermath of drawn out traumatic situations (such as a nasty divorce). Hopefully, the DSM text will be adapted to reflect this sad reality.

Recovery and Healing

Victims of abuse in all its forms - verbal, emotional, financial, physical, and sexual - are often disorientated. They require not only therapy to heal their emotional wounds, but also practical guidance and topical education. At first, the victim is, naturally, distrustful and even hostile. The therapist or case worker must establish confidence and rapport painstakingly and patiently.

The therapeutic alliance requires constant reassurance that the environment and treatment modalities chosen are safe and supportive. This is not easy to do, partly because of objective factors such as the fact that the records and notes of the therapist are not confidential. The offender can force their disclosure in a court of law simply by filing a civil lawsuit against the survivor!

The first task is to legitimize and validate the victim's fears. This is done by making clear to her that she is not responsible for her abuse or guilty for what happened. Victimization is the abuser's fault - it is not the victim's choice. Victims do not seek abuse - although, admittedly some of them keep finding abusive partners and forming relationships of co-dependence. Facing, reconstructing, and reframing the traumatic experiences is a crucial and indispensable first phase.

The therapist should present the victim with her own ambivalence and the ambiguity of her messages - but this ought to be done gently, non-judgementally, and without condemnation. The more willing and able the abuse survivor is to confront the reality of her mistreatment (and the offender), the stronger she would feel and the less guilty.

Typically, the patient's helplessness decreases together with her self-denial. Her self-esteem as well as her sense of self-worth stabilize. The therapist should emphasize the survivor's strengths and demonstrate how they can save her from a recurrence of the abuse or help her cope with it and with her abuser.

Education is an important tool in this process of recovery. The patient should be made aware of the prevalence and nature of violence against women and stalking, their emotional and physical effects, warning signs and red flags, legal redresses, coping strategies, and safety precautions.

The therapist or social worker should provide the victim with lists of contacts: help organizations, law enforcement agencies, other women in her condition, domestic violence shelters, and victims' support groups both online and in her neighbourhood or city. Knowledge empowers and reduces the victim's sense of isolation and worthlessness.

Helping the survivor regain control of her life is the over-riding goal of the entire therapeutic process. With this aim in mind, she should be encouraged to re-establish contact with family, friends, colleagues, and the community at large. The importance of a tightly-knit social support network cannot be exaggerated.

Ideally, after a period of combined tutoring, talk therapy, and (anti-anxiety or antidepressant) medications, the survivor will self-mobilize and emerge from the experience more resilient and assertive and less gullible and self-deprecating.

The Guilt of Others

Question: Am I to blame for my husband's/child's/parent's mental state and behaviour? Is there anything that I can or should do to help him or to reach him?

Answer: Self-flagellation is a characteristic of those who choose to live with a narcissist (for a choice it is). Constant feelings of guilt, self-reproach, self-recrimination and, thus, self-punishment characterize the relationships formed between the sadist-narcissist and the masochistic-dependent mate or partner.

435   The narcissist is sadistic because, early on, he was forced into expressing his own guilt and self-reproach in this manner. His Superego is unpredictable, capricious, arbitrary, judgemental, cruel, and self-annihilating (suicidal). Externalizing these internal voices is a way of alleviating internal conflicts and fears generated by the narcissist's inner turmoil.

The narcissist projects this "civil war" and drags everyone around him into a swirl of bitterness, suspiciousness, meanness, aggression and pettiness. His life is a reflection of his psychological landscape: barren, paranoiac, tormented, guilt-ridden. He feels compelled to do unto others what he inflicts upon himself. He gradually transforms his closest, nearest and dearest into replicas of his conflictive, punishing personality structure.

Some narcissists are more subtle than others. They disguise their sadism. For instance, they undertake to "educate" their family members or friends. This "education" is compulsive, obsessive, incessantly, harshly, and unduly critical. Its effect is to erode the subject, to humiliate, to create dependence, to intimidate, to restrain, to control, to paralyse.

The victim of such "edification" internalizes the endless hectoring and humiliating criticism and makes them her own. She begins to see justice where there is only twisted logic based on crooked assumptions. She begins to self-punish, to withhold, to request approval prior to any action, to forgo her preferences and priorities, to erase her own identity - hoping to thus avoid the excruciating pains of the narcissist's destructive analyses.

Other narcissists are less sophisticated and they use all manner of abuse to domesticate their kin and partners in life. These include physical violence, verbal violence (during intensive rage attacks), psychological abuse, brutal "honesty", sick or offending humour, sexual degradation, and so on.

But both categories of narcissists employ very simple deceptive mechanisms to achieve their goals. Usually such abusive practice is not a well thought out, previously planned campaign by the average narcissist. His behaviour is dictated by forces that he cannot master.

Most of the time the narcissist is not even conscious of why he is doing what he is doing. When he is self-aware, he can't seem to be able to predict the outcomes of his actions. Even when he can foretell them, he feels powerless to modify his behaviour. The narcissist is a pawn in the chess game played between the structures of his fragmented, fluid personality. So, in a strictly classical juridical sense, the narcissist has diminished capacity because he is not fully responsible or aware of what he is doing to others.

This seems to contradict my answer to FAQ 75 where I write:

"The narcissist knows to tell right from wrong. He is perfectly capable of anticipating the results of his actions and their influence on his milieu. The narcissist is very perceptive and sensitive to the subtlest nuances. He has to be: the very integrity of his personality depends upon input from others... A person suffering from NPD must be subjected to the same moral treatment and judgement as the rest of us. The courts do not recognize NPD as a mitigating circumstance - why should we?"

But, the contradiction is only apparent. The narcissist is perfectly capable of both distinguishing right from wrong and of foreseeing the outcomes of his actions. In this sense, the narcissist should be held liable for his misdeeds and exploits. If he so chooses, the narcissist can fight his compulsive inclination to behave the way he does.

This self-imposed restraint would come at a great psychological price, though. Avoidance or suppression of a compulsive act result in increased anxiety. The narcissist prefers his own psychological well-being to that of others. Even when confronted with the great misery that he fosters, he hardly feels responsible (for instance, he rarely attends couples therapy or individual psychotherapy).

To put it more plainly, the (average) narcissist is unable to answer the question: "Why did you do what you did?" or "Why did you choose this mode of action over others available to you under the same circumstances?" These decisions are arrived at unconsciously.

But once the course of action is (unconsciously) selected, the narcissist has a perfect grasp of what he is doing, whether it is right or wrong and what will be the price others are likely to pay for his actions and choices. And he can then decide to reverse course (for instance, to refrain from doing anything). On the one hand, therefore, the narcissist is not to blame - on the other hand, he is very guilty.

The narcissist deliberately confuses responsibility with guilt. The concepts are so close that the distinctions often get blurred. By provoking in others guilt, the narcissist transforms life with him into a constant trial. Actually, this continuous trial itself is a form of punishment.

Failures, for instance, induce guilt. The narcissist always labels his victim's efforts as "failures" and then proceeds to shift the responsibility for said failures to his victim so as to maximize the opportunity to chastise and castigate her.

The logic is two-phased. First, every responsibility imputed to the victim is bound to lead to failure, which, in turn, induces in the victim guilt feelings, self-recrimination and self-punishment. Second, more and more responsibilities are shifted away from the narcissist and onto his mate, so that, as time goes by, an asymmetry of failures is established. Burdened with less and less responsibilities and tasks, the narcissist fails less often. It preserves the narcissist's sense of superiority, on the one hand and legitimizes his sadistic attacks on his victim, on the other hand.

The narcissist's partner is often a willing participant in this shared psychosis. Such folie-a-deux can never take place without the full collaboration of a voluntarily subordinated victim. Such partners have a wish to be punished, to be eroded through constant, biting criticisms, unfavourable comparisons, veiled and not so veiled threats, acting out, betrayals and humiliations. It makes them feel cleansed, "holy", whole, and sacrificial.

Many of these partners, when they realize their situation (it is very difficult to discern it from the inside) abandon the narcissist and dismantle the relationship. Others prefer to believe in the healing power of love or some such other nonsense. It is nonsense not because love has no therapeutic power - it is by far the most powerful weapon in the healing arsenal. It is nonsense because it is wasted on a human shell, incapable of feeling anything but negative emotions, which vaguely filter through the dense veil of his dreamlike existence. The narcissist is unable to love, his emotional apparatus ruined by years of deprivation, abuse, misuse and disuse.

The narcissist-victim dyad is a conspiracy, a collusion of victim and mental tormentor, a collaboration of two needy people who find solace and supply in each other's deviations. Only by breaking loose, by aborting the game, by ignoring the rules can the victim be transformed (and by the way, acquire the newly found appreciation of the narcissist).

The narcissist also stands to benefit from such a move. But both the narcissist and his partner do not really think about each other. Gripped in the arms of an all-consuming dance macabre, they follow the motions morbidly, semiconscious, desensitized, exhausted, concerned only with survival. Living with a narcissist is very much like being in a maximum security prison.

The narcissist's partner should not feel guilty or responsible and should not seek to change what only time (not even therapy) and (difficult) circumstances may change. She should not strive to please and to appease, to be and not to be, to barely survive as a superposition of pain and fear. Releasing herself from the chains of guilt and from the throes of a debilitating relationship is the best help that a loving mate can provide to her ailing narcissistic partner.

Narcissistic Confinement

Question: Do narcissists have friends?

Answer: "Who's the fairest of them all?" - asks the Bad Queen in the fairy tale. Having provided the wrong answer, the mirror is smashed to smithereens. Not a bad allegory for how the narcissist treats his "friends".

Literature helps us grasp the intricate interactions between the narcissist and members of his social circle.

439 Both Sherlock Holmes and Hercules Poirot, the world's most renowned fiction detectives, are quintessential narcissists. Both are also schizoids: they have few friends and are largely confined to their homes, engaged in solitary activities. Both have fatuous, sluggish, and anodyne sidekicks who slavishly cater to their whims and needs and provide them with an adulating gallery - Holmes' Dr. Watson and Poirot's poor Hastings.

Both Holmes and Poirot assiduously avoid the "competition" - equally sharp minds who seek their company for a fertilizing intellectual exchange among equals. They feel threatened by the potential need to admit to ignorance and confess to error. Both gumshoes are self-sufficient and consider themselves peerless.

The Watsons and Hastings of this world provide the narcissist with an obsequious, unthreatening, audience and with the kind of unconditional and unthinking obedience that confirms to him his omnipotence. They are sufficiently vacuous to make the narcissist look sharp and omniscient - but not so asinine as to be instantly discernible as such. They are the perfect backdrop, never likely to attain centre stage and overshadow their master.

Moreover, both Holmes and Poirot sadistically - and often publicly - taunt and humiliate their Sancho Panzas, explicitly chastising them for being dim-witted. Narcissism and sadism are psychodynamic cousins and both Watson and Hastings are perfect victims of abuse: docile, understanding, malignantly optimistic, self-deluding, and idolizing.

Narcissists can't empathize or love and, therefore, have no friends. The narcissist is one track minded. He is interested in securing Narcissistic Supply from Narcissistic Supply Sources. He is not interested in people as such. He is a solipsist, and recognizes only himself as human. To the narcissist, all others are three dimensional cartoons, tools and instruments in the tedious and Sisyphean task of generating Narcissistic Supply and consuming it.

The narcissist over-values people (when they are judged to be potential sources of such supply), uses them, devalues them (when no longer able to supply him) and discards them nonchalantly. This behaviour pattern tends to alienate and to distance people from him.

Gradually, the social circle of the narcissist dwindles (and ultimately vanishes). People around him who are not turned off by the ugly succession of his acts and attitudes are rendered desperate and fatigued by the turbulent nature of the narcissist's life.

Those few still loyal to him, gradually abandon him because they can no longer withstand and tolerate the ups and downs of his career, his moods, his confrontations and conflicts with authority, his chaotic financial state and the dissolution of his emotional affairs. The narcissist is a human roller coaster - fun for a limited time, nauseating in the long run.

This is one aspect of the process of narcissistic confinement.

Ever sensitive to outside opinion, the narcissist's behaviour, choices, acts, attitudes, beliefs, interests, in short: his very life is curtailed by it. The narcissist derives his ego functions from observing his reflection in other people's eyes. Gradually, he homes in on the right mixture of texts and actions, which elicit Narcissistic Supply from his environment.

Anything which might - however remotely - endanger the availability or the quantity of the narcissist's Narcissistic Supply is excised. The narcissist avoids certain situations (for instance: where he is likely to encounter opposition, or criticism, or competition). He refrains from certain activities and actions (which are incompatible with his projected False Self). And he steers clear of people he deems insufficiently amenable to his charms.

To avoid narcissistic injury, the narcissist employs a host of Emotional Involvement Prevention Measures (EIPMs). He becomes rigid, repetitive, predictable, boring, limits himself to "safe subjects" (such as, endlessly, himself) and to "safe conduct", and often rages hysterically when confronted with unex-

pected situations or with the slightest resistance to his precon-
ceived course of action.

The narcissist's rage is not so much a reaction to offended
grandiosity as it is the outcome of panic. The narcissist maintains a precarious balance, a mental house of cards, poised on
a precipice. His equilibrium is so delicate that anything and anyone can upset it: a casual remark, a disagreement, a slight criticism, a hint, or a fear.

The narcissist magnifies it all into monstrous, ominous, proportions. To avoid these (not so imagined) threats, the narcissist
prefers to "stay at home". He limits his social intercourse. He
abstains from daring, trying, or venturing out. He is crippled.
This, indeed, is the very essence of the malignancy that is at the
heart of narcissism: the fear of flying.

Narcissistic Allocation

Question: What is the mechanism behind the cycles of over-valuation (idealization) and devaluation in the narcissist's life?

Answer: Cycles of over-valuation (idealization) followed by devaluation characterize many personality disorders (they are even more typical of the Borderline Personality Disorder, for instance). They reflect the need to be protected against the whims, needs, and choices of others, shielded from the hurt that they can inflict on the narcissist.

The ultimate and only emotional need of the narcissist is to be the subject of attention and, thus, to regulate his labile sense of self-worth. The narcissist is dependent on others for the performance of critical ego functions. While healthier people overcome disappointment or disillusionment with relative ease, to the narcissist these can mean the difference between Being and Nothingness.

The quality and reliability of Narcissistic Supply are, therefore, of paramount importance. The more the narcissist convinces himself that his sources are perfect, grand, comprehensive, authoritative, omniscient, omnipotent, beautiful, powerful, rich, brilliant, and so on, the better he feels. The narcissist has to idealize his Supply Sources in order to highly value the supply that he derives from them. This leads to over-valuation. The narcissist forms a fantastic picture of his Sources of Narcissistic Supply.

The fall is inevitable. Disillusionment and disappointment set in. The slightest criticism, disagreement, or differences of opinion with these Sources of Narcissistic Supply are interpreted by the narcissist as an all out assault against the foundations of his existence. The previous appraisal is sharply reversed: the same people are judged stupid who were previously deemed to possess genius, for instance.

442

MALIGNANT SELF LOVE

SAM VAKNIN

This is the devaluation part of the cycle and it is very painful to both the narcissist and the devalued (for very different reasons, of course). The narcissist mourns the loss of a promising "investment opportunity" (Source of Narcissistic Supply). The "investment opportunity" mourns the loss of the narcissist.

But what is the mechanism behind this cycling? What drives the narcissist to such extremes? Why doesn't the narcissist develop a better (more efficient) coping technique?

The answer is that the over-valuation-devaluation mechanism is the most efficient one available. To understand why, one needs to take stock of the narcissist's store of energy, or, rather, the lack thereof.

The narcissist's personality is a precariously balanced affair and it requires inordinate amounts of energy to maintain. So overwhelmingly dependent on the environment for mental sustenance, the narcissist must optimize (rather, maximize) the use of the scarce psychological and objective resources at his disposal.

Not one iota of effort, time and emotion must be wasted lest the narcissist finds his emotional balance severely upset. The narcissist attains this goal by sudden and violent shifts between foci of attention. This is a highly efficacious mechanism of allocation of resources in constant pursuit of the highest available emotional yields.

After emitting a narcissistic signal [see FAQ 29: The Narcissistic Mini-Cycle], the narcissist receives a host of narcissistic stimuli. The latter are, simply, messages from people who are willing to provide the narcissist with Narcissistic Supply. But mere readiness is not sufficient.

The narcissist now faces the daunting task of evaluating the potential content, quality, and extent of Narcissistic Supply each and every one of the potential collaborators has to offer. He does so by rating each one of them. The stimulus with the highest rating is, naturally, selected. It represents "the best value for money", the most cost/reward efficient proposition.

The narcissist immediately over-values and idealizes this source. It is the narcissistic equivalent of getting emotionally involved. The narcissist "bonds" with the new source. The narcissist feels attracted, interested, curious, magically rewarded, reawakened. Healthier people recognize this phenomenon: it is called infatuation.

To remove doubt: the Source of Narcissistic Supply thus chosen need not be human. The narcissist is equally interested in inanimate objects (for example: as status symbols), in groups of people (the nation, the Church, the army, the police), and even in the abstract ("history", "destiny", "mission").

A process of courting then commences. The narcissist knows how to charm, how to simulate emotions, how to flatter. Many narcissists are gifted thespians, having acted the role of their False Self for so long. They wine the targeted Supply Source (whether Primary or Secondary) and dine it. They compliment and sweet-talk, intensely present, deeply interested.

Their genuine and keen (though selfish) immersion in the other, their overt high regard for him or her (a result of idealization), their almost submissiveness are alluring. It is nigh impossible to resist a narcissist on the prowl for Sources of Supply. At this stage, his energies are all focused and dedicated to the task, like a laser beam.

During this phase of narcissistic courting or narcissistic pursuit, the narcissist is manic: he is full of vitality, of dreams and hopes and plans and vision. And his energy is not dissipated. He attempts (and in many cases, succeeds to achieve) the impossible. Example: if he targeted a publishing house, or a magazine, as his future Source of Supply (by publishing his work), he produces copious amounts of material in a short period of time.

If it is a potential mate, he floods her with attention, gifts and inventive gestures. If it is a group of people that he wishes to impress, he fanatically identifies with their goals and beliefs. The narcissist has the frightening capacity to turn himself into a weapon: focused, powerful, and lethal.

He lavishes all his energies, capabilities, talents, charms and emotions on the newly selected Source of Supply. This has a great effect on the intended source and on the narcissist. This also serves to maximize the narcissist's returns in the short run.

Once the Source of Supply is captured, preyed upon and depleted, the reverse process (of devaluation) sets in. The narcissist instantaneously (and startlingly abruptly) loses all interest in his former (and now useless or judged to be so) Source of Narcissistic Supply. He dumps and discards it.

He becomes bored, lazy, slow, devoid of energy, absolutely uninterested. He conserves his energies in preparation for the attack on, and the siege of, the next selected Source of Supply. These tectonic shifts are hard to contemplate, still harder to believe.

The narcissist has no genuine interests, loves, or hobbies. He likes that which yields the most Narcissistic Supply. A narcissist can be a gifted artist for as long as his art rewards him with fame and adulation. Once public interest wanes, or once criticism mounts, the narcissist, in a typical act of cognitive dissonance, immediately ceases to create, loses interest in art, and does not miss his old vocation for a second. He is likely to turn around and criticize his erstwhile career even as he pursues another, totally unrelated one.

The narcissist has no genuine emotions. He can be madly in "love" with a woman (Secondary Narcissistic Supply Source) because she is famous, or wealthy, or a native and can help him obtain legal residence through marriage, or because she comes from the right family, or because she is unique in a manner positively reflecting on the narcissist's perceived uniqueness, or because she had witnessed past successes of the narcissist, or merely because she admires him.

Yet, this "love" dissipates immediately when her usefulness runs its course or when a better "qualified" Source of Supply presents herself.

The over-valuation and devaluation cycles are mere reflections and derivatives of these ups and downs of the narcissist's pools of energy and flows of supply. Efficient (that is, abrupt) energy shifts are more typical of automata than of human beings. But then the narcissist likes to brag of his inhumanity and machine-like qualities.

Narcissistic Immunity

"We permit all things to ourselves and that which we call sin in others is experiment for us, for there is no crime to the intellect."
[Ralph Waldo Emerson, Poet and Philosopher]

Question: Aren't narcissists deterred by the consequences of their actions and behaviour?

Answer: Narcissists, like children, have magical thinking. They feel omnipotent. They feel that there is nothing they couldn't do or achieve if they only were to really want and apply themselves to it.

They feel omniscient: they rarely admit to ignorance in any field. They believe that they are in possession of all relevant and useful knowledge. They are haughtily convinced that introspection is a more important and more efficient (not to mention easier to accomplish) method of edification than the systematic study of outside sources of information in accordance with strict (read: tedious) curricula.

To some extent, they believe that they are omnipresent because they are either famous or about to become famous. Deeply immersed in their delusions of grandeur, they are firmly convinced that their acts have - or will have - a great influence on Mankind, on their firm, on their country, on others. Having learned to manipulate their human environment, they believe that they will always "get away with it".

Narcissistic immunity is the narcissist's (erroneous) feeling that he is immune to the consequences of his actions; that he will never be effected by the outcomes of his own decisions, opinions, beliefs, deeds and misdeeds, acts, inaction, or by being a member of certain groups; that he is above reproach and punishment (though not above being feared and notorious);

446

that, magically, he is protected and will miraculously be saved at the last moment.

What are the sources of this fantastic appraisal?

The first and foremost source is, of course, the False Self. It is constructed as a childish response to abuse and trauma. It is possessed of everything that the child wishes he had in order to retaliate: power, wisdom, magic - all of them unlimited and instantaneously available.

The False Self, this Superman, is indifferent to abuse and punishment. It shields the vulnerable True Self from the harsh realities experienced by the child. This artificial, maladaptive separation between a vulnerable (but not punishable) True Self and a punishable (but invulnerable) False Self is an effective mechanism. It isolates the child from an unjust, capricious, emotionally dangerous world. But, at the same time, it fosters a false sense of "nothing can happen to me, because I am not there, I cannot be punished because I am immune".

The second source is the sense of entitlement possessed by every narcissist. In his grandiose delusions, the narcissist is sui generis (unique), a gift to humanity, a precious, fragile, object. Moreover, the narcissist is convinced both that this uniqueness is immediately discernible and that it gives him special rights.

The narcissist feels that he is sheltered by some cosmological law pertaining to "endangered species". He is convinced that his future contribution to humanity should (and does) exempt him from the mundane: daily chores, boring jobs, recurrent tasks, personal exertion, orderly investment of resources and efforts, or even aging and death.

The narcissist is entitled to "special treatment": high living standards, constant and immediate catering to his ever shifting needs, the avoidance of the mundane and the routine, an absolution of his sins, fast track privileges (to higher education, or in his encounters with the bureaucracy). Punishment is for ordinary people (where no great loss to humanity is involved). Narcissists feel that they are above the law and that they are a law unto themselves.

The third source has to do with the narcissist's ability to manipulate his (human) environment. The typical narcissist develops his manipulative skills to the level of an art form because that is the only way he could survive his poisoned and dangerous childhood. Yet, narcissists use this "gift" long after its "expiry date".

Narcissists are possessed of inordinate abilities to charm, to convince, to seduce and to persuade. They are gifted orators.

In many cases, they are intellectually endowed. They put all this to the limited use of obtaining Narcissistic Supply with startling results.

They become pillars of society and members of the upper class. They mostly do get exempted many times by virtue of their standing in society, their charisma, or their ability to find willing scapegoats. Having "got away with it" so many times, they develop a theory of personal immunity, which rests on some kind of societal and even cosmic "order of things". Some people are just above punishment, the "special ones", the "endowed or gifted ones". This is the "narcissistic hierarchy".

But there is a fourth, simpler, explanation:

The narcissist just does not know what he is doing. Divorced from his True Self, unable to empathize (to understand what it is like to be someone else), unwilling to act empathically (to constrain his actions in accordance with the feelings and needs of others), the narcissist is in a constant dreamlike state.

He experiences his life like a movie, autonomously unfolding, guided by a sublime (even divine) director. The narcissist is a mere spectator, mildly interested, greatly entertained at times. He does not feel that he owns his actions. He, therefore, emotionally, cannot understand why he should be punished and when he is, he feels grossly wronged.

To be a narcissist is to be convinced of a great, inevitable personal destiny. The narcissist is preoccupied with ideal love, the construction of brilliant, revolutionary scientific theories, the composition or authoring or painting of the greatest work of art ever, the founding of a new school of thought, the attainment of fabulous wealth, the reshaping of the fate of a nation, becoming immortalized and so on.

The narcissist never sets realistic goals to himself. He is forever floating amidst fantasies of uniqueness, record breaking, or breathtaking achievements. His speech is verbose and florid and reflects this grandiosity.

So convinced is the narcissist that he is destined to great things, that he refuses to acknowledge setbacks, failures and punishments. He regards them as temporary, as someone else's errors, as part of the future mythology of his rise to power, brilliance, wealth, ideal love, etc. To accept punishment is to divert scarce energy and resources from the all-important task of fulfilling his mission in life.

That the narcissist is destined to greatness is a divine certainty: a higher order or power has pre-ordained him to achieve something lasting, of substance, of import in this world, in this life. How could mere mortals interfere with the cosmic, the divine, the very scheme of things? Therefore, punishment is impossible and will not happen is the narcissist's conclusion.

The narcissist is pathologically envious of people and projects his aggression unto them. He is always vigilant, ready to fend off an imminent attack. When inevitable punishment does come, the narcissist is shocked and irritated by the nuisance. Being punished also proves to him and validates what he suspected all along: that he is being persecuted.

Strong forces are poised against him. People are envious of his achievements, angry at him, out to get him. He constitutes a threat to the accepted order. When required to account for his (mis)deeds, the narcissist is always disdainful and bitter. He feels like Gulliver, a giant, chained to the ground by teeming dwarves while his soul soars to a future, in which people recognize his greatness and applaud it.

Narcissists, Love and Healing

Question: Why do narcissists react with rage to gestures or statements of love?

Answer: Nothing is more hated by some narcissists than the sentence "I Love You". It evokes in the narcissist almost primordial reactions. It provokes him to uncontrollable rage. Why is that?

a. The narcissist hates women virulently and vehemently. A misogynist, he identifies being loved with being possessed, encroached upon, shackled, transformed, reduced, exploited, weakened, engulfed, digested and excreted. To him love is a dangerous pursuit.

b. Being loved means being known intimately. The narcissist likes to think that he is so unique and deep that he can never be fathomed. The narcissist believes that he is above mere human understanding and empathy, that he is one of a kind (sui generis). To say to him "I love you", means to negate this feeling, to try to drag him to the lowest common denominator, to threaten his sense of uniqueness. After all, everyone is capable of loving and everyone, even the basest human beings, fall in love. To the narcissist loving is an animalistic and pathological behaviour, as is sex.

c. The narcissist knows that he is a con artist, a fraud, an elaborate hoax, a script, hollow and really non-existent. The person who claims to love him is either lying (what is there to love in a narcissist?) - or is a self-deceiving, clinging, and immature co-dependent. The narcissist cannot tolerate the thought that he has chosen a liar or an idiot for a mate. Indirectly, her declaration of love is a devastating critique of the narcissist's own powers of discernment.

The narcissist hates love, however and wherever it is manifested.

450

SAM VAKNIN   MALIGNANT SELF LOVE

Thus, for instance, when his spouse demonstrates her love to their children, he wishes them all ill. He is so pathologically envious of his spouse that he wishes she never existed. Being a tad paranoid, he also nurtures the growing conviction that she is showing love to her children demonstrably and on purpose, to remind him how miserable he is, how deficient, how deprived and discriminated against.

He regards her interaction with their children to be a provocation, an assault on his emotional welfare and balance. Seething envy, boiling rage and violent thoughts form the flammable concoction in the narcissist's mind whenever he sees other people happy.

Many people naively believe that they can cure the narcissist by engulfing him with love, acceptance, compassion and empathy. This is not so. The only time a transformative healing process occurs is when the narcissist experiences a severe narcissistic injury, a life crisis, when he hits rock bottom.

Forced to shed his malfunctioning defences, an ephemeral window of vulnerability is formed through which therapeutic intervention can try and sneak in.

The narcissist is susceptible to treatment only when his defences are down because they had failed to secure a steady stream of Narcissistic Supply. The narcissist's therapy aims to wean him off Narcissistic Supply.

But the narcissist perceives other people's love and compassion as forms of Narcissistic Supply!

It is a lose-lose proposition:

If therapy is successful and the narcissist is rid of his addiction to Narcissistic Supply, he is rendered incapable of giving and receiving love, which he regards as a variety of said supply.

The roles of Narcissistic Supply should be clearly distinguished from those of an emotional bond (such as love), though.

Narcissistic Supply has to do with the functioning of the narcissist's primitive defence mechanisms. The emotional component in the narcissist's psyche is repressed, dysfunctional, and deformed. It is subconscious: the narcissist is not aware of his emotions and is out of touch with his feelings.

The narcissist pursues Narcissistic Supply as a junkie seeks drugs. Junkies can form emotional "bonds" but these are always subordinate to their habit. Their emotional interactions are the victims of their habits, as their children and spouses can attest.

It is impossible to have any real, meaningful, or lasting emotional relationship with the narcissist until his primitive defence mechanisms crumble and are discarded. Dysfunctional interpersonal relationships are one of the hallmarks of other personality disorders as well.

To help the narcissist:

1. Cut him from his Sources of Supply and thus precipitate a narcissistic crisis or injury;
2. Use this window of opportunity and convince the narcissist to attend structured therapy in order to help him mature emotionally;
3. Encourage him in his emotional, self-forming baby steps.

"Emotional" liaisons which co-exist with the narcissist's narcissistic defence mechanisms are part of the narcissistic theatrical repertoire, fake and doomed. The narcissist's defence mechanisms render him a serial monogamist or a non-committal playboy.

The narcissist is unlikely to get rid of his defence mechanisms on his own. He does not employ them because he needs them, but because he knows no different. They proved useful in his infancy. They were adaptive in an abusive environment. Old tricks and old habits die hard.

The narcissist has disorganized personality (Kernberg). He may improve and emotionally mature in order to avoid the pain of certain or recurrent narcissistic injuries.

452

When narcissists do attend therapy, it is in order to try and alleviate some of what has become an intolerable pain. None of them goes to therapy because he wants to better interact with others. Love is important, but to fully enjoy its emotional benefits, first the narcissist must heal.

Vindictive Narcissists

Question: Are narcissists vindictive? Do they stalk and harass?

Answer: Narcissists are often vindictive and they often stalk and harass. The narcissist feels entitled to other people's time, attention, admiration, and resources. He interprets every rejection as an act of aggression which leads to a narcissistic injury. The narcissist reacts with sustained rage and vindictiveness and can turn violent because he feels omnipotent and immune to the consequences of his actions.

453 Basically, there are only four ways of coping with vindictive narcissists:

I. To Frighten Them

Narcissists live in a state of constant rage, repressed aggression, envy and hatred. They firmly believe that everyone else is precisely like them. As a result, they are paranoid, suspicious, scared, labile, and unpredictable. Frightening the narcissist is a powerful behaviour modification tool. When sufficiently deterred, the narcissist promptly disengages, gives up everything he fought for and sometimes makes amends.

To act effectively, one has to identify the vulnerabilities and susceptibilities of the narcissist and strike repeated, escalating blows at them until the narcissist lets go and vanishes.

Example: If a narcissist has a secret, one should use this fact to threaten him. One should drop cryptic hints that there are mysterious witnesses to the events and recently revealed evidence. The narcissist has a very vivid imagination. Let it do the rest.

The narcissist may have been involved in tax evasion, in malpractice, in child abuse, in infidelity - there are so many possibilities, which offer a rich vein of attack. If these insinuations are done cleverly, noncommittally, gradually, legally, and incrementally, the narcissist crumbles, disengages and disappears. He lowers his profile thoroughly in the hope of avoiding hurt and pain.

Many narcissists have been known to disown and abandon a whole Pathological Narcissistic Space in response to a well-focused campaign by their victims. Thus, the narcissist may leave town, change his job, abandon a field of professional interest, avoid friends and acquaintances only to relieve the unrelenting pressure exerted on him by his victims.

I repeat: most of the drama takes place in the paranoid mind of the narcissist. His imagination runs amok. He finds himself snarled by horrifying scenarios, pursued by the vilest "certainties". The narcissist is his own worst persecutor and prosecutor.

You don't have to do much except utter a vague reference, make an ominous allusion, delineate a possible turn of events. The narcissist will do the rest for you. He is like a small child in the dark, generating the very monsters that paralyse him with fear.

Needless to add that all these activities have to be pursued legally, preferably through the good services of law offices and in broad daylight. Done the wrong way, they might constitute extortion or blackmail, harassment and a host of other criminal offences.

II. To Lure Them

Another way to neutralize a vindictive narcissist is to offer him continued Narcissistic Supply until the war is over and won by you. Dazzled by the drug of Narcissistic Supply, the narcissist immediately becomes tamed, forgets his vindictiveness and triumphantly takes over his "property" and "territory".

Under the influence of Narcissistic Supply, the narcissist is unable to tell when he is being manipulated. He is blind, dumb and deaf. You can make a narcissist do anything by offering, withholding, or threatening to withhold Narcissistic Supply (adulation, admiration, attention, sex, awe, subservience, etc.).

III. Threaten Him with Abandonment

The threat to abandon need not be explicit or conditional ("If you don't do something or if you do it, I will ditch you"). It is sufficient to confront the narcissist, to completely ignore him, to insist on respect for one's boundaries and wishes, or to shout back at him. The narcissist takes these signs of personal autonomy to be harbingers of impending separation and reacts with anxiety.

The narcissist is a living emotional pendulum. If he gets too close to someone emotionally, if he becomes intimate with someone, he fears ultimate and inevitable abandonment. He, thus, immediately distances himself, acts cruelly and brings about the very abandonment that he fears in the first place. This is called the Approach-Avoidance Repetition Complex.

In this paradox lies the key to coping with the narcissist. If, for instance, he is having a rage attack - rage back. This will provoke in him fears of being abandoned and calm him down instantaneously (and eerily).

Mirror the narcissist's actions and repeat his words. If he threatens - threaten back and credibly try to use the same language and content. If he leaves the house - do the same, disappear on him. If he is suspicious - act suspicious. Be critical, denigrating, humiliating, go down to his level - because that's the only way to penetrate his thick defences. Faced with his mirror image - the narcissist always recoils.

You will find that if you mirror him consistently and constantly, the narcissist becomes obsequious and tries to make amends, moving from one (cold and bitter, cynical and misanthropic, cruel and sadistic) pole to another (warm, even "loving", fuzzy, engulfing, emotional, maudlin, and saccharine).

IV. Manipulate Him

By playing on the narcissist's grandiosity and paranoia, it is possible to deceive and manipulate him effortlessly. Just offer him Narcissistic Supply - admiration, affirmation, adulation - and he is yours. Harp on his insecurities and his persecutory delusions - and he is likely to trust only you and cling to you for dear life. But be careful not to overdo it!

Note: School Shootings

Healthy narcissism is common in adolescents. Their narcissistic defences help them cope with the anxieties and fears engendered by the demands and challenges of modern society: leaving home, going to college, sexual performance, marriage, and other rites of passage. There is nothing wrong with healthy narcissism. It sustains the adolescent in a critical time of his life and shields him from emotional injuries.

Still, in certain circumstances, healthy narcissism can transform into a malignant form, destructive to self and to others.

Adolescents who are consistently mocked and bullied by peers, role models, and socialization agents (such as teachers, coaches, and parents) are prone to find succour in grandiose fantasies of omnipotence and omniscience. To sustain these personal myths, they may resort to violence and counter-bullying.

The same applies to youths who feel deprived, underestimated, discriminated against, or at a dead end. They are likely to evoke narcissistic defences to fend off the constant hurt and to achieve self-sufficient and self-contained emotional gratification.

Finally, pampered adolescents, who serve as mere extensions of their smothering parents and their unrealistic expectations are equally liable to develop grandiosity and a sense of entitlement incommensurate with their real-life achievements. When frustrated they become aggressive.

This propensity to other-directed violence is further exacerbated by what Lasch called "The Culture of Narcissism". We live in a civilization which condones and positively encourages malignant individualism, bad hero worship (remember the movie "Born Killers"?), exploitativeness, inane ambitiousness, and the anomic atomization of social structures and support networks. Alienation is a hallmark of our age, not only among youngsters.

456

Narcissists as Mass and Serial Killers

Countess Erszebet Bathory was a breathtakingly beautiful, unusually well-educated woman, married to a descendant of Vlad Dracula of Bram Stoker fame. In 1611, she was tried - though, being a noblewoman, not convicted - in Hungary for slaughtering 612 young girls. The true figure may have been 40-100, though the Countess recorded in her diary more than 610 girls and 50 bodies were found in her estate when it was raided.

457 The girls were not killed outright. They were kept in a dungeon and repeatedly pierced, prodded, pricked, and cut. The Countess may have bitten chunks of flesh off their bodies while they were alive. She is said to have bathed and showered in their blood in the mistaken belief that she could thus slow down the aging process.

The Countess was notorious as an inhuman sadist long before her hygienic fixation. She once ordered the mouth of a talkative servant sewn. It is rumoured that in her childhood she witnessed a gypsy being sewn into a horse's stomach and left to die.

Her servants were executed, their bodies burnt and their ashes scattered. Being royalty, she was merely confined to her bedroom until she died in 1614. For a hundred years after her death, by royal decree, mentioning her name in Hungary was a crime.

Cases like Barothy's give the lie to the assumption that serial killers are a modern - or even post-modern - phenomenon, a cultural-societal construct, a by-product of urban alienation, Althusserian interpellation, and media glamorization. Serial killers are, indeed, largely made, not born. But they are spawned by every culture and society, moulded by the idiosyncrasies of every period as well as by their personal circumstances and genetic makeup.

Still, every crop of serial killers mirrors and reifies the pathologies of the milieu, the depravity of the Zeitgeist, and the malignancies of the Leitkultur. The choice of weapons, the identity and range of the victims, the methodology of murder, the disposal of the bodies, the geography, the sexual perversions and paraphilias - are all informed and inspired by the slayer's environment, upbringing, community, socialization, education, peer group, sexual orientation, religious convictions, and personal narrative. Movies like "Born Killers", "Man Bites Dog", "Copycat", and the Hannibal Lecter series capture this truth.

Serial killers are the quiddity and quintessence of malignant narcissism.

Yet, to some degree, we all are narcissists. Primary narcissism is a universal and inescapable developmental phase. Narcissistic traits are common and often culturally condoned. To this extent, serial killers are merely our reflection through a glass darkly.

In their book "Personality Disorders in Modern Life", Theodore Millon and Roger Davis attribute pathological narcissism to *"a society that stresses individualism and self-gratification at the expense of community... In an individualistic culture, the narcissist is 'God's gift to the world'. In a collectivist society, the narcissist is 'God's gift to the collective'."*

Lasch described the narcissistic landscape thus [in "The Culture of Narcissism: American Life in an age of Diminishing Expectations", 1979]:

"The new narcissist is haunted not by guilt but by anxiety. He seeks not to inflict his own certainties on others but to find a meaning in life."

The narcissist's pronounced lack of empathy, off-handed exploitativeness, grandiose fantasies and uncompromising sense of entitlement make him treat all people as though they were objects (he "objectifies" people). The narcissist regards others either as useful conduits for and Sources of Narcissistic Supply (attention, adulation, etc.) - or as extensions of himself.

Similarly, serial killers often mutilate their victims and abscond with trophies - usually, body parts. Some of them have been known to eat the organs they have ripped - an act of merging with the dead and assimilating them through digestion. They treat their victims as some children do their rag dolls.

Killing the victim - often capturing him or her on film before the murder - is a form of exerting unmitigated, absolute, and irreversible control over it. The serial killer aspires to "freeze time" in the still perfection that he has choreographed. The victim is motionless and defenceless. The killer attains long sought "object permanence". The victim is unlikely to run on the serial assassin, or vanish as earlier objects in the killer's life (e.g., his parents) have done.

In malignant narcissism, the True Self of the narcissist is replaced by a false construct, imbued with omnipotence, omniscience, and omnipresence. The narcissist's thinking is magical and infantile. He feels immune to the consequences of his own actions. Yet, this very source of apparently superhuman fortitude is also the narcissist's Achilles heel.

The narcissist's personality is chaotic. His defence mechanisms are primitive. The whole edifice is precariously balanced on pillars of denial, splitting, projection, rationalization, and Projective Identification. Narcissistic injuries - life crises, such as abandonment, divorce, financial difficulties, incarceration, public opprobrium - can bring the whole thing tumbling down. The narcissist cannot afford to be rejected, spurned, insulted, hurt, resisted, criticized, or disagreed with.

Likewise, the serial killer is trying desperately to avoid a painful relationship with his object of desire. He is terrified of being abandoned or humiliated, exposed for what he is and then discarded. Many killers often have sex - the ultimate form of intimacy - with the corpses of their victims. Objectification and mutilation allow for unchallenged possession.

Devoid of the ability to empathize, permeated by haughty feelings of superiority and uniqueness, the narcissist cannot put himself in someone else's shoes, or even imagine what it means. The very experience of being human is alien to the narcissist whose invented False Self is always to the fore, cutting him off from the rich panoply of human emotions.

Thus, the narcissist believes that all people are narcissists. Many serial killers believe that killing is the way of the world. Everyone would kill if they could or were given the chance to do so. Such killers are convinced that they are more honest and open about their desires and, thus, morally superior. They hold others in contempt for being conforming hypocrites, cowed into submission by an overweening establishment or society.

The narcissist seeks to adapt society in general - and meaningful others in particular - to his needs. He regards himself as the epitome of perfection, a yardstick against which he measures everyone, a benchmark of excellence to be emulated. He acts the guru, the sage, the "psychotherapist", the "expert", the objective observer of human affairs. He diagnoses the "faults" and "pathologies" of people around him and "helps" them "improve", "change", "evolve", and "succeed" - i.e., conform to the narcissist's vision and wishes.

Serial killers also "improve" their victims - slain, intimate objects - by "purifying" them, removing "imperfections", depersonalizing and dehumanizing them. This type of killer saves its victims from degeneration and degradation, from evil and from sin, in short: from a fate worse than death.

The killer's megalomania manifests at this stage. He claims to possess, or have access to, higher knowledge and morality. The killer is a special being and the victim is "chosen" and should be grateful for it. The killer often finds the victim's ingratitude irritating, though sadly predictable.

In his seminal work, "Aberrations of Sexual Life" (originally: "Psychopathia Sexualis"), quoted in the book "Jack the Ripper" by Donald Rumbelow, Kraft-Ebbing offers this observation:

"The perverse urge in murders for pleasure does not solely aim at causing the victim pain and - most acute injury of all - death, but that the real meaning of the action consists in, to a certain extent, imitating, though perverted into a monstrous and ghastly form, the act of defloration. It is for this reason that an essential component ... is the employment of a sharp cutting weapon; the victim has to be pierced, slit, even chopped up... The chief wounds are inflicted in the stomach region and, in many cases, the fatal cuts run from the vagina into the abdomen. In boys an artificial vagina is even made... One can connect a fetishistic element too with this process of hacking ... inasmuch as parts of the body are removed and ... made into a collection."

Yet, the sexuality of the serial, psychopathic, killer is self-directed. His victims are props, extensions, aides, objects, and symbols. He interacts with them ritually and, either before or after the act, transforms his diseased inner dialog into a self-consistent extraneous catechism. The narcissist is equally auto-erotic. In the sexual act, he merely masturbates with other - living - people's bodies.

The narcissist's life is a giant Repetition Complex. In a doomed attempt to resolve early conflicts with significant others, the narcissist resorts to a restricted repertoire of coping strategies, defence mechanisms, and behaviours. He seeks to recreate his past in each and every new relationship and interaction. Inevitably, the narcissist is invariably confronted with the same outcomes. This recurrence only reinforces the narcissist's rigid reactive patterns and deep-set beliefs. It is a vicious, intractable, cycle.

Correspondingly, in some cases of serial killers, the murder ritual seemed to have recreated earlier conflicts with meaningful objects, such as parents, authority figures, or peers. The outcome of the replay is different to the original, though. This time, the killer dominates the situation.

The killings allow him to inflict abuse and trauma on others rather than be abused and traumatized. He outwits and taunts figures of authority - the police, for instance. As far as the killer is concerned, he is merely "getting back" at society for what it did to him. It is a form of poetic justice, a balancing of the books, and, therefore, a "good" thing. The murder is cathartic and allows the killer to release hitherto repressed and pathologically transformed aggression - in the form of hate, rage, and envy.

But repeated acts of escalating gore fail to alleviate the killer's overwhelming anxiety and depression. He seeks to vindicate his negative introjects and sadistic Superego by being caught and punished. The serial killer tightens the proverbial noose around his neck by interacting with law enforcement agencies and the media and thus providing them with clues as to his identity and whereabouts. When apprehended, most serial assassins experience a great sense of relief.

Serial killers are not the only objectifiers - people who treat others as objects. To some extent, leaders of all sorts - political, military, or corporate - do the same. In a range of demanding professions - surgeons, medical doctors, judges, law enforcement agents - objectification efficiently fends off attendant horror and anxiety.

Yet, serial killers are different. They represent a dual failure - of their own development as full-fledged, productive individuals - and of the culture and society they grow in. In a pathologically narcissistic civilization - social anomies proliferate. Such societies breed malignant objectifiers - people devoid of empathy - also known as "narcissists".

First published on the Suite 101 Narcissistic Personality Disorders Topic.

Narcissists, Narcissistic Supply
And Sources of Supply

Question: What is Narcissistic Supply?

Answer: We all search for positive cues from people around us. These cues reinforce in us certain behaviour patterns. There is nothing special in the fact that the narcissist does the same. However there are two major differences between the narcissistic and the normal personality.

The first is quantitative. The normal person is likely to welcome a moderate amount of attention - verbal and non-verbal - in the form of affirmation, approval, or admiration. Too much attention, though, is perceived as onerous. Though constructive criticism is accepted, destructive and negative criticism is avoided altogether.

The narcissist, in contrast, is the mental equivalent of an alcoholic. He is insatiable. He directs his whole behaviour, in fact his life, to obtaining pleasurable titbits of attention. He embeds them in a coherent, completely biased, picture of himself. He uses them to regulate his labile sense of self-worth and self-esteem.

To elicit constant interest, he projects to others a confabulated, fictitious version of himself, known as the False Self. The False Self is everything the narcissist is not: omniscient, omnipotent, charming, intelligent, rich, or well-connected.

The narcissist then proceeds to harvest reactions to this projected image from family members, friends, co-workers, neighbours, business partners and from colleagues. If these - the adulation, admiration, attention, fear, respect, applause, affirmation - are not forthcoming, the narcissist demands them, or extorts them. Money, compliments, a favourable critique, an appearance in the media, a sexual conquest are all converted into the same currency in the narcissist's mind. This currency is

462

SAM VAKNIN   MALIGNANT SELF LOVE

what I call Narcissistic Supply. The narcissist uses these inputs to regulate his fluctuating sense of self-worth.

The narcissist cathexes (emotionally invests) with grandiosity everything he owns or does: his nearest and dearest, his work, his environment. But, as time passes, this pathologically intense aura fades. The narcissist finds fault with things and people he had first thought impeccable. He energetically berates and denigrates that which he equally zealously exulted and praised only a short while before.

This inexorable and (to the outside world) disconcerting roller-coaster is known as the "Idealization-Devaluation Cycle". It involves serious cognitive and emotional deficits and a formidable series of triggered defence mechanisms.

It is important to distinguish between the various components of the process of Narcissistic Supply:

1. The *Trigger of Supply* is the person or object that provokes the source into yielding Narcissistic Supply by confronting the source with information about the narcissist's False Self.
2. The *Source of Narcissistic Supply* is the person that provides the Narcissistic Supply.
3. *Narcissistic Supply* is the reaction of the source to the trigger.

Publicity (celebrity or notoriety, being famous or being infamous) is a Trigger of Narcissistic Supply because it provokes people to pay attention to the narcissist (in other words, it moves sources to provide the narcissist with Narcissistic Supply). Publicity can be obtained by exposing oneself, by creating something, or by eliciting attention. The narcissist resorts to all three repeatedly (as drug addicts do to secure their daily dose). A mate or a companion is one such Source of Narcissistic Supply.

The narcissist homes in on Triggers and Sources of Narcissistic Supply - people, possessions, creative works, money - and imbues these sources and triggers with imputed uniqueness, perfection, brilliance, and grandiose qualities (omnipotence, omnipresence, omniscience). He filters out any data that contradict these fantastic misperceptions. He rationalizes, intellectualizes, denies, represses, projects and, in general, defends against contrarian information.

But the picture is more complicated. There are two categories of Narcissistic Supply and their Sources (NSSs):

The *Primary Narcissistic Supply* is attention, in both its public forms (fame, notoriety, infamy, celebrity) and its private, interpersonal, forms (adoration, adulation, applause, fear, repulsion). It is important to understand that attention of any kind -

positive or negative - constitutes Primary Narcissistic Supply. Infamy is as sought after as fame, being notorious is as good as being renowned.

To the narcissist his "achievements" can be imaginary, fictitious, or only apparent, as long as others believe in them. Appearances count more than substance, what matters is not the truth but its perception.

Triggers of Primary Narcissistic Supply include, apart from being famous (celebrity, notoriety, fame, infamy), having an air of mystique (when the narcissist is considered to be mysterious), having sex and deriving from it a sense of masculinity/virility/femininity, and being close or connected to political, financial, military, or spiritual power or authority or actually yielding them.

Sources of Primary Narcissistic Supply are all those who provide the narcissist with Narcissistic Supply on a casual, random basis.

Secondary Narcissistic Supply includes: leading a normal life (a source of great pride for the narcissist), having a secure existence (economic security, social acceptability, upward mobility), and obtaining companionship.

Thus, having a mate, possessing conspicuous wealth, being creative, running a business (transformed into a Pathological Narcissistic Space), possessing a sense of anarchic freedom, being a member of a group or collective, having a professional or other reputation, being successful, owning property and flaunting one's status symbols all constitute Secondary Narcissistic Supply.

Sources of Secondary Narcissistic Supply are all those who provide the narcissist with Narcissistic Supply on a regular basis: spouse, friends, colleague, business partners, teachers, neighbours, and so on.

Both these Primary and Secondary Narcissistic Supply and their triggers and sources are incorporated in a *Narcissistic Pathological Space*.

Question: What are the functions of Narcissistic Supply in the narcissistic pathology?

Answer: The narcissist internalizes a "bad" object (typically, his mother) in his childhood. He harbours socially forbidden emotions towards this object: hatred, envy, and other forms of aggression. These feelings reinforce the narcissist's self-image as bad and corrupt. Gradually he develops a dysfunctional sense of self-worth. His self-confidence and self-image become unrealistically low and distorted.

In an effort to repress these "bad" feelings, the narcissist also suppresses all emotions. His aggression is channelled to fantasies or to socially legitimate outlets (dangerous sports, gambling, reckless driving, compulsive shopping). The narcissist views the world as a hostile, unstable, unrewarding, unjust, and unpredictable place.

He defends himself by loving a completely controllable object (himself), by projecting to the world an omnipotent and omniscient False Self, and by turning others to functions or to objects so that they pose no emotional risk. This reactive pattern is what we call pathological narcissism.

To exorcise his demons, the narcissist needs the world: its admiration, its adulation, its attention, its applause, even its penalties. The lack of a functioning personality on the inside is balanced by importing ego functions and boundaries from the outside.

The Primary Narcissistic Supply reaffirms the narcissist's grandiose fantasies, buttresses his False Self and, thus allows him to regulate his fluctuating sense of self-worth. The Narcissistic Supply contains information which pertains to the way the False Self is perceived by others and allows the narcissist to "calibrate" and "fine tune" it. The Narcissistic Supply also serves to define the boundaries of the False Self, to regulate its contents and to substitute for some of the functions normally reserved for a True, functioning, Self.

While it is easy to understand the function of the Primary Supply, Secondary Supply is a more complicated affair.

Interacting with the opposite sex and "doing business" are the two main Triggers of Secondary Narcissistic Supply (SNS). The narcissist mistakenly interprets his narcissistic needs as emotions. To him, pursuing a woman (a Source of Secondary Narcissistic Supply - SSNS), for instance, is what others call "love" or "passion".

Narcissistic Supply, both Primary and Secondary, is perishable goods. The narcissist consumes it and has to replenish it. As is the case with other drug addictions, to produce the same effect, he is forced to increase the dosage as he goes.

While the narcissist uses up his supply, his partner serves as a silent (and admiring) witness to the narcissist's "great moments" and "achievements". Thus, the narcissist's female friend "accumulates" the narcissist's "grand" and "illustrious past". When Primary Narcissistic Supply is low, she "releases" the supply she had accumulated. This she does by reminding the narcissist of those moments of glory that she had witnessed. She helps the narcissist to regulate his sense of self-worth.

This function - of Narcissistic Supply accumulation and release - is performed by all SSNSs, male or female, inanimate or institutional. The narcissist's co-workers, bosses, colleagues, neighbours, partners, and friends are all potential SSNSs. They all witness the narcissist's past accomplishments and can remind him of them when new supply runs dry.

Question: Why does the narcissist devalue his Source of Secondary Narcissistic Supply (SSNS)?

Answer: The narcissist realizes and resents his dependence on Narcissistic Supply. Moreover, deep inside, he is aware of the fact that his False Self is an untenable sham. Still, omnipotent as he holds himself to be, the narcissist believes in his ability to make it all come true, to asymptotically approximate his grandiose fantasies. He is firmly convinced that, given enough time and practice, he can and will become his lofty and ideal False Self.

Hence the narcissist's idea of progress: the frustrating and masochistic pursuit of an ever-receding mirage of perfection, brilliance, omniscience, omnipresence, and omnipotence. The narcissist dumps old Sources and Triggers of Supply because he is convinced that he is perpetually improving and that he deserves better and that "better" is just around the corner. He is driven by his own impossible Ego Ideal.

466

Narcissists are forever in pursuit of Narcissistic Supply. They are oblivious to the passage of time and are not constrained by any behavioural consistency, "rules" of conduct, or moral considerations. Signal to the narcissist that you are a willing source, and he is bound to try to extract Narcissistic Supply from you by any and all means.

This is a reflex. The narcissist would have reacted absolutely the same way to any other source because, to him, all sources are interchangeable.

Some Sources of Supply are ideal (from the narcissist's point of view): sufficiently intelligent, sufficiently gullible, submissive, reasonably (but not overly) inferior to the narcissist, in possession of a good memory (with which to regulate the flow of Narcissistic Supply), available but not imposing, not explicitly or overtly manipulative, undemanding, attractive (if the narcissist is somatic). In short: a Galathea-Pygmallion type.

But then, often abruptly and inexplicably, it is all over. The narcissist is cold, uninterested and remote.

One of the reasons is, as Groucho Marx put it, that the narcissist doesn't like to belong to those clubs which would accept him as a member. The narcissist devalues his Sources of Supply for the very qualities that made them such sources in the first place: their gullibility, their submissiveness, their (intellectual or physical) inferiority.

But there are many other reasons. For instance, the narcissist resents his dependency. He realizes that he is hopelessly and helplessly addicted to Narcissistic Supply and is in hock to its sources. By devaluing the sources of said supply (his spouse, his employer, his colleague, his friends) he ameliorates the dissonance.

Moreover, the narcissist perceives intimacy and sex as a threat to his uniqueness. Everyone needs sex and intimacy: it is the great equalizer. The narcissist resents this commonness. He rebels by striking out at the perceived founts of his frustration and "enslavement": his Sources of Narcissistic Supply.

Sex and intimacy are usually also connected to unresolved past conflicts with important Primary Objects (parents or caregivers). By constantly invoking these conflicts, the narcissist encourages transference and provokes the onset of approach-avoidance cycles. He blows hot and cold on his relationships.

Additionally, narcissists simply get tired of their sources. They get bored. There is no mathematical formula which governs this. It depends on numerous variables. Usually, the relationship lasts until the narcissist "gets used" to the source and its stimulating effects wear off or until a better Source of Supply presents itself.

Question: Could negative input serve as Narcissistic Supply (NS)?

Answer: Yes, it can. NS includes all forms of attention, both positive and negative: fame, notoriety, adulation, fear, applause, approval. Whenever the narcissist gets attention, positive or negative, whenever he is in the "limelight", it constitutes NS. If he can manipulate people or influence them - positively or negatively - it qualifies as NS.

Even quarrelling with people and confronting them constitute NS. Perhaps not the conflict itself, but the narcissist's ability to influence other people, to make them feel the way he wants, to manipulate them, to make them do something or refrain from doing it all count as forms of Narcissistic Supply. Hence the phenomenon of "serial litigators".

Question: Does the narcissist want to be liked?

Answer: Would you wish to be liked by your television set? To the narcissist, people are mere tools, Sources of Supply. If, in order to secure this supply, he must be liked by them, he acts likable, helpful, collegial, and friendly. If the only way is to be feared, he makes sure they fear him. He does not really care either way as long as he is being attended to. Attention - whether in the form of fame or infamy - is what it's all about. His world revolves around this constant mirroring. I am seen therefore I exist is his motto.

But the classic narcissist also craves punishment. His actions are aimed to elicit social opprobrium and sanctions. His life is a Kafkaesque, ongoing trial and the never-ending proceedings are in themselves the punishment. Being penalized (reprimanded, incarcerated, abandoned) serves to vindicate and validate the internal damning voices of the narcissist's sadistic, ideal and immature Superego (really, the erstwhile voices of his parents or other caregivers). It confirms his worthlessness. It relieves him from the inner conflict he endures when he is successful: the conflict between the gnawing feelings of guilt, anxiety, and shame and the need to relentlessly secure Narcissistic Supply.

Question: How does the narcissist treat his past Sources of Narcissistic Supply? Does he regard them as enemies?

Answer: One should be careful not to romanticize the narcissist. His remorse and good behaviour are always linked to fears of losing his sources.

Narcissists have no enemies. They have only Sources of Narcissistic Supply. An enemy means attention means supply. One holds sway over one's enemy. If the narcissist has the power to provoke emotions in you, then you are still a Source of Supply to him, regardless of which emotions are provoked.

The narcissist seeks out his old Sources of Narcissistic Supply when he has absolutely no other NS Sources at his disposal. Narcissists frantically try to recycle their old and wasted sources in such a situation. But the narcissist would not do even that had he not felt that he could still successfully extract a modicum of NS from the old source (even to attack the narcissist is to recognize his existence and to attend to him!!!).

If you are an old Source of Narcissistic Supply, first, get over the excitement of seeing the narcissist again. It may be flattering, perhaps sexually arousing. Try to overcome these feelings.

Then, simply ignore him. Don't bother to respond in any way to his offer to get together. If he talks to you - keep quiet, don't answer. If he calls you - listen politely and then say goodbye and hang up. Return his gifts unopened. Indifference is what the narcissist cannot stand. It indicates a lack of attention and interest that constitutes the kernel of negative NS to be avoided.

How to Cope with a Narcissist?

No one should feel responsible for the narcissist's predicament. As far as he is concerned, others hardly exist - so enmeshed he is in himself and in the resulting misery of this very self-preoccupation. Others are objects on which he projects his wrath, rage, suppressed and mutating aggression and, finally, ill disguised violence. How should his closest, nearest and dearest cope with his eccentric vagaries?

The short answer is by abandoning him or by threatening to abandon him.

The threat to abandon need not be explicit or conditional ("If you don't do something or if you do it, I will ditch you"). It is sufficient to confront the narcissist, to completely ignore him, to insist on respect for one's boundaries and wishes, or to shout back at him. The narcissist takes these signs of personal autonomy to be harbingers of impending separation and reacts with anxiety.

The narcissist is tamed by the very same weapons that he uses to subjugate others. The spectre of being abandoned looms large over everything else. In the narcissist's mind, every discordant note presages solitude and the resulting confrontation with his orphaned self.

The narcissist is a person who is irreparably traumatized by the behaviour of the most important people in his life: his parents, role models, or peers. By being capricious, arbitrary, and sadistically judgemental, they moulded him into an adult, who fervently and obsessively tries to recreate the trauma in order to, this time around, resolve it (Repetition Complex).

Thus, on the one hand, the narcissist feels that his freedom depends upon re-enacting these early unsavoury experiences. On the other hand, he is terrified by this prospect. Realizing that he is doomed to go through the same traumas over and over again, the narcissist distances himself by using his aggression to alienate others, to humiliate people, and in general, to be emotionally absent.

This behaviour brings about the very consequence that the narcissist so fears: abandonment. But, this way, at least, the narcissist is able to convince himself (and others) that HE was the one who fostered the separation, that it was fully his choice and that he was not surprised. The truth is that, governed by his internal demons, the narcissist has no real choice. The dismal future of his relationships is preordained.

The narcissist is a binary person: the carrot is the stick in his case. If he gets too close to someone emotionally, he fears ultimate and inevitable abandonment. He, thus, distances himself, acts cruelly and brings about the very abandonment that he feared in the first place.

In this paradox lies the key to coping with the narcissist. If, for instance, he is having a rage attack - rage back. This will provoke in him fears of being abandoned and the resulting calm will be so total that it might seem eerie. Narcissists are known for these sudden tectonic shifts in mood and in behaviour.

Mirror the narcissist's actions and repeat his words. If he threatens - threaten back and credibly try to use the same language and content. If he leaves the house - leave it as well, disappear on him. If he is suspicious - act suspicious. Be critical, denigrating, humiliating, go down to his level - because that's the only way to penetrate his thick defences. Faced with his mirror image, the narcissist always recoils.

We must not forget that the narcissist behaves the way he does in order to engender and encourage abandonment. When mirrored, the narcissist dreads imminent and impending desertion, which is the inevitable result of his actions and words. This prospect so terrifies him that it induces in him an incredible alteration of behaviour.

He instantly succumbs and obsequiously tries to make amends, moving from one (cold and bitter, cynical and misanthropic, cruel and sadistic) pole to another (warm, even loving, fuzzy, engulfing, emotional, maudlin, and saccharine).

The other coping strategy is to give up on him.

Dump him and go about reconstructing your own life. Very few people deserve the kind of investment that is an absolute prerequisite to living with a narcissist. To cope with a narcissist is a full time, energy and emotion-draining job, which reduces people around him to insecure nervous wrecks. Who deserves such a sacrifice?

No one, to my mind, not even the most brilliant, charming, breathtaking, suave narcissist. The glamour and trickery wear thin and underneath them a monster lurks which irreversibly and adversely influences the lives of those around it for the worse.

Narcissists are incorrigibly and notoriously difficult to change. Thus, trying to "modify" them is doomed to failure. You should either accept them as they are or avoid them altogether. If one accepts the narcissist as he is, one should cater to his needs. His needs are part of who he is. Would you have ignored a physical handicap in another intimate partner? Would you not have assisted a quadriplegic? The narcissist is an emotional cripple. He needs constant adulation. He cannot help it. So, if one chooses to accept him, it is a package deal, the incessant provision of Narcissistic Supply included.

Narcissists and Women

Question: Do narcissists hate women?

Answer: Primary Narcissistic Supply (PNS) is any kind of Narcissistic Supply (NS) provided by people who are not "meaningful" or "significant" others. Adulation, attention, affirmation, fame, notoriety, sexual conquests are all forms of PNS.

Secondary NS (SNS) emanates from people who are in repetitive or continuous touch with the narcissist. It includes the important roles of Narcissistic Accumulation and Narcissistic Regulation, among others.

Narcissists abhor and dread getting emotionally intimate. The cerebral ones regard sex as a maintenance chore, something they have to do in order to keep their Source of Secondary Supply. The somatic narcissist treats women as objects and sex as a means to obtaining Narcissistic Supply.

Moreover, many narcissists tend to frustrate women. They refrain from having sex with them, tease them and then leave them, resist flirtatious and seductive behaviours and so on. Often, they invoke the existence of a girlfriend/fiancйe/spouse as the "reason" why they cannot have sex or develop a relationship. But this is not out of loyalty and fidelity in the empathic and loving sense. This is because they wish (and often succeed) to sadistically frustrate the interested party.

But, this latter behaviour pertains only to cerebral narcissists not to somatic narcissists and to histrionics (Histrionic Personality Disorder - HPD) who use their body, sexuality, and seduction/flirtation to extract Narcissistic Supply from others.

Narcissists are misogynists. They team up with women who serve as Sources of SNS (Secondary Narcissistic Supply). The woman's chores are to accumulate past Narcissistic Supply (by witnessing the narcissist's "moments of glory") and release it in

472

SAM VAKNIN   MALIGNANT SELF LOVE

an orderly manner in order to regulate the fluctuating flow of primary supply and compensate for times of deficient supply.

Otherwise, cerebral narcissists are not interested in women.

Most of them are asexual (desire sex very rarely, if at all). They hold women in contempt and abhor the thought of being really intimate with them. Usually, they choose for partners submissive women whom they disdain for being well below their intellectual level.

This leads to a vicious cycle of neediness and self-contempt ("How come I am dependent on this inferior woman"). Hence the abuse. When Primary NS is available, the woman is hardly tolerated, as one would reluctantly pay the premium of an insurance policy.

Narcissists of all stripes do regard the "subjugation" of an attractive woman to be a Source of Narcissistic Supply, though.

Such conquests are status symbols, proofs of virility, and they allow the narcissist to engage in "vicarious" narcissistic behaviours, to express his narcissism through the "conquered" women, transforming them into instruments at the service of his narcissism, into his extensions. This is done by employing defence mechanisms such as Projective Identification.

473 The narcissist believes that being in love is actually merely going through the motions. To him, emotions are mimicry and pretence. He says: "I am a conscious misogynist. I fear and loathe women and tend to ignore them to the best of my ability. To me they are a mixture of hunter and parasite."

Most male narcissists are misogynists. After all, they are the warped creations of women. Women gave birth to them and moulded them into what they are: dysfunctional, maladaptive, and emotionally dead. They are angry at their mothers and, by extension, at all women.

The narcissist's attitude to women is, naturally, complex and multi-layered but it can be described using four axes:

1. The Holy Whore
2. The Hunter Parasite
3. The Frustrating Object of Desire
4. Uniqueness Roles

The narcissist divides all women to saints (Madonnas) and whores. He finds it difficult to have sex ("dirty", "forbidden", "punishable", "degrading") with feminine significant others (spouse, intimate girlfriend). To him, sex and intimacy are mutually exclusive rather than mutually expressive or mutually reinforcing propositions.

Sex is reserved to "whores" (all other women in the world). This division resolves the narcissist's constant cognitive dissonance ("I want her but...", "I don't need anyone but..."). It also legitimizes his sadistic urges (abstaining from sex is a major and recurrent narcissistic "penalty" inflicted on female "transgressors"). It tallies well with the frequent idealization-devaluation cycles the narcissist goes through. The idealized females are sexless, the devalued ones "deserving" of their degradation (sex) and the contempt that, inevitably, follows thereafter.

The narcissist believes firmly that women are out to "hunt" men by genetic predisposition. As a result, he feels threatened (as any prey would). This, of course, is an intellectualization of the real state of affairs: the narcissist feels threatened by women and tries to justify this irrational fear by imbuing them with "objective", menacing qualities. The narcissist frequently "pathologizes" others in order to control them.

The narcissist believes that, once their prey is secured, women assume the role of "body snatchers". They abscond with the male's sperm, generate an endless stream of demanding children, and financially bleed the men in their lives to cater to their needs and to the needs of their dependants.

Put differently, women are parasites, leeches, whose sole function is to suck dry every man they find and tarantula-like decapitate him once no longer useful. This, of course, is exactly what the narcissist does to people. Thus, his view of women is a projection.

Heterosexual narcissists desire women as any other red-blooded male does or even more so due to their special symbolic nature in the narcissist's universe. Humbling a woman in acts of faintly sado-masochistic sex is a way of getting back at mother. But the narcissist is frustrated by his inability to meaningfully interact with women, by their apparent emotional depth and powers of psychological penetration (real or attributed) and by their sexuality.

Women's incessant demands for intimacy are perceived by the narcissist as threats. He recoils instead of getting closer. The cerebral narcissist also despises and derides sex, as we said before. Thus, caught in a seemingly intractable Repetition Complex, in approach-avoidance cycles, the narcissist becomes furious at the source of his frustration.

Some narcissists set out to do some frustrating of their own. They tease (passively or actively), or they pretend to be asexual and, in any case, they turn down, rather cruelly, any feminine attempt to court them and to get closer. Sadistically, they tremen-

474

dously enjoy their ability to frustrate the desires, passions and sexual wishes of women. It makes them feel omnipotent and self-righteous. Narcissists regularly frustrate all women sexually and significant women in their lives both sexually and emotionally.

Somatic narcissists simply use women as objects and then discard them. They masturbate, using women as "flesh and blood sex dolls". The emotional background is identical. While the cerebral narcissist punishes through abstention, the somatic narcissist penalizes through excess.

The narcissist's mother kept behaving as though the narcissist was and is not special (to her). The narcissist's whole life is a pathetic and pitiful effort to prove her wrong. The narcissist constantly seeks confirmation from others that he is special: in other words that he is, that he actually exists.

Women threaten this quest. Sex is "bestial" and "common". There is nothing "special or unique" about sex. Women's sexual needs threaten to reduce the narcissist to the lowest common denominator: intimacy, sex and human emotions. Everybody and anybody can feel, copulate and breed. There is nothing in these activities to set the narcissist apart and above others. And yet women seem to be interested only in these pursuits. Thus, the narcissist emotionally believes that women are the continuation of his mother by other means and in different guises.

The narcissist hates women virulently, passionately and uncompromisingly. His hate is primal, irrational, the progeny of mortal fear and sustained abuse. Granted, most narcissists learn how to disguise, even repress these untoward feelings. But their hatred does get out of control and erupt from time to time.

Living with a narcissist is an arduous and eroding task. Narcissists are infinitely pessimistic, bad-tempered, paranoid and sadistic in an absent-minded and indifferent manner. Their daily routine is a rigmarole of threats, complaints, hurts, eruptions, moodiness and rage.

The narcissist rails against slights true and imagined. He alienates people. He humiliates them because this is his only weapon against his own humiliation wrought by their indifference. Gradually, wherever he is, the narcissist's social circle dwindles and then vanishes. Every narcissist is also a schizoid, to some extent. A schizoid is not a misanthrope. The narcissist does not necessarily hate people - he simply does not need them. He regards social interactions as a nuisance to be minimized.

The narcissist is torn between his need to obtain Narcissistic Supply (from others) and his fervent wish to be left alone. This wish springs from contempt and overwhelming feelings of superiority.

In the narcissist's psyche, there are fundamental conflicts between dependence, counter-dependence and contempt, neediness and devaluation, seeking and avoiding, turning on the charm to attract adulation and reacting wrathfully to the minutest "provocations". These conflicts lead to rapid cycling between gregariousness and self-imposed ascetic seclusion.

Such an unpredictable but always bilious and festering ambience, typical of the narcissist's "romantic" liaisons is hardly conducive to love or sex. Gradually, both become extinct. Relationships are hollowed out. Imperceptibly, the narcissist switches to asexual co-habitation.

But the vitriolic environment that the narcissist creates is only one hand of the equation. The other hand involves the woman herself.

As we said, heterosexual narcissists are attracted to women, but simultaneously repelled, horrified, bewitched and provoked by them. They seek to frustrate and humiliate them. Psychodynamically, the narcissist probably visits upon them his mother's sins, but such simplistic explanation does this complex subject great injustice.

Most narcissists are misogynists. Their sexual and emotional lives are perturbed and chaotic. They are not able to love in any true sense of the word, nor are they capable of developing any measure of intimacy. Lacking empathy, they are unable to offer to their partners emotional sustenance.

Do narcissists miss loving, would they have liked to love and are they angry with their parents for crippling them in this respect?

To the narcissist, these questions are incomprehensible. There is no way they can answer them. Narcissists have never loved. They do not know what is it that they are supposedly missing. Observing it from the outside, love seems to them to be a risible pathology.

Narcissists equate love with weakness. They hate being weak and they hate and despise weak people (e.g., the sick, the old and the young). They do not tolerate what they consider to be stupidity, disease and dependence and love seems to consist of all three. These are not sour grapes. They really feel this way.

Narcissists are angry men - but not because they never experienced love and probably never will. They are angry because they are not as powerful, awe inspiring and successful as they

476

wish they were and, to their mind, deserve to be. Because their daydreams refuse so stubbornly to come true. Because they are their worst enemy. And because, in their unmitigated paranoia, they see adversaries plotting everywhere and they feel discriminated against and contemptuously ignored.

Many of them (the borderline narcissists) cannot conceive of life in one place with one set of people, doing the same thing, in the same field with one goal within a decades-old game plan. To them, this is the equivalent of death. They are most terrified of boredom and whenever faced with its daunting prospect, they inject drama or even danger into their lives. This way they feel alive.

The narcissist is a lonely wolf. He is a shaky platform, indeed, on which to base a family, or plans for the future.

The Spouse/Mate/Partner of the Narcissist

Question: What kind of a spouse/mate/partner is likely to be attracted to a narcissist?

Answer:

The Victims

On the face of it, there is no partner or mate, who typically "binds" with a narcissist. They come in all shapes and sizes. The initial phases of attraction, infatuation and falling in love are pretty normal. The narcissist puts on his best face - the other party is blinded by budding love. A natural selection process occurs only much later, as the relationship develops and is put to the test.

Living with a narcissist can be exhilarating, is always onerous, often harrowing. Surviving a relationship with a narcissist indicates, therefore, the parameters of the personality of the survivor. She (or, more rarely, he) is moulded by the relationship into The Typical Narcissistic Mate/Partner/Spouse.

First and foremost, the narcissist's partner must have a deficient or a distorted grasp of her self and of reality. Otherwise, she (or he) is bound to abandon the narcissist's ship early on. The cognitive distortion is likely to consist of belittling and demeaning herself, while aggrandizing and adoring the narcissist.

The partner is, thus, placing herself in the position of the eternal victim: undeserving, punishable, a scapegoat. Sometimes, it is very important to the partner to appear moral, sacrificial and victimized. At other times, she is not even aware of this predicament. The narcissist is perceived by the partner to be a person in the position to demand these sacrifices from her because he is superior in many ways (intellectually, emotionally, morally, professionally, or financially).

478

SAM VAKNIN   MALIGNANT SELF LOVE

The status of professional victim sits well with the partner's tendency to punish herself, namely: with her masochistic streak. She feels that the tormented life with the narcissist is just what she deserves. In this respect, the partner is the mirror image of the narcissist. By maintaining a symbiotic relationship with him, by being totally dependent upon her source of masochistic supply (which the narcissist most reliably constitutes and most amply provides), the partner enhances certain traits and encourages certain behaviours, which are at the very core of narcissism.

The narcissist is never whole without an adoring, submissive, available, self-denigrating partner. His very sense of superiority, indeed his False Self, depends on it. His sadistic Superego switches its attentions from the narcissist (in whom it often provokes suicidal ideation) to the partner, thus finally obtaining an alternative source of sadistic satisfaction.

It is through self-denial that the partner survives. She denies her wishes, hopes, dreams, aspirations, sexual, psychological and material needs, choices, preferences, values, and much else besides. She perceives her needs as threatening because they might engender the wrath of the narcissist's God-like supreme figure.

The narcissist is rendered in her eyes even more superior through and because of this self-denial. Self-denial undertaken to facilitate and ease the life of a "great man" is more palatable. The "greater" the man (the narcissist), the easier it is for the partner to ignore her own self, to dwindle, to degenerate, to turn into an appendix of the narcissist and, finally, to become nothing but an extension, to merge with the narcissist to the point of oblivion and of merely dim memories of herself.

The two collaborate in this macabre dance. The narcissist is formed by his partner inasmuch as he forms her. Submission breeds superiority and masochism breeds sadism. The relationship is characterized by emergentism: within the couple, roles are allocated almost from the start and any deviation meets with an aggressive, even violent reaction.

The predominant state of the partner's mind is utter confusion. Even the most basic relationships - with husband, children, or parents - remain bafflingly obscured by the giant shadow cast by the intensive interaction with the narcissist. A suspension of judgement is part and parcel of a suspension of individuality, which are both prerequisites to and the outcomes of living with a narcissist. The partner no longer knows what is true and right and what is wrong and forbidden.

The narcissist recreates for the partner the sort of emotional ambience that led to his own formation in the first place: capriciousness, fickleness, arbitrariness, emotional (and physical or sexual) abandonment. The world becomes hostile and ominous and the partner has only one thing left to cling to: the narcissist.

And cling she does. If there is anything which can safely be said about those who emotionally team up with narcissists, it is that they are overtly and overly dependent.

The partner doesn't know what to do - and this is only too natural in the mayhem that is the relationship with the narcissist. But the typical partner also does not know what she wants and, to a large extent, who she is and what she wishes to become.

These unanswered questions hamper the partner's ability to gauge reality. Her primordial sin is that she fell in love with an image, not with a real person. It is the voiding of the image that is mourned when the relationship ends.

The break-up of a relationship with a narcissist is, therefore, very emotionally charged. It is the culmination of a long chain of humiliations and of subjugation. It is the rebellion of the functioning and healthy parts of the partner's personality against the tyranny of the narcissist.

The partner is likely to have totally misread and misinterpreted the whole interaction (I hesitate to call it a relationship). This lack of proper interface with reality might be labelled "pathological".

Why is it that the partner seeks to prolong her pain? What is the source and purpose of this masochistic streak? Upon the break-up of the relationship, the partner (but not the narcissist, who usually refuses to provide closure) engage in a tortuous and drawn out post mortem.

But the question who did what to whom (and even why) is irrelevant. What is relevant is to stop mourning oneself, start smiling again and love in a less subservient, hopeless, and pain-inflicting manner.

The Abuse

Abuse is an integral, inseparable part of the Narcissistic Personality Disorder.

The narcissist idealizes and then DEVALUES and discards the object of his initial idealization. This abrupt, heartless devaluation IS abuse. The narcissist exploits, lies, insults, demeans, ignores (the "silent treatment"), manipulates, and controls others.

There are many forms of abuse. To love too much is to abuse. It is tantamount to treating someone as one's extension, an object, or an instrument of gratification. To be over-protective, not to respect privacy, to be brutally honest, with a morbid sense of humour, or consistently tactless is to abuse. To expect too much, to denigrate, to ignore someone are all modes of abuse. There is physical abuse, verbal abuse, psychological abuse, sexual abuse. The list is long.

Narcissists are masters of abusing surreptitiously ("ambient abuse"). They are "stealth abusers". You have to actually live with one in order to witness the abuse.

There are two important categories of abuse:

1. *Overt Abuse* - The open and explicit abuse of another person. Threatening, coercing, battering, lying, berating, demeaning, chastising, insulting, humiliating, exploiting, ignoring ("silent treatment"), devaluing, unceremoniously discarding, verbal abuse, physical abuse and sexual abuse are all forms of overt abuse.

2. *Covert or Controlling Abuse* - Narcissism is almost entirely about control. It is a primitive and immature reaction to the circumstances of the narcissist's life (usually in his childhood) in which he was rendered helpless. It is about re-asserting one's identity, re-establishing predictability, mastering the environment, both human and physical.

The bulk of narcissistic behaviours can be traced to this panicky reaction to the potential for loss of control. Narcissists are hypochondriacs (and difficult patients) because they are afraid to lose control over their body, their appearance, and their proper functioning. They are obsessive-compulsive in their efforts to subdue their physical habitat and render it foreseeable. They stalk people and harass them as a means of "being in touch": another form of narcissistic control.

But why the panic?

The narcissist is a solipsist. To him, nothing exists except himself. Meaningful others are his extensions, assimilated by him, they are internal objects - not external ones. Thus, losing control of a significant other is equivalent to losing the use of a limb, or of one's brain. It is terrifying.

Independent or disobedient people evoke in the narcissist the realization that something is wrong with his worldview, that he is not the centre of the world or its prime mover and that he cannot control what, to him, are internal representations.

To the narcissist, losing control means going insane. Because other people are mere elements in the narcissist's mind, being unable to manipulate them literally means losing it (his mind). Imagine, if you suddenly were to find out that you cannot manipulate your memories or control your thoughts... It would have felt nightmarish!

Moreover, it is often only through manipulation and extortion that the narcissist can secure his Narcissistic Supply (NS). Controlling his Sources of Narcissistic Supply is a (mental) life or death question for the narcissist. The narcissist is a drug addict (his drug being Narcissistic Supply) and he goes to great lengths to obtain the next dose.

In his frantic efforts to maintain control or re-assert it, the narcissist resorts to a myriad of fiendishly inventive stratagems and mechanisms. Here is a partial list:

Unpredictability

The narcissist acts unpredictably, capriciously, inconsistently and irrationally. This serves to demolish in others their carefully crafted worldview. They become dependent upon the next twist and turn of the narcissist, his inexplicable whims, his outbursts, denial, or smiles.

In other words: the narcissist makes sure that HE is the only stable entity in the lives of others by shattering the rest of their world through his seemingly insane behaviour. He guarantees his presence in their lives by destabilizing them.

In the absence of a self, there are no likes or dislikes, preferences, predictable behaviour or characteristics. It is not possible to know the narcissist. There is no one there.

The narcissist was conditioned from an early age of abuse and trauma to expect the unexpected. His was a world in which (sometimes sadistic) capricious caretakers and peers often behaved arbitrarily. He was trained to deny his True Self and nurture a False one.

Having invented himself, the narcissist sees no problem in re-inventing that which he designed in the first place. The narcissist is his own repeated creator - hence his grandiosity.

Moreover, the narcissist is a man for all seasons, forever adaptable, constantly imitating and emulating role models, a human sponge, a perfect mirror, a chameleon, a non-entity that is, at the same time, all entities combined.

The narcissist is best described by Heidegger's phrase: "Being and Nothingness". Into this reflective vacuum, this sucking black hole, the narcissist attracts the Sources of his Narcissistic Supply.

To an observer, the narcissist appears to be fractured or discontinuous.

Pathological narcissism has been compared to the Dissociative Identity Disorder (formerly the Multiple Personality Disorder). By definition, the narcissist has at least two selves, the True and False ones. His personality is very primitive and disorganized. Living with a narcissist is a nauseating experience not only because of what he is, but because of what he is NOT. He is not a fully formed human, but a dizzyingly kaleidoscopic gallery of ephemeral images, which melt into each other seamlessly. It is incredibly disorienting.

It is also exceedingly problematic. Promises made by the narcissist are easily disowned by him. His plans are transient. His emotional ties a simulacrum. Most narcissists have one island of stability in their life (spouse, family, their career, a hobby, their religion, country, or idol) pounded by the turbulent currents of an otherwise stochastic existence.

The narcissist does not keep agreements, does not adhere to laws or social norms, and regards consistency and predictability as demeaning traits. Thus, to invest in a narcissist is a purposeless, futile and meaningless activity. To the narcissist, every day is a new beginning, a hunt, a new cycle of idealization or devaluation, a newly invented self. There is no accumulation of credits or goodwill because the narcissist has no past and no future. He occupies an eternal and timeless present. He is a fossil caught in the frozen ashes of a volcanic childhood.

What to do?

Refuse to accept such behaviour. Demand reasonably predictable and rational actions and reactions. Insist on respect for your boundaries, predilections, preferences, and priorities.

Disproportional Reactions

One of the favourite tools of manipulation in the narcissist's arsenal is the disproportionality of his reactions. He reacts with supreme rage to the slightest slight. He punishes severely for what he perceives to be an offence against him, no matter how minor. He throws a temper tantrum over any discord or disagreement, however gently and considerately expressed. Immediately thereafter, he may act attentive, charming and seductive (even over-sexed, if need be). This ever-shifting emotional landscape ("affective dunes") coupled with an inordinately harsh and arbitrarily applied "penal code" are both promulgated by the narcissist. Neediness and dependence on the source of all justice meted - the narcissist - are thus guaranteed.

What to do?

Demand a just and proportional treatment. Reject or ignore unjust and capricious behaviour.

If you are up to the inevitable confrontation, react in kind. Let him taste some of his own medicine.

Dehumanisation and Objectification

People have a need to believe in the empathic skills and basic good-heartedness of others. By dehumanizing and objectifying people the narcissist attacks the very foundations of the social treaty. This is the "alien" aspect of narcissists: they may be excellent imitations of fully formed adults but they are emotionally non-existent, or, at best, immature.

This is so horrid, so repulsive, so phantasmagoric that people recoil in terror. It is then, with their defences absolutely down, that they are the most susceptible and vulnerable to the narcissist's control. Physical, psychological, verbal and sexual abuse are all forms of dehumanization and objectification.

What to do?

Never show your abuser that you are afraid of him. Do not negotiate with bullies. They are insatiable. Do not succumb to blackmail.

If things get rough - disengage, involve law enforcement officers, friends and colleagues, or threaten him (legally).

Do not keep your abuse a secret. Secrecy is the abuser's weapon.

Never give him a second chance. React with your full arsenal to the first transgression.

Abuse of Information

From the first moments of an encounter with another person, the narcissist is on the prowl. He collects information with the intention of abusing it later in order to extract Narcissistic Supply. The more he knows about his potential Source of Supply, the better able he is to coerce, manipulate, charm, extort or convert her "to the cause". The narcissist does not hesitate to misuse the information he gleaned, regardless of its intimate nature or the circumstances in which he obtained it. This is a powerful tool in his armoury.

What to do?

Be guarded. Don't be too forthcoming in a first or casual meeting. First, gather intelligence on your interlocutor.

Be yourself. Don't misrepresent your wishes, boundaries, preferences, priorities, and red lines.

Do not behave inconsistently. Do not go back on your word. Be firm and resolute.

Impossible Situations

The narcissist engineers impossible, dangerous, unpredictable, unprecedented, or highly specific situations in which he is sorely and indispensably needed. The narcissist's knowledge, his skills or his traits become the only ones applicable, or the most useful to coping with these artificial predicaments. It is a form of control by proxy.

What to do?

Stay away from such quagmires. Scrutinize every offer and suggestion, no matter how innocuous.

Prepare back-up plans. Keep others informed of your whereabouts and appraised of your situation.

Be vigilant and doubting. Do not be gullible and suggestible. Better safe than sorry.

Control by Proxy

If all else fails, the narcissist recruits friends, colleagues, mates, family members, the authorities, institutions, neighbours, or the media - in short, third parties - to do his bidding. He uses them to cajole, coerce, threaten, stalk, offer, retreat, tempt, convince, harass, communicate and otherwise manipulate his target. He controls these unaware instruments exactly as he plans to control his ultimate prey. He employs the same mechanisms and devices. And he dumps his props unceremoniously when the job is done.

Another form of control by proxy is to engineer situations in which abuse is inflicted upon another person. Such carefully crafted scenarios involve embarrassment and humiliation as well as social sanctions (condemnation, opprobrium, or even physical punishment). Society, or a social group become the instruments of the narcissist.

What to do?

Often the abuser's proxies are unaware of their role. Expose him. Inform them. Demonstrate to them how they are being abused, misused, and plain used by the abuser.

Trap your abuser. Treat him as he treats you. Involve others. Bring it into the open. Nothing like sunshine to disinfest abuse.

Ambient Abuse

Gaslighting or stealth or ambient abuse is the fostering, propagation and enhancement of an atmosphere of fear, intimidation, instability, unpredictability and irritation. There are no acts of traceable or provable explicit abuse, nor any manipulative settings of control. Yet, the irksome feeling remains, a disagreeable foreboding, a premonition, a bad omen.

In the long-term, such an environment erodes one's sense of self-worth and self-esteem. Self-confidence is shaken badly. Often, the victims become paranoid or schizoid and thus are exposed even more to criticism and judgement. The roles are thus reversed: the victim is considered mentally disordered and the narcissist the suffering soul or the victim.

What to do?

Run! Get away! Ambient abuse often develops into overt and violent abuse.

You don't owe anyone an explanation but you owe yourself a life. Bail out of the relationship. Leave him now.

Indifference and Decompensation in Pathological Narcissism

The narcissist lacks empathy. Consequently, he is not really interested in the lives, emotions, needs, preferences, and hopes of people around him. Even his nearest and dearest are, to him, mere instruments of gratification. They require his undivided attention only when they "malfunction" - when they become disobedient, independent, or critical. He loses all interest in them if they cannot be "fixed" (for instance, when they are terminally ill or develop a modicum of personal autonomy and independence).

Once he gives up on his erstwhile Sources of Supply, the narcissist proceeds to promptly and peremptorily devalue and discard them. This is often done by simply ignoring them - a facade of indifference that is known as the "silent treatment" and is, at heart, hostile and aggressive. Indifference is, therefore, a form of devaluation. People find the narcissist "cold", "inhuman", "heartless", "clueless", "robotic or machine-like".

Early on in life, the narcissist learns to disguise his socially-unacceptable indifference as benevolence, equanimity, cool-headedness, composure, or superiority. "It is not that I don't care about others" - he shrugs off his critics - "I am simply more level-headed, more resilient, more composed under pressure... They mistake my equanimity for apathy."

The narcissist tries to convince people that he is compassionate. His profound lack of interest in his spouse's life, vocation, interests, hobbies, and whereabouts he cloaks as benevolent altruism. "I give her all the freedom she can wish for!" - he protests - "I don't spy on her, follow her, or nag her with endless questions. I don't bother her. I let her lead her life the way she sees fit and don't interfere in her affairs!" He makes a virtue out of his emotional truancy.

All very commendable but when taken to extremes such benign neglect turns malignant and signifies the voidance of true love and attachment. The narcissist's emotional (and, often, physical) absence from all his relationships is a form of aggression and a defence against his own thoroughly repressed feelings.

In rare moments of self-awareness, the narcissist realizes that without his input - even in the form of feigned emotions - people will abandon him. He then swings from cruel aloofness to maudlin and grandiose gestures intended to demonstrate the "larger than life" nature of his sentiments. This bizarre pendulum only proves the narcissist's inadequacy at maintaining adult relationships. It convinces no one and repels many.

The narcissist's guarded detachment is a sad reaction to his unfortunate formative years. Pathological narcissism is thought to be the result of a prolonged period of severe abuse by primary caregivers, peers, or authority figures. In this sense, pathological narcissism is, therefore, a reaction to trauma. Narcissism IS a form of Post-Traumatic Stress Disorder that got ossified and fixated and mutated into a personality disorder.

All narcissists are traumatized and all of them suffer from a variety of post-traumatic symptoms: abandonment anxiety, reckless behaviours, anxiety and mood disorders, somatoform disorders, and so on. But the presenting signs of narcissism rarely indicate post-trauma. This is because pathological narcissism is an EFFICIENT coping (defence) mechanism. The narcissist presents to the world a facade of invincibility, equanimity, superiority, skilfulness, cool-headedness, invulnerability, and, in short: indifference.

This front is penetrated only in times of great crises that threaten the narcissist's ability to obtain Narcissistic Supply. The narcissist then "falls apart" in a process of disintegration known as decompenzation. The dynamic forces which render him paralyzed and fake - his vulnerabilities, weaknesses, and fears - are starkly exposed as his defences crumble and become dysfunctional. The narcissist's extreme dependence on his social milieu for the regulation of his sense of self-worth is painfully and pitifully evident as he is reduced to begging and cajoling.

At such times, the narcissist acts out self-destructively and anti-socially. His mask of superior equanimity is pierced by displays of impotent rage, self-loathing, self-pity, and crass attempts at manipulation of his friends, family, and colleagues. His ostensible benevolence and caring evaporate. He feels caged and threatened and he reacts as any animal would do - by striking back at his perceived tormentors, at his hitherto "nearest" and "dearest".

The Malignant Optimism of the Abused

I often come across sad examples of the powers of self-delusion that the narcissist provokes in his victims. It is what I call "malignant optimism". People refuse to believe that some questions are unsolvable, some diseases incurable, some disasters inevitable. They see a sign of hope in every fluctuation. They read meaning and patterns into every random occurrence, utterance, or slip of tongue. They are deceived by their own pressing need to believe in the ultimate victory of good over evil, health over sickness, order over disorder. Life appears otherwise so meaningless, so unjust and so arbitrary...

So, they impose upon it a design, progress, aims, and paths. This is magical thinking.

"If only he tried hard enough", "If he only really wanted to heal", "If only we found the right therapy", "If only his defences were down", "There MUST be something good and worthy under his hideous facade", "NO ONE can be that evil and destructive", "He must have meant it differently", "God, or a higher being, or the spirit, or the soul is the solution and the answer to our prayers", "He is not responsible for what he is - his narcissism is the product of a difficult childhood, of abuse, and of his monstrous parents."

The Pollyanna defences of the abused are aimed against the emerging and horrible understanding that humans are mere specks of dust in a totally indifferent universe, the playthings of evil and sadistic forces, of which the narcissist is one and that finally the victims' pains means nothing to anyone but themselves.

The narcissist holds such malignant optimism in barely disguised contempt. To him, it is a sign of weakness. It gives off the scent of prey. It is a gaping vulnerability. He uses and abuses this human need for order, good, and meaning as he uses and abuses all other human needs. Gullibility, selective blindness, malignant optimism - these are the weapons of the beast. And the abused are hard at work to provide it with its arsenal.

Investing in a Narcissist

Question: In what type of narcissist is it worthwhile to invest emotionally?

Answer: This, obviously, is a matter of value judgement. Narcissism is a powerful force, akin to the psychological element in drug addiction. The narcissist is sustained by ever increasing amounts of Narcissistic Supply. Adoration, approval, attention and the maintenance of an audience are the nourishment without which the narcissist shrivels.

489   Depending on how talented the narcissist is, Narcissistic Supply could be the by-product of real achievements. The narcissist usually applies his skills and exploits his natural advantages where they provide him with the highest narcissistic rewards. For instance: he writes books to gain public acclaim not because he has something to say or because he cannot contain his emotions or his message - but in order to garner the attention of the public and the media. Still, narcissists are, mostly, gifted and, therefore, are able to contribute to society at large. They become artists, authors, political leaders, business leaders, or entertainers in order to bask in the limelight.

Some narcissists could be judged "worthy of sacrifice". They benefit their community "more" than they harm it. Those nearest and dearest pay a price - which is deemed more than amply compensated for by the contributions of the narcissist to the well-being of his community. But it is always a close call.

The Double Reflection

Narcissistic Couples and Narcissistic Types

Question: Can two narcissists establish a long-term, stable relationship?

Answer: Two narcissists of the same type (somatic, cerebral, classic, compensatory, or inverted) cannot maintain a stable, long-term, full-fledged, and functional relationship.

Consider two types of narcissists: the somatic narcissist and the cerebral narcissist. The somatic type relies on his body and sexuality as Sources of Narcissistic Supply. The cerebral narcissist uses his intellect, his intelligence and his professional achievements to obtain the same.

Narcissists are either predominantly cerebral or overwhelmingly somatic. In other words, they either generate their Narcissistic Supply by using their bodies or by flaunting their minds.

The somatic narcissist flashes his sexual conquests, parades his possessions, puts his muscles on ostentatious display, brags about his physical aesthetics or sexual prowess or exploits, is often a health freak and a hypochondriac. The cerebral narcissist is a know-it-all, haughty and intelligent "computer". He uses his awesome intellect, or knowledge (real or pretended) to secure adoration, adulation and admiration. To him, his body and its maintenance are a burden and a distraction.

Both types are autoerotic (psychosexually in love with themselves, with their bodies or with their brains). Both types prefer masturbation to adult, mature, interactive, multi-dimensional and emotion-laden sex.

The cerebral narcissist is often celibate (even when he has a girlfriend or a spouse). He prefers pornography and sexual autostimulation to the real thing. The cerebral narcissist is sometimes a latent (hidden, not yet outed) homosexual.

The somatic narcissist uses other people's bodies to masturbate. Sex with him - pyrotechnics and acrobatics aside - is likely to be an impersonal and emotionally alienating and draining experience. The partner is often treated as an object, an extension of the somatic narcissist, a sex toy or a sex slave.

It is a mistake to assume type-constancy. In other words, all narcissists are both cerebral and somatic. In each narcissist, one of the types is dominant. So, the narcissist is either largely cerebral - or dominantly somatic. But the other, recessive (manifested less frequently) type, is there. It is lurking, waiting to erupt.

The narcissist swings between his dominant type and his recessive type which manifests mainly after a major narcissistic injury or life crisis.

The cerebral narcissist brandishes his brainpower, exhibits his intellectual achievements, basks in the attention given to his mind and to its products. He hates his body and neglects it. It is a nuisance, a burden, a derided appendix, an inconvenience, a punishment. The cerebral narcissist is asexual (rarely has sex, often years apart). He masturbates regularly and very mechanically. His fantasies are homosexual or paedophiliac or tend to objectify his partner (rape, group sex). He stays away from women because he perceives them to be ruthless predators who are out to consume him.

The cerebral narcissist typically goes through a few major life crises. He gets divorced, goes bankrupt, does time in prison, is threatened, harassed and stalked, is often devalued, betrayed, denigrated and insulted. He is prone to all manner of chronic illnesses.

Invariably, following every life crisis, the somatic narcissist in him takes over. The cerebral narcissist suddenly becomes a lascivious lecher. When this happens, he maintains a few relationships - replete with abundant and addictive sex - going simultaneously. He sometimes participates in and initiates group sex and mass orgies. He exercises, loses weight and hones his body into an irresistible proposition.

This outburst of unrestrained, primordial lust wanes in a few months and he settles back into his cerebral ways. No sex, no women, no body.

These total reversals of character stun his mates. His girlfriend or spouse finds it impossible to digest this eerie transformation from the gregarious, darkly handsome, well-built and sexually insatiable person that swept her off her feet - to the bodiless, bookwormish hermit with not an inkling of interest in either sex or other carnal pleasures.

The cerebral narcissist misses his somatic half, but finding a balance is a doomed quest. The satyr that is the somatic narcissist is forever trapped in the intellectual cage of the cerebral one, the Brain.

Thus, if both members of the couple are cerebral narcissists, for instance if both of them are scholars, the resulting competition prevents them from serving as ample Sources of Narcissistic Supply to each other. Finally the mutual admiration society crumbles.

Consumed by the pursuit of their narcissistic gratification, they have no time or energy or will left to cater to the narcissistic needs of their partner. Moreover, the partner is perceived as a dangerous and vicious contender for a scarce resource: extant Sources of Narcissistic Supply. This may be less true if the two narcissists work in totally unrelated academic or intellectual fields.

But if the narcissists involved are of different types, if one of them is cerebral and the other one somatic, a long-term partnership based on the mutual provision of Narcissistic Supply can definitely survive.

Example: if one of the narcissists is somatic (uses his/her body as a source of narcissistic gratification) and the other one cerebral (uses his intellect or his professional achievements as such a source), there is nothing to destabilize such collaboration. It is even potentially emotionally rewarding.

The relationship between these two narcissists resembles the one that exists between an artist and his art or a collector and his collection. This can and does change, of course, as the narcissists involved grow older, flabbier and less agile intellectually. The somatic narcissist is also prone to multiple sexual relationships and encounters intended to support his somatic and sexual self-image. These may subject the relationship to fracturing strains. But, all in all, a stable and enduring relationship can - and often does - develop between dissimilar narcissists.

Narcissistic Parents

Question: What are the effects that narcissistic parents have on their offspring?

Answer: At the risk of over-simplification: narcissism tends to breed narcissism - but only a minority of the children of narcissistic parents become narcissists. This may be due to a genetic predisposition or to different life circumstances (like being the firstborn). Still, MOST narcissists have one or more narcissistic parents or caregivers.

493   The narcissistic parent regards his or her child as a multi-faceted Source of Narcissistic Supply. The child is considered to be and treated as an extension of the narcissist parent. It is through the child that the narcissist seeks to settle "open scores" with the world. The child is supposed to realize the unfulfilled dreams, wishes, and fantasies of the narcissistic parent.

This "life by proxy" can develop in two ways: the narcissist can either merge with his child or be ambivalent about him. The ambivalence is the result of a conflict between the narcissist's wish to attain his narcissistic goals through the child and his pathological (destructive) envy of the child and his accomplishments.

To ameliorate the unease bred by this emotional ambivalence, the narcissistic parent resorts to a myriad control mechanisms. These can be grouped into: *guilt-driven* ("I sacrificed my life for you..."), *co-dependent* ("I need you, I cannot cope without you..."), *goal-driven* ("We have a common goal which we can and must achieve") and *explicit* ("If you do not adhere to my principles, beliefs, ideology, religion, values, if you do not obey my instructions - I will punish you").

This exercise of control helps to sustain the illusion that the child is a part of the narcissist. But maintaining the illusion calls for extraordinary levels of control (on the part of the parent) and obedience (on the part of the child). The relationship is typically symbiotic and emotionally turbulent.

The child fulfils another important narcissistic function: the provision of Narcissistic Supply. There is no denying the implied (though imaginary) immortality in having a child. The early (natural) dependence of the child on his caregivers serves to assuage their abandonment anxiety.

The narcissist tries to perpetuate this dependence, using the aforementioned control mechanisms. The child is the ultimate Secondary Narcissistic Source of Supply. He is always present, he admires the narcissist, he witnesses the narcissist's moments of triumph and grandeur.

Owing to his wish to be loved, the child can be extorted into constant giving. To the narcissist, a child is a dream come true, but only in the most egotistical sense. When the child is perceived as "reneging" on his main obligation (to provide his narcissistic parent with a constant supply of attention), the parent's emotional reaction is harsh and revealing.

It is when the narcissistic parent is disenchanted with his child that we see the true nature of this pathological relationship. The child is totally objectified. The narcissist reacts to a breach in the unwritten contract between them with wells of aggression and aggressive transformations: contempt, rage, emotional and psychological abuse, and even physical violence. He tries to annihilate the real "disobedient" child and substitute it with the subservient, edifying, former version.

Narcissists and Children

Question: My husband positively detests children. When a child enters the room, I can see him arching like a cat, ready to do battle. Needless to say we are childless.

Answer: The narcissist sees in children feigned innocence, relentless and ruthless manipulation, the cunning of the weak. They are ageless. Their narcissism is disarming in its directness, in its cruel and absolute lack of empathy. They demand with insistence, punish absent-mindedly, idealize and devalue capriciously. They have no loyalty. They do not love, they cling. Their dependence is a mighty weapon and their neediness - a drug. They have no time, neither before, nor after. To them, existence is a play, they are the actors, and we all are but the props. They raise and drop the curtain of their mock emotions at will. The bells of their laughter often tintinnabulate. They are the fresh abode of good and evil, and pure they are.

495

Children, to the narcissist, are both mirrors and competitors. They reflect authentically the narcissist's constant need for adulation and attention. Their grandiose fantasies of omnipotence and omniscience are crass caricatures of his internal world. The way they abuse others and mistreat them hits close to home. Their innocuous charm, their endless curiosity, their fount of energy, their sulking, nagging, boasting, bragging, lying, and manipulating are mutations of the narcissist's own behaviour. He recognizes his thwarted self in them. When they make their entrance, all attention is diverted. Their fantasies endear them to their listeners. Their vainglorious swagger often causes smiles. Their trite stupidities are invariably treated as pearls of wisdom. Their nagging is yielded to, their threats provoke to action, their needs accommodated urgently. The narcissist stands aside, an abandoned centre of attention, the dormant eye of an intellectual storm, all but ignored and neglected. He watches the child with envy, with rage, with wrath. He hates the child's effortless ability to defeat him.

Children are loved by their mothers, as the narcissist was not. They are bundled emotions, and happiness and hope. The narcissist is jealous of them, infuriated by his deprivation, fearful of the sadness and hopelessness that they provoke in him. Like music, they reify a threat to the precariously balanced emotional black hole that is the narcissist. They are his past, his dilapidated and petrified True Self, his wasted potentials, his self-loathing and his defences. They are his pathology projected.

The narcissist revels in his Orwellian narcissistic newspeak. Love is weakness, happiness is a psychosis, hope is malignant optimism. Children defy all this. They are proof positive of how different it could all have been.

But what the narcissist consciously experiences is disbelief. He cannot understand how anyone can love these thuggish brats, their dripping noses, gelatinous fat bodies, whitish sweat, and bad breath. How can anyone stand their cruelty and vanity, their sadistic insistence and blackmail, their prevarication and deceit? In truth, no one except their parents can.

As far as the narcissist knows, children are always derided by everyone except their parents. To him, there is something sick and sickening in a mother's affections. There is a maddening blindness involved, an addiction, a psychotic episode, it's sick, this bond, it's nauseous. The narcissist hates children. He hates them for being him.

The Narcissist and His Family

Question: Is there a typical relationship between the narcissist and his family?

Answer: We are all members of a few families in our lifetime: the one that we are born to and the one(s) that we create. We all transfer hurts, attitudes, fears, hopes and desires - a whole emotional baggage - from the former to the latter. The narcissist is no exception.

497 The narcissist has a dichotomous view of humanity: people are either Sources of Narcissistic Supply (and, then, idealized and over-valued) or do not fulfil this function (and, therefore, are valueless, devalued). The narcissist gets all the love that he needs from himself. From the outside he requires approval, affirmation, admiration, adoration, attention - in other words, externalized ego boundary functions. He does not require - nor does he seek - his parents' or his siblings' love, or to be loved by his children. He casts them as the audience in the theatre of his inflated grandiosity. He wishes to impress them, shock them, threaten them, infuse them with awe, inspire them, attract their attention, subjugate them, or manipulate them.

He emulates and simulates an entire range of emotions and employs every means to achieve these effects. He lies (narcissists are pathological liars: their very Self is a False one). He acts the pitiful, or, its opposite, the resilient and reliable. He stuns and shines with outstanding intellectual brilliance or physical capacities and achievements, or he adopts behaviour patterns appreciated by other members of the family. When confronted with (younger) siblings or with his own children, the narcissist is likely to go through three phases:

At first, he perceives his offspring or siblings as a threat to his Narcissistic Supply, competitors for the attention of his spouse, or mother, as the case may be. They intrude on his turf and invade the Pathological Narcissistic Space. The narcissist does his best to belittle them, hurt (even physically) and humiliate them and then, when these reactions prove ineffective or counterproductive, he retreats into an imaginary world of omnipotence. A period of emotional absence and detachment ensues.

His aggression having failed to elicit Narcissistic Supply, the narcissist proceeds to indulge himself in daydreaming, delusions of grandeur, planning of future coups, nostalgia and hurt (the Lost Paradise Syndrome). The narcissist reacts this way to the birth of his children or to the introduction of new foci of attention to the family cell (even to a new pet!).

Whoever the narcissist perceives to be in competition with for scarce Narcissistic Supply is relegated to the role of the enemy. Where the uninhibited expression of the aggression and hostility aroused by this predicament is illegitimate or impossible, the narcissist prefers to stay away. Rather than attack his offspring or siblings, he sometimes immediately disconnects, detaches himself emotionally, becomes cold and uninterested, or directs transformed anger at his mate or at his parents (the more "legitimate" targets).

Other narcissists see the opportunity in the "mishap". They seek to manipulate their parents (or their mate) by "taking over" the newcomer. Such narcissists monopolize their siblings or their newborn children. This way, indirectly, they benefit from the attention directed at the infants. The sibling or offspring become vicarious Sources of Narcissistic Supply and proxies for the narcissist.

An example: by being a good father to his offspring or a good brother to his siblings, the narcissist secures the grateful admiration of the mother ("What an outstanding father/brother he is"). He also assumes part of or all the credit for baby's/sibling's achievements. This is a process of annexation and assimilation of the other, a strategy that the narcissist makes use of in most of his relationships.

As siblings or progeny grow older, the narcissist begins to see their potential for becoming edifying, reliable and satisfactory Sources of Narcissistic Supply. His attitude, then, is completely transformed. The former threats have now become promising potentials. He cultivates those whom he trusts to be the most rewarding. He encourages them to idolize him, to adore him, to be awed by him, to admire his deeds and capabilities, to learn to blindly trust and obey him, in short to surrender to his charisma and to become submerged in his folie-de-grandeur.

It is at this stage that the risk of child abuse - up to and including outright incest - is heightened. The narcissist is auto-erotic. He is the preferred object of his own sexual attraction. His siblings and his children share his genetic material. Molesting or having intercourse with them is as close as the narcissist gets to having sex with himself.

Moreover, the narcissist perceives sex in terms of annexation. The sexual partner is "assimilated" and becomes an extension of the narcissist, a fully controlled and manipulated object. Sex, to the narcissist, is the ultimate act of depersonalization and objectification of the other. He actually masturbates with other people's bodies.

Minors pose little danger of criticizing the narcissist or confronting him. They are perfect, malleable and abundant Sources of Narcissistic Supply. The narcissist derives gratification from having coital relations with adulating, physically and mentally inferior, inexperienced and dependent "bodies".

These roles - allocated to them explicitly and demandingly or implicitly and perniciously by the narcissist - are best fulfilled by ones whose mind is not yet fully formed and independent. The older the siblings or offspring, the more they become critical, even judgemental, of the narcissist. They are better able to put into context and perspective his actions, to question his motives, to anticipate his moves. As they mature, they often refuse to continue to play the mindless pawns in his chess game. They hold grudges against him for what he has done to them in the past, when they were less capable of resistance. They can gauge his true stature, talents and achievements - which, usually, lag far behind the claims that he makes.

This brings the narcissist a full cycle back to the first phase. Again, he perceives his siblings or sons/daughters as threats. He quickly becomes disillusioned and devaluing. He loses all interest, becomes emotionally remote, absent and cold, rejects any effort to communicate with him, citing life's pressures and the preciousness and scarceness of his time.

He feels burdened, cornered, besieged, suffocated, and claustrophobic. He wants to get away, to abandon his commitments to people who have become totally useless (or even damaging) to him. He does not understand why he has to support them, or to suffer their company and he believes himself to have been deliberately and ruthlessly trapped.

He rebels either passively-aggressively (by refusing to act or by intentionally sabotaging the relationships) or actively (by being overly critical, aggressive, unpleasant, verbally and psychologically abusive and so on). Slowly - to justify his acts to himself - he gets immersed in conspiracy theories with clear paranoid hues.

To his mind, the members of the family conspire against him, seek to belittle or humiliate or subordinate him, do not understand him, or stymie his growth. The narcissist usually finally gets what he wants and the family that he has created disintegrates to his great sorrow (due to the loss of the Narcissistic Space) - but also to his great relief and surprise (how could they have let go someone as unique as he?).

This is the cycle: the narcissist feels threatened by arrival of new family members - he tries to assimilate or annex his siblings or offspring - he obtains Narcissistic Supply from them - he over-values and idealizes these newfound sources - as sources grow older and independent, they adopt anti narcissistic behaviours - the narcissist devalues them - the narcissist feels stifled and trapped - the narcissist becomes paranoid - the narcissist rebels and the family disintegrates.

This cycle characterizes not only the family life of the narcissist. It is to be found in other realms of his life (his career, for instance). At work, the narcissist, initially, feels threatened (no one knows him, he is a nobody). Then, he develops a circle of admirers, cronies and friends which he "nurtures and cultivates" in order to obtain Narcissistic Supply from them. He over-values them (he regards them as the brightest, the most loyal, with the biggest chances to climb the corporate ladder and other superlatives).

But following some anti-narcissistic behaviours on their part (a critical remark, a disagreement, a refusal, however polite, to do the narcissist's bidding), the narcissist devalues all these previously idealized individuals. Now that they have dared oppose him, they are judged by him to be stupid, cowardly, lacking in ambition, skills and talents, common (the worst expletive in the narcissist's vocabulary), with an unspectacular career ahead of them.

The narcissist feels that he is misallocating his scarce and invaluable resources (for instance, his time). He feels besieged and suffocated. He rebels and erupts in a serious of self-defeating and self-destructive behaviours, which lead to the disintegration of his life.

Doomed to build and to ruin, attach and detach, appreciate and depreciate, the narcissist is predictable in his "death wish". What sets him apart from other suicidal types is that his wish is granted to him in small, tormenting doses throughout his anguished life.

Custody and Visitation

A parent diagnosed with full-fledged Narcissistic Personality Disorder (NPD) should be denied custody and should be granted only restricted rights of visitation under supervision.

Narcissists accord the same treatment to children and adults. They regard both as Sources of Narcissistic Supply, mere instruments of gratification: they idealize them at first and then devalue them in favour of alternative, safer and more subservient, sources. Such treatment is traumatic and can have long-lasting emotional effects.

The narcissist's inability to acknowledge and abide by the personal boundaries set by others puts the child at heightened risk of abuse - verbal, emotional, physical, and, often, sexual. His possessiveness and panoply of indiscriminate negative emotions - transformations of aggression, such as rage and envy - hinder the narcissist's ability to act as a "good enough" parent. His propensities for reckless behaviours, substance abuse, and sexual deviance endanger the child's welfare, or even his or her life.

501 The Roots of Paedophilia

Paedophiles are attracted to prepubescent children and act on their sexual fantasies. It is a startling fact that the aetiology of this paraphilia is unknown. Paedophiles come from all walks of life and have no common socio-economic background. Contrary to media-propagated myths, most of them had not been sexually abused in childhood and the vast majority of paedophiles are also drawn to adults of the opposite sex (are heterosexuals).

Only a few belong to the Exclusive Type: the ones who are tempted solely by kids. Nine tenths of all paedophiles are male. They are fascinated by preteen females, teenage males, or (more rarely) both.

Moreover, at least one fifth (and probably more) of the population have paedophiliac fantasies. The prevalence of child pornography and child prostitution prove it. Paedophiles start out as "normal" people and are profoundly shocked and distressed to discover their illicit sexual preference for the prepubertal. The process and mechanisms of transition from socially acceptable sexuality to much-condemned (and criminal) paedophilia are still largely mysterious.

Paedophiles seem to have narcissistic and antisocial (psychopathic) traits. They lack empathy for their victims and express no remorse for their actions. They are in denial and, being pathological confabulators, they rationalize their transgressions, claiming that the children were merely being educated for their own good and, anyhow, derived great pleasure from it.

The paedophile's ego-syntony rests on his alloplastic defences. He generally tends to blame others (or the world or the "system") for his misfortunes, failures, and deficiencies. Paedophiles frequently accuse their victims of acting promiscuously, of "coming on to them", of actively tempting, provoking, and luring (or even trapping) them.

The paedophile - similar to the autistic patient - misinterprets the child's body language and inter-personal cues. His social communication skills are impaired and he fails to adjust information gained to the surrounding circumstances (for instance, to the kid's age and maturity).

Coupled with his lack of empathy, this recurrent inability to truly comprehend others causes the paedophile to objectify the targets of his lasciviousness. Paedophilia is, in essence, auto-erotic. The paedophile uses children's bodies to masturbate with. Hence the success of the Internet among paedophiles: it offers disembodied, anonymous, masturbatory sex. Children in cyberspace are mere representations - often nothing more than erotic photos and screen names.

It is crucial to realize that paedophiles are not enticed by the children themselves, by their bodies, or by their budding and nubile sexuality (remember Nabokov's Lolita?). Rather, paedophiles are drawn to what children symbolize, to what preadolescents stand for and represent.

To the paedophile...

Sex with Children is "Free" and "Daring"

Sex with sub-teens implies freedom of action with impunity. It enhances the paedophile's magical sense of omnipotence and immunity. By defying the authority of the state and the edicts of his culture and society, the paedophile experiences an adrenaline rush to which he gradually becomes addicted. Illicit sex becomes the outlet for his urgent need to live dangerously and recklessly.

The paedophile is on a quest to reassert control over his life. Studies have consistently shown that paedophilia is associated with anomic states (war, famine, epidemics) and with major life crises (failure, relocation, infidelity of spouse, separation, divorce, unemployment, bankruptcy, illness, death of the offender's nearest and dearest). It is likely - though hitherto unsubstantiated by research - that the typical paedophile is depressive and with a borderline personality (low organization and fuzzy personal boundaries). Paedophiles are reckless and emotionally labile. The paedophile's sense of self-worth is volatile and dysregulated. He is likely to suffer from abandonment anxiety and be a co-dependent or counter-dependent.

Paradoxically, it is by seemingly losing control in one aspect of his life (sex) that the paedophile re-acquires a sense of mastery. The same mechanism is at work in the development of eating disorders. An inhibitory deficit is somehow magically perceived as omnipotence.

Sex with Children is Corrupt and Decadent

The paedophile makes frequent (though unconscious) use of projection and Projective Identification in his relationships with children. He makes his victims treat him the way he views himself - or attributes to them traits and behaviours that are truly his.

The paedophile is aware of society's view of his actions as vile, corrupt, forbidden, evil, and decadent (especially if the paedophiliac act involves incest). He derives pleasure from the sleazy nature of his pursuits because it tends to sustain his view of himself as "bad", "a failure", "deserving of punishment", and "guilty".

In extreme (mercifully uncommon) cases, the paedophile projects these torturous feelings and self-perceptions onto his victims. The children defiled and abused by his sexual attentions thus become "rotten", "bad objects", guilty and punishable. This leads to sexual sadism, lust rape, and snuff murders.

Sex with Children is a Re-Enactment of a Painful Past

Many paedophile truly bond with their prey. To them, children are the reification of innocence, genuineness, trust, and faithfulness - qualities that the paedophile wishes to nostalgically recapture.

The relationship with the child provides the paedophile with a "safe passage" to his own, repressed and fearful, inner child. Through his victim, the paedophile gains access to his suppressed and thwarted emotions. It is a fantasy-like second chance to re-enact his childhood, this time benignly. The paedophile's dream to make peace with his past comes true transforming the interaction with the child to an exercise in wish fulfilment.

Sex with Children is a Shared Psychosis

The paedophile treats "his" chosen child as an object, an extension of himself, devoid of a separate existence and denuded of distinct needs. He finds the child's submissiveness and gullibility gratifying. He frowns on any sign of personal autonomy and regards it as a threat. By intimidating, cajoling, charming, and making false promises, the abuser isolates his prey from his family, school, peers, and from the rest of society and, thus, makes the child's dependence on him total.

To the paedophile, the child is a "transitional object" - a training ground on which to exercise his adult relationship skills. The paedophile erroneously feels that the child will never betray and abandon him, therefore guaranteeing "object constancy".

The paedophile - stealthily but unfailingly - exploits the vulnerabilities in the psychological makeup of his victim. The child may have low self-esteem, a fluctuating sense of self-worth, primitive defence mechanisms, phobias, mental health problems, a disability, a history of failure, bad relations with parents, siblings, teachers, or peers, or a tendency to blame herself, or to feel inadequate (autoplastic neurosis). The kid may come from an abusive family or environment - which conditioned her or him to expect abuse as inevitable and "normal". In extreme and rare cases the victim is a masochist, possessed of an urge to seek ill-treatment and pain.

The paedophile is the guru at the centre of a cult. Like other gurus, he demands complete obedience from his "partner". He feels entitled to adulation and special treatment by his child-mate. He punishes the wayward and the straying lambs. He enforces discipline.

The child finds himself in a twilight zone. The paedophile imposes on him a shared psychosis, replete with persecutory delusions, "enemies", mythical narratives, and apocalyptic scenarios if he is flouted. The child is rendered the joint guardian of a horrible secret.

The paedophile's control is based on ambiguity, unpredictability, fuzziness, and ambient abuse. His ever-shifting whims exclusively define right versus wrong, desirable and unwanted, what is to be pursued and what to be avoided. He alone determines rights and obligations and alters them at will.

The typical paedophile is a micro-manager. He exerts control over the minutest details and behaviours. He punishes severely and abuses withholders of information and those who fail to conform to his wishes and goals.

The paedophile does not respect the boundaries and privacy of the (often reluctant and terrified) child. He ignores his or her wishes and treats children as objects or instruments of gratification. He seeks to control both situations and people compulsively.

The paedophile acts in a patronizing and condescending manner and criticises often. He alternates between emphasizing the minutest faults (devaluation) and exaggerating the looks, talents, traits, and skills (idealization) of the child. He is wildly unrealistic in his expectations - which legitimizes his subsequent abusive conduct when he is inevitably disappointed or frustrated.

Narcissistic paedophiles claim to be infallible, superior, talented, skilful, omnipotent, and omniscient. They often lie and confabulate to support these unfounded claims and to justify their actions. Most paedophiles suffer from cognitive deficits and reinterpret reality to fit their fantasies.

In extreme cases, the paedophile feels above the law - any kind of law. This grandiose and haughty conviction leads to criminal acts, incestuous or polygamous relationships, and recurrent friction with the authorities.

The Paedophile Regards Sex with Children As an Ego-Booster

Sub-teen children are, by definition, "inferior". They are physically weaker, dependent on others for the fulfilment of many of their needs, cognitively and emotionally immature, and easily manipulated. Their fund of knowledge is limited and their skills restricted. His relationships with children buttress the paedophile's twin grandiose delusions of omnipotence and omniscience. Compared to his victims, the paedophiles is always the stronger, the wiser, the most skilful and well-informed.

Sex with Children Guarantees Companionship

Inevitably, the paedophile considers his child-victims to be his best friends and companions. Paedophiles are lonely, erotomanic, people.

The paedophile believes that he is in love with (or simply loves) the child. Sex is merely one way to communicate his affection and caring. But there are other venues.

To show his keen interest, the common paedophile keeps calling the child, dropping by, writing e-mails, giving gifts, providing services, doing unsolicited errands "on the kid's behalf", getting into relationships with the preteen's parents, friends, teachers, and peers, and, in general, making himself available (stalking) at all times. The paedophile feels free to make legal, financial, and emotional decisions for the child.

The paedophile intrudes on the victim's privacy, disrespects the child's express wishes and personal boundaries and ignores his or her emotions, needs, and preferences. To the paedophile, "love" means enmeshment and clinging coupled with an over-powering separation anxiety (fear of being abandoned).

Moreover, no amount of denials, chastising, threats, and even outright hostile actions convince the erotomaniac that the child is not in love with him. He knows better and will make the world see the light as well. The child and his guardians are simply unaware of what is good for the kid. The paedophile determinedly sees it as his task to bring life and happiness into the child's dreary and unhappy existence.

Thus, regardless of overwhelming evidence to the contrary, the paedophile is convinced that his feelings are reciprocated - in other words, that the child is equally infatuated with him or her. He interprets everything the child does (or refrains from doing) as coded messages confessing to and conveying the child's interest in and eternal devotion to the paedophile and to the "relationship".

Some (by no means all) paedophiles are socially-inapt, awkward, schizoid, and suffer from a host of mood and anxiety disorders. They may also be legitimately involved with the child (e.g., stepfather, former spouse, teacher, gym instructor, sibling) - or with his parents (for instance, a former boyfriend, a one night stand, colleagues or co-workers). They are driven by their all-consuming loneliness and all-pervasive fantasies.

Consequently, paedophiles react badly to any perceived rejection by their victims. They turn on a dime and become dangerously vindictive, out to destroy the source of their mounting frustration. When the "relationship" looks hopeless, some paedophiles violently embark on a spree of self-destruction or criminal acts, such as kidnapping and worse..

Paedophilia is to some extent a culture-bound syndrome, defined as it is by the chronological age of the child involved. Ephebophilia, for instance - the exclusive sexual infatuation with teenagers - is not considered to be a form of paedophilia (or even paraphilia).

In some cultures, societies and countries (Afghanistan, for instance) the age of consent is as low as 12. The marriageable age in Britain until the end of the nineteenth century was 10. Paedophilia is a common and socially-condoned practice in certain tribal societies and isolated communities (the Island of Pitcairn).

It would, therefore, be wise to redefine paedophilia as an attraction to or sexual acts with prepubescent children or with people of the equivalent mental age (e.g., retarded) in contravention of socially, legally, and culturally accepted practices.

Narcissists, Sex and Fidelity

The Somatic and the Cerebral Narcissist

Question: Are narcissists mostly hyperactive or hypoactive sexually and to what extent are they likely to be unfaithful in marriage?

Answer: Broadly speaking, there are two types of narcissists, loosely corresponding to the two categories mentioned in the question.

507   Sex, to the narcissist, is an instrument designed to increase the number of Sources of Narcissistic Supply. If it happens to be the most efficient weapon in the narcissist's arsenal, he makes profligate use of it. In other words: if the narcissist cannot obtain adoration, admiration, approval, applause, or any other kind of attention by other means (e.g., intellectually), he resorts to sex.

He then becomes a satyr (or a nymphomaniac) and indiscriminately engages in sex with multiple partners. His sex partners are considered by him to be objects - Sources of Narcissistic Supply. It is through the processes of successful seduction and sexual conquest that the narcissist derives his badly needed narcissistic "fix".

The narcissist is likely to perfect his techniques of courting and regard his sexual exploits as a form of art. He usually discloses this side of him - in great detail - to others, to an audience, expecting to win their approval and admiration. Because the Narcissistic Supply in his case is in the very act of conquest and (what he perceives to be) subordination, the narcissist is forced to hop from one partner to another.

Some narcissists prefer "complicated" situations. If men - they prefer virgins, married women, frigid or lesbian women, etc.

The more "difficult" the target, the more rewarding the narcissistic outcome. Such a narcissist may be married, but he does not regard his extra-marital affairs as either immoral or a breach of any explicit or implicit contract between him and his spouse.

He keeps explaining to anyone who cares to listen that his other sexual partners are nothing to him, meaningless, that he is merely taking advantage of them and that they do not constitute a threat to his great marriage and should not be taken seriously by his spouse. In his mind a clear separation exists between the honest "woman of his life" (really, a Madonna-saint) and the "whores" that he is having sex with.

With the exception of the meaningful women in his life, he tends to view all females in a bad light. His behaviour, thus, achieves a dual purpose: securing Narcissistic Supply, on the one hand and re-enacting old, unresolved conflicts and traumas (abandonment by Primary Objects and the Oedipal Conflict, for instance).

When inevitably abandoned by his spouse, the narcissist is veritably shocked and hurt. This is the sort of crisis, which might drive him to psychotherapy. Still, deep inside, he feels compelled to continue to pursue precisely the same path. His abandonment is cathartic, purifying. Following a period of deep depression and suicidal ideation, the narcissist is likely to feel cleansed, invigorated, unshackled, ready for the next round of hunting.

But there is another type of narcissist. The cerebral narcissist also has bouts of sexual hyperactivity in which he trades sexual partners and tends to regard them as objects. However, with him, this is a secondary behaviour. It appears mainly after major narcissistic traumas and crises.

A painful divorce, a devastating and disgraceful personal or financial upheaval - and this type of narcissist adopts the view that the "old" (intellectual) solutions do not work anymore. He frantically gropes and searches for new ways to attract attention, to restore his False Self (his grandiosity) and to secure a subsistence level of Narcissistic Supply.

Sex is handy and is a great source of the right kind of supply: it is immediate, sexual partners are interchangeable, the solution is comprehensive (it encompasses all the aspects of the narcissist's being), natural, highly charged, adventurous, and pleasurable. Thus, following a life crisis, the cerebral narcissist is likely to be deeply immersed in sexual activities, very frequently and almost to the exclusion of all other matters.

However, as the memories of the crisis fade, as the narcissistic wounds heal, as the Narcissistic Cycle re-commences and the balance is restored, this second type of narcissist reveals his true colours. He abruptly loses interest in sex and in all his sexual partners. The frequency of his sexual activities deteriorates from a few times a day to a few times a year. He reverts to intellectual pursuits, sports, politics, voluntary activities - anything but sex.

This kind of narcissist is afraid of encounters with the opposite sex and is even more afraid of emotional involvement or commitment that he fancies himself prone to develop following a sexual encounter. In general, such a narcissist withdraws not only sexually, but also emotionally. If married - he loses all overt interest in his spouse, sexual or otherwise. He confines himself to his world and makes sure that he is sufficiently busy to preclude any interaction with his nearest (and supposedly dearest).

He becomes completely entangled in "big projects", lifelong plans, a vision, or a cause - all very rewarding narcissistically and all very demanding and time consuming. In such circumstances, sex inevitably becomes an obligation, a necessity, or a maintenance chore reluctantly undertaken to preserve his Sources of Supply (e.g., his marriage).

The cerebral narcissist does not enjoy sex and by far prefers masturbation or "objective", emotionless sex, like going to prostitutes. Actually, he uses his mate or spouse as an "alibi", a shield against the attentions of other women, an insurance policy which preserves his virile image while making it socially and morally commendable for him to avoid any intimate or sexual contact with others.

Ostentatiously ignoring women other than his wife (a form of aggression) he feels righteous in saying: "I am a faithful husband". At the same time, he feels hostility towards his spouse for ostensibly preventing him from freely expressing his sexuality, for depriving him of carnal pleasures he could have had with others.

The narcissist's inner dialog goes something like this: "I am married/attached to this woman. Therefore, I am not allowed to be in any form of contact with other women which might be interpreted as more than casual or businesslike. This is why I refrain from having anything to do with women - because I am being faithful, as opposed to immoral men. However, I do not like this situation. I envy my free peers. They can have as much sex and romance as they want to, while I am confined to this marriage, chained by my wife, my freedom curbed. I am angry at her and I will punish her by abstaining from having sex with her."

Thus frustrated, the narcissist minimizes all manner of intercourse with his close circle (spouse, children, parents, siblings, very intimate friends): sexual, verbal, or emotional. He limits himself to the rawest exchanges of information and isolates himself socially.

His reclusion insures against a future hurt and skirts the intimacy that he so dreads. But, again, this way he also secures abandonment and the replay of old, unresolved, conflicts. Finally, he really is left alone by everyone, with no Secondary Sources of Supply.

In his quest to find new sources, he again embarks on ego-mending bouts of sex, followed by the selection of a spouse or a mate (a Secondary Narcissistic Supply Source). Then the cycle re-commence: a sharp drop in sexual activity, emotional absence and cruel detachment leading to abandonment.

Most cerebral narcissists, though, are sexually faithful to their spouses. The typical cerebral narcissist alternates between what appears to be hyper-sexuality and asexuality (really, forcefully repressed sexuality). In the second phase, he feels no sexual urges, bar the most basic. He is, therefore, not compelled to "cheat" upon his mate, betray her, or violate the marital vows. He is much more interested in preventing a worrisome dwindling of the kind of Narcissistic Supply that really matters. Sex, he says to himself, contentedly, is for those who can do no better.

Somatic narcissists lean towards verbal exhibitionism. They tend to brag in graphic details about their conquests and exploits. In extreme cases, they might introduce "live witnesses" and revert to total, classical exhibitionism. This sits well with their tendency to "objectify" their sexual partners, to engage in emotionally-neutral sex (group sex, for instance) and to indulge in autoerotic sex.

The exhibitionist sees himself reflected in the eyes of his beholders. This constitutes the main sexual stimulus, this is what turns him on. This outside "look" is also what defines the narcissist. There is bound to be a connection. One (the exhibitionist) may be the culmination, the "pure case" of the other (the narcissist).

The Extra-Marital Narcissist

Question: My husband has a liaison with another woman. He has been diagnosed with Narcissistic Personality Disorder. What should I do?

Answer: Narcissists are people who fail to maintain a stable sense of self-worth. Very often somatic narcissists (narcissistic who use their bodies and their sexuality to secure Narcissistic Supply) tend to get involved in extra-marital affairs. The new "conquests" sustain their grandiose fantasies and their distorted and unrealistic self-image.

It is, therefore, nigh impossible to alter this particular behaviour of a somatic narcissist. Sexual interactions serve as a constant, reliable, easy to obtain Source of Narcissistic Supply. It is the only Source of such Supply if the narcissist is not cerebral (does not rely on his intellect, intelligence, or professional achievements for Narcissistic Supply).

You should set up rigid, strict and VERY WELL DEFINED rules of engagement. Ideally, all contacts between your spouse and his lover should be immediately and irrevocably severed. But this is usually too much to ask for. So, you should make crystal clear when is she allowed to call, whether she is allowed to write to him at all and in which circumstances, what are the subjects she is allowed to broach in her correspondence and phone calls, when is he allowed to see her and what other modes of interaction are permissible.

CLEAR AND PAINFUL SANCTIONS in case the above rules are violated must be promulgated. Both rules and sanctions MUST BE APPLIED RIGOROUSLY AND MERCILESSLY and MUST BE SET IN WRITING IN UNEQUIVOCAL TERMS.

The problem is that the narcissist never really separates from his Sources of Narcissistic Supply until and unless they cease to be ones. Narcissists never really say good-bye. His lover is likely to still have an emotional hold on him.

Help him by telling him what will be the price that he stands to pay if he does not obey the rules and sanctions you have agreed on. Tell him that you cannot live like this any longer, that if he does not get rid of this presence - of the echoes of his past, really - he will be squandering his present, he will be forfeiting you. Don't be afraid to lose him. If he prefers this woman to you, it is important for you to know it. If he prefers you to her, your nightmare is over (at least until the next round).

If you insist on staying with him, you must also be prepared to serve as a Source of Narcissistic Supply, an alternative to the supply provided by his former lover. You must brace yourself: serving as a Narcissistic Supply Source is an onerous task, a full time job and a very ungrateful one at that. The narcissist's thirst for adulation, admiration, worship, approval, and attention is unquenchable. It is a Sisyphean, mind-numbing effort, which heralds only additional demands and disgruntled, critical, humiliating tirades by the narcissist.

That you are afraid to confront reality is normal. You are afraid to set clear alternatives and boundaries. You are afraid that he will leave you. You are afraid that he will prefer her to you. AND YOU MAY WELL BE RIGHT. But if this is the case and you go on living with him and tormenting yourself, it is unhealthy.

If you find it difficult to confront the fact that it is all over between you, that your relationship is an empty shell, that your husband is with another woman, do not hesitate to seek help from professionals and non-professionals alike. But do not let this situation fester into psychological gangrene. Amputate now while you can.

FREQUENTLY ASKED QUESTION # 100

Mourning the Narcissist

Question: If the narcissist is as abusive as you say, why do we react so badly when he leaves?

Answer: At the commencement of the relationship, the narcissist is a dream-come-true. He is often intelligent, witty, charming, good looking, an achiever, empathetic, in need of love, loving, caring, attentive and much more besides. He is the perfect bundled answer to the nagging questions of life: finding meaning, companionship, compatibility, and happiness. He is, in other words, ideal.

It is difficult to let go of this idealized figure. Relationships with narcissists inevitably and invariably end with the dawn of a double realization. The first is that one has been (ab)used by the narcissist and the second is that one was regarded by the narcissist as a disposable, dispensable and interchangeable instrument (object).

The assimilation of this new gained knowledge is an excruciating process, often unsuccessfully completed. People get fixated at different stages. They fail to come to terms with their rejection as human beings - the most total form of rejection there is.

We all react to loss. Loss makes us feel helpless and objectified. When our loved ones die, we feel that Nature or God or Life treated us as playthings. When we divorce (especially if we did not initiate the break-up), we often feel that we have been exploited and abused in the relationship, that we are being "dumped", that our needs and emotions are ignored. In short, we again feel objectified.

Losing the narcissist is no different to any other major loss in life. It provokes a cycle of bereavement and grief (as well as some kind of mild Post-Traumatic Stress Syndrome in cases of severe abuse). This cycle has four phases: denial, rage, sadness and acceptance.

513

Denial can assume many forms. Some go on pretending that the narcissist is still a part of their life, even going to the extreme of "interacting" with the narcissist by pretending to "communicate" with him or to "meet" him (through others, for instance). Extreme cases of such denial are known as erotomania.

Others develop persecutory delusions, thus incorporating the narcissist into their life and psyche as an ominous and dark presence, as a "bad object". This ensures "his" continued "interest" in them - however malevolent and threatening that "interest" is perceived to be. These are radical denial mechanisms, which border on the psychotic and often resolve into brief psychotic micro-episodes.

More benign and transient forms of denial include the development of ideas of reference. The narcissist's every move or utterance is interpreted as directed at the suffering person, his ex, and to carry a hidden message which can be "decoded" only by the recipient.

Others deny the very narcissistic nature of the narcissist. They attribute his abusive conduct to ignorance, mischief, lack of self-control (due to childhood abuse or trauma), or benign intentions. This denial mechanism leads them to believe that the narcissist is really not a narcissist at all but someone who is merely not aware of his "true" essence, or someone who innocently enjoys mind games and toying with people's lives, or an unwitting part of a dark conspiracy to defraud and abuse gullible victims.

Often the narcissist is depicted as obsessed or possessed - imprisoned by his "invented" condition and, really, deep inside, a nice and gentle and lovable person.

At the healthier end of the spectrum of denial reactions we find the classical denial of loss: the disbelief, the hope that the narcissist may return, the suspension and repression of all information to the contrary.

Denial in mentally healthy people quickly evolves into rage. There are a few types of rage. Rage can be focussed and directed at the narcissist, at other facilitators of the loss, such as the narcissist's lover, or at specific circumstances. It can be directed at oneself - which often leads to depression, suicidal ideation, self-mutilation and, in some cases, suicide. Or, it can be diffuse, all-pervasive, all-encompassing and engulfing. Such loss-related rage can be intense and in bursts or osmotic and permeate the whole emotional landscape.

Rage gives place to sadness. It is the sadness of the trapped animal, an existential angst mixed with acute depression. It involves dysphoria (inability to rejoice, to be optimistic, or expectant) and anhedonia (inability to experience pleasure or to find meaning in life). It is a paralyzing sensation, which slows one down and enshrouds everything in the grey veil of randomness. Everything suddenly looks meaningless and empty.

This, in turn, gives place to gradual acceptance, renewed energy, and bouts of activity. The narcissist is gone both physically and mentally. The void left in his wake still hurts and pangs of regret and hope still exist. But, on the whole, the narcissist is transformed into a narrative, a symbol, another life experience, or a (tedious) clichй. He is no longer omnipresent and his former victim entertains no delusions as to the one-sided and abusive nature of the relationship or as to the possibility and desirability of its renewal.

The Three Forms of Closure

For her traumatic wounds to heal, the victim of abuse requires closure - one final interaction with her tormentor in which he, hopefully, acknowledges his misbehaviour and even tenders an apology. Fat chance. Few abusers - especially if they are narcissistic - are amenable to such weakling pleasantries. More often, the abused are left to wallow in a poisonous stew of misery, self-pity, and self-recrimination.

Depending on the severity, duration, and nature of the abuse, there are three forms of effective closure:

Conceptual Closure

This most common variant involves a frank dissection of the abusive relationship. The parties meet to analyse what went wrong, to allocate blame and guilt, to derive lessons, and to part ways cathartically cleansed. In such an exchange, a compassionate offender (quite the oxymoron, admittedly) offers his prey the chance to rid herself of cumulating resentment.

He also disabuses her of the notion that she, in any way, was guilty or responsible for her maltreatment, that it was all her fault, that she deserved to be punished, and that she could have saved the relationship (malignant optimism). With this burden gone, the victim is ready to resume her life and to seek companionship and love elsewhere.

Retributive Closure

When the abuse has been "gratuitous" (sadistic), repeated, and protracted, conceptual closure is not enough. Retribution is called for, an element of vengeance, of restorative justice and a restored balance. Recuperation hinges on punishing the delinquent and merciless party. The penal intervention of the Law is often therapeutic to the abused.

Regrettably, the victim's understandable emotions often lead to abusive (and illegal) acts. Many of the tormented stalk their erstwhile abusers and take the law into their own hands. Abuse tends to breed abuse all around, in both prey and predator.

Dissociative Closure

Absent the other two forms of closure, victims of egregious and prolonged mistreatment tend to repress their painful memories. In extremis, they dissociate. The Dissociative Identity Disorder (DID) - formerly known as "Multiple Personality Disorder" - is thought to be such a reaction. The harrowing experiences are "sliced off", tucked away, and attributed to "another personality".

Sometimes, the victim "assimilates" his or her tormentor, and even openly and consciously identifies with him. This is the narcissistic defence. In his own anguished mind, the victim becomes omnipotent and, therefore, invulnerable. He or she develops a False Self. The True Self is, thus, shielded from further harm and injury.

According to psychodynamic theories of psychopathology, repressed content rendered unconscious is the cause of all manner of mental health disorders. The victim thus pays a hefty price for avoiding and evading his or her predicament.

Back to La-la Land

Relationships with narcissists peter out slowly and tortuously. Narcissists do not provide closure. They stalk. They cajole, beg, promise, persuade, and, ultimately, succeed in doing the impossible yet again: sweep you off your feet, though you know better than to succumb to their spurious and superficial charms.

So, you go back to your "relationship" and hope for a better ending. You walk on eggshells. You become the epitome of submissiveness, a perfect Source of Narcissistic Supply, the ideal mate or spouse or partner or colleague. You keep your fingers crossed.

But how does the narcissist react to the resurrection of the bond?

It depends on whether you have re-entered the liaison from a position or strength, or of vulnerability and weakness.

The narcissist casts all interactions with other people in terms of conflicts or competitions to be won. He does not regard you as a partner - but as an adversary to be subjugated and defeated. Thus, as far as he is concerned, your return to the fold is a triumph, proof of his superiority and irresistibility.

If he perceives you as autonomous, dangerously independent, and capable of bailing out and abandoning him - the narcissist acts the part of the sensitive, loving, compassionate, and empathic counterpart. Narcissists respect strength, they are awed by it. As long as you maintain a "no nonsense" attitude, placing the narcissist on probation, he is likely to behave himself.

If, on the other hand, you have resumed contact because you have capitulated to his threats or because you are manifestly dependent on him financially or emotionally - the narcissist will pounce on your frailty and exploit your fragility to the maximum. Following a perfunctory honeymoon, he will immediately seek to control and abuse you.

In both cases, the narcissist's thespian reserves are ultimately exhausted and his true nature and feelings emerge. The facade crumbles and beneath it lurks the same old heartless falsity that is the narcissist. His gleeful smugness at having bent you to his wishes and rules, his all-consuming sense of entitlement, his sexual depravity, his aggression, pathological envy, and rage - all erupt uncontrollably.

The prognosis for the renewed affair is far worse if it follows a lengthy separation in which you have made a life for yourself with your own interests, pursuits, set of friends, needs, wishes, plans, and obligations, independent of your narcissistic ex.

The narcissist cannot countenance your separateness. To him, you are a mere instrument of gratification or an extension of his bloated False Self. He resents your pecuniary wherewithal, is insanely jealous of your friends, refuses to accept your preferences or compromise his own, in envious and dismissive of your accomplishments.

Ultimately, the very fact that you have survived without his constant presence seems to deny him his much-needed Narcissistic Supply. He rides the inevitable cycle of idealization and devaluation. He berates you, humiliates you publicly, threatens you, destabilizes you by behaving unpredictably, fosters ambient abuse, and uses others to intimidate and humble you ("abuse by proxy").

You are then faced with a tough choice:

To leave again and give up all the emotional and financial investments that went into your attempt to resurrect the relationship - or to go on trying, subject to daily abuse and worse?

It is a well-known landscape. You have been here before. But this familiarity doesn't make it less nightmarish.

Surviving the Narcissist

Question: Is there a point in waiting for the narcissist to heal? Can he ever get better?

Answer: The victims of the narcissist's abusive conduct resort to fantasies and self-delusions to salve their pain.

Rescue Fantasies

"It is true that he is a chauvinistic narcissist and that his behaviour is unacceptable and repulsive. But all he needs is a little love and he will be straightened out. I will rescue him from his misery and misfortune. I will give him the love that he lacked as a child. Then his narcissism will vanish and we will live happily ever after."

Loving a Narcissist

I believe in the possibility of loving the narcissist if one accepts him unconditionally, in a disillusioned and expectation-free manner.

Narcissists are narcissists. Take them or leave them. Some of them are lovable. Most of them are highly charming and intelligent. The source of the misery of the victims of the narcissist is their disappointment, their disillusionment, their abrupt and tearing and tearful realization that they fell in love with an ideal of their own making, a phantasm, an illusion, a fata morgana. This "waking up" is traumatic. The narcissist always remains the same. It is the victim who changes.

It is true that narcissists present a luring facade in order to captivate Sources of Narcissistic Supply. But this facade is easy to penetrate because it is inconsistent and too perfect. The cracks are evident from day one but often ignored. Then there are those who KNOWINGLY and WILLINGLY commit their emotional wings to the burning narcissistic candle.

This is the catch-22. To try to communicate emotions to a narcissist is like discussing atheism with a religious fundamentalist.

Narcissists have emotions, very strong ones, so terrifyingly overpowering and negative that they hide them, repress, block and transmute them. They employ myriad defence mechanisms to cope with their repressed emotions: Projective Identification, splitting, projection, intellectualization, rationalization.

Any effort to relate to the narcissist emotionally is doomed to failure, alienation and rage. Any attempt to "understand" (in retrospect or prospectively) narcissistic behaviour patterns, reactions, or the narcissist's inner world in emotional terms is equally hopeless. Narcissists should be regarded as a force of nature or an accident waiting to happen.

The Universe has no master-plot or mega-plan to deprive anyone of happiness. Being born to narcissistic parents, for instance, is not the result of a conspiracy. It is a tragic event, for sure. But it cannot be dealt with emotionally, without professional help, or haphazardly. Stay away from narcissists, or face them aided by your own self-discovery through therapy. It can be done.

Narcissists have no interest in emotional or even intellectual stimulation by significant others. Such feedback is perceived as a threat. Significant others in the narcissist's life have very clear roles: the accumulation and dispensation of past Primary Narcissistic Supply in order to regulate current Narcissistic Supply. Nothing less but definitely nothing more. Proximity and intimacy breed contempt. A process of devaluation is in full operation throughout the life of the relationship.

A passive witness to the narcissist's past accomplishments, a dispenser of accumulated Narcissistic Supply, a punching bag for his rages, a co-dependent, a possession (though not prized but taken for granted) and nothing much more. This is the ungrateful, FULL TIME, draining job of being the narcissist's significant other.

But people are not instruments. To regard them as such is to devalue them, to reduce them, to restrict them, to prevent them from realizing their potential. Inevitably, narcissists lose interest in their instruments, these truncated versions of full-fledged humans, once they cease to serve them in their pursuit of glory and fame.

Consider "friendship" with a narcissist as an example of such thwarted relationships. One cannot really get to know a narcissist "friend". One cannot be friends with a narcissist and one cannot love a narcissist. Narcissists are addicts. They are no different to drug addicts. They are in pursuit of gratification through the drug known as Narcissistic Supply. Everything and EVERYONE around them is an object, a potential source (to be idealized) or not (and, then to be cruelly discarded).

Narcissists home in on potential suppliers like cruise missiles. They are excellent at imitating emotions, at exhibiting the right behaviours on cue, and at manipulating.

All generalizations are false, of course, and there are bound to be some happy relationships with narcissists [I discuss the narcissistic couple in FAQ 94]. One example of a happy marriage is when a somatic narcissist teams up with a cerebral one or vice versa.

Narcissists can be happily married to submissive, subservient, self-deprecating, echoing, mirroring and indiscriminately supportive spouses. They also do well with masochists. But it is difficult to imagine that a healthy, normal person would be happy in such a folie-a-deux ("madness in twosome" or shared psychosis).

It is also difficult to imagine a benign and sustained influence on the narcissist of a stable, healthy mate/spouse/partner. [One of my FAQs is dedicated to this issue The Narcissist's Spouse/Mate/Partner]

BUT many a spouse/friend/mate/partner like to BELIEVE that, given sufficient time and patience, they will be the ones to rid the narcissist of his inner demons. They think that they can "rescue" the narcissist, shield him from his (distorted) self, as it were.

The narcissist makes use of this naiveté and exploits it to his benefit. The natural protective mechanisms, which are provoked in normal people by love are cold bloodedly used by the narcissist to extract yet more Narcissistic Supply from his writhing victim.

The narcissist affects his victims by infiltrating their psyches, by penetrating their defences. Like a virus, it establishes a new genetic strain within his/her victims. It echoes through them, it talks through them, it walks through them. It is like the invasion of the body snatchers.

You should be careful to separate your self from the narcissist's seed inside you, this alien growth, this spiritual cancer that is the result of living with a narcissist. You should be able to tell apart the real you and the parts assigned to you by the narcissist. To cope with him/her, the narcissist forces you to "walk on eggshells" and develop a False Self of your own. It is nothing as elaborate as his False Self, but it is there, in you, as a result of the trauma and abuse inflicted upon you by the narcissist.

Thus, perhaps we should talk about VoNPD, another mental health diagnostic category: Victims of NPD.

They experience shame and anger at their past helplessness and submissiveness. They are hurt and sensitized by the harrowing experience of sharing a simulated existence with a simulated person, the narcissist. They are scarred and often suffer from Post-Traumatic Stress Disorder (PTSD). Some of them lash out at others, offsetting their frustration with bitter aggression.

Like his disorder, the narcissist is all-pervasive. Being the victim of a narcissist is a condition no less pernicious than being a narcissist. Great mental efforts are required to abandon a narcissist and physical separation is only the first (and least important) step.

One can abandon a narcissist - but the narcissist is slow to abandon his victims. He is there, lurking, rendering existence unreal, twisting and distorting with no respite, an inner, remorseless voice, lacking in compassion and empathy for its victim.

The narcissist is there in spirit long after he had vanished in the flesh. This is the real danger that the victims of the narcissist face: that they become like him, bitter, self-centred, lacking in empathy. This is the last bow of the narcissist, his curtain call, by proxy as it were.

Narcissistic Tactics

The narcissist tends to surround himself with his inferiors (in some respect: intellectually, financially, physically). He limits his interactions with them to the plane of his superiority. This is the safest and fastest way to sustain his grandiose fantasies of omnipotence and omniscience, brilliance, ideal traits, perfection and so on.

People are interchangeable and the narcissist does not distinguish one individual from another. To him they are all inanimate elements of "his audience" whose job is to reflect his False Self. This generates a perpetual and permanent cognitive dissonance:

The narcissist despises the very people who sustain his ego boundaries and functions. He cannot respect people so expressly and clearly inferior to him - yet he can never associate with people evidently on his level or superior to him, the risk of narcissistic injury in such associations being too great. Equipped with a fragile Ego, precariously teetering on the brink of narcissistic injury, the narcissist prefers the safe route. But he feels contempt for himself and for others for having preferred it.

Some narcissists are also psychopaths (suffer from the Antisocial Personality Disorder) and/or sadists. Antisocials don't really enjoy hurting others - they simply don't care one way or the other. But sadists do enjoy it.

Classical narcissists do not enjoy wounding others - but they do enjoy the sensation of unlimited power and the validation of their grandiose fantasies when they do harm others or are in the position to do so. It is more the POTENTIAL to hurt others than the actual act that turns them on.

The Never-Ending Story

Even the official termination of a relationship with a narcissist is not the end of the affair. The ex "belongs" to the narcissist. She is an inseparable part of his Pathological Narcissistic Space. This possessive streak survives the physical separation.

Thus, the narcissist is likely to respond with rage, seething envy, a sense of humiliation and invasion and violent-aggressive urges to an ex's new boyfriend, or new job (to her new life without him). Especially since it implies a "failure" on his part and, thus negates his grandiosity.

But there is a second scenario:

If the narcissist firmly believes (which is very rare) that the ex does not and will never represent any amount, however marginal and residual, of any kind (Primary or Secondary) of Narcissistic Supply, he remains utterly unmoved by anything she does and anyone she may choose to be with.

Narcissists do feel bad about hurting others and about the unsavoury course their lives tend to assume. Their underlying (and subconscious) ego-dystony (feeling bad about themselves) was only recently discovered and described. But the narcissist feels bad only when his Supply Sources are threatened because of his behaviour or following a narcissistic injury in the course of a major life crisis.

The narcissist equates emotions with weakness. He regards the sentimental and the emotional with contempt. He looks down on the sensitive and the vulnerable. He derides and despises the dependent and the loving. He mocks expressions of compassion and passion. He is devoid of empathy. He is so afraid of his True Self that he would rather disparage it than admit to his own faults and "soft spots".

He likes to talk about himself in mechanical terms ("machine", "efficient", "punctual", "output", "computer"). He suppresses his human side diligently and with dedication. To him being human and survival are mutually exclusive propositions. He must choose and his choice is clear. The narcissist never looks back, unless and until forced to by life's circumstances.

All narcissists fear intimacy. But the cerebral narcissist deploys strong defences against it: "scientific detachment" (the

narcissist as the eternal observer), intellectualizing and rationalizing his emotions away, intellectual cruelty [see FAQ 21
regarding inappropriate affect], intellectual "annexation" (he
regards others as his extension, property, or turf), objectifying
the other, and so on. Even emotions that he does express
(pathological envy, rage) have the not wholly unintended effect
of alienating rather than creating intimacy.

Abandoning the Narcissist

The narcissist initiates his own abandonment because of his fear
of it. He is so terrified of losing his Sources of Narcissistic Supply
(and of being emotionally hurt) that he would rather "control",
"master", or "direct" the potentially destabilizing situation.
Remember: the personality of the narcissist has a low level of
organization. It is precariously balanced.

Being abandoned could cause a narcissistic injury so grave
that the whole edifice can come crumbling down. Narcissists
usually entertain suicidal ideation in such cases. But, if the narcissist had initiated and directed his own abandonment, if it is
perceived as a goal he had set to himself - he can and does avoid
all these untoward consequences.

[See the section about Emotional Involvement Prevention
Mechanisms in the Essay]

The Dynamics of the Relationship

The narcissist lives in a fantasized world of ideal beauty, incom-
parable (imaginary) achievements, wealth, brilliance and unmitigated success. The narcissist denies his reality constantly. This
is what I call the Grandiosity Gap: the abyss between his sense
of entitlement grounded in his inflated grandiose fantasies - and
his incommensurate reality and meagre accomplishments.

The narcissist's partner is perceived by him to be merely a
Source of Narcissistic Supply, an instrument, an extension of
himself. It is inconceivable that - blessed by the constant presence of the narcissist - such a tool would malfunction. The needs
and grievances of the partner are perceived by the narcissist as
threats and slights. The narcissist considers his very presence in
the relationship as nourishing and sustaining. He feels entitled
to the best others can offer without investing in maintaining his
relationships or in catering to the well-being of his "suppliers".

To rid himself of deep-set feelings of (rather justified) guilt
and shame, he pathologizes the partner. He projects his own
mental illness unto her. Through the intricate mechanism of
Projective Identification he forces her to play an emergent role

of "the sick" or "the weak" or "the naive" or "the dumb" or "the no good". What he denies in himself, what he is loath to face in his own personality, he attributes to others and moulds them to conform to his prejudices against himself.

The narcissist must have the best, the most glamorous, stunning, talented, head turning, mind-boggling spouse in the entire world. Nothing short of this fantasy will do. To compensate for the shortcomings of his real life spouse, he invents an idealized figure and relates to it instead.

Then, when reality conflicts too often and too evidently with this figment, he reverts to devaluation. His behaviour turns on a dime and becomes threatening, demeaning, contemptuous, berating, reprimanding, destructively critical and sadistic - or cold, unloving, detached, and "clinical". He punishes his real life spouse for not living up to his fantasy, for "refusing" to be his Galatea, his Pygmalion, his ideal creation. The narcissist then plays a wrathful and demanding God.

Moving On

To preserve one's mental health - one must abandon the narcissist. One must move on.

Moving on is a process, not a decision or an event. First, one has to acknowledge and accept painful reality. Such acceptance is a volcanic, shattering, agonizing series of nibbling thoughts and strong resistances. Once the battle is won, and harsh and agonizing realities are assimilated, one can move on to the learning phase.

Learning

We label. We educate ourselves. We compare experiences. We digest. We have insights.

Then we decide and we act. This is "to move on". Having gathered sufficient emotional sustenance, knowledge, support and confidence, we face the battlefields of our relationships, fortified and nurtured. This stage characterizes those who do not mourn - but fight; do not grieve - but replenish their self-esteem; do not hide - but seek; do not freeze - but move on.

Grieving

Having been betrayed and abused, we grieve. We grieve for the image we had of the traitor and abuser - the image that was so fleeting and so wrong, yet so dear to us. We mourn the damage. We experience the fear of never being able to love or to trust again - and we grieve this loss, too. At one stroke, we lost someone we trusted and even loved, we lost our trusting and loving selves and we lost the trust and love that we felt. Can anything be worse?

The emotional process of grieving has many phases.

At first, we are dumbfounded, shocked, inert, immobile. We play dead to avoid our inner monsters. We are ossified in our pain, cast in the mould of our reticence and fears. Then we feel enraged, indignant, rebellious and hateful. Then we accept. Then we cry. And then - some of us - learn to forgive and to pity. And this is called healing.

All stages are absolutely necessary and good for you. It is bad not to rage back, not to shame those who shamed us, to deny, to pretend, to evade. But it is equally bad to get fixated on our rage. Permanent grieving is the perpetuation of our abuse by other means.

By endlessly recreating our harrowing experiences, we unwillingly collaborate with our abuser to perpetuate his or her evil deeds. It is by moving on that we defeat our abuser, minimizing him and his importance in our lives. It is by loving and by trusting anew that we annul that which was done to us. To forgive is never to forget. But to remember is not necessarily to re-experience.

Forgiving and Forgetting

Forgiving is an important capability. It does more for the forgiver than for the forgiven. But it should not be a universal, indiscriminate behaviour. It is legitimate not to forgive sometimes. It depends, of course, on the severity or duration of what was done to you.

In general, it is unwise and counterproductive to apply to life "universal" and "immutable" principles. Life is too chaotic to succumb to rigid edicts. Sentences which start with "never" or "always" are not very credible and often lead to self-defeating, self-restricting and self-destructive behaviours.

Conflicts are an important and integral part of life. One should never seek them out, but when confronted with a conflict, one should not avoid it. It is through conflicts and adversity as much as through care and love that we grow.

Human relationships are dynamic. We must assess our friendships, partnerships, even our marriages periodically. In and by itself, a common past is insufficient to sustain a healthy, nourishing, supportive, caring and compassionate relationship. Common memories are a necessary but not a sufficient condition. We must gain and regain our friendships on a daily basis. Human relationships are a constant test of allegiance and empathy.

Remaining Friends with the Narcissist

Can't we act civilized and remain on friendly terms with our narcissist ex? Never forget that narcissists (full fledged ones) are nice and friendly only when:

a. They want something from you - Narcissistic Supply, help, support, votes, money... They prepare the ground, manipulate you and then come out with the "small favour" they need or ask you blatantly or surreptitiously for Narcissistic Supply ("What did you think about my performance...", "Do you think that I really deserve the Nobel Prize?");

b. They feel threatened and they want to neuter the threat by smothering it with oozing pleasantries;

c. They have just been infused with an overdose of Narcissistic Supply and they feel magnanimous and magnificent and ideal and perfect. To show magnanimity is a way of flaunting one's impeccable divine credentials. It is an act of grandiosity. You are an irrelevant prop in this spectacle, a mere receptacle of the narcissist's overflowing, self-contented infatuation with his False Self.

This beneficence is transient. Perpetual victims often tend to thank the narcissist for "little graces". This is the Stockholm Syndrome: hostages tend to emotionally identify with their captors rather than with the police. We are grateful to our abusers and tormentors for ceasing their hideous activities and allowing us to catch our breath.

Some people say that they prefer to live with narcissists, to cater to their needs and to succumb to their whims because this is the way they have been conditioned in early childhood. It is only with narcissists that they feel alive, stimulated and excited. The world glows in Technicolor in the presence of a narcissist and decays to sepia colours in his absence.

I see nothing inherently "wrong" with that. The test is this: if someone were to constantly humiliate and abuse you verbally using Archaic Chinese, would you have felt humiliated and abused? Probably not. Some people have been conditioned by the narcissistic Primary Objects in their lives (parents or caregivers) to treat narcissistic abuse as Archaic Chinese, to turn a deaf ear.

This technique is effective in that it allows the inverted narcissist (the narcissist's willing mate) to experience only the good aspects of living with a narcissist: his sparkling intelligence, the constant drama and excitement, the lack of intimacy and emotional attachment (some people prefer this). Every now and then the narcissist breaks into abuse in Archaic Chinese. So what, who understands Archaic Chinese anyway, says the inverted narcissist to herself.

I have only one nagging doubt, though:

If the relationship with a narcissist is so rewarding, why are inverted narcissists so unhappy, so ego-dystonic, so in need of help (professional or otherwise)? Aren't they victims who are simply experiencing the Stockholm Syndrome (Trauma Bonding, identifying with the kidnapper rather than with the Police) and who are then in denial of their own torment?

Narcissists and Abandonment

Narcissists are terrified of being abandoned exactly as are co-dependents and borderlines.

But their solution is different.

Co-dependents cling. Borderlines are emotionally labile and react disastrously to the faintest hint of being abandoned.

Narcissists facilitate their own abandonment. They make sure that they are abandoned.

This way they achieve two goals:

1. Getting it over with - The narcissist has a very low threshold of tolerance to uncertainty and inconvenience, emotional or material. Narcissists are very impatient and "spoiled". They cannot delay gratification or impending doom. They must have it all now, good or bad.

2. By bringing the feared abandonment about, the narcissist can lie to himself persuasively. "She didn't abandon me, it is I who abandoned her. I controlled the situation. It was all my doing, so I was really not abandoned, was I now?" In time, the narcissist adopts this "official version" as the truth. He might say: "I abandoned her emotionally and sexually long before she left."

[This is one of the important Emotional Involvement Prevention Mechanisms (EIPM) that I write about in the Essay]

Why the Failing Relationships?

Narcissists hate happiness and joy and ebullience and vivaciousness - in short, they hate life itself.

The roots of this bizarre propensity can be traced to a few psychological dynamics, which operate concurrently (it is very confusing to be a narcissist).

First, there is pathological envy.

The narcissist is constantly envious of other people: their successes, their property, their character, their education, their children, their ideas, the fact that they are capable of feeling, their good moods, their past, their future, their present, their spouses, their mistresses or lovers, their location...

Almost anything can be the trigger of a bout of biting, acidulous envy. But there is nothing, which reminds the narcissist more of the totality of his envious experiences than happiness. Narcissists lash out at happy people out of their own nagging sense of deprivation.

Then there is narcissistic hurt.

The narcissist regards himself as the centre of the world and the epicentre of the lives of his closest, nearest and dearest. He is the source of all emotions, responsible for all developments, positive and negative alike, the axis, the prime cause, the only cause, the mover, the shaker, the broker, the pillar, forever indispensable.

It is therefore a bitter and sharp rebuke to this grandiose fantasy to see someone else happy for reasons that have nothing to do with the narcissist. It painfully serves to illustrate to him that he is but one of many causes, phenomena, triggers and catalysts in other people's lives; that there are things happening outside the orbit of his control or initiative; that he is not privileged or unique.

The narcissist uses Projective Identification. He channels his negative emotions through other people, his proxies. He induces unhappiness and gloom in others to enable him to experience his own misery. Inevitably, he attributes the source of such sadness either to himself, as its cause - or to the "pathology" of the sad person.

"You are constantly depressed, you should really see a therapist", is a common advice he doles out.

The narcissist - in an effort to maintain the depressive state until it serves some cathartic purpose - strives to perpetuate it by constantly reminding the depressed person of its existence. "You look sad/bad/pale today. Is anything wrong? Can I help you? Things haven't been going so well lately?"

Last but not least is the exaggerated fear of losing control.

The narcissist feels that he controls his human environment mostly by manipulation and mainly by emotional extortion and distortion. This is not far from reality. The narcissist suppresses any sign of emotional autonomy. He feels threatened and belittled by an emotion not directly or indirectly fostered by him or by his actions. Counteracting someone else's happiness is the narcissist's way of reminding everyone: "I am here, I am omnipotent, you are at my mercy and you will feel happy only when I tell you to."

Living with a Narcissist

You cannot change people, at least not in the real, profound, deep sense. You can only adapt to them and adapt them to you. If you do find your narcissist rewarding at times - you should consider doing these:

1. Determine your limits and boundaries. How much and in which ways can you adapt to him (i.e., accept him AS HE IS) and to which extent and in which ways would you like him to adapt to you (i.e., accept you as you are). Act accordingly. Accept what you have decided to accept and reject the rest. Change in you what you are willing and able to change - and ignore the rest. Conclude an unwritten contract of co-existence (could be written if you are more formally inclined).

2. Try to maximize the number of times that "...his walls are down", that you "...find him totally fascinating and everything I desire". What makes him be and behave this way? Is it something that you say or do? Is it preceded by events of a specific nature? Is there anything you can do to make him behave this way more often?

Remember, though:

Sometimes we mistake guilt and self-assumed blame for love.

Committing suicide for someone else's sake is not love.

Sacrificing yourself for someone else is not love.

It is domination through co-dependence.

You control your narcissist by giving, as much as he controls you through his pathology.

Your unconditional generosity sometimes prevents him from facing his True Self and thus healing.

It is impossible to have a relationship with a narcissist that is meaningful to the narcissist.

It is, of course, possible to have a relationship with a narcissist that is meaningful to you [see FAQ 50].

You modify your behaviour in order to secure the narcissist's continuing love, not in order to be abandoned.

This is the root of the perniciousness of this phenomenon:

The narcissist is a meaningful, crucially significant figure ("object") in the inverted narcissist's life.

This is the narcissist's leverage over the inverted narcissist. And since the inverted narcissist is usually very young when making the adaptation to the narcissist - it all boils down to fear of abandonment and death in the absence of care and sustenance.

The inverted narcissist's accommodation of the narcissist is as much a wish to gratify one's narcissist (parent) as the sheer terror of forever withholding gratification from one's self.

The Need to be Hopeful

I understand the need to be hopeful.

There are gradations of narcissism. This book deals with the extreme and ultimate form of narcissism, the Narcissistic Personality Disorder (NPD). The prognosis for those merely with narcissistic traits or a narcissistic style is far better than the healing prospects of a full-fledged narcissist.

We often confuse shame with guilt.

Narcissists feel shameful when confronted with a failure. They feel (narcissistically) injured. Their omnipotence is threatened, their sense of perfection and uniqueness is questioned. They are enraged, engulfed by self-reprimand, self-loathing and internalized violent urges.

The narcissist punishes himself for failing to be God - not for mistreating others.

The narcissist makes an effort to communicate his pain and shame in order to elicit the Narcissistic Supply he needs to restore and regulate his failing sense of self-worth. In doing so, the narcissist resorts to the human vocabulary of empathy. The narcissist will say anything to obtain Narcissistic Supply. It is a manipulative ploy - not a confession of real emotions or an authentic description of internal dynamics.

Yes, the narcissist is a child - but a very young one.

Yes, he can tell right from wrong - but is indifferent to both.

Yes, a process of "re-parenting" (what Kohut called a "self-object") is required to foster growth and maturation. In the best of cases, it takes years and the prognosis is dismal.

Yes, some narcissists make it. And their mates or spouses or children or colleagues or lovers rejoice.

But is the fact that people survive tornadoes a reason to go out and seek one?

The narcissist is very much attracted to vulnerability, to unstable or disordered personalities or to his inferiors. Such people constitute secure Sources of Narcissistic Supply. The inferior offer adulation. The mentally disturbed, the traumatized, the abused become dependent and addicted to him. The vulnerable can be easily and economically manipulated without fear of repercussions.

"A healed narcissist" is a contradiction in terms, an oxymoron (though there may be exceptions, of course).

Still, healing (not only of narcissists) is dependent upon and derived from a sense of security in a relationship.

The narcissist is not particularly interested in healing. He tries to optimize his returns, taking into consideration the scarcity and finiteness of his resources. Healing, to him, is simply a bad business proposition.

In the narcissist's world being accepted or cared for (not to mention loved) is a foreign language. It is meaningless.

One might recite the most delicate haiku in Japanese and it would still remain meaningless to a non-Japanese.

That non-Japanese are not adept at Japanese does not diminish the value of the haiku or of the Japanese language, needless to say.

Narcissists damage and hurt but they do so offhandedly and naturally, as an after-thought and reflexively.

They are aware of what they are doing to others - but they do not care.

Narcissists feel that they are entitled to their pleasure and gratification (Narcissistic Supply is often obtained by subjugating and subsuming others).

They feel that others are less than human, mere extensions of the narcissist, or instruments to fulfil the narcissist's wishes and obey his often capricious commands.

The narcissist feels that no evil can be inflicted on machines, instruments, or extensions. He feels that his needs justify his actions.

The Dead Parents

Question: How do narcissists react to the death of their parents?

Answer: The narcissist has a complicated relationship with his parents (mainly with his mother, but, at times, also with his father). As Primary Objects, the narcissist's parents are often a source of frustration which leads to repressed or to self-directed aggression. They traumatize the narcissist during his infancy and childhood and thwart his healthy development well into his late adolescence.

Often, they are narcissists themselves. Always, they behave capriciously, reward and punish the narcissist arbitrarily, abandon him or smother him with ill-regulated emotions. They instil in him a demanding, rigid, idealistic and sadistic Superego. Their voices continue to echo in him as an adult and to adjudicate, convict and punish him in a myriad ways.

Thus, in most important respects, the narcissist's parents never die. They live on to torment him, to persecute and prosecute him. Their criticism, verbal and other forms of abuse, and berating go on long after their physical demise. Their objectification of the narcissist lasts longer than any corporeal reality.

Naturally, the narcissist has a mixed reaction to the passing away of his parents. It is composed of elation and a sense of overwhelming freedom mixed with grief. The narcissist is attached to his parents in much the same way as a hostage gets "attached" to his captors (the Stockholm Syndrome, or Trauma Bonding), the tormented to his tormentors, the prisoner to his wardens. When this bondage ceases, the narcissist feels lost and released, saddened and euphoric, empowered and drained.

Additionally, the narcissist's parents are typically Secondary Narcissistic Supply Sources (SNSSs). They fulfil the roles of Accumulation of Narcissistic Supply (witnessing the narcissist's

532

SAM VAKNIN   MALIGNANT SELF LOVE

grand moments, they function as his "biographers") and Regulation of Narcissistic Supply (they provide the narcissist with Narcissistic Supply on a regular and reliable basis). Their death represents the loss of the narcissist's best and most veteran sources and, therefore, constitutes a devastating blow to the narcissist's mental composure.

But beneath these evident losses lies a more disturbing reality. The narcissist has unfinished business with his parents. All of us do - but his is more fundamental. Unresolved conflicts, traumas, fears and hurts seethe under the surface and the resulting pressure deforms the narcissist's personality.

The death of his parents denies the narcissist the closure he so craves and needs. It seals his inability to come to terms with the very sources of his invalidity, with the very poisonous roots of his disorder. These are grave and disconcerting news, indeed. Moreover, the death of his parents virtually secures a continuation of the acrimonious debate between the narcissist's Superego and the other structures of his personality.

Unable to contrast the ideal parents in his mind with the real (less than ideal) ones, unable to communicate with them, unable to defend himself, to accuse, even to pity them, the narcissist finds himself trapped in a time capsule, forever re-enacting his childhood and its injustice and abandonment.

The narcissist needs his parents alive mostly in order to get back at them, to accuse and punish them for what they have done to him. This attempt at reciprocity ("settling the scores") represents to him justice and order, it introduces sense and logic into an otherwise totally chaotic mental landscape. It is a triumph of right over wrong, weak over strong, law and order over chaos and capriciousness.

The demise of his parents is perceived by him to be a cosmic joke at his expense. He feels "stuck" for the rest of his life with the consequences of events and behaviour not of his own making or fault. The villains evade responsibility by leaving the stage, ignoring the script and the director's (the narcissist's) orders.

The narcissist goes through a final big cycle of helpless rage when his parents die. He then feels, once again, belittled, ashamed and guilty, worthy of condemnation and punishment (for being angry at his parents as well as elated at their death). It is when his parents pass away that the narcissist becomes a child again. And, like the first time round, it is not a pleasant or savoury experience.

533

Malignant Self Love

Narcissism Revisited

The Mind of the Narcissist

This section contains professional terms.

CHAPTER I

The Soul of a Narcissist
The State of the Art

We all love ourselves. That seems to be such an instinctively true statement that we do not bother to examine it more thoroughly. In our daily affairs - in love, in business, in other areas of life - we act on this premise. Yet, upon closer inspection, it looks shakier.

Some people explicitly state that they do not love themselves at all (they are ego-dystonic). Others confine their lack of self-love to certain of their traits, to their personal history, or to some of their behaviour patterns. Yet others feel content with who they are and with what they are doing (ego-syntonic).

But one group of people seems distinct in its mental constitution - narcissists.

According to the legend of Narcissus, this Greek boy fell in love with his own reflection in a pond. In a way, this amply sums up the nature of his namesakes: narcissists. The mythological Narcissus rejected the advances of the nymph Echo and was punished by the goddess Nemesis. He was consigned to pine away as he fell in love with his own reflection - exactly as Echo had pined away for him. How apt. Narcissists are punished by echoes and reflections of their problematic personalities up to this very day.

Narcissists are said to be in love with themselves.

But this is a fallacy. Narcissus is not in love with HIMSELF. He is in love with his REFLECTION.

There is a major difference between one's True Self and reflected-self.

Loving your True Self is healthy, adaptive, and functional.

Loving a reflection has two major drawbacks:

1. One depends on the existence and availability of the reflection to produce the emotion of self-love.

2. The absence of a "compass", an "objective and realistic yardstick", by which to judge the authenticity of the reflection. In other words, it is impossible to tell whether the reflection is true to reality and, if so, to what extent.

The popular misconception is that narcissists love themselves. In reality, they direct their love at other people's impressions of them. He who loves only impressions is incapable of loving people, himself included.

But the narcissist does possess the in-bred desire to love and to be loved. If he cannot love himself, he must love his reflection. But to love his reflection, it must be loveable. Thus, driven by the insatiable urge to love (which we all possess), the narcissist is preoccupied with projecting a loveable image, albeit compatible with his self-image (the way he "sees" himself).

The narcissist maintains this projected image and invests resources and energy in it, sometimes depleting him to the point of rendering him vulnerable to external threats.

But the most important characteristic of the narcissist's projected image is its lovability.

To a narcissist, love is interchangeable with other emotions, such as awe, respect, admiration, attention, or even being feared (collectively known as Narcissistic Supply). Thus, to him, a projected image, which provokes these reactions in others, is both "loveable and loved". It also feels like self-love.

The more successful this projected image (or series of successive images) is in generating Narcissistic Supply (NS), the more the narcissist becomes divorced from his True Self and married to the image.

I am not saying that the narcissist does not have a central nucleus (a "self"). All I am saying is that he prefers his image - with which he identifies unreservedly - to his True Self. The True Self becomes serf to the Image. The narcissist, therefore, is not selfish because his True Self is paralyzed and subordinate.

The narcissist is not attuned exclusively to his needs. On the contrary: he ignores them because many of them conflict with his ostensible omnipotence and omniscience. He does not put himself first - he puts his self last. He caters to the needs and wishes of everyone around him because he craves their love and admiration. It is through their reactions that he acquires a sense of distinct self. In many ways he annuls himself only to re-invent himself through the look of others. The narcissist is the person most insensitive to his true needs.

The narcissist drains himself of mental energy in this process. This is why he has none left to dedicate to others. This fact, as well as his inability to love human beings in their many dimensions and facets, ultimately transform him into a recluse. He guards its territory jealously and fiercely. He protects what he perceives to constitute his independence.

Why should people indulge the narcissist? And what is the "evolutionary", survival value of preferring one kind of love (directed at an image) to another (directed at one's self)?

These questions torment the narcissist. His convoluted mind comes up with the most elaborate contraptions in lieu of answers.

Why should people indulge the narcissist, divert time and energy, give him attention, love and adulation? The narcissist's answer is simple: because he is entitled to it. He feels that he deserves whatever he succeeds to extract from others and much more besides. Actually, he feels betrayed, discriminated against and underprivileged because he believes that he is not being treated fairly, that he should get more than he does.

There is a discrepancy between his infinite certainty that his is a special status which renders him worthy of recurrent praise and adoration, replete with special benefits and prerogatives and the actual state of his affairs. To the narcissist, his uniqueness is bestowed upon him not by virtue of his achievements, but merely because he exists.

The narcissist's deems his mere existence as sufficiently unique to warrant the kind of treatment that he expects to get from the world. This is the paradox, which haunts the narcissist: he derives his sense of uniqueness from the very fact that he exists and he derives his sense of existence from his belief that he is unique.

Clinical data show that there is rarely any realistic basis for these grandiose notions of greatness and uniqueness.

Some narcissists are high achievers with proven track records. Some of them are pillars of their communities. Mostly, they are dynamic and successful. Still, they are ridiculously pompous and inflated personalities, bordering on the farcical and provoking resentment.

The narcissist is forced to use other people in order to feel that he exists. It is trough their eyes and through their behaviour that he obtains proof of his uniqueness and grandeur. He is a habitual "people-junkie". With time, he comes to regard those around him as mere instruments of gratification, as two-dimensional cartoon figures with negligible lines in the script of his magnificent life.

He becomes unscrupulous, never bothered by the constant exploitation of his milieu, indifferent to the consequences of his actions, to the damage and the pain that he inflicts on others and even to the social condemnation and sanctions that he often has to endure.

When a person persists in a dysfunctional, maladaptive or plain useless behaviour despite grave repercussions to himself and to others, we say that his acts are compulsive. The narcissist is compulsive in his pursuit of Narcissistic Supply. This linkage between narcissism and obsessive-compulsive disorders sheds light on the mechanisms of the narcissistic psyche.

The narcissist does not suffer from a faulty sense of causation. He is not oblivious to the likely outcomes of his actions and to the price he may have to pay. But he doesn't care.

A personality whose very existence is a derivative of its reflection in other people's minds is perilously dependent on these people's perceptions. They are the Sources of Narcissistic Supply (NSS). Criticism and disapproval are interpreted by the narcissist as a sadistic withholding of said supply and as a direct threat to the narcissist's mental house of cards.

The narcissist lives in a world of all or nothing, of a constant "to be or not be". Every discussion that he holds, every glance of every passer-by reaffirm his existence or cast it in doubt. This is why the reactions of the narcissist seem so disproportionate: he reacts to what he perceives to be a danger to the very cohesion of his self. Thus, every minor disagreement with a Source of Narcissistic Supply - another person - is interpreted as a threat to the narcissist's very self-worth.

This is such a crucial matter, that the narcissist cannot take chances. He would rather be mistaken then remain without Narcissistic Supply. He would rather discern disapproval and unjustified criticism where there are none then face the consequences of being caught off-guard.

The narcissist has to condition his human environment to refrain from expressing criticism and disapproval of him or of his actions and decisions. He has to teach people around him that these provoke him into frightful fits of temper and rage attacks and turn him into a constantly cantankerous and irascible person. His exaggerated reactions constitute a punishment for their inconsiderateness and their ignorance of his true psychological state.

The narcissist blames others for his behaviour, accuses them of provoking him into his temper tantrums and believes firmly that "they" should be punished for their "misbehaviour".

Apologies - unless accompanied by verbal or other humiliation - are not enough. The fuel of the narcissist's rage is spent mainly on vitriolic verbal send-offs directed at the (often imaginary) perpetrator of the (oft innocuous) offence.

The narcissist - wittingly or not - utilises people to buttress his self-image and to regulate his sense of self-worth. As long and in as much as they are instrumental in achieving these goals, he holds them in high regard, they are valuable to him. He sees them only through this lens. This is a result of his inability to love others: he lacks empathy, he thinks utility, and, thus, he reduces others to mere instruments.

If they cease to "function", if, no matter how inadvertently, they cause him to doubt his illusory, half-baked, self-esteem, they are subjected to a reign of terror. The narcissist then proceeds to hurt these "insubordinates". He belittles and humiliates them. He displays aggression and violence in myriad forms. His behaviour metamorphoses, kaleidoscopically, from over-valuing (idealizing) the useful person to a severe devaluation of same. The narcissist abhors, almost physiologically, people judged by him to be "useless".

These rapid alterations between absolute overvaluation (idealization) and complete devaluation make long-term interpersonal relationships with the narcissist all but impossible.

The more pathological form of narcissism - the Narcissistic Personality Disorder (NPD) - was defined in successive versions of the American DSM (Diagnostic and Statistical Manual published by the American Psychiatric Association) and the international ICD (International Classification of Diseases, published by the World Health Organization). It is useful to scrutinize these geological layers of clinical observations and their interpretation.

In 1977 the DSM-III criteria included:
- An inflated valuation of oneself (exaggeration of talents and achievements, demonstration of presumptuous self-confidence);
- Interpersonal exploitation (uses others to satisfy his needs and desires, expects preferential treatment without undertaking mutual commitments);
- Possesses expansive imagination (externalizes immature and non-regimented fantasies, "prevaricates to redeem self-illusions");
- Displays supercilious imperturbability (except when the narcissistic confidence is shaken), nonchalant, unimpressed and cold-blooded;

• Defective social conscience (rebels against the conventions of common social existence, does not value personal integrity and the rights of other people).

Compare the 1977 version with the one adopted 10 years later (in the DSM-III-R) and expanded upon in 1994 (in the DSM-IV) and in 2000 (the DSM-IV-TR). [You can find the criteria on: http://behavenet.com/capsules/disorders/narcissisticpd.htm]

The narcissist is portrayed as a monster, a ruthless and exploitative person. Yet, inside, the narcissist suffers from a chronic lack of confidence and is fundamentally dissatisfied. This applies to all narcissists. The distinction between "compensatory" and "classic" narcissists is spurious. All narcissists are walking scar tissue, the outcomes of various forms of abuse.

On the outside, the narcissist may appear to be labile and unstable. But, this does not capture the barren landscape of misery and fears that is his soul. His brazen and reckless behaviour covers up for a depressive, anxious interior.

How can such contrasts coexist?

Freud (1915) offered a trilateral model of the human psyche, composed of the Id, the Ego, and the Superego.

According to Freud, narcissists are dominated by their Ego to such an extent that the Id and Superego are neutralized. Early in his career, Freud believed narcissism to be a normal developmental phase between autoeroticism and object-love. Later on, he concluded that linear development can be thwarted by the very efforts we all make in our infancy to evolve the capacity to love an object (another person).

Some of us, thus Freud, fail to grow beyond the phase of self-love in the development of our libido. Others refer to themselves and prefer themselves as objects of love. This choice - to concentrate on the self - is the result of an unconscious decision to give up a consistently frustrating and unrewarding effort to love others and to trust them.

The frustrated and abused child learns that the only "object" he can trust and that is always and reliably available, the only person he can love without being abandoned or hurt is himself.

So, is pathological narcissism the outcome of verbal, sexual, physical, or psychological abuse - or, on the contrary, the sad result of spoiling the child and idolizing it?

This debate is easier to resolve if one agrees to adopt a more comprehensive definition of "abuse". Overweening, smothering, spoiling, overvaluing, and idolizing the child are also forms of parental abuse.

This is because, as Horney pointed out, the smothered and spoiled child is dehumanized and instrumentalized. His parents love him not for what he really is but for what they wish and imagine him to be: the fulfilment of their dreams and frustrated wishes. The child becomes the vessel of his parents' discontented lives, a tool, the magic airbrush with which they seek to retouch their failures into successes, their humiliation into victory, their frustrations into happiness.

The child is taught to give up on reality and adopt the parental fantasies. Such an unfortunate child feels omnipotent and omniscient, perfect and brilliant, worthy of adoration and entitled to special treatment. The faculties that are honed by constantly brushing against bruising reality - empathy, compassion, a realistic assessment of one's abilities and limitations, realistic expectations of oneself and of others, personal boundaries, team work, social skills, perseverance and goal-orientation, not to mention the ability to postpone gratification and to work hard to achieve it - are all deficient or missing altogether.

This kind of child turned adult sees no reason to invest resources in his skills and education, convinced that his inherent genius should suffice. He feels entitled for merely being, rather than for actually doing (rather as the nobility in days gone by felt entitled not by virtue of its merits but as the inevitable, foreordained outcome of its birth right). The narcissist is not meritocratic but aristocratic.

Such a mental structure is brittle, susceptible to criticism and disagreement, vulnerable to the incessant encounter with a harsh and intolerant world. Deep inside, narcissists of both kinds (those wrought by "classic" abuse and those yielded by being idolized) feel inadequate, phoney, fake, inferior, and deserving of punishment.

Millon makes a distinction between several types of narcissists. He wrongly assumes that the "classic" narcissist is the outcome of parental overvaluation, idolization, and spoiling and, thus, is possessed of supreme, unchallenged, self-confidence, and is devoid of all self-doubt.

According to Millon, it is the "compensatory" narcissist that falls prey to nagging self-doubts, feelings of inferiority, and a masochistic desire for self-punishment.

Yet, this distinction is both wrong and unnecessary. Psychodynamically, there is only one type of pathological narcissism - though there are two developmental paths to it. And all narcissists are besieged by deeply ingrained (though at times not conscious) feelings of inadequacy, fears of failure, masochistic desires to be penalized, a fluctuating sense of self-worth (regulated by Narcissistic Supply), and an overwhelming sensation of fraudulence.

In the early childhood of all narcissists, meaningful others are inconsistent in their acceptance of the child. They pay attention to the narcissist only when they wish to satisfy their needs. They tend to ignore him - or actively abuse him - when these needs are no longer pressing.

The narcissist's past of abuse teaches him to avoid deeper relationships in order to escape this painful approach-avoidance pendulum. Protecting himself from hurt and from abandonment, he insulates himself from people around him. He digs in rather than spring out.

We all put people around us (the aforementioned objects) to recurrent tests. This is the "primary narcissistic stage". A positive relationship with one's parents or caregivers (Primary Objects) secures the smooth transition to "object love". The child then forgoes his narcissism.

Giving up one's narcissism is tough. Narcissism is alluring, soothing, warm and dependable. It is always present and all-pervasive. It is custom tailored to the needs of the individual. To love oneself is to have the perfect lover. Good reasons and strong forces - collectively known as "parental love" - are required to motivate the child to give up its narcissism.

The child progresses beyond its primary narcissism in order to be able to love his parents. If they are narcissists, they subject him to idealization (over-valuation) and devaluation cycles. They do not reliably satisfy the child's needs. In other words, they frustrate him. He gradually realizes that he is no more than a toy, an instrument, a means to an end: his parents' gratification.

This shocking revelation deforms the child's budding Ego. The child forms a strong dependence (as opposed to attachment) on his parents. This dependence is really the outcome of fear, the mirror image of aggression. In Freud-speak (psychoanalysis) we say that the child is likely to develop accentuated oral fixations and regressions. In plain terms, we are likely to see a lost, phobic, helpless, raging child. But a child is still a child and his relationship with his parents is of ultimate importance to him.

He, therefore, resists his natural reactions to his abusive caregivers, and tries to defuse his libidinal and aggressive sensations and emotions. This way, he hopes to rehabilitate the damaged relationship with his parents (which never really existed). Hence the primordial confabulation, the mother of all future narcissistic fantasies. In his embattled mind, the child transforms the Superego into an idealized, sadistic parent-child. His Ego, in turn, becomes a hated, devalued child-parent.

The family is the mainspring of support of every kind. It mobilizes psychological resources and alleviates emotional burdens. It allows for the sharing of tasks, provides material supplies coupled with cognitive training. It is the prime socialization agent and encourages the absorption of information, most of it useful and adaptive.

This division of labour between parents and children is vital both to personal growth and to proper adaptation. The child must feel, as he does in a functional family, that he can share his experiences without being defensive and that the feedback that he is getting is open and unbiased. The only "bias" acceptable (often because it is consonant with feedback from the outside) is the family's set of beliefs, values and goals that are finally internalized by the child by way of imitation and unconscious identification.

So, the family is the first and the most important source of identity and emotional support. It is a greenhouse, where the child feels loved, cared for, accepted, and secure - the prerequisites for the development of personal resources. On the material level, the family should provide the basic necessities (and, preferably, beyond), physical care and protection, and refuge and shelter during crises.

The role of the mother (the Primary Object) has often been discussed. The father's part is mostly neglected, even in professional literature. However, recent research demonstrates his importance to the orderly and healthy development of the child.

The father participates in the day-to-day care, is an intellectual catalyst who encourages the child to develop his interests and to satisfy his curiosity through the manipulation of various instruments and games. He is a source of authority and discipline, a boundary setter, enforcing and encouraging positive behaviours and eliminating negative ones.

The father also provides emotional support and economic security, thus stabilizing the family unit. Finally, he is the prime source of masculine orientation and identification to the male child and gives warmth and love as a male to his daughter, without transgressing the socially permissible limits.

We can safely say that the narcissist's family is as severely disordered as he is. Pathological narcissism is largely a reflection of this dysfunction. Such an environment breeds self-deception.

The narcissist's internal dialogue is "I do have a relationship with my parents. It is my fault - the fault of my emotions, sensations, aggressions and passions - that this relationship is not working. It is, therefore, my responsibility to make amends. I will construct a narrative in which I am both loved and punished. In this script, I will allocate roles to myself and to my parents. This way, everything will be fine and we will all be happy."

Thus starts the cycle of over-valuation (idealization) and devaluation. The dual roles of sadist and punished masochist (Superego and Ego), parent and child, permeate all the narcissist's interactions with other people.

The narcissist experiences a reversal of roles as his relationships progress. At the beginning of a relationship he is the child in need of attention, approval and admiration. He becomes dependent. Then, at the first sign of disapproval (real or imaginary), he is transformed into an avowed sadist, punishing and inflicting pain.

It is commonly agreed that a loss (real or perceived) at a critical junction in the psychological development of the child forces him to refer to himself for nurturing and for gratification. The child ceases to trust others and his ability to develop object love, or to idealize is hampered. He is constantly haunted by the feeling that only he can satisfy his emotional needs.

He exploits people, sometimes unintentionally, but always ruthlessly and mercilessly. He uses them to obtain confirmation of the accuracy of his grandiose self-portrait.

The narcissist is usually above treatment. He knows best. He feels superior to his therapist in particular and to the science of psychology in general. He seeks treatment only following a major life crisis, which directly threatens his projected and perceived image. Even then he only wishes to restore the previous balance.

Therapy sessions with the narcissist resemble a battlefield. He is aloof and distanced, demonstrates his superiority in a myriad ways, resents what he perceives to be an intrusion on his innermost sanctum. He is offended by any hint regarding defects or dysfunctions in his personality or in his behaviour. A narcissist is a narcissist is a narcissist - even when he asks for help with his world and worldview shattered.

Appendix: Object Relations Theories and Narcissism

Otto Kernberg (1975, 1984, 1987) disagrees with Freud. He regards the division between an "object libido" (energy directed at objects, meaningful others, people in the immediate vicinity of the infant) and a "narcissistic libido" (energy directed at the self as the most immediate and satisfying object), which precedes it as spurious.

Whether a child develops normal or pathological narcissism depends on the relations between the representations of the self (roughly, the image of the self that the child forms in his mind) and the representations of objects (roughly, the images of other people that the child forms in his mind, based on all the emotional and objective information available to him). It is also dependent on the relationship between the representations of the self and real, external, "objective" objects.

Add to these instinctual conflicts related to both the libido and to aggression (these very strong emotions give rise to strong conflicts in the child) and a comprehensive explanation concerning the formation of pathological narcissism emerges.

Kernberg's concept of Self is closely related to Freud's concept of Ego. The self is dependent upon the unconscious, which exerts a constant influence on all mental functions. Pathological narcissism, therefore, reflects a libidinal investment in a pathologically structured self and not in a normal, integrative structure of the self.

547 The narcissist suffers because his self is devalued or fixated on aggression. All object relations of such a self are distorted: it detaches from real objects (because they hurt it often), dissociates, represses, or projects. Narcissism is not merely a fixation on an early developmental stage. It is not confined to the failure to develop intra psychic structures.

Franz Kohut regarded narcissism as the final product of the failing efforts of parents to cope with the needs of the child to idealize and to be grandiose (for instance, to be omnipotent).

Idealization is an important developmental path leading to narcissism. The child merges the idealized aspects of the images of his parents (Imagos, in Kohut's terminology) with those wide segments of the image of the parent which are cathected (infused) with object libido (in which the child invests the energy that he reserves for objects).

This exerts an enormous and all-important influence on the processes of re-internalization (the processes in which the child re-introduces the objects and their images into his mind) in each of the successive phases.

Through these processes, two permanent nuclei of the personality are constructed:

a. The basic, neutralizing texture of the psyche, and
b. The ideal Superego

Both of them are characterized by an invested instinctual narcissistic cathexis (invested energy of self-love which is instinctual). At first, the child idealizes his parents. As he grows up, he begins to notice their shortcomings and vices. He withdraws part of the idealizing libido from the images of the parents, which is conducive to the natural development of the Superego. The narcissistic part of the child's psyche remains vulnerable throughout its development. This is largely true until the "child" re-internalizes the ideal parent image.

Also, the very construction of the mental apparatus can be tampered with by traumatic deficiencies and by object losses right through the Oedipal period (and even in latency and in adolescence).

The same effect can be attributed to traumatic disappointment by objects.

Disturbances leading to the formation of Narcissistic Personality Disorder (NPD) can be thus grouped into:

1. *Very early disturbances in the relationship with an ideal object*. These lead to a structural weakness of the personality, which develops a deficient and/or dysfunctional stimuli-filtering mechanism. The ability of the individual to maintain a basic narcissistic homeostasis of the personality is damaged. Such a person suffers from diffusive narcissistic vulnerability.

2. *A disturbance occurring later in life - but still pre-Oedipally* - affects the pre-Oedipal formation of the basic mechanisms for controlling, channelling, and neutralizing drives and urges. The nature of the disturbance has to be a traumatic encounter with the ideal object (such as a major disappointment). The symptomatic manifestation of this structural defect is the propensity to re-sexualize drive derivatives and internal and external conflicts, either in the form of fantasies or in the form of deviant acts.

3. *A disturbance formed in the Oedipal or even in the early latent phases* - inhibits the completion of the Superego idealization. This is especially true of a disappointment related to an ideal object of the late pre-Oedipal and the Oedipal stages, where the partly idealized external parallel of the newly internalized object is traumatically destroyed.

Such a person possesses a set of values and standards, but he is always on the lookout for ideal external figures from whom he aspires to derive the affirmation and the leadership that he cannot get from his insufficiently idealized Superego.

548

SAM VAKNIN   MALIGNANT SELF LOVE

CHAPTER II

Being Special

We all fear the loss of our identity and uniqueness. We seem to be acutely aware of this fear in a crowd of people. "Far from the madding crowd" is not only the title of a book, it is also an apt description of one of the most ancient recoil mechanisms.

This wish to be distinct, "special" in the most primitive sense is universal. It crosses cultural barriers and spans different periods in human history. We use hairdressing, clothing, behaviour, lifestyles and products of our creative mind to differentiate ourselves.

549

The sensation of "being unique or special" is of paramount importance. It is behind many a social custom. People feel indispensable, one of a kind, in a loving relationship, for instance. One's uniqueness is reflected by one's spouse and this provides one with an "independent, external and objective" affirmation of one's specialness.

This sounds very close to pathological narcissism, as we defined it in the Introduction to this essay. Indeed, the difference is in measure not in substance.

Healthy people "use" others to confirm their sense of distinctiveness, but they do not over-dose or over-do it. Feeling unique is to the average bloke of secondary importance. He derives the bulk of his sense of identity from his well-developed, differentiated Ego. The clear-cut boundaries of his Ego and his thorough acquaintance with a beloved figure - his self - are enough.

Only people whose Ego is underdeveloped, immature, and relatively undifferentiated, need ever larger quantities of external Ego boundary setting, of affirmation through reflection. Such people make no distinction between significant and less meaningful others. Everyone carries the same weight and fulfils the same functions: reflection, affirmation, recognition, adulation, or attention. This is why, to them, everyone is interchangeable and dispensable.

The narcissist employs the following mechanisms in his relationships (say, in a marriage):

1. He "merges" with his spouse/mate and contains him/her as a representation of the outside world.
2. He exerts absolute dominion over the spouse (again in her symbolic capacity as The World).

These two mechanisms substitute for the healthier forms of relationship, where the two members of the couple maintain their distinctiveness, while, at the same time, creating a new "being of togetherness".

- To ensure a constant flow of Narcissistic Supply, the narcissist seeks to "replicate" his projected self. He becomes addicted to publicity, fame, and celebrity. Merely observing his "replicated self" - on billboards, TV screens, book covers, or newspapers - sustains the narcissist's feelings of omnipotence and omnipresence, akin to what he experienced in his early childhood. The "replicated self" provides the narcissist with an "existential substitute", proof that he exists - functions normally carried out by a healthy, well-developed Ego through its interactions with the outside world (the "reality principle").
- In extreme cases of deprivation, when Narcissistic Supply is nowhere to be found, the narcissist decompensates and disintegrates, even up to the point of having psychotic microepisodes. The narcissist also forms or participates in hermetic or exclusive, cult-like, social circles, whose members share his delusions (Pathological Narcissistic Space). The function of these acolytes is to serve as a psychological entourage and to provide "objective" proof of the narcissist's self-importance and grandeur.

When these devices fail, it leads to an all-pervasive feeling of annulment and alienation.

An abandoning spouse or a business failure, for instance, are crises whose magnitude and meaning cannot be suppressed. This usually moves the narcissist to seek treatment. Therapy starts where self-delusion leaves off, but it takes a massive disintegration of the very fabric of the narcissist's life and personality organization to bring about this limited concession of defeat. Even then the narcissist merely seeks to be "fixed" in order to continue his life as before.

The boundaries (and the very existence) of the narcissist's Ego are defined by others. In times of crisis, the inner experience of the narcissist - even when he is surrounded by people - is that of rapid, uncontrollable dissolution.

This feeling is life threatening. This existential conflict forces the narcissist to fervently seek or improvise solutions, optimal or suboptimal, at any cost. The narcissist proceeds to find a new spouse, to secure publicity, or to get involved with new "friends", who are willing to accommodate his desperate need for Narcissistic Supply (NS).

This sense of overwhelming urgency causes the narcissist to suspend all judgement. In these circumstances, the narcissist is likely to misjudge the traits and abilities of a prospective spouse, the quality of his own work, or his status within his social milieu. He is liable to make indiscriminate use of all his defence mechanisms to justify and rationalize this hot pursuit.

Many narcissists reject treatment even in the direst circumstances. Feeling omnipotent, they seek the answers themselves and in themselves, and then venture to "fix" and "maintain" themselves. They gather information, philosophise, "creatively innovate", and contemplate. They do all this single-handedly and even when they are forced to seek other people's counsel, they are unlikely to admit it and are prone to devalue their helpers.

551 The narcissist dedicates a lot of his time and energy to establish his own specialness. He is concerned with the degree of his uniqueness and with various methods to substantiate, communicate and document it.

The narcissist's frame of reference is nothing less than posterity and the entirety of the human race. His uniqueness must be immediately and universally recognized. It must (potentially, at least) be known by everyone at all times - or it loses its allure. It is an all or nothing situation.

CHAPTER III

Uniqueness and Intimacy

Uniqueness and intimacy are strong rivals.

Intimacy implies a certain acquaintance of one's partner with privileged information. Yet, it is exactly such partially or wholly withheld information that buttresses one's sense of superiority, uniqueness, and mystery which, inevitably, vanish with disclosure and intimacy.

Additionally, intimacy is a common and universal pursuit. It does not confer uniqueness on its seeker.

When you get to know people intimately, they all seem unique to you. Personal idiosyncrasies surface with intimate acquaintance. Intimacy makes unique beings out of us all. It, therefore, negates the self-perceived uniqueness of the truly and exclusively unique - the narcissist.

Finally, the very process of getting intimate creates (false) sensations of uniqueness. Two people getting to intimately know each other are made unique to one another.

These traits of intimacy negate the narcissist's notion of uniqueness. Intimacy may help distinguish us to our loved ones - but it also makes us common and indistinguishable to all others. If everyone is distinct, then no one is unique. Widespread acts or behaviours are anathema to uniqueness. Intimacy eliminates information asymmetries, obviates superiority and demystifies.

The narcissist does his damnedest to avoid intimacy. He constantly lies about every aspect of his life: his self, his history, his vocations and avocations, and his emotions. These false data guarantee an informative lead, asymmetry, or "advantage" in his relationships. They foster disintimization. They cast a pall of cover up, separateness, mystery over the narcissist's affairs.

The narcissist lies even in therapy. He obscures the truth by ﹘ing "psycho-babble", or professional lingo. It makes him feel that he "belongs", that he is a "Renaissance man". By demonstrating his control of several professional jargons he almost proves (to himself) that he is superhuman. In therapy, this has the effect of "objectifying" and emotional detachment.

The narcissist's behaviour is experienced by his mate as frustrating and growth-cramping. To live with him is akin to living with an emotionally-absent non-entity, or with an "alien", a form of "artificial intelligence". The partners of the narcissist often complain of overwhelming feelings of imprisonment and punishment.

The psychological source of this kind of behaviour could well involve transference. Most narcissists fall prey to unresolved conflicts with their Primary Objects (parents or caregivers), especially with the parent of the opposite sex. The development of the narcissist's intimacy skills is hindered at an early stage. Punishing and frustrating the partner or spouse is a way of getting back at the abusive parent. It is a way of avoiding the narcissistic injury brought on by inevitable abandonment.

The narcissist, it seems, is still the hurt child. His attitude serves a paramount need: not to be hurt again. The narcissist anticipates his abandonment and, by trying to avoid it, he precipitates it. Maybe he does it to demonstrate that - having been the cause of his own abandonment - he is in sole and absolute control of his relationships.

To be in control - this unconquerable drive - is a direct reaction to having been abandoned, ignored, neglected, avoided, smothered, or abused at an early stage in life. "Never again" - vows the narcissist - "If anyone will do the abandoning, it will be me."

The narcissist is devoid of empathy and incapable of intimacy with others as well as with himself. To him, lying is a second nature. A False Self takes over. The narcissist begins to believe his own lies. He makes himself to be what he wants to be and not what he really is.

To the narcissist, life is a jumbled amalgam of "cold" facts: events, difficulties, negative externalities, and predictions and projections. He prefers this "objective and quantifiable" mode of relating to the world to the much-disdained "touchy-feely" alternative. The narcissist is so afraid of the cesspool of negative emotions inside him that he would rather deny them and thus refrain from knowing himself.

The narcissist is predisposed to maintaining asymmetric relationships, where he both preserves and exhibits his superiori Even with his mate or spouse, he is forever striving to be

Guru, the Lecturer, the Teacher (even the Mystic), the Psychologist, the Experienced Elder.

The narcissist never talks - he lectures. He never moves - he poses. He is patronizing, condescending, forgiving, posturing, or teaching. This is the more benign form of narcissism. In its more malignant variants, the narcissist is hectoring, humiliating, sadistic, impatient, and full of rage and indignation. He is always critical and torments all around him with endless, bitter cynicism and with displays of disgust and repulsion.

There is no way out of the narcissistic catch: the narcissist despises the submissive and fears the independent, the strong (who constitute a threat) and the weak (who are, by definition, despicable).

Asked to explain his lack of ability to make contact in a true sense of the word, the narcissist comes up with a host of superbly crafted explanations. These are bound to include some "objective" difficulties, which have to do with the narcissist's traits, his history and the characteristics of his environment (both human and non-human).

The narcissist is the first to admit the difficulties experienced by others in trying to adapt or relate to him. To his mind, these difficulties make him unique and amply explain the gap between his grandiose theories about himself and the grey, shabby pattern that is his life (the Grandiosity Gap). The narcissist has no doubt who should adapt to whom: the world should adjust itself to the narcissist's superior standards and requirements (and, thus, incidentally, make itself a better place).

Inevitably, the sexuality of the narcissist is as disturbed as his emotional landscape.

We distinguish three types of Sexual Communicators (and hence, the same number of modes of sexual communications):

1. *The Emotional-Sexual Communicator* - is, first, attracted sexually to his potential mate. He then proceeds to examine how compatible they are and only then does he fall in love and have sexual intercourse.

   He forms a relationship that is based on a perception of the other as a whole, as an amalgam of attributes and traits, good and bad.

   His relationships last reasonably long and they disintegrate as incremental changes in the psychological makeup of the two parties encroach upon their mutual appreciation and create emotional deficiencies and hunger which can be satisfied only by resorting to new partners.

2. *The Transactional Sexual Communicator* - first examines whether he and the prospective mate are mutually compatible. If he finds compatibility, he proceeds to test the mate sexually and then forms habits, which, put together, present a fair semblance of love, though a dispassionate one.

He forms relationships with people he judges to be reliable partners and good friends. Only a modicum of desire and passion form ingredients of this brew - but its mettle is, usually, very strong and relationships founded on these bases last the longest.

3. *The Purely Sexual Communicator* - is first, attracted sexually to his potential mate.

He then proceeds to sexually explore and test the counterparty.

This interaction leads to the development of an emotional correlate, partly the result of a forming habit.

This communicator has the shortest, most disastrous relationships. He treats his mate as he would an object or a function. His problem is a saturation of experiences.

As any addict does, he increases the dose (of sexual encounters) as he proceeds and this tends to severely destabilize his relationships.

Notes to the Table:

The narcissist is almost always the Purely Sexual Communicator. This, obviously, is a gross over-simplification. Still, it provides insights into the mating mechanism of the narcissist.

The narcissist's mate-seeking behaviour is usually infantile, either because of a fixation (pre-genital or genital) or due to an unresolved Oedipal Conflict.

The narcissist tends to separate the sexual from the emotional. He can have great sex as long as it is devoid of emotional content.

The narcissist's sexual life is likely to be highly irregular or even abnormal. He sometimes leads an asexual life with a partner who is merely a platonic "friend". This is the result of what I call "approach avoidance infantilism".

There are grounds to believe that many narcissists are latent homosexuals. Conversely, there are grounds to believe that many homosexuals are repressed or outright pathological narcissists. At the extreme, homosexuality may be a private case of (somatic) narcissism. The homosexual makes love to himself and loves himself in the form of a same-gender object.

The narcissist treats others as objects. His "meaningful" other performs ego substitution functions for the narcissist. This is not love. Indeed, the narcissist is incapable of loving anyone, especially not himself.

In his relationships, the narcissist is hard-pressed to maintain both continuity and availability. He promptly develops acutely felt saturation points (both sexual and emotional). He feels shackled and trapped and escapes, either physically or by becoming emotionally and sexually absent. Thus, one way or the other, he is never there for his significant other.

Moreover, he prefers sex with objects or object representations. Some narcissists prefer masturbation (objectifying the body and reducing it to a penis), group sex, fetish sex, paraphilias, or paedophilia to normal sex.

The narcissist treats his mate as a sex object, or a sex slave. Often a verbal, or emotional, or physical abuser, he tends to mistreat his partner sexually as well.

This separation of the emotional from the sexual makes it difficult for the narcissist to have sex with people that he believes that he loves (though he never really does love). He is terrified and repelled by the idea that he has to objectify the subject of his emotions. He separates his sexual objects from his emotional partners - they can never be the same people.

The narcissist is thus conditioned to deny his nature (as a Purely Sexual Communicator) and a cycle of frustration-aggression is set in motion.

Narcissists brought up by conservative parents, who castigated sex as dirty and forbidden, adopt the ways of the Transactional Communicator. They tend to look for someone "stable, to set up a home with". But this sometimes negates their true, repressed, nature.

True partnership, a veritable, equitable transaction, does not allow for the objectification of the partner. To succeed in a partnership, the two partners must share an insightful and multidimensional view of each other: strengths and weaknesses, fears and hopes, joy and sadness, needs and choices. Of this the narcissist is incapable.

So, he feels inadequate, frustrated, and, consequently, fearful that he might be abandoned. He transforms this internal turmoil into deep-seated aggression. Once in a while the conflict reaches critical levels and the narcissist has fits of rage, emotionally deprives the partner, or humiliates her/him. Acts of violence - verbal or physical - are not uncommon.

Summary Table: Types of Communicators

Type of Communicator / Characteristics	Purely Sexual	Emotional-Sexual	Transactional
Strength of relationship	WEAK: alternation, strong motivation, low stimulus threshold	MEDIUM: emotion decays. New, strong, stimulus required	STRONG: rare compatibility ensures negative results of severed relationship
Main plane and means of examination	PHYSICAL: looks, scents, colours, voice, sex	EMOTIONAL: interaction, introspection and observation	COMPATIBILITY: preferences, opinions, sex, future plans, conversations
Filtering	Sex-Emotion-Compatibility	Emotion-Sex-Compatibility	Compatibility-Sex-Emotion
Compromise zones	Compatibility (fragility of relationships)	Compatibility (equilibrium between emotion and compatibility upstaged during decay of relationship)	Sex (sexual compromises do not affect compatibility and emotions)
Control, regulation and examination axes	External-External (2 human bodies, sexual technique)	Internal-External (bodily contact - another way to express emotions)	Internal-Internal
Decay pattern	Interest wanes when alternative found	Emotional predictability, ennui, decay of interest, alternative found	Change in a determining parameter of member of the couple
Plane of interaction	Conscious, bodily parameters, signal communication	Near conscious and unconscious, mixed (bodily and verbal) parameters, mixed (signal and verbal) communication	Conscious, verbal parameters, verbal communication
Types of communicators	Primary: Sexual Secondary: Emotional	Primary: Emotional Secondary: Sexual or Transactional (rare)	Primary: Transactional Secondary: Sexual or Emotional (rare)

The narcissist's position is untenable and unenviable. He knows - albeit he normally represses this information - that his partner disagrees with being treated as an object, sexual or emotional. Merely gratifying the narcissist does not form an edifice for a long lasting relationship.

But the narcissist is in dire need of stability and emotional certainty. He craves not to be abandoned or abused again. So, he denies his nature in a desperate plea to cheat both himself and his partner. He pretends - and sometimes he succeeds in misleading himself into believing - that he is interested in a true partnership. He really does his best, careful not to broach thorny issues, always consulting the partner when making decisions, and so on.

But inside, he harbours growing resentment and frustration. His "lone wolf" nature is bound to manifest itself, sooner or later. This conflict between the act that the narcissist puts on in order to secure the longevity of his relationships and his true character is likely more often than not to result in an eruption. The narcissist is bound to become aggressive, if not violent. The shift from benevolent lover-partner to a raging maniac - a "Dr. Jekyll and Mr. Hyde" effect - is terrifying.

Gradually, the trust between the partners is shattered and the way to the narcissist's worst fears - abandonment, emotional desolation and the dissolution of the relationship - is paved by the narcissist himself!

It is this sorry paradox - the narcissist is the instrument of his own punishment - that comprises the essence of narcissism. The narcissist is Sisyphically doomed to repeat the same cycle of pretension, wrath and hatred.

The narcissist is afraid to introspect. For, were he to do so, he would have discovered a both dismaying and comforting truth: he is in need of no one on a long-term basis. Other people are, to him, just short-term solutions.

Avid protestations to the contrary notwithstanding, the narcissist is expedient and exploitative in his relationships. Denying this, he often marries for the wrong reasons: to calm his troubled soul, to pacify himself by conforming socially.

But the narcissist does not need companionship or emotional support, let alone true partnership. There is no beast on earth more self-sufficient than a narcissist. Years of unpredictability in his relationships with meaningful others, early on abuse, sometimes decades of violence, aggression, instability and humiliation have eroded the narcissist's trust in others to the point of

vanishing. The narcissist knows that he can rely only ⌐
ble, unconditional source of love and nurturance: or

True, when in need of reassurance (e.g., in crisis ⌐
the narcissist seeks friendship. But while normal people ⌐
friends for companionship and support, the narcissist uses up his
friends the way the sick consume medication or the hungry
food. Here, too, a basic pattern emerges: to the narcissist,
other people are objects to be used and tossed away. Here, too,
he proves discontinuous and unavailable.

Moreover, the narcissist can make do with very little. If he has
a spouse - why should he seek the added burden of friends?
Other people to the narcissist are what a yoke is to the ox. He
cannot fathom reciprocity in human relations. He is easily bored
with other people's lives, their problems and solicitations. The
need to maintain his relationships drains him.

Having fulfilled their function (by listening to the narcissist,
by asking for his advice in an ego-inflating manner, by admiring
him), others would do well to vanish until they are needed
again. The narcissist feels encumbered when asked to reciprocate. Even the most basic human interaction requires a display
of his grandiosity and consumes time and energy in careful dramatic preparations.

559

The narcissist limits his social encounters to situations which
yield net energy contributions (Narcissistic Supply). Interacting
with others involves the expenditure of energy. Narcissists are
willing to oblige on condition that they are able to extract
Narcissistic Supply (attention, adulation, celebrity, sex) sufficient to outweigh the energy they had expended.

This "perpetuum mobile" cannot be maintained for long. The
narcissist's milieu (really, entourage) feel drained and bored and
his social circle dwindles. When this happens, the narcissist
springs to life and, using the vast resources of his undeniable
personal charm, he recreates a social circle, knowing full well
that it - in due course - will also take its leave and dissolve in
disgust and acrimony.

The narcissist is either terrified by the thought of children or
absolutely fascinated by it. A child, after all, is the ultimate
Source of Narcissistic Supply. It is unconditionally adoring, worshipping and submissive. But it is also a demanding thing and it
tends to divert attention from the narcissist. A child devours
time, energy, emotions, resources, and attention. The narcissist
can easily be converted to the view that a child is a competitive
menace, a nuisance, utterly unnecessary.

These make for a very shaky foundation of marital life. The narcissist does not need or seek companionship or friendship. He does not mix sex and emotions. He finds it hard to make love to someone that he "loves". He ultimately abhors his children and tries to limit and confine them to the role of Narcissistic Supply Sources. He is a bad friend, lover and father. He is likely to divorce many times (if he ever gets married) and to end up in a series of monogamous (if he is cerebral) or polygamous (if he is somatic) relationships.

Most narcissists had a functioning parent, but one that was indifferent to them and used them for his or her own narcissistic ends. Narcissists tend to breed narcissists and perpetuate their condition. The conflict with the frustrating parent is carried forward and reconstructed in intimate relationships. The narcissist directs all the major transformations of aggression at his spouse, partner, and friends. He hates, hates to admit it, sublimates and explodes in an occasional outburst of rage.

The more intimate the relationship, the more the other party has to lose by severing it, the more dependent the narcissist's partner is on the relationship and on the narcissist - the more likely is the narcissist to be aggressive, hostile, envious, and hating. This serves a dual function: as an outlet for pent-up aggression and as a kind of test.

The narcissist is putting meaningful people in his life to a constant test: will they accept him "as he is", however obnoxious? In other words, do people love him for what he really is - or are they infatuated with the image that he so elaborately projects? The narcissist cannot understand - or believe - that as far as normal people go, the difference between who they "really" are and their public persona is negligible. In his case, the gap between the two is so substantial that he resorts to extreme means to ascertain WHICH of the two people around him really love - or, rather, who is it that they profess to love: the False Self or the real person.

The fact that people choose to hang on to their relationships with him, despite his intolerable behaviour, proves to the narcissist his uniqueness and superiority. The narcissist's aggression thus serves to reassure him.

When he doesn't have access to willing victims, the narcissist indulges in fantasies of unmitigated aggression and sadism. He might find himself identifying with figures of outstanding cruelty in human history or with periods, which represent peaks of human degradation.

So, the narcissist's intimate relationship are fraught with ambivalence and contradiction: love-hate, well-wishing and envy, fear of being abandoned with a desire to be left alone, control-freakery and paranoid fears of persecution. The narcissist's psyche is torn in an all-pervasive conflict which never ceases to torment him, regardless of external or extenuating circumstances.

Mental Map # 1

Bad, unpredictable, inconsistent, threatening object
leads to defective internalisation (introjection of bad objects)
and to an unresolved Oedipal Conflict.
Damaged object relations aggression, envy, hatred
Low self-esteem
Fear that these emotions will erupt
Narcissistic defence mechanisms
Repression of all emotions, good and bad (the self as object)
Compensatory functions
Redirection of negative emotions at the self
Grandiosity, fantasies
Avoidance of emotional situations
Uniqueness, demands adulation, "I deserve" (entitlement)
Intellectual compensation, exploitativeness, envy,
lack of empathy, haughtiness.
Objectification of the OTHER
Formation of False Self (FS)
Defective interpersonal relationships
(transference relationships)
Narcissistic Supply Sources (NSSs)
Fear that the (potentially) meaningful other
(external reinforcement of FS):
1. Will invoke deep emotions and provoke negative ones
2. Fear of abandonment
(result of malnourished True Self - TS)
3. Narcissistic vulnerability: True Self (TS)
a. Negation of uniqueness
b. Ego hurt when abandoned
Anhedonia and dysphoria
Feeling of annulment, disintegration (of TS)
Fear of exposure, condemnation, persecution (FS)
Ego-dystonia (stress)

561

The above mental map includes three basic building blocks of the psyche of a typical narcissist: the True Self, the False Self and the Narcissistic Sources of Supply.

Appendix: Libido and Aggression

Narcissism is a direct result of the aggression the narcissist experienced in early life. To better understand the narcissist's intimate relationships, we must first analyse this facet of narcissism: aggression.

Emotions are instincts. They form part of human behaviour. Interactions with other people provide a framework, an organizational structure into which emotions fit nicely. Emotions are organized by object relations to the libido (the positive pole) or to aggression (which is negative and associated with hurt).

Anger is the basic emotion underlying aggression. As it fluctuates, it is transformed. Janus-like, it has two faces: hatred and envy. The libido has sexual excitation as its basic emotion. It is an ancient tactile remembrance of the mother's skin and the wholesome feeling and smell of her breasts that provoke this excitement. So important are these early experiences, that an early age pathology of object relations - a traumatic experience, physical or psychological abuse, abandonment - move aggression to a dominant position over the libido. Whenever aggression rules over libidinal drives, we have a psychopathology.

The emotional twins - libido and aggression - are inseparable. They characterize all references of the self to objects. A world of emotionally-invested object relations is formed with each such reference.

The dynamic unconscious is made of basic mental experiences, which are really dyadic relations between self-representations and object representations in either of two contexts: elation or rage.

A subconscious fantasy of merging or unification of self and object prevails in symbiotic relationships - both in euphoric moods and in aggressive and wrathful ones.

Anger has evolutionary and adaptive functions. It is intended to alert the individual to a source of pain and irritation and to motivate him to eliminate it. It is the beneficial outcome of frustration and pain. It is also instrumental in the removal of barriers to the satisfaction of needs.

As most sources of bad feelings are human, aggression (in the form of rage) is directed at (human) "bad" objects - people around us who are perceived by us to be deliberately frustrating our wishes to satisfy our needs. At the furthest end of this range we find the will and wish to make such a frustrating object suffer. But such desire is a different ball game: it combines aggression and pleasure, therefore it is sadistic.

Rage can easily convert to hatred. There is a wish to control the bad object in order to avoid persecution or fear. This control is achieved by the development of obsessive control mechanisms, which psychopathologically regulate the repression of aggression in such an individual.

Aggression can assume many forms, depending on the sublimatory venues of the aggressive reaction. Biting humour, excessive candour, the search for autonomy and personal enhancement, a compulsive effort to secure the absence of any kind of outside intervention are all sublimations of aggression.

Hatred is a derivative of anger which is intended to facilitate the destruction of the bad object, to make it suffer and to control it. Yet, the process of transformation alters the characteristics of rage in its manifestation as hatred. The former is acute, passing and disruptive - the latter is chronic, stable and connected to character. Hatred seems justified on the grounds of revenge against the frustrating object. The wish to avenge is very typical of hatred. Paranoid fears of retaliation accompany hatred. Hatred thus has paranoid, sadistic and vengeful characteristics.

Another transformation of aggression is envy. This is a greedy wish to incorporate the object, even to destroy it. Yet, this very object which the envious mind seeks to eliminate by incorporation or by destruction is also an object of love, THE object of love without which life itself will not have existed or will have lost its taste and impetus.

The narcissist's mind is pervaded by conscious and unconscious transformations of enormous amounts of aggression into envy. The more severe cases of Narcissistic Personality Disorder (NPD) display partial control of their drives, anxiety intolerance and rigid sublimatory channels. The magnitude of hatred in such individuals is so great, that they deny both the emotion and any awareness of it. Alternatively, aggression is converted to action or to acting out.

This denial affects normal cognitive functioning as well. Such an individual has intermittent bouts of arrogance, curiosity and pseudo-stupidity, all transformations of aggression taken to the extreme. It is difficult to tell envy from hatred in these cases.

The narcissist is constantly envious of people. He begrudges others their success, or brilliance, or happiness, or good fortune. He is driven to excesses of paranoia, guilt, and fear that subside only after he "acts out" or punishes himself. It is a vicious cycle in which he is entrapped.

The New Oxford Dictionary of English defines envy as:

"A feeling of discontented or resentful longing aroused by someone else's possessions, qualities, or luck."

And an earlier version (The Shorter Oxford English Dictionary) adds:

"Mortification and ill-will occasioned by the contemplation of another's superior advantages."

Pathological envy - the second deadly sin - is a compounded emotion. It is brought on by the realization of some lack, deficiency, or inadequacy in oneself. It is the result of unfavourably comparing oneself to others: to their success, their reputation, their possessions, their luck, or their qualities. It is misery and humiliation and impotent rage and a tortuous, slippery path to nowhere. The effort to break the padded walls of this self-visited purgatory often leads to attacks on the perceived source of frustration.

There is a spectrum of reactions to this pernicious and cognitively distorting emotion:

Subsuming the Object of Envy through Imitation

Some narcissists seek to imitate or even emulate their (ever changing) role models. It is as if by imitating the object of his envy, the narcissist BECOMES that object. So, narcissists are likely to adopt their boss' typical gestures, the vocabulary of a successful politician, the dress code of a movie star, the views of an esteemed tycoon, even the countenance and actions of the (fictitious) hero of a movie or a novel.

In his pursuit of peace of mind, in his frantic effort to alleviate the burden of consuming jealousy, the narcissist often deteriorates to conspicuous and ostentatious consumption, impulsive and reckless behaviours, and substance abuse.

In my essay "The Dance of Jael", [Vaknin, Sam. After the Rain - How the West Lost the East. Prague and Skopje, Narcissus Publications, 2000 - p. 76-81] I wrote:

"In extreme cases, to get rich quick through schemes of crime and corruption, to out-wit the system, to prevail, is thought by these people to be the epitome of cleverness (providing one does not get caught), the sport of living, a winked-at vice, a spice."

Destroying the Frustrating Object

Other narcissists "choose" to destroy the object that gives them so much grief by provoking in them feelings of inadequacy and frustration. They display obsessive, blind animosity and engage in compulsive acts of rivalry often at the cost of self-destruction and self-isolation.

From my essay "The Dance of Jael":

"This hydra has many heads. From scratching the paint of new cars and flattening their tyres, to spreading vicious gossip, to media-hyped arrests of successful and rich businessmen, to wars against advantaged neighbours.

The stifling, condensed vapours of envy cannot be dispersed. They invade their victims, their rageful eyes, their calculating souls, they guide their hands in evil doings and dip their tongues in vitriol... (The envious narcissist's existence is) a constant hiss, a tangible malice, the piercing of a thousand eyes. The imminence and immanence of violence. The poisoned joy of depriving the other of that which you don't or cannot have."

Self-Deprecation

From my essay, "The Dance of Jael":

"There are those narcissists who idealize the successful and the rich and the lucky. They attribute to them super-human, almost divine, qualities...

In an effort to justify the agonizing disparities between themselves and others, they humble themselves as they elevate the others. They reduce and diminish their own gifts, they disparage their own achievements, they degrade their own possessions and look with disdain and contempt upon their nearest and dearest, who are unable to discern their fundamental shortcomings. They feel worthy only of abasement and punishment. Besieged by guilt and remorse, voided of self-esteem, perpetually self-hating and self-deprecating - this is by far the more dangerous species of narcissist.

For he who derives contentment from his own humiliation cannot but derive happiness from the downfall of others. Indeed, most of them end up driving the objects of their own devotion and adulation to destruction and decrepitude..."

Cognitive Dissonance

"...But the most common reaction is the good old cognitive dissonance. It is to believe that the grapes are sour rather than to admit that they are craved.

These people devalue the source of their frustration and envy. They find faults, unattractive features, high costs to pay, immorality in everything they really most desire and aspire to and in everyone who has attained that which they so often can't. They walk amongst us, critical and self-righteous, inflated with a justice of their making and secure in the wisdom of being what they are rather than what they could have been and really wish to be. They make a virtue of jejune abstention, of wishful constipation, of judgemental neutrality, this oxymoron, the favourite of the disabled."

Avoidance – The Schizoid Solution

And then, of course, there is avoidance. To witness the success and joy of others is too painful and too high a price to pay. So, the narcissist stays away, alone and incommunicado. He inhabits the artificial bubble that is his world where he is king and country, law and yardstick, the one and only. The narcissist becomes the resident of his own burgeoning delusions. There, he is happy and soothed.

But the narcissist must justify to himself - on those rare occasions that he does catch a glimpse of his internal turmoil - why all this hatred and why the envy. The object of envy and hatred has to be magnified, glorified, idealized, demonized or elevated to superhuman levels to account for the narcissist's strong negative emotions. Outstanding qualities, skills and abilities are imputed to it and the object of these emotions is perceived to possess all the traits that the narcissist would have liked to have but doesn't.

This is very different from the purer, healthier, forms of hate directed at an object, which is genuinely - or is genuinely perceived to be - ominous, dangerous, or sadistic. In this healthy reaction, the properties of the hated object are not ones the person doing the hating would have liked to possess!

Hatred is therefore used to eliminate a source of frustration, which sadistically attacks the self. Jealousy is aimed at another person, who sadistically - or provocatively - prevents the jealous self from obtaining what it desires.

CHAPTER IV

The Workings of a Narcissist
A Phenomenology

We all face a choice: we can become horizontal expanders or vertical climbers. We can either select a profession, a vocation, an avocation, a geographic region, a spouse, a lifestyle, stick to them and climb up the proverbial ladder. This calls for incessant studies, specialization, focused energy, in depth involvement. Such people are the achiever (A) types.

The alternative is to frequently change professions, travel, accumulate experiences, memories, and encounters with people and with landscapes. In short, to learn a little about a lot. The price to pay: lack of socially recognized accomplishments.

Most narcissists belong to the second type in most fields of their life. They often maintain one island of stability (for instance, their marriage or career), but other realms of their life are highly unstable. To invest hard work and study in depth and laboriously is to admit that one is imperfect, less than omniscient and omnipotent. Narcissists don't admit to difficulties, challenges, ignorance, or shortcomings.

Narcissists cannot delay gratification. They are creatures of the here and now, because they feel boundlessly entitled. When forced to specialize or persist, they feel stagnation and "death". It is not a matter of choice but a structural constraint. This is the way a narcissist is built, this is his modus operandi, and his vacillating style of life and dizzying array of activities are written into his operations manual.

As a direct result, the narcissist cannot form a stable marital relationship, or reasonably devote himself to his family, or maintain an on going business, or reside in one place for long, or dedicate himself to a single profession or to one career, or complete his academic studies, or accumulate material wealth.

Narcissists are often described as indolent, labile, unstable, unreliable, unable and unwilling to undertake long-term commitments and obligations, or to maintain a job, or a career path. The narcissist's life is characterized by jerky, episodic careers, relationships, marriages, and domiciles. He is volatile, erratic, flexible, and ephemeral.

Hitherto we have touched upon the less malignant dimensions. There is worse to come.

The narcissist is possessed of a low self-esteem. In public, the narcissist presents himself as the quintessential winner. But deep inside, he judges himself to be a good-for-nothing loser, a permanent, irreversible failure. He hates himself for being so, and he constantly envies everyone around him for various reasons.

His discontent is often transformed into depression. Unable to love himself, the narcissist is unable to love another. He regards and treats people as though they were objects: exploits and discards them. He mistreats people around him by asserting his superiority at all times, by being emotionally cold or absent, by constantly bickering, verbally humiliating, incessantly (mostly unjustly) criticizing, and by actively rejecting or ignoring them, thus provoking uncertainty.

The narcissist's interpersonal relationships are deformed and sick. The longer the relationship, the more it is tinted by the pathological hue of narcissism. In his marriage, the narcissist recreates the conflicts with his Primary Objects (parents or caregivers). He is immature in every walk of life, sex included. He tends to select the wrong partners or spouse. He does everything to bring about his greatest horror: abandonment. Even his staunchest supporters and lovers ultimately desert him.

In the wake of such abandonment, the narcissist experiences the horrifying and complete breakdown of his defences. He feels lonely, but his loneliness is of the existential, almost solipsist type. The whole world seems unreal to him, possessed of a nightmarish quality. He either feels disproportionately guilty and assumes all the burden of blame, allocating none to his partner - or blames her for everything, denying any personal responsibility.

These moments of crisis may be the only occasions in which the narcissist is in touch with his emotions - an experience he has been trying to avoid all his life and at a great cost to his mental health. Learning the truth about his emotional infirmity, the narcissist often entertains suicidal ideation. He cannot countenance deforming his body, so he is inclined to use sleeping pills.

But, soon enough, the narcissist recovers and escapes into a new psychosexual liaison. Another toy, another object of gratification enters his world. His emotional wounds are shallow and they heal fast. Only his Ego is scarred, a memory that the narcissist represses.

Because he is detached from his self, the narcissist tends to ignore his body altogether - or to idolize and idealize it. The cerebral narcissist may indulge in smoking, abuse drugs, consume unhealthy foods, and lead a sedentary life. Though often unfit, he treats himself medically only when and if it is absolutely inevitable.

The somatic narcissist worships his body, cultivating it like a rare flower, feeding it a special diet, refraining from any hint of bodily malpractice. Such a narcissist wastes hours inspecting himself in mirrors and applying a myriad of lotions, creams and medicines to his precious shrine. He is also likely to be a hypochondriac.

The narcissist always prefers his image to his self. He goes a long way towards inventing himself, lying if needed, believing his own lies where expedient. To maintain this spectre, the narcissist resorts to chronic, pathological, misrepresentations and non-truths ("pseudologica fantastica").

The narcissist tries to compulsively replicate this invented image by becoming famous, a celebrity. Like his other obsessive-compulsive acts, it does not make the narcissist happier by any lasting measure, neither does it alleviate his anxiety. When faced with the choice, the narcissist always prefers his invented self to his true one. For instance, he draws attention to figments of his imagined rather to his real biography.

The narcissist engages in a host of self-defeating and reckless behaviours. He might, for instance, gamble or shop compulsively and lose all his possessions, time and again. Ironically, this lands him in economic uncertainty - which is what he dreads and loathes most.

These behaviours - pathological gambling, compulsive shopping, reckless driving, substance abuse - result in great personal and financial instability. Such a narcissist seems always to be in debt and harried, no matter how much money he makes. This, sometimes, is compounded by frequent changes of profession and by the lack of a stable career. Some narcissists, though, are at the top of their profession and earn the money, which goes with such a professional status.

Money is not the narcissist's only compulsion. Many narcissists are inordinately orderly and clean, or they may be addicted to knowledge, or obsessed with time. Some suffer from compulsive ticks and more complex repetitive, ritualistic movements. They might even become criminally compulsive, kleptomaniacs, for instance.

Narcissists are very misleading. They are possessed of undeniable personal charm and, usually, of sparkling intellect. Other people tend to associate these traits with maturity, authority and responsibility. Yet, as far as narcissists go, this association is a grave mistake.

The Dorian Grays of this world are eternal children (puer aeternus, Peter Pans), immature, puerile even, irresponsible, morally inconsistent (and in certain areas of life, morally non-existent). Narcissists actively encourage people to form expectations of them - only to disappoint and frustrate them later. They lack many adult skills and tend to rely on people around them to makeup for these deficiencies.

That people will obey him, cater to his needs, and comply with his wishes is taken for granted by the narcissist, as a birth right. At times the narcissist socially isolates himself, exuding an air of superiority, expressing disdain, or a patronizing attitude. At times he verbally lashes his nearest and dearest. Yet the narcissist expects total allegiance, loyalty, and submissiveness in all circumstances.

Abuse has many forms apart from the familiar ones: sexual, verbal, emotional, psychological, and physical (battering and assault). Some narcissists are the outcomes of insufficient or erratic love - others the sad consequences of too much love.

Forcing a child into adult pursuits is one of the subtlest varieties of soul murder. Very often we find that the narcissist was deprived of his childhood. He may have been a Wunderkind, the answer to his mother's prayers and the salve to her frustrations. A human computing machine, a walking-talking encyclopaedia, a curiosity, a circus freak - he may have been observed by developmental psychologists, interviewed by the media, endured the envy of his peers and their pushy mothers.

Consequently, such narcissists constantly clash with figures of authority because they feel entitled to special treatment, immune to prosecution, with a mission in life, destined for greatness, and, therefore, inherently superior.

The narcissist refuses to grow up. In his mind, his tender age formed an integral part of the precocious miracle that he once was. One looks much less phenomenal and one's exploits and achievements are much less awe-inspiring at the age of 40 than at the age of 4. Better stay young forever and thus secure one's Narcissistic Supply.

So, the narcissist refuses to grow up. He never takes out a driver's licence. He does not have children. He rarely has sex. He never settle-down in one place. He rejects intimacy. In short, he refrains from adulthood and adult chores. He has no adult skills. He assumes no adult responsibilities. He expects indulgence from others. He is petulant and haughtily spoiled. He is capricious, infantile and emotionally labile and immature. The narcissist is frequently a 40 years-old brat.

Narcissists suffer from repetition complexes. Like certain mythological figures, they are doomed to repeat their mistakes and failures, and the faulty behaviours which led to them. They refrain from planning and conceive of the world as a menacing, unpredictable, failure-prone, and hostile place, or, at best, a nuisance.

This culminates in self-destruction. Narcissists engage in conscious - and unconscious - acts of violence and aggression aimed at restricting their choices, gains, and potentials. Some of them end up as criminals.

Their criminality usually satisfies two conditions:

1. It is Ego enhancing. The act(s) are - or must be perceived as - sophisticated, entailing the use of special traits or skills, incredible, memorable, unique. The narcissist is very likely to be involved in "white collar crime". He harnesses his leadership charisma, personal charm, and natural intelligence to do the "job".

2. The criminal act includes a mutinous and contumacious element. The narcissist, after all, is mostly recreating the relationship that he has had with his parents. He rejects authority the way an adolescent does. He regards any kind of intrusion on his privacy and his autonomy - however justified and called for - as a direct and total threat to his psychic integrity. He tends to interpret the most mundane and innocuous gestures, sentences, exclamations, or offers as such threats. The narcissist is paranoiac when it comes to a breach of his splendid isolation. He reacts with disproportionate aggression and is thought of by his environment to be a dangerous type or, at the very least, odd and eccentric.

Any offer of help is immediately interpreted by the narcissist to imply that he is not omnipotent and omniscient. The narcissist reacts with rage to such impudent allegations and, thus, rarely asks for succour, unless he finds himself in a critical condition.

A narcissist can roam the streets for hours, looking for an address, before conceding his inferiority by asking a passer-by for guidance. He prefers to suffer physical pain, hunger and fear, rather than ask for help. The mere ability to help is considered proof of superiority and the mere need for help a despicable state of inferiority and weakness.

This is precisely why narcissists appear, at times, to be outstanding altruists. They enjoy the sense of power which goes with giving. They feel superior when they are needed. They encourage dependence of any kind. They know - sometimes, intuitively - that help is the most addictive drug and that relying on someone dependable fast becomes an indispensable habit.

Their exhibitionistic and "saintly" altruism disguises their thirst for admiration and accolades, and their propensity to play God. They pretend that they are interested only in the well-being of the happy recipients of their unconditional giving. But this kind of representation is patently untrue and misleading. No other kind of largesse comes with more strings attached. The narcissist gives only if and when he receives adulation and attention.

If not applauded or adulated by the beneficiaries of his charity, the narcissist loses interest, or deceives himself into believing that he is, in fact, revered. Mostly, the narcissist prefers to be feared or admired rather than loved. He describes himself as a "strong, no nonsense" man, who is able to successfully weather extraordinary losses and exceptional defeats and to recuperate. He expects other people to respect this image that he projects.

Thus, the beneficiaries are objects, silent witnesses to the narcissist's grandiosity and magnanimity, the audience in his one-man show. He is inhuman in that he needs no one and nothing - and he is superhuman in that he showers and shares the cornucopia of his wealth or talents abundantly and unconditionally. Even the narcissist's charity reflects his sickness.

Even so, the narcissist is more likely to donate what he considers to be the greatest gift of all - himself, his presence. Where other altruists contribute money - he avails of his time and of his knowledge. He needs to be in personal touch with those aided by him, so as to be immediately rewarded (narcissistically) for his efforts.

When the narcissist volunteers, he is at his best. He is often cherished as a pillar of civic behaviour and a contributor to community life. Thus, he is able to act, win applause, and reap Narcissistic Supply - and all with full social legitimacy.

CHAPTER V

The Tortured Self

The Inner World of the Narcissist

We dealt until now only with appearances. The narcissist's behaviour is indicative of a severe pathology which lies at the heart of his psyche and which deforms almost all his mental processes. A permanent dysfunction permeates and pervades all the strata of his mind and all his interactions with others and with himself.

What makes a narcissist tick? What is his hidden psychodynamic landscape like?

It is a terrain guarded zealously by defence mechanisms as old as the narcissist himself. More than to others, entrance to this territory is barred to the narcissist himself. Yet, to heal, however marginally, he needs this access most.

Narcissists are bred by other narcissists. To treat others as objects, one must first be treated as such. To become a narcissist, one must feel that one is nothing but an instrument used to satisfy the needs of a meaningful (maybe the most meaningful) figure in his life. One must feel that the only source of reliable, unconditional, total love is himself. One must, thus, lose faith in the existence or in the availability of other sources of emotional gratification.

This is a sorry state to which the narcissist is driven by long years of denial of his separate existence and his boundaries, by a volatile, or arbitrary milieu, and by constant emotional self-reliance. The narcissist - not daring to face the imperfection of the frustrating figure (usually, his mother), not able to direct his aggression at it - resorts to destroying himself.

The narcissist thus catches two birds with one stone of self-directed aggression: he vindicates the meaningful figure and her negative judgement of himself and he relieves his anxiety.

Narcissistic parents tend to perniciously mould their offspring in the formative years of early infanthood, well into the sixth year of age.

An adolescent, while still applying the finishing touches to his or to her personality, is already out of harm's way. The 10 year olds are more susceptible to narcissistic pathology, but not in the subtle irreversible manner which is the precondition for the formation of a Narcissistic Personality Disorder. The seed of pathological narcissism is planted earlier than that.

It often happens that children are exposed to only one narcissistic parent. If you are the other parent, you would do well to simply be yourself. Do not directly confront or counteract the narcissistic parent. This will transform him or her into a martyr or a role model (especially to rebellious teenagers). Simply show them that there is another way. They will make the right choice. All people do - except narcissists.

Narcissists are born to narcissistic, depressive, obsessive-compulsive, alcoholic, drug addicted, hypochondriac, passive-aggressive and, in general, mentally disturbed parents. Alternatively, they may be born into chaotic circumstances. Delinquent parents are not the exclusive vehicle of deprivation. War, disease, famine, a particularly nasty divorce, or sadistic peers and role models (teachers, for instance) can do the job as efficiently.

It is not the quantity of deprivation but its quality that breeds narcissism. The most important questions are: is the child accepted and loved as he is, unconditionally? Is his treatment consistent, predictable and just? Capricious behaviour and arbitrary judgement, contradicting directives, or emotional absence are the elements which constitute the narcissist's menacing, whimsically unexpected, dangerously cruel world.

In such a world, emotions are negatively rewarded. The development of emotions requires long-term, repeated, and safe interactions. Such interactions call for stability, predictability and a lot of goodwill. When these prerequisites are absent, the child prefers to escape into a world of his own making to minimize the hurt. Such a world combines an "analytical ratio" coupled with repressed emotions.

This invented, highly elaborate, universe is not devoid of emotions. Quite the contrary: it is infused with them, they colour every act, however automatic and basic. But they are tagged differently. The narcissist does not lose his ability to feel - he loses his ability to realize that he is feeling and to recognize his feelings as such. In other words: he is out of touch with his emotions. At best, the narcissist experiences a "binary", shallow, emotional state: (generally) good - as opposed to (generally) bad, or relative calm contrasted with unease.

The narcissist objectifies himself as well. He invests an enormous amount of psychic energy in this conversion process and - to avoid a destructive dissonance - he feels proud of his achievements. He brags about his "razor-like, totally unbiased, absolutely objective" judgement, which is expressly unaffected by emotions. He might nickname himself "the brain", or "the machine", and call himself a "wondrous instrument". It is as though his analytic skills acquire a life of their own and shield him from his labile emotions.

The narcissist, out of touch with his emotions, finds it impossible to communicate them. He disavows their very existence and the existence or prevalence or incidence of emotions in others. He finds the task of emoting so daunting, that he repudiates his feelings and their content and denies that he is capable of feeling at all.

When forced to communicate his emotions - usually by some kind of threat to his image or to his imaginary world, or by a looming abandonment - the narcissist uses an alienating and alienated, "objective" language. He makes profligate use of this emotionless speech also in therapy sessions, where direct contact is made with his feelings.

The narcissist does everything not to express directly and in plain language what he feels. He generalizes, compares, analyses, justifies, uses objective or objective-looking data, theorizes, intellectualizes, rationalizes, hypothesizes - anything but acknowledge his emotions.

Even when genuinely attempting to convey his feelings, the narcissist, who is normally verbally adept, sounds mechanic, hollow, disingenuous, or as though he is referring to someone else. This "observer stance" is favoured by narcissists. In an attempt to help the inquirer (the therapist, for instance) they assume a detached, "scientific" poise and talk about themselves in the third person.

Some of them even go to the extent of getting acquainted with psychological jargon to sound more convincing (though a few actually go to the trouble of studying psychology in-depth). Another narcissistic ploy is to pretend to be a "tourist" in one's own internal landscape: politely and mildly interested in the geography and history of the place, sometimes amazed, at times amused - but always uninvolved.

All this makes it difficult to penetrate the impregnable: the narcissist's inner world.

The narcissist himself has limited access to it. Humans rely on communication to get to know each other and they empathize through comparison. Communication absent or lacking, we cannot truly feel the "humanness" of the narcissist.

The narcissist is, thus, often described by others as "robotic", "machine-like", "inhuman", "emotionless", "android", "vampire", "alien", "automatic", "artificial", and so on. People are deterred by the narcissist's emotional absence. They are wary of him and keep their guard up at all times.

Certain narcissists are good at simulating emotions and can easily mislead people around them. Yet, their true colours are exposed when they lose interest in someone because he no longer serves a narcissistic (or other) purpose. Then they no longer invest energy in what, to others, comes naturally: emotional communication.

This is the essence of the narcissist's exploitativeness. To a certain degree, we all exploit each other. But, the narcissist abuses people. He misleads them into believing that they mean something to him, that they are special and dear to him, and that he cares about them. When they discover that it was all a sham and a charade, they are devastated.

The narcissist's problem is exacerbated by being constantly abandoned. It is a vicious cycle: the narcissist alienates people and they leave him. This, in turn, convinces him that he was always right in thinking that people are selfish and always prefer their self-interest to his welfare. His antisocial and asocial behaviours are, thus, amplified, leading to yet more serious emotional ruptures with his closest, nearest, and dearest.

CHAPTER VI

The Emotional Involvement
Preventive Measures

The narcissist is typically born into a dysfunctional family. It is characterized by massive denial, both internal ("You do not have a real problem, you are only pretending") and external ("You must never reveal the family's secrets to anyone"). Such emotional illness leads to affective and other personality disorders shared by all the members of the family and ranging from obsessive-compulsive disorders to hypochondriasis and depression.

577   Dysfunctional families are often reclusive and autarkic (self-sufficient). They actively reject and encourage abstention from social contacts. This inevitably leads to defective or partial socialization and differentiation, and to problems of sexual, gender, and self identity. This monastic attitude is sometimes applied even to the extended family. The members of the nuclear family feel emotionally or financially deprived or threatened by the world at large. They react with envy, rejection, self-isolation and rage in a kind of shared psychosis.

Constant aggression and violence are permanent features of such families. The violence and abuse can be verbal (degradation, humiliation), psychological-emotional, physical, or sexual.

Trying to rationalize and intellectualize its unique position and to justify it, the dysfunctional family emphasizes some superior logic it allegedly possesses and its efficiency. It adopts a transactional approach to life and it regards certain traits (e.g., intelligence) as an expression of superiority and as an advantage. These families encourage excellence - mainly cerebral and academic - but only as means to an end. The end is usually highly narcissistic (to be famous/rich/to live well, etc.).

Some narcissists, bred in such households, react by creatively escaping into rich, imagined worlds in which they exercise total physical and emotional control over their environment. But all of them divert libido, which should have been object-oriented, to their own self.

The source of all the narcissist's problems is the belief that human relationships invariably end in humiliation, betrayal, pain and abandonment. This conviction is the outcome of indoctrination in early childhood by parents, peers, or role models.

Moreover, the narcissist always generalizes. To him, any emotional interaction and any interaction with an emotional component is bound to end ignominiously. Getting attached to a place, a job, an asset, an idea, an initiative, a business, or a pleasure is certain to end as badly as getting involved in a relationship with another person.

This is why the narcissist avoids intimacy, real friendships, love, other emotions, commitment, attachment, dedication, perseverance, planning, emotional or other investment, morale or conscience (which are only meaningful if one believes in one's future), developing a sense of security, or pleasure.

The narcissist emotionally invests in the only in thing that he feels that he is in full, unmitigated control of: himself.

But the narcissist cannot ignore the fact that there is emotional content and residual affect even in the most basic activities. To protect himself from these remnants of emotions, these remote threats, he constructs a False Self, grandiose, and fantastic.

The narcissist uses his False Self in all his interactions, letting it get "tainted" by emotions in the process. Thus the False Self insulates the narcissist from the risks of emotional "contamination".

When even this fails, the narcissist has a more powerful weapon in his arsenal: the Wunderkind (wonder-boy) mask.

The narcissist creates two masks, which serve to hide him from the world and to force the world to cater to his needs and desires.

The first mask is the old, worn-out False Self.

The False Self is a special type of Ego. It is grandiose (and, in this sense, fantastic), invulnerable, omnipotent, omniscient, and "unattached". This kind of Ego prefers adulation or being feared to love. This Ego learns the truth about itself and its boundaries by being reflected. Other people's constant feedback (Narcissistic Supply) helps the narcissist to modulate and fine tune his False Self.

But the second mask is as important. This is the mask of the Wunderkind.

The narcissist, wearing this mask, broadcasts to the world that he is both a child (and therefore vulnerable, susceptible, and subject to adult protection) and a genius (and therefore worthy of special treatment and of admiration).

Inwardly this mask makes the narcissist less emotionally vulnerable. A child does not fully comprehend and grasp events and circumstances, does not commit himself, waltzes through life, and does not have to deal with emotionally charged problems or situations such as sex or child rearing.

Being a child, the narcissist is exempt from assuming responsibility and develops a sense of immunity and security. No one is likely to hurt a child or to severely punish him. The narcissist is a dangerous adventurer because - like a child - he feels that he is immune to the consequences of his actions, that his possibilities are unlimited, that everything is allowed without paying an attendant price.

The narcissist hates adults and is repelled by them. In his mind, he is forever innocent and loveable. Being a child, he feels no need to acquire adult skills or adult qualifications. Many narcissists do not complete their academic studies, refuse to marry or have children, or even get a driver's license. They feel that people should adore them as they are and cater to all the needs that they, as children, cannot themselves secure.

It is precisely because of this precociousness, the built-in contradiction between his (mental) age and his (adult) knowledge and intelligence, that the narcissist is able to sustain a grandiose self at all! Only a child with this kind of intelligence and with this kind of biography and with this kind of knowledge is entitled to feel superior and grandiose. The narcissist must remain a child if he is to feel superior and grandiose.

The problem is that the narcissist uses these two masks indiscriminately. There are situations in his life when one or both of them prove to be dysfunctional, even detrimental to his well-being.

Example: the narcissist dates a woman. At first, he makes use of the False Self in order to convert her into a Secondary Narcissistic Supply Source (SNSS) and to put her to the test (will she abandon/humiliate/betray him once she discovers that his self is confabulated?).

This phase successfully over, she is by now a full-fledged SNSS and is committed to sharing her life with the narcissist. But he is unlikely to believe her. His False Self, gratified by the SNSS, "exits". It is not likely to re-enter unless there is a problem with the flow of Narcissistic Supply.

The Wunderkind mask takes over. Its main goal is to avoid or to mitigate the consequences of a guaranteed emotional injury in the future. It permits the development of emotional involvement but in such a distorted and warped manner that this combination (Wunderkind mask in front - False Self in the background) does indeed lead to betrayal and to the abandonment of the narcissist.

The bridge connecting the two - the False Self and Wunderkind mask - is made of their common preference. They both prefer adulation to love.

Another example: the narcissist gets a job in a new workplace or meets a new group of people in social circumstances. At first, he uses his False Self with the aim of obtaining Primary Narcissistic Supply Source (PNSS) by demonstrating his superiority and uniqueness. This he does by putting on display his intellect and knowledge.

This phase over, the narcissist believes that his superiority is established, securing a constant flow of Narcissistic Supply and Narcissistic Accumulation. His False Self is satisfied and exits the scene. It will not reappear unless the supply is threatened.

It is the turn of the Wunderkind mask. Its goal is to allow the narcissist to establish some emotional involvement without suffering the results of an assured ultimate narcissistic injury or trauma. Again this underlying falsity, this infantilism, provoke rejection, the dismantling of the narcissist's social frameworks and groups, and the abandonment of the narcissist by friends and colleagues.

To summarize:

The narcissist has a post-traumatic personality with a tough, sadistic, and rigidly punishing ideal Superego (SEGO).

This contributes to the weakening and subsequent disintegration of the True Ego (TEGO).

The same pathology makes the narcissist create a "mask": the False Ego (FEGO).

The FEGO's aim is to ensure emotional autarky (self-sufficiency) and to avoid inevitable emotional injuries.

The FEGO prefers adulation, attention, or even fear to a mature adult love relationship.

FEGO is responsible to obtain PNSS and SNSS.

Adulation is secured by displaying superior qualities: intellect and knowledge, in the case of the cerebral narcissist - physical and sexual prowess in the case of his somatic counterpart.

Love and intimacy are perceived as threats by both types of narcissist.

When the target selected by the FEGO is successfully converted into a Narcissistic Source of Supply (NSS) and does not abandon ship after the first few encounters, the narcissist begins to develop a kind of emotional attachment and investment in the object.

But this attachment comes with a corollary: guaranteed hurt in the future. The narcissist's sadistic SEGO always attacks the object and makes it abandon the narcissist. The SEGO does it to punish the narcissist.

Anticipating this painful and (potentially) life-threatening phase, the narcissist activates another mask: the Wunderkind mask. This mask does allow for emotions to infiltrate the narcissistic fortress while maintaining impenetrable and successful defences against emotional injury.

Put together, though, these masks cause the very conflicts that they are intended to prevent, the very losses that they are intended to fend off, the very dysphoria, which they were supposed to eliminate.

Their combined actions lead to the necessity to allocate libido to FEGO to obtain new PNSS and SNSS - and the cycle begins anew.

Mental Map # 2

SEGO (ideal, sadistic, tough, punishing, offensive)
interacts with a HYPERCONSTRUCT one
of whose components is: the TEGO (really a child).
The SEGO interacts with TEGO
by exporting to the TEGO its aggression
and importing from it obsessive-compulsive behaviours.
SEGO employs EIPM to ensure punishment
through loss and hurt.
Another component of the Hyperconstruct is the FEGO.
FEGO employs the intellect
and an array of defence mechanisms.
FEGO imports libido from the ID
(another component of the Hyperconstruct).
FEGO imports drives from the ID.
FEGO exports PNSSs and SNSSs to the OBJECTS (partner,
spouse, business, money, friends, social framework, etc.).
FEGO imports hurt-free losses from OBJECTS (the hurt
is neutralized by initiating these losses and abandonment).
FEGO ("Wonder") and TEGO ("Boy") form Wonderboy, a Mask.
The WUNDERKIND MASK deflects the hurt
provoked by the SEGO following losses and abandonment.

When PNSSs/SNSSs are lost, FEGO experiences Loss Dysphoria and Deficiency Dysphoria. FEGO activates the Reactive Repertoire to escape the hurt. Libido is allocated to FEGO to look for new PNSSs and SNSSs.

But what happens if the NSSs (spouse, workplace) insist upon having a meaningful emotional involvement (e.g., the spouse insists upon being loved and upon more intimacy)?

In other words, what happens if someone close wants to penetrate the masks, to see what is (rather who is) behind them?

At this stage the Wunderkind mask is already active. It allows the narcissist to receive without giving, or investing, emotionally. But if the mask is bombarded with emotional demands from the outside, it ceases to function. It becomes a perfect child on the one hand (totally helpless and frightened) and a perfect, machine-like, genius on the other hand (with a defective reality test). The weakening of the mask permits direct contact between SEGO and object, which is subjected now to transformations of aggression.

The object is stunned by the apparently inexplicable change in the narcissist's mood and behaviour. It tries to weather the storm in the hope that this is a transient phenomenon. Only when the aggression persists does the object abandon the narcissist, thus causing a severe narcissistic injury and forcing upon the narcissist a painful transition to a new situation in which he is bereft of his SNSS. The object flees the SEGO. The narcissist is left feeling very envious of the object because she can avoid the monster that lurks inside him.

The failure of the masks means full emotional involvement, SEGO-originated aggression, and the certainty of abandonment with a full-fledged narcissistic injury, which could even threaten the narcissist's life.

Another thing to learn from this model is how the narcissist's attitude to objects changes when he senses a dwindling of the PNSS. The narcissist begins then to rely more heavily on the supply accumulated by the SNSS. He rehashes and recycles the information regarding his accomplishments and his grand moments stored in the SNSS's memory until they have lost most of their freshness and meaning.

As no new supply is forthcoming because of the gradual disappearance of PNSS, the reservoir is not replenished and becomes stale. The FEGO becomes weakened and undernourished. Its growing infirmity allows for a direct contact between SEGO and objects. This has the same consequences as before.

Only this time the SEGO's aggression is directed at the TEGO as well.

SEGO and the Hyperconstruct (which is the TEGO, the FEGO, the ID, together with the Wunderkind mask) are engaged in constant, energy consuming, warfare to obtain access to objects. The Hyperconstruct gains the upper hand when the FEGO is fortified by Narcissistic Supply coming from a variety of PNSSs and SNSSs.

When SEGO wins, a deep emotional involvement is formed, anxiety is aroused because of the anticipation of the SEGO's future sadistic actions, and the narcissist engages in compulsive acts to channel the anxiety and to neutralize it. SEGO directs aggression and its transformations at the objects and they react by fighting back, injuring the narcissist in the process. Finally the objects, hurt and dejected, abandon the narcissist, or the common framework (the business, the workplace, the family unit), or change to such a degree that it amounts to emotional abandonment.

The FEGO then experiences a thorough and hazardous narcissistic injury.

To avoid the emotional consequences of a possible victory of the SEGO, the Hyperconstruct activates a series of mechanisms, attitudes, and behaviour patterns. They are all intended to assist the narcissist in "keeping his emotional distance" in order to protect him from emotional hurt. The Wunderkind mask causes a considerable (and discernible) infantilization of the narcissist and a gradual loss of his grasp on reality. When the objects abandon him, the narcissistic injury is thus made more tolerable.

But there is a deeply embedded conflict in the narcissist's personality.

The SEGO hates the narcissist and wishes to destroy him. It, therefore, wants the narcissist to have a meaningful emotional involvement. Its externalized aggression transformations are most effective precisely when the narcissist is emotionally involved. The effectiveness of its punishment is thus enhanced and the pain is bound to be larger and life threatening.

Deep inside, the SEGO "believes" that the narcissist does not deserve to live. The aggression that the narcissist transforms and stores is of lethal proportions. In his childhood, the narcissist wanted the most sacred figures in his life dead and he believes that he deserves to die for it. The SEGO is a constant reminder of this and, thus, it is the narcissist's executioner.

The Hyperconstruct is assembled by the narcissist at a very early stage in his life precisely to confront this kind of self-destructive impulse. While the self-loathing cannot be eliminated, it can at least be ameliorated and its potentially fatal consequences can be prevented.

The Hyperconstruct protects the narcissist from being emotionally devastated, from carrying the consequences of inevitable betrayal and abandonment too far. It achieves this by putting a distance between the narcissist and his objects so that when the predictable abandonment transpires, it is less intolerable. It prevents emotional involvement to avoid potentially dangerous reactions to abandonment.

When the Hyperconstruct weakens (because of the insistence of an object to get emotionally involved), or diverted (when most of the libido is dedicated to looking for PNSS), or when the PNSS reservoir is dilapidated, emotional involvement does develop together with transformed aggression directed at the object and which can be traced back to the SEGO.

The fate of the narcissist's relationships is preordained. The behavioural pair "emotional involvement-aggression" is constant and it always leads to abandonment. Only two components can be regulated in this trio (emotional involvement - aggression - abandonment) and they are emotional involvement and abandonment. The narcissist can choose to precipitate and anticipate an act of abandonment by initiating it - or he can choose to fight against emotional involvement and thus avoid being aggressive.

The Hyperconstruct does this by employing a series of ingeniously deceptive Emotional Involvement Preventive Measures (EIPM).

Emotional Involvement Preventive Measures

Personality and Conduct

Lack of enthusiasm, anhedonia, and constant boredom
A wish to "vary", to "be free",
to hop from one subject matter or object to another.
Laziness, constantly present fatigue
Dysphoria to the point of depression
leads to reclusiveness, detachment, low energies.
Repression of the affect and uniform emotional "hues"
Self-hatred disables capacity to love or
to develop emotional involvement.

Externalized transformations of aggression:
Envy, rage, cynicism, vulgar honesty, black humour
(all lead to disintimization and distancing
and to pathological emotional and sexual communication)

Narcissistic compensatory and defence mechanisms:
Grandiosity and grandiose fantasies
(Feelings of) uniqueness
Lack of empathy,
or the existence of functional empathy,
or empathy by proxy.
Demands for adoration and adulation
A feeling that he deserves everything ("entitlement")
Exploitation of objects
Objectification/symbolization (abstraction)
and fictionalization of objects.
Manipulative behaviour
(using personal charm, ability to
psychologically penetrate the object, ruthlessness,
and knowledge and information regarding the object
obtained, largely, by interacting with the object)
Intellectualization through generalization,
differentiation and categorization of objects.
Feelings of omnipotence and omniscience
Perfectionism and performance anxiety (repressed)
These mechanisms lead to emotional substitution
(adulation and adoration instead of love),
to the distancing and repulsion of objects, to disintimization
(not possible to interact with the "real" narcissist).

The results:
Narcissistic vulnerability to narcissistic injury
(more bearable than emotional vulnerability
and can be more easily recovered from)
"Becoming a child" and infantilism
(the narcissist's inner dialogue: "No one will hurt me",
"I am a child and I am loved unconditionally, unreservedly,
non-judgementally, and disinterestedly")
Adults don't expect such unconditional love and acceptance
and they constitute a barrier to mature, adult relationships.
Intensive denial of reality
(perceived by others as innocence, naiveтй,
or pseudo-stupidity)
Constant lack of confidence
concerning matters not under full control
leads to hostility towards objects and towards emotions.
Compulsive behaviours intended to neutralize
a high level of anxiety and compulsive seeking
of love substitutes (money, prestige, power)...

Instincts and Drives

The Cerebral Narcissist

Sexual abstinence, low frequency of sexual activity
lead to less emotional involvement.
Frustration of emotional objects through sex avoidance
encourages abandonment by the object.
Sexual disintimization by preferring autoerotic,
anonymous sex with immature or incompatible objects
(who do not represent an emotional threat or pose demands).
Sporadic sex with long intervals
and drastic alterations of sexual behaviour patterns.

Dissociation of pleasure centres:
Pleasure avoidance (unless "for and on behalf" of the object)
Refraining from child rearing or family formation
Using the object as an "alibi" not to form new sexual
and emotional liaisons, extreme marital and monogamous
faithfulness, to the point of ignoring all other objects
leads to object inertia.
This mechanism defends the narcissist
from the need to make contact with other objects.
Sexual frigidity with significant other
and sexual abstinence with others.

The Somatic Narcissist

The somatic narcissist treats others as sex objects
or sex slaves or masturbatory aides.
High frequency of unemotional sex,
lacking in intimacy and warmth.

Object Relations

Manipulative attitudes, which in conjunction with
feelings of omnipotence and omniscience,
create a mystique of infallibility and immunity.
Partial reality test
Social friction leads to social sanctions (up to imprisonment)
Refraining from intimacy
Absence of emotional investment or presence
Reclusive life, avoiding neighbours, family
(both nuclear and extended), spouse and friends.
The narcissist is often a schizoid
Active misogyny (women-hatred)
with sadistic and anti-social elements.
Narcissistic dependence serves as
substitute for emotional involvement.

Immature emotional dependence and habit
Object interchangeability
(dependence upon ANY object - not upon a specific object)...
Limitation of contacts with objects
to material and "cold" transactions.
The narcissist prefers fear, adulation, admiration
and Narcissistic Accumulation to love.
To the narcissist, objects have no autonomous existence
except as PNSSs and SNSSs
(Primary and Secondary Sources of Narcissistic Supply).
Knowledge and intelligence serve as control mechanisms and
extractors of adulation and attention (Narcissistic Supply).
The object is used to re-enact early life conflicts:
The narcissist is bad and asks to be punished anew
and thus obtain confirmation that people are angry at him.
The object is kept emotionally distant through deterrence
and is constantly tested by the narcissist
who reveals his negative sides to the object.
The aim of negative, off-putting behaviours
is to check whether the narcissist's uniqueness will
override and offset them in the mind of the object.

The object experiences emotional absence,
repulsion, deterrence and insecurity.
It is thus encouraged not to develop
emotional involvement with the narcissist
(emotional involvement requires
a positive emotional feedback).
The erratic and demanding relationship with the narcissist
is experienced as an energy-depleting burden.
It is punctuated by a series of "eruptions" followed by relief
The narcissist is imposing, intrusive,
compulsive and tyrannical.
Reality is interpreted cognitively so that negative aspects,
real and imagined, of the object are highlighted.
This preserves the emotional distance
between the narcissist and his objects,
fosters uncertainty, prevents emotional involvement
and activates narcissistic mechanisms
(such as grandiosity) which, in turn,
increase the repulsion and the aversion of the partner.
The narcissist claims to have chosen the object because of
an error/circumstances/pathology/loss of control/
immaturity/partial or false information, etc.

Functioning and Performance

A grandiosity shift:
A preference to be emotionally invested
in grandiose career-related fantasies
in which the narcissist does not have to
face practical, rigorous and consistent demands.
The narcissist avoids success in order to avoid
emotional involvement and investment.
He shuns success because it obliges him to follow through
and to identify himself with some goal or group.
He emphasizes areas of activity
in which he is unlikely to succeed.
The narcissist ignores the future and does not plan
Thus he is never emotionally committed
The narcissist invests the necessary minimum
in his job (emotionally).
He is not thorough and under-performs,
his work is shoddy and defective or partial.
He evades responsibility and tends to pass it on to others
while exercising little control.
His decision-making processes are ossified and rigid
(he presents himself as a man of "principles" -
usually referring to his whims and moods)
The narcissist reacts very slowly to
a changing environment (change is painful).
He is a pessimist,
knows that he will lose his job/business -
so, he is constantly engaged in seeking alternatives
and constructing plausible alibis.
This yields a feeling of temporariness,
which prevents engagement, involvement, commitment,
dedication, identification and emotional hurt
in case of change or failure.
The alternative to having a spouse/companion:
Solitary life (with vigorous emphasis on PNSS)
or frequent changes of partners.
Serial vocations prevent the narcissist from having
a clear career path and obviate the need to persevere.
All the initiatives adopted by the narcissist are egocentric,
sporadic and discrete (they focus on one skill or trait of
the narcissist, are randomly distributed in space and in time,
and do not form a thematic or other continuum
- they are not goal or objective oriented).

Sometimes, as a substitute,
the narcissist engages in performance shifting:
He comes up with imaginary, invented goals
with no correlation to reality and its constraints.
To avoid facing performance tests
and to maintain grandiosity and uniqueness
the narcissist refrains from acquiring skills and training
(such as a driver's licence, technical skills,
any systematic - academicor non-academic - knowledge).
The "child" in the narcissist is reaffirmed this way -
because he avoids adult activities and attributes.
The gap between the image projected by the narcissist
(charisma, unusual knowledge, grandiosity, fantasies)
and his actual achievements - create in him
permanent feelings that he is a crook, a hustler,
that his life is unreal life and movie-like
(derealization and depersonalization).
This gives rise to ominous feelings of imminent threat
and, concurrently, to compensatory assertions
of immunity and omnipotence.
The narcissist is forced to become a manipulator

589   **Locations and Environment**

A feeling of not belonging and of detachment
Bodily discomfiture
(the body feels as depersonalized, alien and a nuisance,
its needs are totally ignored, its signals re-routed
and re-interpreted, its maintenance neglected)
Keeping his distance from relevant communities
(his neighbourhood, coreligionists,
his nation and countrymen)
Disavowing his religion, his ethnic background, his friends
The narcissist often adopts the stance
of a "scientist-observer".
This is narcissistic detachment - the feeling that
he is a director or an actor in a movie about his own life.
The narcissist avoids "emotional handles":
photographs, music identified with a certain period in his life,
familiar places, people he knew,
mementoes and emotional situations.
The narcissist lives on borrowed time in a borrowed life
Every place and period are transitory
and lead to the next, unfamiliar environment.
The narcissist feels that the end is near

He lives in rented apartments, is an illegal alien,
is fully mobile on a short notice,
does not buy real estate or immovables.
He travels light and he likes to travel
He is peripatetic and itinerant
The narcissist cultivates feelings of incompatibility
with his surroundings.
He considers himself superior to others
and keeps criticizing people, institutions and situations.
The above behaviour patterns constitute a denial of reality
The narcissist defines a rigid,
impenetrable, personal territory
and is physically revolted when it is breached.

The narcissist does get sometimes emotionally attached to his money and to his belongings, though.

Money and possessions represent power, they are love substitutes, they are mobile and disposable on short notice. They constitute an inseparable part of a Pathological Narcissistic Space and are a determinant of FEGO. The narcissist assimilates them and identifies with them. This is why he is so traumatized by their loss or depreciation. They provide him with the certainty and safety that he feels nowhere else. They are familiar, predictable, and controllable. There is no danger involved in emotionally investing in them.

Suzanne Forward distinguishes the narcissist from the sadist, the sociopath and the misogynist with respect to their attitudes towards women. She says that the narcissist "goes through" many women in order to replenish his SNSS (to use my terminology).

The narcissist lives with his spouse only as long as she fully caters to his narcissistic needs through accumulation and adoration. The narcissist's misogyny and his sadism are a result of his fear of being abandoned (the recreation of earlier traumas) and not the result of his narcissism. A narcissist with an ideal, sadistic, rigid, primitive, and punishing Superego inevitably becomes antisocial and lacks morals and a working conscience.

Here lies the difference. The narcissist treats women the way he does in order to weaken them and to make them dependent on him so as to prevent them from abandoning him. He uses a variety of techniques to undermine the sources of his partner's strengths: her healthy sexuality, her supportive family, thriving career, self-esteem and self-image, sound mental health, proper reality test, good friends, income, savings, assets, and social circle.

Once deprived of all these, the narcissist remains his partner's only available source of authority, interest, meaning, feeling and hope. A woman thus denuded of her network of support is highly unlikely to abandon the narcissist. Her state of dependence is fostered by his unpredictable behaviours, which cause her to react with fear and phobic hesitation.

The narcissist needs women and that's why he hates them. It is his dependence on women that he resents and detests. The misogynist hates women, humiliates them, scorns them and despises them - but he does not need them.

One last point: sex leads to intimacy. However minimal this intimacy is, the narcissist is bound to experience as abandonment every interruption of a sexual relationship. He feels lonely and annulled. This has to do with the absence of the SNSS's defining look. The longing is so great that the narcissist is driven to finding a substitute. This substitute is another SNSS.

Each narcissist has a profile of his preferred SNSS. It reflects the predilections of the narcissist and the matrix of his pathological needs. But a few things are common to all potential women SNSS:

They must not be garrulous, they must be slow, inferior in some important respect, submissive, with an aesthetic appearance, intelligent but passive, admiring, emotionally available, dependent and either simple or femme fatale. They are not the narcissist's type if they are critical, independently thinking, demonstrate superiority, sophistication, personal autonomy, or provide unsolicited advice or opinions. The narcissist forms no relationships with such women, though the somatic narcissist often seeks to "subjugate" them by "conquering" them sexually.

Having spotted the "right profile", the narcissist sees if he is sexually attracted to the woman. If he is, he proceeds to condition her using a variety of measures: sex, money, assumption of responsibilities, fostering sexual, emotional, existential and operational uncertainties (followed by bouts of relief on her part as conflicts are resolved), grandiose gestures, expressions of interest, of need and of dependence (mistakenly interpreted by the woman to mean deep emotions), grandiose plans, idealization, demonstrations of unlimited trust (but no sharing of decision making powers), encouraging feelings of uniqueness and of pseudo-intimacy, and childlike behaviour.

Ultimately, dependence is formed and a new SNSS is born.

The last phase is the *SNSS transaction*. The narcissist extracts from his partner adulation, Narcissistic Accumulation and submissiveness. In turn, he undertakes to continue to condition his partner using the same measures. Concurrently, he activates the Wunderkind mask in anticipation of abandonment.

In this sort of relationship, the narcissist does not ensure stability, emotional or sexual exclusivity, or emotional and spiritual sharing. He is not intimate with his partner and there is no real exchange of trust, information, experience, or opinions. Such relationships are limited to sexual compatibility, common decision-making, cohabitation, long-term planning, and common property. Narcissists rarely have children WITH their spouses - rather they make children FOR their spouses.

All this leads to the inevitable: a depletion of the energy of the SNSS (who keeps giving of herself emotionally without receiving much in return), pain and hurt, the end of sexual and emotional exclusivity and abandonment.

The narcissist always prefers a woman to any other type of SNSS (example: to business). She requires less long-term investment and is easier to "train". Moreover, she is often motivated to be conditioned. She wants to supply the narcissist and, thus, to keep the flame burning.

The world of business, in contrast, is indifferent to the narcissist and to his often marginal activities. Additionally, women are far better at reliably regulating the narcissist's flow of Narcissistic Supply.

Both functions (stabilization-accumulation and adulation) are thus found in one and the same NSS: a woman. This allows the narcissist to focus his efforts on a single object. Naturally, this creates greater dependence and greater risk of abandonment but the savings in energy are worth it as far as the narcissist is concerned.

THE AUTHOR

Shmuel (Sam) Vaknin
Curriculum Vitae

Born in 1961 in Qiryat-Yam, Israel.
Served in the Israeli Defence Force (1979-1982) in training and education units.

Education

Graduated a few semesters in the Technion – Israel Institute of Technology, Haifa.

Ph.D. in Philosophy (major: Philosophy of Physics) – Pacific Western University, California, USA.
Graduate of numerous courses in Finance Theory and International Trading.
Certified E-Commerce Concepts Analyst by Brainbench.
Certified in Psychological Counselling Techniques by Brainbench.
Certified Financial Analyst by Brainbench.
Full proficiency in Hebrew and in English.

Business Experience

1980 to 1983

Founder and co-owner of a chain of computerized information kiosks in Tel-Aviv, Israel.

1982 to 1985

Senior positions with the Nessim D. Gaon Group of Companies in Geneva, Paris and New-York (NOGA and APROFIM SA):
– Chief Analyst of Edible Commodities in the Group's Headquarters in Switzerland
– Manager of the Research and Analysis Division
– Manager of the Data Processing Division
– Project Manager of the Nigerian Computerized Census

- Vice President in charge of RND and Advanced Technologies
- Vice President in charge of Sovereign Debt Financing

1985 to 1986

Represented Canadian Venture Capital Funds in Israel.

1986 to 1987

General Manager of IPE Ltd. in London. The firm financed international multi-lateral countertrade and leasing transactions.

1988 to 1990

Co-founder and Director of "Mikbats-Tesuah", a portfolio management firm based in Tel-Aviv.
Activities included large-scale portfolio management, underwriting, forex trading and general financial advisory services.

1990 to Present

Freelance consultant to many of Israel's Blue-Chip firms, mainly on issues related to the capital markets in Israel, Canada, the UK and the USA.
Consultant to foreign RND ventures and to governments on macro-economic matters.
Freelance journalist and analyst for various media in the USA.

1990 to 1995

President of the Israel chapter of the Professors World Peace Academy (PWPA) and (briefly) Israel representative of the "Washington Times".

1993 to 1994

Co-owner and Director of many business enterprises:
- The Omega and Energy Air-Conditioning Concern
- AVP Financial Consultants
- Handiman Legal Services - Total annual turnover of the group: 10 million USD.
Co-owner, Director and Finance Manager of COSTI Ltd. - Israel's largest computerized information vendor and developer. Raised funds through a series of private placements locally in the USA, Canada and London.

1993 to 1996

Publisher and Editor of a Capital Markets Newsletter distributed by subscription only to dozens of subscribers countrywide.
In a legal precedent in 1995 - studied in business schools and law faculties across Israel - was tried for his role in an attempted take-over of Israel's Agriculture Bank.
Was interned in the State School of Prison Wardens.

MALIGNANT SELF LOVE   SAM VAKNIN

Managed the Central School Library, wrote, published and lectured on various occasions.
Managed the Internet and International News Department of an Israeli mass media group, "Ha-Tikshoret and Namer".
Assistant in the Law Faculty in Tel-Aviv University (to Prof. S.G. Shoham).

1996 to 1999

Financial consultant to leading businesses in Macedonia, Russia and the Czech Republic.
Economic commentator in "Nova Makedonija", "Dnevnik", "Makedonija Denes", "Izvestia", "Argumenti i Fakti", "The Middle East Times", "The New Presence", "Central Europe Review", and other periodicals, and in the economic programs on various channels of Macedonian Television.
Chief Lecturer in Macedonia in courses organized by the Agency of Privatization, by the Stock Exchange, and by the Ministry of Trade.

1999 to 2002

Economic Advisor to the Government of the Republic of Macedonia and to the Ministry of Finance.

2001 to 2003

595 Senior Business Correspondent for United Press International (UPI).

Web and Journalistic Activities

Author of extensive Web sites in:
- Psychology ("Malignant Self-Love") – An Open Directory Cool Site,
- Philosophy ("Philosophical Musings"),
- Economics and Geopolitics ("World in Conflict and Transition").
Owner of the Narcissistic Abuse Study List and the Abusive Relationships Newsletter (more than 6000 members).
Owner of the Economies in Conflict and Transition Study List, the Toxic Relationships Study List, and the Link and Factoid Study List.
Editor of mental health disorders and Central and Eastern Europe categories in various Web directories (Open Directory, Search Europe, Mentalhelp.net).
Editor of the Personality Disorders, Narcissistic Personality Disorder, the Verbal and Emotional Abuse, and the Spousal (Domestic) Abuse and Violence topics on Suite 101 and Bellaonline.
Columnist and commentator in "The New Presence", United Press International (UPI), InternetContent, eBookWeb, PopMatters, "Global Politician", eBookNet, and "Central Europe Review".

Publications and Awards

"Managing Investment Portfolios in States of Uncertainty", Limon Publishers, Tel-Aviv, 1988

"The Gambling Industry", Limon Publishers, Tel-Aviv, 1990

"Requesting My Loved One - Short Stories", Yedioth Aharonot, Tel-Aviv, 1997

"The Suffering of Being Kafka" (electronic book of Hebrew and English Short Fiction), Prague and Skopje, 1998-2004

"The Macedonian Economy at a Crossroads - On the Way to a Healthier Economy" (dialogues with Nikola Gruevski), Skopje, 1998

"The Exporters' Pocketbook", Ministry of Trade, Republic of Macedonia, Skopje, 1999

"Malignant Self Love - Narcissism Revisited", Narcissus Publications, Prague and Skopje, 1999-2007

The Narcissism Series (e-books regarding relationships with abusive narcissists), Skopje, 1999-2007

"After the Rain - How the West Lost the East", Narcissus Publications in association with Central Europe Review/CEENMI, Prague and Skopje, 2000

Winner of numerous awards, among them Israel's Council of Culture and Art Prize for Maiden Prose (1997), The Rotary Club Award for Social Studies (1976), and the Bilateral Relations Studies Award of the American Embassy in Israel (1978).

Hundreds of professional articles in all fields of finances and the economy, and numerous articles dealing with geopolitical and political economic issues published in both print and Web periodicals in many countries.

Many appearances in the electronic media on subjects in philosophy and the sciences, and concerning economic matters.

Write to Me:

samvaknin@gmail.com
narcissisticabuse-owner@yahoogroups.com

My Web Sites:

Economy/Politics: http://ceeandbalkan.tripod.com/

Psychology: http://www.narcissistic-abuse.com/

Philosophy: http://philosophos.tripod.com/

Poetry: http://samvak.tripod.com/contents.html

Fiction: http://samvak.tripod.com/sipurim.html

Abused? Stalked? Harassed? Bullied? Victimized?
Afraid? Confused? Need HELP? DO SOMETHING ABOUT IT!

Had a Narcissistic Parent?
Married to a Narcissist - or Divorcing One?
Afraid your children will turn out the same?
Want to cope with this pernicious, baffling condition?
OR
Are You a Narcissist - or suspect that You are one...
This book will teach you how to...
Cope, Survive, and Protect Your Loved Ones!
You should read...

Eight additional e-books, All NEW Editions, JUST RELEASED!!!

Toxic Relationships, Pathological Narcissism FAQs, Coping with Divorce, The Narcissist and Psychopath in the Workplace - and MORE!!!

Copy-paste this link to your browser window to purchase the eight e-books:

http://www.narcissistic-abuse.com/thebook.html

Personality Disorders Revisited - click on this link to purchase:

http://www.ccnow.com/cgi-local/cart.cgi?vaksam_PERSONALITY

Free excerpts from the EIGHTH, Revised Impression of **"Malignant Self Love - Narcissism Revisited"** are available as well as a free NEW EDITION of the Narcissism Book of Quotes

Copy-paste this link to your browser window to download the files:

http://www.narcissistic-abuse.com/freebooks.html

"After the Rain - How the West Lost the East"

The history, cultures, societies, and economies of countries in transition in the Balkans.

Copy-paste this link to your browser window to purchase this print book:

http://www.ccnow.com/cgi-local/cart.cgi?vaksam_ATR

Electronic Books (e-books) from the Publisher

An *electronic book* is a computer file, sent to you as an attachment to an e-mail message. Just save it to your hard disk and click on the file to open, read, and learn!

1. **"Malignant Self Love - Narcissism Revisited"**
Eighth, Revised Edition (January 2007)

The e-book version of Sam Vaknin's "Malignant Self - Love - Narcissism Revisited". Contains the entire text: essays, frequently asked questions (FAQs) and appendices regarding pathological narcissism and the Narcissistic Personality Disorder (NPD).

Copy-paste this link to your browser window to purchase the e-book:

http://www.ccnow.com/cgi-local/cart.cgi?vaksam_MSL-EBOOK

2. **"The Narcissism Series"**
Eighth, Revised Edition (January 2007)

EIGHT e-books (more than 2500 pages), including the full text of "Malignant Self Love - Narcissism Revisited", regarding Pathological Narcissism, relationships with abusive narcissists and psychopaths, and the Narcissistic Personality Disorder (NPD).

Copy-paste this link to your browser window to purchase the EIGHT e-books:

http://www.ccnow.com/cgi-local/cart.cgi?vaksam_SERIES

3. **"Toxic Relationships - Abuse and its Aftermath"**
Fourth Edition (February 2006)

How to identify abuse, cope with it, survive it, and deal with your abuser and with the system in divorce and custody issues.

Copy-paste this link to your browser window to purchase the e-book:

http://www.ccnow.com/cgi-local/cart.cgi?vaksam_ABUSE

4. **"The Narcissist and Psychopath in the Workplace"**
(September 2006)

Identify abusers, bullies, and stalkers in the workplace (bosses, colleagues, suppliers, and authority figures) and learn how to cope with them effectively.

Copy-paste this link to your browser window to purchase the e-book:

http://www.ccnow.com/cgi-local/cart.cgi?vaksam_WORKPLACE

5. **"Abusive Relationships Workbook"** - (February 2006)

Self-assessment questionnaires, tips, and tests for victims of abusers, batterers, and stalkers in various types of relationships.

Copy-paste this link to your browser window to purchase the e-book:

http://www.ccnow.com/cgi-local/cart.cgi?vaksam_WORKBOOK

6. **"Pathological Narcissism FAQs"**
Eighth, Revised Edition (January 2007)

Dozens of Frequently Asked Questions regarding Pathological Narcissism, relationships with abusive narcissists, and the Narcissistic Personality Disorder.

Copy-paste this link to your browser window to purchase the e-book:

http://www.ccnow.com/cgi-local/cart.cgi?vaksam_FAQS

7. **"The World of the Narcissist"**
Eighth, Revised Edition (January 2007)

A book-length psychodynamic study of pathological narcissism, relationships with abusive narcissists, and the Narcissistic Personality Disorder, using a new vocabulary.

Copy-paste this link to your browser window to purchase the e-book:

http://www.ccnow.com/cgi-local/cart.cgi?vaksam_ESSAY

8. **"Excerpts from the Archives of the Narcissism List"**

Hundreds of excerpts from the archives of the Narcissistic Abuse Study List regarding Pathological Narcissism, relationships with abusive narcissists, and the Narcissistic Personality Disorder (NPD).

Copy-paste this link to your browser window to purchase the e-book:

http://www.ccnow.com/cgi-local/cart.cgi?vaksam_EXCERPTS

9. **"Diary of a Narcissist"** - (November 2005)

The anatomy of one man's mental illness - its origins, its unfolding, its outcomes.

Copy-paste this link to your browser window to purchase the e-book:

http://www.ccnow.com/cgi-local/cart.cgi?vaksam_JOURNAL

10. **"After the Rain - How the West Lost the East"**

The history, cultures, societies, and economies of countries in transition in the Balkans.

Copy-paste this link to your browser window to purchase the e-book:

http://www.ccnow.com/cgi-local/cart.cgi?vaksam_ATR-EBOOK

Download Free Electronic Books

Copy-paste this link to your browser window:

http://www.narcissistic-abuse.com/freebooks.html

Testimonials and Additional Resources

You can read Readers' Reviews at the Barnes and Noble Web page dedicated to "Malignant Self Love"

Copy-paste this link to your browser window:

http://search.barnesandnoble.com/bookSearch/isbnInquiry.asp?r=1&ISBN=9788023833843

Dozens of Links and Resources

Copy-paste these links into your browser window:

The Narcissistic Abuse Study List
http://groups.yahoo.com/group/narcissisticabuse
The Toxic Relationships Study List
http://groups.yahoo.com/group/toxicrelationships
Abusive Relationships Newsletter
http://groups.google.com/group/narcissisticabuse/

Participate in Discussions about Abusive Relationships

http://personalitydisorders.suite101.com/discussions.cfm
http://groups.yahoo.com/group/Narcissistic_Personality_Disorder
http://groups.msn.com/NARCISSISTICPERSONALITYDISORDER

Links to Therapist Directories, Psychological Tests, NPD Resources, Support Groups for Narcissists and Their Victims, and Tutorials

http://www.suite101.com/links.cfm/npd

Support Groups for Victims of Narcissists and Narcissists

http://dmoz.org/Health/Mental_Health/Disorders/Personality/Narcissistic

BE WELL, SAFE AND WARM WHEREVER YOU ARE!

Sam Vaknin